COLLECTIONS

A Harcourt Reading / Language Arts Program

Get ready to explore the times of discovery!

COLLECTIONS
A Harcourt Reading / Language Arts Program

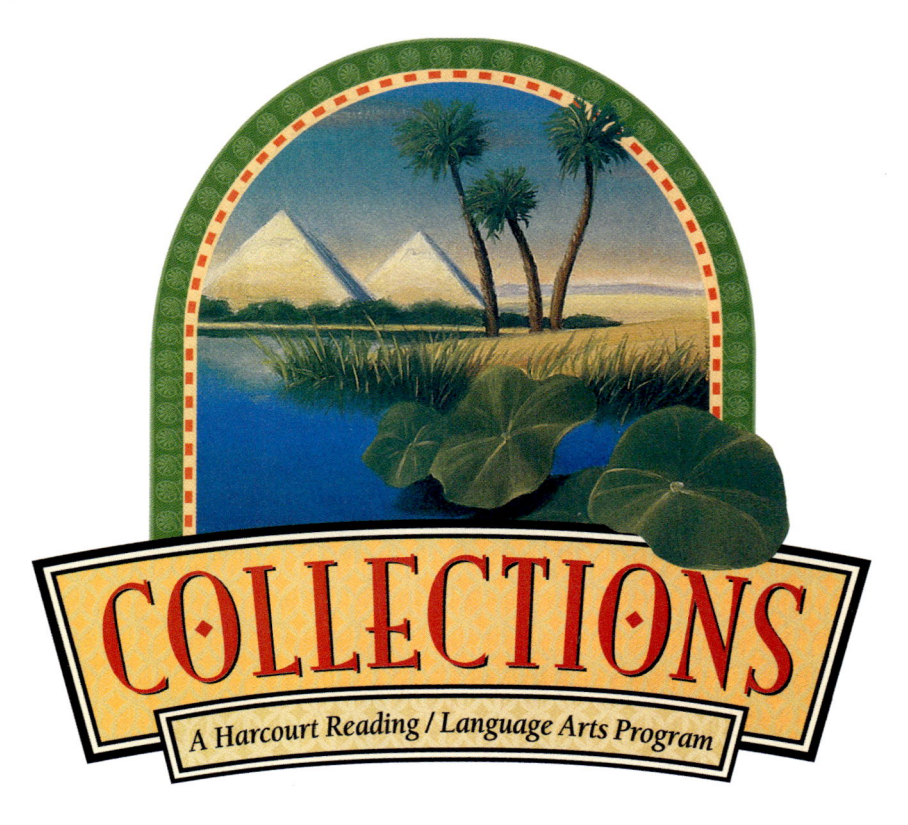

TIMES OF DISCOVERY

SENIOR AUTHORS
Roger C. Farr • Dorothy S. Strickland • Isabel L. Beck

AUTHORS
Richard F. Abrahamson • Alma Flor Ada • Bernice E. Cullinan • Margaret McKeown • Nancy Roser
Patricia Smith • Judy Wallis • Junko Yokota • Hallie Kay Yopp

SENIOR CONSULTANT
Asa G. Hilliard III

CONSULTANTS
Karen S. Kutiper • David A. Monti • Angelina Olivares

Harcourt

Orlando   Boston   Dallas   Chicago   San Diego

Visit *The Learning Site!*

www.harcourtschool.com

Copyright © 2001 by Harcourt, Inc.

All rights reserved. No part of this publication may be reproduced or transmitted in any form or by any means, electronic or mechanical, including photocopy, recording, or any information storage and retrieval system, without permission in writing from the publisher.

Requests for permission to make copies of any part of the work should be mailed to the following address: School Permissions, Harcourt, Inc., 6277 Sea Harbor Drive, Orlando, Florida 32887-6777.

HARCOURT and the Harcourt Logo are trademarks of Harcourt, Inc.

Acknowledgments appear in the back of this work.

Printed in the United States of America

ISBN 0-15-312051-7

3 4 5 6 7 8 9 10   048   2003 2002 2001

Times of Discovery

Dear Reader,

Every day, we make new discoveries about the world we live in. Some we make by exploring new ideas and places, while others come from our personal experiences and our relationships with people.

In **Times of Discovery,** you will meet many unique characters and discover the special talents of real people. You will unlock mysteries of the past as you read your way through the secret passageways and hidden rooms of Egypt's pyramids. You will cheer for two courageous brothers as they struggle to invent and fly the first airplane. Speaking of flying, you will learn what it takes to become an astronaut and explore space.

So, get ready to read about times of discovery in the past, the present, and the future!

Sincerely,

The Authors

The Authors

THEME
PERSONAL BEST

CONTENTS

Using Reading Strategies 16
Theme Opener 18
Reader's Choice 20

The Best School Year Ever 22
Realistic Fiction/Social Studies
written by Barbara Robinson
illustrated by Tom Newson
Author Feature

FOCUS SKILL:
Prefixes, Suffixes, and Roots 38

The View from Saturday 40
Realistic Fiction/Social Studies
written by E. L. Konigsburg
illustrated by Marc Burckhardt
Author Feature

FOCUS SKILL:
Vocabulary in Context 58

Knots in My Yo-yo String 60
Autobiography/Physical Education
written by Jerry Spinelli
illustrated by Gary Davis
and Kathy Lengyel
Author Feature

From the Autograph Album.......72
　Poetry/Physical Education
　Anonymous
　Good Sportsmanship
　written by Richard Armour
　illustrated by Mike Gardner

The Marble Champ....................76
　Short Story/Physical Education
　written by Gary Soto
　illustrated by David Diaz
　Author and Illustrator Features

So Long, Michael......................90
　Magazine Article/Physical Education
　from *Sports Illustrated for Kids*

Darnell Rock Reporting.............94
　Realistic Fiction/Social Studies
　written by Walter Dean Myers
　illustrated by James Ransome
　Author and Illustrator Features

**Saving the Day
(and the Lake)**........................110
　Electronic Text/Science
　from *Tomorrow's Morning*

Theme Wrap-Up........................114

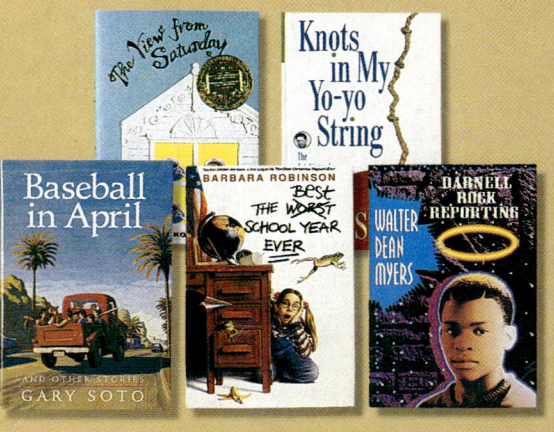

THEME

FRIENDS
TO THE
RESCUE

CONTENTS

Theme Opener......................116

Reader's Choice 118

Number the Stars...............120
Historical Fiction/Social Studies
written by Lois Lowry
illustrated by Russ Wilson
Author Feature

FOCUS SKILL:
Sequence/Cause and Effect............144

The Summer of the Swans.......146
Realistic Fiction/Social Studies
written by Betsy Byars
illustrated by Lori Lohstoeter
Author Feature

Old Yeller........................166
Realistic Fiction/Social Studies
written by Fred Gipson
illustrated by David Moreno
Author and Illustrator Features

FOCUS SKILL:
Author's Purpose and Perspective......................182

Saving Shiloh....................184
Realistic Fiction/Social Studies
written by Phyllis Reynolds Naylor
illustrated by Murray Kimber
Author Feature

Puppies with a Purpose...........204
Magazine Article/Social Studies
from *National Geographic World*

Flood: Wrestling with the Mississippi..................208
Nonfiction/Science
written by Patricia Lauber
Author Feature

Smoke Jumpers....................224
Magazine Article
from *National Geographic World*

Theme Wrap-Up 230

THEME
UNLOCKING THE PAST

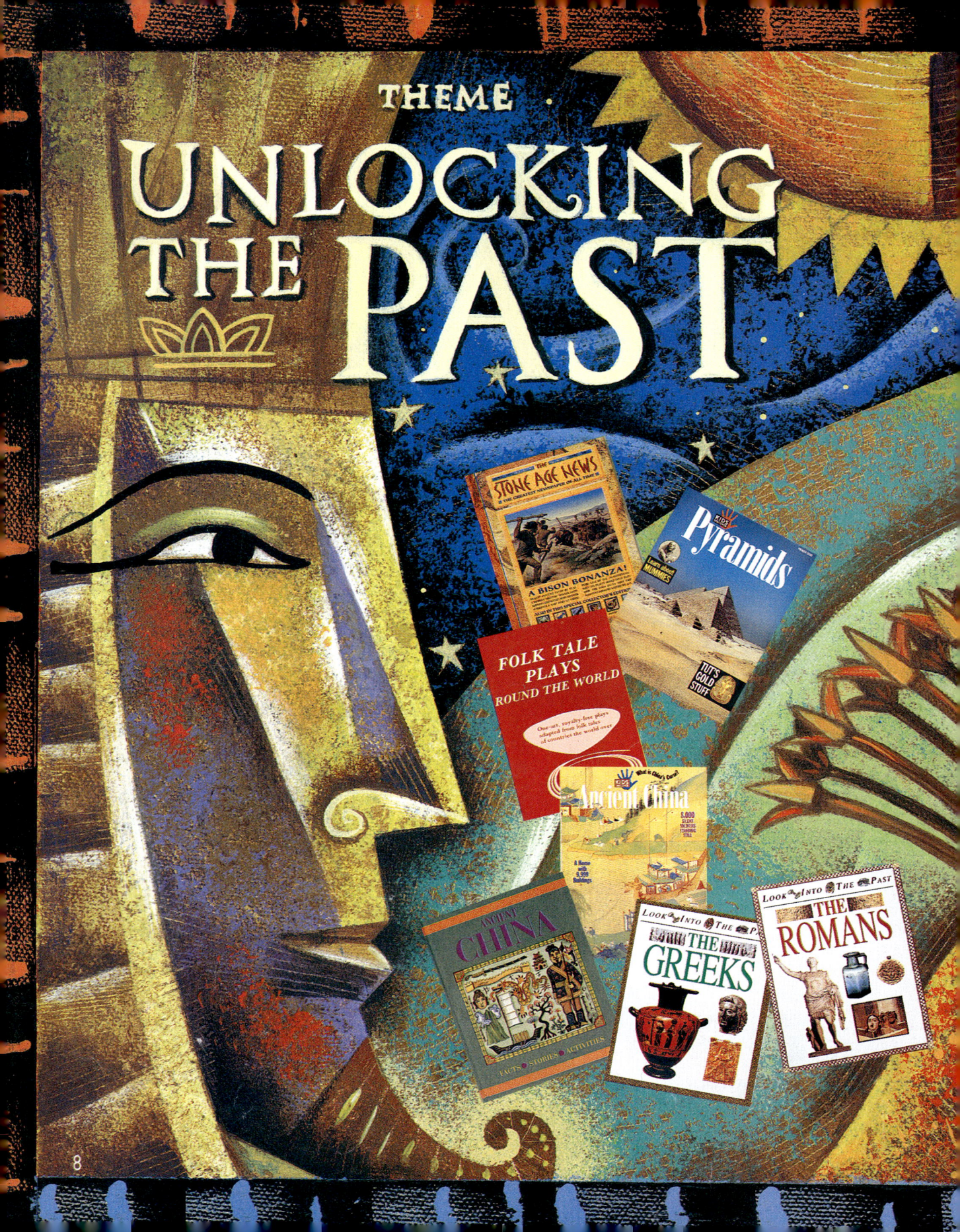

CONTENTS

Theme Opener..........................232

Reader's Choice......................234

The Stone Age News...........236
    Informational Text/Social Studies
    written by Fiona Macdonald
    Author Feature

FOCUS SKILL:
Fact and Opinion....................254

Ancient China.......................256
    Nonfiction/Social Studies
    written by Robert Nicholson
    and Claire Watts

The Chinese Dynasties.........270
    Time Line and Graph/Social Studies
    from *Kids Discover*

Pyramids..............................274
    Magazine Article/Social Studies
    from *Kids Discover*

FOCUS SKILL:
Graphic Sources....................292

**Look Into the Past:
The Greeks and
the Romans**...........................294
    Nonfiction/Social Studies
    written by A. Susan Williams
    and Peter Hicks

The Skill of Pericles.............314
    Play/Social Studies
    written by Paul T. Nolan
    illustrated by David Scott Meier
    Illustrator Feature

A Song of Greatness..............328
    Song/Music
    transcribed by Mary Austin
    illustrated by Bernie Fuchs

Theme Wrap-Up.....................332

Theme

Creative Solutions

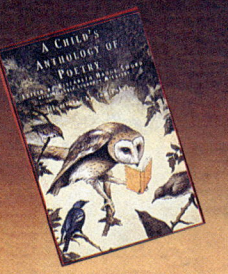

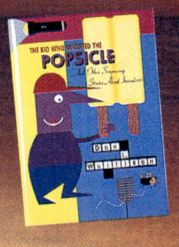

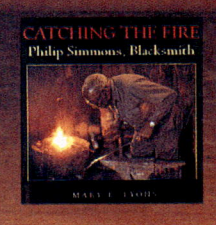

CONTENTS

Theme Opener......................334

Reader's Choice....................336

**My Side of the
Mountain**...........................338
- **Realistic Fiction/Science**
- written by Jean Craighead George
- illustrated by Allen Garns
- Author Feature

FOCUS SKILL:
Predict Outcomes...................352

Febold Feboldson..............354
- **Tall Tale/Social Studies**
- retold by Mary Pope Osborne
- illustrated by Michael McCurdy
- Author Feature

Dividing the Horses............364
- **Folktale/Math**
- retold by George Shannon
- illustrated by Peter Sís

Aesop's Fables....................366
- **Fables/Social Studies/Science**
- retold by Margaret Clark
- illustrated by Charlotte Voake

**The Kid Who Invented
the Popsicle**......................370
- **Nonfiction/Social Studies**
- written by Don L. Wulffson
- illustrated by Chris Wood
- Author Feature

FOCUS SKILL:
Draw Conclusions..................386

A Do-It-Yourself Project......388
- **Realistic Fiction/Science**
- written by Anilú Bernardo
- illustrated by Karen Blessen
- Author Feature

Some Like It Wet................404
- **Magazine Article/Science**
- from *Contact Kids*

**Catching the Fire:
Philip Simmons,
Blacksmith**........................408
- **Biography/Social Studies**
- written by Mary E. Lyons
- Author Feature

The Road Not Taken..........422
- **Poem**
- written by Robert Frost

Theme Wrap-Up...................426

11

THEME
MAKING A

DIFFERENCE

CONTENTS

Theme Opener.........................428
Reader's Choice......................430

Seventh Grade....................432
Realistic Fiction/Social Studies
written by Gary Soto
illustrated by Stephanie Garcia
Author and Illustrator Features

FOCUS SKILL:
**Narrative Elements:
Plot, Character, Setting**............448

Fall Secrets......................450
Realistic Fiction/Performing Arts
written by Candy Dawson Boyd
illustrated by Floyd Cooper
Author and Illustrator Features

Kids Did It!......................464
Magazine Article/Social Studies
from *National Geographic World*

**Out of Darkness:
The Story of Louis Braille**.....468
Biography/Social Studies
written by Russell Freedman
illustrated by Glenn Harrington
Author and Illustrator Features

FOCUS SKILL:
Make Generalizations..............482

Anne of Green Gables..........484
Play/Social Studies
written by Lucy Maud Montgomery
adapted by Jamie Turner
illustrated by Mitchell Heinze
Author Feature

Tea Biscuits......................504
Recipe/Math
written by Carolyn Strom Collins
and Christina Wyss Erikksson

**Cowboys: Roundup
on an American Ranch**........508
Nonfiction/Social Studies
written by Joan Anderson
photographs by George Ancona
Author and Photographer Features

Home on the Range.............522
Song/Music
Traditional Cowboy Song

Theme Wrap-Up...................526

13

THEME

EXPANDING WORLDS

In The Next Three Seconds...

Four Ancestors

I Want to Be... An Astronaut

The Wright Brothers: How They Invented the Airplane

Voyager

CONTENTS

Theme Opener..................528

Reader's Choice 530

The Wright Brothers: How They Invented the Airplane..............532
Biography/Social Studies
written by Russell Freedman
Author Feature

FOCUS SKILL:
Main Idea and Supporting Details 548

I Want to Be an Astronaut 550
Nonfiction/Science
written by Stephanie Maze and Catherine O'Neill Grace

FOCUS SKILL:
Summarize/Paraphrase 564

Voyager: An Adventure to the Edge of the Solar System 566
Nonfiction/Science
written by Sally Ride and Tam O'Shaughnessy
Author Feature

The Three Hunters and the Great Bear 584
Myth/Science
retold by Joseph Bruchac
illustrated by S. S. Burrus

CyberSurfer..................590
Nonfiction/Social Studies
written by Nyla Ahmad
illustrated by Martha Newbigging
Author Feature

In the Next Three Seconds..606
Nonfiction/Social Studies
compiled by Rowland Morgan
illustrated by Rod and Kira Josey

The Fun They Had 612
Science Fiction/Science
written by Isaac Asimov
illustrated by A. J. Garces
Author Feature

To Dark Eyes Dreaming.......622
Poem
written by Zilpha Keatley Snyder
illustrated by Jui Ishida

Theme Wrap-Up 626

Glossary 628

Index of Titles and Authors 638

Using Reading Strategies

A strategy is a plan for doing something well.

You probably already use some strategies as you read. For example, you may **look at the title and illustrations before you begin reading** a story. You may **think about what you want to find out while reading.** Using strategies like these can help you become a better reader.

Look at the list of strategies on page 17. You will learn about and use these strategies as you read the selections in this book. As you read, look back at the list to remind yourself of the **strategies good readers use.**

Strategies Good Readers Use

- Use Prior Knowledge
- Make and Confirm Predictions
- Adjust Reading Rate
- Self-Question
- Create Mental Images
- Use Context to Confirm Meaning
- Use Text Structure and Format
- Use Graphic Aids
- Use Reference Sources
- Read Ahead
- Reread
- Summarize and Paraphrase

Here are some ways to check your own comprehension:

✔ Make a copy of this list on a piece of construction paper shaped like a bookmark.

✔ Have it handy as you read.

✔ After reading, talk with a classmate about which strategies you used and why.

THEME
PERSONAL BEST

CONTENTS

The Best School Year Ever 22
by Barbara Robinson

FOCUS SKILL:
Prefixes, Suffixes, and Roots 38

The View from Saturday 40
by E. L. Konigsburg

FOCUS SKILL:
Vocabulary in Context 58

Knots in My Yo-yo String 60
by Jerry Spinelli

From the Autograph Album 72
Anonymous

Good Sportsmanship
by Richard Armour

The Marble Champ 76
by Gary Soto

So Long, Michael 90
from *Sports Illustrated for Kids*

Darnell Rock Reporting 94
by Walter Dean Myers

**Saving the Day
(and the Lake)** 110
from *Tomorrow's Morning*

18

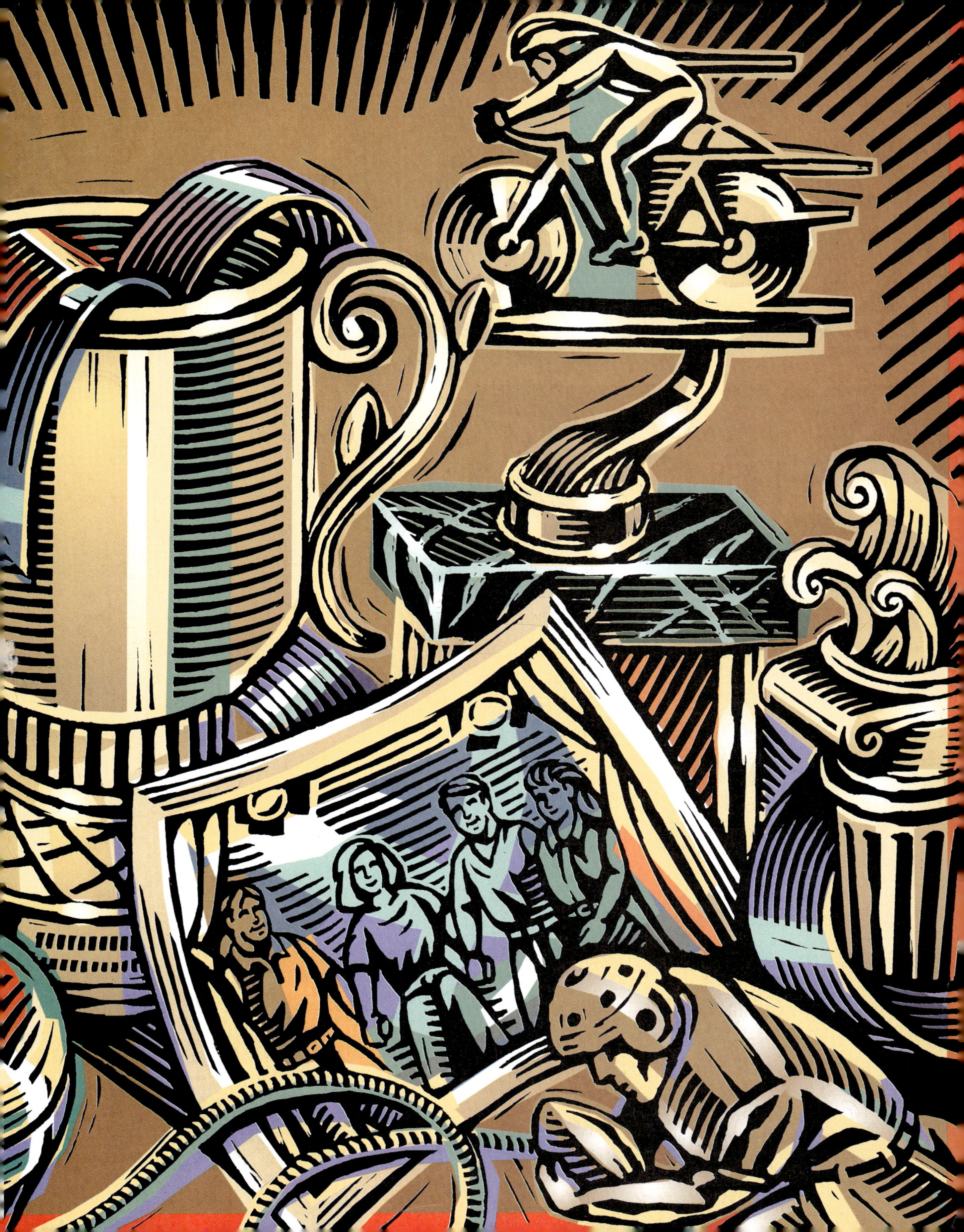

READER'S CHOICE

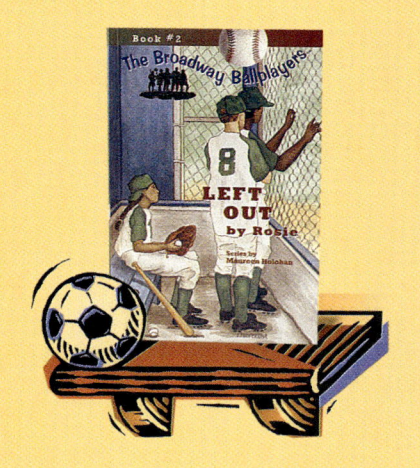

Left Out
by Maureen Holohan

REALISTIC FICTION

Eleven-year-old Rosie Jones is one of the best baseball players in the city. When she makes the all-star team, Rosie finds out the importance of the bonds of friendship and the support of family.

READER'S CHOICE LIBRARY

Wilma Rudolph
by Wayne Coffey

BIOGRAPHY

This is the story of a young woman from Tennessee who overcame crippling illnesses and other problems to become the fastest female athlete in the world.

READER'S CHOICE LIBRARY

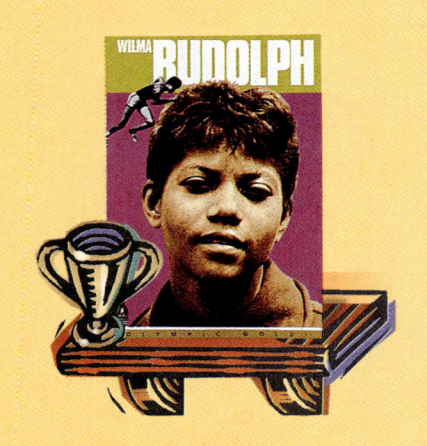

Mariah Loves Rock

by Mildred Pitts Walter

REALISTIC FICTION

Mariah is happy with her life. She does well in school and is a big fan of rock star Sheik Bashara. She is worried, though, that the arrival of her stepsister will change her life forever.

Small Steps

by Peg Kehret

AUTOBIOGRAPHY

This is the touching autobiography of a young girl's struggle with polio. Through courage and perseverance, she is able to overcome her illness.

ALA NOTABLE BOOK

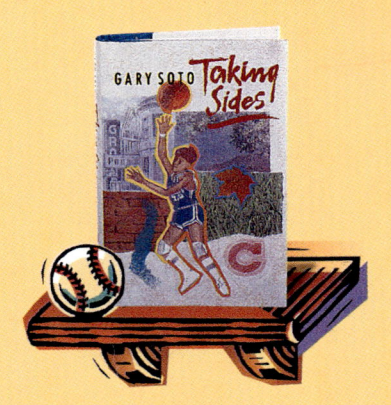

Taking Sides

by Gary Soto

REALISTIC FICTION

Lincoln Mendoza is struggling to fit in at his new school. He finds his loyalties divided, though, when he plays in a basketball game against his former teammates.

22

The Best School Year Ever

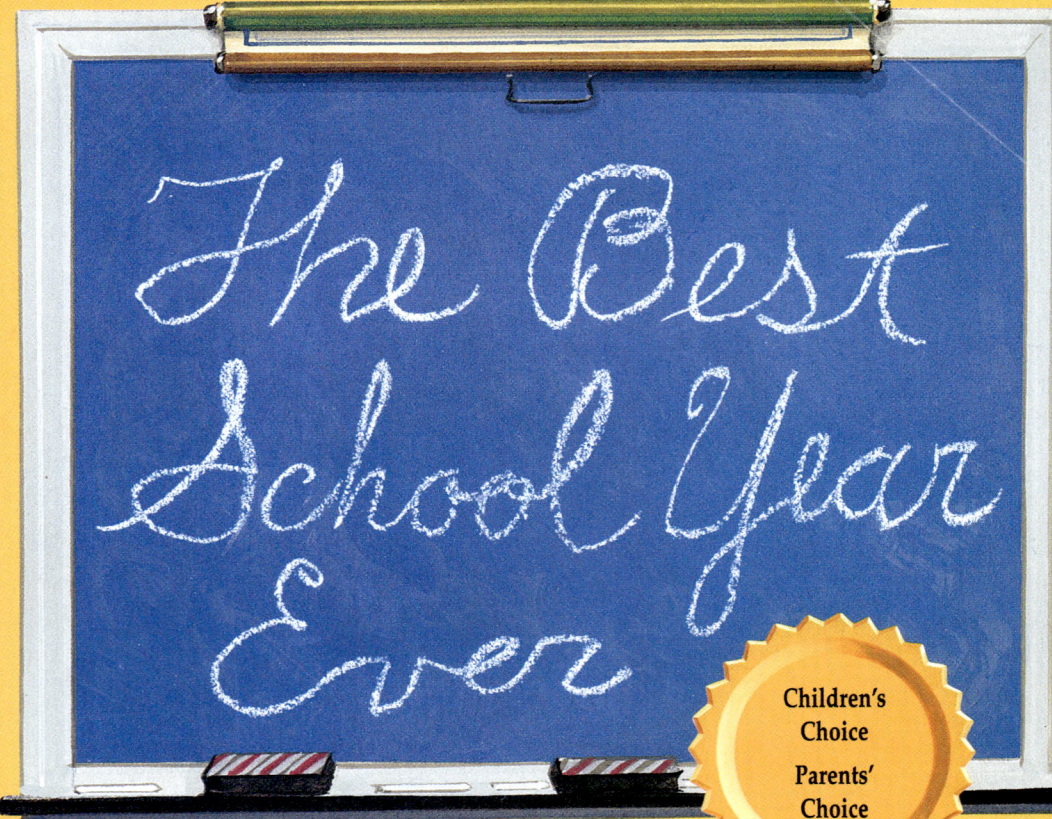

by Barbara Robinson
illustrated by Tom Newson

All the students in Miss Kemp's sixth-grade class have had the same assignment all year long: to think of at least one compliment for each of their fellow classmates. Now, on the last day of school, they must each draw a name and shower that person with compliments. Unfortunately, Beth draws the name Imogene Herdman, a member of the rowdiest family of kids in town. How can Beth find anything positive to say about Imogene?

This year there was no big surprise about what we would do on the last day. It was up on the blackboard—Compliments for Classmates—and we had each drawn a name from a hat and had to think of more compliments for that one person.

"We've been thinking about this all year," Miss Kemp said. She probably knew that some kids had but most kids hadn't—but now everybody would think about it in a hurry. "And on the last day of school," she went on, "we're going to find out what we've learned about ourselves and each other."

courage

I had finally thought of a word for Albert. Once you get past thinking *fat* you can see that Albert's special quality is optimism, because Albert actually believes he will be thin someday, and says so. Another word could be *determination,* or even *courage.* There were lots of good words for Albert, so I really hoped I would draw his name.

I didn't. The name I drew was Imogene Herdman, and I had used up the one and only compliment I finally thought of for Imogene—*patriotic.*

"Patriotic?" my mother said. "What makes you think Imogene is especially patriotic?"

"When we do the Pledge of Allegiance," I said, "she always stands up."

"Everybody stands up," Charlie said. "If everybody sat down and *only* Imogene stood up, that would be patriotic."

"That would be brave," I said.

"Well, she would do that," Charlie said. "I mean, she would do whatever everybody else didn't do."

Would that make Imogene brave? I didn't really think so, but I had to have some more compliments, so I wrote it down—*patriotic, brave.*

Two days later I still had just *patriotic* and *brave* while other people had big long lists. I saw the bottom of Joanne Turner's list, sticking out of her notebook: "Cheerful, good sport, graceful, fair to everybody." I wondered who *that* was.

Maxine Cooper asked me how to spell *cooperative* and *enthusiastic,* so obviously she had a terrific list. Boomer must have drawn a boy's name, because all his compliments came right out of the Boy Scout Rules—*thrifty, clean, loyal.*

cheerful
good sport
graceful
fair to everybody

I kept my eye on Imogene as much as possible so if she did something good I wouldn't miss it, but it was so hard to tell, with her, what was good.

I thought it was good that she got Boyd Liggett's head out of the bike rack, but Mrs. Liggett didn't think so.

Mrs. Liggett said it was all the Herdmans' fault in the first place. "Ollie Herdman told Boyd to do it," she said, "and then that Gladys got him so scared and nervous that he couldn't get out, and then along came Imogene . . ."

I could understand how Boyd got his head *into* the bike rack—he's only in the first grade, plus he has a skinny head—but at first I didn't know why he couldn't get it *out*.

Then I saw why. It was his ears. Boyd's ears stuck right straight out from his head like handles, so his head and his ears were on one side of the bike rack and the rest of him was on the other side, and kids were hollering at him and telling him what to do. "Turn your head upside down!" somebody said, and somebody else told him to squint his eyes and squeeze his face together.

Boyd's sister Jolene tried to fold his ears and push them through but that didn't work, even one at a time. Then she wanted half of us to get in front of him and push and the other half to get in back and pull. "He got his head through there," she said. "There must be some way to get it back out."

I didn't think pushing and pulling was the way but Boyd looked ready to try anything.

Then Gladys Herdman really cheered him up. "Going to have to cut off your ears, Boyd," she said. "But maybe just one ear. Do you have a favorite one? That you like to hear out of?"

You could tell that he believed her. If you're in the first grade with your head stuck through the bike rack, this is the very thing you think will happen.

Several teachers heard Boyd yelling, "Don't cut my ears off!" and they went to tell Mr. Crabtree. Mr. Crabtree called

26

27

the fire department, and while he was doing that the kindergarten teacher stuck her head out the window and called to Boyd, "Don't you worry, they're coming to cut you loose."

But she didn't say who, or how, and Gladys told him they would probably leave a little bit of ear in case he ever had to wear glasses, so Boyd was a total wreck when Imogene came along.

She wanted to know how he got in there—in case she ever wanted to shove somebody else in the bike rack, probably—but Boyd was too hysterical to tell her, and nobody else knew for sure, so I guess she decided to get him loose first and find out later.

Imogene Scotch-taped his ears down and buttered his whole head with soft margarine from the lunchroom, and then she just pushed on his head—first one side and then the other—and it slid through.

Of course Boyd was a mess, with butter all over his eyes and ears and up his nose, so Jolene had to take him home. She made him walk way away from her and she told him, "As soon as you see Mother, you yell, 'I'm all right. I'm all right.'" She looked at him again. "You better tell her who you are, too."

Even so, Mrs. Liggett took one look and screamed and would have fainted, Jolene said, except she heard Boyd telling her that he was all right.

"What do you think of that?" Mother asked my father that night. "She buttered his head!"

"I think it was resourceful," my father said. "Messy, but resourceful."

"That's like a compliment, isn't it?" I asked my father. "It's good to be resourceful?"

"Certainly," he said. So I wrote that down, along with *patriotic* and *brave.*

I thought we would just hand in our compliment papers on the last day of school, but Alice thought Miss Kemp would read three or four out loud—"Some of the best ones," Alice said, meaning, of course, her own—and Boomer thought she would read the different compliments and we would have to guess the person. So when Miss Kemp said, "Now we're going to share these papers," it was no big surprise.

28

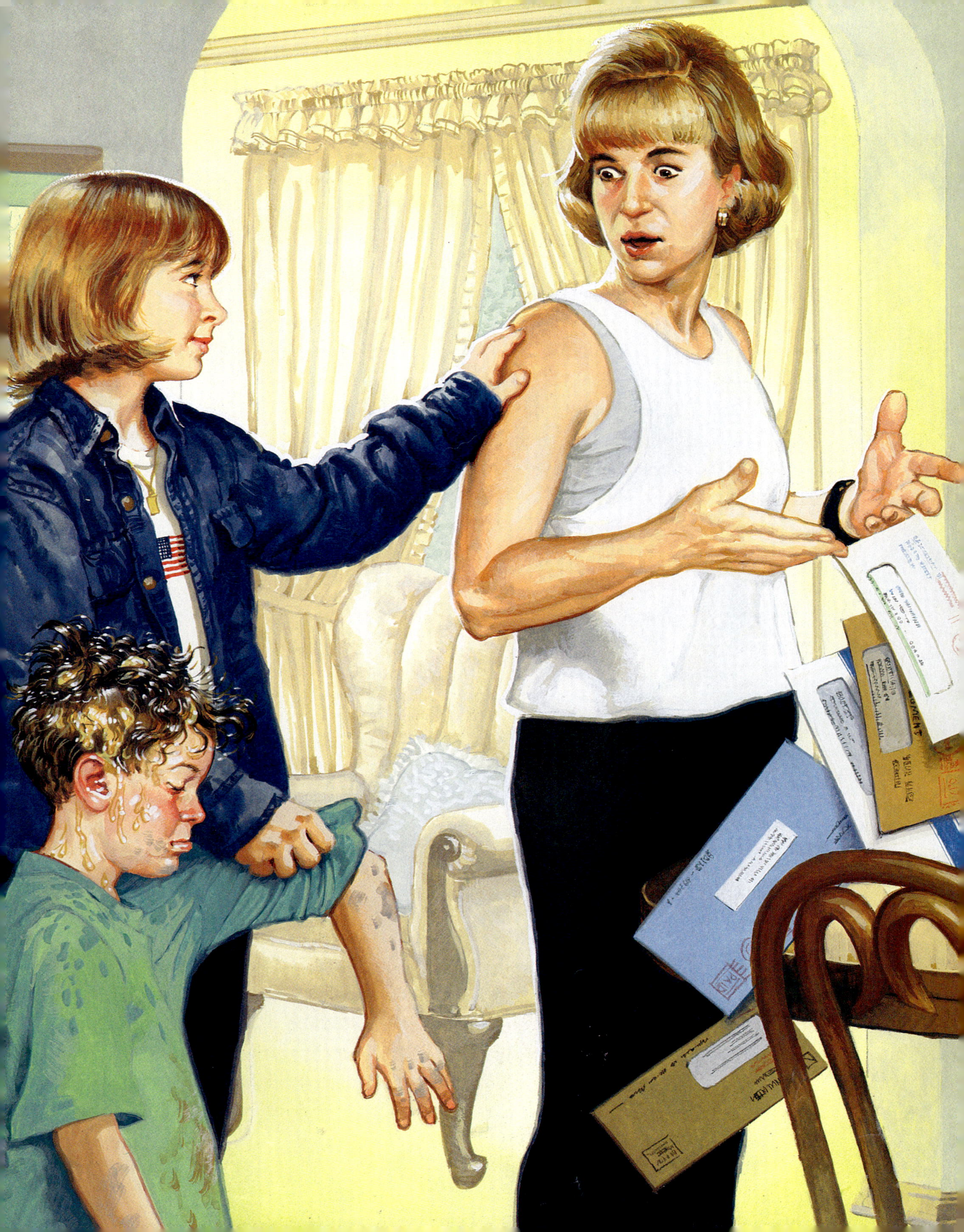

But then she said, "I think we'll start with Boomer. LaVerne Morgan drew your name, Boomer. I want you to sit down in front of LaVerne and listen to what she says about you."

LaVerne squealed and Boomer turned two or three different shades of red and all over the room kids began to check their papers in case they would have to read out loud some big lie or, worse, some really personal compliment.

LaVerne said that Boomer was smart and good at sports—but not stuck up about it—and friendly, and two or three other normal things. "And I liked when you took the gerbil back to the kindergarten that time," she said, "in case they wanted to bury it. That was nice."

It *was* nice, I thought, and not everybody would have done it, either. To begin with, not everybody would have *picked up* the gerbil by what was left of its tail, let alone carry it all the way down the hall and down the stairs to the kindergarten room.

"Good, Boomer," I said when he came back to his seat—glad to get there, I guess, because he was all sweaty with embarrassment from being told nice things about himself face to face and in front of everybody.

Next came Eloise Albright and then Louella and then Junior Jacobs and then Miss Kemp said, "Let's hear about you, Beth. Joanne Turner drew your name."

I remembered Joanne Turner's paper—"Cheerful, good sport, graceful, fair to everybody." I had wondered who that was.

It was me.

"I know we weren't supposed to say things about how you look," Joanne said, "but I put down graceful anyway because I always notice how you stand up very straight and walk like some kind of dancer. I don't know if you can keep it up, but if you can I think people will always admire the way you stand and walk."

It was really hard, walking back to my seat now that I was famous for it—but I knew if I did it now, with everybody watching, I *could* probably keep it up for the rest of my life and, if Joanne was right, be admired forever. This made me feel strange and loose and light, like when you press your hands hard against the sides of a door, and

30

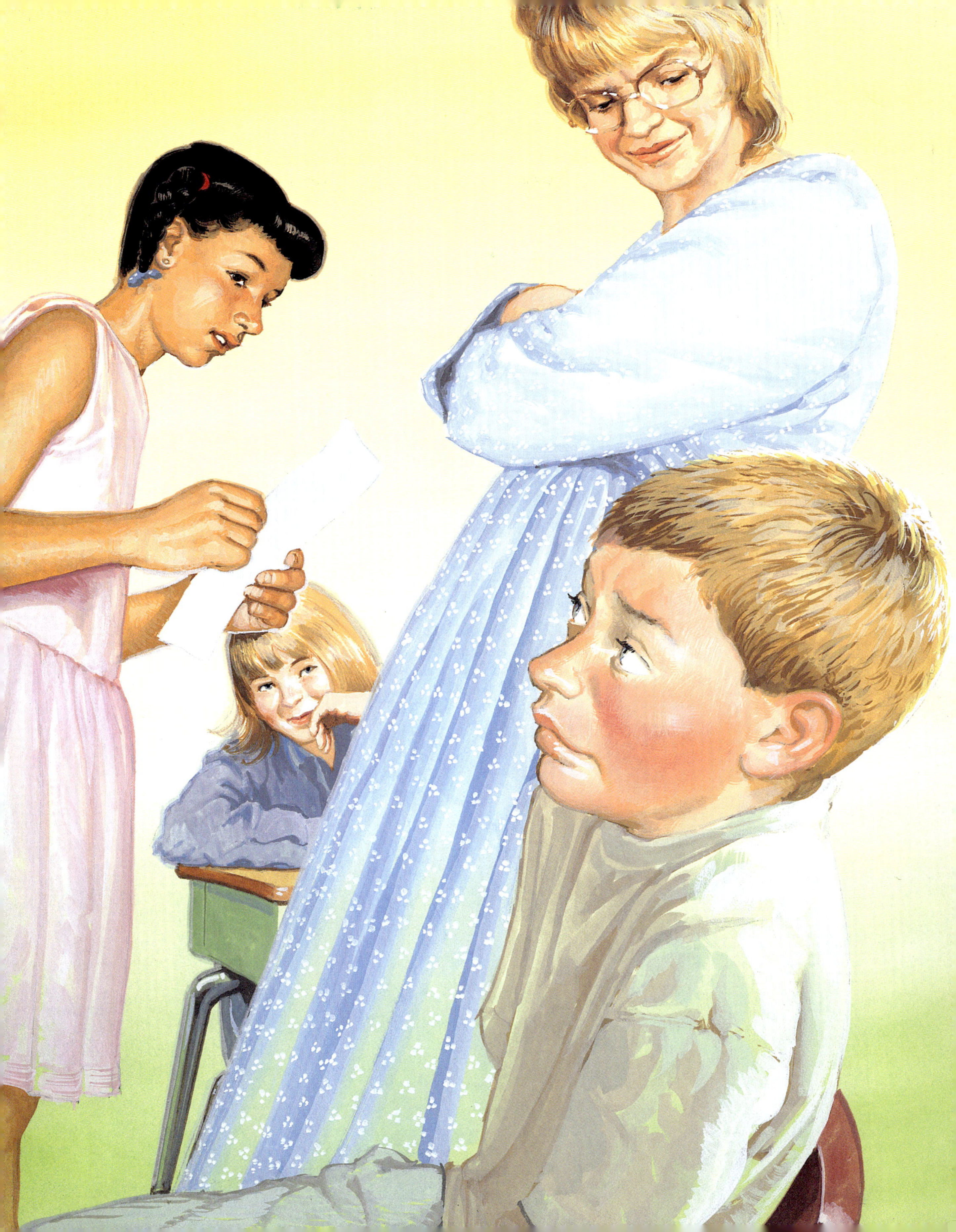

when you walk away your hands float up in the air all by themselves.

I was still feeling that way three people later when Miss Kemp said it was Imogene's turn.

"To do what?" Imogene said.

"To hear what Beth has to say about you. She drew your name."

Imogene gave me this dark, suspicious look. "No, I don't want to."

"You're going to hear *good* things, you know, Imogene," Miss Kemp said, but you could tell Miss Kemp wasn't too sure about that, and Imogene probably never *heard* any good things about herself, so she wasn't too sure, either.

"That's okay," I said. "I mean, if Imogene doesn't want to, I don't care."

This didn't work. I guess Miss Kemp was curious like everybody else. "Imogene Herdman!" Louella had just whispered. "That's whose name you drew? How could you think of compliments for Imogene Herdman?"

"Well, you had to think of *one*," I said. "We had to think of one compliment for everybody."

Louella rolled her eyes. "I said she was healthy. I didn't know anything else to say."

Louella wasn't the only one who wanted to hear my Imogene words. The whole room got very quiet and I was glad, now, that at the last minute I had looked up *resourceful* in the dictionary.

"I put down that you're patriotic," I told Imogene, "and brave and resourceful . . . and cunning and shrewd and creative, and enterprising and sharp and inventive . . ."

"Wait!" she yelled. "Wait a minute! Start over!"

"Oh, honestly!" Alice put in. "You just copied that out of the dictionary! They're all the same thing!"

"And," I went on, ignoring Alice, "I think it was good that you got Boyd's head out of the bike rack."

"Oh, honestly!" Alice said again, but Miss Kemp shut her up.

Of course she didn't say, "Shut up, Alice"—she just said that no one could really comment on what anybody else said because it was very personal and individual. "That's how Beth sees Imogene," she said.

Actually, it wasn't. Alice was right about the words. I did copy them out of the dictionary so I wouldn't be the only person with three dumb compliments, and I didn't exactly connect them with Imogene, except *sharp* because of her knees and elbows which she used like weapons to leave you black and blue.

But now, suddenly, they all turned out to fit. Imogene *was* cunning and shrewd. She *was* inventive. Nobody else thought of buttering Boyd's head or washing their cat at the Laundromat. She was creative, if you count drawing pictures on Howard . . . and enterprising, if you count charging money to look at him. She was also powerful enough to keep everybody away from the teachers' room forever, and human enough to give Howard her blanket.

Imogene *was* all the things I said she was, and more, and they were good things to be—depending on who it was doing the inventing or the creating or the enterprising. If Imogene could keep it up, I thought, till she got to be civilized, if that ever happened, she could be almost anything she wanted to be in life.

She could be Imogene Herdman, President . . . or, of course, Imogene Herdman, Jailbird. It would be up to her.

33

At the end of the day Miss Kemp said, "Which was harder—to give compliments or to receive them?" and everyone agreed that it was really uncomfortable to have somebody tell you, in public, about the best hidden parts of you. Alice, however, made this long, big-word speech about how it was harder for her to *give* compliments because she wanted to be very accurate and truthful, "and not make things up," she said, looking at me.

Resourceful

"I didn't make things up," I told her later, "except, maybe, brave. I don't know whether Imogene is brave."

"You made her sound like some wonderful person," Alice said, "and if that's not making things up, what is?"

When the bell rang everybody whooped out to get started on summer, but Imogene grabbed me in the hall, shoved a Magic Marker in my face, and told me to write the words on her arm.

"On your arm?" I said.

"That's where I keep notes," she said, and I could believe it because I could still see the remains of several messages—something pizza . . . big rat . . . get Gladys . . .

Get Gladys something? I wondered. No, probably just get Gladys.

There was only room for one word on her skinny arm, so Imogene picked *resourceful*. "It's the best one," she said. "I looked it up and I like it. It's way better than graceful, no offense." She turned her arm around, admiring the word. "I like it a lot."

Think About It

1. What does Beth learn about giving and receiving compliments?

2. Would you like to hear compliments about yourself in front of your class? Why or why not?

3. How does the author use humor to tell the story?

34

MEET THE AUTHOR

Barbara Robinson

Barbara Robinson introduced readers to the rowdy Herdman kids in her book *The Best Christmas Pageant Ever*. This popular novel was later made into a TV special and a play.

What if your teacher told you to think of compliments for Barbara Robinson? You might come up with these:

- ✓ **hardworking**—She has written many books and short stories for young readers.
- ✓ **funny**—Her books make people laugh.
- ✓ **interested in kids**—She often visits schools to meet with young readers like you.

Now let's think of compliments for *The Best School Year Ever*:

- ✓ **zany**—The characters get themselves into outrageous situations.
- ✓ **original**—The Herdman kids are unusual and interesting characters.
- ✓ **realistic**—Beth's feelings about school and her relationships with her classmates are similar to those of real students.

Visit *The Learning Site!*
www.harcourtschool.com

Response

Compliments Galore

MAKE A LIST Skim the story to find at least six compliments that Beth and her classmates collect. Use a synonym finder or a thesaurus to find one or more synonyms for each compliment. Share your list with the class. Discuss the fact that synonyms have meanings beyond the dictionary meaning.

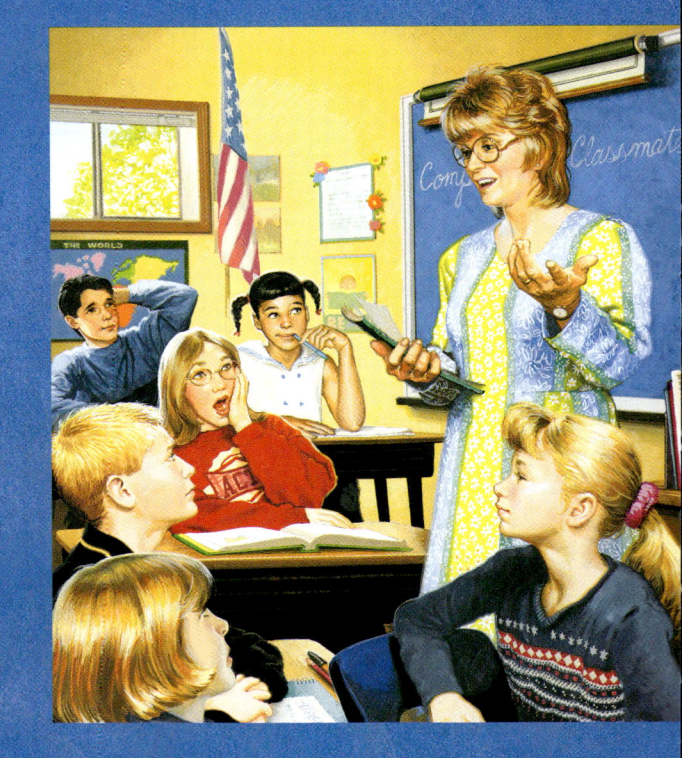

The Next Adventure

DRAW A PICTURE Imagine that you are friends with a character in the story. Draw a picture of something you did with him or her that illustrates one of your good qualities. Write a brief caption, and display your picture in the classroom.

Activities

After-School Enterprises

WRITE A PARAGRAPH
Beth calls Imogene *enterprising* because she charges classmates money to look at drawings on Howard's head. Think of a different way someone your age can be enterprising, and write a paragraph about your enterprising idea.

Solving Tricky Problems

MAKE PROBLEM-SOLUTION CHARTS
Imogene finds an interesting solution to Boyd's problem. Write three new problems for Imogene or another character to solve. Exchange papers with a partner, and write your own solutions to the problems.

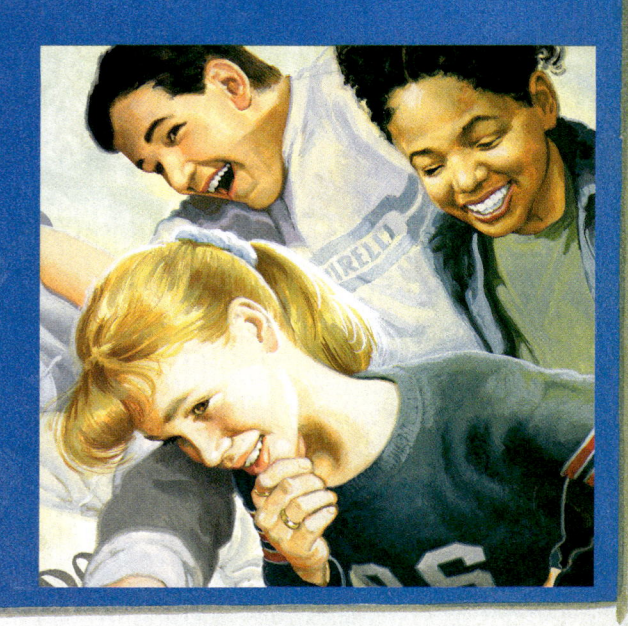

FOCUS SKILL: Prefixes, Suffixes, and Roots

The story words on the board are some of the words students in "The Best School Year Ever" use to compliment their classmates. Each one ends with a word part called a **suffix**. Notice that the suffixes have changed the base words from nouns into adjectives.

Base Word	Story Word	Meaning of Story Word	Meaning of Suffix
cheer	cheerful	"full of cheer"	"full of"
thrift	thrifty	"having the quality of thrift"	"having the quality of"
friend	friendly	"like a friend"	"like"

A **prefix** is a word part added to the beginning of a word that changes its meaning. What does each of these words mean with the prefix added?

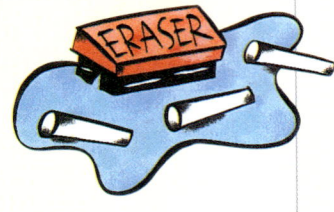

unfriendly   defrost   disloyal   foreground   preview

In the story, Beth looked up the meaning of a word in a dictionary. The word *dictionary* is itself made up of parts. The first part, *dict-*, is called a root. A **root** is the basic part of any word that gives it its meaning. English word roots often come from other languages; for example, Greek and Latin. In this case, *dict-* is a Latin root that means "speak." How does this root's meaning help you understand the meaning of the word *dictionary*?

Some words have more than one prefix and more than one suffix. If you know the meanings of prefixes, suffixes, and roots, you have the key to the meanings of many words. Understanding their meanings will help you become a better reader. The chart below may help you unlock the meanings of some words.

Read the paragraph below. Identify the prefixes, suffixes, and roots in the underlined words. Then tell what the words mean.

Prefixes and Meanings		Roots and Meanings		Suffixes and Meanings	
de-	"down"	act	"do"	-or	"one who"
super-	"over"	port	"carry"	-en	"make"
mid-	"middle"	vid, vis	"see"	-ful	"full of"

Molly <u>used</u> the remote control to <u>sharpen</u> the <u>video</u> picture. She was watching one of her favorite movies. She enjoyed the <u>powerful</u> performance by the <u>actor</u> playing the <u>supervisor</u>. She hoped her friend Jenny could come over at <u>midday</u> to watch this movie with her.

WHAT HAVE YOU LEARNED?

1. What other words with suffixes can you find in the selection? What do the suffixes mean?

2. Read this sentence: *The doctor used a tongue depressor when she examined my throat.* Use the prefix, suffix, and root to explain the meaning of the underlined word.

TRY THIS • TRY THIS • TRY THIS

Make a personal book of prefixes, suffixes, and roots. On separate pages, list as many words as you can using each prefix, suffix, and root listed on the chart above. Then write five words that have both prefixes and suffixes.

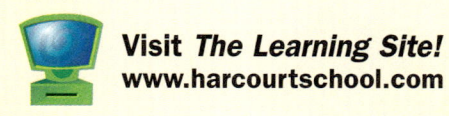

Visit *The Learning Site!*
www.harcourtschool.com

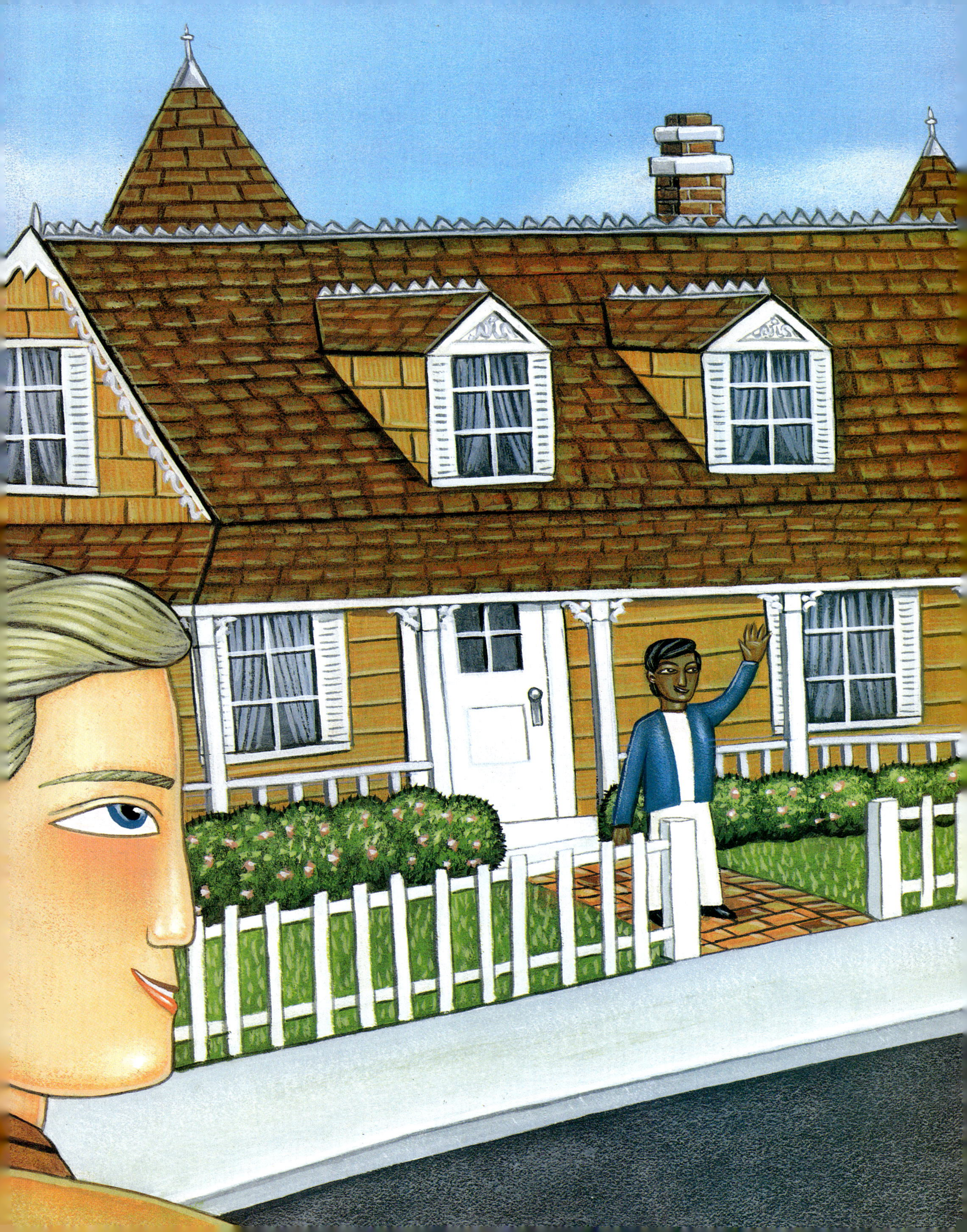

The View from Saturday

by E. L. Konigsburg
illustrated by Marc Burckhardt

Newbery Medal
ALA Notable Book
***SLJ* Best Book**

*E*than, a sixth grader in Epiphany, New York, has homeroom with three bright kids named Noah, Nadia, and Julian. Julian has just moved to Epiphany. His father has bought a historic landmark building, the Sillington house, and he plans to turn it into a bed-and-breakfast inn. Ethan doesn't know Noah, Nadia, and Julian very well. Then Julian invites them all to a party at the Sillington house in a very unusual way.

The time of year had come when the after-school hours were growing shorter and shorter, and I had pumpkins to attend to. Every Saturday morning from June until mid-November, I went with Mother to the Farmers' Market and helped her sell her fresh produce and free range eggs. In September and October we sold a lot of pumpkins. Mother paid me, and I saved almost all of it.

I was the son who was scheduled to inherit the farm because Luke was scheduled for greater things. I knew that as soon as I announced to my family what I wanted to do, I would have to be prepared to pay my own way.

There was no one in Epiphany to whom I could tell my plans. No one in Epiphany would believe that Ethan Potter wanted to go to New York City to work in the theater. I didn't want to be an actor. I wanted to design costumes or stage sets, but I could not tell anyone. In mental mileage, Epiphany, New York, is farther from New York City, New York, than the road mileage from New York to Hollywood.

Last summer Nadia Diamondstein's father took us to see *The Phantom of the Opera*. I had seen high school plays and plays that Clarion U. had put on, but I had never seen something like that. When that chandelier came down from the ceiling, my throat went dry. No one I knew was sitting by me, and I squeezed the arms of my chair to keep myself from getting up to cheer. I had seen football fans act the way I felt. I dream about that show. I bought a souvenir booklet that cost ten dollars, and I had looked at it so often that I was wearing the gloss off its pages. Someday I'm going to design costumes for a show like that.

But first I had to harvest pumpkins.

On the third Saturday after school began, Julian and his father appeared at market. I saw them first from a distance. They did not stand out in that crowd because the Clarion County Farmers' Market attracts a lot of people from the college, and the college in turn attracts a lot of dark-skinned people. Julian's father was carrying a basket over his arm. A lot of the college people and suburbanites believe it is the ecological thing to do. I saw Julian pointing me out to his father before they made their way to our booth.

Julian introduced his father to both Mother and me.

43

Mr. Singh sang the praises of the quality of the goods at the market. (Everyone does. There is a rule that you cannot sell anything at the market that you do not grow or make yourself.) He said that as soon as his B and B opened for business, he would become a regular customer.

When they left, Mother asked about them. She had never before expressed a friendly interest in the fate of the Sillington house. I told her as much as I knew.

On the following Saturday, Julian and his father came to our booth again. Mr. Singh took forever to select four pumpkins from the $2.50 pile. They were not very big, but they were so similar in shape and size that they looked like clones. Julian handed me a ten-dollar bill. I hated that. I don't know why I hate taking money from someone my age even though it isn't charity. I took the money, which was folded in half, and said, "Thank you." A lot of the booth operators say, "Have a nice day." I never do. Mother never does either. Sometimes she'll say, "Enjoy," but never "Have a nice day." Except for Uncle Lew who was in politics, Potters are famous for not saying anything they don't mean.

I waited until Julian and his father were on the far side of the next booth before I unfolded the ten-dollar bill. A small Post-it note was attached inside the fold. I glanced at it, couldn't understand it, looked at it harder, and decided to pocket the money with the note instead of putting it in the cashbox. I'd make it up with Mother.

Business was brisk the entire morning, and that was good. It meant that there would be fewer pumpkins to reload. I didn't have a chance to give Julian's note a second glance or a second thought. Well, maybe I did give it a second thought but not a third and not for long.

At home I waited until I was alone in my room before taking the ten-dollar bill from my pocket. I peeled the Post-it from inside the fold.

Alice's Adventures in Wonderland
Chapter VII Title

I found the book on the shelf in the living room and carried it upstairs. I closed my bedroom door, sat on the edge of my bed, and turned the pages until I came to Chapter VII, the chapter called "A Mad Tea Party."

This was obviously an invitation. The strangest I had ever received. I not only had never been invited to a tea party before but had never before been invited to a party where I was not told the time and the place. Either the mystery would clear up, or it wouldn't. Either way, I wouldn't give it a second thought or discuss it with anyone.

Including Julian Singh.

Having established my habit of not speaking to Julian on the bus, it was easy to avoid talking about the message in the ten-dollar bill. And, to his credit, Julian gave no hint—no secret smiles or glances out of the corner of his eye—to indicate that he was waiting for a response. Instead, he boarded the bus, walked to the back, said "Good morning" just as he always did and said nothing for the rest of the way. And he did not wait for me at the foot of the bus steps.

I once again managed to be the last one off the bus. As I picked up my backpack, I found a Post-it note attached to the underside of the left shoulder strap. I pulled it off and read it.

Tea Time is always 4:00 P.M.
World Atlas
Map 4: D–16

I put it in my shirt pocket.

Our class would be in the school media center after lunch. We were allowed to browse for the first fifteen minutes. I found the atlas. Map 4 was New York State. D–16 of Map 4 was Clarion County. On the page facing Map 4 was a drawing of a house with a lacy wraparound porch. The address, 9424 Gramercy Road, was written beneath it. I took the drawing from the book and put it in my shirt pocket with the other two notes. I now knew the what, the where, and part of the when. I still didn't know the date.

As I returned to my study table, I passed Nadia Diamondstein among the stacks. She was in the fiction section, removing a book from the D's. *D for Dodgson*, Lewis Carroll's real name. I watched Nadia quickly leaf through the book she held in her hand, then go check it out. It was *Alice's Adventures in Wonderland*.

That evening as I was undressing, I removed the notes from my shirt pocket. Behind the Post-its and the small sketch of the Sillington House there was a fourth piece of paper: a small page from a pocket calendar. The month of October. The fourteenth was circled. Now I knew everything I needed to know except how Julian had slipped that into my pocket.

F or the first time since I started school—no, even longer than that—for the first time ever, I was looking forward to a party. And I knew that part of the reason I was looking forward to it was because Julian had not made it public. Whenever someone makes out a guest list, the people not on it become officially uninvited, and that makes them the enemies of the invited. Guest lists are just a way of choosing sides. The way Julian had done the inviting, I didn't know who else was coming—although I strongly suspected that Nadia Diamondstein would be, and that thought did not displease me.

I wondered if I should bring a gift. It was always better to bring something. I didn't know what. I suspected that sports equipment was out. Books: He probably had as many books as the library. Video game? Wrong. Clothes: NO! Then, when I was in the shower, a word dropped from the showerhead. *Puzzle.* That was it. That was exactly it. A puzzle would be the perfect present for Julian Singh. The video store at the mall had dozens of different puzzles that were not electronic. I had seen three-dimensional puzzles and jigsaw puzzles that had a different picture printed on either side.

I didn't want to tell anyone that I was going to a party. A *tea* party of all things. I hardly believed it myself. I needed a way to get to the mall, so on the Saturday of the party, I asked Mother to please drop me off at the mall on the way home from market. She asked why, as I knew she would,

PUZZLES

and I told her that I had to buy a present for a party I was going to later that afternoon. Mother was not pleased. She liked to get home right after market so that we could unload the truck and straighten out the accounts. She said all right—not gladly—and told me that she would wait in the truck while I made my purchase.

Why couldn't she come into the mall and browse like a normal woman? Why? Because she knew there was no better way to get me to hurry.

I hopped down from the truck and ran to the video game store. As luck would have it, no salesperson pounced on me the minute I entered. If I had been there to browse, not buy, they would have. Now, I had to practically beg for attention. High on top of the shelves stocked with closed cartons of games of every sort was a display of jigsaw puzzles. There were picture puzzles of waterfalls, 1,000 pieces. There was another one that was a painting of water lilies done in a very loose way. Still another had a picture of a waterfall on one side and a picture of a koala bear on the other. One was a totally white circle. That would be tough because there would be no pattern to help a person line up the pieces. I decided on that one. Two salesclerks were standing at one end of the counter talking. I walked toward them and had to say "Excuse me" twice. I pointed to the puzzle I wanted and said I would like it gift wrapped.

"That's number four-sixty-two. We're all out."

"Then why do you have it on display?"

"It's very popular. We're expecting another shipment next week."

"I need it today," I said. "It's all right with me if you sell me the sample."

"I can't."

"Why? I don't need a discount or anything just because it's the

GALORE

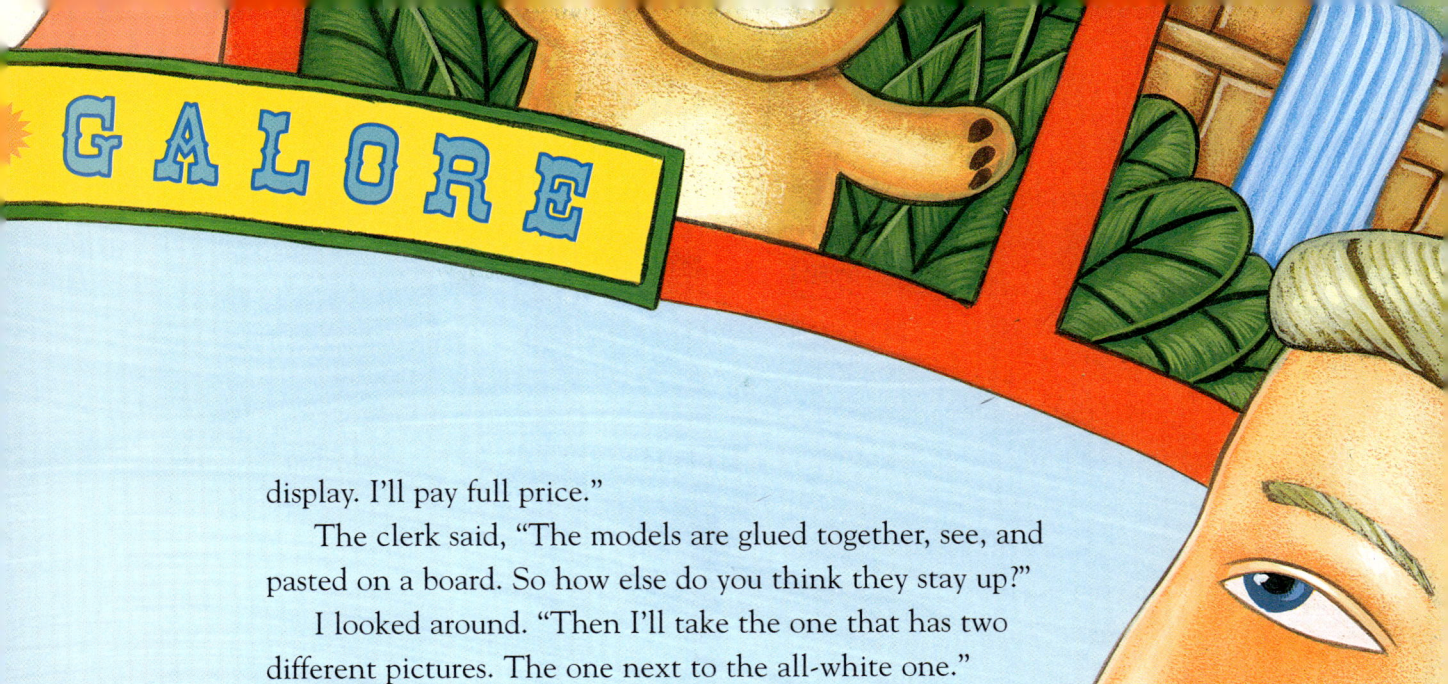

display. I'll pay full price."

The clerk said, "The models are glued together, see, and pasted on a board. So how else do you think they stay up?"

I looked around. "Then I'll take the one that has two different pictures. The one next to the all-white one."

"We're out of that one, too."

"Could you please check your stock in the back?"

"I checked this morning. We don't have it. We have the heart-shaped one in stock."

I looked it over. Instead of a circle, it was shaped like a heart. It was all pink except for a small red heart within the large pink one. Although it wouldn't be quite as difficult as the all-white circle, it, too, would be hard. But it was pink. Pink! Even on Valentine's Day, for a Valentine's Day party, I wouldn't consider giving a pink heart to another guy. "I'll take the water lilies then."

"That's one of our most popular puzzles," the clerk said. "It's a reproduction of a famous painting by an impressionistic French artist who was famous."

"Does that mean you are out of it, too?"

"'Fraid so."

I thought of Mother waiting in the truck. "Okay," I said, "give me the heart-shaped one. And gift wrap it, please." How could a store that seemed so un-busy be sold out of all the good stuff?

"That will take a while," the clerk said.

"Can you hurry? Please?"

"Not if you want me to do a good job."

"Medium," I said. "Can you do a medium job in a hurry?"

The salesclerk smiled and called to her fellow worker. She asked him to do the gift wrap as she rang up the sale. Then while we both waited, she asked, "Is that a present for your girlfriend?"

I knew it. I knew it. My choice was not half wrong; it was all wrong. I was on the verge of asking her to take it back and give me a refund when the clerk emerged from the back room carrying the puzzle box all wrapped in pink paper. I thought I would die. Then I thought of Mother waiting in the truck and asked for a bag to carry it in.

Mother folded the newspaper she was reading. She turned the key in the ignition even before she asked, "What did you get?"

"A puzzle."

"Good idea," she replied.

"Yeah, about twenty minutes ago, I thought so, too."

"By the way, where is this party?"

"The Sillington house."

"Well," Mother said, "I'll bet you'll have good food. I hear that Mr. Singh is a wonderful cook."

"I don't guess I'll be finding that out. I'm only going for tea."

"For tea?" Mother asked, a broad smile breaking across her face. *"Tea?"* she repeated.

I wished I could bite off my tongue. How in the world had I let that piece of information escape? "Yes," I said. "For tea. It's a tea party, and tea is always at four."

It would be a good walk—a mile and a half. I could cover three miles in forty-five minutes, so I guessed that I would need a half hour to make it to the Sillington House without a sweat. I was not about to ask Mother to drive me there. I put on a plaid flannel shirt and my best sweater. At the last minute, I put on a necktie. I don't know why I did, and I didn't want to think about it.

Nadia and Julian were on the front porch. They were bending over a small ball of fur. It was a puppy.

"She is Ginger's child," Nadia explained.

"Neat," I replied. I hated saying *Neat*. Nadia's red hair in the autumn light made me forget not to say it.

Mr. Singh came out onto the porch, and Julian made a formal introduction. We shook hands. "How do you like Julian's present from Nadia?" he asked.

I said "awesome" and immediately wished I hadn't.

Mr. Singh held his hand over his brow to make a sunshade and looked into the distance. "That looks like our other guest. Let us welcome him." Then he turned to me and Nadia and asked if we would please excuse him and Julian for a minute.

Nadia and I stood there on the front porch and said nothing to each other. No one would guess that we were almost relatives. We watched Noah Gershom get out of the car and start walking up the brick path to the house. In one hand he held a beautifully wrapped present. I watched Mr. Singh with his white turban and long blue apron over his trousers and Julian at his side walk down the path to greet him. Silhouetted against the sky, they looked like a travel poster for a distant land.

Mr. Singh stepped aside to allow Julian and Noah to precede him up the walk.

Julian took Noah's gift and said, "I believe you know everyone here except Alice."

"Who's Alice?" Noah asked.

Nadia answered. "She is Ginger's daughter. Ginger is my dog, and I have given Julian one of her puppies."

"Did you ask if Julian can have a pet?" Noah asked.

"No," she replied.

"I've never heard of someone giving someone a pet for a present without permission."

"I could not believe that anyone would not want one of Ginger's puppies."

"What if Julian has an allergy?"

"If Julian had an allergy—which he does not—he would still want one of Ginger's pups. Ginger is a genius." She looked at me and added, "She is a hybrid genius of unknown I.Q.," and I knew that she was acknowledging our conversation of last summer.

"Oh," Noah said. He hit his forehead with the palm of his hand. "Of course. Of course. I almost forgot. Ginger is the dog that invented $E = mc^2$."

"$E = mc^2$ was not invented. It was discovered, and Einstein discovered it. Ginger is a genius of her genus. She is the best there is of *Canis familiaris*, and Alice is the best of her litter."

"Alice," Noah repeated. "Who named her that?"

"I did," Nadia said. "I thought Julian would like the name because he sent me the invitation to tea in the book, *Alice's Adventures in Wonderland*."

"I've never heard of someone giving someone a pet for a present without permission and then choosing that pet's name without even asking."

Nadia said, "Well, Noah, now you have. In a single afternoon you have heard of both."

The large center hall of the Sillington house had a staircase that curved upward like a stretch of DNA. To the right of the hall was a living room that had a huge fireplace on the end wall; there was no furniture in the room, and the wallpaper was peeling from the walls. On the left of the center hall was the long dining room. I did not remember its having a fireplace, but it did. I was drawn into the room by the large, framed poster hanging over the fireplace mantel.

Extraordinaire
Simonetta
Chanteuse

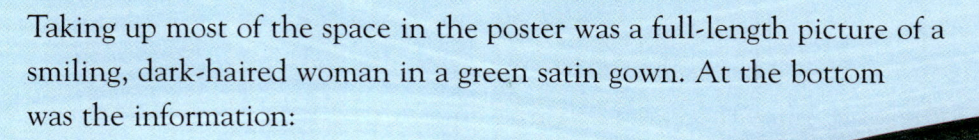

Taking up most of the space in the poster was a full-length picture of a smiling, dark-haired woman in a green satin gown. At the bottom was the information:

Appearing Nightly
November 14–29
The Stardust Room

Julian came up behind me. "That is my mother," he said.

"Your mother is a chanteuse?"

"Yes, she was a chanteuse," he said, pronouncing it *shawn-tewz*.

"What does a shawn-tewz do?"

"She sings."

"I saw The Phantom of the Opera last summer. There was a wonderful chanteuse in that show."

Julian smiled but said nothing.

"Has she retired?" I asked.

"No," he said. "She died."

"Oh," I said, embarrassed. "I'm sorry."

Julian looked up at the poster. "That poster is quite old. From before my birth. The Stardust Room mentioned there is on a cruise ship. Mother performed there and on other cruise ships. Before it was necessary for me to start school, I used to travel with Mother and Father. Then I went to boarding school in the north of England in the fall and winter and traveled with them during one of the summer months. Until this year."

"Are you an alien?" I asked.

"Actually, no," he said. "Mother was an American by birth; Father is by naturalization. I was born on the high seas. That makes me American."

"As American as apple pie," I said.

Julian smiled. "Not quite," he said. "Let us say that I am as American as pizza pie. I did not originate here, but I am here to stay." He extended his arm in the direction of Nadia and Noah and took a small step back so that I could pass in front of him. "I think we must join our other guests," he said. "Please," he said. I crossed in front of him, and as I did so, I felt that I was crossing from stage right to stage left and wearing a tuxedo, and I did not mind the feeling at all.

Think About It

1 What is unusual about Julian's invitation?

2 Do you think Ethan feels comfortable at the party? Tell why you think as you do.

3 What do Ethan's plans for the future tell you about him?

Meet the Author
E. L. Konigsburg

E. L. (Elaine) Konigsburg is the author of many popular books, including the Newbery Medal winner *From the Mixed-Up Files of Mrs. Basil E. Frankweiler*. Over the years, Konigsburg has kept a file of articles that interest her. Some of these have provided the ideas behind her books.

Konigsburg says that when she begins to work on a book, she starts a "movie" in her head. The characters in *The View from Saturday* took shape one day while she was walking along the beach. She had an idea about a boy named Ethan meeting a boy named Julian on the school bus on their first day of sixth grade. Then Konigsburg thought about some of the articles she had saved. Konigsburg realized that the characters had something in common. "I knew that kids would love meeting one character, then two and three," she says.

Throughout her career, E. L. Konigsburg has created interesting characters that young readers love to meet.

Visit *The Learning Site!*
www.harcourtschool.com

Response Activities

A Funny Thing Happened...

WRITE A SONG Ethan has a funny experience when he goes to buy a gift for Julian's party. Think of a funny shopping experience you have had, or make one up. Write a song about the experience, using a new or a borrowed melody.

You're Invited

WRITE PARTY CLUES Julian uses clues to tell his classmates about his tea party. Make an invitation to another party, using new clues. Then exchange invitations with a partner. See if you can figure out when and where the other person's party will take place.

A Note of Thanks

WRITE A NOTE
Imagine you were one of the students at Julian's party. Write a note thanking him for his hospitality. Be sure to tell him what a great success his party was.

Picture This

WRITE A DESCRIPTION
The author compares the staircase at Sillington House to a curving stretch of DNA. Choose an unusual building or structure in your community, or find one in an encyclopedia. Write a creative description of the building or structure, using figurative language.

FOCUS SKILL: Vocabulary in Context

In "The View from Saturday," Ethan is looking for a party gift to buy. He asks the store clerk about the store's *stock* of a certain puzzle. Their conversation follows:

"We're out of that one, too."

"Could you please check your stock in the back?"

Stock is a word with multiple meanings. You can understand which meaning is intended by using the **context** of nearby words and sentences. In the sentence above, *stock* means "a quantity of something kept for use or sale." *Stock* can also have the following meanings:

Meaning	Sentence Example
"livestock"	Farmer Brown's stock includes pigs and sheep.
"to lay in supplies"	The Produce Barn stocks pineapples and bananas.
"commonly used"	"Once upon a time" is a stock opening for fairy tales.
"part ownership of a business divided into shares"	Mom owns stock in a software company.
"the liquid from boiling meat or vegetables"	Please save the stock for chicken soup.

Read the paragraph below. Then make and fill in a chart like the one shown to identify the multiple meanings of the underlined words. The first one has been done for you.

The farmers' market in the town square does a brisk business on Sundays. Every Sunday my aunt and I board a bus and go there to shop. We buy lettuce and vine-ripened tomatoes at a produce stand. To their credit, the farmers charge very reasonable prices. I gave one woman a ten-dollar bill for goat cheese, and she gave me change.

Multiple-Meaning Word	Meaning in the Paragraph	Additional Meanings
brisk	"fast-moving"	"cool and stimulating"

WHAT HAVE YOU LEARNED?

1. What is the story meaning of these underlined words from the selection? "I had seen football fans act the way I felt." What additional meanings do these words have?

2. Write two sentences that show different meanings for the word check.

TRY THIS • TRY THIS • TRY THIS

Word meanings can change over time. What words do you use often that have more than one meaning?

Visit *The Learning Site!*
www.harcourtschool.com

KNOTS
in Yo-Yo
String
by Jerry

Knots in My Yo-yo String

The Autobiography of a Kid

by Newbery Medalist
Jerry Spinelli

Award-Winning Author

Giants

Willie Mays

WILLIE MAYS outfield NEW YORK GIANTS

ERNIE BANKS shortstop CHICAGO CUBS

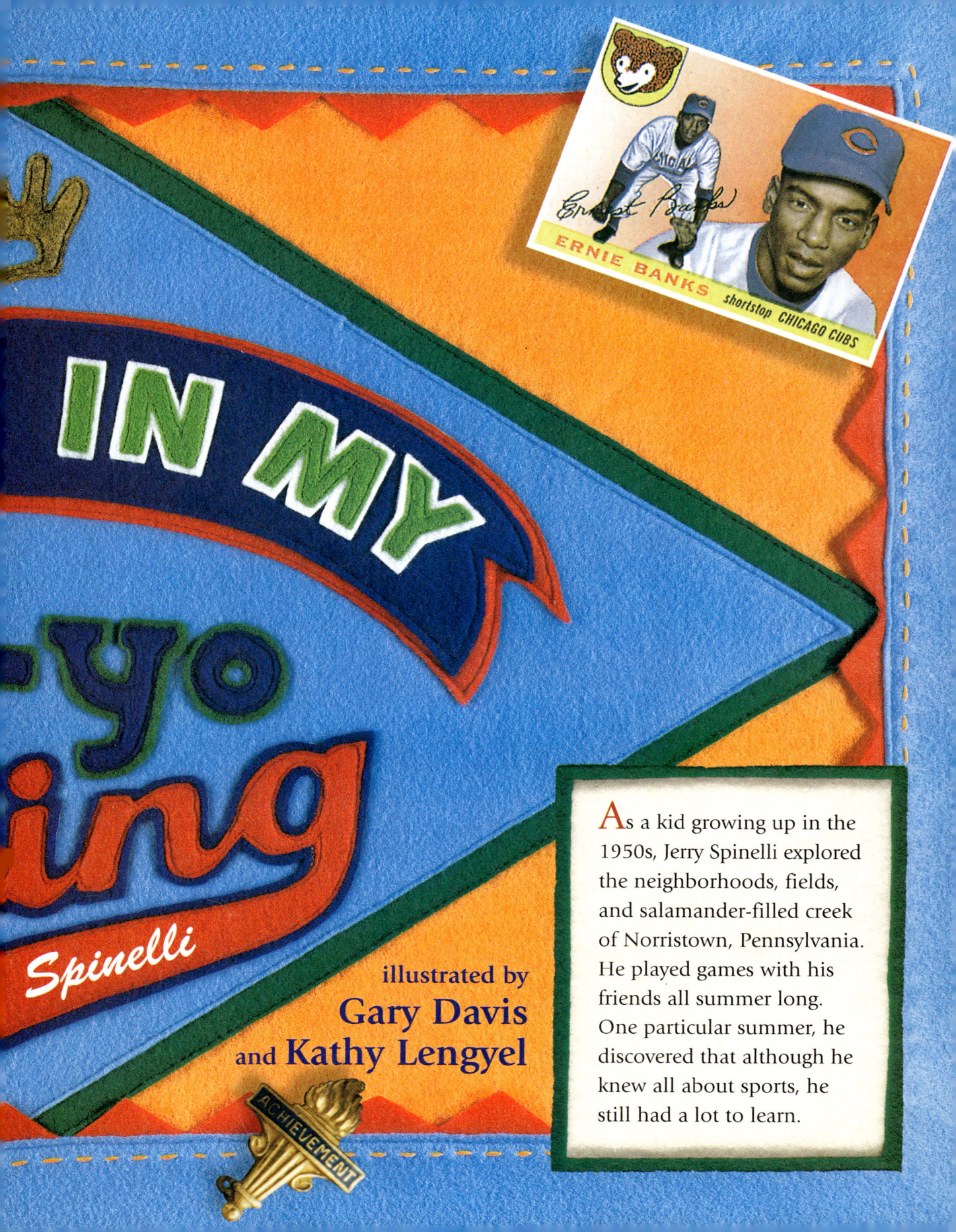

IN MY

-yo
ing

Spinelli

illustrated by
Gary Davis
and **Kathy Lengyel**

As a kid growing up in the 1950s, Jerry Spinelli explored the neighborhoods, fields, and salamander-filled creek of Norristown, Pennsylvania. He played games with his friends all summer long. One particular summer, he discovered that although he knew all about sports, he still had a lot to learn.

In a green metal box in a bedroom closet, tucked into a fuzzy gray cotton pouch, lies the most cherished memento of my grade-school days. It is a gold-plated medal no bigger than a postage stamp. Inscribed on the back are the words "50-YARD DASH—CHAMPION."

The medal came from the only official race I ever participated in. There were many unofficial ones . . .

"Race you to the store!"

"Last one in's a monkey!"

"Ready . . . Set . . . Go!"

Like kids the world over, we raced to determine the fastest. In the early 1950s on the 800 block of George Street in the West End of Norristown, Pennsylvania, that was me. I was usually the winner, and never the monkey.

I reached my peak at the age of twelve. That summer I led the Norristown Little League in stolen bases. In an all-star playoff game I did something practically unheard of: I was safe at first base on a ground ball to the pitcher.

Some days I pulled my sneaker laces extra tight and went down to the railroad tracks. The cinders there had the feel of a running track. I measured off fifty or a hundred yards and sprinted the distance, timing myself with my father's stopwatch. Sometimes, heading back to the starting line, I tried to see how fast I could run on the railroad ties. Sometimes I ran on the rail.

It was during that year that I won my medal. I represented Hartranft in the fifty-yard dash at the annual track-and-field meet for the Norristown grade schools. The meet was held at Roosevelt Field, where the high school track and football teams played.

Favored to win the race was Laverne Dixon of Gotwals Elementary. "Froggy," as he was known to everyone but his teachers, had won the fifty-yard dash the year before

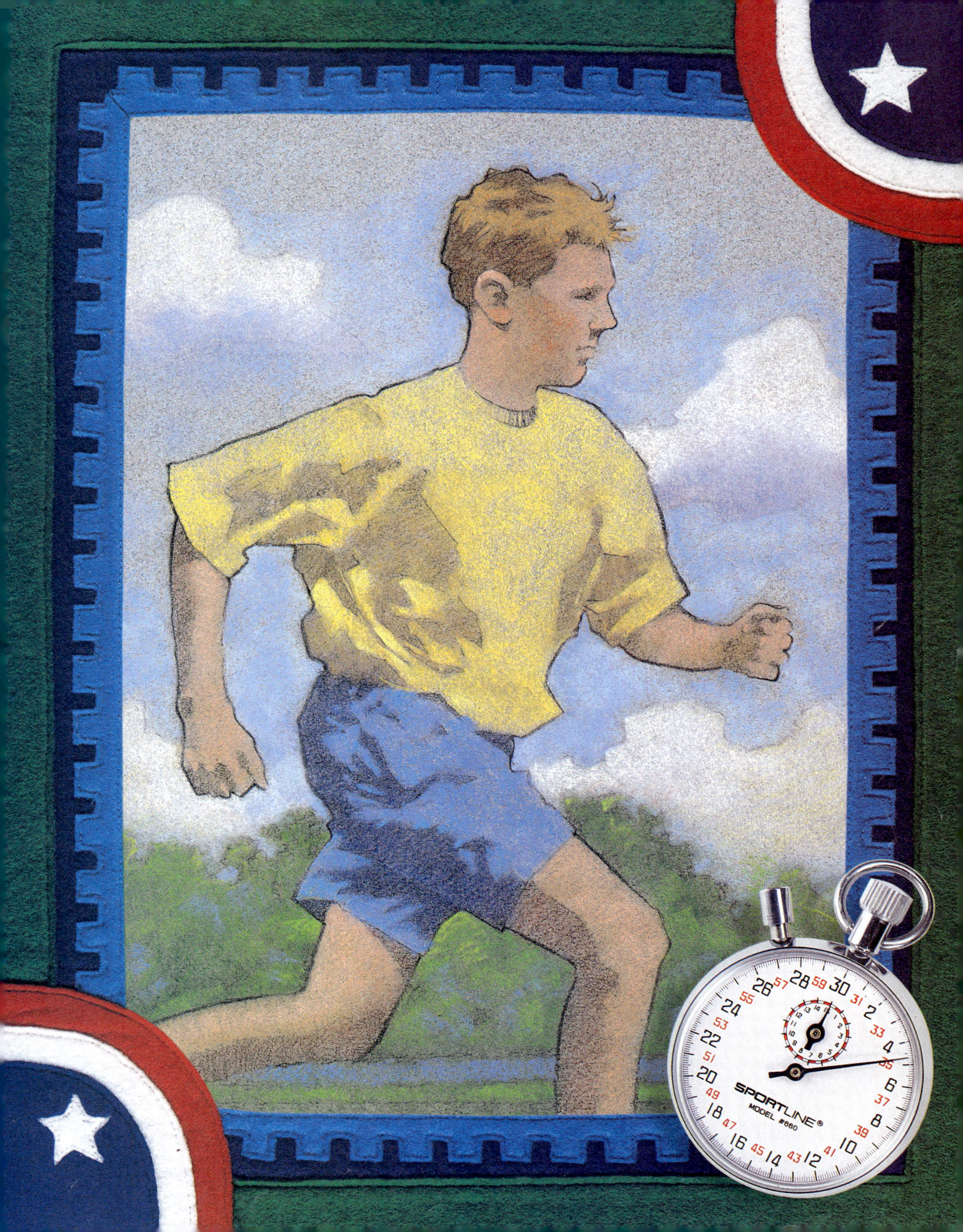
SPORTLINE®
MODEL #660

as a mere fifth grader. Surely he would win again. My goal was to place second.

When the starter barked, "Ready!" I got into position: one knee and ten fingertips on the cinder track. I knew what to do from the many meets I had attended with my father. I glanced to my left and right and saw nothing but shins—everyone else was standing. I could not have known it then, but the race was already mine.

I was off with the gun. My memory of those fifty yards has nothing to do with sprinting but rather with two sensations. The first was surprise that I could not see any other runners. This led to a startling conclusion: *I must be ahead!* Which led to the second sensation: an anxious expectation, a waiting to be overtaken.

I never was. I won.

Froggy Dixon didn't even come in second. That went to Billy Steinberg, a stranger then, who would become my best friend in junior high school. He would also grow to be faster than I, as would many of my schoolmates. But that was yet to come. For the moment, as I slowed down and trotted into a sun the color and dazzle of the medal I was about to receive, I knew only the wonder of seven astounding seconds when no one was ahead of me.

From ages eleven to sixteen, if someone asked me what I wanted to be when I grew up, I gave one of two answers: "A baseball player" or "A shortstop."

Major league baseball—that was the life for me. And I wanted to live it only as a shortstop. When I trotted onto a diamond, I instinctively headed for the dusty plain between second and third. I never wanted to play any other position. When we got up sandlot games, no one else occupied shortstop. They knew it was mine.

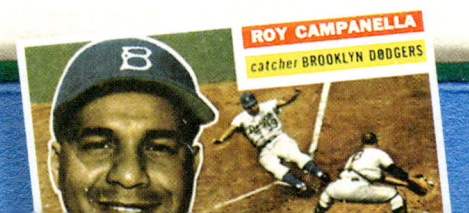

I was eleven when I first played Little League baseball. To give as many kids as possible a chance to participate, the Little League declared that some of us would share uniforms with others. And so the season was exactly half over when I pedaled my bike up to Albert Pascavage's house to pick up his uniform: green socks, green cap, gray woolen shirt, and pants with green trim. I packed my precious cargo into my bike basket and drove it carefully home. I was a member of the Green Sox.

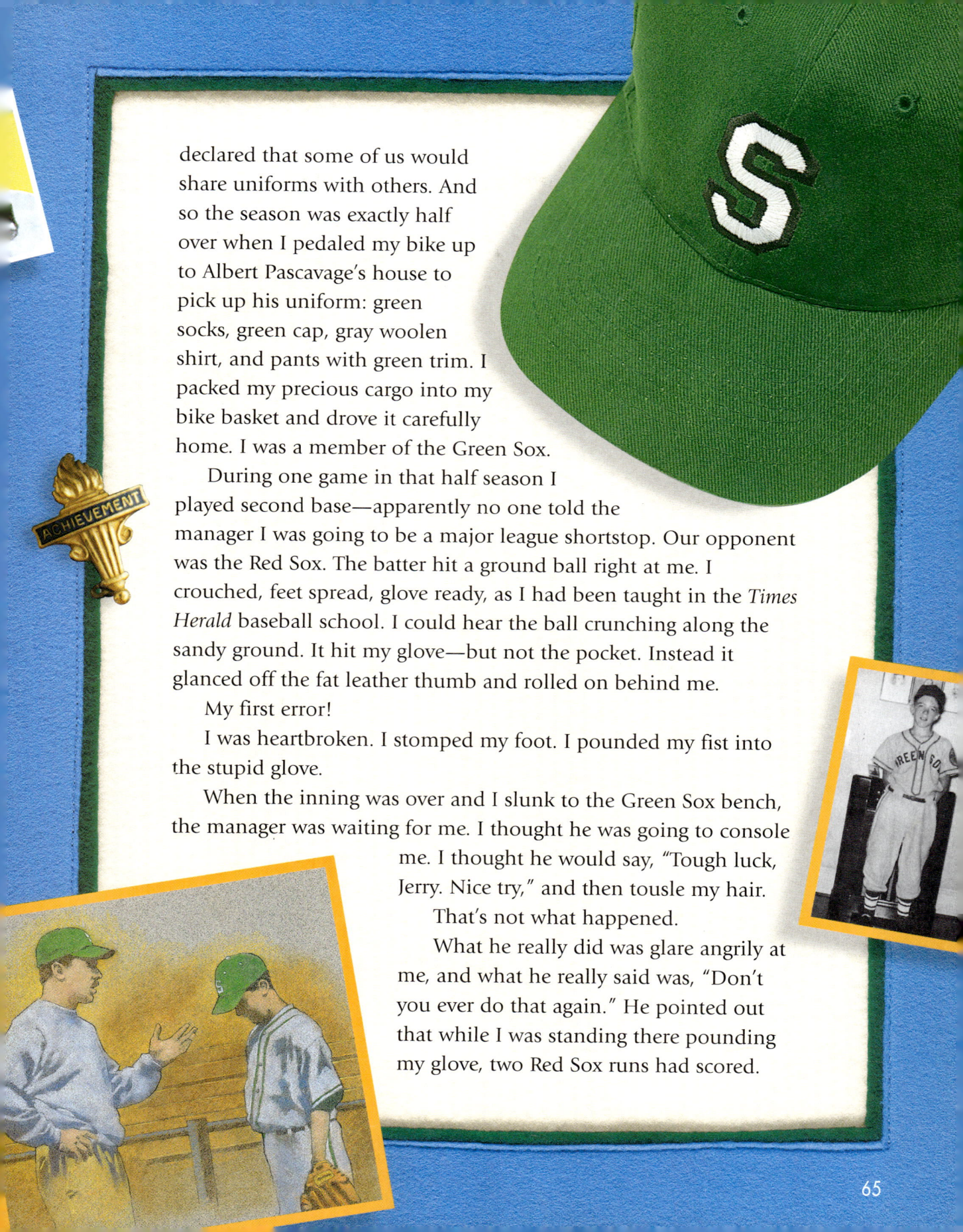

During one game in that half season I played second base—apparently no one told the manager I was going to be a major league shortstop. Our opponent was the Red Sox. The batter hit a ground ball right at me. I crouched, feet spread, glove ready, as I had been taught in the *Times Herald* baseball school. I could hear the ball crunching along the sandy ground. It hit my glove—but not the pocket. Instead it glanced off the fat leather thumb and rolled on behind me.

My first error!

I was heartbroken. I stomped my foot. I pounded my fist into the stupid glove.

When the inning was over and I slunk to the Green Sox bench, the manager was waiting for me. I thought he was going to console me. I thought he would say, "Tough luck, Jerry. Nice try," and then tousle my hair.

That's not what happened.

What he really did was glare angrily at me, and what he really said was, "Don't you ever do that again." He pointed out that while I was standing there pounding my glove, two Red Sox runs had scored.

"Next time you miss the ball, you turn around and chase it down. You don't just stand there feeling sorry for yourself. Understand?"

I nodded. And I never forgot.

Like most of the kids in my class, I got better at sports simply by growing older. I went from being one of the worst players in Little League as an eleven-year-old to making the all-star team as a twelve-year-old. The following year I was the only seventh grader to start on the Stewart Junior High School team—at shortstop, of course. It mattered little that I was not very good at hitting a curve ball, since most pitchers threw only fastballs.

During the summer of junior high school I played in a baseball league called Connie Mack Knee-Hi, for thirteen- to fifteen-year-olds. Before each game, one team would line up along the first-base line, the other team along third base. The umpire stood on the pitcher's mound, took off his cap, and read aloud the Sportsmanship Pledge, pausing after each line so the rest of us could repeat it in chorus. We pledged ourselves to be loyal to, among other things, "clean living and clean speech." In the final line we promised to be "a generous victor and a gracious loser."

In the Knee-Hi summer of 1955, I had little chance to be a gracious loser. My team, Norristown Brick Company, swept through the local league undefeated, winning our games by an average score of 12–1. One score was 24–0. One team simply refused to show up. Our pitchers threw four no-hitters, three by Lee Holmes. Opposing batters could no more hit Bill Bryzgornia's fastball than spell his name. We were a powerhouse.

We beat Conshohocken two out of three to gain the state playoffs. Three wins there put us into the title game. On a bright Saturday afternoon at War Memorial Field in Doylestown,

1955

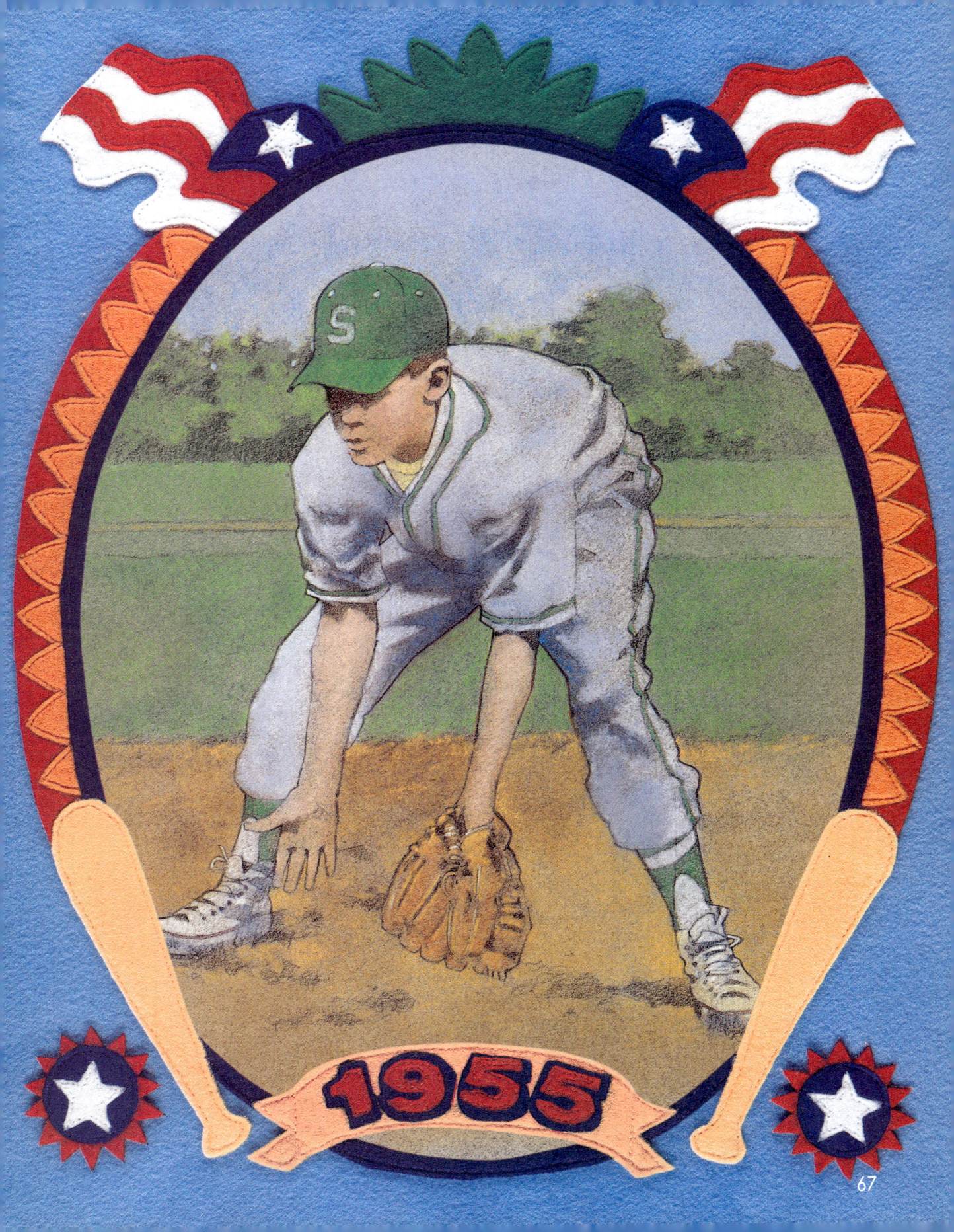

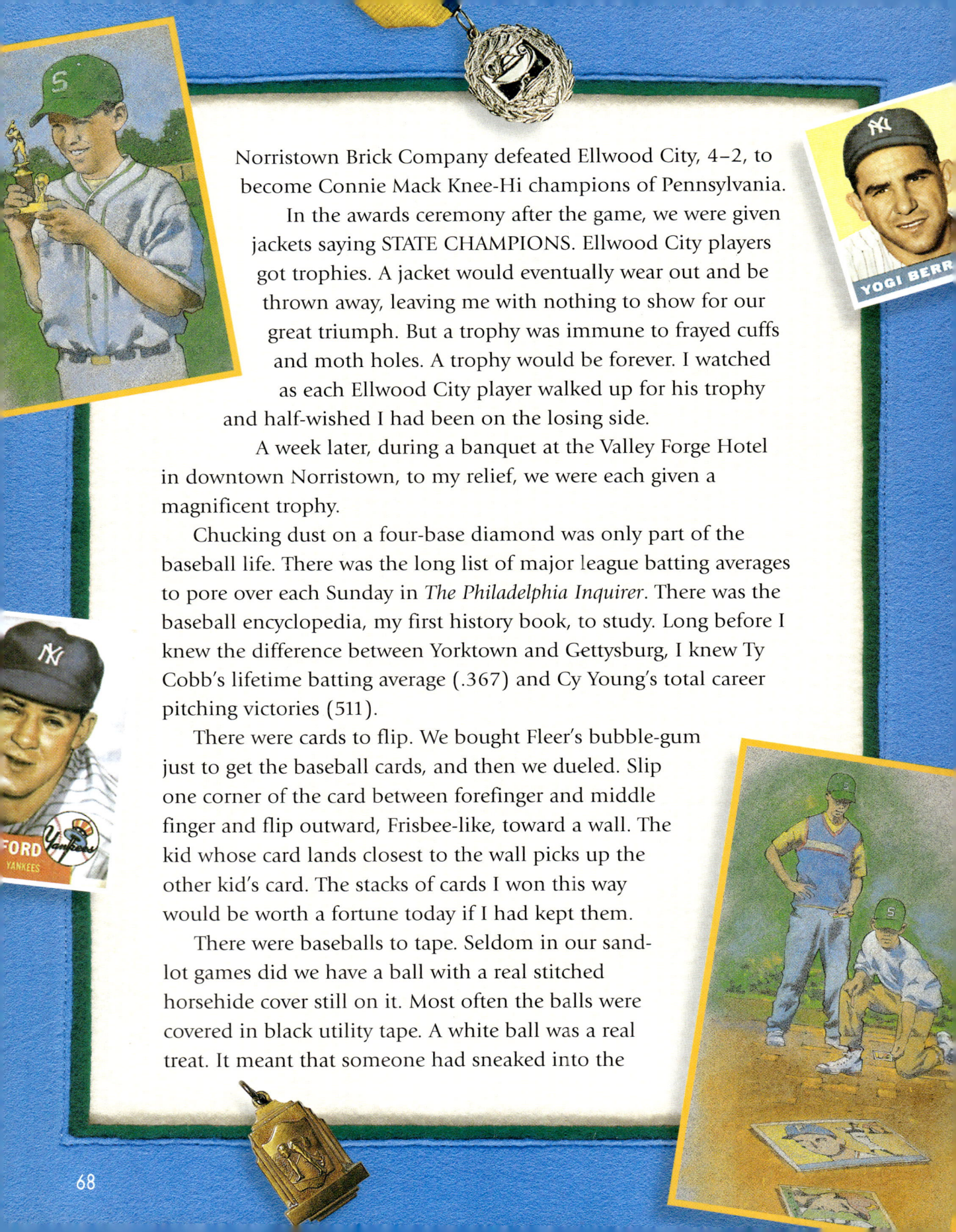

Norristown Brick Company defeated Ellwood City, 4–2, to become Connie Mack Knee-Hi champions of Pennsylvania. In the awards ceremony after the game, we were given jackets saying STATE CHAMPIONS. Ellwood City players got trophies. A jacket would eventually wear out and be thrown away, leaving me with nothing to show for our great triumph. But a trophy was immune to frayed cuffs and moth holes. A trophy would be forever. I watched as each Ellwood City player walked up for his trophy and half-wished I had been on the losing side.

A week later, during a banquet at the Valley Forge Hotel in downtown Norristown, to my relief, we were each given a magnificent trophy.

Chucking dust on a four-base diamond was only part of the baseball life. There was the long list of major league batting averages to pore over each Sunday in *The Philadelphia Inquirer*. There was the baseball encyclopedia, my first history book, to study. Long before I knew the difference between Yorktown and Gettysburg, I knew Ty Cobb's lifetime batting average (.367) and Cy Young's total career pitching victories (511).

There were cards to flip. We bought Fleer's bubble-gum just to get the baseball cards, and then we dueled. Slip one corner of the card between forefinger and middle finger and flip outward, Frisbee-like, toward a wall. The kid whose card lands closest to the wall picks up the other kid's card. The stacks of cards I won this way would be worth a fortune today if I had kept them.

There were baseballs to tape. Seldom in our sandlot games did we have a ball with a real stitched horsehide cover still on it. Most often the balls were covered in black utility tape. A white ball was a real treat. It meant that someone had sneaked into the medicine chest at home and used up half a roll of first-aid tape.

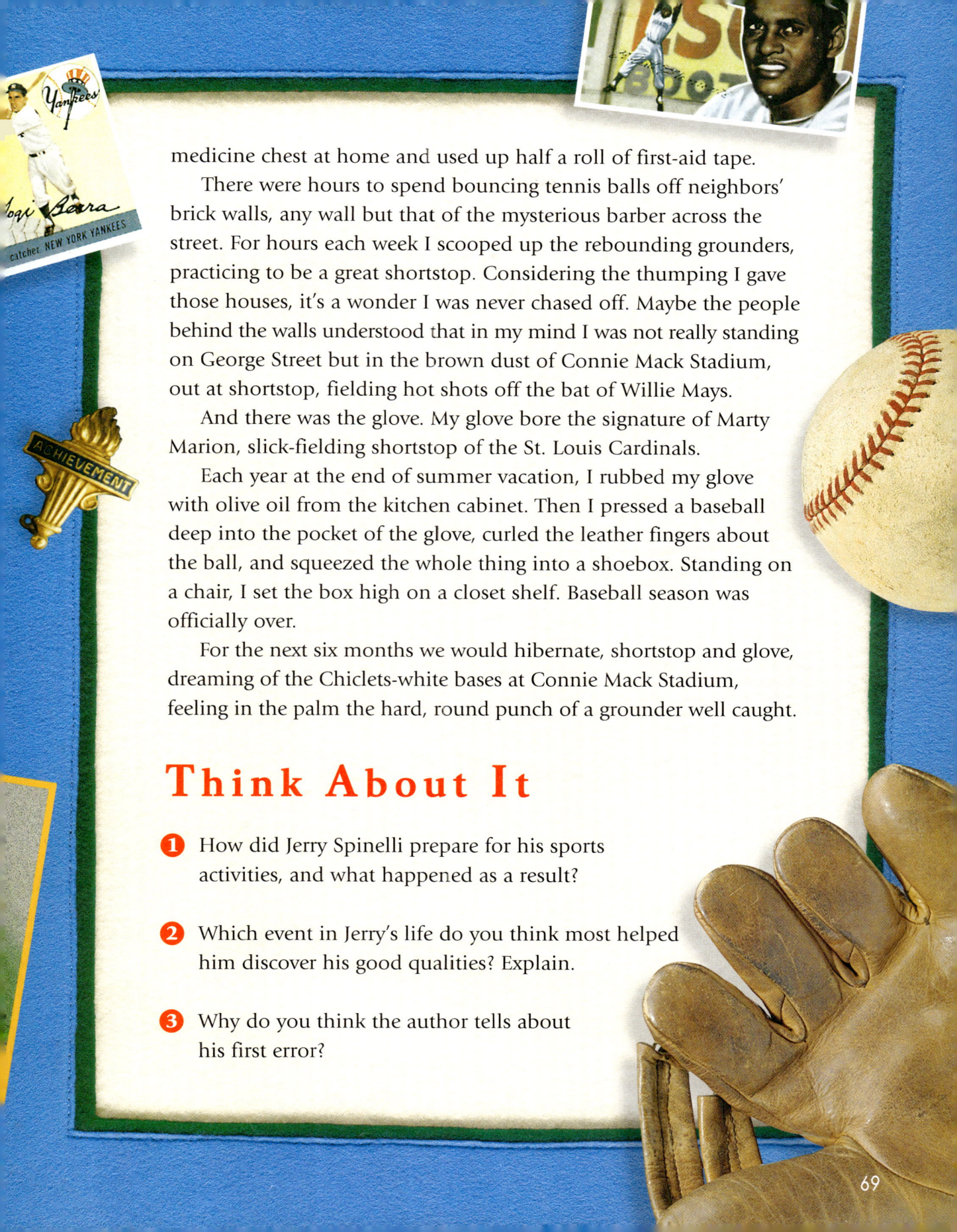

There were hours to spend bouncing tennis balls off neighbors' brick walls, any wall but that of the mysterious barber across the street. For hours each week I scooped up the rebounding grounders, practicing to be a great shortstop. Considering the thumping I gave those houses, it's a wonder I was never chased off. Maybe the people behind the walls understood that in my mind I was not really standing on George Street but in the brown dust of Connie Mack Stadium, out at shortstop, fielding hot shots off the bat of Willie Mays.

And there was the glove. My glove bore the signature of Marty Marion, slick-fielding shortstop of the St. Louis Cardinals.

Each year at the end of summer vacation, I rubbed my glove with olive oil from the kitchen cabinet. Then I pressed a baseball deep into the pocket of the glove, curled the leather fingers about the ball, and squeezed the whole thing into a shoebox. Standing on a chair, I set the box high on a closet shelf. Baseball season was officially over.

For the next six months we would hibernate, shortstop and glove, dreaming of the Chiclets-white bases at Connie Mack Stadium, feeling in the palm the hard, round punch of a grounder well caught.

Think About It

1. How did Jerry Spinelli prepare for his sports activities, and what happened as a result?

2. Which event in Jerry's life do you think most helped him discover his good qualities? Explain.

3. Why do you think the author tells about his first error?

Green Sox

JERRY SPINELLI

Meet the Author

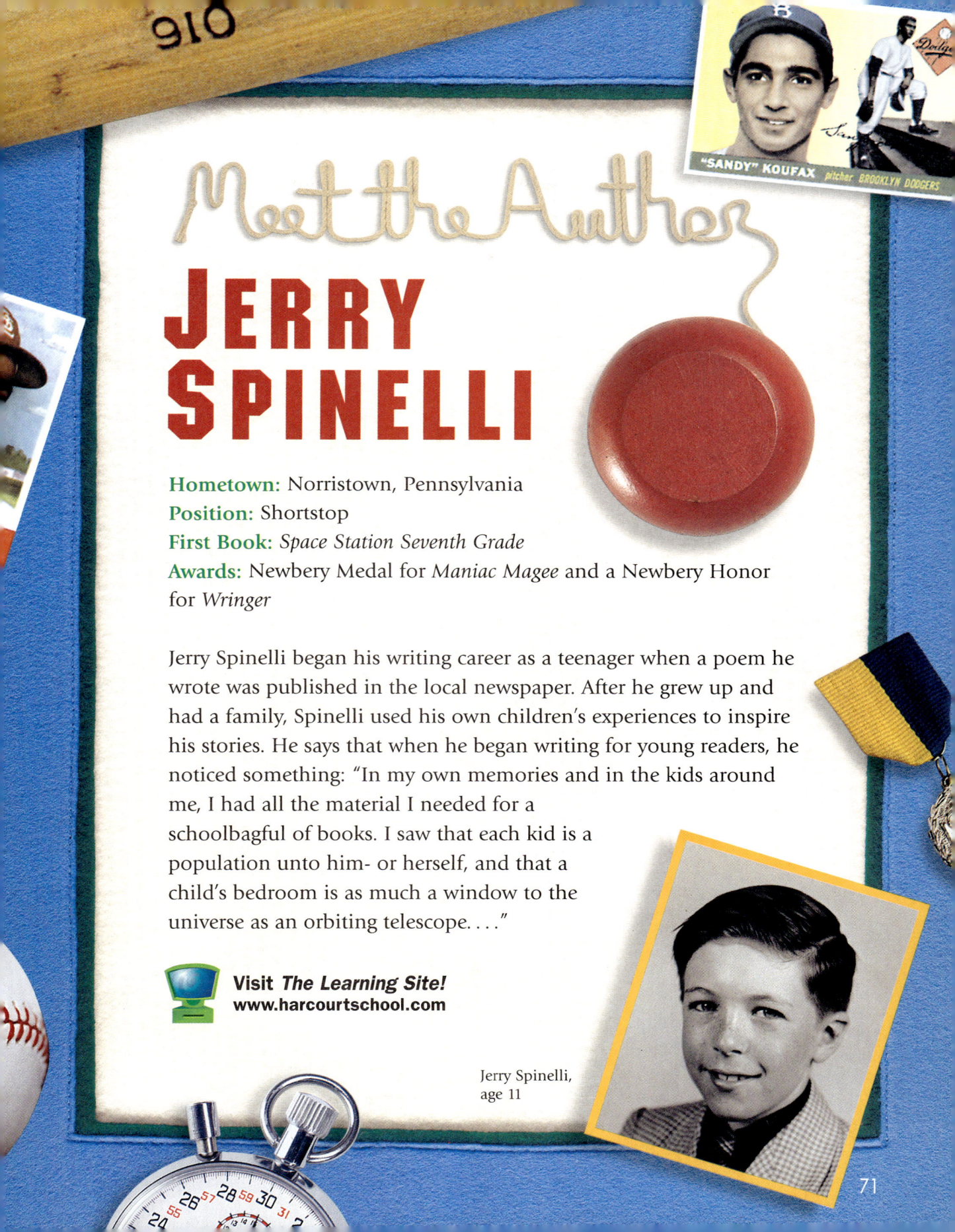

JERRY SPINELLI

Hometown: Norristown, Pennsylvania
Position: Shortstop
First Book: *Space Station Seventh Grade*
Awards: Newbery Medal for *Maniac Magee* and a Newbery Honor for *Wringer*

Jerry Spinelli began his writing career as a teenager when a poem he wrote was published in the local newspaper. After he grew up and had a family, Spinelli used his own children's experiences to inspire his stories. He says that when he began writing for young readers, he noticed something: "In my own memories and in the kids around me, I had all the material I needed for a schoolbagful of books. I saw that each kid is a population unto him- or herself, and that a child's bedroom is as much a window to the universe as an orbiting telescope...."

Visit **The Learning Site!**
www.harcourtschool.com

Jerry Spinelli, age 11

71

FROM THE AUTOGRAPH ALBUM
(Anonymous)

If at first you don't succeed,
Slide for second.

In curve, out curve,
Slow ball, drop.
Don't forget Jim
The star shortstop.

Life and baseball
Are just the same;
You must strike hard
To win the game.

Good Sportsmanship

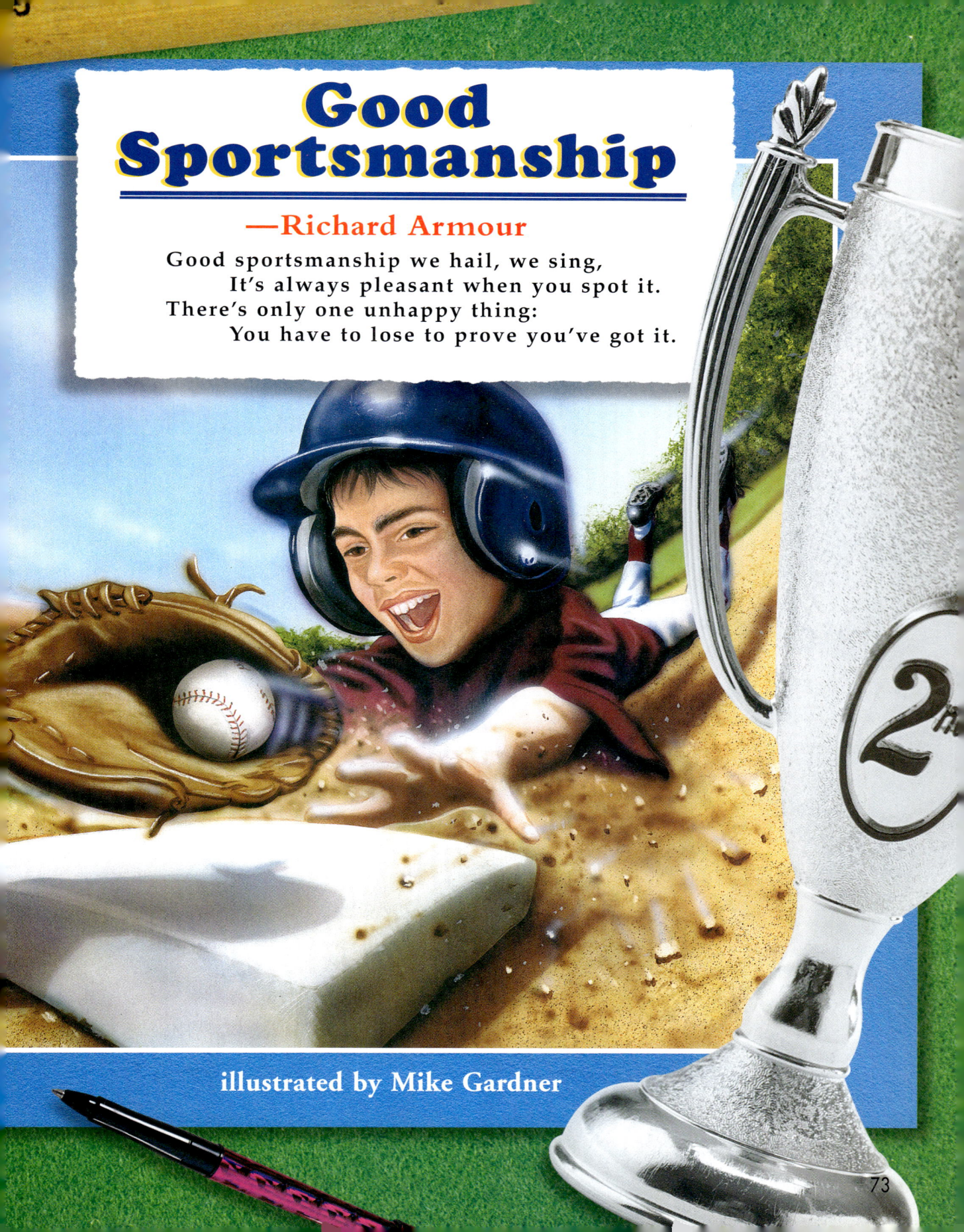

—**Richard Armour**

Good sportsmanship we hail, we sing,
   It's always pleasant when you spot it.
There's only one unhappy thing:
   You have to lose to prove you've got it.

illustrated by Mike Gardner

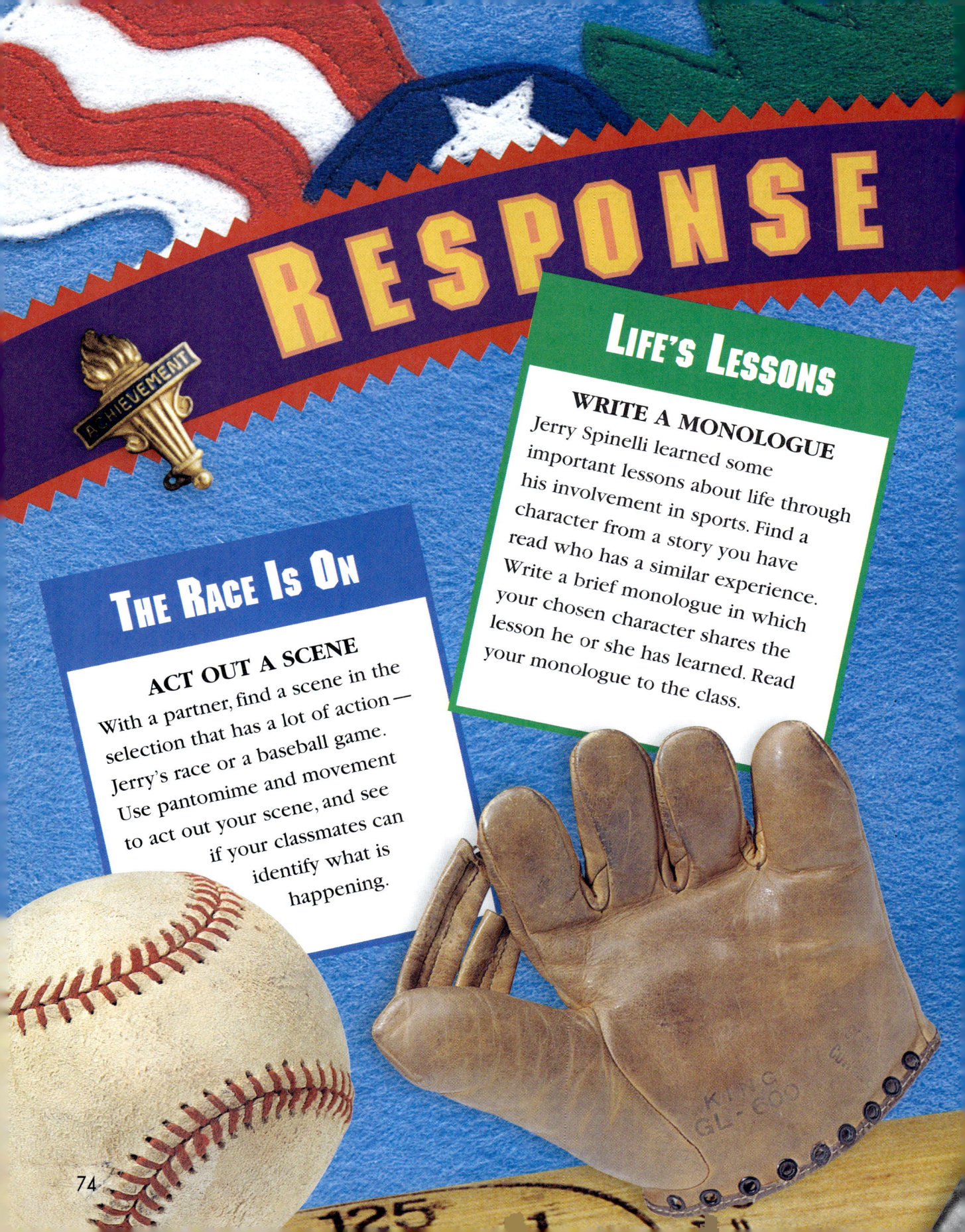

RESPONSE

LIFE'S LESSONS

WRITE A MONOLOGUE

Jerry Spinelli learned some important lessons about life through his involvement in sports. Find a character from a story you have read who has a similar experience. Write a brief monologue in which your chosen character shares the lesson he or she has learned. Read your monologue to the class.

THE RACE IS ON

ACT OUT A SCENE

With a partner, find a scene in the selection that has a lot of action—Jerry's race or a baseball game. Use pantomime and movement to act out your scene, and see if your classmates can identify what is happening.

ACTIVITIES

SPORTS REPORT

INTERVIEW AN ATHLETE

People compete in sports for many different reasons. Interview a friend or family member who is an athlete. Ask how the person prepares for competition and why he or she enjoys competing. Share your new knowledge with the rest of the class.

MAKING CONNECTIONS

WRITE A PARAGRAPH

Suppose young Jerry Spinelli read the poems "From the Autograph Album" and "Good Sportsmanship" after he made a baseball error. Write a paragraph from his point of view in which he tells which poem he likes better and why.

75

The Marble Champ

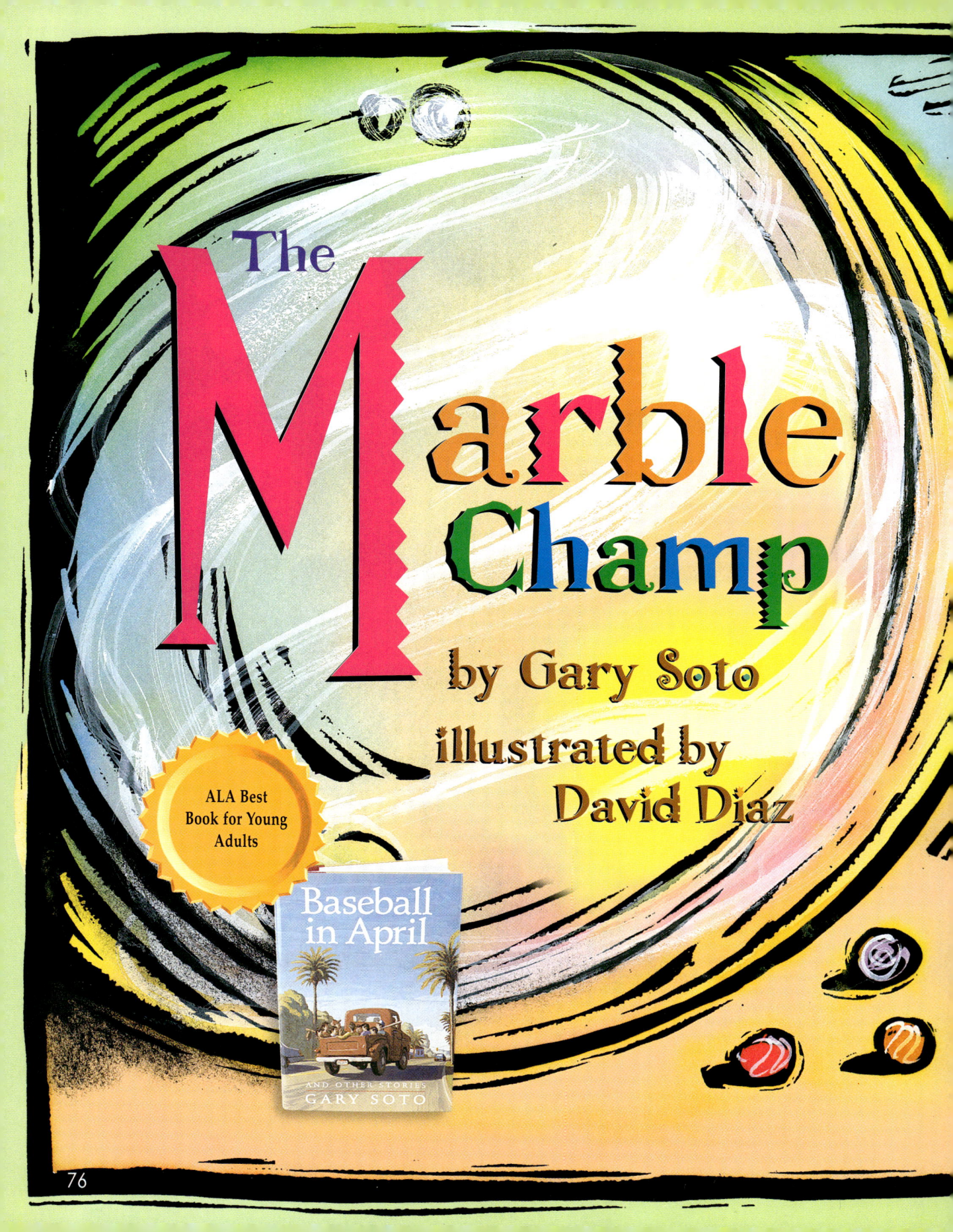

by Gary Soto

illustrated by David Diaz

ALA Best Book for Young Adults

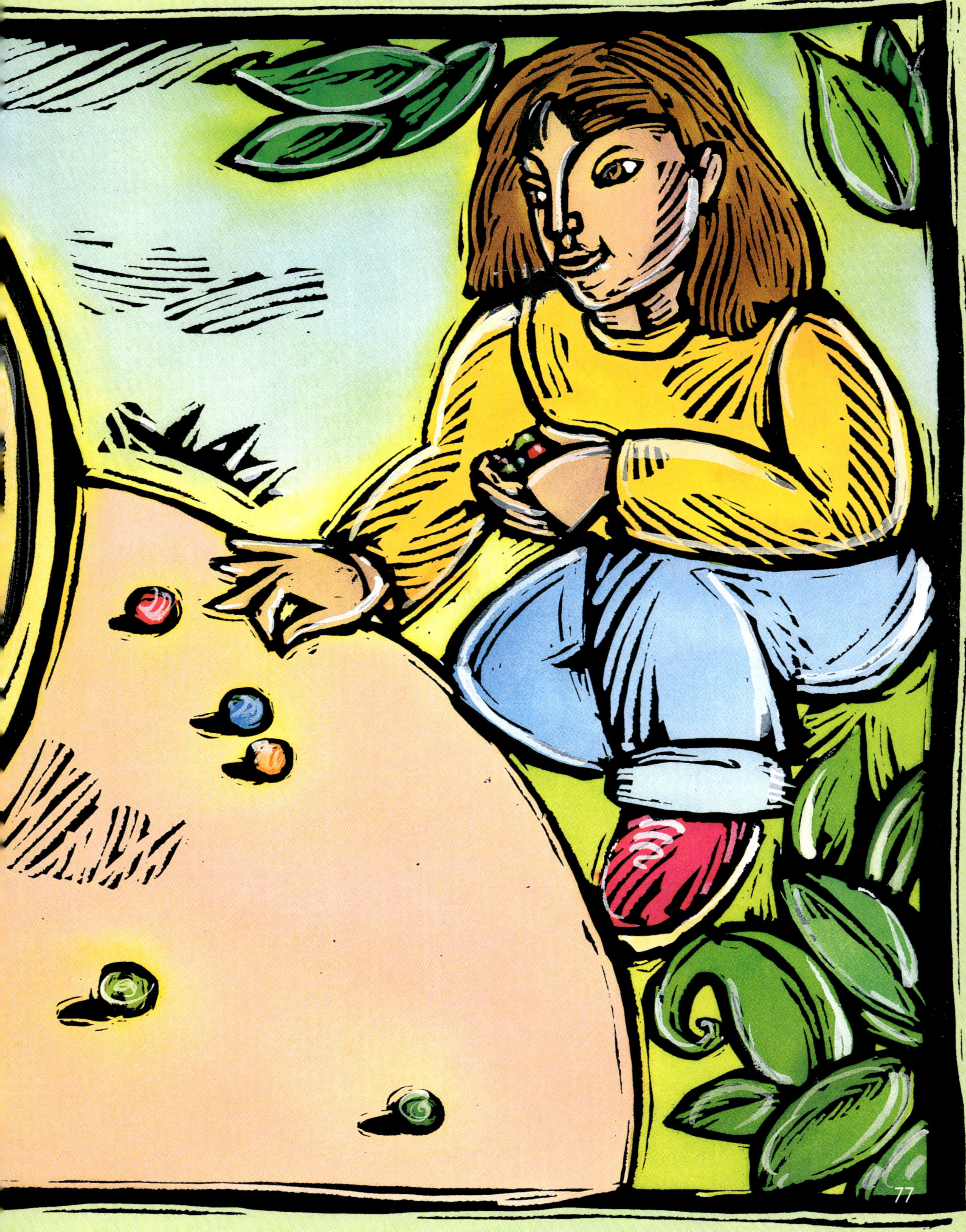

Lupe Medrano, a shy girl who spoke in whispers, was the school's spelling bee champion, winner of the reading contest at the public library three summers in a row, blue ribbon awardee in the science fair, the top student at her piano recital, and the playground grand champion in chess. She was a straight-A student and—not counting kindergarten, when she had been stung by a wasp—had never missed one day of elementary school. She had received a small trophy for this honor and had been congratulated by the mayor.

But though Lupe had a razor-sharp mind, she could not make her body, no matter how much she tried, run as fast as the other girls'. She begged her body to move faster, but could never beat anyone in the fifty-yard dash.

The truth was that Lupe was no good in sports. She could not catch a pop-up or figure out in which direction to kick the soccer ball. One time she kicked the ball at her own goal and scored a point for the other team. She was no good at baseball or basketball either, and even had a hard time making a hula hoop stay on her hips.

It wasn't until last year, when she was eleven years old, that she learned how to ride a bike. And even then she had to use training wheels. She could walk in the swimming pool but couldn't swim, and chanced roller skating only when her father held her hand.

"I'll never be good at sports," she fumed one rainy day as she lay on her bed gazing at the shelf her father had made to hold her awards. "I wish I could win something, anything, even marbles."

At the word "marbles," she sat up. "That's it. Maybe I could be good at playing marbles." She hopped out of bed and rummaged through the closet until she found a can full of her brother's marbles. She poured the rich glass treasure on her bed and picked five of the most beautiful marbles.

She smoothed her bedspread and practiced shooting, softly at first so that her aim would be accurate. The marble rolled from her thumb and clicked against the targeted marble. But the target wouldn't budge. She tried again and again. Her aim became accurate, but the power from her thumb made the marble move only an inch or

79

two. Then she realized that the bedspread was slowing the marbles. She also had to admit that her thumb was weaker than the neck of a newborn chick.

She looked out the window. The rain was letting up, but the ground was too muddy to play. She sat cross-legged on the bed, rolling her five marbles between her palms. Yes, she thought, I could play marbles, and marbles is a sport. At that moment she realized that she had only two weeks to practice. The playground championship, the same one her brother had entered the previous year, was coming up. She had a lot to do.

To strengthen her wrists, she decided to do twenty push-ups on her fingertips, five at a time. "One, two, three..." she groaned. By the end of the first set she was breathing hard, and her muscles burned from exhaustion. She did one more set and decided that was enough push-ups for the first day.

She squeezed a rubber eraser one hundred times, hoping it would strengthen her thumb. This seemed to work because the next day her thumb was sore. She could hardly hold a marble in her hand, let alone send it flying with power. So Lupe rested that day and listened to her brother, who gave her tips on how to shoot: get low, aim with one eye, and place one knuckle on the ground.

"Think 'eye and thumb'—and let it rip!" he said.

After school the next day she left her homework in her backpack and practiced three hours straight, taking time only to eat a candy bar for energy. With a popsicle stick, she drew an odd-shaped circle and tossed in four marbles. She used her shooter, a milky agate with hypnotic swirls, to blast them. Her thumb *had* become stronger.

After practice, she squeezed the eraser for an hour. She ate dinner with her left hand to spare her shooting hand and said nothing to her parents about her dreams of athletic glory.

Practice, practice, practice. Squeeze, squeeze, squeeze. Lupe got better and beat her brother and Alfonso, a neighbor kid who was supposed to be a champ.

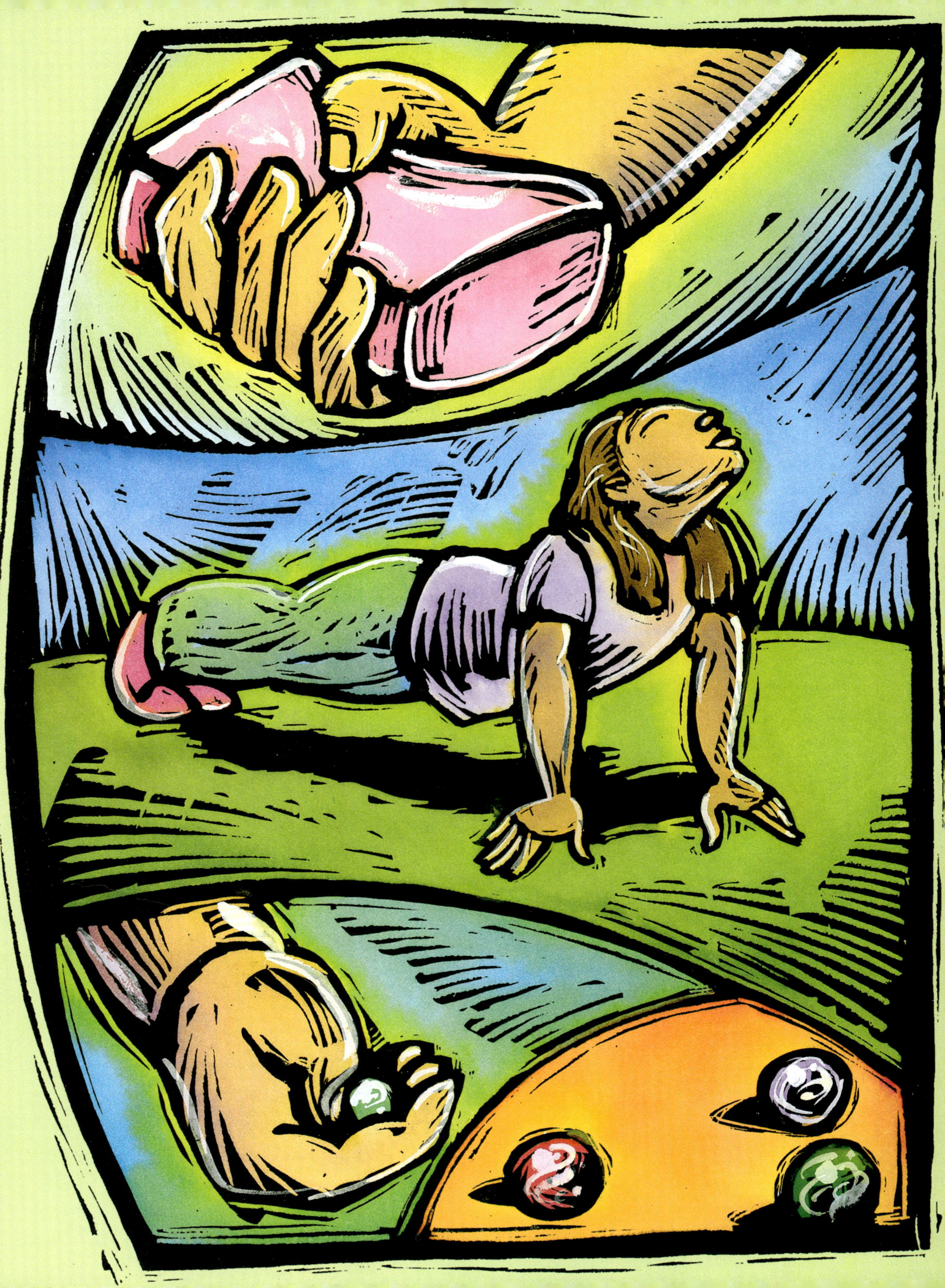

"Man, she's bad!" Alfonso said. "She can beat the other girls for sure. I think."

The weeks passed quickly. Lupe worked so hard that one day, while she was drying dishes, her mother asked why her thumb was swollen.

"It's muscle," Lupe explained. "I've been practicing for the marbles championship."

"You, honey?" Her mother knew Lupe was no good at sports.

"Yeah. I beat Alfonso, and he's pretty good."

That night, over dinner, Mrs. Medrano said, "Honey, you should see Lupe's thumb."

"Huh?" Mr. Medrano said, wiping his mouth and looking at his daughter.

"Show your father."

"Do I have to?" an embarrassed Lupe asked.

"Go on, show your father."

Reluctantly, Lupe raised her hand and flexed her thumb. You could see the muscle.

The father put down his fork and asked, "What happened?"

"Dad, I've been working out. I've been squeezing an eraser."

"Why?"

"I'm going to enter the marbles championship."

Her father looked at her mother and then back at his daughter. "When is it, honey?"

"This Saturday. Can you come?"

The father had been planning to play racquetball with a friend Saturday, but he said he would be there. He knew his daughter thought she was no good at sports and he wanted to encourage her. He even rigged some lights in the backyard so she could practice after dark. He squatted with one knee on the ground, entranced by the sight of his daughter easily beating her brother.

The day of the championship began with a cold blustery sky. The sun was a silvery light behind slate clouds.

"I hope it clears up," her father said, rubbing his hands together as he returned from getting the newspaper. They ate breakfast, paced nervously around the house waiting for 10:00 to arrive, and walked the two blocks to the playground (though Mr. Medrano wanted to drive so Lupe wouldn't get tired). She signed up and was assigned her first match on baseball diamond number three.

Lupe, walking between her brother and her father, shook from the cold, not nerves. She took off her mittens, and everyone stared at her thumb. Someone asked, "How can you play with a broken thumb?" Lupe smiled and said nothing.

She beat her first opponent easily, and felt sorry for the girl because she didn't have anyone to cheer for her. Except for her sack of marbles, she was all alone. Lupe invited the girl, whose name was Rachel, to stay with them. She smiled and said, "OK." The four of them walked to a card table in the middle of the outfield, where Lupe was assigned another opponent.

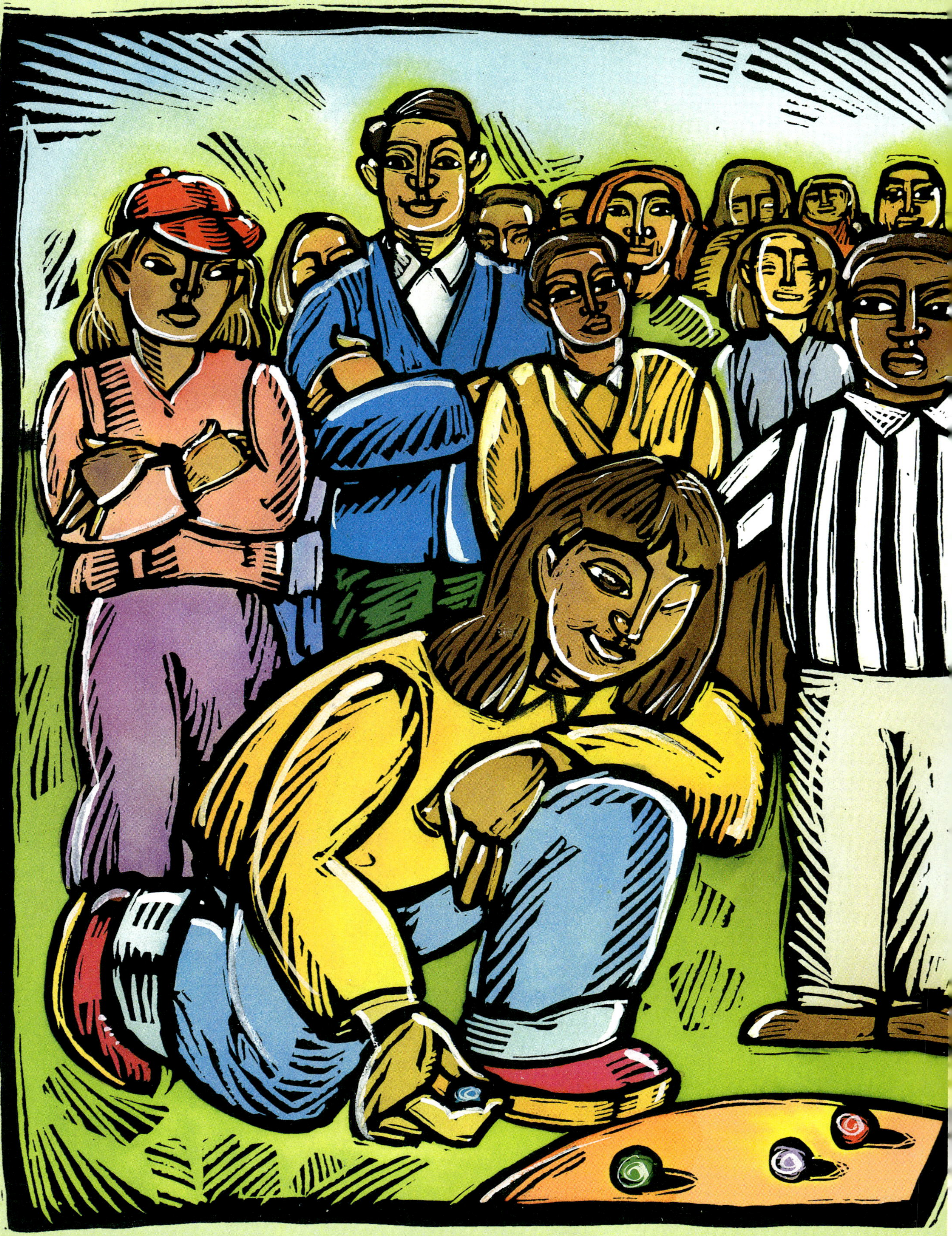

She also beat this girl, a fifth-grader named Yolanda, and asked her to join their group. They proceeded to more matches and more wins, and soon there was a crowd of people following Lupe to the finals to play a girl in a baseball cap. This girl seemed dead serious. She never even looked at Lupe.

"I don't know, Dad, she looks tough."

Rachel hugged Lupe and said, "Go get her."

"You can do it," her father encouraged. "Just think of the marbles, not the girl, and let your thumb do the work."

The other girl broke first and earned one marble. She missed her next shot, and Lupe, one eye closed, her thumb quivering with energy, blasted two marbles out of the circle but missed her next shot. Her opponent earned two more before missing. She stamped her foot and said "Shoot!" The score was three to two in favor of Miss Baseball Cap.

The referee stopped the game. "Back up, please, give them room," he shouted. Onlookers had gathered too tightly around the players.

Lupe then earned three marbles and was set to get her fourth when a gust of wind blew dust in her eyes and she missed badly. Her opponent quickly scored two marbles, tying the game, and moved ahead six to five on a lucky shot. Then she missed, and Lupe, whose eyes felt scratchy when she blinked, relied on instinct and thumb muscle to score the tying point. It was now six to six, with only three marbles left. Lupe blew her nose and studied the angles. She dropped to one knee, steadied her hand, and shot so hard she cracked two marbles from the circle. She was the winner!

"I did it!" Lupe said under her breath. She rose from her knees, which hurt from bending all day, and hugged her father. He hugged her back and smiled.

Everyone clapped, except Miss Baseball Cap, who made a face and stared at the ground. Lupe told her she was a great player, and they shook hands. A newspaper photographer took pictures of the two girls standing shoulder-to-shoulder, with Lupe holding the bigger trophy.

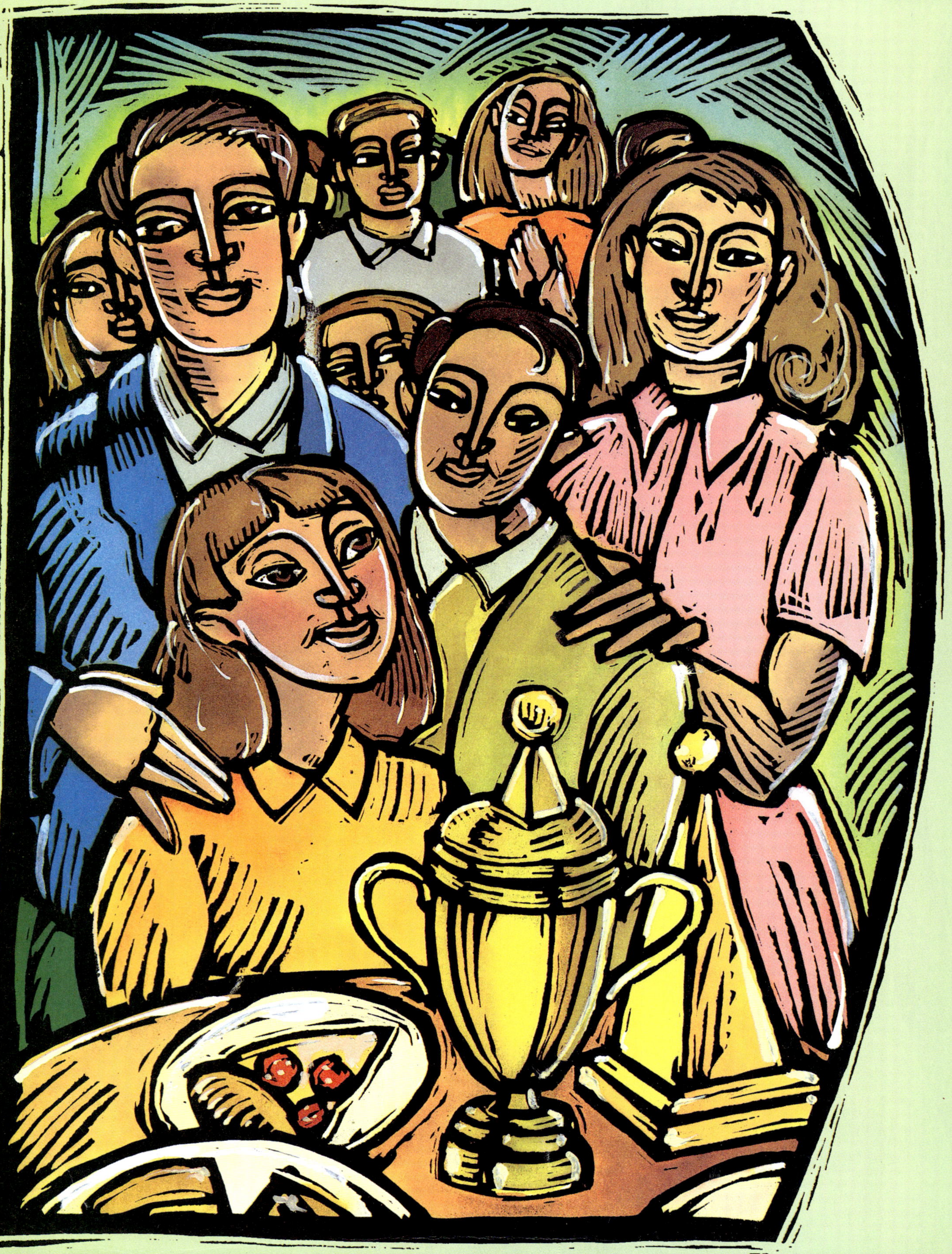

Lupe then played the winner of the boys' division, and after a poor start beat him eleven to four. She blasted the marbles, shattering one into sparkling slivers of glass. Her opponent looked on glumly as Lupe did what she did best—win!

The head referee and the President of the Fresno Marble Association stood with Lupe as she displayed her trophies for the newspaper photographer. Lupe shook hands with everyone, including a dog who had come over to see what the commotion was all about.

That night, the family went out for pizza and set the two trophies on the table for everyone in the restaurant to see. People came up to congratulate Lupe, and she felt a little embarrassed, but her father said the trophies belonged there.

Back home, in the privacy of her bedroom, she placed the trophies on her shelf and was happy. She had always earned honors because of her brains, but winning in sports was a new experience. She thanked her tired thumb. "You did it, thumb. You made me champion." As its reward, Lupe went to the bathroom, filled the bathroom sink with warm water, and let her thumb swim and splash as it pleased. Then she climbed into bed and drifted into a hard-won sleep.

Think About It

1. What problem does Lupe want to solve, and how does she solve it?
2. What do you think are Lupe's best qualities? Explain.
3. How is Lupe's father important to the story?

Meet the Author

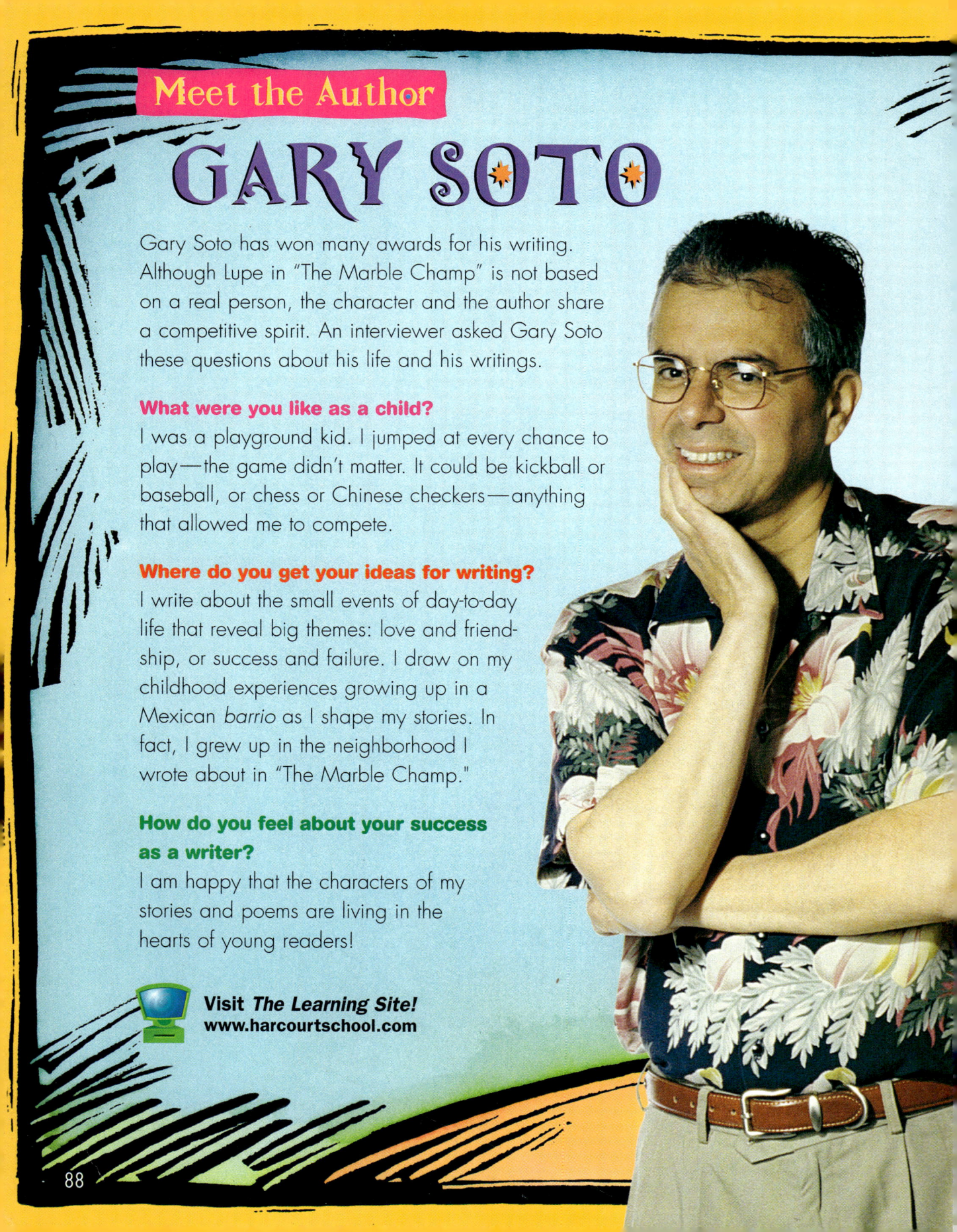

GARY SOTO

Gary Soto has won many awards for his writing. Although Lupe in "The Marble Champ" is not based on a real person, the character and the author share a competitive spirit. An interviewer asked Gary Soto these questions about his life and his writings.

What were you like as a child?
I was a playground kid. I jumped at every chance to play—the game didn't matter. It could be kickball or baseball, or chess or Chinese checkers—anything that allowed me to compete.

Where do you get your ideas for writing?
I write about the small events of day-to-day life that reveal big themes: love and friendship, or success and failure. I draw on my childhood experiences growing up in a Mexican *barrio* as I shape my stories. In fact, I grew up in the neighborhood I wrote about in "The Marble Champ."

How do you feel about your success as a writer?
I am happy that the characters of my stories and poems are living in the hearts of young readers!

Visit *The Learning Site!*
www.harcourtschool.com

Meet the Illustrator

DAVID DIAZ

Like Lupe, David Diaz is no stranger to competition. His high school art teacher encouraged his students to enter art competitions. Diaz soon realized that he could be successful *and* make a living doing something he loved. Over the years, he experimented with different techniques until he developed his own unique style. David Diaz's hard work and competitive spirit have helped him become an award-winning illustrator.

So Long,

Michael Jordan retired after 13 seasons with the Chicago Bulls (1984–93; 1995–98). His career was full of incredible thrills. Here's a look at a few of them. Thanks, Michael. We'll miss you!

★ Hello, Chicago!
Michael was awesome as a rookie (1984–85). He finished third in the league in scoring (28.2 points per game) and was the NBA Rookie of the Year. The Bulls reached the playoffs but lost in the first round. Michael was just getting warmed up!

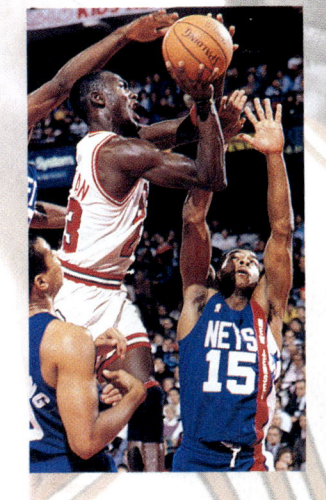

★ Non-Stop Scoring Machine
Michael won the first of his 10 NBA scoring titles in the 1986–87 season. He averaged 37.1 points per game, an NBA record for a guard. Michael scored 3,041 points that season. Only legendary 7' 1" center Wilt Chamberlain had scored more than 3,000 points in a single season.

★ Olympian
Michael led the U.S. "Dream Team" at the 1992 Summer Olympics. He was one of 11 NBA stars on the team. It was the first time pro players were allowed to play at the Olympics. Michael's teammates included Karl Malone, Charles Barkley, and Larry Bird. The U.S. won the gold medal. Michael averaged 14.9 points per game.

Michael

from *Sports Illustrated for Kids*

★ Baseball Dreams
Michael retired from basketball on October 6, 1993. He decided to play pro baseball. He joined the Chicago White Sox' Class AA minor league team, the Birmingham Barons. He batted .202 as a rightfielder in 127 games during the 1994 season.

★ Back to the Basket
On March 18, 1995, Michael announced that he was returning to basketball. His number 23 jersey had already been retired, so he wore number 45. His older brother Larry had worn that number in high school. In just his fifth game back, Michael burned the New York Knicks for 55 points.

★ Michael Makes a Movie
The movie *Space Jam* opened in theaters in November 1996. Michael starred in the film, along with Porky Pig, Bugs Bunny, Daffy Duck, and the rest of the Looney Tunes cartoon characters. NBA players Charles Barkley and Patrick Ewing were in the movie too. The movie was a hit!

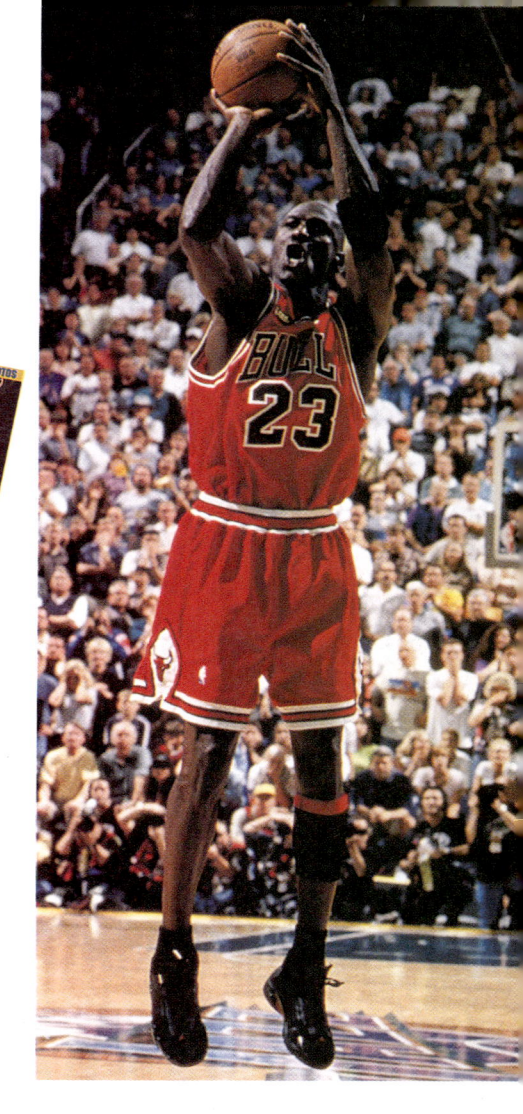

★ What a Way to Go!
The Bulls beat the Utah Jazz, four games to two, in the 1998 NBA Finals. It was Chicago's sixth NBA championship in eight seasons. Michael scored 45 points in Game 6. His thrilling 17-foot jump shot with 6.9 seconds left in the game gave Chicago an 87–86 victory. The shot was Michael's last.

Think About It
How would you describe Michael Jordan? Why would you use those words?

91

RESPONSE

BECOME AN ILLUSTRATOR

DRAW A PICTURE Draw a picture for a story scene that is not already illustrated, or draw a new interpretation of a scene that is shown. Use story details to capture the action. Display your picture in the classroom.

DEAR DIARY,...

WRITE JOURNAL ENTRIES Imagine that you are Lupe, keeping a diary during the competition. Write three or four entries about how you feel and what you are learning about yourself. Set a new goal, and tell how you might achieve it.

ACTIVITIES

AND THE WINNER IS . . .

INTERVIEW A CLASSMATE Interview a classmate who has won an award during a sports, school, or music competition. Ask how he or she prepared for the contest and what happened during it. Write a paragraph based on your discussion.

MAKING CONNECTIONS

DO RESEARCH Both Lupe and Michael Jordan work hard to be the best at what they do. Choose one person you admire who has worked hard to reach his or her personal best. Look for some facts about this person in your school library or on the Internet. Organize what you learn in a chart. Post your chart on a bulletin board in the classroom.

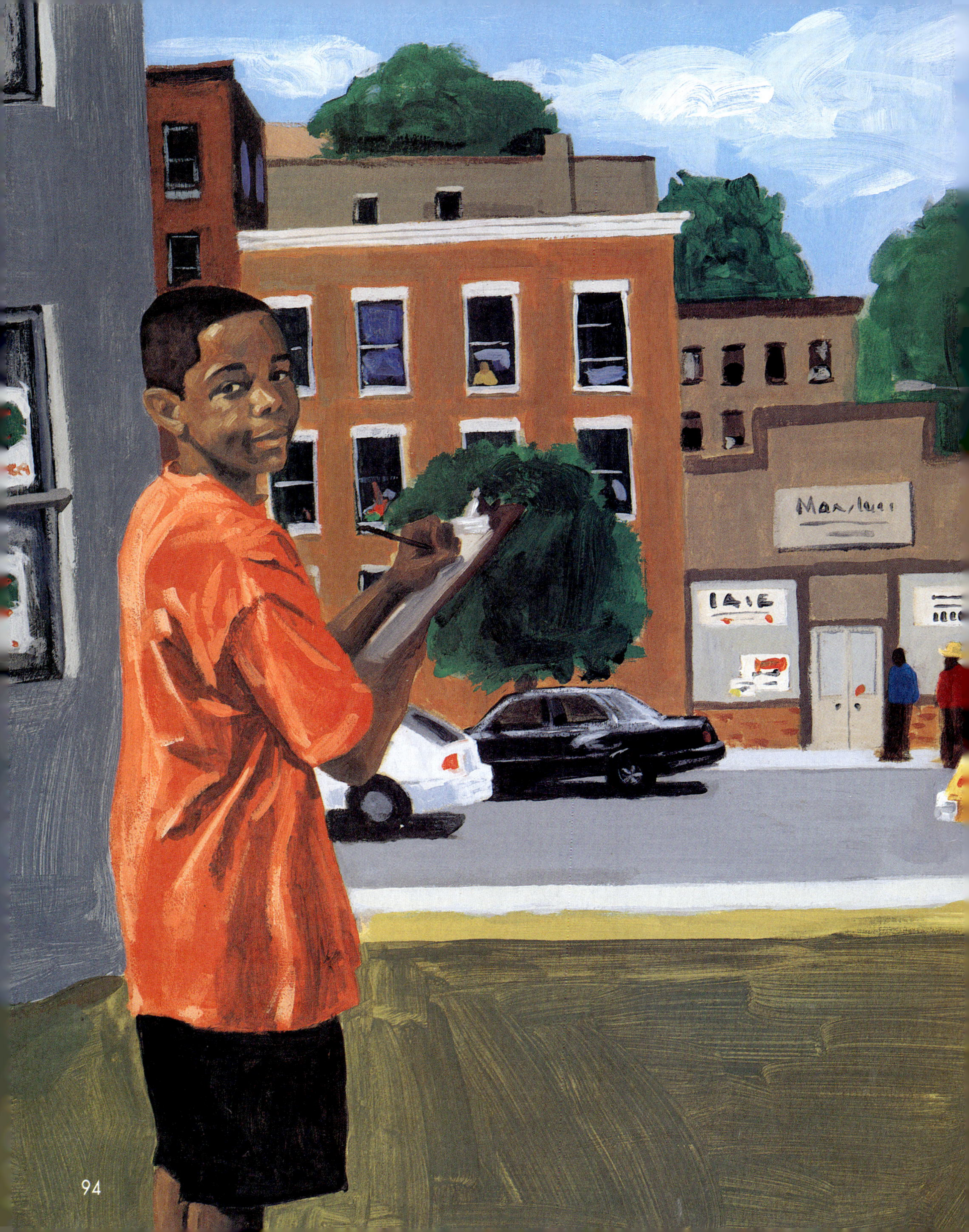

Darnell Rock Reporting

by Walter Dean Myers
illustrated by James Ransome

To prove to the principal, Mr. Baker, that he is not a failure, Darnell Rock joins the school newspaper. His first assignment is to interview a homeless man named Sweeby Jones. Darnell writes an article suggesting that an empty lot near his school be turned into a garden for homeless people. When his article is reprinted in the *Oakdale Journal*, another student, Linda Gold, writes an opposing article. Darnell and Linda are given a chance to speak at a City Council meeting, where the issue will be decided.

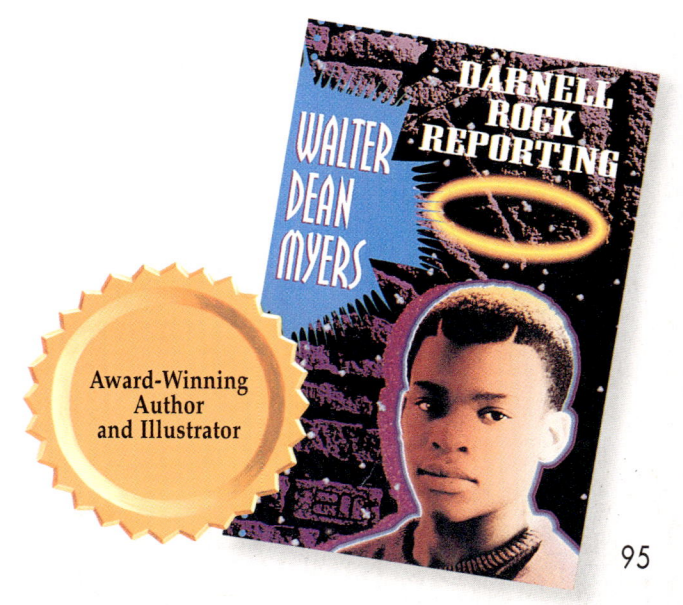

Award-Winning Author and Illustrator

City Garden offers a chance to help community.

by Darnell Rock

"Nobody wants to be homeless," Sweeby Jones said. He is a homeless man who lives in our city of Oakdale. It is for him and people like him that I think we should build a garden where the basketball courts were, near the school. That way the homeless people can help themselves by raising food.

"You see a man or woman that's hungry and you don't feed them, or help them feed themselves, then you got to say you don't mind people being hungry," Mr. Jones said. "And if you don't mind people being hungry, then there is something wrong with you."

This is what Mr. Sweeby Jones said when I spoke to him. I don't want to be the kind of person who says it's all right for some people to be hungry. I want to do something about it. But I think there is another reason to have the garden. Things can happen to people that they don't plan. You can get sick, and not know why, or even homeless. But sometimes there are things you can do to change your life or make it good. If you don't do anything to make your life good, it will probably not be good.

"I was born poor and will probably be poor all my life," Mr. Sweeby Jones said.

I think maybe it is not how you were born that makes the most difference, but what you do with your life. The garden is a chance for some people to help their own lives.

Empty lot should benefit local teachers

by Linda Gold

Teaching is a difficult profession. Teachers need as much support as they can possibly get. After all, we are dependent on them for our future. Education is the key to a good and secure future, and teachers help us to get that education. We must give them all the support we can. This is why I am supporting the idea of building a parking lot near the school.

There are some people in our school who think it is a good idea to build a garden so that the homeless can use it. Use it for what? Homeless people don't have experience farming and could not use the land anyway. This is just a bad idea that will help nobody and will hurt the teachers. The teachers give us good examples on how we should live and how we should conduct ourselves. The homeless people, even though it is no fault of theirs, don't give us good examples.

On Friday evening, at 7:00 p.m., the City Council will meet to make a final decision. I urge them to support the teachers, support education, and support the students at South Oakdale.

"You see anybody from the school?" Larry looked over the large crowd at the Oakdale Court building.

"There goes Mr. Derby *and* Mr. Baker." Tamika pointed toward the front of the building.

Darnell felt a lump in the pit of his stomach. There were at least a hundred people at the City Council meeting.

Tamika led them through the crowd to where she had spotted Mr. Derby and South Oakdale's principal. The large, high-ceilinged room had rows of benches that faced the low platform for the City Council. Linda Gold was already sitting in the front row. Darnell saw that her parents were with her.

He had brought a copy of the *Journal* with him and saw that a few other people, grown-ups, also had copies of the paper.

The nine members of the City Council arrived, and the meeting was called to order. The city clerk said that there were five items on the agenda, and read them off. The first three items were about Building Code violations. Then came something about funding the city's library.

"The last item will be the use of the basketball courts as a parking lot at South Oakdale Middle School," the clerk said. "We have three speakers scheduled."

Linda turned and smiled at Darnell.

"You want me to run up there and punch her out?" Tamika whispered to Darnell.

Darnell didn't know what Building Code violations were but watched as building owners showed diagrams explaining why there were violations. The first two weren't that interesting, but the third one was. A company had built a five-story building that was supposed to be a minimum of twenty feet from the curb, but it was only fifteen feet.

98

"You mean to tell me that your engineers only had fifteen-foot rulers?" one councilman asked.

"Well, er, we measured it right the first time"—the builder shifted from one foot to the other—"but then we made some changes in the design and somehow we sort of forgot about the er . . . you know . . . the other five feet."

To Darnell the builder sounded like a kid in his homeroom trying to make an excuse for not having his homework.

"Can you just slide the building back five or six feet?" the councilman asked.

Everybody laughed and the builder smiled, but Darnell could tell he didn't think it was funny.

Somebody touched Darnell on the shoulder, and he turned and saw his parents.

"We have this ordinance for a reason," a woman on the Council was saying. "I don't think we should lightly dismiss this violation. An exception granted here is just going to encourage others to break the law."

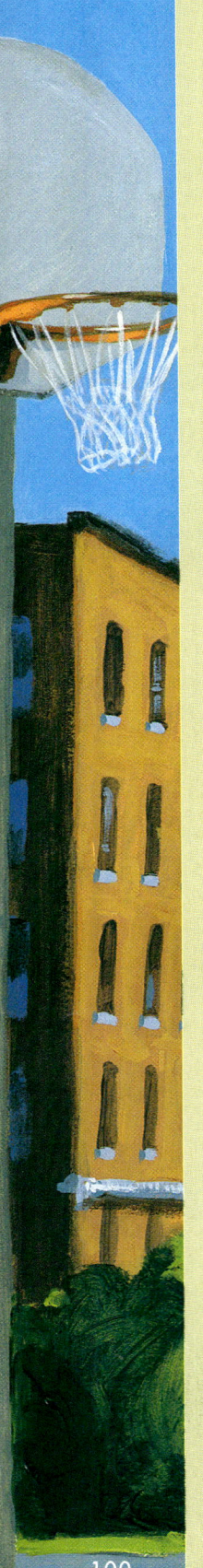

"This is going to ruin me," the builder said. "I've been in Oakdale all of my life and I think I've made a contribution."

"Let's have a vote." The head of the Council spoke sharply.

"Let's have a vote to postpone a decision," the woman who had spoken before said. "We'll give Mr. Miller an opportunity to show his good faith."

"What do you want me to do?" the builder asked.

"That's up to you," the woman said.

"Next time you'd better get it right!" Tamika called out.

"She's right," the councilwoman said.

There was a vote, and the decision was postponed. The builder gave Tamika a dirty look as he pushed his papers into his briefcase.

The city library funding was next, and eight people, including Miss Seldes, spoke for the library, but the Council said it didn't have any more money. There was some booing, including some from Tamika and Larry. Darnell knew that if he didn't have to speak he would have enjoyed the meeting.

"The issue at South Oakdale is should the old basketball courts be used as a parking lot, or should they be used as a community garden?"

"Who's going to pay for paving the lot?" a councilman asked. "Does it have to be paved?"

"It's my understanding that it doesn't have to be paved," the head of the Council answered. "Am I right on that?"

"Yes, you are," Miss Joyner spoke up from the audience.

"We have two young people from the school to speak," the councilwoman said. "The first is a Miss Gold."

Linda went into the middle aisle, where there was a microphone. She began reading her article in the snootiest voice that Darnell had ever heard. He felt a knot in his stomach. He turned to look at his mother, and she was smiling. On the stage some of the councilmen were looking at some papers.

"I hope I don't mess up," he whispered to Tamika.

"You won't," Tamika said.

Linda finished reading her article and then turned toward Darnell.

"Although everybody would like to help the homeless," she said, "schools are supposed to be for kids, and for those who teach kids! Thank you."

There was applause for Linda, and Miss Joyner stood up and nodded toward her. Darnell felt his hands shaking.

Darnell's name was called, and he made the long trip to the microphone.

"When I first thought about having a garden instead of a parking lot, I thought it was just a good idea," Darnell said. "Then, when the *Journal* asked me to send them a copy of my interview with Mr. Jones, I was thinking that it was mainly a good idea to have a garden to help out the homeless people. But now I think it might be a good idea to have the garden to help out the kids— some of the kids—in the school.

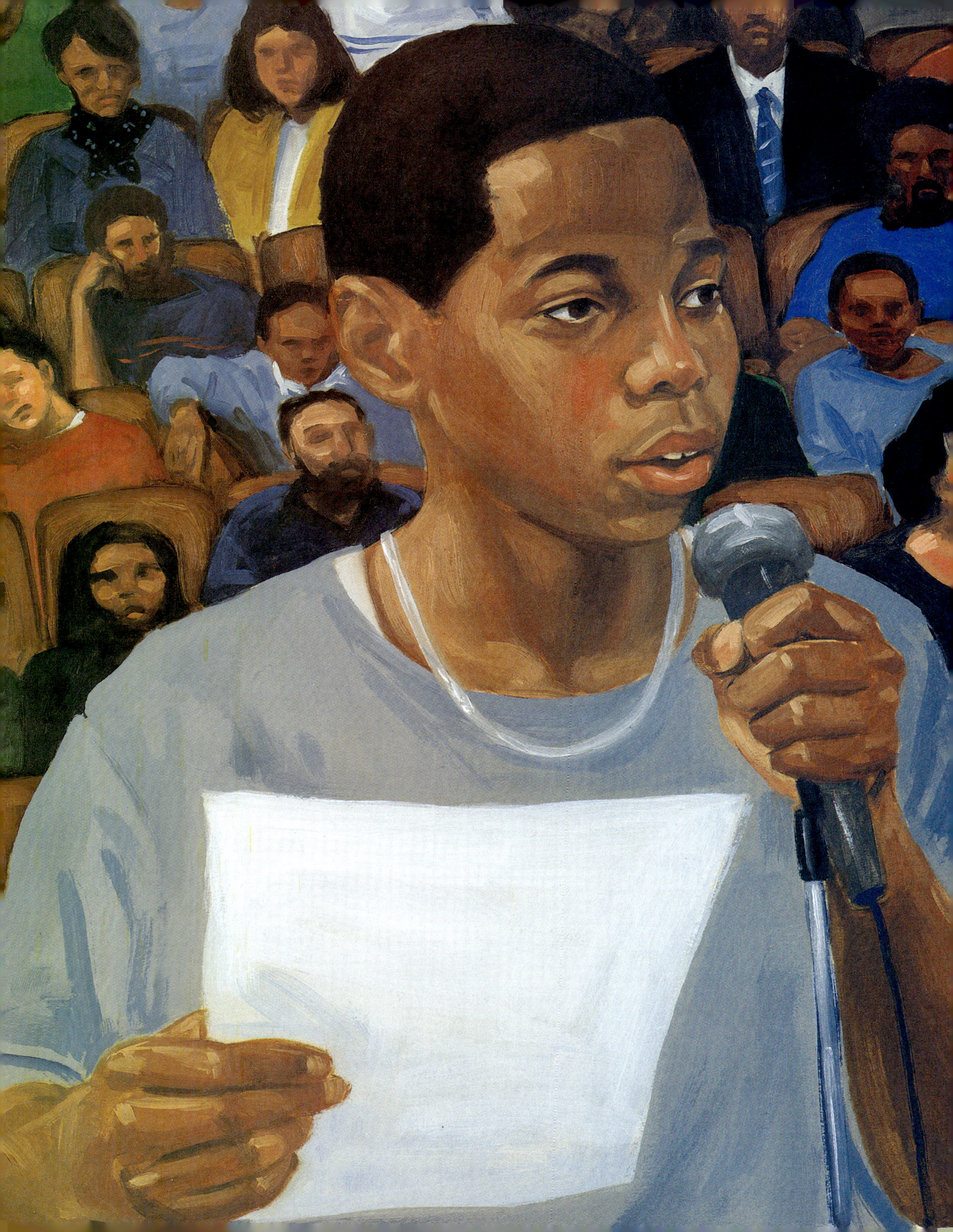

"Sometimes, when people go through their life they don't do the things that can make them a good life. I don't know why they don't do the right thing, or maybe even if they know what the right thing is sometimes.

"But I see the same thing in my school, South Oakdale. Some of the kids always do okay, but some of us don't. Maybe their parents are telling them something, or maybe they know something special. But if you're a kid who isn't doing so good, people start off telling you what you should be doing, and you know it, but sometimes you still don't get it done and mess up some more. Then people start expecting you to mess up, and then *you* start expecting you to mess up. Teachers get mad at you, or the principal, or your parents, and they act like you're messing up on purpose. Like you want to get bad marks and stuff like that. Then you don't want people getting on your case all the time so you don't do much because the less you do the less they're going to be on your case. Only that doesn't help anything, and everybody knows it, but that's the way it goes."

"You seem to be doing all right, young man," the head of the City Council said.

"I wasn't doing too hot before," Darnell said, taking a quick look over to where Mr. Baker sat. " But when I got on the paper and the *Journal* printed my article, then everybody started treating me different. People came up to me and started explaining their points of view instead of just telling me what to do. And you people are listening to me. The kids I hung out with, they called us the Corner Crew, are mostly good kids but you wouldn't listen to them unless they got into trouble.

"In South Oakdale some kids have bad things happen to them—like they get sick—and I don't know why that happens, but all they can do is to go to the hospital. And some kids just get left out of the good things and can't find a way of getting back into them. People get mad at them the same way they get mad at the homeless people or people who beg on the street.

Maybe the garden will be a way for the homeless people to get back into some good things, and maybe seeing the homeless people getting back into a better life will be a way for some of the kids to think about what's happening to them. Thank you."

There was some applause as Darnell turned to go back to his seat.

"Just a minute, young man," one of the councilmen called to him. "The girl said that these people don't know anything about raising a garden. Is that true?"

"It doesn't matter," someone said from the audience. "I'm from the college, and we can help with technical advice."

"I didn't ask you," the councilman said.

"I'm telling you anyway," the man said.

"I don't know how effective a community garden would be," the councilman said. "You can't feed people from a garden."

"You could sell what you grow," Darnell heard himself saying.

"I think bringing people who are . . . nonschool people into that close a contact with children might not be that good an idea," the councilman said. "Who's the last speaker?"

"A Mr. Jones," the clerk said.

Sweeby came into the middle aisle, and a lot of people began to talk among themselves. There were a lot of things they were interested in, and most of them were not interested in the school parking lot.

"I just want to ask you why you don't want to listen to this boy," Sweeby asked.

"You have four minutes to speak," the councilman said. He seemed angry. "We don't have to answer your questions."

"You don't have to answer my questions," Sweeby said. "And you don't have to have the garden. You don't have to think about us—what you call us?—nonschool people?

"But it's a shame you don't want to listen to this boy. I wish he had been my friend when I was his age. Maybe I would be sitting in one of your seats instead of being over here."

"Is there anything more?" the councilman asked.

"No, you can just forget about the whole thing now," Sweeby said. "Go on back to your papers."

"I think we can vote on this issue now," the councilman said.

"I think Mr."—the councilman looked at the agenda to find Darnell's name—"Mr. Darnell Rock had some good points, but it's still a tough issue. Let's get on with the vote."

The vote went quickly. Three councilpeople decided not to vote, five voted against the garden, and only one voted for it.

Darnell took a deep breath and let it out slowly. Tamika patted him on his hand. When he looked at her she had tears in her eyes.

Darnell felt he had let Sweeby down. His father patted him on his back, and Miss Seldes came over.

"You did a good job," she said. "Really good."

"I lost," Darnell said.

"Sometimes you lose," Miss Seldes said. "But you still did a good job."

Sweeby and some of his friends were waiting outside the Council meeting, and they shook hands with Darnell. Sweeby was telling him how the members of the Council didn't really care about people when Darnell saw Linda through the crowd. She waved and he waved back. She was smiling.

Larry's mother came over and asked his father for a lift home, and they were waiting for Larry when Peter Miller from the *Journal* came over.

"Hey, you want to write another article for the paper?" he said. "There's a guy who wants to donate a couple of lots for a garden in another location. My boss wants to run it as a human interest piece."

"Yeah, sure," Darnell said. "You want a long article or a short one?"

"I don't know. Call the paper tomorrow and ask for the city desk," the reporter said. "My editor will give you the word count."

"Okay," Darnell said. "But first I have to check with my editor to see what she wants."

Darnell was disappointed that the Jackson Avenue garden was as small as it was, but as Sweeby said, it was a start. It was located between two abandoned buildings and was fifty feet deep by thirty-five feet wide. A flatbed truck was parked in front of it and was being used as a platform for the mayor as he made his speech about how some kids from South Oakdale had "made things happen."

"And as long as I'm mayor, I'll always listen to the kids, for they are the future!" he said. Then he got down from the truck, got into a limousine, and was gone.

"They should have named it after you!" Larry said.

"When they name stuff after you it means you're dead!" Darnell said.

"Darnell!" It was Linda Gold.

"What?"

"They want you to be in a picture breaking the ground," Linda said.

"Doing what?"

"Breaking the ground," Linda said. "Just come over here and hold the shovel."

Linda reached over and took Darnell's hand and started toward where a small knot of reporters was gathered in one corner.

When they reached the reporters, Darnell was told to put his hand on the shovel.

"You the man of the hour," Sweeby said. He had his hand right next to Darnell's.

They all put one hand on the shovel, as if they were all digging with it at the same time, and had their picture taken. When that was finished, a reporter asked Sweeby how he felt.

"I feel good," Sweeby said. "A young brother like Darnell here has put his mind to a problem of his people. How you going to feel bad when something like that happens?"

"Do you really think this garden is going to make a difference?" the reporter asked.

"It's going to make a big difference," Sweeby said. "Because every time somebody walks by this place they're going to remember that there are people who need some help, and there are some people who are willing to help. You can't see that?"

"Yeah, I guess so," the reporter said, closing his notebook. He shook Sweeby's hand before walking away.

"Looka that," Sweeby said to Darnell after the reporter had left. "When's the last time you think he shook the hand of a used-to-be homeless man?"

"You got a place to stay now?" Darnell asked.

"You got me so excited about being down at the City Council and in the newspapers that I had to do something," Sweeby said. "And me being in the newspapers helped because the hospital offered me a job. Like this garden, it's small, but it's a start. Now, you take care of yourself. I got about a half hour to get to work."

Think About It

1. How does Darnell make a difference in his community?

2. Who do you think presents the better speech to the City Council, Darnell or Linda? Explain.

3. How does Darnell discover the good in himself? Explain.

Meet the Author
Walter Dean Myers

NEW YORK, N.Y. — Like his fictional character Darnell Rock, award-winning author Walter Dean Myers has discovered the good in himself through writing. He says he "wrote fiction on a regular basis from the time I was ten or eleven, filling up notebooks." However, he "never knew writing was a job." He worked at several jobs after leaving the army at age twenty, but none was as rewarding to him as writing.

In the late 1960s Walter Dean Myers won a writing contest. He started writing novels for and about teenagers a few years later. His best-known books are about African American teenagers who live in Harlem, a neighborhood of New York City. He has also written science fiction, nonfiction, and mystery adventure stories.

I wrote fiction on a regular basis from the time I was ten or eleven, filling up notebooks.
—Walter Dean Myers

Meet the Illustrator
James Ransome

POUGHKEEPSIE, N.Y. — James Ransome describes himself as a "visual storyteller." He believes that "the pictures should tell the story that the writer has written." Ransome became interested in art at a very early age when he began watching television and reading comic books. By the time he was a teenager, he was writing and illustrating his own stories. Ransome feels that his work is successful when readers feel as if they are part of the story.

Visit *The Learning Site!*
www.harcourtschool.com

TOMORROW'S MORNING

Volume 6 Number 240

Internet Edition

Goodworks

SAVING THE DAY (and the lake)

Do you have a goal? Maybe it's to learn a new sport. Maybe it's to get that math grade up, do a better job of cleaning up your room (just what was that stuff under the bed?)—or to try to get along better with your brother or sister.

Well, about two years ago, Jason Phillips, 12, made a New Year's resolution, to accomplish a goal. Jason decided he wanted to do something to help the environment. His first thought was to try to save the rainforest, but his parents said that might be a little too big to attempt to solve. They suggested he try to do something closer to home. And that's when Jason decided to save the town's lake, for which his town is named.

Palmer Lake, of Palmer Lake, Colorado, is drying up. Originally 14–15 feet deep, it's now only about 4–5 feet deep.

"Too much sludge is clogging the natural springs that feed the lake," explained Jason. "What I decided to do is go get more information about the lake, to learn how I could help it."

Jason, a third-grader at the time, spoke with a woman at the town's museum and she gave Jason lots of information about the history of the lake. He also went to speak to the town's finance (money) person to learn what the town was trying to do to save the lake.

"After getting the information together, I wrote a speech about the need to save our lake and gave it to other grades in my school. I got coffee cans and asked the school kids to make contributions to the lake's rejuvenation (bringing-it-back-to-life) project," said Jason. The first year, $383 was collected at the school.

"I formed a kids' committee last year of 13 kids to help in my project of saving the lake. Kids had to give me three reasons why they wanted to help me, and from there I got my committee together," explained Jason. More coffee cans were placed in each classroom, as well as in many local businesses. Other fund-raising activities have included selling pasta—and also buttons with a picture of the lake. Jason is currently working with the owner of the local T-shirt company to make up shirts to sell with a logo of the lake on them.

His speeches and fund-raising projects have been very successful. So far, Jason's efforts have raised about $10,000.

In addition to saving the namesake of the town, Jason said that it's important to save the lake because of the environment. "It's a major drinking area for the wildlife—deer, mountain lions, bears, birds and ducks. They all use the lake. I am concerned that the wildlife will be hurt if the lake isn't fixed."

Jason's efforts have awakened the town to save the lake. And now, they're building nature trails around the lake, as well as soccer and baseball fields for the townspeople to enjoy.

Jason, who's now in sixth grade, says kids can make a difference at any age. "You just have to believe in yourself and if there is something really important to you, just step up and make a difference in some way."

Think About It

Do you agree with Jason that "kids can make a difference at any age"? Why or why not?

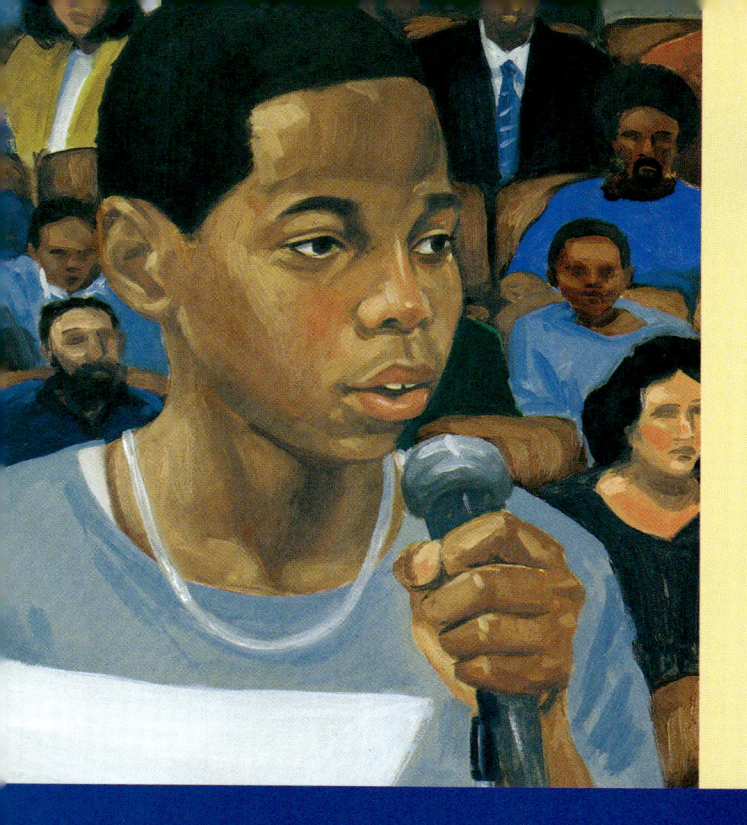

Junior Reporter

ROLE-PLAY A JOB INTERVIEW
Imagine that Darnell wants a summer writing job at the *Journal*. With a partner, role-play a newspaper editor interviewing Darnell. Darnell might talk about how his experience has helped him find the good in himself.

★ Response

The Way I See It

WRITE A PERSUASIVE ESSAY
Darnell writes an article telling why he thinks the basketball court should be a made into a community garden. List the facts he gives to support his opinion. Then think of another way to use the court. Write a persuasive essay that includes your opinion and supporting reasons.

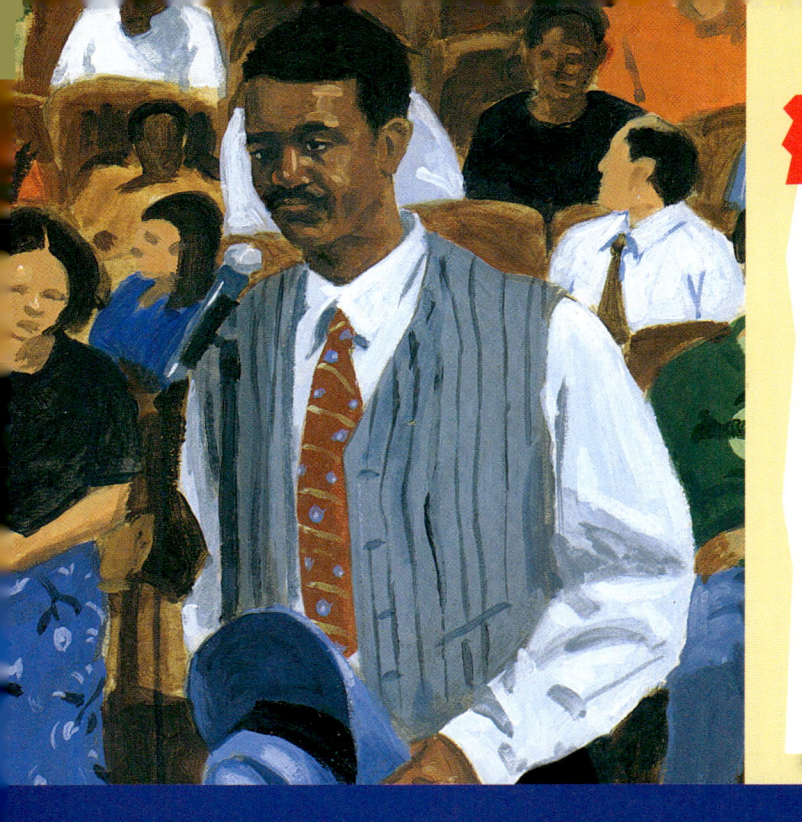

Making Connections

WRITE A NEWSPAPER ARTICLE Imagine that Darnell from "Darnell Rock Reporting" and Jason from "Saving the Day" work together to solve a problem at your school. Write a newspaper article that answers the questions *who*, *what*, *where*, *when*, and *how*. Include a headline and a photo idea. If possible, use a word-processing program to type your article.

Activities ★

Green Thumb

PLAN A COMMUNITY GARDEN Think of what you would grow in a community garden. You might contact a local nursery for ideas. Draw a garden map. Include symbols, a key, and a guide to when to plant, weed, water, prune, and harvest. Display your plan on a bulletin board.

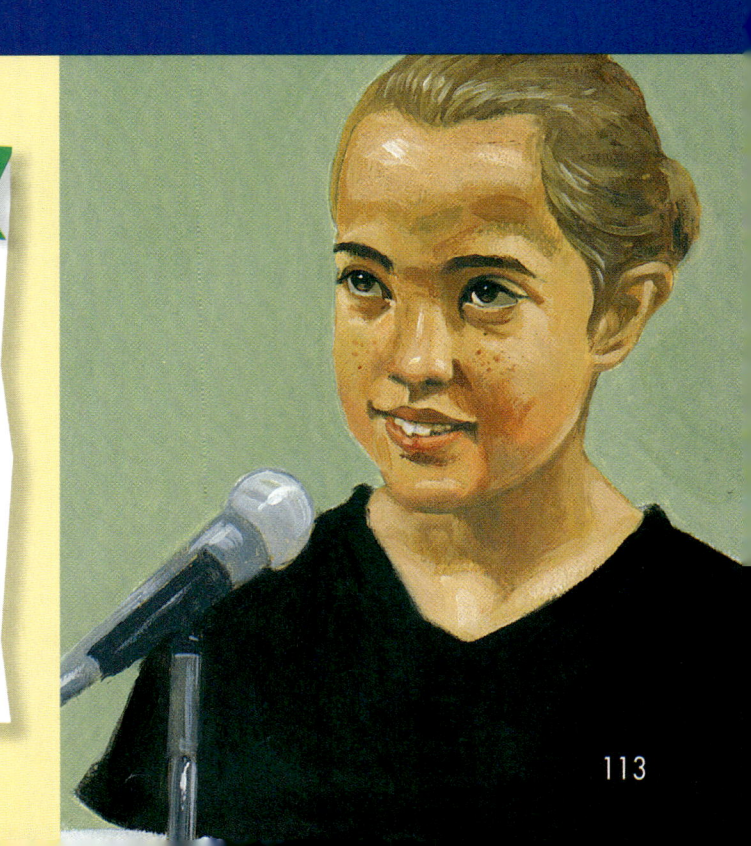

Good Points

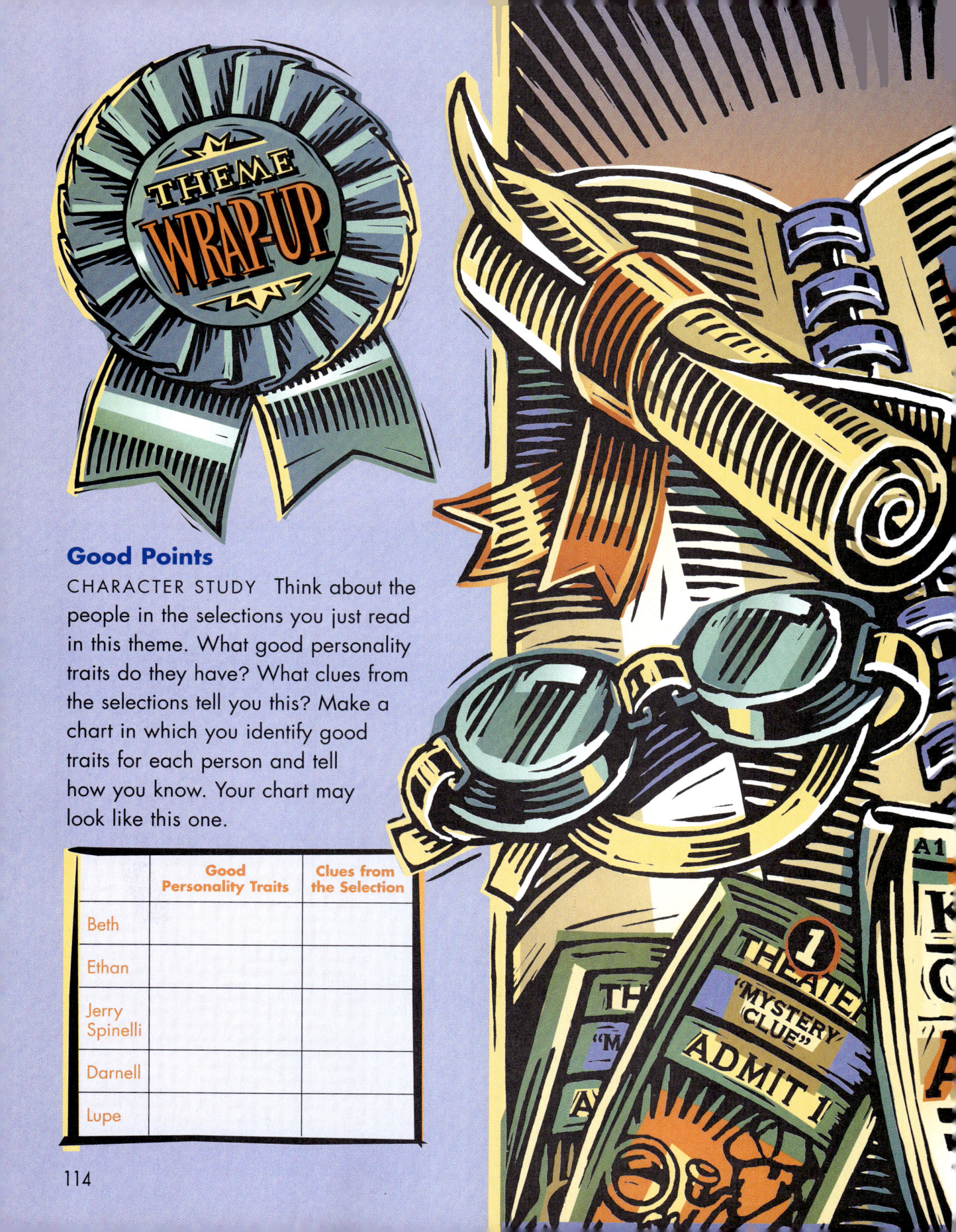

CHARACTER STUDY Think about the people in the selections you just read in this theme. What good personality traits do they have? What clues from the selections tell you this? Make a chart in which you identify good traits for each person and tell how you know. Your chart may look like this one.

	Good Personality Traits	Clues from the Selection
Beth		
Ethan		
Jerry Spinelli		
Darnell		
Lupe		

A Very Important Person

WRITE A CONVERSATION This theme features fictional main characters and real people who all succeed by finding the good in themselves and others. Write an imaginary conversation held by three people from three selections. Have them tell each other about an important person in their lives. Read your conversation aloud, playing the part of each person.

Vote for Your Favorite

CONDUCT A SURVEY With a partner, make a list of five questions about the selections in the theme. You might write questions such as these:

- What is your favorite selection?
- Which character would you most like to have as a friend?

Use your list to survey your classmates. Compile the results and show them in a bar graph.

THEME

FRIENDS
TO THE
RESCUE

CONTENTS

Number the Stars 120
by Lois Lowry

FOCUS SKILL:
Sequence/Cause and Effect 144

The Summer of the Swans .. 146
by Betsy Byars

Old Yeller 166
by Fred Gipson

FOCUS SKILL:
**Author's Purpose
and Perspective** 182

Saving Shiloh 184
by Phyllis Reynolds Naylor

Puppies with a Purpose 204
from *National Geographic World*

**Flood: Wrestling with
the Mississippi** 208
by Patricia Lauber

Smoke Jumpers 224
from *National Geographic World*

117

READER'S

Mrs. Frisby and the Rats of NIMH
by Robert C. O'Brien

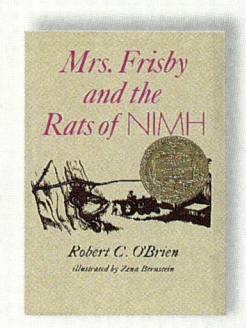

FICTION

Mrs. Frisby, a widowed mouse with a sick child, seeks help from a strange group of ex-laboratory rats. Sworn to secrecy, she discovers some amazing truths, not only about the rats but about her late husband as well.

Newbery Medal/ALA Notable Book
READER'S CHOICE LIBRARY

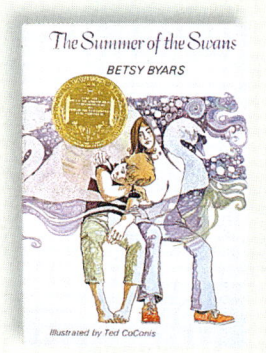

The Summer of the Swans
by Betsy Byars

REALISTIC FICTION

Sara sees herself as ugly and is tired of her everyday routine. But when her ten-year-old brother Charlie is missing, Sara begins to realize her true worth.

Newbery Medal/ALA Notable Book
READER'S CHOICE LIBRARY

CHOICE

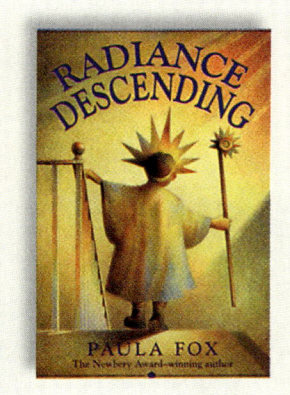

Radiance Descending
by Paula Fox

REALISTIC FICTION

Paul's younger brother, Jacob, has Down's syndrome. At first, Paul is embarrassed by Jacob, but with the help of his wise grandfather, he comes to love and appreciate him.

Notable Children's Book in Language Arts

Make Like a Tree and Leave
by Paula Danziger

REALISTIC FICTION

When an accident leaves their volunteer helper with heavy medical expenses, Mrs. Stanton's class decides to hold a pet wash to raise money.

Passage to Freedom
by Ken Mochizuki

NONFICTION

This is the true story of the only Asian to receive the "Righteous Among the Nations" award for his courage during the Holocaust.
ALA Notable Book
Notable Children's Book in Language Arts
Notable Social Studies Trade Book for Young People
Teacher's Choice

Number the Stars

by Lois Lowry
Illustrated by Russ Wilson

**Newbery Medal
ALA Notable Book
Teachers' Choice**

By 1943, German troops had occupied Denmark for about a year. Annemarie Johansen, her little sister, Kirsti, and her best friend, Ellen, could remember when the tall German soldier, "the Giraffe," and his partner didn't stand watch on the street corner near the school. As the Germans began to "relocate" all the Jews in Denmark, the Johansens had to act heroically during a time of terror and war.

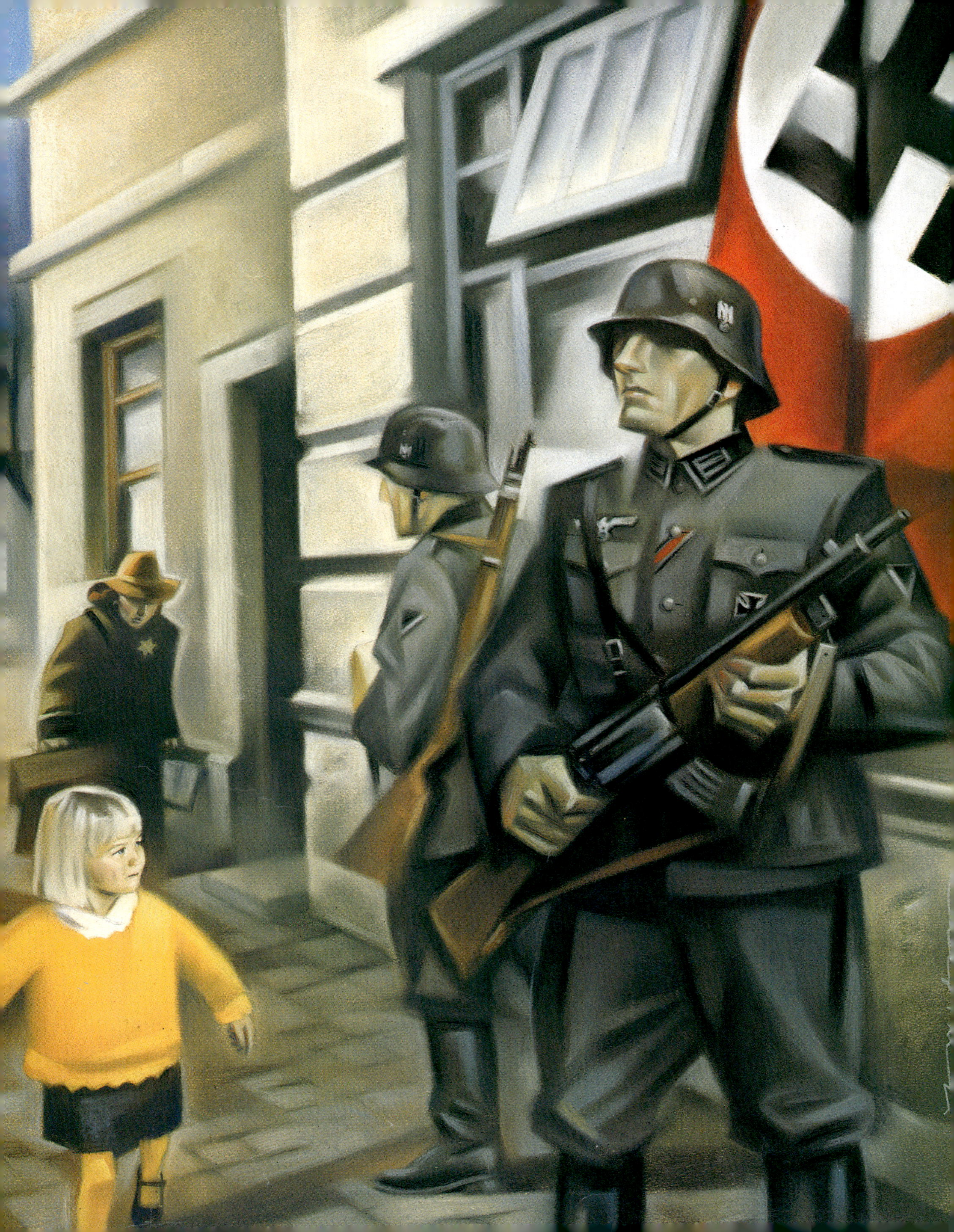

Alone in the apartment while Mama was out shopping with Kirsti, Annemarie and Ellen were sprawled on the living room floor playing with paper dolls. They had cut the dolls from Mama's magazines, old ones she had saved from past years. The paper ladies had old-fashioned hair styles and clothes, and the girls had given them names from Mama's very favorite book. Mama had told Annemarie and Ellen the entire story of *Gone With the Wind*, and the girls thought it much more interesting and romantic than the king-and-queen tales that Kirsti loved.

"Come, Melanie," Annemarie said, walking her doll across the edge of the rug. "Let's dress for the ball."

"All right, Scarlett, I'm coming," Ellen replied in a sophisticated voice. She was a talented performer; she often played the leading roles in school dramatics. Games of the imagination were always fun when Ellen played.

The door opened and Kirsti stomped in, her face tear-stained and glowering. Mama followed her with an exasperated look and set a package down on the table.

"I won't!" Kirsti sputtered. "I won't ever, *ever* wear them! Not if you chain me in a prison and beat me with sticks!"

Annemarie giggled and looked questioningly at her mother. Mrs. Johansen sighed. "I bought Kirsti some new shoes," she explained. "She's outgrown her old ones."

"Goodness, Kirsti," Ellen said, "I wish my mother would get *me* some new shoes. I love new things, and it's so hard to find them in the stores."

"Not if you go to a *fish* store!" Kirsti bellowed. "But most mothers wouldn't make their daughters wear ugly *fish* shoes!"

"Kirsten," Mama said soothingly, "you know it wasn't a fish store. And we were lucky to find shoes at all."

Kirsti sniffed. "Show them," she commanded. "Show Annemarie and Ellen how ugly they are."

Mama opened the package and took out a pair of little girl's shoes. She held them up, and Kirsti looked away in disgust.

"You know there's no leather anymore," Mama explained. "But they've found a way to make shoes out of fish skin. I don't think these are too ugly."

Annemarie and Ellen looked at the fish skin shoes. Annemarie took one in her hand and examined it. It was odd-looking; the fish scales were visible. But it was a shoe, and her sister needed shoes.

"It's not so bad, Kirsti," she said, lying a little.

Ellen turned the other one over in her hand. "You know," she said, "it's only the color that's ugly."

"Green!" Kirsti wailed. "I will never, *ever* wear green shoes!"

"In our apartment," Ellen told her, "my father has a jar of black, black ink. Would you like these shoes better if they were black?"

Kirsti frowned. "Maybe I would," she said, finally.

"Well, then," Ellen told her, "tonight, if your mama doesn't mind, I'll take the shoes home and ask my father to make them black for you, with his ink."

Mama laughed. "I think that would be a fine improvement. What do you think, Kirsti?"

Kirsti pondered. "Could he make them shiny?" she asked. "I want them shiny."

Ellen nodded. "I think he could. I think they'll be quite pretty, black and shiny."

Kirsti nodded. "All right, then," she said. "But you mustn't tell anyone that they're *fish*. I don't want anyone to know." She took her new shoes, holding them disdainfully, and put them on a chair.

Then she looked with interest at the paper dolls.

"Can I play, too?" Kirsti asked. "Can I have a doll?" She squatted beside Annemarie and Ellen on the floor.

Sometimes, Annemarie thought, Kirsti was such a pest, always butting in. But the apartment was small. There was no other place for Kirsti to play. And if they told her to go away, Mama would scold.

"Here," Annemarie said, and handed her sister a cut-out little girl doll. "We're playing *Gone With the Wind*. Melanie and Scarlett are going to a ball. You can be Bonnie. She's Scarlett's daughter."

Kirsti danced her doll up and down happily. "I'm going to the ball!" she announced in a high, pretend voice.

Ellen giggled. "A little girl wouldn't go to a ball. Let's make them go someplace else. Let's make them go to Tivoli!"

"Tivoli!" Annemarie began to laugh. "That's in Copenhagen! *Gone With the Wind* is in America!"

"Tivoli, Tivoli, Tivoli," little Kirsti sang, twirling her doll in a circle.

"It doesn't matter, because it's only a game anyway," Ellen pointed out. "Tivoli can be over there, by that chair. 'Come, Scarlett,'" she said, using her doll voice, "'we shall go to Tivoli to dance and watch the fireworks, and maybe there will be some handsome men there! Bring your silly daughter Bonnie, and she can ride on the carousel'."

Annemarie grinned and walked her Scarlett toward the chair that Ellen had designated as Tivoli. She loved Tivoli Gardens, in the heart of Copenhagen; her parents had taken her there, often, when she was a little girl. She remembered the music and the brightly colored lights, the carousel and ice cream and especially the magnificent fireworks in the evenings: the huge colored splashes and bursts of lights in the evening sky.

"I remember the fireworks best of all," she commented to Ellen.

"Me too," Kirsti said. "I remember the fireworks."

"Silly," Annemarie scoffed. "You never saw the fireworks." Tivoli Gardens was closed now. The German occupation forces had burned part of it, perhaps as a way of punishing the fun-loving Danes for their lighthearted pleasures.

Kirsti drew herself up, her small shoulders stiff. "I did too," she said belligerently. "It was my birthday. I woke up in the night and I could hear

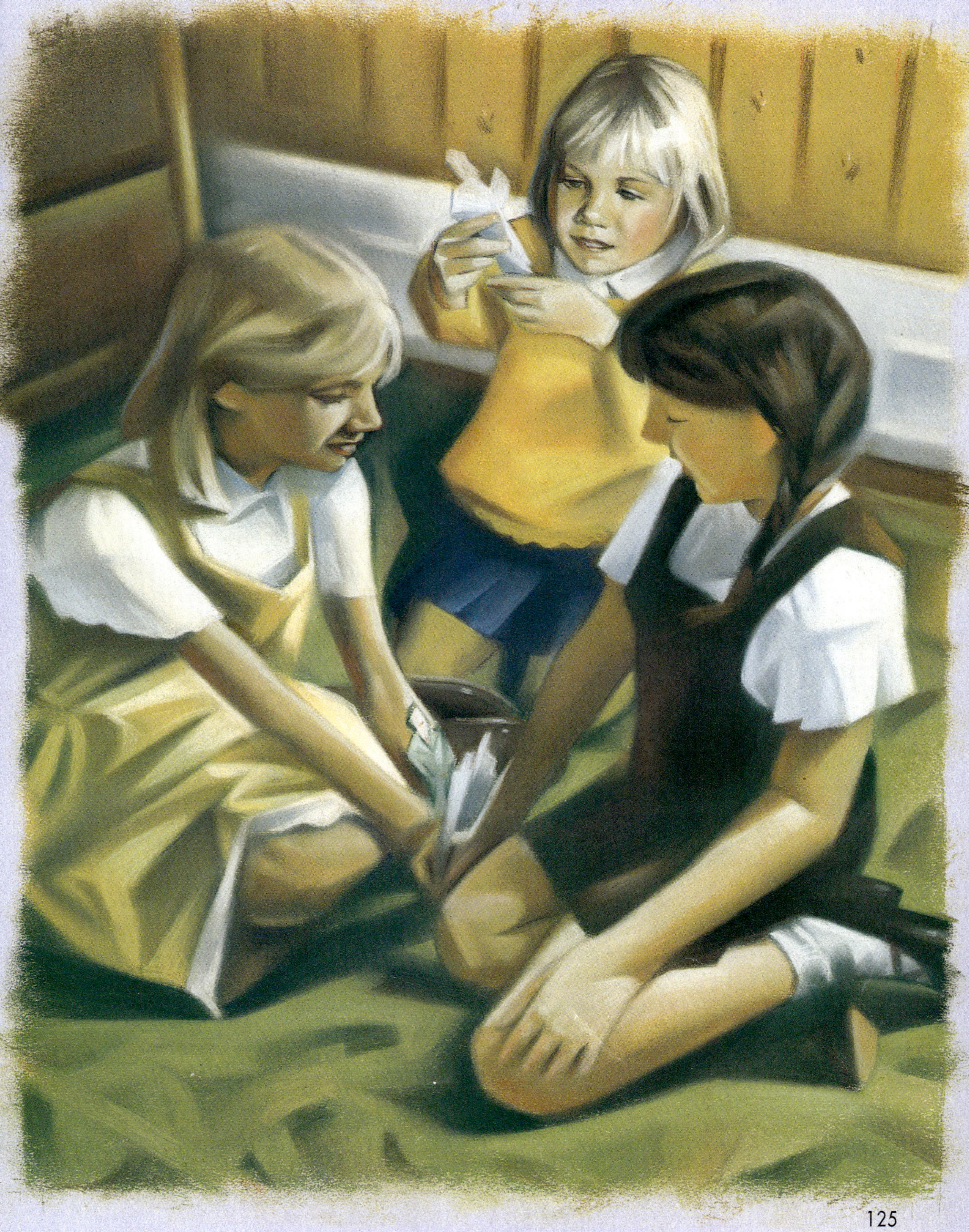

the booms. And there were lights in the sky. Mama said it was fireworks for my birthday!"

Then Annemarie remembered. Kirsti's birthday was late in August. And that night, only a month before, she, too, had been awakened and frightened by the sound of explosions. Kirsti was right — the sky in the southeast had been ablaze, and Mama had comforted her by calling it a birthday celebration. "Imagine, such fireworks for a little girl five years old!" Mama had said, sitting on their bed, holding the dark curtain aside to look through the window at the lighted sky.

The next evening's newspaper had told the sad truth. The Danes had destroyed their own naval fleet, blowing up the vessels one by one, as the Germans approached to take over the ships for their own use.

"How sad the king must be," Annemarie had heard Mama say to Papa when they read the news.

"How proud," Papa had replied.

It had made Annemarie feel sad and proud, too, to picture the tall, aging king, perhaps with tears in his blue eyes, as he looked at the remains of his small navy, which now lay submerged and broken in the harbor.

"I don't want to play anymore, Ellen," she said suddenly, and put her paper doll on the table.

"I have to go home, anyway," Ellen said. "I have to help Mama with the housecleaning. Thursday is our New Year. Did you know that?"

"Why is it yours?" asked Kirsti. "Isn't it our New Year, too?"

"No. It's the Jewish New Year. That's just for us. But if you want, Kirsti, you can come that night and watch Mama light the candles."

Annemarie and Kirsti had often been invited to watch Mrs. Rosen light the Sabbath candles on Friday evenings. She covered her head with a cloth and said a special prayer in Hebrew as she did so. Annemarie always stood very quietly, awed, to watch; even Kirsti, usually such a chatterbox, was always still at that time. They didn't understand the words or the meaning, but they could feel what a special time it was for the Rosens.

"Yes," Kirsti agreed happily. "I'll come and watch your mama light the candles, and I'll wear my new black shoes."

But this time was to be different. Leaving for school on Thursday with her sister, Annemarie saw the Rosens walking to the synagogue early in the morning, dressed in their best clothes. She waved to Ellen, who waved happily back.

"Lucky Ellen," Annemarie said to Kirsti. "She doesn't have to go to school today."

"But she probably has to sit very, very still, like we do in church," Kirsti pointed out. "*That's* no fun."

That afternoon, Mrs. Rosen knocked at their door but didn't come inside. Instead, she spoke for a long time in a hurried, tense voice to Annemarie's mother in the hall. When Mama returned, her face was worried, but her voice was cheerful.

"Girls," she said, "we have a nice surprise. Tonight Ellen will be coming to stay overnight and to be our guest for a few days! It isn't often we have a visitor."

Kirsti clapped her hands in delight.

"But, Mama," Annemarie said, in dismay, "it's their New Year. They were going to have a celebration at home! Ellen told me that her mother managed to get a chicken someplace, and she was going to roast it — their first roast chicken in a year or more!"

"Their plans have changed," Mama said briskly. "Mr. and Mrs. Rosen have been called away to visit some

127

relatives. So Ellen will stay with us. Now, let's get busy and put clean sheets on your bed. Kirsti, you may sleep with Mama and Papa tonight, and we'll let the big girls giggle together by themselves."

Kirsti pouted, and it was clear that she was about to argue. "Mama will tell you a special story tonight," her mother said. "One just for you."

"About a king?" Kirsti asked dubiously.

"About a king, if you wish," Mama replied.

"All right, then. But there must be a queen, too," Kirsti said.

Though Mrs. Rosen had sent her chicken to the Johansens, and Mama made a lovely dinner large enough for second helpings all around, it was not an evening of laughter and talk. Ellen was silent at dinner. She looked frightened. Mama and Papa tried to speak of cheerful things, but it was clear that they were worried, and it made Annemarie worry, too. Only Kirsti was unaware of the quiet tension in the room. Swinging her feet in their newly blackened and shiny shoes, she chattered and giggled during dinner.

"Early bedtime tonight, little one," Mama announced after the dishes were washed. "We need extra time for the long story I promised, about the king and queen." She disappeared with Kirsti into the bedroom.

"What's happening?" Annemarie asked when she and Ellen were alone with Papa in the living room. "Something's wrong. What is it?"

Papa's face was troubled. "I wish that I could protect you children from this knowledge," he said quietly. "Ellen, you already know. Now we must tell Annemarie."

He turned to her and stroked her hair with his gentle hand. "This morning, at the synagogue, the rabbi told his congregation that the Nazis have taken the synagogue lists of all the Jews. Where they live, what their names are. Of course the Rosens were on that list, along with many others."

"Why? Why did they want those names?"

"They plan to arrest all the Danish Jews. They plan to take them away. And we have been told that they may come tonight."

"I don't understand! Take them where?"

Her father shook his head. "We don't know where, and we don't really know why. They call it 'relocation.' We don't even know what that means. We

128

only know that it is wrong, and it is dangerous, and we must help."

Annemarie was stunned. She looked at Ellen and saw that her best friend was crying silently.

"Where are Ellen's parents? We must help them, too!"

"We couldn't take all three of them. If the Germans came to search our apartment, it would be clear that the Rosens were here. One person we can hide. Not three. So Peter has helped Ellen's parents to go elsewhere. We don't know where. Ellen doesn't know either. But they are safe."

Ellen sobbed aloud, and put her face in her hands. Papa put his arm around her. "They are safe, Ellen. I promise you that. You will see them again quite soon. Can you try hard to believe my promise?"

Ellen hesitated, nodded, and wiped her eyes with her hand.

"But, Papa," Annemarie said, looking around the small apartment, with its few pieces of furniture: the fat stuffed sofa, the table and chairs, the small bookcase against the wall. "You said that we would hide her. How can we do that? Where can she hide?"

Papa smiled. "That part is easy. It will be as your mama said: you two will sleep together in your bed, and you may giggle and talk and tell secrets to each other. And if anyone comes —"

Ellen interrupted him. "Who might come? Will it be soldiers? Like the ones on the corners?" Annemarie remembered how terrified Ellen had looked the day when the soldier had questioned them on the corner.

"I really don't think anyone will. But it never hurts to be prepared. If anyone should come, even soldiers, you two will be sisters. You are together so much, it will be easy for you to pretend that you are sisters."

He rose and walked to the window. He pulled the lace curtain aside and looked down into the street. Outside, it was beginning to grow dark. Soon they would have to draw the black curtains that all Danes had on their windows; the entire city had to be completely darkened at night. In a nearby tree, a bird was singing; otherwise it was quiet. It was the last night of September.

"Go, now, and get into your nightgowns. It will be a long night."

Annemarie and Ellen got to their feet. Papa suddenly crossed the room and put his arms around them both. He kissed the top of each head: Annemarie's blond one, which reached to his shoulder, and Ellen's dark hair, the thick curls braided as always into pigtails.

"Don't be frightened," he said to them softly. "Once I had three daughters. Tonight I am proud to have three daughters again."

• • •

"Do you really think anyone will come?" Ellen asked nervously, turning to Annemarie in the bedroom. "Your father doesn't think so."

"Of course not. They're always threatening stuff. They just like to scare people." Annemarie took her nightgown from a hook in the closet.

"Anyway, if they did, it would give me a chance to practice acting. I'd just pretend to be Lise. I wish I were taller, though." Ellen stood on tiptoe, trying to make herself tall. She laughed at herself, and her voice was more relaxed.

"You were great as the Dark Queen in the school play last year," Annemarie told her. "You should be an actress when you grow up."

"My father wants me to be a teacher. He wants *everyone* to be a teacher, like him. But maybe I could convince him that I should go to acting school." Ellen stood on tiptoe again, and made an imperious gesture with her arm. "I am the Dark Queen," she intoned dramatically. "I have come to command the night!"

"You should try saying, 'I am Lise Johansen!'" Annemarie said, grinning. "If you told the Nazis that you were the Dark Queen, they'd haul you off to a mental institution."

131

Ellen dropped her actress pose and sat down, with her legs curled under her, on the bed. "They won't really come here, do you think?" she asked again.

Annemarie shook her head. "Not in a million years." She picked up her hairbrush.

The girls found themselves whispering as they got ready for bed. There was no need, really, to whisper; they were, after all, supposed to be normal sisters, and Papa had said they could giggle and talk. The bedroom door was closed.

But the night did seem, somehow, different from a normal night. And so they whispered.

"How did your sister die, Annemarie?" Ellen asked suddenly. "I remember when it happened. And I remember the funeral — it was the only time I have ever been in a Lutheran church. But I never knew just what happened."

"I don't know *exactly*," Annemarie confessed. "She and Peter were out somewhere together, and then there was a telephone call, that there had been an accident. Mama and Papa rushed to the hospital — remember, your mother came and stayed with me and Kirsti? Kirsti was already asleep and she slept right through everything, she was so little then. But I stayed up, and I was with your mother in the living room when my parents came home in the middle of the night. And they told me Lise had died."

"I remember it was raining," Ellen said sadly. "It was still raining the next morning when Mama told me. Mama was crying, and the rain made it seem as if the whole *world* was crying."

Annemarie finished brushing her long hair and handed her hairbrush to her best friend. Ellen undid her braids, lifted her dark hair away from the thin gold chain she wore around her neck — the chain that held the Star of David — and began to brush her thick curls.

"I think it was partly because of the rain. They said she was hit by a car. I suppose the streets were slippery, and it was getting dark, and maybe the driver just couldn't see," Annemarie went on, remembering. "Papa looked so angry. He made one hand into a fist, and he kept pounding it into the other hand. I remember the noise of it: slam, slam, slam."

Together they got into the wide bed and pulled up the covers. Annemarie blew out the candle and drew the dark curtains aside so that the open window near the bed let in some air. "See that blue trunk in the corner?" she said, pointing through the darkness. "Lots of Lise's things are in there. Even her wedding dress. Mama and Papa have never looked at those things, not since the day they packed them away."

Ellen sighed. "She would have looked so beautiful in her wedding dress. She had such a pretty smile. I used to pretend that she was *my* sister, too."

"She would have liked that," Annemarie told her. "She loved you."

"That's the worst thing in the world," Ellen whispered. "To be dead so young. I wouldn't want the Germans to take my family away — to make us live someplace else. But still, it wouldn't be as bad as being dead."

Annemarie leaned over and hugged her. "They won't take you away," she said. "Not your parents, either. Papa promised that they were safe, and he always keeps his promises. And you are quite safe, here with us."

For a while they continued to murmur in the dark, but the murmurs were interrupted by yawns. Then Ellen's voice stopped, she turned over, and in a minute her breathing was quiet and slow.

Annemarie stared at the window where the sky was outlined and a tree branch moved slightly in the breeze. Everything seemed very familiar, very comforting. Dangers were no more than odd imaginings, like ghost stories that children made up to frighten one another: things that couldn't possibly happen. Annemarie felt completely safe here in her own home, with her parents in the next room and her best friend asleep beside her. She yawned contentedly and closed her eyes.

It was hours later, but still dark, when she was awakened abruptly by the pounding on the apartment door.

Annemarie eased the bedroom door open quietly, only a crack, and peeked out. Behind her, Ellen was sitting up, her eyes wide.

She could see Mama and Papa in their nightclothes, moving about. Mama held a lighted candle, but as Annemarie watched, she went to a lamp and switched it on. It was so long a time since they had dared to use the strictly rationed electricity after dark that the light in the room seemed startling to Annemarie, watching through the slightly opened bedroom door. She saw her mother look automatically to the blackout curtains, making certain that they were tightly drawn.

Papa opened the front door to the soldiers.

"This is the Johansen apartment?"

A deep voice asked the question loudly, in the terribly accented Danish.

"Our name is on the door, and I see you have a flashlight," Papa answered. "What do you want? Is something wrong?"

"I understand you are a friend of your neighbors the Rosens, Mrs. Johansen," the soldier said angrily.

"Sophy Rosen is my friend, that is true," Mama said quietly. "Please, could you speak more softly? My children are asleep."

"Then you will be so kind as to tell me where the Rosens are." He made no effort to lower his voice.

"I assume they are at home, sleeping. It is four in the morning, after all," Mama said.

Annemarie heard the soldier stalk across the living room toward the kitchen. From her hiding place in the narrow sliver of open doorway, she could see the heavy uniformed man, a holstered pistol at his waist, in the entrance to the kitchen, peering in toward the sink.

Another German voice said, "The Rosens' apartment is empty. We are wondering if they might be visiting their good friends the Johansens."

"Well," said Papa, moving slightly so that he was standing in front of Annemarie's bedroom door, and she could see nothing except the dark blur of his back, "as you see, you are mistaken. There is no one here but my family."

"You will not object if we look around." The voice was harsh, and it was not a question.

"It seems we have no choice," Papa replied.

"Please don't wake my children," Mama requested again. "There is no need to frighten little ones."

The heavy, booted feet moved across the floor again and into the other bedroom. A closet door opened and closed with a bang.

Annemarie eased her bedroom door closed silently. She stumbled through the darkness to the bed.

"Ellen," she whispered urgently, "take your necklace off!"

Ellen's hands flew to her neck. Desperately she began trying to unhook the tiny clasp. Outside the bedroom door, the harsh voices and heavy footsteps continued.

"I can't get it open!" Ellen said frantically. "I never take it off — I can't

135

even remember how to open it!"

Annemarie heard a voice just outside the door. "What is here?"

"Shhh," her mother replied. "My daughters' bedroom. They are sound asleep."

"Hold still," Annemarie commanded. "This will hurt." She grabbed the little gold chain, yanked with all her strength, and broke it. As the door opened and light flooded into the bedroom, she crumpled it into her hand and closed her fingers tightly.

Terrified, both girls looked up at the three Nazi officers who entered the room.

One of the men aimed a flashlight around the bedroom. He went to the closet and looked inside. Then with a sweep of his gloved hand he pushed to the floor several coats and a bathrobe that hung from pegs on the wall.

There was nothing else in the room except a chest of drawers, the blue decorated trunk in the corner, and a heap of Kirsti's dolls piled in a small rocking chair. The flashlight beam touched each thing in turn. Angrily the officer turned toward the bed.

"Get up!" he ordered. "Come out here!"

Trembling, the two girls rose from the bed and followed him, brushing past the two remaining officers in the doorway, to the living room.

Annemarie looked around. These three uniformed men were different from the ones on the street corners. The street soldiers were often young, sometimes ill at ease, and Annemarie remembered how the Giraffe had, for a moment, let his harsh pose slip and had smiled at Kirsti.

But these men were older and their faces were set with anger.

Her parents were standing beside each other, their faces tense, but Kirsti was nowhere in sight. Thank goodness that Kirsti slept through almost everything. If they had wakened her, she would be wailing — or worse, she would be angry, and her fists would fly.

"Your names?" the officer barked.

"Annemarie Johansen. And this is my sister —"

"Quiet! Let her speak for herself. Your name?" He was glaring at Ellen.

Ellen swallowed. "Lise," she said, and cleared her throat. "Lise Johansen."

The officer stared at them grimly.

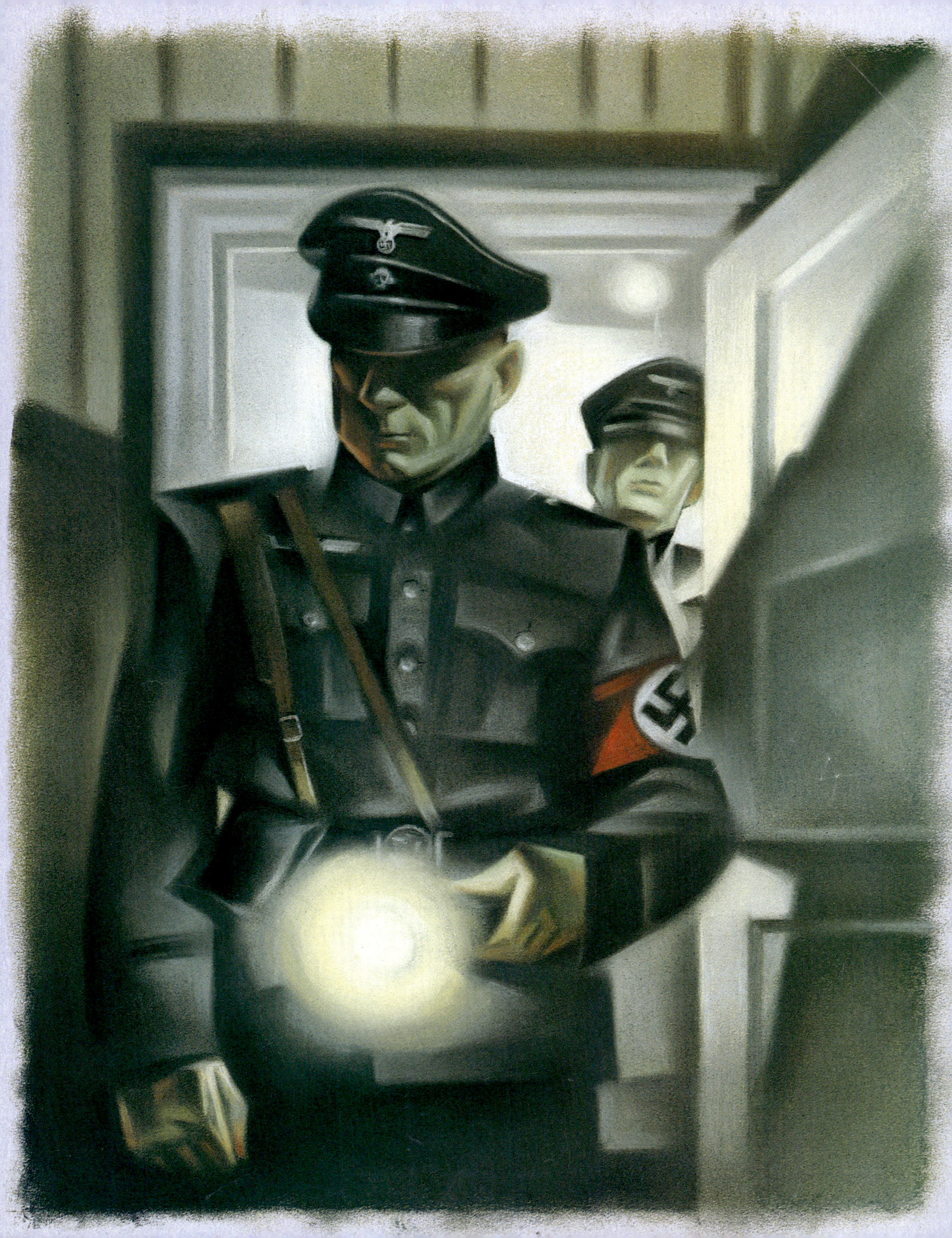

"Now," Mama said in a strong voice, "you have seen that we are not hiding anything. May my children go back to bed?"

The officer ignored her. Suddenly he grabbed a handful of Ellen's hair. Ellen winced.

He laughed scornfully. "You have a blond child sleeping in the other room. And you have this blond daughter —" He gestured toward Annemarie with his head. "Where did you get the dark-haired one?" He twisted the lock of Ellen's hair. "From a different father? From the milkman?"

Papa stepped forward. "Don't speak to my wife in such a way. Let go of my daughter or I will report you for such treatment."

"Or maybe you got her someplace else?" the officer continued with a sneer. "From the Rosens?"

For a moment no one spoke. Then Annemarie, watching in panic, saw her father move swiftly to the small bookcase and take out a book. She saw that he was holding the family photograph album. Very quickly he searched through its pages, found what he was looking for, and tore out three pictures from three separate pages.

He handed them to the German officer, who released Ellen's hair.

"You will see each of my daughters, each with her name written on the photograph," Papa said.

Annemarie knew instantly which photographs he had chosen. The album had many snapshots — all the poorly focused pictures of school events and birthday parties. But it also contained a portrait, taken by a photographer, of each girl as a tiny infant. Mama had written, in her delicate handwriting, the name of each baby daughter across the bottom of those photographs.

She realized too, with an icy feeling, why Papa had torn them from the book. At the bottom of each page, below the photograph itself, was written the date. And the real Lise Johansen had been born twenty-one years earlier.

"Kirsten Elisabeth," the officer read, looking at Kirsti's baby picture. He let the photograph fall to the floor.

"Annemarie," he read next, glanced at her, and dropped the second photograph.

"Lise Margrete," he read finally, and stared at Ellen for a long, unwavering moment. In her mind, Annemarie pictured the photograph that he held: the baby, wide-eyed, propped against a pillow, her tiny hand holding a silver teething ring, her bare feet visible below the hem of an embroidered dress. The wispy curls. Dark.

The officer tore the photograph in half and dropped the pieces on the floor. Then he turned, the heels of his shiny boots grinding into the pictures, and left the apartment. Without a word, the other two officers followed. Papa stepped forward and closed the door behind him.

Annemarie relaxed the clenched fingers of her right hand, which still clutched Ellen's necklace. She looked down, and saw that she had imprinted the Star of David into her palm.

Think About It

1. How does Annemarie's family work together to help save Ellen from the German soldiers?
2. Do you think the Johansen family should have hidden Ellen? Explain why you feel as you do.
3. How does the author use dialogue and actions to make the German soldiers seem powerful and threatening?

Meet the Author
Lois Lowry

Lois Lowry has written many award-winning books for young readers. Here, Lowry talks about her Newbery Award-Winning *Number the Stars*.

Q: What inspired you to write *Number the Stars*?

A: I went on vacation with a Danish friend of mine. We talked about her childhood. As we talked, I began to get an idea of what it was like for her during World War II. Although the incident in the story did not happen to her, she was able to tell me what it felt like when the Jewish families in her neighborhood started disappearing.

Q: Did you do any special research while writing the book?

A: After I started writing, I saw that I would need to do a great deal of research for the story, and I eventually went to Denmark. I spoke to people who lived through the war, and I went to the Holocaust Museum, which is dedicated to the role Denmark played. That was where I saw the shoes of fish skin that I used in the story.

Q: The Danes were very good about protecting Jewish people from the Nazis.

A: Yes. Like all Danes, my friend is proud of her country and its role in the war. For example, Danish doctors put Jewish people in hospitals, pretending they were patients, in order to save them. Of course, the doctors had to fill out medical papers for them, and as a sort of bitter joke, they put down German measles as a diagnosis. As my friend told me these stories, I began to see that they would make a wonderful children's book.

Visit *The Learning Site!*
www.harcourtschool.com

Lois Lowry

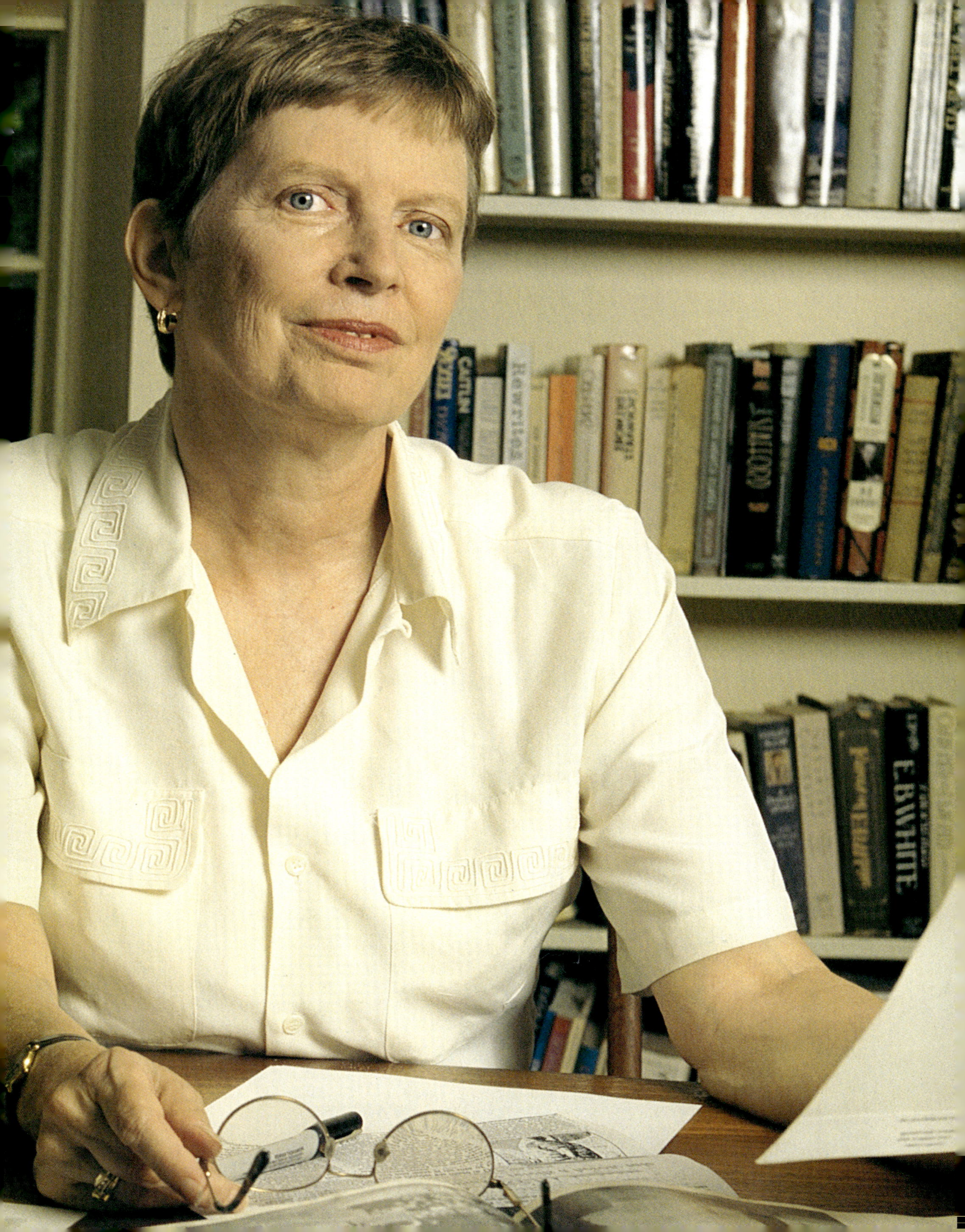
E.B.WHITE

Seeing Poetry

WRITE A POEM

Personification means "giving objects human characteristics." Lois Lowry uses personification to create powerful images. For instance, Ellen says about Lise's death, "The rain made it seem as if the whole world was crying." Write a poem using personification. Share your poem with your classmates.

RESPONSE

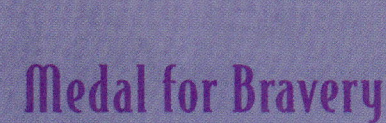

Medal for Bravery

CREATE AN AWARD

Annemarie, Ellen, and their families have to depend on each other during the Nazi occupation. Design a special medal of courage to be presented to them. Write a short statement acknowledging their bravery. Display your medal, and read your statement to the class.

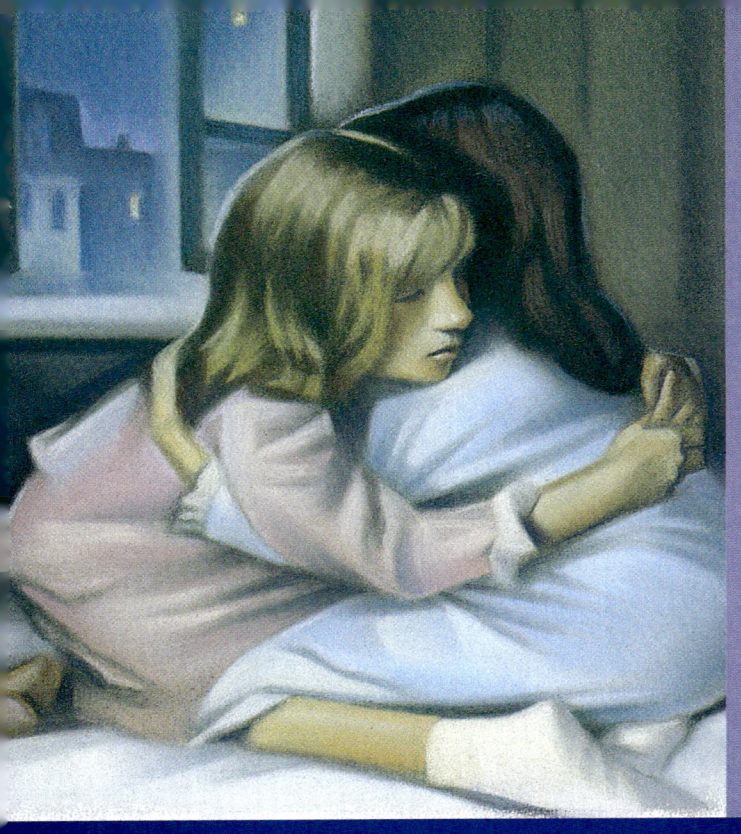

ACTIVITIES

What Happened Next?

WRITE A NEW SCENE
Think about what happens to Annemarie, Ellen, and their families in the story. Write a new scene from the point of view of one of the characters. Act out your scene with your classmates.

Happy New Year!

CREATE A CLASS BOOKLET
Ellen and her family celebrate the Jewish New Year. Interview a partner about how his or her family celebrates the new year. Write a paragraph about that celebration, and draw an illustration to go with it. Add your work to a class booklet called "New Year Celebrations."

FOCUS SKILL: Sequence/Cause and Effect

In "Number the Stars," the Nazis begin to gather the Jews to relocate them. To protect Ellen, the Johansens hide her and pretend she is Annemarie's older sister. The first event is a **cause**; the second event is the **effect**.

Cause	→	Effect
Nazis' actions		Johansens hide Ellen.

The event that makes another event happen is a cause. The event or action it leads to is an effect. Identifying causes and effects in a story helps you follow the **sequence** of events.

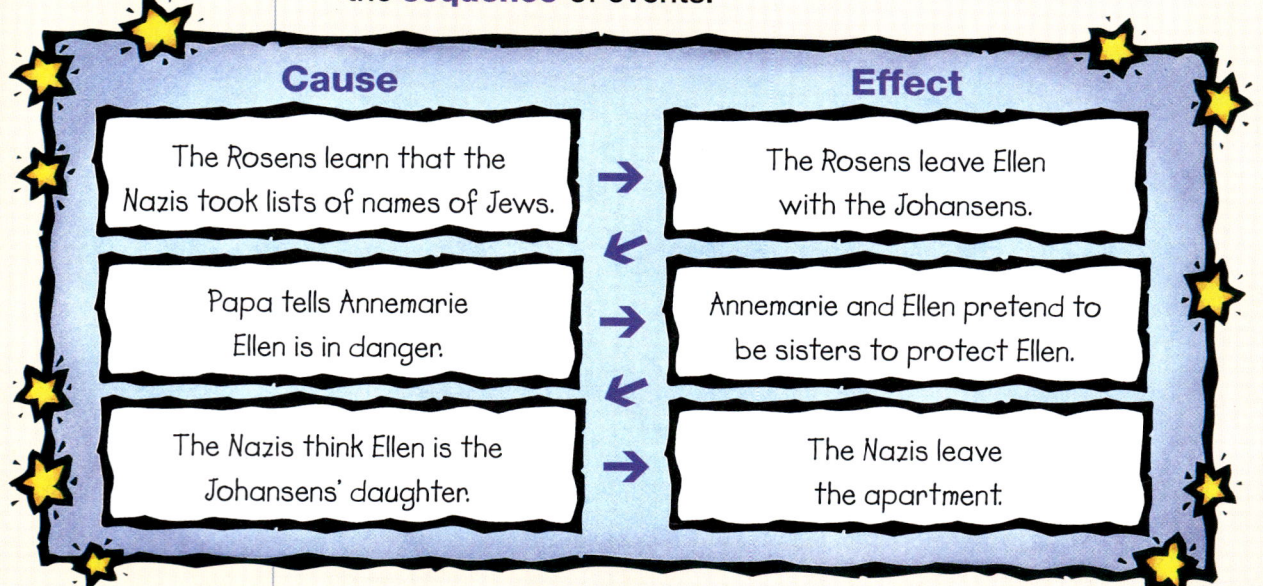

Cause		Effect
The Rosens learn that the Nazis took lists of names of Jews.	→	The Rosens leave Ellen with the Johansens.
Papa tells Annemarie Ellen is in danger.	→	Annemarie and Ellen pretend to be sisters to protect Ellen.
The Nazis think Ellen is the Johansens' daughter.	→	The Nazis leave the apartment.

Writers don't always show causes and effects in order. In "Number the Stars," Mrs. Rosen comes to the Johansens' door (effect) before you know the cause. Later, you read the cause: the Rosens have learned that the Nazis have lists with names of all the Danish Jews.

144

In most stories, a cause leads to an effect, and then that effect becomes the cause of the next effect. This chain of related events becomes the story sequence.

Below is part of a cause-and-effect chart for "Number the Stars." On a seperate piece of paper, finish the chart with causes and effects to the end of the story.

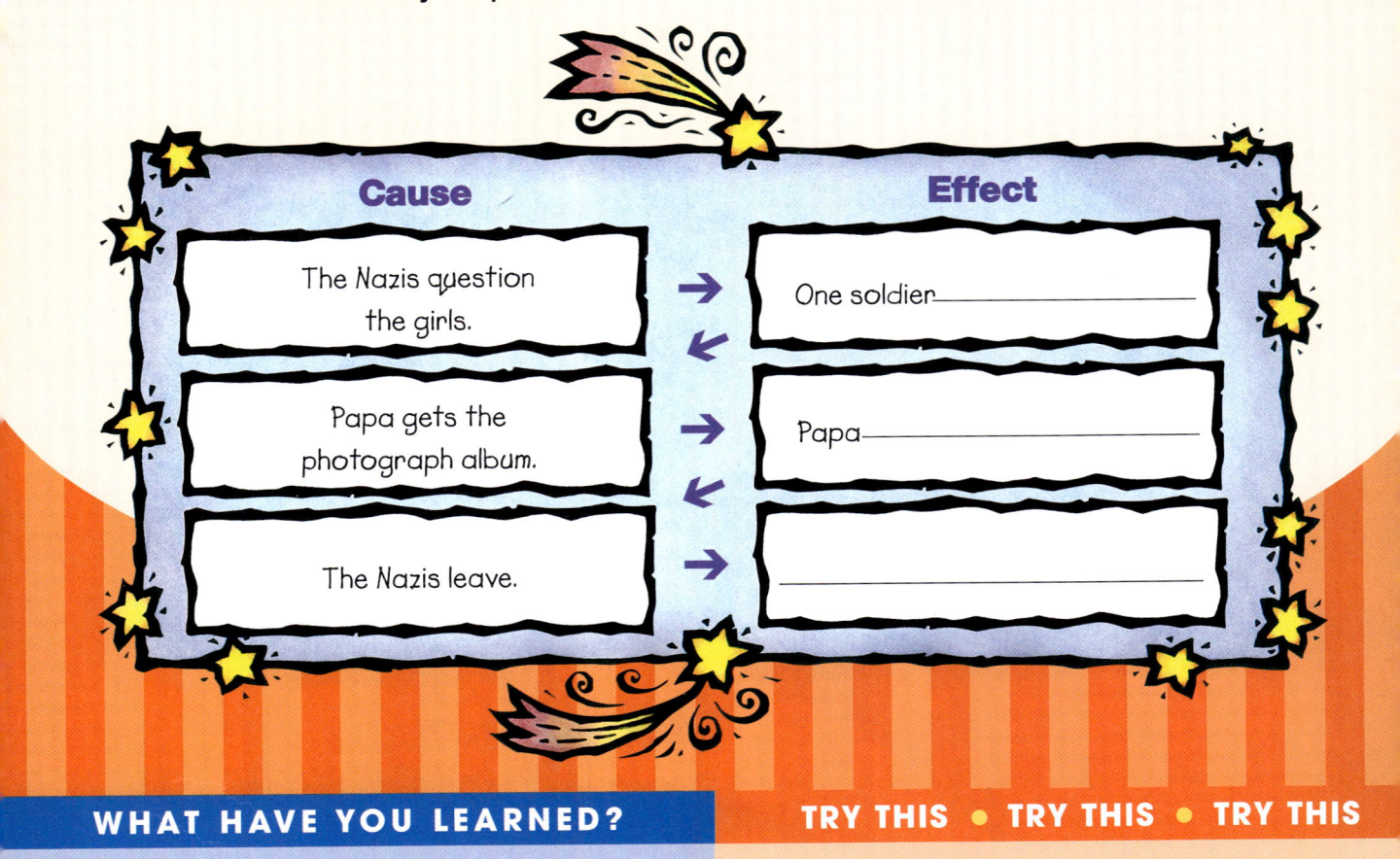

Cause		Effect
The Nazis question the girls.	→	One soldier _____
Papa gets the photograph album.	→	Papa _____
The Nazis leave.	→	_____

WHAT HAVE YOU LEARNED?

1. What caused the king of Denmark to destroy his fleet?

2. Name the cause and its effect shown in the illustration below. Then write a chain of three events that this cause could bring about. Give reasons for your choices.

TRY THIS • TRY THIS • TRY THIS

Think of a problem that a character had in another story you have read. Think about how you might have helped that character. Consider the sequence of events that might have taken place if you had helped. Then make a cause-and-effect chart like the ones on these pages to show what might have happened.

Visit *The Learning Site!*
www.harcourtschool.com

145

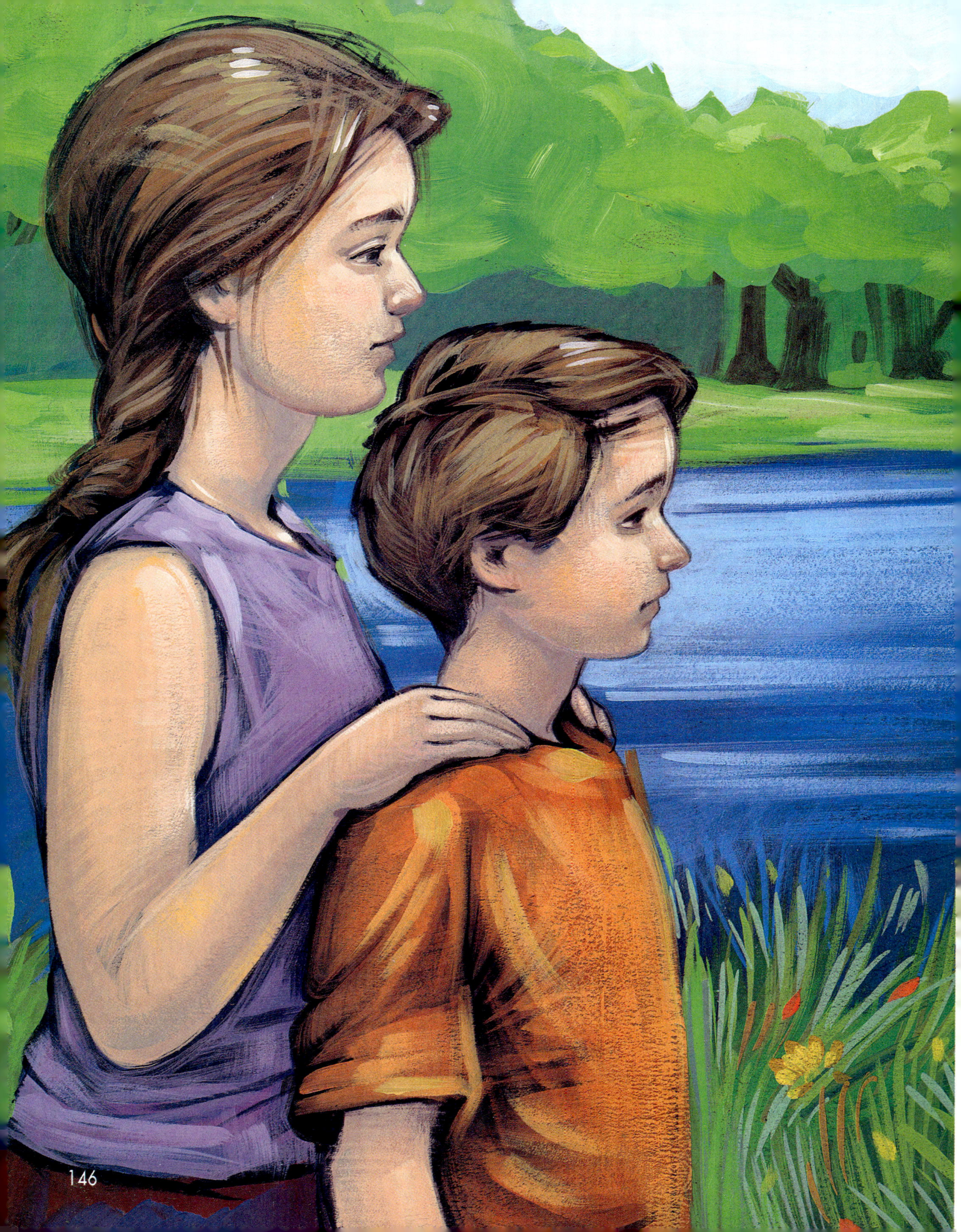

The Summer of the Swans

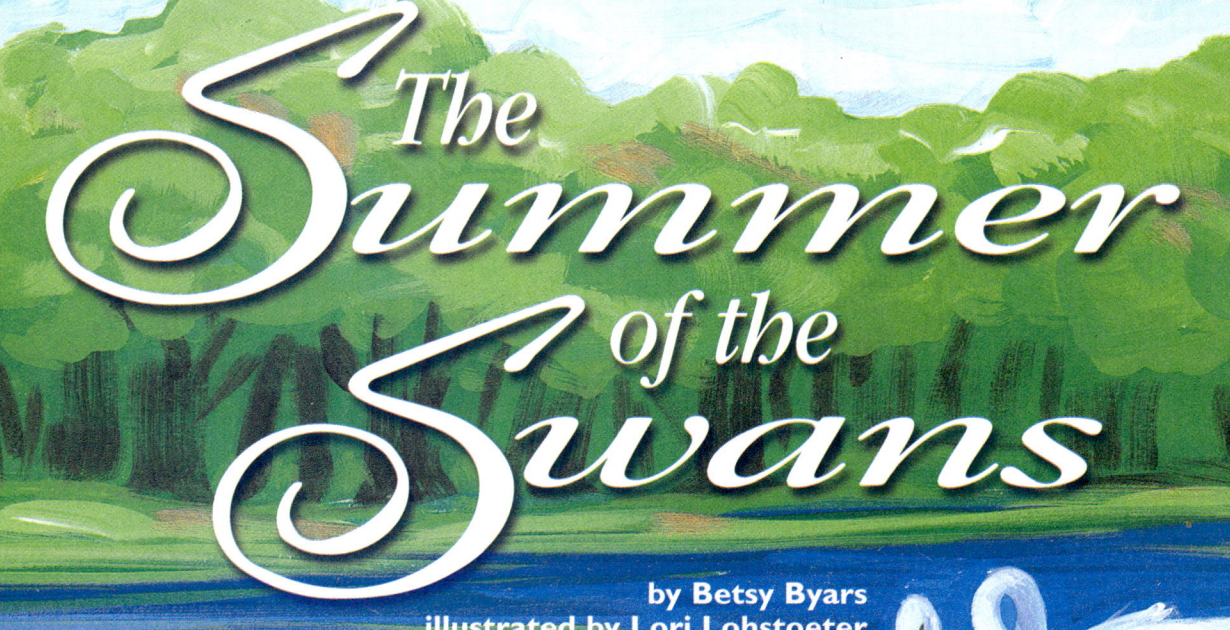

by Betsy Byars
illustrated by Lori Lohstoeter

**Newbery Medal
ALA Notable Book**

Charlie is a ten-year-old boy who is developmentally disabled and unable to speak. He leaves his house one night, looking for the swans he has seen that day. He soon becomes lost in the nearby woods and is very frightened.

The next day, when his older sister, Sara, discovers he is missing, she and her classmate Joe search for him. After searching for hours, though, all they have found is Charlie's slipper.

There was a ravine in the forest, a deep cut in the earth, and Charlie had made his way into it through an early morning fog. By chance, blindly stepping through the fog with his arms outstretched, he had managed to pick the one path that led into the ravine, and when the sun came out and the fog burned away, he could not find the way out.

All the ravine looked the same in the daylight, the high walls, the masses of weeds and wild berry bushes, the trees. He had wandered around for a while, following the little paths made by dirt washed down from the hillside, but finally he sat down on a log and stared straight ahead without seeing.

After a while he roused enough to wipe his hands over his cheeks where the tears and dirt had dried together and to rub his puffed eyelids. Then he looked down, saw his bare foot, put it on top of his slipper, and sat with his feet overlapped.

There was a dullness about him now. He had had so many scares, heard so many frightening noises, started at so many shadows, been hurt so often that all his senses were worn to a flat hopelessness. He would just sit here forever.

It was not the first time Charlie had been lost, but never before had there been this finality. He had become separated from Aunt Willie once at the county fair and had not even known he was lost until she had come bursting out of the crowd screaming, "Charlie, Charlie," and enveloped him. He had been lost in school once in the hall and could not find his way back to his room, and he had walked up and down the halls, frightened by all the strange children looking out of every door, until one of the boys was sent out to lead him to his room. But in all his life there had never been an experience like this one.

He bent over and looked down at his watch, his eyes on the tiny red hand. For the first time he noticed it was no longer moving. Holding his breath in his concern, he brought the watch closer to his face. The hand was still. For a moment he could not believe it. He watched it closely, waiting. Still the hand did not move. He shook his hand back and forth, as if he were trying to shake the watch off his wrist. He had seen Sara do this to her watch.

Then he held the watch to his ear. It was silent. He had had the watch for five months and never before had it failed him. He had not even known it could fail. And now it was silent and still.

He put his hand over the watch, covering it completely. He waited. His breathing had begun to quicken again. His hand on the watch was almost clammy. He waited, then slowly, cautiously, he removed his hand and looked at the tiny red hand on the dial. It was motionless. The trick had not worked.

Bending over the watch, he looked closely at the stem. Aunt Willie always wound the watch for him every morning after breakfast, but he did not know how she did this. He took the stem in his fingers, pulled at it clumsily, then harder, and it came off. He looked at it. Then, as he attempted to put it back on the watch, it fell to the ground and was lost in the leaves.

A chipmunk ran in front of him and scurried up the bank. Distracted for a moment, Charlie got up and walked toward it. The chipmunk paused and then darted into a hole, leaving Charlie standing in the shadows trying to see where it had gone. He went closer to the bank and pulled at the leaves, but he could not even find the place among the roots where the chipmunk had disappeared.

Suddenly something seemed to explode within Charlie, and he began to cry noisily. He threw himself on the bank and began kicking, flailing at the ground, at the invisible chipmunk, at the silent watch. He wailed, yielding in helplessness to his anguish, and his piercing screams, uttered again and again, seemed to hang in the air so that they overlapped. His fingers tore at the tree roots and dug beneath the leaves and scratched, animal-like, at the dark earth.

His body sagged and he rolled down the bank and was silent. He looked up at the trees, his chest still heaving with sobs, his face strangely still. After a moment, his eyelids drooped and he fell asleep.

"Charlie! Charlie!"

The only answer was the call of a bird in the branches overhead, one long tremulous whistle.

"He's not even within hearing distance," Sara said.

For the past hour she and Joe Melby had been walking deeper and deeper into the forest without pause, and now the trees were so thick that only small spots of sunlight found their way through the heavy foliage.

"Charlie, oh, Charlie!"

She waited, looking down at the ground.

Joe said, "You want to rest for a while?"

Sara shook her head. She suddenly wanted to see her brother so badly that her throat began to close. It was a tight feeling she got sometimes when she wanted something, like the time she had

had the measles and had wanted to see her father so much she couldn't even swallow. Now she thought that if she had a whole glass of ice water—and she was thirsty—she probably would not be able to drink a single drop.

"If you can make it a little farther, there's a place at the top of the hill where the strip mining is, and you can see the whole valley from there."

"I can make it."

"Well, we can rest first if— "

"I can make it."

She suddenly felt a little better. She thought that if she could stand up there on top of the hill and look down and see, somewhere in that huge green valley, a small plump figure in blue pajamas, she would ask for nothing more in life. She thought of the valley as a relief map where everything would be shiny and smooth, and her brother would be right where she could spot him at once. Her cry, "There he is!" would ring like a bell over the valley and everyone would hear her and know that Charlie had been found.

She paused, leaned against a tree for a moment, and then continued. Her legs had begun to tremble.

It was the time of afternoon when she usually sat down in front of the television and watched game shows, the shows where the married couples tried to guess things about each other and where girls had to pick out dates they couldn't see. She would sit in the doorway to the hall where she always sat and Charlie would come in and watch with her, and the living room would be dark and smell of the pine-scented cleaner Aunt Willie used.

Then "The Early Show" would come on, and she would sit through the old movie, leaning forward in the doorway, making fun, saying things like, "Now, Charlie, we'll have the old Convict Turning Honest scene," and Charlie, sitting on the stool closer to the television, would nod without understanding.

She was good, too, at joining in the dialogue with the actors. When the cowboy would say something like, "Things are quiet around here tonight," she would join in with, "Yeah, *too* quiet," right on cue. It seemed strange to be out here in the woods with Joe Melby instead of in the living room with Charlie, watching *Flame of Araby*, which was the early movie for that afternoon.

Her progress up the hill seemed slower and slower. It was like the time she had won the slow bicycle race, a race in which she had to go as slow as possible without letting a foot touch the ground, and she had gone slower and slower, all the while feeling a strong compulsion to speed ahead and cross the finish line first. At the end of the race it had been she and T.R. Peters, and they had paused just before the finish line, balancing motionless on their bicycles. The time had seemed endless, and then T.R. lost his balance and his foot touched the ground and Sara was the winner.

She slipped on some dry leaves, went down on her knees, straightened, and paused to catch her breath.

"Are you all right?"

"Yes, I just slipped."

She waited for a moment, bent over her knees, then she called, "Charlie! Charlie," without lifting her head.

"Oh, Charleeeeee," Joe shouted above her.

Sara knew Charlie would shout back if he heard her, the long wailing cry he gave sometimes when he was frightened during the night. It was such a familiar cry that for a moment she thought she heard it.

She waited, still touching the ground with one hand, until she was sure there was no answer.

"Come on," Joe said, holding out his hand.

He pulled her to her feet and she stood looking up at the top of the hill. Machines had cut away the earth there to get at the veins of coal, and the earth had been pushed down the hill to form a huge bank.

"I'll never get up that," she said. She leaned against a tree whose leaves were covered with the pale fine dirt which had filtered down when the machines had cut away the hill.

"Sure you will. I've been up it a dozen times."

He took her hand and she started after him, moving sideways up the steep bank. The dirt crumbled beneath her feet and she slid, skinned one knee, and then slipped again. When she had regained her balance she laughed wryly and said, "What's going to happen is that I'll end up pulling you all the way down the hill."

"No, I've got you. Keep coming."

She started again, putting one foot carefully above the other, picking her way over the stones. When she paused, he said, "Keep coming. We're almost there."

"I think it's a trick, like at the dentist's when he says, 'I'm almost through drilling.' Then he drills for another hour and says, 'Now, I'm really almost through drilling,' and he keeps on and then says, 'There's just one more spot and then I'll be practically really through.'"

"We must go to the same dentist."

"I don't think I can make it. There's no skin at all left on the sides of my legs."

"Well, we're really almost practically there now, in the words of your dentist."

She fell across the top of the dirt bank on her stomach, rested for a moment, and then turned and looked down the valley.

She could not speak for a moment. There lay the whole valley in a way she had never imagined it, a tiny finger of civilization set in a sweeping expanse of dark forest. The black treetops seemed to crowd against the yards, the houses, the roads, giving the impression that at any moment the trees would close over the houses like waves and leave nothing but an unbroken line of black-green leaves waving in the sunlight.

Up the valley she could see the intersection where they shopped, the drugstore, the gas station where her mother had once won a set of twenty-four stemmed glasses which Aunt Willie would not allow them to use, the grocery store, the lot where the yellow school buses were parked for the summer. She could look over the valley and see another hill where white cows were all grouped together by a fence and beyond that another hill and then another.

She looked back at the valley and she saw the lake and for the first time since she had stood up on the hill she remembered Charlie.

Raising her hand to her mouth, she called, "Charlie! Charlie! Charlie!" There was a faint echo that seemed to waver in her ears.

"Charlie, oh, Charlie!" Her voice was so loud it seemed to ram into the valley.

Sara waited. She looked down at the forest, and everything was so quiet it seemed to her that the whole valley, the whole world was waiting with her.

"Charlie, hey, Charlie!" Joe shouted.

"Charleeeeee!" She made the sound of it last a long time. "Can you hear meeeeee?"

With her eyes she followed the trail she knew he must have taken—the house, the Akers' vacant lot, the old pasture, the forest. The forest that seemed powerful enough to engulf a whole valley, she thought with a sinking feeling, could certainly swallow up a young boy.

"Charlie! Charlie! Charlie!" There was a waver in the last syllable that betrayed how near she was to tears. She looked down at the Indian slipper she was still holding.

"Charlie, oh, Charlie."

She waited. There was not a sound anywhere. "Charlie, where are you?"

"Hey, Charlie!" Joe shouted.

They waited in the same dense silence. A cloud passed in front of the sun and a breeze began to blow through the trees. Then there was silence again.

"Charlie, Charlie, Charlie, Charlie, Charlie."

She paused, listened, then bent abruptly and put Charlie's slipper to her eyes. She waited for the hot tears that had come so often this summer, the tears that had seemed so close only a moment before. Now her eyes remained dry.

I have cried over myself a hundred times this summer, she thought, I have wept over my big feet and my skinny legs and my nose, I have even cried over my stupid shoes, and now when I have a true sadness there are no tears left.

She held the felt side of the slipper against her eyes like a blindfold and stood there, feeling the hot sun on her head and the wind wrapping around her legs, conscious of the height and the valley sweeping down from her feet.

"Listen, just because you can't hear him doesn't mean anything. He could be — "

"Wait a minute." She lowered the slipper and looked down the valley. A sudden wind blew dust into her face and she lifted her hand to shield her eyes.

"I thought I heard something. Charlie! Answer me right this minute."

She waited with the slipper held against her breasts, one hand to her eyes, her whole body motionless, concentrating on her brother. Then she stiffened. She thought again she had heard something—Charlie's long high wail. Charlie could sound sadder than anyone when he cried.

In her anxiety she took the slipper and twisted it again and again as if she were wringing water out. She called, then stopped abruptly and listened. She looked at Joe and he shook his head slowly.

156

She looked away. A bird rose from the trees below and flew toward the hills in the distance. She waited until she could see it no longer and then slowly, still listening for the call that didn't come, she sank to the ground and sat with her head bent over her knees.

Beside her, Joe scuffed his foot in the dust and sent a cascade of rocks and dirt down the bank. When the sound of it faded, he began to call, "Charlie, hey, Charlie," again and again.

Charlie awoke, but he lay for a moment without opening his eyes. He did not remember where he was, but he had a certain dread of seeing it.

There were great parts of his life that were lost to Charlie, blank spaces that he could never fill in. He would find himself in a strange place and not know how he had got there. Like the time Sara had been hit in the nose with a baseball at the Dairy Queen, and the blood and the sight of Sara kneeling on the ground in helpless pain had frightened him so much that he had turned and run without direction, in a frenzy, dashing headlong up the street, blind to cars and people.

By chance Mr. Weicek had seen him, put him in the car, and driven him home, and Aunt Willie had put him to bed, but later he remembered none of this. He had only awakened in bed and looked at the crumpled bit of ice-cream cone still clenched in his hand and wondered about it.

His whole life had been built on a strict routine, and as long as this routine was kept up, he felt safe and well. The same foods, the same bed, the same furniture in the same place, the same seat on the school bus, the same class procedure were all important to him. But always there could be the unexpected, the dreadful surprise that would topple his carefully constructed life in an instant.

The first thing he became aware of was the twigs pressing into his face, and he put his hand under his cheek. Still he did not open his eyes. Pictures began to drift into his mind; he saw Aunt Willie's cigar box which was filled with old jewelry and buttons and knickknacks, and he found that he could remember every item in that box — the string of white beads without a clasp, the old earrings, the tiny book with souvenir fold-out pictures of New York, the plastic decorations from cakes, the turtle made of sea shells. Every item was so real that he opened his eyes and was surprised to see, instead of the glittering contents of the box, the dull and unfamiliar forest.

He raised his head and immediately felt the aching of his body. Slowly he sat up and looked down at his hands. His fingernails were black with earth, two of them broken below the quick, and he got up slowly and sat on the log behind him and inspected his fingers more closely.

Then he sat up straight. His hands dropped to his lap. His head cocked to the side like a bird listening. Slowly he straightened until he was standing. At his side his fingers twitched at the empty air as if to grasp something. He took a step forward, still with his head to the side. He remained absolutely still.

Then he began to cry out in a hoarse excited voice, again and again, screaming now, because he had just heard someone far away calling his name.

At the top of the hill Sara got slowly to her feet and stood looking down at the forest. She pushed the hair back from her forehead and moistened her lips. The wind dried them as she waited.

Joe started to say something but she reached out one hand and took his arm to stop him. Scarcely daring to believe her ears, she stepped closer to the edge of the bank. Now she heard it unmistakably—the sharp repeated cry—and she knew it was Charlie.

"Charlie!" she shouted with all her might.

She paused and listened, and his cries were louder and she knew he was not far away after all, just down the slope, in the direction of the ravine.

"It's Charlie, it's Charlie!"

A wild joy overtook her and she jumped up and down on the bare earth and she felt that she could crush the whole hill just by jumping if she wanted.

She sat and scooted down the bank, sending earth and pebbles in a cascade before her. She landed on the soft ground, ran a few steps, lost her balance, caught hold of the first tree trunk she could find, and swung around till she stopped.

She let out another whoop of pure joy, turned and ran down the hill in great strides, the puce tennis shoes slapping the ground like rubber paddles, the wind in her face, her hands grabbing one tree trunk after another for support. She felt like a wild creature who had traveled through the forest this way for a lifetime. Nothing could stop her now.

At the edge of the ravine she paused and stood gasping for breath. Her heart was beating so fast it pounded in her ears, and her throat was dry. She leaned against a tree, resting her cheek against the rough bark.

She thought for a minute she was going to faint, a thing she had never done before, not even when she broke her nose. She hadn't even believed people really did faint until this minute when she clung to the tree because her legs were as useless as rubber bands.

There was a ringing in her ears and another sound, a wailing siren-like cry that was painfully familiar.

"Charlie?"

Charlie's crying, like the sound of a cricket, seemed everywhere and nowhere.

She walked along the edge of the ravine, circling the large boulders and trees. Then she looked down into the ravine where the shadows lay, and she felt as if something had turned over inside her because she saw Charlie.

He was standing in his torn pajamas, face turned upward, hands raised, shouting with all his might. His eyes were shut tight. His face was streaked with dirt and tears. His pajama jacket hung in shreds about his scratched chest.

He opened his eyes and as he saw Sara a strange expression came over his face, an expression of wonder and joy and disbelief, and Sara knew that if she lived to be a hundred no one would ever look at her quite that way again.

She paused, looked down at him, and then, sliding on the seat of her pants, went down the bank and took him in her arms.

"Oh, Charlie."

His arms gripped her like steel.

"Oh, Charlie."

She could feel his fingers digging into her back as he clutched her shirt. "It's all right now, Charlie, I'm here and we're going home." His face was buried in her shirt and she patted his head, said again, "It's all right now. Everything's fine."

She held him against her for a moment and now the hot tears were in her eyes and on her cheeks and she didn't even notice.

"I know how you feel," she said. "I know. One time when I had the measles and my fever was real high, I got lost on my way back from the bathroom, right in our house, and it was a terrible feeling, terrible, because I wanted to get back to my bed and I couldn't find it, and finally Aunt Willie heard me and came and you know where I was? In the kitchen. In our kitchen and I couldn't have been more lost if I'd been out in the middle of the wilderness."

She patted the back of his head again and said, "Look, I even brought your bedroom slipper. Isn't that service, huh?"

She tried to show it to him, but he was still clutching her, and she held him against her, patting him. After a moment she said again, "Look, here's your slipper. Let's put it on." She knelt, put his foot into the shoe, and said, "Now, isn't that better?"

He nodded slowly, his chest still heaving with unspent sobs.

"Can you walk home?"

He nodded. She took her shirttail and wiped his tears and smiled at him. "Come on, we'll find a way out of here and go home."

"Hey, over this way," Joe called from the bank of the ravine. Sara had forgotten about him in the excitement of finding Charlie, and she looked up at him for a moment.

"Over this way, around the big tree," Joe called. "That's probably how he got in. The rest of the ravine is a mass of brier bushes."

She put one arm around Charlie and led him around the tree. "Everybody in town's looking for you, you know that?" she said. "Everybody. The police came and all the neighbors are out—there must be a hundred people looking for you. You were on the radio. It's like you were the President of the United States or something. Everybody was saying, 'Where's Charlie?' and 'We got to find Charlie.' "

Suddenly Charlie stopped and held up his hand and Sara looked down. "What is it?"

He pointed to the silent watch.

She smiled. "Charlie, you are something, you know that? Here we are racing down the hill to tell everyone in great triumph that you are found, found, and we have to stop and wind your watch first."

161

She looked at the watch, saw that the stem was missing, and shook her head. "It's broken, Charlie, see, the stem's gone. It's broken."

He held it out again.

"It's *broken*, Charlie. We'll have to take it to the jeweler and have it fixed."

He continued to hold out his arm.

"Hey, Charlie, you want to wear my watch till you get yours fixed?" Joe asked. He slid down the bank and put his watch on Charlie's arm. "There."

Charlie bent his face close and listened.

"Now can we go home?" Sara asked, jamming her hands into her back pockets.

Charlie nodded.

Think About It

1. What do you think Sara learns about herself as she searches for Charlie?

2. Would you recommend this story to a friend? Explain why or why not.

3. Why do you think the author shows readers both Charlie's and Sara's thoughts during the story?

MEET THE AUTHOR

Betsy Byars

Award-winning author Betsy Byars's novels have been made into TV movies, and her books have been translated into nine languages. She is so popular with young readers that she receives about 200 fan letters a week.

Byars got the story idea for *The Summer of the Swans* while volunteering to teach children with learning disabilities. The children she met sparked ideas for the book. "Although the character Charlie is not one of the children I tutored—he is purely a fictitious character—he was an outgrowth of the experience," she says.

Byars's children helped her learn how to write for young readers. "Living with my own teenagers taught me that not only must I not write down to my readers, I must write up to them," Byars says. She also learns from students. "When I visit classrooms and talk with students, I am always impressed to find how many of them are writing stories and how knowledgeable they are about writing."

Visit *The Learning Site!*
www.harcourtschool.com

Response

Movie Soundtrack

CHOOSE SONGS

Think about how Charlie and Sara feel during the story. Choose some songs that would work well as a soundtrack to a scene in the story. Play the songs as you read the scene aloud, or describe in writing why the music fits the mood of the scene.

View from Above

WRITE A DESCRIPTION

Reread the description of the valley on page 154. Then write a description of your own. Share a bird's-eye view of your favorite outdoor place. Include sensory details describing what you see, hear, and feel when you are in this place.

Activities

Lost and Found

WRITE A REPORT

Sara and Joe thought that if they walked to the top of a hill, they could spot Charlie more easily. Research how professionals approach the task of rescuing people. Write a brief report outlining a typical day of a rescue worker.

Words into Action

PANTOMIME A SCENE

Reread the section on pages 150–154 that describes Sara and Joe searching for Charlie in the forest. Pantomime their actions in front of a partner. Try to make your movements match the descriptions in the story.

OLD YELLER

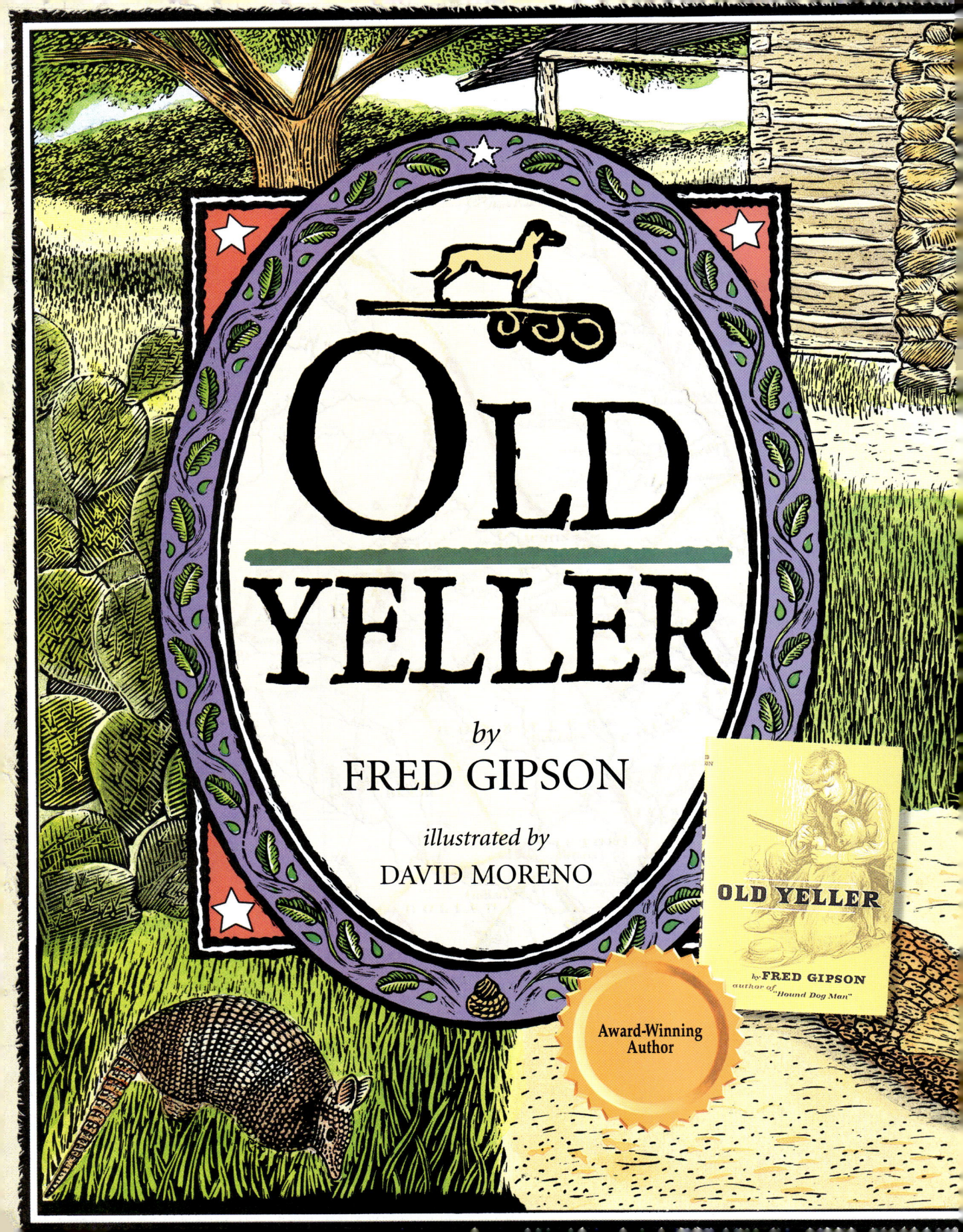

by
FRED GIPSON

illustrated by
DAVID MORENO

Award-Winning Author

OLD YELLER
by FRED GIPSON
author of "Hound Dog Man"

Papa, Mama, and their sons, Travis and Arliss, are settlers in the Texas hill country. To earn money, Papa has left on a year-long cattle run, leaving fourteen-year-old Travis to hunt for food, work on the farm, and guard the family.

One night, a stray yellow dog steals the family's deer meat. Travis does not like the dog, whom he names Old Yeller, but Arliss immediately loves him. Over time, Old Yeller proves to be a good addition to the family in many ways.

That Little Arliss! If he wasn't a mess! From the time he'd grown up big enough to get out of the cabin, he'd made a practice of trying to catch and keep every living thing that ran, flew, jumped, or crawled.

Every night before Mama let him go to bed, she'd make Arliss empty his pockets of whatever he'd captured during the day. Generally, it would be a tangled-up mess of grasshoppers and worms and praying bugs and little rusty tree lizards. One time he brought in a horned toad that got so mad he swelled out round and flat as a Mexican *tortilla* and bled at the eyes. Sometimes it was stuff like a young bird that had fallen out of its nest before it could fly, or a green-speckled spring frog or a striped water snake. And once he turned out of his pocket a wadded-up baby copperhead that nearly threw Mama into spasms. We never did figure out why the snake hadn't bitten him, but Mama took no more chances on snakes. She made me spend better than a week, taking him out and teaching him to throw rocks and kill snakes.

That was all right with Little Arliss. If Mama wanted him to kill his snakes first, he'd kill them. But that still didn't keep him from sticking them in his pockets along with everything else he'd captured that day. The snakes might be stinking by the time Mama called on him to empty his pockets, but they'd be dead.

Then, after the yeller dog came, Little Arliss started catching even bigger game. Like cottontail rabbits and chaparral birds and a baby possum that sulked and lay like dead for the first several hours until he finally decided that Arliss wasn't going to hurt him.

Of course, it was Old Yeller that was doing the catching. He'd run the game down and turn it over to Little Arliss. Then Little Arliss could come in and tell Mama a big fib about how he caught it himself.

I watched them one day when they caught a blue catfish out of Birdsong Creek. The fish had fed out into water so shallow that his top fin was sticking out. About the time I saw it, Old Yeller and Little Arliss did, too. They made a run at it. The fish went scooting away toward deeper water, only Yeller was too fast for him. He pounced on the fish and shut his big mouth down over it and went romping to the bank, where he dropped it down on the grass and let it flop. And here came Little Arliss to fall on it like I guess he'd been doing everything else. The minute he got his hands on it, the fish finned him and he went to crying.

But he wouldn't turn the fish loose. He just grabbed it up and went running and squawling toward the house, where he gave the fish to Mama. His hands were all bloody by then, where the fish had finned him. They swelled up and got mighty sore; not even a mesquite thorn hurts as bad as a sharp fish fin when it's run deep into your hand.

But as soon as Mama had wrapped his hands in a poultice of mashed-up prickly-pear root to draw out the poison, Little Arliss forgot all about his hurt. And that night when we ate the fish for supper, he told the biggest windy I ever heard about how he'd dived 'way down into a deep hole under the rocks and dragged that fish out and nearly got drowned before he could swim to the bank with it.

But when I tried to tell Mama what really happened, she wouldn't let me. "Now, this is Arliss's story," she said. "You let him tell it the way he wants to."

I told Mama then, I said: "Mama, that old yeller dog is going to make the biggest liar in Texas out of Little Arliss."

But Mama just laughed at me, like she always laughed at Little Arliss's big windies after she'd gotten off where he couldn't hear her. She said for me to let Little Arliss alone. She said that if he ever told a bigger whopper than the ones I used to tell, she had yet to hear it.

Well, I hushed then. If Mama wanted Little Arliss to grow up to be the biggest liar in Texas, I guessed it wasn't any of my business.

All of which, I figure, is what led up to Little Arliss's catching the bear. I think Mama had let him tell so many big yarns about his catching live game that he'd begun to believe them himself.

When it happened, I was down the creek a ways, splitting rails to fix up the yard fence where the bulls had torn it down. I'd been down there since dinner, working in a stand of tall slim post oaks. I'd chop down a tree, trim off the branches as far up as I wanted, then cut away the rest of the top. After that I'd start splitting the log.

I'd split the log by driving steel wedges into the wood. I'd start at the big end and hammer in a wedge with the back side of my axe. This would start a little split running lengthways of the log. Then I'd take a second wedge and drive it into this split. This would split the log further along and, at the same time, loosen the first wedge. I'd then knock the first wedge loose and move it up in front of the second one.

Driving one wedge ahead of the other like that, I could finally split a log in two halves. Then I'd go to work on the halves, splitting them apart. That way, from each log, I'd come out with four rails.

Swinging that chopping axe was sure hard work. The sweat poured off me. My back muscles ached. The axe got so heavy I could hardly swing it. My breath got harder and harder to breathe.

An hour before sundown, I was worn down to a nub. It seemed like I couldn't hit another lick. Papa could have lasted till past sundown, but I didn't see how I could. I shouldered my axe and started toward the cabin, trying to think up some excuse to tell Mama to keep her from knowing I was played clear out.

That's when I heard Little Arliss scream.

Well, Little Arliss was a screamer by nature. He'd scream when he was happy and scream when he was mad and a lot of times he'd scream just to hear himself make a noise. Generally, we paid no more mind to his screaming than we did to the gobble of a wild turkey.

But this time was different. The second I heard his screaming, I felt my heart flop clear over. This time I knew Little Arliss was in real trouble.

I tore out up the trail leading toward the cabin. A minute before, I'd been so tired out with my rail splitting that I couldn't have struck a trot. But now I raced through the tall trees in that creek bottom, covering ground like a scared wolf.

Little Arliss's second scream, when it came, was louder and shriller and more frantic-sounding than the first. Mixed with it was a whimpering crying sound that I knew didn't come from him. It was a sound I'd heard before and seemed like I ought to know what it was, but right then I couldn't place it.

Then, from way off to one side came a sound that I would have recognized anywhere. It was the coughing roar of a charging bear. I'd just heard it once in my life. That was the time Mama had shot and wounded a hog-killing bear and Papa had had to finish it off with a knife to keep it from getting her.

My heart went to pushing up into my throat, nearly choking off my wind. I strained for every lick of speed I could get out of my running legs. I didn't know what sort of fix Little Arliss had got himself into, but I knew that it had to do with a mad bear, which was enough.

The way the late sun slanted through the trees had the trail all cross-banded with streaks of bright light and dark shade. I ran through these bright and dark patches so fast that the changing light nearly blinded me. Then suddenly, I raced out into the open where I could see ahead. And what I saw sent a chill clear through to the marrow of my bones.

There was Little Arliss, down in that spring hole again. He was lying half in and half out of the water, holding onto the hind leg of a little black bear cub no bigger than a small coon. The bear cub was out on the bank, whimpering and crying and clawing the rocks with all three of his other feet, trying to pull away. But Little Arliss was holding on for all he was worth, scared now and screaming his head off. Too scared to let go.

How come the bear cub ever to prowl close enough for Little Arliss to grab him, I don't know. And why he didn't turn on him and bite loose, I couldn't figure out, either. Unless he was like Little Arliss, too scared to think.

But all of that didn't matter now. What mattered was the bear cub's mama. She'd heard the cries of her baby and was coming to save him. She was coming so fast that she had the brush popping and breaking as she crashed through and over it. I could see her black heavy figure piling off down the slant on the far side of Birdsong Creek. She was roaring mad and ready to kill.

And worst of all, I could see that I'd never get there in time!

Mama couldn't either. She'd heard Arliss, too, and here she came from the cabin, running down the slant toward the spring, screaming at Arliss, telling him to turn the bear cub loose. But Little Arliss wouldn't do it. All he'd do was hang with that hind leg and let out one shrill shriek after another as fast as he could suck in a breath.

Now the she-bear was charging across the shallows in the creek. She was knocking sheets of water high in the bright sun, charging with her fur up and her long teeth bared, filling the canyon with that awful coughing roar. And no matter how fast Mama ran or how fast I ran, the she-bear was going to get there first!

I think I nearly went blind then, picturing what was going to happen to Little Arliss. I know that I opened my mouth to scream and not any sound came out.

Then, just as the bear went lunging up the creek bank toward Little Arliss and her cub, a flash of yellow came streaking out of the brush.

It was that big yeller dog. He was roaring like a mad bull. He wasn't one-third as big and heavy as the she-bear, but when he piled into her from one side, he rolled her clear off her feet. They went down in a wild, roaring tangle of twisting bodies and scrambling feet and slashing fangs.

As I raced past them, I saw the bear lunge up to stand on her hind feet like a man while she clawed at the body of the yeller dog hanging to her throat. I didn't wait to see more. Without ever checking my stride, I ran in and jerked Little Arliss loose from the cub. I grabbed him by the wrist and yanked him up out of that water and slung him toward Mama like he was a half-empty sack of corn. I screamed at Mama. "Grab him, Mama! Grab him and run!" Then I swung my chopping axe high and wheeled, aiming to cave in the she-bear's head with the first lick.

But I never did strike. I didn't need to. Old Yeller hadn't let the bear get close enough. He couldn't handle her; she was too big and strong for that. She'd stand there on her hind feet,

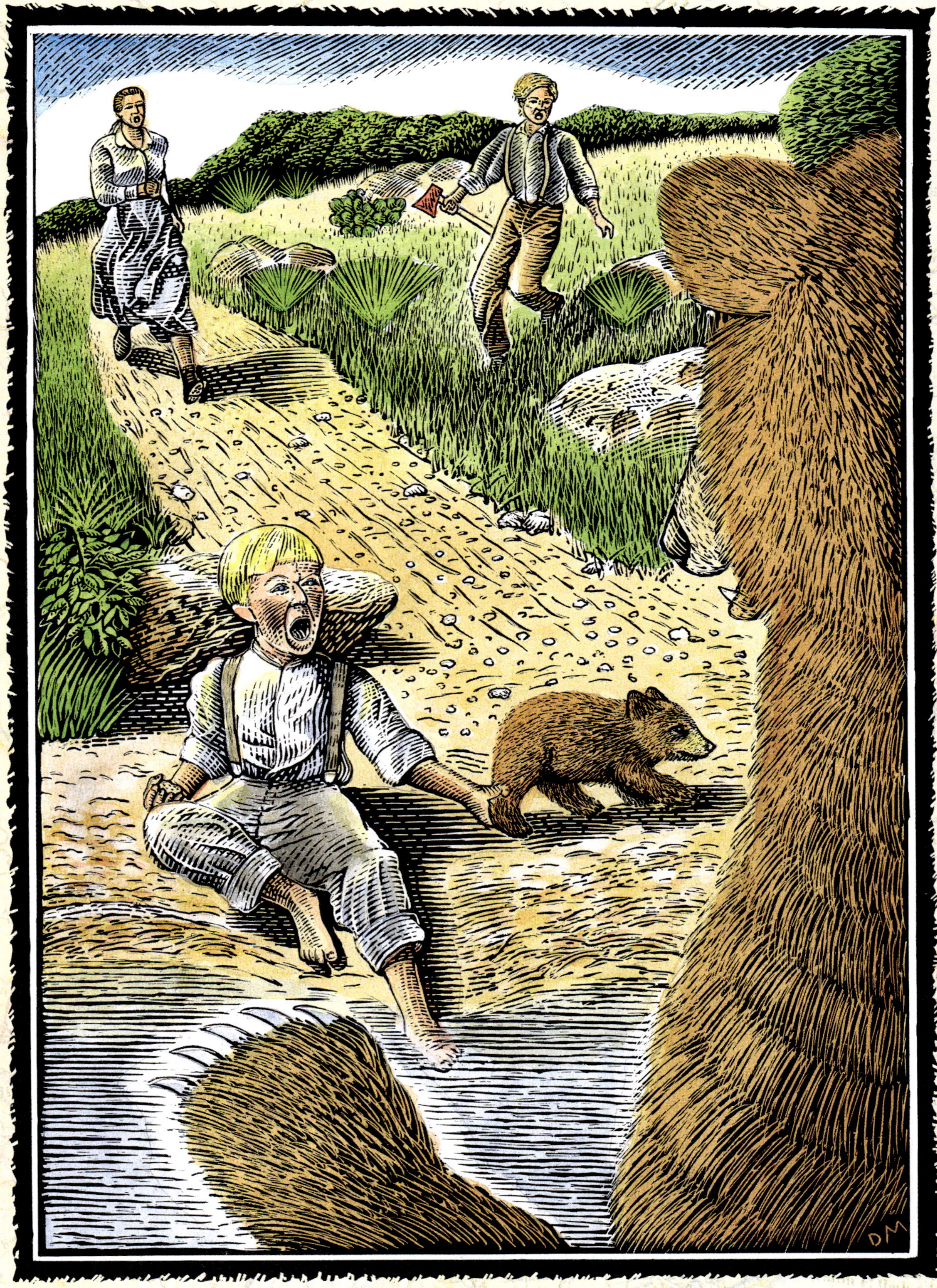

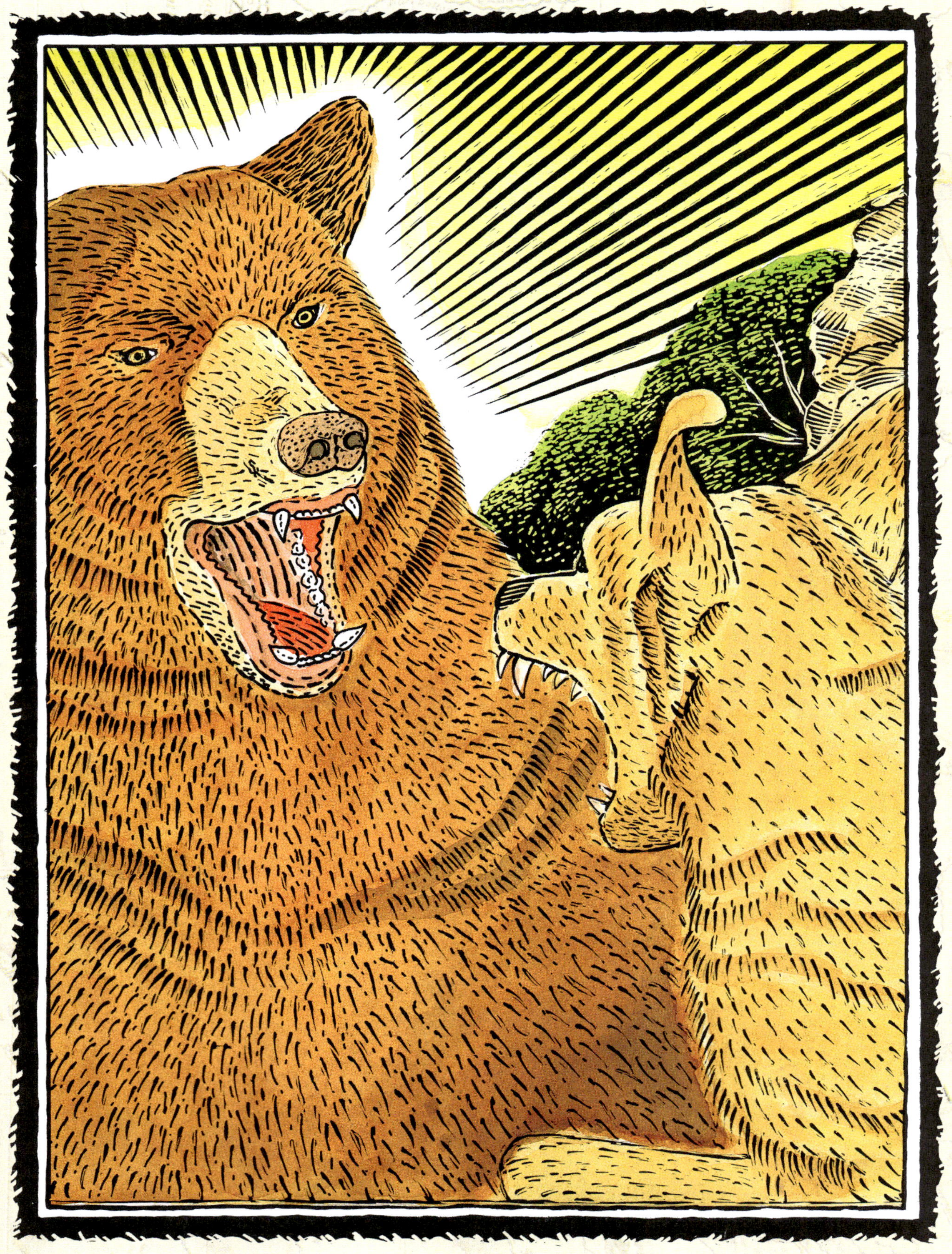

hunched over, and take a roaring swing at him with one of those big front claws. She'd slap him head over heels. She'd knock him so far that it didn't look like he could possibly get back there before she charged again, but he always did. He'd hit the ground rolling, yelling his head off with the pain of the blow; but somehow he'd always roll to his feet. And here he'd come again, ready to tie into her for another round.

I stood there with my axe raised, watching them for a long moment. Then from up toward the house, I heard Mama calling: "Come away from there, Travis. Hurry, son! Run!"

That spooked me. Up till then, I'd been ready to tie into that bear myself. Now, suddenly, I was scared out of my wits again. I ran toward the cabin.

But like it was, Old Yeller nearly beat me there. I didn't see it, of course; but Mama said that the minute Old Yeller saw we were all in the clear and out of danger, he threw the fight to that she-bear and lit out for the house. The bear chased him for a little piece, but at the rate Old Yeller was leaving her behind, Mama said it looked like the bear was backing up.

But if the big yeller dog was scared or hurt in any way when he came dashing into the house, he didn't show it. He sure didn't show it like we all did. Little Arliss had hushed his screaming, but he was trembling all over and clinging to Mama like he'd never let her go. And Mama was sitting in the middle of the floor, holding him up close and crying like she'd never stop. And me, I was close to crying, myself.

Old Yeller, though, all he did was come bounding in to jump on us and lick us in the face and bark so loud that there, inside the cabin, the noise nearly made us deaf.

The way he acted, you might have thought that bear fight hadn't been anything more than a rowdy romp that we'd all taken part in for the fun of it.

Till Little Arliss got us mixed up in that bear fight, I guess I'd been looking on him about like most boys look on their little brothers. I liked him, all right, but I didn't have a lot of use for him. What with his always playing in our drinking water and getting in the way of my chopping axe and howling his head off and chunking me with rocks when he got mad, it didn't seem to me like he was hardly worth the bother of putting up with.

But that day when I saw him in the spring, so helpless against the angry she-bear, I learned different. I knew then that I loved him as much as I did Mama and Papa, maybe in some ways even a little bit more.

So it was only natural for me to come to love the dog that saved him.

Think About It

1. How do Travis's feelings about Old Yeller change? What causes this change?

2. Suppose you lived by Birdsong Creek with your family. Describe what you would like or dislike about being a pioneer.

3. What do you think is the most dramatic part of the story? How does the author help you picture what is happening?

About the Author
FRED GIPSON

As a young boy, Fred Gipson (1908–1973) worked on his family's farm in Mason, Texas. Back then, Fred's father used to entertain the family by telling stories. When Fred grew up, he found work as a reporter. When he started writing fiction, he used his Texas background to inspire his stories.

Fred Gipson's most popular book was *Old Yeller*. He later wrote the screenplay for the movie based on the story. In an interview, he explained why he enjoyed creating exciting, realistic stories. "I've always liked true adventure tales and have always felt that I learned more about the history of my country from these tales than I ever did from the history books."

Meet the Illustrator
DAVID MORENO

David Moreno lives in Central Texas, the setting of *Old Yeller*. In fact, the story takes place near his hometown. This made it very easy for Moreno to research the area and take photographs. When he is not at work photographing, designing, or illustrating, Moreno relaxes by biking, windsurfing, or horseback riding.

Visit *The Learning Site!*
www.harcourtschool.com

RESPONSE ACTIVITIES

Creatures of Birdsong Creek

MAKE A POSTER
Reread the story to find an interesting creature that lives in or around Birdsong Creek. Research the creature's appearance and habitat. Use the information to make a poster. Display your work, and then act as a nature guide by answering viewers' questions.

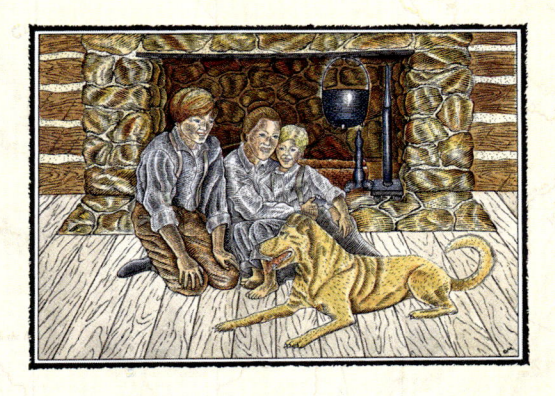

In Arliss's Words

WRITE A CONVERSATION
In the story, everything you learn about Arliss is told from Travis's point of view. Suppose Arliss greets his father when he returns. Write a conversation between Arliss and his father. Have Arliss tell about an adventure that happened while his father was away and how it made him feel.

180

Pioneer Days

RESEARCH PIONEERS

Travis and his family face many challenges as Texas pioneers. With a partner, find out about a group of early settlers of your region. Write a conversation between two imaginary settlers. Have them discuss how they help each other during difficult times.

New Home

CONDUCT AN INTERVIEW

Many people move to a new home at some time in their lives. Interview a family member or friend about a move to a different place. Find out what he or she liked or disliked about starting over in a new place.

FOCUS SKILL: Author's Purpose and Perspective

Authors often present their own perspectives on life in their writing. An author's **perspective** is his or her view of something. It shows what he or she values. Through their choice of words and the actions and words of their characters, authors express their perspectives.

Authors also have a purpose in mind when they write. An author's **purpose** can be to entertain, to inform, or to persuade. While carrying out their purposes, authors try to influence their audiences to agree with their perspectives on things.

Through events in "Old Yeller," readers come to understand the author's perspective on families — that members show through their words and actions how much they care about one another. Notice how the following incidents show the author's perspective.

Events

Mama wraps Arliss's hand when he is hurt.

+

She stands up for his right to tell stories his way.

+

She runs to save him from the bear.

⬇

Author's Perspective

Family members show they care by helping each other.

182

Readers can figure out the author's perspective on families from Travis's words and actions, too. What story details about Travis and Arliss help you interpret the author's perspective? On a seperate sheet of paper, add details to the chart below.

> Travis teaches Arliss how to kill snakes to be safe.
>
> +
>
>
>
> +
>
>
>
> ↓
>
> Family members show they care by helping each other.

WHAT HAVE YOU LEARNED?

1. What is the author's perspective on hard work? What does the author have the characters in "Old Yeller" do and say to show this perspective? What is the author's purpose in writing a story with this perspective?

2. Think about your perspective on teamwork. Write a brief outline of a story plot that shows your perspective. What would be your purpose in writing the story you describe?

TRY THIS • TRY THIS • TRY THIS

Write down a perspective of yours that you'd like to get across to people. It might be on family responsibilities, treatment of animals, or something else. If you wrote another adventure about Travis and Arliss, what things could you have them say or do to persuade readers to think or feel as you do? Put your ideas in a story web.

Visit *The Learning Site!*
www.harcourtschool.com

SAVING

Shiloh

by Phyllis Reynolds Naylor
illustrated by Murray Kimber

Marty's constant companion is a clever beagle named Shiloh. Marty had rescued Shiloh from Judd Travers, a neighbor known to mistreat his hunting dogs. Ever since Judd was injured in a car accident, though, he has tried to mend his ways. When a dangerous accident happens, Marty is forced to trust Judd, and both must test their courage.

Award-Winning Author

Saving SHILOH
PHYLLIS REYNOLDS NAYLOR

The last Saturday in March, Dad picks me up after my job at the vet's and then we pick up David. Been raining all week, off and on, and the water's right high, lapping at the side of the road through the Narrows. When we get to the Shiloh bridge, we see there're only ten layers of stones showing on the supports between the floor of the bridge and the top of the water.

"It's close," Dad says.

He drops us off at the driveway and goes on to deliver the rest of his mail, and David and I run up to the house where Ma's got grilled cheese sandwiches and tomato soup waiting.

"Da-vid!" sings out Becky, all smiles, when she sees him. Girls always like to show off for David.

"Hi, Popcorn," says David.

Then Dara Lynn has to be her usual nuisance, and keeps kickin' us under the table and pretending it was Becky did it.

"Dara Lynn, will you stop it?" I snap, almost sorry I'm savin' that kitten for her.

"Dara Lynn, I'm not tellin' you again! Behave!" says Ma, and I notice she's holding her cheek. "I got no patience with you today." And then she gives this little half smile to David and says, "Sorry I'm not more cheery, but I got a toothache that is making my whole face sore."

I take a good look at Ma. "It's swelling up some, too," I say.

She feels with her hand, then goes and looks in the mirror.

186

"Guess I ought to have gone to the dentist like your dad said," she tells me.

She goes back in the bedroom and lies down, and we try to keep it quiet in the living room. We spread out my Monopoly set on the floor and let Dara Lynn play, but when you get down on the rug like that, Shiloh thinks it's playtime, and he wiggles and rolls and tries to lick our faces, and soon the houses on Park Place are all over the board. Becky thinks it's funny, but Dara Lynn gets mad.

"Stupid old dog!" she yells, and hits at him hard. Shiloh gives this little yelp and comes around behind me. I swoop all Dara Lynn's houses and money off the board, and tell her the game's over. "Don't you ever, never, hit my dog!" I say.

"Oh, who wants to play Monopoly, anyway? Come on, Becky," she says, and the girls go off to their bedroom, get down the box of old jewelry Grandma Preston give them once, and try on all the pieces.

It's raining lightly outside, and David and me are waiting for it to stop. Then we're going back to the old Shiloh schoolhouse to see if we can find any more stuff those men left behind—keep it for a souvenir.

We horse around a little, try to teach Shiloh to help David take his jacket off, make himself useful. But Shiloh yanks too hard on one sleeve and a seam pulls out at the shoulder.

Ma comes out of the bedroom and makes some calls in the kitchen, then comes over to me.

"Marty, I've called the dentist and he says if I can get down there right now, he'll take me today. This toothache's gettin' worse and worse. I called Mrs. Sweeney, and she said she and her daughter are going to Sistersville and they think they can squeeze me in the cab of their pickup, too. Mrs. Ellison is going to come up here and watch you kids till I get back."

"We don't need a sitter!" I say, embarrassed.

"Maybe not, but the girls do, and I want you to behave for her now. Hear?"

She goes in the bathroom to brush her teeth, and by the time she's got her coat on, we can see Mrs. Sweeney's pickup coming up the drive. Ma goes out and gets in.

Great! I'm thinking. David comes for an overnight, and we get a baby-sitter! Mrs. Ellison's nice, though. Always leaves a little something in her mailbox for Dad when she bakes, and I'm thinking she might show up with a chocolate cake. At least Dara Lynn and Becky are having a fine time in their bedroom, and are leaving David and me alone for a change. We open a pop and watch a basketball game on TV.

Fifteen minutes go by, though, and Mrs. Ellison still hasn't come. Phone rings and she says, "Marty, your ma still there?" I tell her she's gone, and Mrs. Ellison says, "Well, the water here in Little is higher than I thought, and I'm afraid if I get over to your place in our Buick, I might not make it back again. Sam's on his way home right now, and he's going to drive me to your house in the four by four. Everything okay there?"

"Everything's fine," I tell her.

No sooner hang up than it rings again, and this time it's Michael Sholt.

"Marty!" he says. "I'm up at my cousin's, and there's a dead man floating down the creek! He just went by! Should be by your place in five minutes. Go see who he is!"

I drop that phone and David and me grab our jackets and run

outside, Shiloh at our heels. The rain's tapered off, but there's mud everywhere. We don't care, though. We run up on the bridge and wait right in the middle, looking upstream. That is one wild-looking creek!

"You suppose dead men float on their backs or their stomachs?" I ask David.

"Stomachs," he says. "That's the way they do in the movies, anyway."

Who could it be? I wonder. Bet someone's called the sheriff already and there'll be men waiting down at the bend where the water slows—see if they can snag him, pull him in. Wouldn't it be something if David and me could find out who he is, and be the first to call the paper? And then the thought come to me: What if it's Judd Travers?

Don't know what made me think that, but it just crossed my mind.

We stand out there on the bridge watching that muddy water come rushing at us and disappear under our feet. No one in the *world* would think Middle Island Creek was anything but a river now.

"You figure five minutes are up?" I ask David.

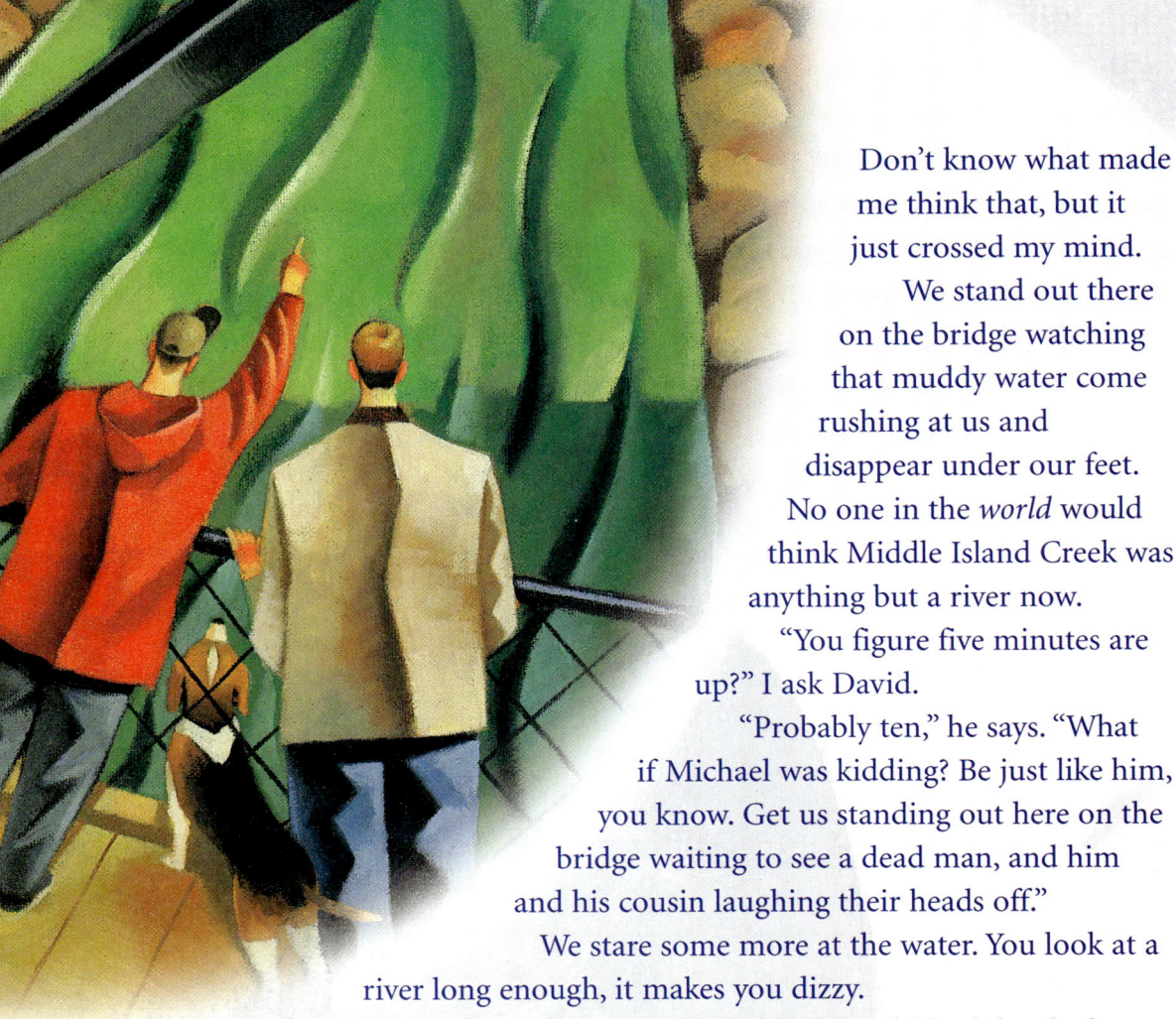

"Probably ten," he says. "What if Michael was kidding? Be just like him, you know. Get us standing out here on the bridge waiting to see a dead man, and him and his cousin laughing their heads off."

We stare some more at the water. You look at a river long enough, it makes you dizzy.

"There's something!" David yells suddenly, and I look hard where he's pointing. Sure enough, bobbing around the curve ahead is something about the size of a man. When it bumps a rock, we see an arm fly up.

"Jiminy!" breathes David.

We run to the far side of the bridge where it looks like the body is heading. Can't tell what color his hair is—can't even see his hair, just the shape of his head, and then his feet, tossing about on the current like the feet of Becky's rag doll.

"Here he comes!" yells David, just as I see Dara Lynn and Becky cross the road.

"Go on back!" I yell. "We're comin' right up." I turn toward the water again, and next I know, the body's coming smack toward us, sliding under the bridge, and we see it's no dead man at all, it's one

190

of those dummies left over from Halloween.

"Ah, shoot!" says David, as we turn and watch it pop out from under the bridge on the other side, its straw-stuffed legs flopping this way and that. Even Shiloh's been fooled—runs across to the other side and barks.

"What was *that*?" Dara Lynn demands, hurrying over. She and Becky got their shoes on, but the laces are flopping, and Becky's jacket's inside out.

"It wasn't nothing—just somebody's Halloween dummy," I say. "Go on back to the house, I said!"

"Don't have to!" says Dara Lynn, sticking out her chin. "Ma didn't say I couldn't come down here. I can walk on the bridge same as you."

"We're all goin' back," I tell her.

But David's mad at Michael Sholt. "Bet he knew it was a dummy all along," he's grumbling. "Maybe he and his cousin dropped it in the creek themselves!"

Becky goes over to the edge of the bridge where the railing makes a diamond pattern. She's lookin' at a spiderweb strung in one of those openings. It glistens silver from the rain. I'm thinking that this water is rising faster than I ever seen it before, as though a couple more creeks have suddenly emptied into it up the way, and it's all of them together rushing under the bridge now.

"Come on," I say again, stopping to tie Becky's shoes for her. "We're goin' up to the house. Mrs. Ellison'll be along, wonder where we went."

Becky starts off again, Shiloh trotting ahead of her, and David catches up with me, talking about what he's going to do if Michael starts a story around that he saw a dead man in Middle Island Creek.

"Look at me!" sings out Dara Lynn behind us. I turn and see she's worked her head through one of those diamond openings in the railing, acting like she's a bird, going to sail out over the creek. Her big puffy jacket on one side of the opening, her head on the other, she looks more like a turtle. Girl can't stand not having all the attention on her.

"Dara Lynn, you cut that out and come on," I say. "Get on up to the house."

She just laughs. I grab her by the arm and pull her back through the railing just as the Ellisons' four by four turns in our drive and moves on up to the house.

"I got it!" says David. "If Michael says there was a dead man in the creek, we'll say we saw him, too. Only we'll make it different. Say it was a man with red hair and a blue shirt on."

I laugh. "His face all swole up...."

"And he looked like he'd been shot in the heart!" says David. We both laugh out loud, thinking of Michael's face if we turn that trick around.

"'What'd I miss?' he'll be thinking," I say, "and..."

"Who-eeee!" I hear Dara Lynn whoop. I turn around and my heart shoots up to my mouth, 'cause right at our end of the bridge, Dara Lynn's climbed up on the railing, her skinny legs straddling it, one foot locked behind a metal bar to keep her balance. Both her arms are in the air, like kids do on a roller-coaster.

"Dara Lynn," I bellow, my voice cracking. "Get off there!"

She laughs, and in her hurry to climb up where I can't reach her, wobbles, grabs at the rail to steady herself, but misses. There's this short little scream, and then . . . then she's in the water.

"Dara *Lynn!*"

Stomach feels like I'm on a roller-coaster myself. Can't even swallow. I'm hanging over the rail, but Dara Lynn's too far down to reach. She's lookin' up at me with the wildest, whitest eyes I ever seen, her arms straight out at the sides like the cold of the water has paralyzed her. And then, just like the straw man, she disappears beneath the bridge.

David's shouting something, I don't know what, and Becky's run screaming up our driveway, then turns around and screams some more. I can see Mr. and Mrs. Ellison running down the drive toward her. David is running over to the railing on the other side of the bridge, his face as white as cream.

"Where is she?" he asks, turning to me. "She didn't come back out."

I am running around the end of the bridge, slipping and sliding down the bank toward the high water.

"What happened?" Mrs. Ellison calls.

"Dara Lynn fell in," I yell, and it's more like a sob.

"Oh, Lord, no!" cries Mrs. Ellison in the background, offering up a prayer for all of us.

All I can think of is havin' to tell Ma that Dara Lynn drowned. Of having to remember every last awful thing I ever said to her, like wishin' she'd fall in a hole and pull the dirt in after her. I am praying to Jesus that if he will save my sister I will never say a mean thing to her as long as I live, even while I know it's not humanly possible. "Just don't let her die, please, please!" I whisper. She'll drown without ever knowin' I gave her a kitten.

I squat down, lookin' under the bridge. I see that Dara Lynn's been snagged by the small trees and bushes sticking out of the water near the first support. At that moment she feels herself caught, and her arms come alive, floppin' and flailin' to turn herself around, and finally she's holding on, screamin' herself crazy.

Mr. Ellison's beside me now, and he's shouting instructions to Dara Lynn to pull herself hand over hand toward the bank, to grab on to the next branch and the next, and not let go on any account, while he wades out into that swirling water as far as he can to meet her.

It's when Dara Lynn pulls herself close enough for us to grab her that I think maybe the thumpin' in my chest won't kill me after all. But then it seems my heart stops altogether, for I see Shiloh out there in the water, the current carrying him farther and farther away. I know right off he jumped in to save Dara Lynn, and now he's got to save himself.

All I hear is my scream.

We're haulin' Dara Lynn out, her clothes making a sucking sound as she leaves the water, but I can see my dog trying to paddle toward us; the current's against him, and he can't even keep himself in one place.

Most times Shiloh could throw himself into Middle Island Creek, chasing a stick I'd tossed, and come right out where he'd gone in, the water moves that slow. But when the rains are heavy and the creek swells fast, the water just tumbles around the bend, and Shiloh's never been in nothing like this before. He keeps tryin' to turn himself around in the water and get back to us.

"Shiloh!" I'm yellin', while behind me, back up on the road, Becky sets up a wail of despair.

"Oh, Lord Jesus, that little dog!" cries Mrs. Ellison, praying again, while her husband takes off his coat and wraps it around Dara Lynn. Dara Lynn's crying, too—huge sobs.

Is God puttin' me to some kind of test, I wonder—saving my sister and drowning my dog? Did I trade one for the other? Lord knows I can't swim. Oh, Jesus, why didn't you make me go to the park in Sistersville and take lessons with Sarah Peters? Why'd I get to sixth grade and not even know how to float?

My mouth don't seem connected to my head. Can still hear it screaming. "Shiloh! Shiloh!"

All he's doin' is tirin' himself out tryin' to swim back to us.

I slide farther down the bank, one foot in the water.

"Don't you try to go in there, Marty," Mr. Ellison shouts.

I claw my way back up the bank, eyes stretched wide, thinkin' how I can make better time up on the road, maybe get myself down to the place where the creek narrows, and Shiloh might be close enough I can reach out to him somehow.

David's running beside me. I know I'm cryin' but I don't care. One foot squishes every time my shoe hits the pavement. Run as fast as we can.

And then I see this pickup comin' up the road from Friendly, and I'm like to get myself run over.

Judd Travers stops and leans out the window. "You want to get yourself killed?" he calls, right angry. And then, "What's the matter, Marty?" Sees Mr. Ellison comin' up the road behind me, thinks he's chasin' me, maybe. He gets out of the truck.

I'm gasping. Point to the creek.

"Shiloh! He's in the water, and we can't reach him!"

"Marty, that dog will have to get himself out!" Mrs. Ellison calls from far behind us. "Don't you try to go after him, now."

But Judd crashes through the trees and brush, half sliding down the muddy bank, and I point to the head of my beagle back upstream, out there bobbing around in the current. Once, it looks like he goes under. Now David's cryin', too, squeaky little gasps.

Judd don't say a word. He's scramblin' up the bank again and grabs that rope in his pickup. Hobbles down the road, fast as his two bum legs will carry him, goin' even farther downstream, me and David at his heels. Then he ties one end of that rope to a tree at the edge of the water, the other end around his waist, taking his time to make a proper square knot, and I'm thinkin', Don't worry about knots, Judd—just go!

He's plunging into that cold water—all but his boots, which he leaves by the tree. I see now why he went so far downstream, 'cause if we were back closer to the bridge, Shiloh would have gone past us by now.

Another car stops up on the road. I hear voices.

"What happened?"

"Who's out there?"

And Mr. Ellison's giving the answers: "Judd Travers is going after Marty Preston's dog."

Mrs. Ellison and the girls have reached the spot now. Dara Lynn is dripping water, but she won't hear of going home. Every muscle in my body is straining to keep me as close to the water as I can get, my eyes trained on that muddy yellow surface, looking for Shiloh. Maybe this was a mistake. Maybe I should have stayed back where we saw him last, kept my eye on where he went. What if he's pulled under? What if his strength just gave out, and he can't paddle no more?

197

David gives a shout. We can see Shiloh now. Looks for a time like he's found something to crawl up on out there in that water, a tree limb or something, but while we watch, he's swept away again.

Judd's treading water out in the center of Middle Island Creek, fighting the current himself, and Shiloh's about twenty feet upstream from him. But then—as I stare—I see him turning away from Judd! I wonder if my dog knows how much danger he's in. Wonder if he figures that between the water and Judd Travers, he'll take the water.

"Here, Shiloh! Come here, boy!" Judd calls, his hair all matted down over his eyes.

Shiloh seems spooked. He's lookin' straight ahead, neither to the right nor left. I see his eyes close again, the way he looks lyin' by the stove at night when he's about to fall asleep.

Judd's working his way out farther and farther, trying to get out in the middle of the creek before Shiloh goes by. He's got his head down now, his arms slicing through the water, but it seems like for every three strokes he takes forward, the creek carries him one stroke sideways.

"Don't give up, Shiloh!" I breathe. And then I begin yelling his name. "Come on, Shiloh! Go to Judd. Come on, boy! Come on!"

I wonder if Judd can make it in time. What if Shiloh's too far out and sails on by? What if the rope's not long enough for Judd to reach him? My breath's coming out all shaky.

Judd's out now about as far as he can go, and that rope is stretched taut. One hand is reaching way out, but seems like Shiloh's still trying to paddle away.

"No, Shiloh!" I plead.

Just then Judd gives this whistle. I know that when Shiloh was his, he was taught to come when Judd whistled. Come or else.

I see my dog start to turn. I see Judd's hand go out, and I hear Judd sayin', "Come on, boy. Come on, Shiloh. Ain't going to hurt you none."

And then . . . then my dog's in his arms, and Judd's shoulders go easy. He is just letting that current swing him on downstream and back to the bank. The rope is holding, and Judd don't have to work much—just let the creek do all the carrying.

I slosh along the bank down to where I can see Judd is headed. The Ellisons are going there, too, and a couple of men up on the road.

"Anybody got a blanket?" I hear someone say.

"I got one in my trunk," a man answers.

Arms are reaching out, hands ready. Somebody puts an old blanket around Judd's shoulders soon as he climbs out.

And now Shiloh's against my chest, his rough tongue licking me up one side of my face and down the other, his little body shaking. With Shiloh in one arm, I reach out and put my other around Judd.

"Thanks," I say, my voice all husky. "Thank you, Judd." I'd say more if I could, but I'm all choked up. I just give him a hug with my one free arm, and strangest of all, Judd hugs me back. It's a sort of jerky, awkward hug, like he hadn't had much practice, but it's a start.

I won't repeat what-all my folks said to us later. Dad does the yelling, Ma the crying, and David's got to sit and listen to the whole thing. That me and David went down to that swollen creek in the first place! That we left the girls alone! That Dara Lynn was reckless enough to climb up on that bridge railing....

"Isn't it enough I have the worst toothache of my life without having to come home and find one of my daughters almost drowned?" weeps Ma.

I keep sayin', "I'm sorry"—David, too—but Dad tells us "sorry" wouldn't bring a dead girl back to life. Neither of 'em says anything about Shiloh. That ain't their worry right now.

Dara Lynn hangs her head like the starch has been knocked out of her. Just sits all quiet by the potbellied stove, arms wrapped around her middle. Becky's on the couch, suckin' her thumb. We are the sorriest-looking family right now, but my dog's safe in my arms, and I can't ask for more. Every time he wriggles to get down, I just hold him tighter, and finally he gives up and lays still, knowin' my arms'll get tired by and by.

Next day, though, after Mr. Howard comes for David, my folks are quiet. Seem like every time they walk by one of us, they squeeze a shoulder or pat a head or stroke somebody's hair.

That night after Becky's had her bath and has gone around givin' everyone her butterfly kiss, battin' her lashes against their cheeks, I go out in the kitchen where Dara Lynn's having her graham crackers and milk, and say, "Well, pretty soon you're goin' to have to be sharing that milk with someone else, you know."

She looks at me suspicious-like. "Why?" she says.

" 'Cause we're gettin' another member of the family, that's why."

Dara Lynn's eyes open wide. "Ma's having another baby?"

I laugh. "Not this kind of baby, she ain't. It's gonna be your birthday present from me, Dara Lynn. Somebody brought in a litter of kittens to Doc Collins. You want to come with me some Saturday and pick one out, it's yours."

Dara Lynn leaps off her chair and, with graham cracker crumbs on her fingers, hugs me hard. I hug back—a little jerky and awkward, but it's a start.

Think About It

1. How do people work together to save Dara Lynn and Shiloh?
2. Judd jumps into a raging creek to save Shiloh. Why do you think he does that?
3. How does the author build suspense throughout the story?

Meet the Author
Phyllis Reynolds Naylor

Phyllis Reynolds Naylor has written almost 100 books for young readers. *Saving Shiloh* is the third book in the series she wrote about Marty and his dog. An interviewer asked her these questions about her writing.

How did you start your writing career?
My parents read aloud to us every night. I always loved stories and plots, and I just naturally loved to make up stories myself. When I was 16, a former teacher wrote to me that she was editing a magazine for children. She asked if I would write a story for it. I wrote my first and only baseball story, and she bought it for $4.67.

Where did the idea for the original *Shiloh* come from?
I was in the little community of Shiloh, West Virginia. I came across an abused dog that was too frightened to even allow me to pet her (the real dog was female). I couldn't get her out of my mind. So I did what writers usually do in that situation—I started a book. The real Shiloh is named Clover, and she was adopted by friends of mine in West Virginia.

What do you like to do in your free time?
Even when I'm not writing, I'm thinking about what I'm working on next. But I also take time to swim and hike and snorkel and eat Chinese food and chocolate and go to the theater and play the piano and visit schools to talk about my books.

Phyllis Reynolds Naylor

Visit *The Learning Site!*
www.harcourtschool.com

THE WINDOW Atheneum
FACES
THE WATER Atheneum
SHADOWS
THE WALL Atheneum
FOLLETT
ovel Naylor
Forum
Forum
Forum
Forum
IS REYNOLDS NAYLOR W.H. ALLEN
REYNOLDS NAYLOR W.H. ALLEN
Naylor Atheneum A100 $1.95
Forum
Forum
PHYLLIS REYNOLDS NAYLOR
PHYLLIS REYNOLDS NAYLOR
EYE PHYLLIS REYNOLDS NAYLOR
HERSELF Naylor Atheneum
WATER Naylor
Phyllis Reynolds Naylor
Naylor
Alice the Bra
Alice
Naylor
Naylor
Naylor
Naylor
NIGHT CRY
Phyllis Reynolds Naylor
Naylor The Grand E
NAYLOR Danny's
NAYLOR Wrestle the
NAYLOR Wrestle the
NAYLOR aching
NAYLOR The Treasure of B
sang
NAYLOR sang
The Girls Get Even
The Boys Start the

Puppies with a Purpose

from *National Geographic World*

Training a Dog Guide takes love, patience, and an ability to say goodbye.

Mary Carroll Smith, 15, helps raise Julie, this golden retriever pup, to be a good guide dog like Jamie. That's the German shepherd walking here with Mary Carroll's dad, who is blind. Jamie is his sixth guide dog.

Julie seems like any other lively puppy. She romps and wrestles with other dogs. But unlike most pups, Julie has an important job ahead of her. One day she will serve as substitute eyes for a blind person.

For the first 16 months of her life, Julie is living with Mary Carroll Smith, 15, of Nutley, New Jersey. Mary Carroll is in The Seeing Eye Puppy-Raising Program/4-H Project. The program places future guide dogs with volunteer puppy raisers who start preparing the puppies for the job ahead. Mary Carroll wanted to raise puppies so she could help other people have the same freedom that her blind father has with his guide dog.

Getting Julie used to strangers and new places is Mary Carroll's most important task. She takes Julie to soccer and softball games, into stores and restaurants, and sometimes to school. "At first she was nervous," said Mary Carroll. "But the more I took her out, the better she got. Now she's mellow!"

Playing with Julie is part of Mary Carroll's job, too. Playing helps Julie become a friendly, loving dog. Mary Carroll also teaches her to obey simple commands such as "sit" and "come." "I praise her by talking to her and petting her," explains Mary Carroll. "I correct her by telling her 'no' firmly."

Julie will eventually leave Mary Carroll and return to Seeing Eye headquarters for more guide dog training. Raising a puppy and then giving it up isn't easy. Even so, Mary Carroll says, "It's a good feeling to know you're helping someone else."

Class Act
Every two weeks, Mary Carroll joins other 4-H puppy raisers for talk and training. Here she learns a signal that tells Julie to "rest."

Good Doggies
When the puppy raisers go for an after-class snack, their guide-dogs-in-training are allowed to follow. They learn to stay under the table and not beg.

Think About It
Which of Mary's responsibilities seems most difficult to you?

A Nose for Snooze
Julie waits patiently for Mary Carroll's Latin class to end. Like any good guide dog, she lies still until Mary Carroll signals that it's time to get going.

Response Activities

Cut That Out — With Scissors?

MAKE AN IDIOM GLOSSARY
Marty sometimes uses idioms when he speaks. An idiom is an expression that has a meaning other than a literal one. For example, when Marty says *cut that out,* he means "stop it." Work with a partner to collect idioms from the story and from your conversations. Write glossary entries for them for a class book.

Director's Chair

DRAW A STORYBOARD Create a storyboard that shows how you would film one of the rescues in the story. Sketch each important action in a square, and write the dialogue and directions below the square. Display your storyboard in your classroom.

MAKING CONNECTIONS

WRITE A PARAGRAPH Think about how people depend on Shiloh in the story and on Julie, the golden retriever in "Puppies with a Purpose." Write a paragraph that tells why some dogs are trusty companions and helpers. Include information from the selections and from your own experience.

SAFETY FIRST

WRITE A LIST Think about safety tips that Marty and his sisters should have followed to stay safe. Write a list they could use the next time they are waiting for a baby-sitter to arrive.

FLOOD

WRESTLING WITH THE MISSISSIPPI

BY PATRICIA LAUBER

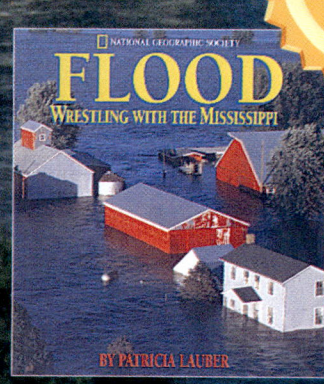

Award-Winning Author

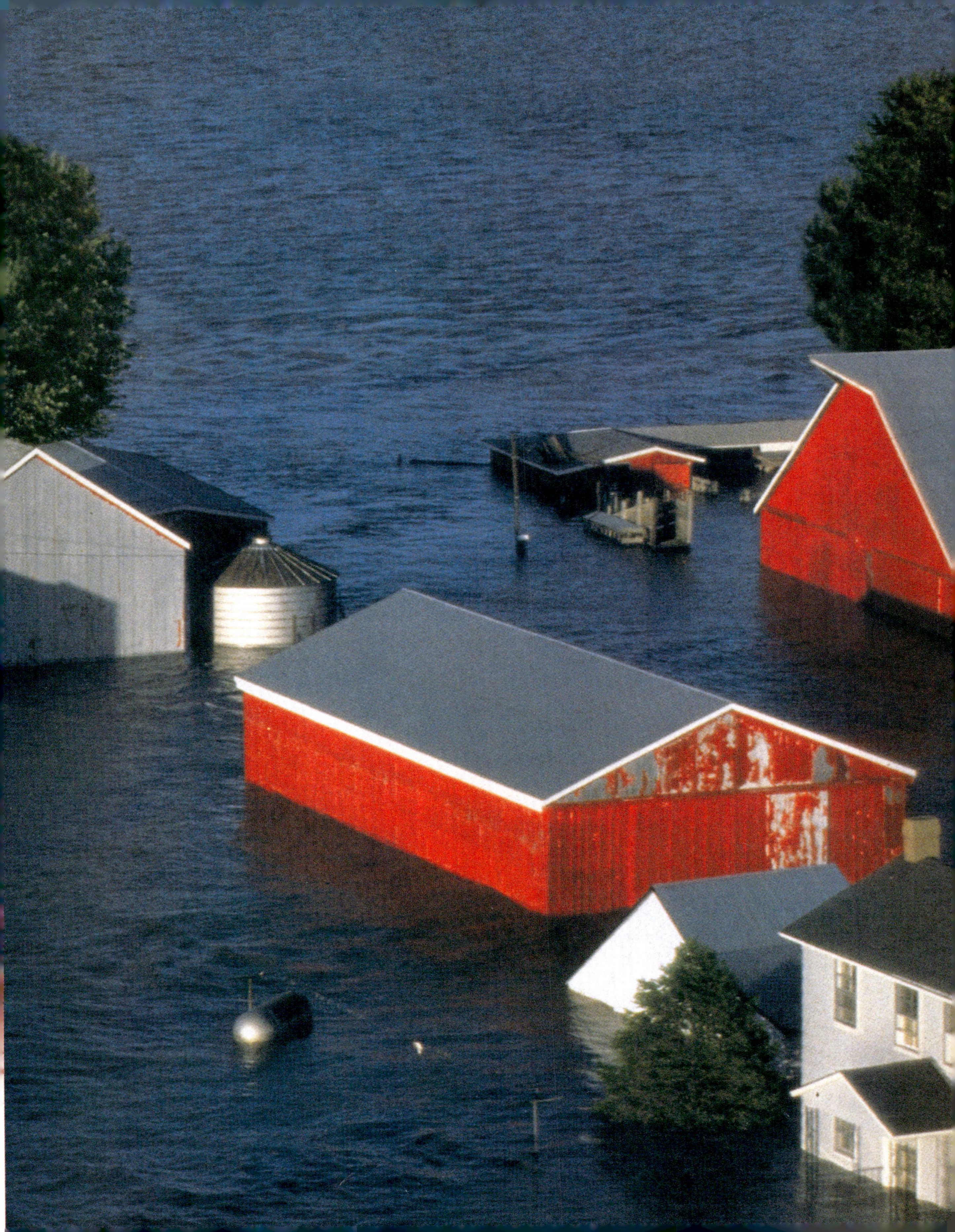

From its beginnings as a small stream in Minnesota, the Mississippi River travels more than 2,000 miles to the Gulf of Mexico. Along the way, the river deposits tons of rich soil and creates thousands of acres of valuable farmland. Farmers all along the way have built levees to try to control the great river. In the summer of 1993, however, the levees were not strong or tall enough to control the Mississippi's raging waters.

Above: St. Louis, with its Gateway Arch, was one of the cities with a floodwall. The 11-mile-long concrete wall was built by the Corps of Engineers.

Right: A levee on the Illinois River near St. Louis forms an arch in this photograph. The barrier stretching across the arch was placed there in case the levee was overtopped during the 1993 flood.

ENDLESS RAIN

Spring of 1992 brought drought. Across Iowa and other states of the upper Middle West, farmland dried into a crumbly crust. In early July, the skies finally darkened and rain began to fall. People rejoiced.

But once started, the rains didn't stop. All summer long, it rained and rained and rained. Summer was also cooler than usual. High above the earth there was haze in the atmosphere, caused by a volcanic eruption in the Philippines. The haze cut off some of the sun's rays. Less water was drawn back into the atmosphere. More stayed on the land, soaking it through and through.

Autumn was rainy.

Winter of 1992–93 brought heavy rains.

Spring brought storms.

As the rain-filled spring crept by, people began to worry. Rivers were rising steadily between their levees. The mighty Mississippi was swollen and rushing. So were its tributaries, the many rivers and streams that added their waters to the big river.

In June worry changed to alarm. The ground had long since soaked up all the water it could hold. The only place rainwater could go was into the rapidly rising creeks, streams, and rivers.

There had been floods before, times when main streets filled with water and farmland turned into lakes. Each time people cleaned up, rebuilt, and went on with their lives. Some flooding, they felt, was a price they had to pay for farming the rich soil of a floodplain.

Over the years defenses had been strengthened. Cities had concrete floodwalls and levees armored with concrete, built by the Corps of Engineers. Earthen levees built by local groups were higher and longer.

Below: A typical Mississippi River Valley levee system

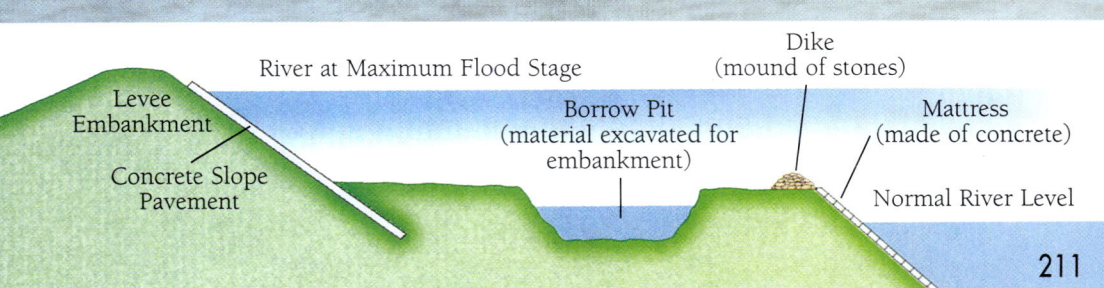

To hold back water, the Corps had built dams and reservoirs on some tributaries of the Mississippi. All this work had one aim: to keep the river in its channel so that people could safely live and work on the floodplain.

Would the defenses hold? In early summer of 1993, people could only wonder—and worry. No one could remember seeing the river rise so high. Nor had anyone ever seen such rain. Even if a day started fair, by afternoon storm clouds were building up again. Nights were shattered by bolts of lightning, claps of thunder, and the drumming of rain on roofs.

Weather scientists could explain what was happening, but they could not offer much hope. Winds high in the atmosphere were steering hot, moist air into the upper Midwest. There the air collided with cold air from Canada. The cold caused moisture to condense out of the warm air and fall as rain. Usually, storms broke up and moved east. In 1993 they could not. They were blocked by a mass of hot, dry air over the East Coast. Until that mass of air moved out to sea, rain would go on falling and falling on the Midwest. Sometimes 5 to 12 inches fell in a single day.

By the middle of July, rain had fallen on the Midwest for 49 straight days. And by then rivers had been bursting through levees, spreading over farms and towns. A satellite picture showed much of Iowa colored blue, as if it were one of the Great Lakes. In eight states, rivers had taken back 15 million acres of farmland and driven 36,000 people from their homes.

Along the Mississippi the worst flooding took place between Davenport, Iowa, and the area south of St. Louis, Missouri. Here there were no reservoirs or lakes to hold back water. And here the Mississippi received the waters of several large tributaries—the Iowa, the Des Moines, the Illinois, and the Missouri. On July 19, there were floods along 464 miles of the Mississippi, from McGregor, Iowa, to St. Louis.

Below: Satellite images show the difference between normal summer water levels of the Mississippi and Missouri rivers (left) and those of the 1993 flood (right). The Mississippi and Illinois rivers are at the top of the images, the Missouri at the left.

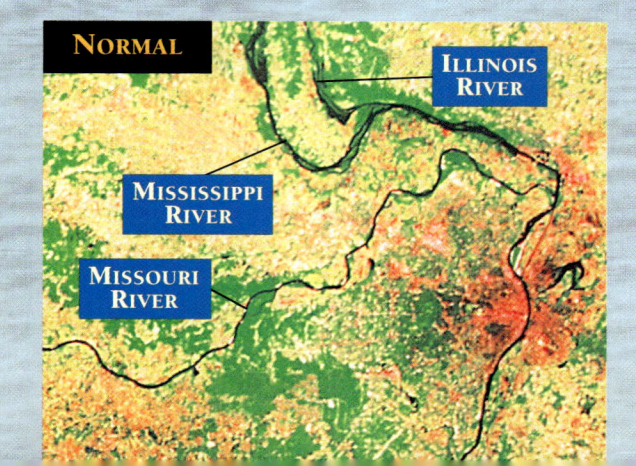

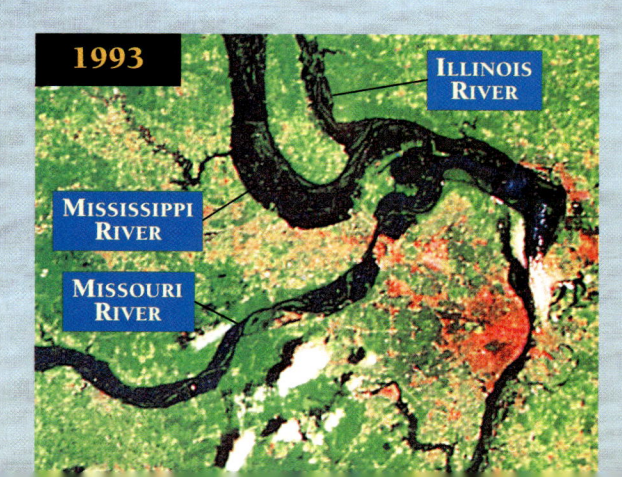

Above: Pigs, rescued from the roof of a barn, are lifted into a boat at Kaskaskia, Illinois. On the Mississippi itself, the worst flooding took place between Davenport, Iowa, and the area south of St. Louis.

THE SNY ISLAND LEVEE

As the Mississippi twists and turns out of Iowa and into Missouri and Illinois, it is fairly narrow—only 1,500 feet wide at some points. Nearing Quincy, Illinois, it can carry 250,000 cubic feet of water a second without flooding. In the summer of 1993, it was carrying more than twice that amount.

The town of Quincy stands on bluffs, high above the Mississippi. It looks out over 110,000 acres of fertile farmlands, up and down the river. All are part of a levee district named Sny Island.

In late spring of 1993, farm buildings and fields of corn and soybeans lay snug behind a 54-mile-long levee. But the men and women who worked and lived there were watching the river. Since April it had been high, as it often was after winter snow had melted. But the water had always gone down as summer arrived. This year it

Above: When this levee gave way, Valmeyer, Illinois, was swamped.

didn't. Instead, it began to rise, slowly but steadily. In late June one of Quincy's two bridges to Missouri was closed. The Missouri end, which had no levees, was underwater.

A thunderstorm raged during the night of Wednesday, June 30. It dumped six inches of rain on Quincy and more to the north. The river rose two feet. People began to wonder whether the levee would hold. In 120 years, it had had only one serious break. But it had never faced a test like this one.

By Thursday morning small creeks had flooded roads, and the river was rising steadily. The Sny levee stood 28 feet above the river channel. The normal height of the river was 11 feet. On the morning of July 1, it was about a foot below the top of the levee and rising an inch an hour. Water was seeping through the base of the levee. And the National Weather Service was predicting that a crest of water 30 feet high would pass Quincy on Saturday, July 3.

People of the floodplain loaded cars

and trucks with their belongings—sofas, TV sets, refrigerators, rugs, desks—to be stored with friends or relatives on higher ground. Farm animals were trucked away to be boarded or sent to market.

A call went out for helpers, trucks, bulldozers, and sandbags. The levee had to be raised and strengthened.

One section was a weak link. During the 1960s most of the Sny was rebuilt, using large amounts of sand. When a levee needs to be raised, wet sand can be bulldozed from its base up the side and will stay in place. Wet earth does not. Bulldozed toward the top, it slides back to the base. For some reason, one mile-long section had not been rebuilt. It was still made of earth. There was only one way to raise it: build a wall of wooden boards along its top and support the wall with beams and sandbags.

Farmers began arriving, some from high ground miles away. Most were strangers, but help was needed and so they came, driving bulldozers and trucks. Over the next three weeks, hundreds of other strangers would also volunteer to help raise the Sny levee and work on the weak link.

All day long that first day, men and women hauled wood, sawed it, and hammered it. They worked in 95° heat, high humidity, swarms of mosquitoes, and never-ending mud. By evening stretches of board were rising on top of the weak link. Work went on into the night, and by 3 a.m. the first section of boards and beams was in place. Now it had to be backed by thousands of sandbags. Each one needed to be filled, moved along the levee, and put in place by hand.

Below: At the Sny, as at other levees, sandbags had to be filled before they could be used.

Above: Kaskaskia is an island that, for a time, appeared as part of the Mississippi.

The river was only inches below the top of the old levee. With no time to waste, everyone was up early and back at work.

Work continued into the night. Somewhere upstream a levee gave way and water poured off the river onto the floodplain. At Sny Island the pressure eased, and the river seemed to be holding steady at just under 28 feet. When work stopped, 42,000 sandbags, each weighing 30 to 40 pounds, had been put in place.

Sunday, July 4, brought heavy rain to the Midwest. The Weather Service forecast that a crest of 31.5 feet would pass Quincy on July 11. That meant the mile-long board fence had to be raised. The governor of Illinois called in the National Guard to help.

Late on the afternoon of July 9, another levee gave way upstream and water rushed over 10,000 acres. At Sny Island the river began to drop, but heavy rains were still falling over Iowa and other parts of the Midwest, draining off the land, swelling rivers, and rushing toward the Mississippi. The Weather Service now forecast a crest of 32.5 feet at Quincy on Wednesday, July 14. The board fence had to be raised again.

By Tuesday morning the fence had been raised. Workers in human chains were passing and placing sandbags—adding to the half million already in place. They felt sure of finishing before the crest arrived. Then the sky turned black, the wind rose, and bolts of lightning streaked the sky. For safety's sake, all workers were pulled off the levee. The river was five inches below the top of the boards.

The battle seemed to be lost, but that night two more levees gave

216

way upstream. The river dropped 2 feet. The Weather Service now forecast that the 32.5-foot crest would pass Quincy on Thursday.

On Thursday night the crest came, 32 feet high. The Sny levee held. The river stayed as high on Friday. The Sny held. Work on the levee now slowed. Workers patrolled, watching for signs of weakness or small leaks. Bulldozers pushed up sand. The river was still pressing against the levee, which was now soggy and weakening.

A week later the river was still at 30 feet. Day and night, farmers watched the Sny. Farmhouses and barns were empty. Corn and soybeans still stretched as far as the eye could see, but it was too early to tell if there would ever be a harvest.

That weekend the rains began again. Slowly the river began to rise. It was one time too many. Part of the Sny levee gave way, not the weak link with the board fence but another part. By evening on Sunday, July 25, 44,000 acres of corn and soybeans lay under 15 feet of water. Only the roofs of houses and barns showed that Sny Island was not a lake. People had done all they could, but it was not enough.

Below: During the summer of 1993, farmers of the floodplain watched anxiously as the Mississippi rose ever higher behind its levees.

Up and Down the Valley

In the upper valley of the Mississippi and along its tributaries, town after town suffered in the summer of 1993. The small river town of Alexandria, Missouri, saw the river rise in spring—and go on rising. On July 8, the levee broke and the town went under for the rest of the summer.

Niota, Illinois, was one of several towns helped by prisoners—young, fit, first offenders sentenced for non-violent crimes. They were city men, most of whom had never seen the Mississippi or a farm. At first, Niota seemed strange to them. But working shoulder-to-shoulder with local people, they soon came to feel that Niota was their town, too, and they worked with a will. For nine straight days, they threw sandbags from 8 a.m. until dark, in rain, sun, heat, humidity, and mud. The townspeople were awed by how hard they worked. The young prisoners were awed by how nice the townspeople were, thanking them, supplying cold drinks, and feeding them roast beef, chicken, catfish, meatloaf, apple pie, and peach cobbler.

At 6 p.m. on July 10, the levee broke. Some of the prisoners cried, as did men and women of Niota. They had done their best, yet the river had won. That last night, the prisoners refused to eat because they had not saved the town.

Davenport, Iowa, had no levees. The city had missed its chance to have the federal government build levees and floodwalls. Later, its citizens decided

Below: Cairo lies on a point of land where the big Ohio River (right) flows in from the east to join the Mississippi.

Above: A family photo and a banjo clock were among the few items saved from a flooded house.

they could not afford to pay for the work themselves. Besides, they did not want to wall off the river and lose their view. The city suffered widespread flooding.

There were also places where defenses did hold. One was Hannibal, Missouri, boyhood home of Mark Twain. The town had built a levee that stood 31 feet higher than the river bottom. As the water rose, townspeople raised the levee 3 feet with sandbags. The river crested at 32 feet, and Hannibal was safe.

Above: Volunteers also helped with the clean-up. This one is shoveling out a house in Hull, Illinois.

The Missouri joins the Mississippi about 20 miles north of St. Louis. St. Louis was the largest city in harm's way. It was also the first to face the floodwaters of both the Missouri and the Mississippi. At one time more than 480 million gallons of water a minute churned past the city. But most of the city stayed dry behind its 11-mile-long concrete floodwall. Damage came chiefly from a small tributary that backed up when forced to take water from the Mississippi.

Downriver from St. Louis was Ste. Genevieve, Missouri, which called itself the first settlement west of the Mississippi. It had stood there for 250 years, but in late July its future did not look bright. Its levee rose 36 to 38 feet above the river bottom; the river was expected to crest at 45 feet. If Ste. Genevieve flooded, it would lose what it most prized: houses made of logs stuck together with clay, animal hair, and straw—the country's best examples of what the French settlers built.

The town's problems began to attract attention on television and in newspapers. From miles away—Colorado, Minnesota, Tennessee, Florida—people decided to help. They piled into buses, cars, and trucks and drove to the small town. All told, some 1,200 volunteers arrived to help. They filled and set in place 1,100,000 sandbags, raising the levee

220

by ten feet. To strengthen it they dumped 100,000 tons of rock behind the sandbags. The old buildings were saved.

Once the floodwaters reached Cape Girardeau and Cairo, they were no longer a problem. The giant lower Mississippi easily swallowed the vast tide that was sweeping south. Its own tributaries were low in the summer of 1993.

As the Waters Fell

There was no one day when the flood of 1993 ended, no one day when people knew they were safe from the river. But in August the weather pattern began slowly to change. People sensed that the worst was over. Those who had been flooded out yearned to go home. Most were living nearby, crammed in with friends or relatives or in mobile homes that the federal government had brought in. But no one could go home until the water drained back into the river. Rain still fell. Some towns went under a second, or even a third, time. In places, farms still lay under muddy water 11 miles wide and 20 feet deep.

Days were spent making the rounds from one government agency to another, applying for loans, grants, and other kinds of help. In early evening, families might

Below: A father and daughter from Taos, Missouri, used a boat to reach their trailer and swam in through the door to save what little they could.

Above: As the waters began to drop, families could visit their towns and farms by boat. This family is looking at the building where it used to store grain.

drive to the edge of the water, park, and talk to neighbors. Ahead was the road that used to lead to home; now it dipped under the water and disappeared. Sometimes people would boat into their towns and float down Main Street. At first there was little to see except a chimney, a TV antenna, the top of a telephone pole. As the water dropped, they began to see the remains of houses—windows blown out, porches sagging.

Finally the time came when they could get into their houses. What many found were mud-caked ruins: eight inches of thick dark mud on the floors, mud on the walls, mud on the ceiling, mud on the furniture. They found mildew, mold, and dead fish. But these were people who had sandbagged for days on end, women who had cooked for hundreds of volunteers and washed their muddy clothes. They were workers. They were people raised to believe that life is good but hard, people raised to believe that you work for what you get. And so they set to work hauling out soggy rugs and couches, ruined refrigerators and TVs, and piling them on lawns covered with slime. With shovels, brooms, and buckets of water and bleach, they attacked the houses that could be repaired. They might still be cleaning up when the first frost came, but they never doubted. They would be back.

Think About It

1. How did people work together to save their communities from flooding? Why weren't they always successful?

2. How does the selection make you feel about the power of nature? Explain your answer.

3. Why do you think the author uses chronological order to tell the story? How does it help you follow what is happening?

Meet The Author
Patricia Lauber

Patricia Lauber has written more than 90 nonfiction and fiction books. She has won many awards, including the Newbery Honor for *Volcano: The Eruption and Healing of Mount St. Helens*. We asked the author about her writing and what inspired her to write about the floods of 1993.

Q: What do you like to write about?
A: I write about the many things that interest me. All of my books are based on what I see around me. I like to stand and stare at things, to talk with people, and to read a lot. By doing these things, I always learn something new.

Q: Where do you get your ideas?
A: My ideas come from everywhere—from things I read and from things people tell me. The things that interest me the most are the things I want to share with others.

Q: Why did you write about the Mississippi floods?
A: The story of the Mississippi, and of the people who use its waters, tugged at my imagination The river often seemed to have a mind of its own. The floods of 1993 moved me to write a book exploring the river and the human lives it impacted.

Visit **The Learning Site!**
www.harcourtschool.com

The noise of the plane's engines is deafening. So is the wind, which rushes past the open door at 110 miles an hour. Inside, men and women wait, taking deep breaths. Then . . . they jump! After five tense seconds their parachutes open. They float to the ground, and everything is perfectly calm—for now.

Smoke Jum

Wherever fires erupt and vehicles cannot reach—that's where you'll find smoke jumpers. They parachute into remote mountain wilderness throughout the western United States, including Alaska. Their mission: to prevent small wildfires from growing into large ones. Employed by the Forest Service and the Bureau of Land Management, smoke jumpers have been fighting fires since 1940.

Smoke jumpers land close to a forest fire. They work to prevent the fire from spreading. They rely on obstacles such as rivers, creeks, lakes, and logging roads to help contain the fire. Sometimes they dig a fire line—a dirt path several feet wide through the surrounding vegetation. Their goal is to let the fire burn out while keeping it from reaching the treetops. If it does reach the treetops, there is no way to put out the fire from the ground. A plane carrying fire retardant might be called in to help.

Once the fire is out, smoke jumpers watch for smoke and feel chunks of timber. They must make sure that no areas are still hot. They call this part of their job mopping up.

Smoke jumpers spend sleepless nights listening to a forest fire roaring in the distance. They breathe thick smoke, work up a terrible sweat, and get covered by dirt and ash. At the end of a mission, smoke jumpers have aching bodies. They may face a 20-mile hike to get home. Smoke jumpers have a dangerous but vital job—they save millions of acres of forestland every year.

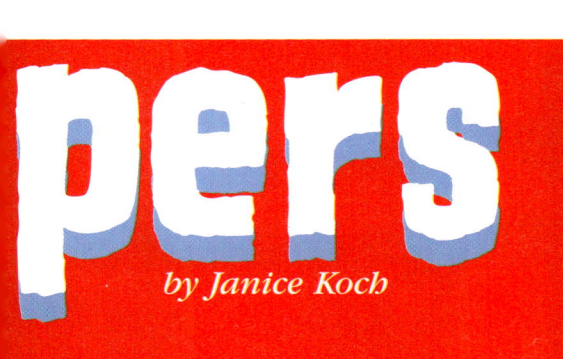

by Janice Koch

Learning to Leap and Land

Jump to It!

Rookie smoke jumpers practice the correct way to land. When they hit the ground, smoke jumpers roll. This distributes the shock of the landing over the entire body.

Stepping Out

A future smoke jumper leaps from a four-story tower. The proper exit technique prevents a smoke jumper from getting tangled in the parachute or hitting the side of the plane.

Wet Landing

In a swimming pool smoke jumpers learn how to free themselves from their parachutes. A gust of wind can carry smoke jumpers over a lake—a dangerous place to land with open parachutes.

All Geared Up and Ready to Go

Smoke jumper Margarita Phillips is well suited to fight a fire. Smoke jumpers put together and repair their own gear—except for their boots and helmets. The equipment Phillips jumps with weighs 85 pounds.

Jumpsuit
The heavily padded jumpsuit is made of the same material as bulletproof vests worn by police officers. Smoke jumpers wear fire-resistant clothing underneath.

Reserve Chute
If the main parachute does not open, the reserve chute gets pulled into service.

Pack-Out Bag
Tucked away in a jumpsuit, this bag is empty at first. Most fire fighting equipment is dropped to the ground in a separate container. Once a fire is out, a smoke jumper puts the equipment in the bag so it can be carried out.

Crosscut Saw
Dropped to the ground in a cargo box, the saw is used to clear timber and branches from a fire line. Here the saw is bent over the pack-out bag and its teeth are covered.

Main Parachute
Within five seconds of leaving the plane, a smoke jumper's parachute opens. It is carried inside a backpack.

Static Line
A yellow nylon strap connects the main parachute to a cable inside the plane. The strap helps pull open the chute, which then disconnects.

Helmet
A motorcycle helmet has a protective metal face guard.

Leg Pockets
Inside go candy bars, long johns, and the "bird's nest"—looped nylon strap (shown on top of the pack-out bag) that smoke jumpers use to descend if they land in a tree. Also inside are signal streamers for communicating with the pilot from the ground.

Rocky Touchdown
A mountain slope presents a challenge to a smoke jumper. This one landed face down. Knowing how to land on different kinds of terrain—thick forests, steep hills, lakes—is an essential smoke jumper skill.

Think About It
How are smoke jumpers and traditional fire fighters alike? How are they different?

RESPONSE ACTIVITIES

Community Rescue Teams

WRITE A PARAGRAPH If disaster struck your town, how might you and the members of your community work together to help? Write a paragraph that tells what you would do.

Rising River

MAKE AN EMERGENCY PLAN People who live in flood zones build levees to help protect their homes. Create a plan to protect your home, school, or community against a natural disaster. Share your plan with your classmates.

River Songs

WRITE A SONG The Mississippi River is one of the most important bodies of water in the United States. In an encyclopedia or a textbook, find some interesting facts about this river. Write a song celebrating the mighty Mississippi.

Making Connections

EXCHANGE POSTCARDS Work with a partner. Imagine that you are either battling rising waters in "Flood" or fighting fires in "Smoke Jumpers." Write a postcard to your partner telling what happened and explaining your feelings. Your partner should respond as if he or she were in the other situation.

FRIENDS TO THE RESCUE

THEME

Coming to the Rescue
PLOT STUDY Think about the exciting events that happen in the theme "Friends to the Rescue." Why are the characters in danger? Who comes to their aid? Where does the action take place? What happens at the end? Make a chart in which you can write short answers to these questions.

May I Quote You?
ROUNDTABLE DISCUSSION From each selection, choose a quote that represents the theme. Write the quote on an index card. On the back of the card, list your reasons for choosing that quote. Then share your quotes in a small group and tell why you chose them.

WRAP-UP

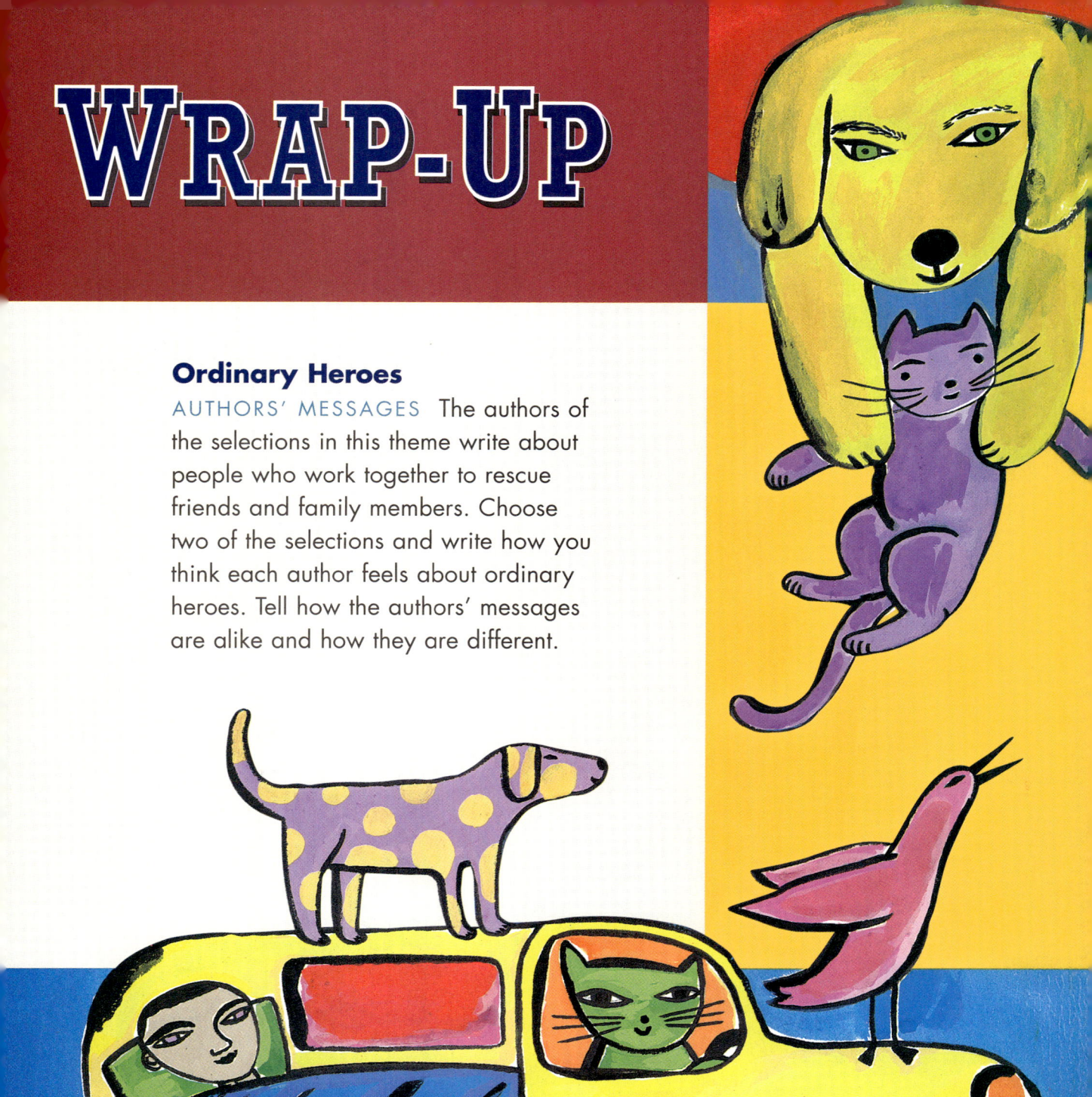

Ordinary Heroes

AUTHORS' MESSAGES The authors of the selections in this theme write about people who work together to rescue friends and family members. Choose two of the selections and write how you think each author feels about ordinary heroes. Tell how the authors' messages are alike and how they are different.

THEME
UNLOCKING THE PAST

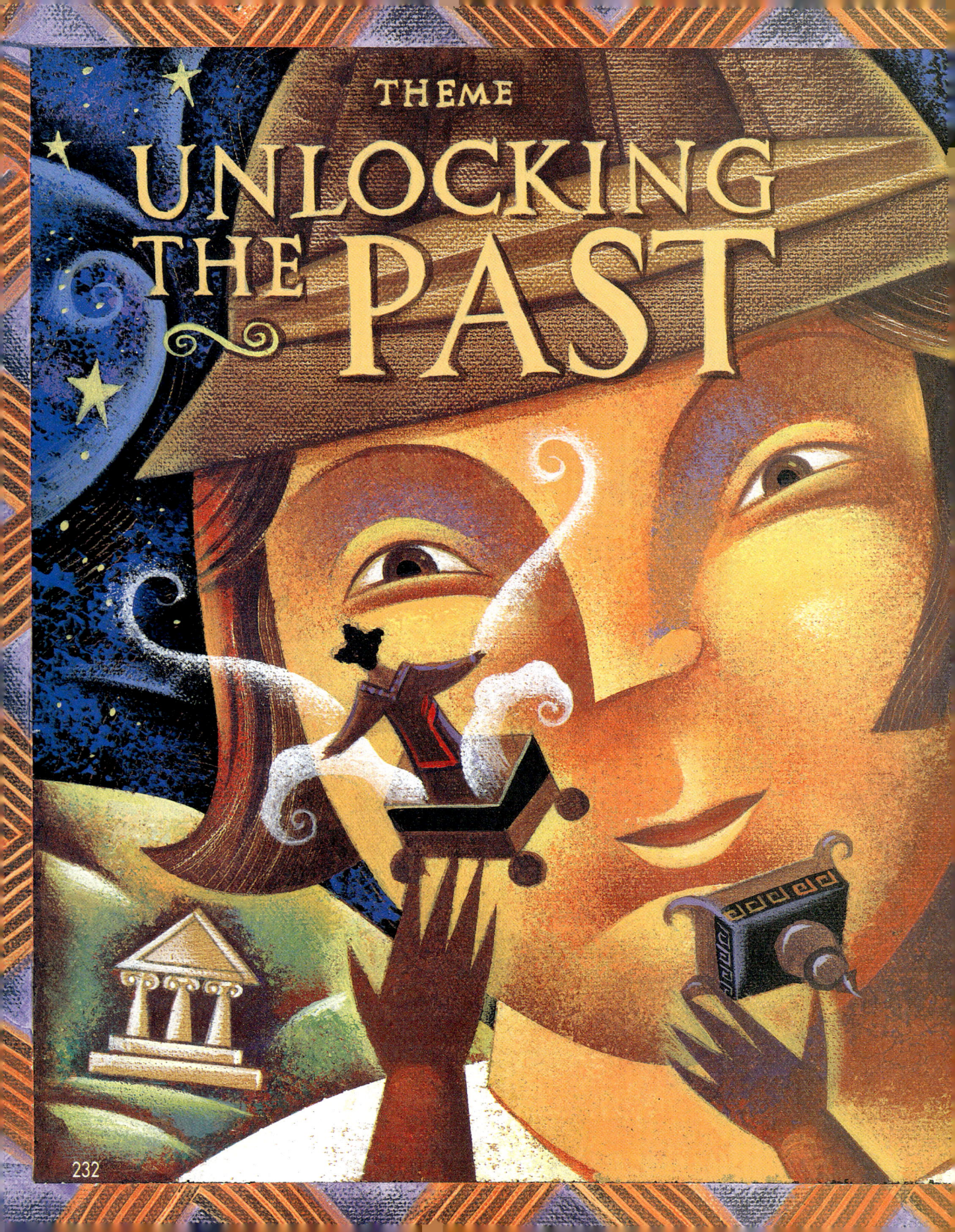

CONTENTS

The Stone Age News...............236
by Fiona Macdonald

FOCUS SKILL:
Fact and Opinion...........................254

Ancient China......................256
by Robert Nicholson
and Claire Watts

The Chinese Dynasties............270
from *Kids Discover*

Pyramids...............................274
from *Kids Discover*

FOCUS SKILL:
Graphic Sources..........................292

**Look Into the Past:
The Greeks and the Romans**...294
by A. Susan Williams
and Peter Hicks

The Skill of Pericles................314
by Paul T. Nolan

A Song of Greatness...............328
transcribed by Mary Austin

READER'S CHOICE

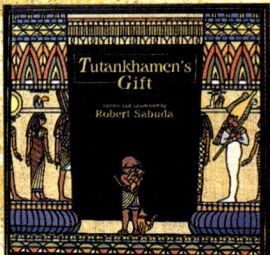

Tutankhamen's Gift
by Robert Sabuda

HISTORICAL FICTION

Colorful illustrations bring the story of Tutankhamen, a young Egyptian pharaoh, to life.

Notable Social Studies Trade Book for Young People
READER'S CHOICE LIBRARY

The Riddle of the Rosetta Stone: Keys to Ancient Egypt
by James Cross Giblin

NONFICTION

The Rosetta Stone is one of the greatest treasures of Ancient Egypt. Find out how scholars translated its mysterious markings to discover the secrets of Egyptian history.

ALA Notable Book
READER'S CHOICE LIBRARY

Tut Tut
by John Scieszka

HISTORICAL FICTION

While Joe, Fred, and Sam are finishing their history projects, Joe's sister opens *The Book*. Suddenly, history comes to life as they all find themselves in ancient Egypt.

The Fool and the Phoenix
by Deborah Nourse Lattimore

FOLKTALE

In this beautifully illustrated book, the author retells the ancient Japanese myth of the Phoenix.

City—A Story of Roman Planning and Construction
by David Macaulay

NONFICTION

The Romans were skilled at city planning. Discover how they designed and built cities that satisfied the needs of the people who lived in them.

ALA Notable Book

The Stone Age News

by Fiona Macdonald

Newspapers did not exist in the Stone Age, but newsworthy events were happening all the time. The Stone Age people's search for a better way of life, their survival during the Ice Age, and the invention of farming are just a few of the stories that would have made headlines.

WORLD EVENTS

ICE CREEPS CLOSER

TIME TO GO: As the weather worsens, people in central Russia head south.
Lee Montgomery

WE ALL MOAN about today's weather, but we've got it easy. There can be nothing worse than living at the peak of an ice age, as this report from 16,000 B.C. shows!

IN ALL MY years as *The Stone Age News*'s weather reporter, I've never known cold quite like this.

The large icecaps that stretch out from the North and South Poles are slowly but surely growing bigger. And there seem to be hardly any regions where the winters aren't getting longer, and the summers, cooler!

Take northeast Europe, for example. No one can remember a time when it wasn't just a barren and icy wasteland. It's hard to believe that all sorts of plants and animals once flourished there.

And now the icecaps are creeping even farther south, over the plains of central Russia.

Recently, I traveled to the Russian plains to find out how people were coping with the ever-worsening climate. It was only late summer, but harsh winter storms were already beginning to beat down upon the land, and there were few living creatures to be seen.

THE STONE AGE NEWS

238

WORLD EVENTS

THE WINTER IS COMING

When at last I found a family group, they were packing up and preparing to move south. Looking thin and drawn, they told me that winter in their lands now lasts for nine months of the year and that even in summer the hunting is barely good enough to keep them alive.

But this is not a new story. The same thing is happening in Germany, Belgium, Britain, and northern France, too—and people are flocking south toward the coast of the Mediterranean.

And the reports from other parts of the globe are just as grim. Icecaps from the South Pole have spread nearly as far as Tasmania. Most of Australia is so cold, dry, and windswept that people have been forced toward the coasts—the only places in Australia where it still rains.

Where will it all end? I wonder. I can't help thinking that if this terrible weather continues, the whole world will turn into a solid block of ice!

ICE AGES: THE COLD FACTS

Maxine Hamil

During an ice age, temperatures around the world are much lower than normal, and even the hottest countries cool down.

As the earth gets colder, vast sheets of ice, up to 10,000 feet thick, spread outward from the icecaps at the North and South Poles, blanketing both land and sea.

Much of the earth's water turns into ice. The oceans shrink and new areas of coastland appear, since large parts of the seabed become uncovered.

Lands not covered by icecaps suffer from drought, as water is absorbed into the icecaps and little rain falls to replace it.

Very few animals can survive in the regions closest to the icecaps and most move on to warmer areas.

Human groups can survive near the icecaps by using clothing and shelters to keep themselves warm. But when the animals that they hunt for food move on, they are forced to follow them.

Ice ages vary in length from several thousand years to just a few hundred. They tend to start very slowly but end rapidly.

No one is certain why ice ages happen, but experts believe they are caused by changes in the way that the earth moves around the sun.

THE STONE AGE NEWS

WORLD EVENTS

NEWFANGLED FARMING

THIS SPECIAL REPORT, first printed in 8400 B.C., broke the hottest news story of recent times. In it, our Middle East reporter describes a new way of gathering food that was developed there—called farming.

I'D HEARD a rumor that some people in Syria were experimenting with a new way of producing food, and that instead of following the herds like the rest of us, they were living in one place; I just had to go and investigate this strange behavior.

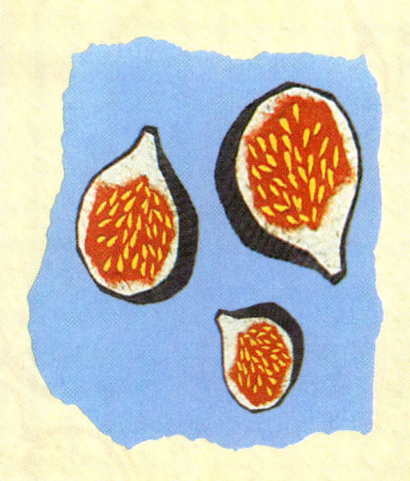

When I arrived, one of the women offered to show me around. She took me to an area where hundreds of tall plants were growing in clusters. I recognized them as wheat, rye, and barley, but I'd never seen so many growing this close together before. Usually, you find just one or two small clumps at a time. I asked my guide to tell me how these big clusters of plants had come about.

SEEDS OF SUCCESS

Apparently, some years ago, the climate in this region became extremely dry. Reliable sources of water were harder and harder to find, so people couldn't roam as widely as they once had. Instead, they were forced to remain close to rivers.

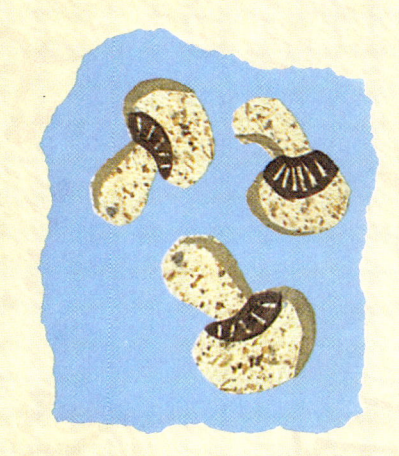

Because they could no longer go far in search of food, they started to build up a store of grains and nuts to last them through the winter months. Then one spring, they noticed how grains that had been dropped on the ground had sprouted.

As an experiment, they tried spilling more seeds, this time on land they had cleared by gathering wild grain the previous year. It

THE STONE AGE NEWS

240

WORLD EVENTS

took several attempts, but at last they managed to grow their own plants. Now they scatter grain each spring.

When the seed heads become ripe, they are cut off using curved flint-bladed knives. The grain is then separated from the husks and spread out to dry in the sun, before being stored in baskets.

I was astounded by all that I had seen. The more I thought about it, the more this "farming" idea made sense. It could change everything—just think, we could settle in one place and grow our own food plants, as the people here do. Then we wouldn't have to spend all those long fall days scouring the land for enough wild food to last through the winter. And whenever animals are scarce and the hunting is poor, there will still be a supply of food at home.

Sharif Tarabay

REAPING THE BENEFITS: Harvesting a field of grain is hard but rewarding work.

Stone Age people can be set in their ways, but you have to move with the times. And I, for one, hope that this newfangled farming catches on!

THE STONE AGE NEWS

241

COOKERY PAGES

BURNING ISSUES

COOKS THESE DAYS have more ways of preparing food than ever before. But can you really beat a good old-fashioned roast? *The Stone Age News* asked a traditional cook and one who prefers to experiment with new recipes to explain their views.

THE FAMILY ROAST: A tradition to be proud of.

Chris Molan

THE TRADITIONALIST

"I'm a firm believer that the old ways are the best. Roasting is a tried and trusted method. Why waste any precious food trying out new ways of cooking that might not even work?

You can roast a piece of meat anywhere. All you need do is skewer it on a wooden spit and find a couple of supports to raise it above a fire.

It's a sociable way of cooking, too. My family group likes nothing better than to gather around the fire for a chat while waiting for the hot, juicy strips of roast meat to be sliced off the joint.

And while the meat is roasting, you can watch to make sure it

THE STONE AGE NEWS

COOKERY PAGES

cooks to perfection. With this new style of cooking, I've heard you put all the food in a bag. It must be nerve-racking not being able to tell if the food inside is raw or cooked."

THE EXPERIMENTER

"It's true that traditional roasting produces good results, but I get bored with cooking the same dish every day. I like to try out new ideas. My favorite at the moment is the 'boil-in-the-bag' approach. It's really easy.

First you need to make a cooking pit by digging a hole in the ground. Then lay a thick piece of hide over the hole and push it down so that it forms a waterproof liner.

Next, carefully clean out an animal stomach, pack it with food, and tie it up very tightly so that nothing can leak out.

Fill up the hole with water and bring it to a boil by dropping in red-hot stones that have been heated in a fire. When the water is boiling, you simply add the parcel of food and let it cook.

The meat boils in its own juices and makes a lovely, rich stew. And you can vary the taste by putting herbs and spices, or even vegetables and fruit, in the parcel, too. Try reindeer and beans, or water bird with berries and garlic!

My family group really looks forward to mealtimes now—everyone loves trying to guess what's in each new dish.

You know what they say, 'Variety is the spice of life.' Well, that's always true with a boil-in-the-bag stew!"

BOIL-IN-THE-BAG: A new way of cooking that's really stirring things up!

Chris Molan

THE STONE AGE NEWS

243

HOME PAGES

HOME SWEET HOME: Caves provide ideal shelter.

Chris Molan

A CAVE OF MY OWN

SOME PEOPLE SEEM to have a knack for making a cozy home out of even the humblest hovel! *The Stone Age News* sent a reporter to the south of France to find out how one woman copes with cave living.

"OUR FAMILY GROUP discovered this cave in late summer and we've spent the entire winter here. The cave's size and location are just perfect.

It has plenty of room for all of us. There's a stream just outside, and as you can see, the trees on the hillside not only supply us with wood for burning and for making tools, but they also shelter the cave from the worst of the wind and snow. Best of all, there's plenty of food—animals to hunt and masses of berries and nuts to pick.

Let me show you around. Watch

THE STONE AGE NEWS

244

HOME PAGES

your head, the entrance is low, but that makes it easier to defend, especially against fierce animals.

We always keep a fire burning in the entrance, too. I like to have a hot fire handy for heating up food. And I find that if you throw on a handful or two of pine needles and fan the smoke into the cave, it freshens the air and also helps to drive out sickness.

Here, you'd better take one of these lamps. It gets quite dark as you go deeper into the cave. I make these lamps myself—they're very simple, just a hollow stone filled with burning fat, with a small thread of moss to act as a wick.

Like most caves, this one is a mixture of large chambers and passages. It stretches back a very long way and has a lot more space than we need to use.

There are a number of passages leading off this main chamber, which in turn lead to more rooms.

HOME COMFORTS

Over here I've built a sleeping shelter—well out of the way of any drafts. It's basically just a wooden frame that I've covered with some dried grass and propped against the wall. You can use turf or dried moss instead, but grass is the best for keeping the warmth in.

Inside the shelter I've put thick hides on the floor—well greased to keep out the damp—as well as a few lighter furs for sleeping under. Most of us don't need shelters, but old people feel the cold more and like the extra warmth and comfort they give.

I've also organized some storage space. I use all the ledges for fragile items, such as baskets of dried berries and various herbs.

I've been so happy here this winter. But, of course, now that spring is coming, we'll all be moving on soon, just as we always do. I'll miss this place, though. It's not always easy turning a cave into a home, but this one has certainly made my task much simpler. We'll definitely be coming back here next winter!"

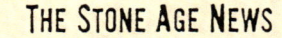

THE STONE AGE NEWS

245

HOME PAGES

PERFECT PITCH

SADLY, ONLY THOSE of us who travel through hilly or mountainous lands can live in caves. But don't forget that tents can be almost as cozy—especially if you follow *The Stone Age News*'s tips for placing and pitching them.

- Choose a sheltered, well-drained site with a good source of water within easy reach.

- For a tepee-shaped tent, arrange wooden stakes in a circle and tie them together at the top. This construction is very stable, and if your poles are properly tied, there will be little chance of your tent collapsing on your head.

- Wind is your greatest enemy—a strong gust can easily leave you homeless! It's a good idea to place your tents side by side in a semicircle to make an effective windbreak.

- Keep out wind and rain by using thick skins, such as bison hides, to cover the tent poles. The weight of the skins will also steady your tent during a gale.

- So the skins won't flap in the wind, put large stones around the bottom.

- Waterproof the skins by rubbing them with animal fat, and coat the seams with pine resin.

- As a quick alternative to a tent, make a lean-to by propping branches against a cliff face or boulder and cover it with hides.

THE STONE AGE NEWS

HUNTING PAGE

A DOG'S LIFE

Today in 8000 B.C., many of us keep hunting dogs. But how many readers know that our friendly pets are related to that ferocious animal, the wolf? This article, from 2,500 years ago, tells how it all began.

IT'S AMAZING, but it's true — humans and wolves, two completely different species, are living side by side!

Hunters in northern Europe have now reared litters of wolves that enjoy human company and even obey their owners' commands.

PUPPY LOVE

The idea of taming wolves happened by chance, when children found some abandoned wolf cubs while out playing. They took the cubs home, fed them scraps, and cuddled and fussed over them.

We're so used to being terrified of wolves that we can't think of them as pets. And yet contact with humans tamed these wild cubs.

Instead of running away as soon as they were old enough to hunt for themselves, these wolves seemed to look upon the children as their "family." They joined in the children's games and even tried to copy some human expressions by curling their lips into a smile. Now, no wild wolf would do that!

When the children grew older and joined in the hunting, their pet wolves went along too.

Naturally, the wolves had very good hunting instincts. Not only did they enjoy the chase, but they could sniff out animals hiding in trees or bushes and then hold them prisoner there for their owners to kill.

Once other hunters had seen how useful these tame wolves were, they got wolf cubs of their own. People and dogs — could this be the beginning of a beautiful friendship?

BEST OF FRIENDS: Children play with their pet wolf cub.

Maxine Hamil

THE STONE AGE NEWS

CRAFT PAGES

MADE IN JAPAN

WE PRIDE OURSELVES on being the first newspaper with the big stories, and here we reprint one of our greatest "scoops." This sensational article appeared back in 9000 B.C., when it broke the news of a brilliant Japanese invention—pottery!

JUST WHEN YOU think life can't get any more exciting, along comes a brand new way of using a familiar old material.

I'm talking about clay. You know the stuff—it's the soft sticky earth that gets stuck between your toes when it rains!

Clay is what bakes into a hard crust beneath your cooking fire. Some artists have made statues and beads out of it, but no one has ever thought up any other use for it.

Not until now, that is! We have

ALL FIRED UP: These new Japanese pots are the best thing since stone knives.

Christian Hook

THE STONE AGE NEWS

CRAFT PAGES

just received news of an amazing invention—pottery, the art of making useful cooking vessels, called pots, out of clay.

The Jomon people of Japan have proved that it's possible to turn lumps of clay into containers that are heatproof, watertight, and strong!

These fantastic Jomon pots are cone-shaped and usually a reddish brown in color. Often they're decorated with scratched patterns.

To cook with them, the Japanese simply fill them with food and water and place them in a fire.

And I'm told that the Jomon specialty—baked fish with herbs and a local vegetable called bamboo shoots—is delicious!

TRADE SECRETS

But I'm not just going to describe this wonderful invention. I can also reveal how the pots are made.

Jomon potters start by kneading a lump of clay until it softens. Then, with the palms of their hands, they shape small balls from the clay.

PERFECT POT: Not just pretty, but practical, too!

Some of these are molded into a cup-shaped base. Others are rolled back and forth to form long sausagelike shapes, which are wound around the base to build up the sides of the pot.

After smoothing the pot's surface by rubbing their fingers across the clay, the potters may decorate it by pressing a pattern into it with a stick or their fingers.

The pots are left for several days, until the clay is completely dry. Then comes the final, most exciting stage—baking the pots in a big bonfire until they are rock hard.

The pots are carefully arranged on the hot ashes of an earlier fire. Then wood is piled over them and set aflame.

Building the fire and keeping it going takes great skill, as any sudden change in temperature will crack the pots.

Finally, after around five hours, the piping-hot pots are pulled out of the glowing embers with a long stick and placed in rows to cool.

So there you have it. There's only one question left unanswered—will this exciting new Japanese idea catch on and spread to other lands? Only time will tell!

THE STONE AGE NEWS

ADVERTISEMENTS

BASKET BARGAINS

Run out of storage space again? On the move and need something light and easy to carry? Come and get one of our beautiful baskets made from willow or alder twigs. Various shapes available.

◇ Better Baskets, Black Forest, Northern Europe ◇

CALLING ALL LEATHER-WORKERS

FOLLOWING OUR RECENT HUGE KILL OF REINDEER, WE NEED SKILLED HELPERS TO SCRAPE, CURE AND DYE THE HIDES, IN RETURN FOR A SHARE OF THE LEATHER.

BOX NO. 8347

FABULOUS FOOTWEAR

Whatever your needs, we can meet them. From cozy slippers to sturdy boots, fur-trimmed or plain. Made to fit feet perfectly.

Best Foot Forward, Black Forest, Europe

EXPERT CARVERS OFFER THEIR SKILLS

Let us decorate your favorite tools and weapons. Our fine carvings in reindeer bone and antler can't be beaten — hunting scenes a speciality.

Visit us in the Dordogne, Southern France.

THINK ABOUT IT

1. How did the Ice Age affect Stone Age people?

2. What is the most interesting thing you learned about the Stone Age? Explain.

3. Does the newspaper format make the selection more interesting to read? Why or why not?

THE STONE AGE NEWS

Meet the Author
Fiona Macdonald

History has always held a special place for award-winning author Fiona Macdonald. Her interest in the history and culture of ancient peoples is reflected in "The Stone Age News." Before she became a full-time writer, she taught history to both children and adults. Macdonald continues to educate through her writing. She has written some 70 books for young readers, mostly on historical subjects.

Fiona Macdonald

Visit *The Learning Site!*
www.harcourtschool.com

Response Activities

A STONE AGE MEETING

PANTOMIME A DISCOVERY Work with a small group to act out a meeting between two groups of Stone Age people who do not speak the same language. Have one group share its knowledge of a new discovery with the other group through movement and facial expressions.

SURVIVAL IN THE PAST

WRITE JOURNAL ENTRIES Imagine that you have traveled back in time to the Stone Age. Write journal entries telling how you feel and what survival skills you are learning. Use information from the selection to add realistic details.

PICTURE THE PAST

MAKE A CAVE PAINTING You are an artist living in the Stone Age. On butcher paper, sketch a cave painting of an important event in your life. Use black crayon over brown paint to make your work look like a real cave painting. Title and display your work. Discuss how real cave paintings bring the ancient past to life.

DAILY SCOOP

MAKE A VENN DIAGRAM Compare and contrast "The Stone Age News" and a daily newspaper. Make a Venn diagram that shows how the two papers are alike and how they are different. Then use your comparison to suggest ways "The Stone Age News" could be improved.

FOCUS SKILL
Fact and Opinion

"The Stone Age News" contains both facts and opinions. A **fact** is something you can prove to be true. An **opinion** is what someone thinks or feels about something. You cannot prove an opinion to be true or false. Read the following passages from the selection. Look for facts and opinions.

When the seed heads become ripe, they are cut off using curved flint-bladed knives. The grain is then separated from the husks and spread out to dry in the sun, before being stored in baskets.

The more I thought about it, the more this "farming" idea made sense.

This chart will help you identify the facts and the opinions in these paragraphs.

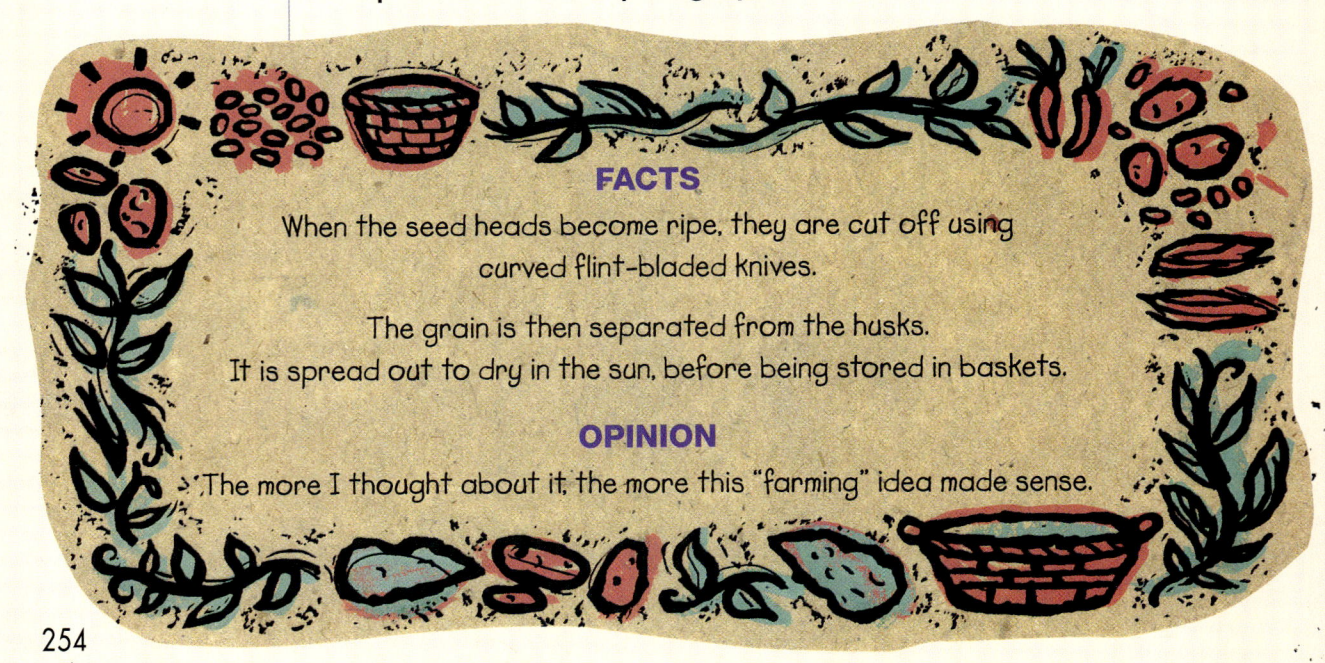

FACTS
When the seed heads become ripe, they are cut off using curved flint-bladed knives.

The grain is then separated from the husks.
It is spread out to dry in the sun, before being stored in baskets.

OPINION
The more I thought about it, the more this "farming" idea made sense.

Being able to tell facts from opinions helps readers make more informed decisions. Use a chart like the one on page 254 to distinguish between the facts and the opinions in the following paragraph.

Whenever we find cattails, we know we're in for a delicious meal. Mama gathers the roots to make cattail stew. She cuts up bison meat, chops wild onions, and adds cattail root. The stew is even more delicious if Mama adds mint. My sisters and I make cattail bread. There's nothing better! First, we collect the pollen in a clay pot. Next, we grind the cattail pollen between stones to make flour. Finally, we mix the flour with a little porcupine fat and water and make balls. Mama fries the flattened balls on hot stones, and we have bread. It's easy!

WHAT HAVE YOU LEARNED?

1. Find at least two opinions in *The Stone Age News* article called "A Dog's Life." Give reasons for calling them opinions.

2. Suppose someone said that early people did not lead comfortable lives. What facts from *The Stone Age News* could help you change that person's opinion?

Visit *The Learning Site!*
www.harcourtschool.com

TRY THIS • TRY THIS • TRY THIS

If you were to tell the story of a day in the life of a Stone Age family, what facts would you include? What opinions would you share with your readers? Make a chart to organize ideas for a story you might write.

Facts

Opinions

ANCIENT CHINA

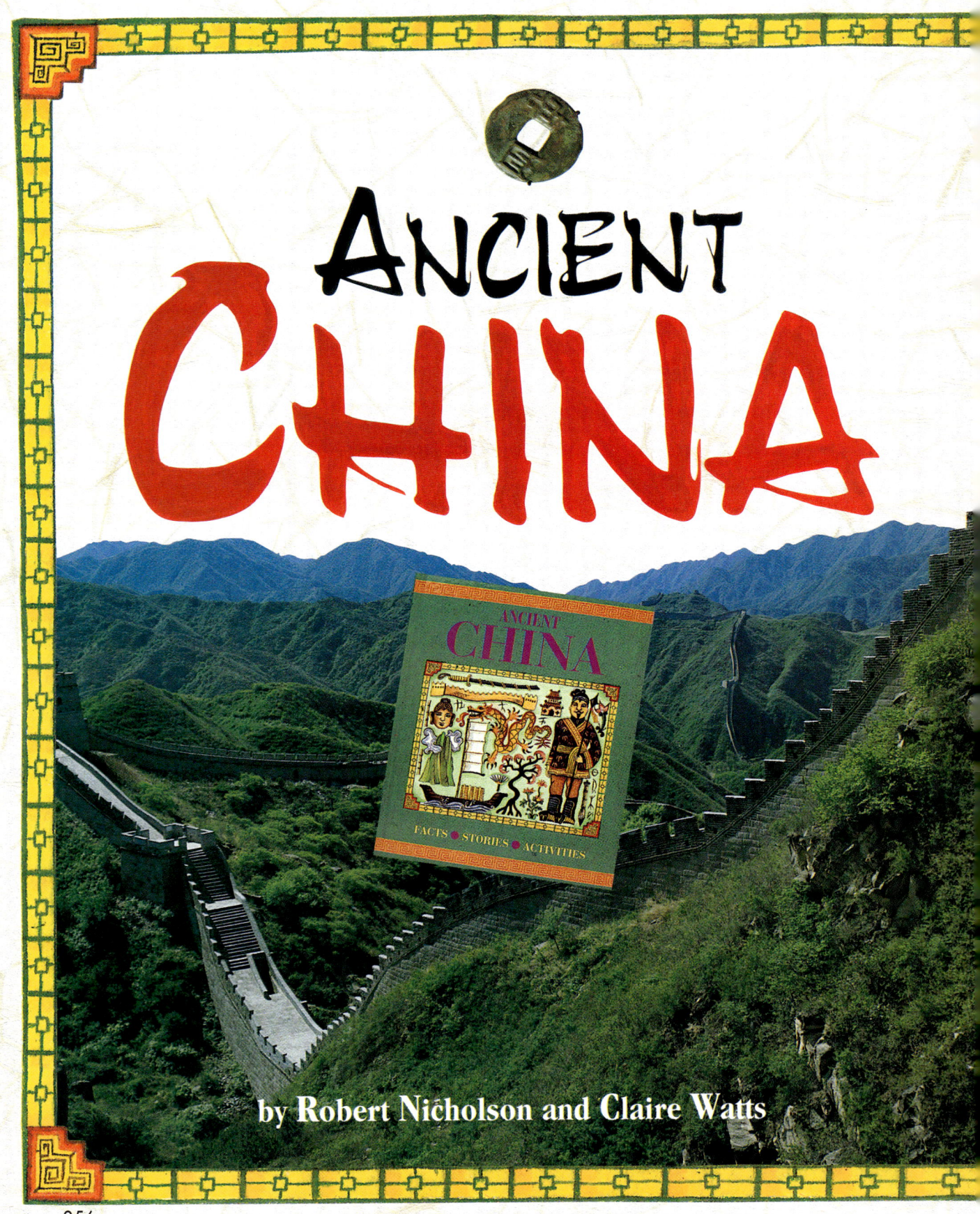

by Robert Nicholson and Claire Watts

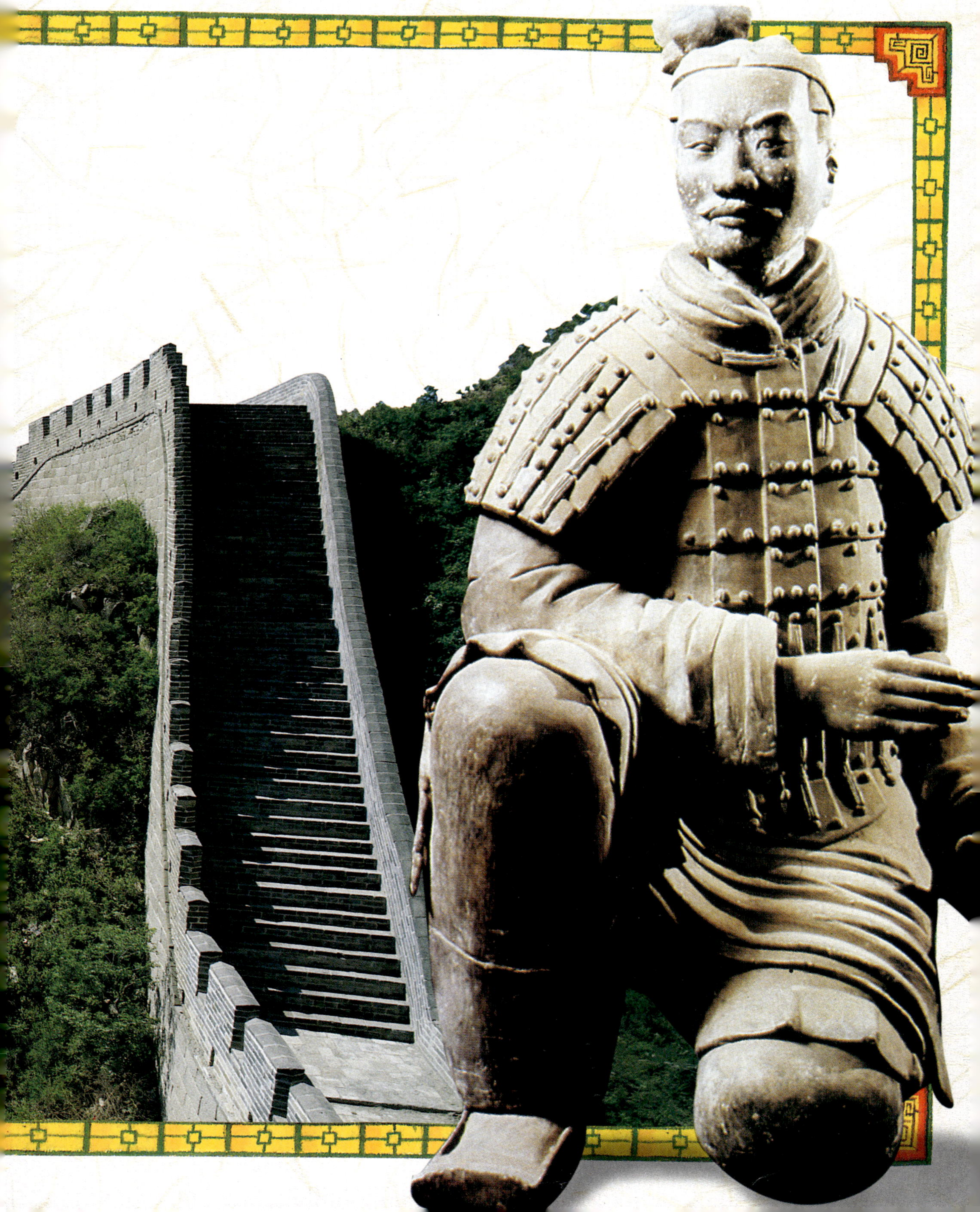

silk route

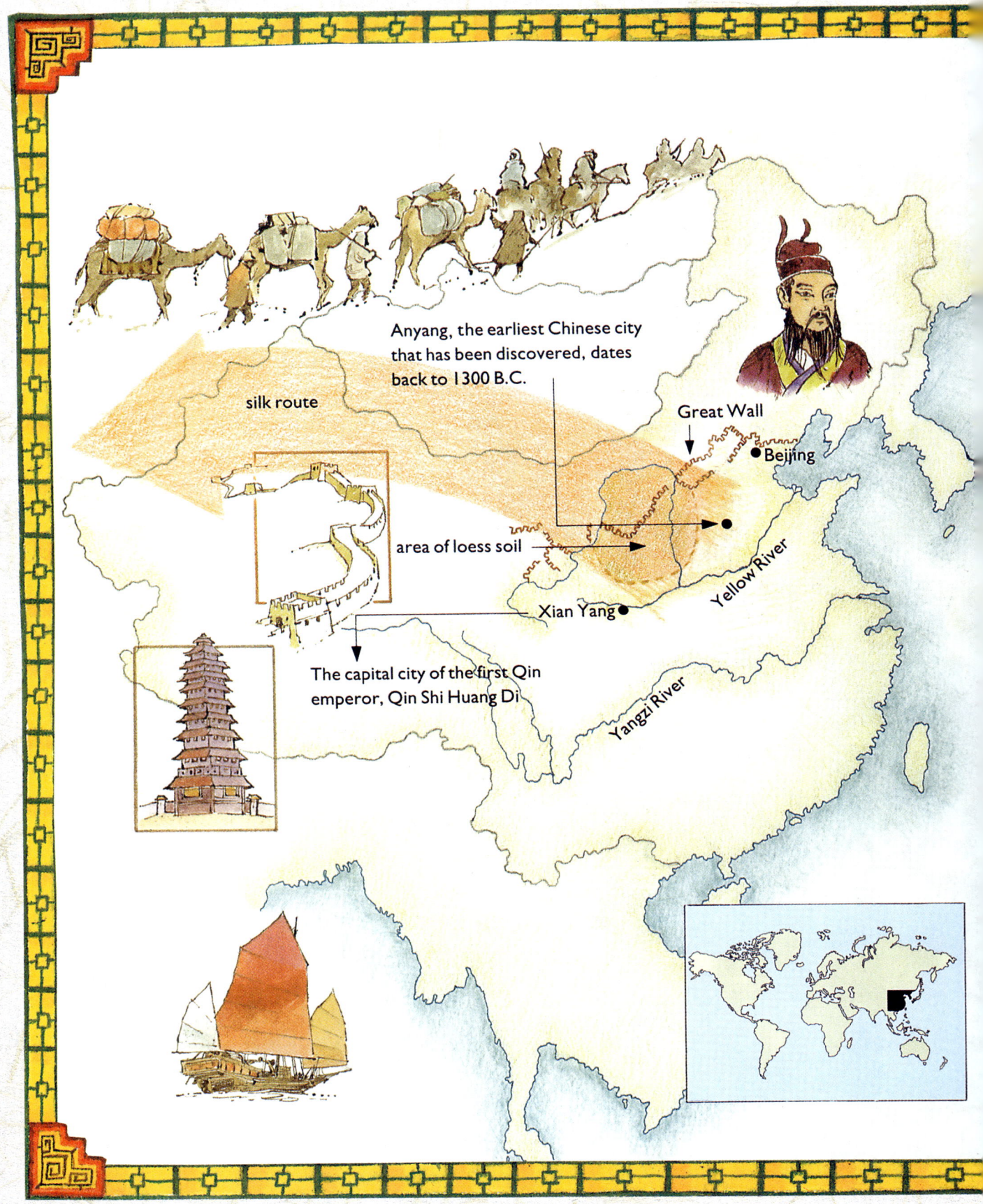

Anyang, the earliest Chinese city that has been discovered, dates back to 1300 B.C.

Great Wall

Beijing

area of loess soil

Xian Yang

Yellow River

The capital city of the first Qin emperor, Qin Shi Huang Di

Yangzi River

China is one of the world's oldest known civilizations. Beginning thousands of years ago, powerful families took control and ruled this enormous region. A family that ruled for a long period of time became known as a dynasty. Influences from many of these great dynasties have survived to this day.

Chinese Lands

China is a huge country, stretching over 1,800 miles from the mountains and ice of Tibet in the west through forests and deserts to the tropical coastline of the east.

Chinese civilization first began around the Yellow River in the center of the country, where the soil is a rich yellow earth called loess. This fertile earth has been blown onto the land by the wind over thousands of years.

The ancient Chinese discovered that they could grow good crops on this loess only if it was kept well watered. They developed a system of terraces cut into the hillsides to make the most of the land. In the north, wheat was the main crop, and in the south, where there was more water, rice was grown in flooded fields called paddies.

Peasant farmers provided food for the entire Chinese empire but usually had scarcely enough to eat themselves. Crops often failed, causing periods of great famine. Sometimes the starving peasants rebelled against the rich landlords.

◀ *Complex irrigation systems were set up to water the fields.*

▲ *Terraces were cut into the hillsides to make the most of every bit of land.*

THE GREAT WALL

The Great Wall of China was built to protect China's northern border from invading tribes. In 221 B.C. the new emperor, Qin Shi Huang Di, (CHIN SHEE HWAHNG·DEE) sent 30,000 men to start building the wall. From then on emperor after emperor extended and rebuilt it right up to this century. The wall was made of pounded earth covered with stones. It was wide at the bottom and narrowed at the top, where there was a walkway for guards. The length of the wall was broken at intervals by watchtowers.

▶ *Traders used to travel along China's northern border, taking their silk to India, the Middle East, and Europe.*

GREAT WALL FACTS
- The wall is between 16 feet and 32 feet high.
- The walkway along the top is 16 feet wide.
- Watchtowers are located every 290 feet to 585 feet along the wall.
- The wall originally stretched for 3,700 miles along China's border.

Cross section of the Great Wall. ▲

The Forbidden City

China was one of the first countries in the world to have large numbers of people living close to one another in cities. Chinese cities were built with walls all around them to protect them from enemies. Inside the most important city, the emperor had a palace which also had high walls, creating a city within a city.

For example, during the Ming dynasty, the emperor Yongle (YUHNG·LEH) rebuilt China's main city, Beijing. By this time Beijing had a million inhabitants. Inside the city walls was a walled imperial city where the important government officials lived and worked. Inside this area was a palace known as the Forbidden City—also surrounded by a high wall—where the emperor lived. At night no man other than the emperor was allowed inside the walls.

▶ *Coins were introduced during the Qin dynasty. The coins were round with holes in the middle.*

Government

The first Chinese emperors gave huge estates all over China to their friends and relatives and enlisted their support to help govern the country. However, these lords often became too powerful for the emperor to control and civil war would break out. In the Qin dynasty, the emperors set up a form of civil service to govern the country instead. People who wanted to join the civil service had to take very difficult exams to prove that they could do the job.

▲ *People walking along the long, straight road to the Forbidden City could be seen long before they arrived at the gates.*

City Life

The Chinese believed that the world was square, so they built their cities to reflect this, laid out in regular patterns, with straight streets crossing each other at right angles. This divided the town into squares, known as *wards*. Usually the houses of the rich would be found at one end, near the palace, and those of the poor at the other end.

The poor people had houses built from mud and thatch. To keep out drafts in winter, the houses were built with floors below ground level, and blankets were hung over the windows and doors. In the center of the house was a sunken pit containing the fire, but there was no chimney to let out the smoke.

Rich people's houses were built around huge courtyards. They were made of painted wood, and roofed with pottery tiles. They contained little furniture—straw mattresses which were rolled up during the day, cushions rather than chairs, and big chests and cupboards.

Festivals

Most Chinese people worked very hard and had no weekends or other days off. Instead there were festivals throughout the year, which were celebrated with processions and dancing in the street. Fireworks would be let off, kites flown, and people would dress up in dragon costumes, because dragons were supposed to represent fun and excitement.

INVENTIONS

Chinese scientists discovered many things that have made great changes to civilization throughout the world. They were interested in medicine, navigation, chemistry and, of course, they were always trying to improve agriculture to feed the enormous population.

THE WHEELBARROW

The Chinese invented all sorts of lifting apparatus, including the wheelbarrow, which they called a wooden ox.

COMPASS

The Chinese discovered magnetism and made compasses by floating magnets in bowls of water. They were used for navigation, and to check that a new building faced in a direction that would bring good fortune.

CLOCKS

Clocks were another Chinese invention. Giant water clocks were invented that rang every 15 minutes to record the passing of the day for the royal officials. The records of this invention were kept so carefully that modern clock makers have been able to use them to reconstruct the clocks.

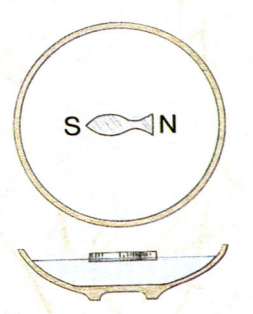

▲ *This huge waterwheel powered the giant water clock.*

Paper

Perhaps the greatest Chinese invention of all was paper and, with it, printing.

The earliest Chinese writing has been found carved on animal bones. After this, the Chinese began to paint on bamboo strips and silk. In about A.D. 100 paper was invented. Wood pulp, hemp and other waste materials were mashed up, mixed with water, rolled, stretched and dried in the sun to form paper. Paper was the cheapest writing material, and it was much quicker and easier to write on than anything people had used before.

Within a few hundred years the Chinese had developed a form of printing. Wooden blocks carved with lines of text were rubbed with ink and then paper was smoothed over them. This was much quicker than writing books by hand and copies could be made very easily.

Chinese Writing

Chinese letters are different from ours. Each of our letters represents a sound, and for them to mean anything we have to combine them to make up a word. Chinese letters are called *characters*. They do not represent sounds but meanings. At first some characters were pictures that could very easily be understood, but gradually the signs became simpler, to make them quicker and easier to write.

EARLY CHARACTERS	MODERN	ENGLISH
ᴟ	山	mountain
⊙	日	sun
☽	月	moon
𦫳	馬	horse

Cutting reeds and soaking them

Mashing the pulp

MAKE YOUR OWN PRINTING BLOCK
The ancient Chinese carved their printing blocks out of wood, but here's an easier way to do it! Draw a design and trace it. Cut several copies of the design out of lightweight cardboard and glue them, one on top of another, to a piece of heavy cardboard, so that the design is raised above the surface. Cover your printing block with ink or paint and press onto a sheet of paper.

Always ask a grown-up to help you when you use sharp scissors.

Heating the pulp

Stretching and drying the paper

Pounding the pulp

CRAFTS

The Chinese were experts in many crafts. They produced beautiful objects in metal, stone, and pottery.

JADE

Jade is a hard, green stone that was considered very valuable by the Chinese. They believed it represented five essential virtues: charity, trustworthiness, courage, wisdom, and fairness. This funeral suit is made from 2,000 pieces of jade threaded together with gold-covered wire.

CHINA

The Chinese invented porcelain, a fine-grained type of ceramic, which we still call *china*. They decorated it with delicate patterns and colors.

SILK

The Chinese kept the secret of silk making to themselves for many years. Silk thread comes from the cocoon of a type of caterpillar, which has to be carefully cared for and fed on mulberry leaves. The cloth made from this thread was the source of China's trade with other countries.

GARDENS

Gardening was regarded as a great art. Chinese cities were designed to include peaceful gardens and parks. Each item in the garden was thought to have a different meaning: water lilies represented truth; chrysanthemums, culture; and bamboo, strength.

How We Know

Have you ever wondered how we know so much about the lives of the ancient Chinese, although they lived thousands of years ago?

Evidence from the Ground

Chinese emperors and important officials were often buried in elaborate tombs that contained many everyday objects. Archaeologists can find out a lot about the way these people lived by studying these objects. One tomb contained a life-sized army—6,000 pottery soldiers and horses, each one with a different face.

Evidence from Books

The Chinese emperors developed a huge administrative system to run their country, and detailed records were made of everything that went on. Many of these records still exist.

Evidence Around Us

Many of the things created by the ancient Chinese survive. The country is still divided into 18 provinces. The Forbidden City and other palaces still stand and tell us much about Chinese architecture.

▲ *The pottery army was an extremely useful find for archaeologists.*

Think About It

1. How did the ancient Chinese use the land and its resources to improve their lives?

2. Do you think you would have enjoyed living in China during ancient times? Explain why you feel as you do.

3. How can examples of Chinese inventions help you understand the past?

THE CHINESE DYNASTIES

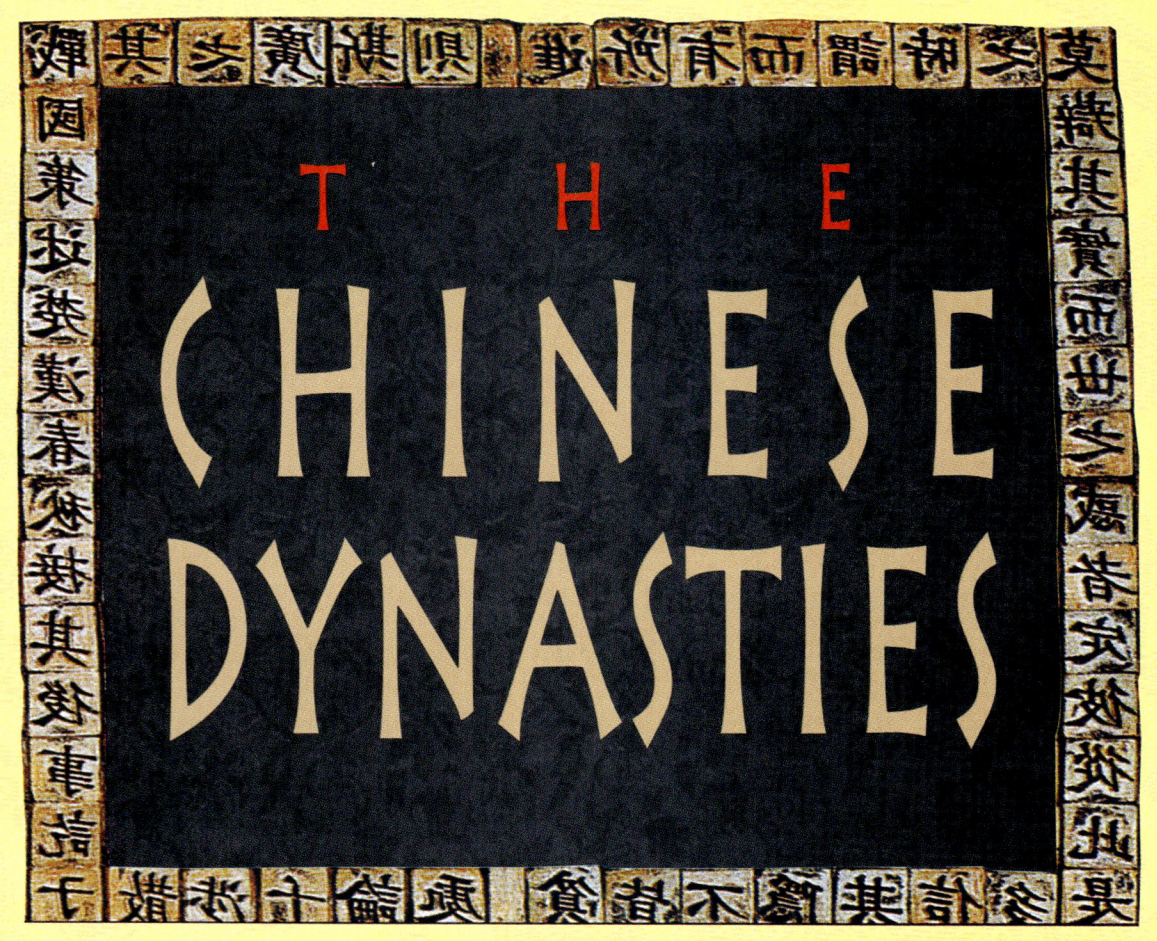

from *Kids Discover*

Ancient China's first dynasty was the Shang. By 1788 B.C. the Shang family had grown so powerful that it was able to take control of much of China. Here are China's major dynasties. A representative piece of art is shown for each.

SHANG	ZHOU	QIN	HAN	SUI
1788–1027 B.C.	1027–256 B.C.	221–207 B.C.	207 B.C.–A.D. 220	589–618

Do this activity on a separate sheet of paper.

How long did China's major dynasties last? Here's how to make a bar graph to compare the length of dynasties. Subtract the lower number from the higher one to find the length of the dynasty (except for the Han dynasty, which spans B.C. and A.D., add the two numbers). Then record the information on the bar graph. Above each dynasty's name, draw a thick line from the bottom of the graph to the nearest number of years of the dynasty's rule. The first one is done for you.

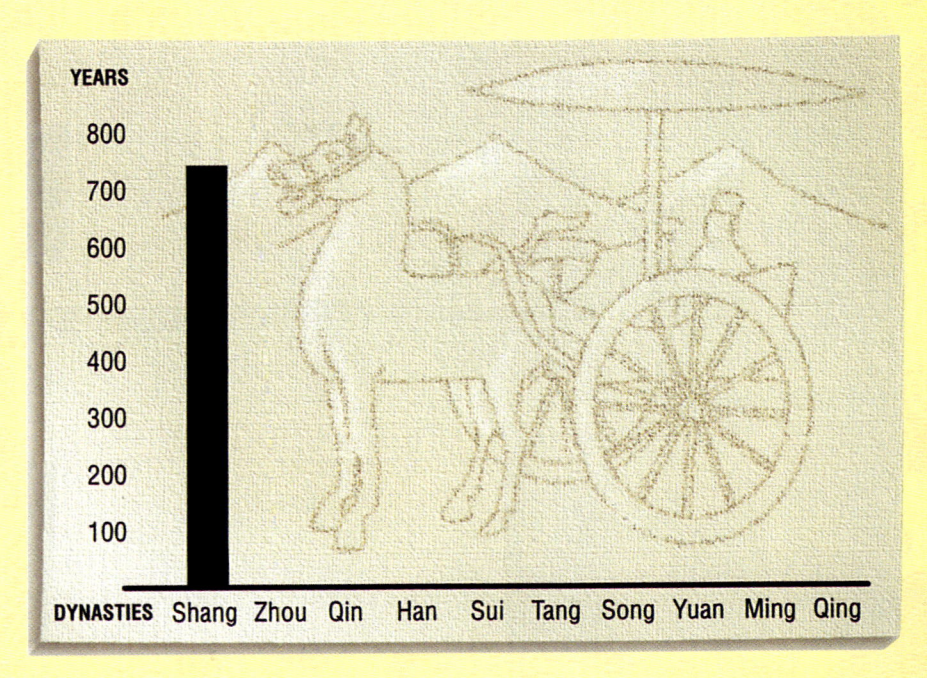

YEARS

800
700
600
500
400
300
200
100

DYNASTIES Shang Zhou Qin Han Sui Tang Song Yuan Ming Qing

THINK ABOUT IT

How many dynasties have ruled China? According to this time line, how long was China ruled by dynasties?

TANG
618–906

SONG
960–1279

YUAN
1279–1368

MING
1368-1644

QING
1644–1912

271

RESPONSE

Royal Festival

PERFORM A DANCE You are living in ancient China and are eager to honor the emperor. With a partner, create a dance for the royal festival. Check out a tape of Chinese folk songs or instrumental music from the library, or perform your dance without music.

View from the Past

WRITE A POEM Imagine that you live in ancient China. Perhaps you enjoy exploring the Forbidden City or standing on top of the Great Wall. Write a short poem describing your feelings. Share your poem with the class. Then discuss how the poem can help people understand ancient China.

ACTIVITIES

Making Connections

WRITE A PARAGRAPH Choose one of the works of art in the Chinese Dynasties time line. Write a paragraph from the viewpoint of the artist. Tell what you like about the piece you created, what its purpose is, and who might want to own it. Use information from "Ancient China" as well as what you know from real life.

Great Inventions

WRITE A LETTER Imagine that as a visitor to ancient China, you learn of a new invention described in the selection. Write a letter to people back home that describes this invention.

PYRA

MIDS
from KIDS DISCOVER

THE OUTSKIRTS OF MODERN-DAY CAIRO, the capital of Egypt, with the Pyramids of Giza in the background. The Giza Pyramids are the only one of the Seven Wonders of the Ancient World still standing.

How Heavy?

The average weight of one of a pyramid's stone blocks is two and a half tons. That's the weight of two medium-sized cars. Some blocks, however, weigh up to 15 tons. That's as much as five elephants!

THE PYRAMIDS OF EGYPT

Egypt's pyramids are the oldest stone buildings in the world. They were built nearly five thousand years ago. These ancient tombs are also among the world's largest structures. The biggest is taller than a *40-story* building and covers an area greater than that of *ten* football fields. Men built these huge structures without the help of equipment that we have today, such as cranes and bulldozers. Sometimes up to 100,000 men worked for 20 seasons on one pyramid.

More than 80 pyramids still stand today. Inside their once-smooth white limestone surfaces, there are secret passageways, hidden rooms, ramps, bridges, and shafts. Most had concealed entrances and false doors. What fun it would be to explore one!

However, the pyramids were not built for exploring. They served a very serious purpose. Ancient Egyptians had a strong belief in life after death. The kings, called pharaohs, wanted their bodies to last forever, so they had pyramids built to protect their bodies after death. Each pyramid housed a pharaoh's preserved body. It also held the goods he would need in the next life to continue living as he had when he was alive.

The pyramids of Egypt are massive monuments to the pharaohs' power. Today they are reminders of a resourceful and creative ancient civilization.

How Tall?
1. Eiffel Tower, 984 feet
2. **Great Pyramid at Giza, 480 feet**
3. Big Ben (Westminster Palace), 316 feet
4. Statue of Liberty, 305 feet
5. Leaning Tower of Pisa, 179 feet

HOW PYRAMIDS GOT THEIR START

EARLIEST TIMES

AROUND 3000 B.C.

AROUND 2700 B.C.

EARLY EGYPTIANS BURIED their dead under a pile of rocks. Bodies were wrapped in goatskin or reed mats. Personal goods were placed around the body.

MASTABA (MAS tuh buh) tombs were made of sunbaked mud bricks, which gave protection against the harmful effects of nature. On the walls of mastabas were carved, painted scenes called *reliefs*. Some reliefs showed rows of people bringing offerings, such as ducks, food, water, milk, and honey.

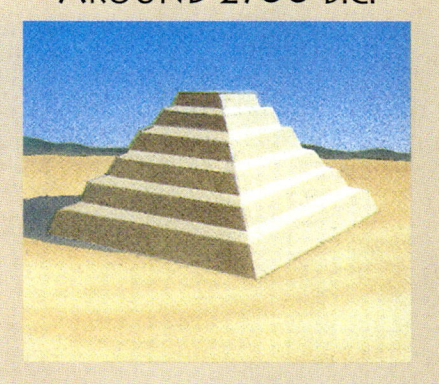

IMHOTEP IS CREDITED with the invention of stone architecture and the design of Egypt's first pyramid, the Step Pyramid. It was begun as a large mastaba tomb, but after going through many changes, it ended up as a pyramid of six steps. The tomb of King Djoser lies under the Step Pyramid.

KING DJOSER

IMHOTEP

PHARAOH TUTANKHAMUN, KNOWN AS KING TUT, WAS buried in the Valley of the Kings. The young king died when he was only 19 years old. Practically untouched by robbers, his tomb contained weapons, furniture, jewelry, musical instruments, clothing, and model boats—many of which were made of solid gold. The king's two stillborn daughters were buried with him, along with a lock of hair from his grandmother, Queen Tiya.

Around 2500 B.C.

Around 1500 B.C.

THE GREAT PYRAMID AT Giza, the largest of the three Giza pyramids, is also one of the largest man-made structures in the world today. Built for Pharaoh Khufu, it was originally 480 feet high. Its base covers approximately 13 acres. The pyramid originally contained over two million blocks of limestone.

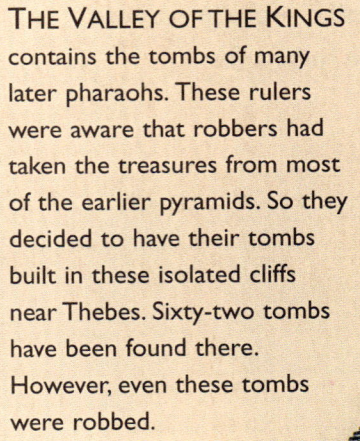

THE VALLEY OF THE KINGS contains the tombs of many later pharaohs. These rulers were aware that robbers had taken the treasures from most of the earlier pyramids. So they decided to have their tombs built in these isolated cliffs near Thebes. Sixty-two tombs have been found there. However, even these tombs were robbed.

PHARAOH KHUFU

ONLY IN EGYPT

Ancient Egypt had a unique combination of ingredients for building pyramids. The country was a long, narrow, fertile strip of land in northeastern Africa. Water came from the mighty Nile River. Natural barriers protected the land from invaders. There were deserts to the east and west. There were dangerous rapids on the Nile to the south. Delta marshes lay to the north. This circle of isolation allowed the Egyptians to work in peace and security.

To build the pyramids, great supplies of raw materials were needed. Ancient Egypt had an abundance of limestone, sandstone, and granite. But these rocks had to be brought from quarries to the building sites. Egypt's most precious resource—the great Nile River—provided the means for transportation.

CAIRO
GIZA
MEMPHIS
SAQQARA
DAHSHUR
TURA (Limestone quarry)
AFRICA
VALLEY OF THE KINGS
ASWAN (Granite quarry)
FIRST CATARACT

THE NILE RIVER IS the longest river in the world. It flows for approximately 4,150 miles. The Nile flooded farmers' lands from July to October until the Aswan Dam was completed in 1970.

DESERTS CUT OFF ancient Egypt from the rest of the world. If you were trying to cross a desert on foot, you would need from four to six gallons of water per day. And, the more water you carried, the more water you would need!

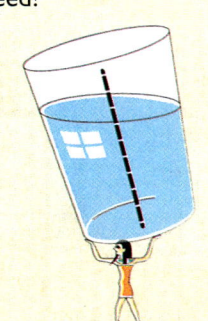

THE NILE RIVER produced fertile farmland. During the flood season, when no farming could be done, farmers paid taxes to the pharaoh in labor, by helping to build the pyramids.

THE STONES WERE levered up and hauled on board. The weighed-down boat then set off for the pyramid site. Oarsmen had to work hard, and the helmsman had to be an expert, since sandbanks could easily destroy a boat.

ANCIENT EGYPTIANS believed that a pharaoh buried in grand style would continue to bless his people. This inspired them to work cheerfully as they built the pyramids—magnificent monuments to their kings.

TWO KINDS OF rocks were used in most pyramids—limestone and small quantities of granite. These rocks were quarried close to the banks of the Nile. They were transported on the Nile in wooden boats.

MASTER BUILDERS

Building a pyramid was difficult and dangerous. It required a highly organized society. Thousands of skilled and unskilled workers were needed. To complete the Great Pyramid at Giza, one huge stone block must have been quarried, shaped, and smoothed every two minutes for 23 years!

Building plans showing how the pyramids were built have never been found. However, experts use present knowledge about construction to make some intelligent guesses. Follow the four steps in the illustration to see how ingenious—and hard working—the ancient Egyptians must have been.

1 THE ENORMOUS limestone blocks were taken off the boats near the pyramid site. If one block accidentally fell, it could crush to death hundreds of people.

2 ONCE UNLOADED, the limestone blocks were hauled on sledges over wooden rollers by gangs of men. Water or milk was poured around the sledges to help them slide.

3 RAMPS, BUILT OF MUD brick, were used to haul the heavy stones to the level where building was going on. To raise the stones higher, spiraling ramps were probably put against the pyramid sides.

4 A CAUSEWAY connected each pyramid to the Nile. Built as a highway for the sledges, it eventually served as a corridor for the funeral procession.

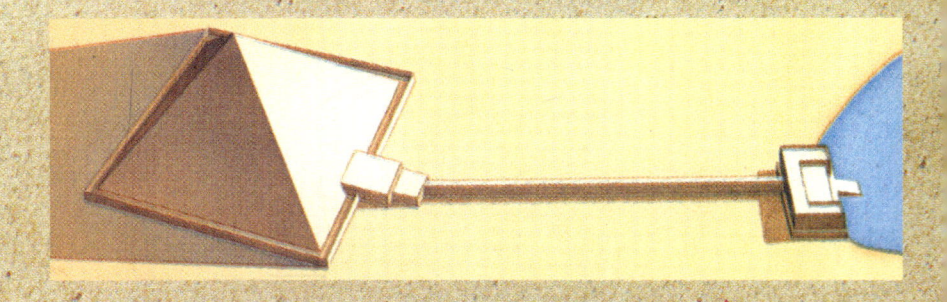

chisels mallet saw drill

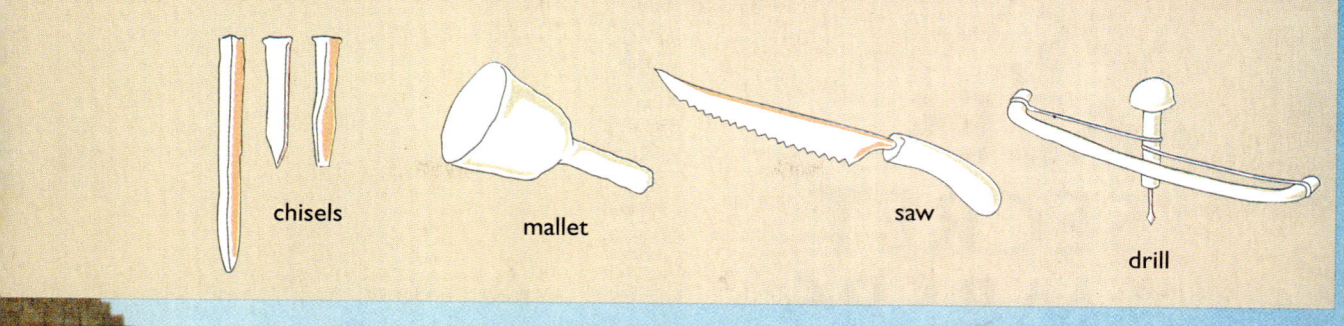

TODAY'S TOOLS ARE MADE OF STEEL. THE ANCIENT EGYPTIANS used tools of copper, a softer metal than steel, and wood. Their tools could cut limestone. Wooden wedges and levers were also used in building the pyramids.

MANPOWER WAS PLENTIFUL IN ancient Egypt. Oxen and other beasts of burden were considered too valuable for the heavy work of building pyramids.

RELIGIOUS AND PRACTICAL REASONS CONTROLLED WHERE THE pyramids had to be built. For religious reasons, the pyramids had to be on the west side of the Nile River, where the sun set. They had to be built close to the Nile so boats could carry the stones to the construction site. They also had to be built high above the level of the river so no damage would occur during the flood season. Each side of the pyramid had to face one of the four cardinal points—north, south, east, and west. Finally, a pyramid had to be close to the pharaoh's palace so he could keep an eye on his "castle of eternity."

TRAPS, MAZES, AND SECRET CHAMBERS

The main purpose of the pyramids was to safeguard the pharaohs' bodies. Granite doors, false passages, and fake burial chambers were constructed in an attempt to confuse and deter robbers. However, in spite of all these precautions, nearly all the pyramids were robbed of their treasures by around 1000 B.C.

Take a trip through the inside of the Great Pyramid of Giza in the illustration and see how skillfully the kings planned for their bodies' final resting places.

THE SPHINX AT GIZA IS 240 FEET LONG and carved out of limestone. Built by Pharaoh Khafre to guard the way to his pyramid, it has a lion's body and the ruler's head.

THE GRAND GALLERY in the Great Pyramid is 150 feet long and 25 feet high. After the king was buried, the entrance to the Grand Gallery was sealed off with enormous blocks that were slid down the gallery.

THE ESCAPE SHAFT let people out of the pyramid after they buried the king.

THE QUEEN'S CHAMBER did not contain the queen. It got its name because people thought the queen was buried there.

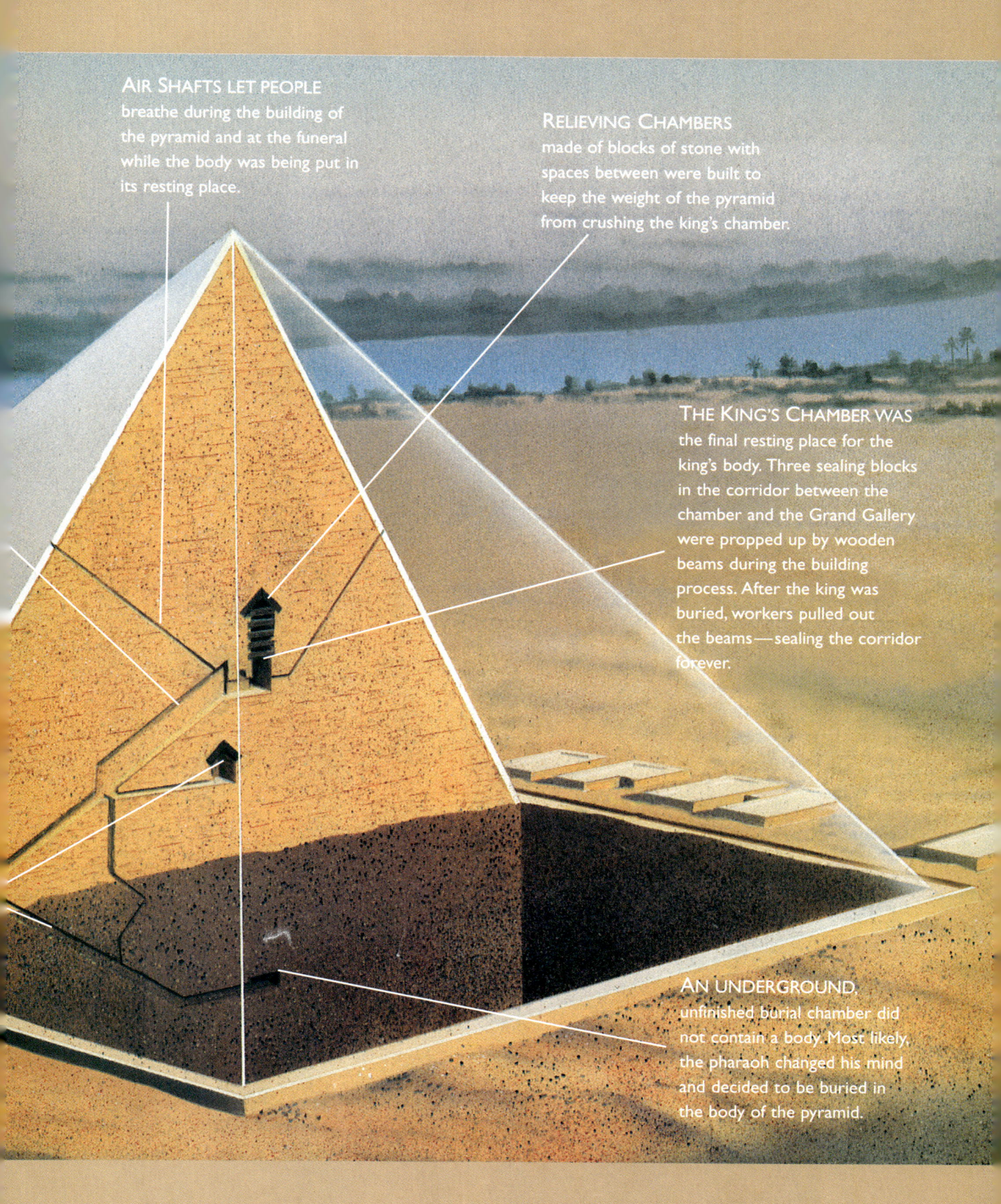

AIR SHAFTS LET PEOPLE breathe during the building of the pyramid and at the funeral while the body was being put in its resting place.

RELIEVING CHAMBERS made of blocks of stone with spaces between were built to keep the weight of the pyramid from crushing the king's chamber.

THE KING'S CHAMBER WAS the final resting place for the king's body. Three sealing blocks in the corridor between the chamber and the Grand Gallery were propped up by wooden beams during the building process. After the king was buried, workers pulled out the beams—sealing the corridor forever.

AN UNDERGROUND, unfinished burial chamber did not contain a body. Most likely, the pharaoh changed his mind and decided to be buried in the body of the pyramid.

ALL ABOUT MUMMIES

The Egyptians believed that life after death was very similar to life on earth. Their dead, therefore, had to be protected and preserved for the next life. The pyramid's job was to protect the body. To preserve the body, a process known as mummification was developed around 2600 B.C. Mummification might take as long as 70 days. The body was dried out for about 40 days. The Egyptians used a salt compound called *natron* to do this. In the next stage, the body was embalmed. That means it was treated with molten resin and perfumed oils. Finally, the body was wrapped in linen bandages.

MUMMIES OF cats, dogs, ibises, crocodiles, and other animals have been found.

THE MUMMY OF Nesmutaatneru shows skillful bandaging. Bandaging took about two weeks. As many as 410 yards of linen could be used. That's about as much material as it would take to go from the top to the bottom of the Empire State Building!

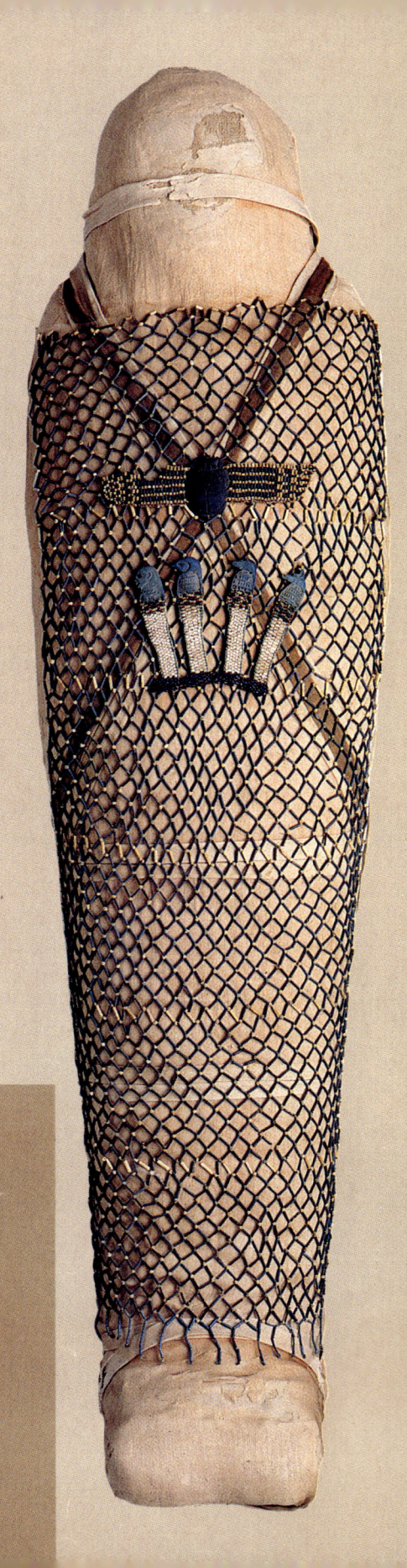

FOUR SEALED JARS, CALLED *CANOPIC* (ca NOH pic) jars, held the liver, lungs, stomach, and intestines. Ancient Egyptians threw away the brain of a dead person because they didn't know what it was. They believed that the heart did all the thinking!

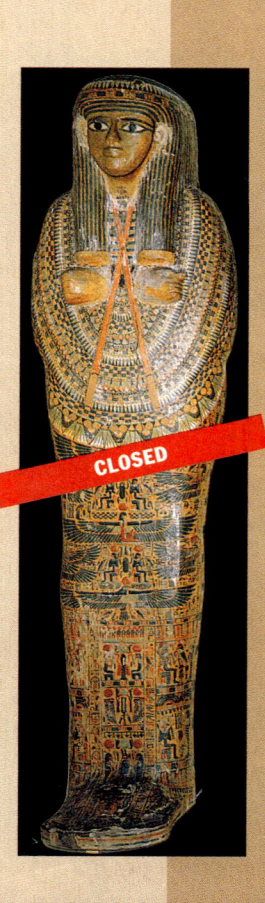

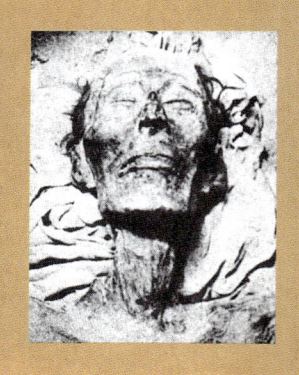

HOLLYWOOD'S BORIS KARLOFF modeled his mummy face and costume in the film *The Mummy* after Rameses III.

MUMMIES TELL US ABOUT LIFE IN ancient Egypt. For example, the decayed teeth in many mummies suggest that ancient Egyptians, like many people today, ate too many sweets.

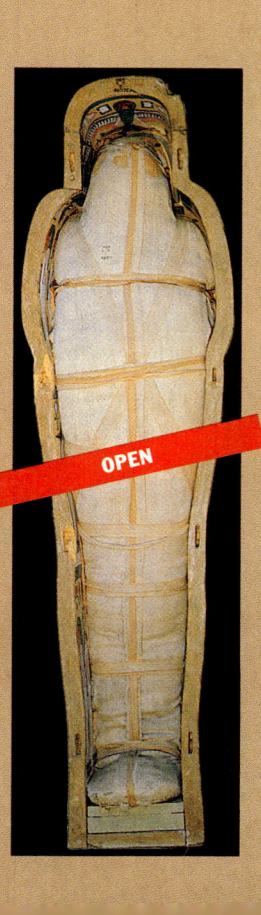

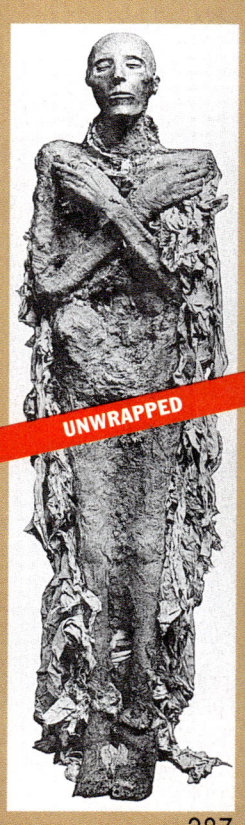

CLOSED   OPEN   UNWRAPPED

287

TREASURES FROM A TOMB

Pharaoh Tutankhamun became king when he was about nine years old (around 1333 B.C.). Ten years later he died. Imagine ruling an entire country when you're only nine!

King Tut's is the only royal burial in the Valley of the Kings that was practically untouched by robbers. In 1922, after many years of excavating, the archaeologist Howard Carter found a sealed entrance to Tut's tomb. In the first room were thrones, vases, chariots, statues, jewelry, and ostrich-feather fans, among other items. Four coffins protected the mummy. The third coffin was made from almost 2,500 pounds of gold!

TREASURES FROM THE TOMBS of the pharaohs are now found in museums around the world.

PYRAMIDS AROUND THE WORLD

THE CASTILLO (THE GREAT pyramid) in Chichén Itzá, Mexico, was probably built some time between A.D. 900 and A.D. 1200.

THE PYRAMID AT THE LOUVRE in Paris, France, is a transparent glass pyramid that rises to 71 feet. Designed by the architecture firm of I. M. Pei & Partners, it serves as an entrance to the museum.

THE GREAT AMERICAN PYRAMID overlooks the Mississippi River in Memphis, Tennessee. It is 321 feet high and covers approximately 6.8 acres. It is a monument to American music.

The pyramids of Egypt were built over a span of one thousand years. The most splendid ones date from about 2700 B.C. to 2200 B.C.

Pyramids, however, have been built in many parts of the world at various times. All of these pyramids contain certain essential elements. They are enormous. They have rectangular bases. Most are made of stone or brick. And most have four sloping sides that meet at a point.

Think About It

1. How did ancient Egyptians work together to build the pyramids?

2. What features of the selection most help bring ancient Egypt to life?

3. How does the author feel about the builders of the pyramids? How can you tell?

Visit *The Learning Site!*
www.harcourtschool.com

RESP ACTIV

PYRAMID PUZZLE

CREATE A MAZE

Draw a large pyramid on a sheet of paper. Inside the pyramid, draw a maze with many pathways. Make sure that only one pathway connects the beginning to the end of the maze. Decorate your maze with pictures of wall paintings and other artifacts. Exchange mazes with a partner. See who can pass through the pyramid first.

HIDDEN TREASURES

WRITE A DESCRIPTION

You are an archaeologist working at a dig on the site of a pyramid. You discover a fantastic artifact. Write a brief, vivid description of your remarkable find, using details from the selection. Read your description to the class, and discuss how artifacts help us understand the past.

ONSE ITIES

TIME-TRAVELING HELPER

WRITE A STORY
Imagine that you travel back in time and find yourself involved in building the Great Pyramid of Giza. What modern technology could you share with the ancient Egyptians? Write a humorous story about your adventure.

A PYRAMID IN YOUR BACKYARD?

MAKE A CHART
Skim the selection to find information about the geography in and around ancient Egypt. Compare it to the geography of your region. You might use an atlas to help you. Present your findings in a chart.

FOCUS SKILL

Graphic Sources

Nonfiction books and articles often include **graphic sources**, such as diagrams, graphs, maps, photographs, and drawings. These graphics help readers understand complicated ideas easily and quickly.

Look at the drawing from "Pyramids." Compare it with the paragraph beside it. Which communicates the information more easily and quickly?

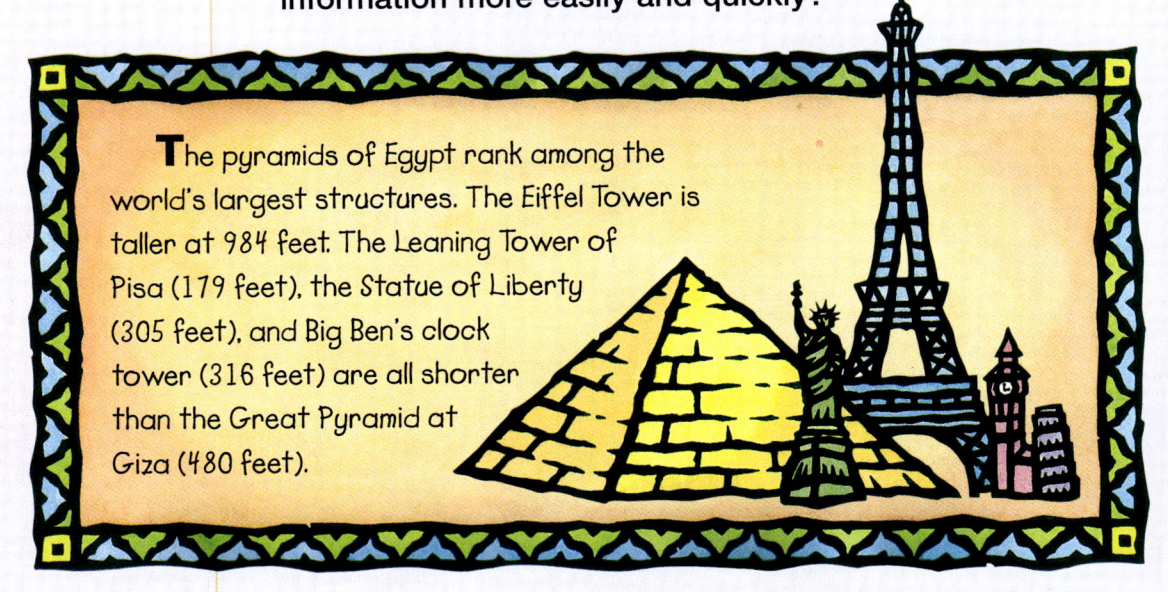

The pyramids of Egypt rank among the world's largest structures. The Eiffel Tower is taller at 984 feet. The Leaning Tower of Pisa (179 feet), the Statue of Liberty (305 feet), and Big Ben's clock tower (316 feet) are all shorter than the Great Pyramid at Giza (480 feet).

A glance at the drawing shows you which structures are taller and which are shorter than the Great Pyramid. You can get this information from the paragraph, but it takes more time. What other kinds of graphic sources might show you this measurement information quickly and easily?

There are many kinds of graphics. The Internet and CD-ROM encyclopedias use graphics. Sometimes the pictures move and the graphics are accompanied by sound.

Since earliest times, people have found ways to use graphics to communicate important information. Below are drawings showing life in Mesoamerica and the Andes Mountains. Explain what you think they communicate.

WHAT HAVE YOU LEARNED?

1. Look at the maps of Africa and the Nile River in the selection. How do they work together to show you where the Egyptian pyramids are located?

2. Think of an educational graphic source you found in a book, in a magazine, on a CD-ROM, or on the Internet. How did it help you? How did it communicate the information more quickly and easily than words would have?

TRY THIS • TRY THIS • TRY THIS

Suppose you were asked to give an oral report about how the Egyptian pyramids were built. What graphics might you use to show information as you presented your report? Create a web as you brainstorm graphics you could use.

Visit *The Learning Site!*
www.harcourtschool.com

LOOK INTO THE GREEKS

BY A. SUSAN WILLIAMS

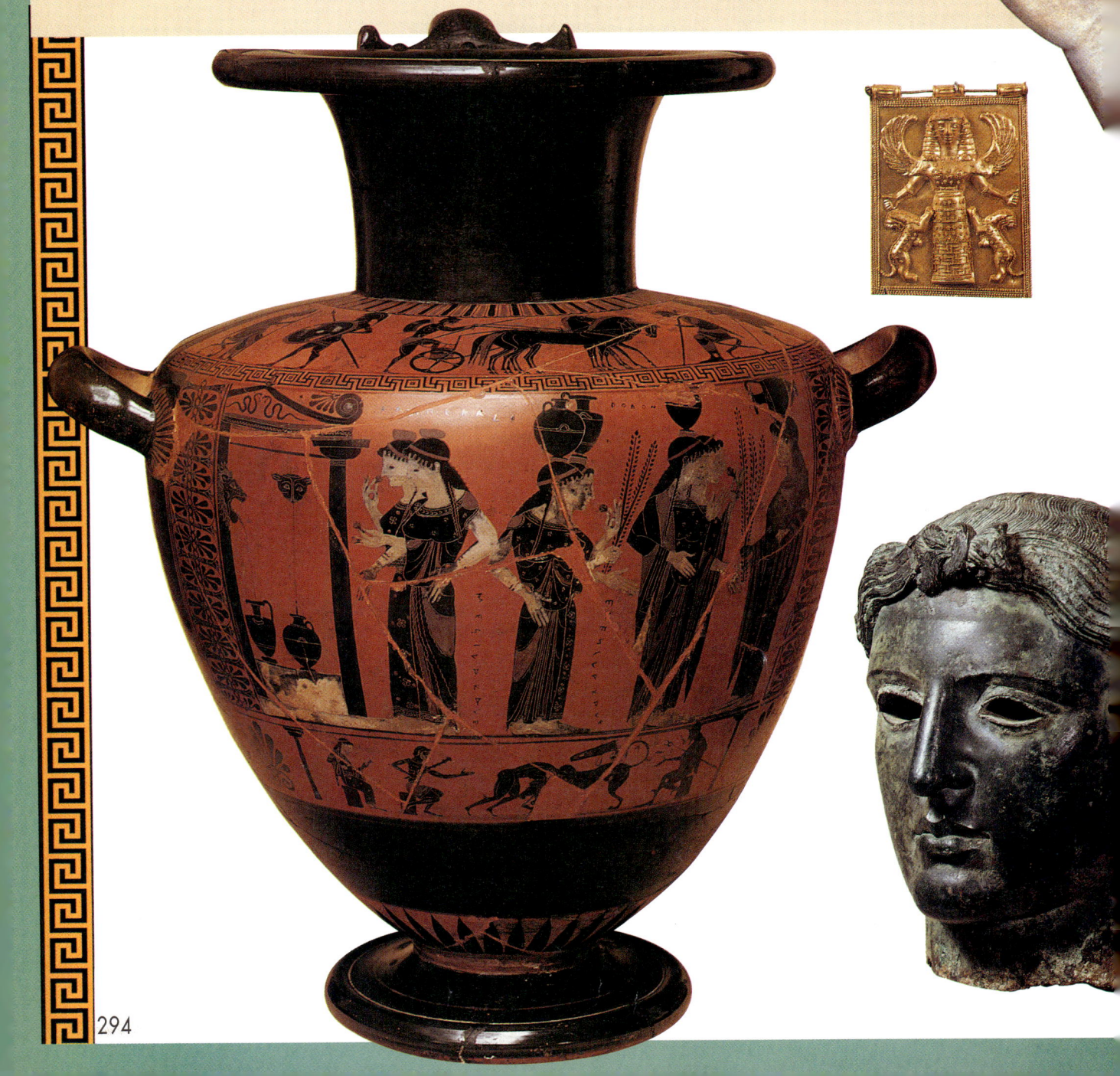

THE PAST
THE ROMANS
BY PETER HICKS

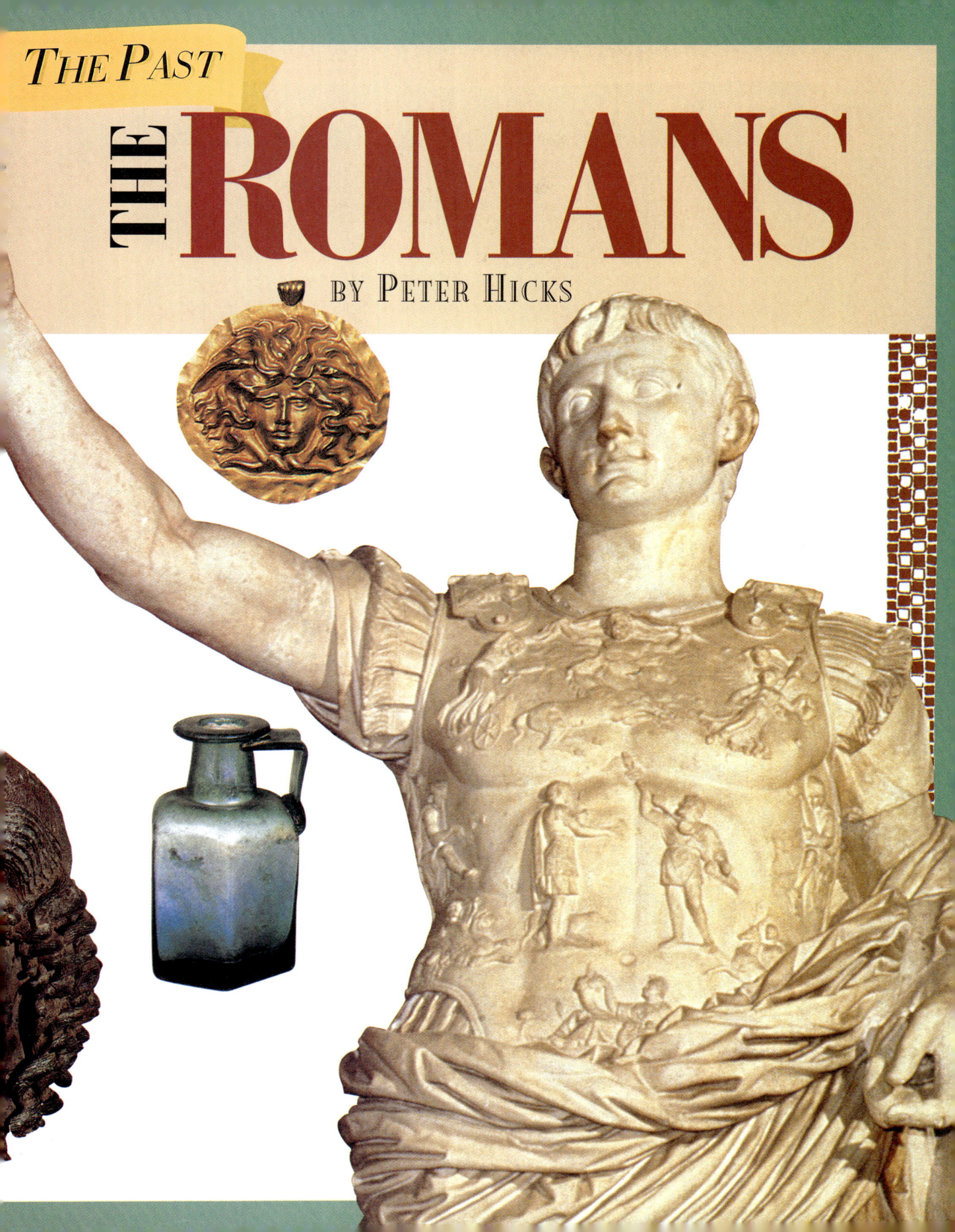

Who Were the Ancient Greeks?

The customs and way of life of the ancient Greeks, who lived more than 2,500 years ago, have affected our lives today. The politics, language, literature, art, and sports of many countries all show links with the Greek civilization in some way. So the more we know about the history of Greece, the more we understand about how we live today.

Archaeologists use remains (called artifacts) that have been found in the area that was ancient Greece to discover how people lived hundreds of years ago.

Pictures on ancient pots, vases, and coins show us how the Greeks used to live. The ruins of buildings and the writings of poets, playwrights, and historians also give us information.

◀ Greece is a land of mountains. In ancient times, the mountains separated groups of people from each other. This led to the development of separate communities, which were called city-states. Athens, Sparta, Argos, and Thebes were four of many city-states.

Today, the different regions of Greece are joined together by such modern inventions as the car and the telephone.

▲ The picture above shows the remains of the entrance to the Minoan palace of Knossos. It had over one thousand rooms, which were built around a courtyard in the middle. The palace was built by a group of people called the Minoans 3,500 years ago, in the fifteenth century B.C., on Crete, a large Greek island. When people talk about the greatest period of Greek civilization, they usually mean the fifth century B.C. (2,500 years ago). This is known as the classical period, which produced the art, politics, and literature that have been admired for so many years.

THE GREEK LANGUAGE

The word "alphabet" comes from the first two letters of the Greek alphabet: alpha and beta. The English alphabet is similar to the Greek alphabet, and many English words are based on Greek words. The word "telephone," for example, is made up of the Greek words for "far off" (tele) and "voice" (phone). The word "hippopotamus" is made up of the words for "horse" (hippos) and "river" (potamos).

Ancient Greek letter	Name of Greek letter
A	alpha
B	beta
Λ	gamma
Δ	delta
E	epsilon
I	zeta
H	eta
Θ	theta
I	iota
K	kappa
L	lambda
M	mu
N	nu
ΧΕ	xi
O	omicron
Π	pi
P	rho
E	sigma
T	tau
V	upsilon
Ø	phi
X	khi
ØE	psi
Ω	omega

▼ In this painting on a vase, a man at a festival in Athens is reciting two long poems written by a blind poet called Homer. Homer's poems are called the *Iliad* and the *Odyssey*. The *Iliad* is about the Trojan War, a war fought between the early Greeks and Troy. The *Odyssey* tells the adventures of Odysseus on his travels after the end of the Trojan War.

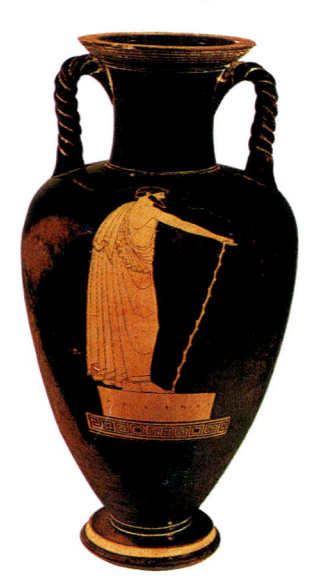

▲ Here is the old Greek alphabet. Some of our letters are different. But you could write your name in Greek letters.

Most men who lived in Athens were able to read, because boys went to school. They learned literature, music, and physical education. Girls in Athens did not go to school but stayed at home to learn how to look after a family. In Sparta, both girls and boys were taught to read and write.

Nearest English letter	
A	
B	
G	
D	
E	(short)
Z	(sd)
E	(long)
Th	
I	
K	
L	
M	
N	
X	(Ks)
O	(short)
P	
R	
S	
T	
U	
Ph, F	
Kh, Ch	
PS	
O	(long)

THE CITY-STATE OF ATHENS

The city-state of Athens was very powerful and ruled a large region. It was a rich city because it owned silver mines nearby, where slaves were made to work very hard. The goddess of Athens was Athena and the emblem of the city was the owl.

▶ This is a bust of Pericles. He was a great leader of Athens in the fifth century B.C. He had the Parthenon and other beautiful temples built and had the port of the city, Piraeus, improved. He led Athens in the war against Sparta, which lasted from 431 B.C. to 404 B.C.

▼ This painting on a vase shows men voting. The people of Athens first invented the idea of democracy, which is the Greek word for "rule by the people." Because Athens was a democracy, the voters of the city could choose their leaders and be asked to serve in government.

However, not everyone was able to take part in elections—women, slaves, and freed slaves were not allowed to vote. Nowadays, most western countries are democracies, in which all adults have the right to vote for the government they prefer.

Homes and Buildings

Greek houses were built with sun-dried bricks and wood and were arranged around an open courtyard. Women and children lived separately from the men in their families. The men lived in the more public areas, where visitors were made welcome. A stranger was not supposed to enter a room containing women, unless he had been invited to do so by the man of the house.

▲ This is a drain at the Minoan palace of Knossos, on the island of Crete, built about 3,500 years ago. The Minoans built an efficient water system to supply water to the palace and to drain it away. The queen even had running water in her bathroom and a toilet that flushed.

◀ This is the porch of the Erechtheion, a temple that was built on the acropolis of Athens, just after the Parthenon. These statues of women take the place of ordinary columns in holding up the roof.

▶ The shape and size of Greek temples were pleasing to the eye. This was because the Greeks knew a lot about mathematics and planned their buildings carefully. The mathematician Pythagoras developed ideas that children learn in school today.

▼ Public buildings were very fine and built of stone and marble. Many were temples to gods and goddesses. This is the Parthenon in Athens. It was built in the classical period and dedicated to Athena, the goddess of the city.

Over 2,000 years later, Greek temples were copied in many parts of the world. Many of the government buildings in Washington, D.C., for example, have columns like those of the temples of ancient Greece.

THE THEATER

The first public performance of a play in Athens took place in the fifth century B.C. Plays soon became very popular and were often performed at festivals. Tragedies were serious plays and had sad endings. Comedies were amusing and had happy endings. A group of dancers and singers called a *chorus* talked about the play as it went along, giving it a broader, deeper meaning.

▼ Like all the theaters built in ancient Greece, the theater at Epidaurus is outdoors. Best preserved of all Greek theaters, it seats some 14,000 people. Because it was cut into a slope, everyone could see the play. It is still in use today.

◀ The actors wore masks like the one worn by this comic actor. Some of the audience would be sitting so far away from the stage that they could not see the expressions on an actor's face. Each mask showed a different emotion very clearly, so that everyone in the audience could see how the characters were feeling. Since women did not perform, men had to play both male and female parts. Many plays were about the gods and their way of dealing with humans.

▶ Plays written in ancient Greece are still performed today. This Greek tragedy is being acted in a modern theater. The Greeks enjoyed going out to see a play, just as we do.

Who Were the Romans?

The story of Rome, its people, and the empire they built is both impressive and exciting. From a city built on the banks of the Tiber River in central Italy sprang a mighty empire that stretched into three continents and lasted nearly 700 years. The Romans built lasting roads, bridges, and towns. They produced great literature and art, strong government, and a powerful army and navy.

▼ Archaeologists have discovered that nearly 4,000 years ago a tribe called the Latini were settled and farming in the region where Rome was built. The land was very fertile and the weather was good, so crops grew well. Farmers grew grain and vegetables and raised animals. The picture below shows a plowman with his team of oxen. The Latini were simple people living in thatched huts. It is believed their small farms gradually developed into villages and towns. The Roman language is called "Latin" because it developed from the language of the Latini.

▼ The area the Latini lived in was called Latium, and two powerful groups of people lived nearby: the Etruscans to the north and Greek settlers to the south. The Latini traded with these people, so it is not surprising that they picked up many ideas from them, including ideas about religion and the use of the alphabet. In fact, many of the ideas that made the Roman Empire so great came from the Etruscans and Greeks.

THE GROWTH OF AN EMPIRE

The cluster of tribal settlements that came together to form the city of Rome was situated on a group of hills above the Tiber River. The high ground and the river protected Rome from enemy attack.

▲ One problem Rome faced was lowland flooding near the Tiber. Once this area was successfully drained, it was made into an open space for meetings called the forum, the remains of which you can see in the picture above. The city council met in a building called the curia at the forum. People also went to the forum to trade goods and to listen to speeches.

305

▶ By A.D. 100, with all the wealth pouring into Rome from the Empire, the city was the largest and most impressive in the world. A million people lived there. The model of Rome gives us a good idea of what the city looked like.

As the model shows, the city was crowded with houses, apartments, public baths, and shops. The huge Colosseum stands on the right and the Circus Maximus is in the foreground. These buildings were where the Roman Games took place.

◀ Huge amounts of grain were needed for the large population and Rome, therefore, depended on receiving plentiful amounts from the Empire. Free grain was given out to the poor and, if this ran out, riots would often take place. This mosaic shows a man measuring grain, a vital crop for the Romans.

▼ By A.D. 100 the Roman Empire was a huge area with an emperor at its head. The Empire was linked by an impressive network of roads. Many Roman roads were long and straight. Straight roads allowed troops to travel quickly and directly to any trouble spots in the Empire. Many of these straight roads built by the Romans still exist today.

▼ The Romans also built roads to cross mountains. Here a road leads twisting and turning over the Alps. This was built by the Romans and shows what excellent engineers they were.

TOWN LIFE

Towns were very important in the growth of the Roman Empire. Roman ideas were spread through the hundreds of towns in the Empire that acted as centers of trade, religion, entertainment, and learning. They were also centers of local government, and they provided protection in times of danger. In the towns of the Empire, the local population could see Roman architecture, fashion, laws, sports, and hygiene. This encouraged them to follow Roman ways.

▲ Romans had very high standards of hygiene, and the sewage systems in their towns were remarkable. There was a plentiful supply of clean water. Since rivers and streams in towns were often polluted, a clean water spring was found, and an aqueduct was built, along which the water was carried. The Romans used more water per person than the people in New York City use today. The picture above shows part of the aqueduct that supplied water to Nîmes in France. Striding dramatically across a valley, this aqueduct carried pure water from 25 miles away.

▼ Most water was used for washing and drinking. It was supplied to fountains, and the excess water was used to flush out the drains. More important, the water was used to feed the public baths built near the town forum. Romans liked to bathe daily and were very clean. Bathing often took place after work when people visited the public baths on the way home. The baths were very cheap and the bath houses provided food and entertainment. The picture at right shows the Roman baths at Bath in England. Although everything above the bases of the pillars was added in the nineteenth century, it is easy to imagine bathers chatting and drinking on the edge or jumping in.

◀ Bathing houses were heated by a furnace and hypocaust system. The hot air from the furnace was channeled into an area under a floor supported by pillars, as shown in the picture. This made the room very hot, so the bathers would sweat before taking their bath. The hypocaust could also heat houses, which was very useful in cold parts of the Empire such as Gaul (present-day France) and Britain. In the picture the air channels are visible at the sides of the walls.

We know a lot about Roman towns from the exciting archaeological discoveries at Pompeii and Herculaneum, near Naples in Italy. Both towns were lost after the volcano Vesuvius erupted in A.D. 79, covering the towns in layers of volcanic mud, ash, and lava. For centuries they lay forgotten, until the area was carefully uncovered. The results were amazing: streets, houses, artifacts, shops, bakeries, barber shops, and laundries were preserved exactly as they were on the day the volcano erupted.

▶ Because archaeologists have found many artifacts, they have been able to reconstruct the rooms from which they came. This is a typical town house kitchen. The large storage containers are called amphorae. There is also a large cooking pot and an oven.

◀ Poor people in Roman towns lived in small apartment buildings, but the rich could afford fine stone town houses with tiled roofs, which tend to be better preserved. Many town houses had luxurious rooms, bath suites, mosaic floors, and beautiful gardens.

THE FALL OF ROME

By the third century A.D. tribes outside the Roman Empire began raiding provinces in the hope of taking rich pickings. In response to this threat, the boundaries of the Empire were strengthened and some cities built walls or added turrets to existing walls. Around the coasts of Gaul and Britain, special forts were built to keep a lookout for Anglo-Saxon raiders, who came in longships from what is now Germany.

▼ The huge towers of this ancient fort helped defenders see along their walls and also improved their fire power. The remains of a defensive ditch are in front of the towers. The ditch would have been much deeper 1,700 years ago.

▶ By the fifth century A.D. tribes from central Europe—the Franks, Vandals, Goths, and Huns—were making serious inroads into Roman territory. One of these tribes, the Huns, was led by Attila, who appears on this medal. The Romans called these tribes barbarians because they lived outside the Empire and were not "civilized." The writing on the medal calls Attila the "*Scourge* of God."

As the attacks on the Empire continued, it became very difficult to collect taxes: people either refused or had no money to pay. This meant that the army could not be paid, so many soldiers deserted, leaving the Empire undefended. Once the army left an area, the Roman way of life collapsed remarkably quickly. Buildings were deserted, pillaged, burned, or left in ruins.

◀ The Roman Empire was very powerful while it was growing; but defending the frontier proved to be too difficult. By A.D. 476 the Empire had broken up. This is the large city wall that bordered Constantinople (now Istanbul in Turkey), around which the Eastern Empire was based. Constantinople survived until the fifteenth century, but the once-mighty Western Empire lay in ruins.

THINK ABOUT IT

❶ How do the lives of people today compare with the lives of the ancient Greeks and Romans?

❷ What would you have liked most about living in ancient Greece or Rome? What would you have liked the least? Explain why you feel as you do.

❸ What is the authors' purpose in writing about these topics? How do you know?

RESPONSE

Eyewitness to History

WRITE A LETTER Imagine that you live in ancient Greece or Rome. Write a letter to a friend or family member telling about an important event that you witnessed. Use details from the selection.

A Roman Mosaic

DESIGN A MOSAIC The selection's photos show a mosaic of a man measuring corn. Use small pieces of colored paper to create a mosaic of another part of ancient Roman life. Display your mosaic in the classroom.

ACTIVITIES

From Democracy to Aqueducts

WRITE A SPEECH Find examples in the selection of ancient Greek and Roman ideas that are still used in our society. Write a short speech about your findings. Tell how knowing about the past can help us understand how we live today.

Name That Building

PLAY A GUESSING GAME Write a detailed description of a building or structure you read about in the selection, but do not name it. Read your description aloud to a small group. The person who correctly guesses the name of the building or structure takes the next turn.

The Skill of

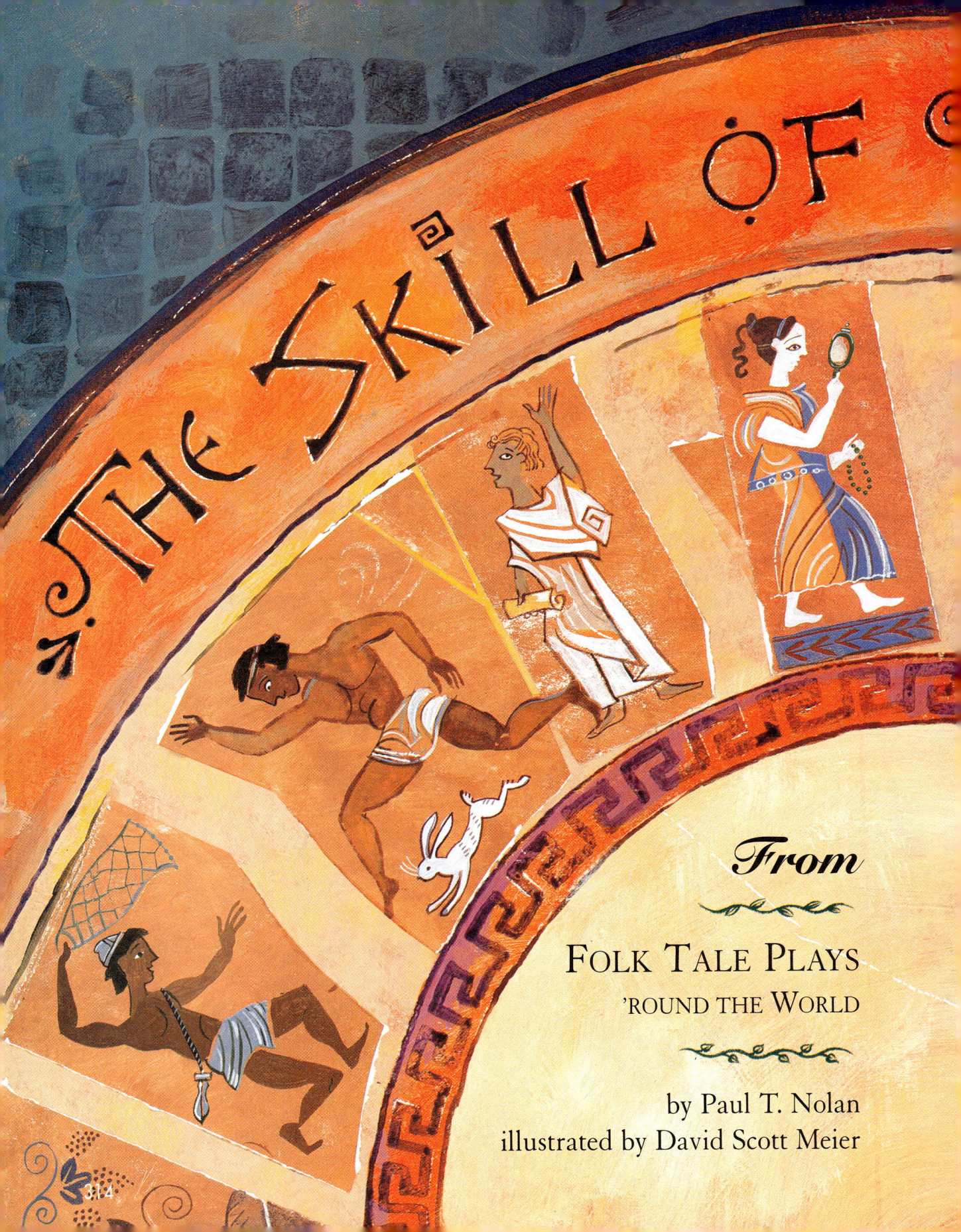

From

Folk Tale Plays
'Round the World

by Paul T. Nolan
illustrated by David Scott Meier

PERICLES

Characters

CIMON *(The Athlete)*
HECTOR *(The Orator)*
AJAX *(The Warrior)*
HELENA *(The Beauty)*
LETA *(The Wise)*
IDA *(The Artful)*
NESTOR *(The Friend)*
THE OLD SAILOR
A MESSENGER
PERICLES
CITIZENS OF ATHENS

TIME: *The fifth century, B.C.*
SETTING: *The market place in Athens.*
AT RISE: THE OLD SAILOR *is telling a story about the voyages he has taken.* THE OLD SAILOR *and the young people—*CIMON, HECTOR, AJAX, HELENA, LETA, IDA, *and* NESTOR—*are downstage left and hold the center of attention, but the* CITIZENS OF ATHENS *can be seen carrying on their business upstage.* THE OLD SAILOR *pretends his tales are true; actually he takes them from the stories of Homer, "The Iliad" and "The Odyssey," but he is very interesting and a favorite with the young people.*

THE SAILOR: And there we were—Odysseus and I—and there was the great big Cyclops. . . .
CIMON: Was the Cyclops as big as ten men?
THE SAILOR: As big as fifty and he had one eye *(Points to the middle of his forehead)* right in the middle of his forehead.
CIMON: I'll bet he could run like the wind.
AJAX: And fight like an army.
HELENA: But he wasn't very pretty.
THE SAILOR: He was ugly all right, and he would have scared any other man to death—except my friend Odysseus and me.
LETA *(Doubting)*: How could you know Odysseus? He lived a long time ago.
THE SAILOR: That's a fact. A long time ago. But I was younger then.
LETA: I thought it was *a thousand years ago*.
THE SAILOR: It may have been. I was a lot younger then.

IDA: Did Homer tell the truth about Odysseus, old sailor?
THE SAILOR: He was a poet and all poets make up stories. But mostly he told the truth.
LETA: Why didn't he mention you?
THE SAILOR: Well, I guess Homer couldn't write down everything.
HELENA: Tell us about your adventures with our leader, Pericles.
THE SAILOR: Ah, yes, Pericles and I.
LETA: Huh. I'll bet you were never at Troy, and you probably don't even know Pericles.
THE SAILOR: Pericles and I have done some big things.
LETA: You made up those stories about Pericles.
NESTOR: What do you want to say that for, Leta? Now he won't tell us any more stories.
LETA: I said it because it's true.
THE SAILOR: Is that so, young girl? Maybe you would believe me if I brought Pericles here and he told you himself?
LETA: Yes, I would. Bring him if you can.
THE SAILOR: Maybe I just don't want to bring him.
LETA: You wouldn't know Pericles even if you saw him.
   (A MESSENGER *enters upstage center and hits a brass gong. All the people stop their business to listen to him.*)
MESSENGER (*Unrolling a scroll and reading it*): Hear ye, hear ye, hear ye. I bring news from our great leader, Pericles. Today Pericles will visit you to pick the youth who best shows he knows the skill of Pericles.
FIRST CITIZEN: The skill of Pericles? What's that?
SECOND CITIZEN: His military skill, of course.
THIRD CITIZEN: Not so. It's his speech-making.
FOURTH CITIZEN: It's his strength.
MESSENGER (*Hitting gong again to silence crowd*): Pericles is already among you, looking and judging. Within the

hour he shall say who best has the skill of Pericles. Parents, prepare your children. Children, be prepared. The one chosen shall win a prize. (MESSENGER *exits*.)

FIRST CITIZEN: Pericles is already among us, judging.

SECOND CITIZEN: Within the hour he will name the winner.

THIRD CITIZEN: I must go home and rouse my lazy son from sleep. But what's the use? Only if sleeping is the skill of Pericles will he win the prize.

FOURTH CITIZEN: Perhaps it is singing. My little girl has the voice of a bird.

FIFTH CITIZEN (*To* 4TH CITIZEN): The voice of a bird all right—a crow. Your daughter cannot sing.

FOURTH CITIZEN: You are jealous. You know it will bring great honor to my house if my child wins the prize. (*During the past several speeches, the* CITIZENS *have been leaving. Now only the seven main characters are left onstage. Upstage center* PERICLES, *disguised as a beggar, sits with his head bent, as though he were half-asleep.*)

CIMON: What is this skill of Pericles? Did anyone ever say?

HELENA: I have never heard of such a thing before.

NESTOR: Wouldn't it be a great honor if one of you should win the prize? I would be very proud to have a friend who has the skill of Pericles.

HECTOR: The old sailor said he knew Pericles well. The sailor can tell us. Where is he?

IDA (*Looking about*): He's gone. Leta made him angry when she said he made up stories.

LETA: I didn't make him angry. He knew that when Pericles came, we would find out his stories were not true.

AJAX: If you think he makes things up, why do you listen to him?

LETA: He tells very good stories. (PERICLES *now comes downstage and joins the group. They pay no attention to him.*)

CIMON: We Greeks are the finest athletes in all the world. We run the fastest, swim the best, hurl the javelin farther than any other people on earth. The skill of Pericles must be in our sports. Nestor, come and race me to the temple and back. If Pericles is watching he will see what a fine runner I am.

NESTOR: Gladly, my friend Cimon, if you think my running with you will help.

CIMON: Hector, tell us when to start.

HECTOR: I don't see why I should help you, Cimon. I, too, would like to win the prize.

NESTOR: Hector, if the prize is for speaking, Pericles will hear your fine voice.

HECTOR: I hadn't thought of that. All right. (CIMON *and* NESTOR *get in a starting position.*) Great runners of Athens, hear my command: Get ready, set, and go! *(The two run off.)* Didn't my voice sound well, Leta?

LETA: Don't be foolish, Hector. How can a voice sound well unless it says something?

HELENA *(Looking off)*: Nestor is almost keeping up with Cimon.

LETA: Nestor is a fine runner, too, but he is more interested in making Cimon a better runner than in winning the race for himself. He will lose.

HELENA: I'm afraid so. And Nestor is nicer than Cimon, too. (NESTOR *and* CIMON *return,* CIMON *leading the race.* HECTOR *takes* CIMON's *hand and raises it.*)

HECTOR: I, Hector, judge: Cimon is the winner.

HELENA: Nestor, you might win a race if you would think about winning instead of trying to make Cimon run faster.

NESTOR: No one can beat my friend Cimon. He is the finest runner in Athens.

CIMON: But you are a great help to me, Nestor. Perhaps Pericles will give a second prize, and you will get it.

HECTOR: You are very quick to take first prize for yourself, Cimon. But I do not think the skill of Pericles is running. Pericles was a great runner in his youth, to be sure. But it takes speaking skill to win men to democracy, not running.

AJAX: Do you think you will win the prize for your speaking, Hector?

HECTOR: I don't say I will win the prize, but I would like to try. Do you remember the story of Admetus, who asked his father to die in his place? Hear me give the father's answer. . . .

LETA *(Breaking in)*: Do we have to listen to that speech again?

HECTOR: Hear me, now. I am the old father speaking. *(Pretending to be an old man)* "Am I slave, son, that you treat me so? Or am I your father, a king and a freeman born? I have given you everything you own. Is it my duty to die for you as well? There is no law of the Greeks that a father must die for his son. . . ."

IDA *(Interrupting)*: Are you going to give the whole speech again?

NESTOR: I think that is a good speech, and Hector gives it very well.

LETA: I don't know what we would do without you, Nestor. You make all our faults sound like virtues: Cimon's bragging and Hector's bellowing, Ajax's prancing about. . . .

AJAX: I do not prance! I walk like a warrior. And that's what I am, a warrior. You will be sorry you have said that, Leta, when I win the prize.

LETA: Do you think you have the skill of Pericles?

AJAX: What is the greatest skill of the Greeks, I ask

you? It is fighting! And who is the greatest warrior here? *(He draws his wooden sword and makes a fake thrust toward* NESTOR, *who pretends to fall dead.)* You see? Victory again. *(He pretends to place a foot on* NESTOR's *body and holds his sword aloft.)* If Pericles has seen what a great warrior I am, I am sure to win the prize.

NESTOR *(Getting to his feet again)*: One of you will win. I am sure of it. No one runs as fast as Cimon, or talks as well as Hector or fights as well as Ajax. We must all have a feast when the prize is given.

PERICLES *(All turn to him as he speaks)*: There is much in what you say, Nestor. We Greeks prize the gifts of your friends here. One of them may well win the prize.

NESTOR: I wish Pericles were here saying that.

IDA: Do you know Pericles, old man?

PERICLES: I have never seen him face to face, but I know something of the way he thinks. *(Turning to girls)* What about you girls? Helena, here, has beauty. Maybe that is the skill of Pericles.

HELENA *(Posing)*: I thought beauty should be the skill of Pericles, but I did not know men would agree with me.

PERICLES: We Athenians are not brutes like the Spartans, Helena. It is our greatness that we know beauty makes life worth living.

HELENA: If I win the prize, I hope it is a lovely necklace for my beautiful neck.

LETA: Do not count the beads until you have won the prize. The Goddess of Beauty won a prize from Paris, but foolish Paris was not as wise as Pericles. I do not think a pretty face will be the skill of Pericles.

PERICLES: That is a good argument for one so young. You are wise, Leta.

NESTOR: Perhaps wisdom is the skill of Pericles, Leta, and then you will win the prize.

LETA: Thank you, Nestor. I am wise enough to know I won't win. All nations have wise people, but all cities are not Athens. I don't know the skill of Pericles, but I do not think it is wisdom.

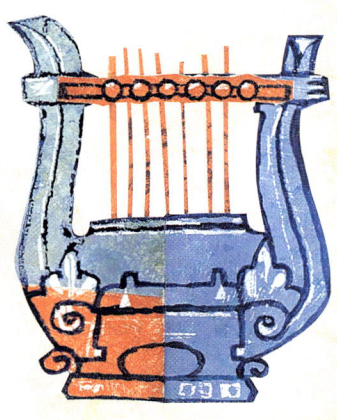

PERICLES: Perhaps it is art. I am told, Ida, that you sing and dance most wonderfully.

NESTOR: She is the finest singer and dancer in all Athens. Sing for us, Ida.

PERICLES: Yes, do, Ida. We Greeks prize our singers. Think of the honor that we have given our poet Homer these many centuries.

IDA: I'll sing if you all join in.

NESTOR: We will join in your singing and in your dancing, too. *(The following song is to be sung to the tune of Bach's "A Song of Praise." IDA sings the first verse alone. The others join her in the second verse. Then IDA and NESTOR do a ballet routine while the others sing the first verse again.)*

IDA:
  We raise a song to isles we love,
  For all the joys that life does bring:
  For freemen's rights and heroes' deeds,
  Our grateful thanks and praise we sing.

OTHERS:
  We raise a song to isles we love,
  For Athens, city that we prize,
  For shining seas and mountains tall,
  In grateful thanks our voices rise.

PERICLES *(Applauding)*: That was very good, Ida. And you did well, too, Nestor.

IDA: Nestor is my favorite partner.

NESTOR: Anyone can dance well with Ida.

PERICLES: But what is your special skill, Nestor? How do you expect to win the prize from Pericles?

NESTOR *(Laughing)*: I will not even be considered. I do not run as well as Cimon, nor talk as well as Hector. I do not fight as well as Ajax. . . .

AJAX: But you are the one I would want at my side in battle.

NESTOR: I thank you for that, Ajax.
HELENA: You are not beautiful, Nestor. But I think you are handsome. Don't you think so, old man?
PERICLES: He has a good face, one I would like in a son or friend.
NESTOR *(Laughing)*: My only skill is the luck to have such good friends. And one of them will win the prize today. I am sure of it. (MESSENGER *enters and strikes the gong again. The* CITIZENS *come onstage again.)*
PERICLES: Well, we shall soon see. Here is the messenger again. *(He leaves the group and goes upstage to the* MESSENGER.*)*
MESSENGER: Citizens of Greece, the time has come to announce the name of the youth with the skill of Pericles.
FIRST CITIZEN: But where is Pericles?
SECOND CITIZEN: We have not seen Pericles yet.
THIRD CITIZEN: He has not heard my lazy son snore.
FOURTH CITIZEN: He has not yet heard my little girl sing.
MESSENGER: Pericles has been with you. He has watched you work and play.
AJAX: Pericles has been here? *(The* OLD SAILOR *comes onstage.)*
HELENA: Look, the old sailor! He's back.
MESSENGER: Pericles has been here, and he is here. He has come disguised. But now he will speak.
IDA: Pericles is here disguised.
CIMON: I'll bet the old sailor is Pericles.
HECTOR: You will not win, Leta, because you said he made up stories.

AJAX: The old sailor said he knew Pericles, and surely a man knows himself. (PERICLES *now steps up beside the* MESSENGER.)

LETA: Look! The old beggar is standing next to the messenger. It is not the old sailor, but the old beggar who is Pericles in disguise.

HECTOR: It can't be. He said he had never seen Pericles face to face.

LETA: No man ever sees himself face to face.

MESSENGER: Citizens of Athens! Pericles! (PERICLES *drops the ragged cloak he has had about him, removes the hood from his head, and stands erect.*)

CITIZENS: Pericles! It is Pericles.

FIRST CITIZEN: I have seen him talking to the children by the river's edge.

SECOND CITIZEN: I have seen him listening to the children sing.

THIRD CITIZEN: He has heard my lazy son snore.

FOURTH CITIZEN *(Pleased)*: He has heard my little girl sing.

PERICLES: Citizens of Athens, I have come disguised not to trick you, but because I wanted to know you as you know each other—as friend knows friend and fellow-citizen knows fellow-citizen.

FIFTH CITIZEN: That is the democratic way.

PERICLES: I have watched and been pleased. Here are many youths with skills and gifts that make life good.

NESTOR *(To his friends)*: You see! He is going to give one of you the prize.

PERICLES: I have seen Cimon race. He will win many palms in the games.

NESTOR: You see, Cimon. He knows.

PERICLES: I have heard Hector speak and seen Ajax fight. With such voices and willing hearts, Athens will long remain free.

NESTOR: Perhaps he will give three prizes.

PERICLES: And I have seen Helena's beautiful face and Ida's grace, and I have heard the wise words of Leta. All our poets will sing of these three.

NESTOR: He's going to give six prizes!

PERICLES: And there are other youths, too. Jason, who works with his father in the olive groves, and Hymen, who sails a boat so well across the waters. Each has skills I wish I had. But my only skill is in knowing that all men have skills.

FIRST CITIZEN: That is true. He knows men have skills that they do not know they have.

PERICLES: Now which youth among you best knows your virtues? What say you, Cimon?

CIMON: My friend, Nestor.

PERICLES: What say you, Hector?

HECTOR: My friend, Nestor.

PERICLES: What say you, Ajax?

AJAX: My friend, Nestor.

PERICLES: What say you, Citizens of Athens?

ALL: Our friend, Nestor.

FIRST CITIZEN: He listens to me when I am sad.

SECOND CITIZEN: He sings with me when I am happy.

THIRD CITIZEN: He is happy when I am fortunate.

PERICLES: Then, my friends, *your* choice is Nestor. He is our friend, and before the sun sets, we will honor him today as he honors us every day of his life. Go to your homes to prepare, and return before the sun sets. (*All except the* OLD SAILOR, PERICLES, *and the seven young people depart, speaking as they go.*)

FIRST CITIZEN: It was a good choice.

SECOND CITIZEN: He has always been a friend to all.

THIRD CITIZEN: And he says my son is not lazy, just thinking, and one day he will be a fine man.

FOURTH CITIZEN: He loves to hear my little girl sing. *(All exit.)*

PERICLES *(Who has made his way down to the seven)*: Well, my young friends, I know you all agree, but what did you learn from this?

LETA: Something we should have known: the first prize in a democracy goes to those who give, not to those who have.

PERICLES: You are wise, Leta, and if you have the wisdom to comfort people, you will be honored all the days of your life. *(The OLD SAILOR attempts to move offstage without being noticed. PERICLES shouts to him.)* Wait a minute, old sailor, my friend. *(To the others)* I must go see my old friend, the sailor. He fought alongside me in many a battle. I must seek his advice on how to make our country better. *(As he is leaving)* He was with Odysseus when they escaped from the Cyclops, you know. *(He goes to the OLD SAILOR and they exit together.)*

CIMON: Did you hear, Leta? The old sailor *was* with Odysseus. You were wrong.

AJAX: You said that he did not even know Pericles. And now you have seen what great friends they are.

LETA: They are now. That is Pericles' skill, to use one's gift to help others. I don't know if the old sailor ever saw Pericles before, but he will never forget him now. *(Curtain)*

THE END

Think About It

❶ Why does Pericles give the prize to Nestor?

❷ Why do you think Pericles disguised himself to judge the contest?

❸ What in this play helps you understand ancient Greek life?

Meet the Illustrator

DAVID SCOTT MEIER

David Scott Meier has been painting since he was four, but he only recently started illustrating children's books. He especially enjoyed illustrating this play because his pet parrot is named Pericles! Meier enjoys collecting artifacts from ancient Greece. He also enjoys traveling, singing, and acting when he can spare the time from his busy illustrating career.

Visit **The Learning Site!**
www.harcourtschool.com

D.S. Meier

A Song of Greatness

A Chippewa song
transcribed by Mary Austin
illustrated by Bernie Fuchs

When I hear the old men
Telling of heroes,
Telling of great deeds
Of ancient days,
When I hear them telling,
Then I think within me
I too am one of these.

When I hear the people
Praising great ones,
Then I know that I too
Shall be esteemed,
I too when my time comes
Shall do mightily.

RESPONSE

SHOW YOUR TALENT

ACT OUT TALENTS

"The Skill of Pericles" describes skills and talents that are important to a democracy. In a small group, brainstorm skills and talents shown by young people your own age. Write them on slips of paper. Take turns choosing one and acting it out.

LEND A HELPING HAND

WRITE A PARAGRAPH

In the last line of the play, Leta says, "That is Pericles' skill, to use one's gift to help others." Write a paragraph explaining what you think Leta means. Use examples from your own experiences to support your opinion.

ACTIVITIES

YOUR PERSONAL BEST

MAKE A LIST

Skim the play and list qualities you admire in the characters. Put a check mark by those you already have and those you would like to develop. Seal the list in an envelope. Open the envelope in six months, and see whether you want to make changes in your list.

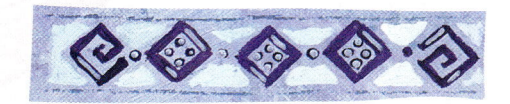

MAKING CONNECTIONS

WRITE A SONG

Nestor's friends admired him very much. Write a "song of greatness" that celebrates Nestor's special talent. Set your song to music, using a well-known melody or a melody of your own. Sing your song for the class.

THEME WRAP-UP

People of the Past

COMPARE CULTURES The peoples of ancient times all had their own unique styles of living and working. With a small group, reread the selections and discuss how the cultures were similar and how they were different. Present your findings to the class.

Surprising, But True!

MAKE A LIST You have just learned a lot of interesting facts about ancient civilizations. Look back at the selections in this theme, and list the facts that surprised you the most. Share your list with your class and tell why those facts surprised you.

What's the Purpose?

COMPARING AUTHORS' PURPOSES For each selection in the theme "Unlocking the Past," think about the author's purpose, or reason for writing. Remember that the author may have more than one purpose. Copy and complete the chart. Below your charts, write sentences explaining why you chose the purposes you did for each selection. Share your chart and reasons with your class.

Author's Purpose				
	To Entertain	To Inform	To Persuade	To Express
The Stone Age News				
Ancient China				
Pyramids				
Look Into the Past: The Greeks and the Romans				
The Skill of Pericles				

Theme

Creative Solutions

CONTENTS

My Side of the Mountain 338
by Jean Craighead George

FOCUS SKILL:
Predict Outcomes 352

Febold Feboldson 354
retold by Mary Pope Osborne

Dividing the Horses 364
retold by George Shannon

Aesop's Fables 366
retold by Margaret Clark

The Kid Who Invented the Popsicle 370
by Don L. Wulffson

FOCUS SKILL:
Draw Conclusions 386

A Do-It-Yourself Project 388
by Anilú Bernardo

Some Like It Wet 404
from Contact Kids

Catching the Fire: Philip Simmons, Blacksmith 408
by Mary E. Lyons

The Road Not Taken 422
by Robert Frost

READER'S

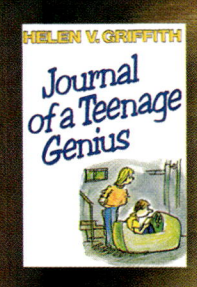

Journal of a Teenage Genius
by Helen V. Griffith

SCIENCE FICTION

Zack, a teenage scientist, meets a girl whose family travels through time in this hilarious science fiction novel.

Award-Winning Author
READER'S CHOICE LIBRARY

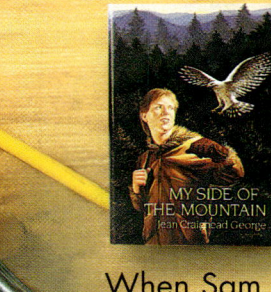

My Side of the Mountain
by Jean Craighead George

REALISTIC FICTION

When Sam Gribley runs away to live in the woods, he must learn to rely on both his inner resources and the natural resources around him.

Newbery Honor/ALA Notable Book
READER'S CHOICE LIBRARY

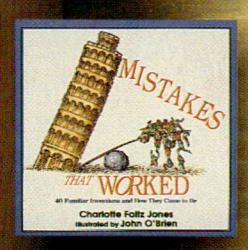

Mistakes That Worked
by Charlotte Foltz Jones

NONFICTION

Many inventions begin as accidents. Find out how the inventors of some familiar products turned their mistakes into successes.

Children's Choice

CHOiCE

My Sister, My Science Report
by Margaret Bechard

REALISTIC FICTION

Tess is upset when her teacher assigns Phoenix, the strangest boy in school, to be her science partner. However, when he suggests an unusual topic for their report, science becomes more interesting than Tess ever imagined.

Women Invent!
by Susan Casey

NONFICTION

Women have invented many of the products that we use every day. Learn about the process of inventing through their inspiring stories.

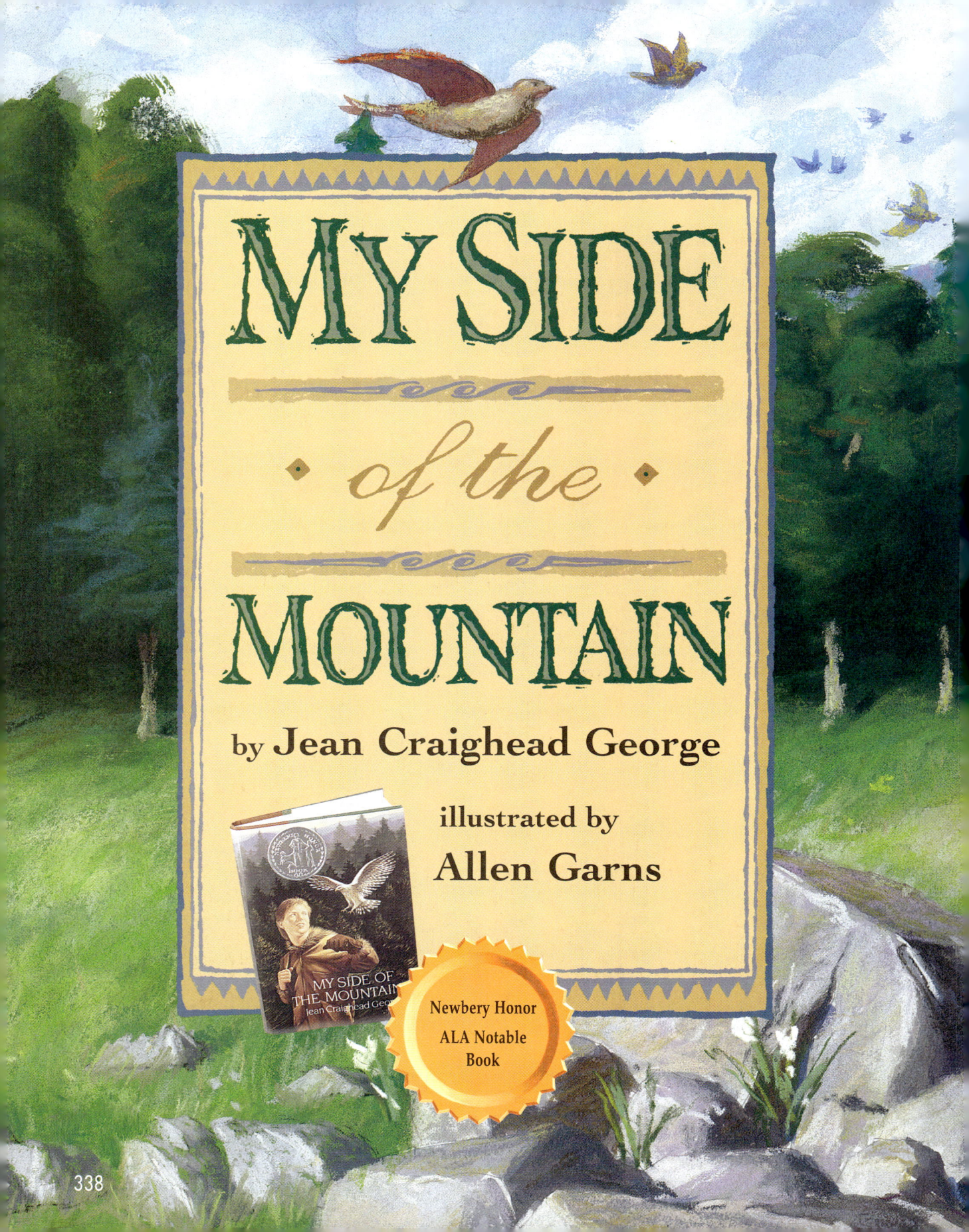

My Side of the Mountain

by Jean Craighead George

illustrated by Allen Garns

Newbery Honor
ALA Notable Book

Sam Gribley leaves crowded New York City for the peace and quiet of the Catskill Mountains. With the help of some maps found by Miss Turner, the local librarian, Sam finds the part of a mountain that once belonged to his great-grandfather. Sam plans to live on this land, using his knowledge of nature and the few supplies he has with him. But how will he find food and shelter, alone on a mountain with fall and winter approaching?

The following morning I stood up, stretched, and looked about me. Birds were dripping from the trees, little birds, singing and flying and pouring over the limbs.

"This must be the warbler migration," I said, and I laughed because there were so many birds. I had never seen so many. My big voice rolled through the woods, and their little voices seemed to rise and answer me.

They were eating. Three or four in a maple tree near me were darting along the limbs, pecking and snatching at something delicious on the trees. I wondered if there was anything there for a hungry boy. I pulled a limb down, and all I saw were leaves, twigs, and flowers. I ate a flower. It was not very good. One manual I had read said to watch what the birds and animals were eating in order to learn what is edible and nonedible in the forest. If the animal life can eat it, it is safe for humans. The book did suggest that a raccoon had tastes more nearly like ours. Certainly the birds were no example.

Then I wondered if they were not eating something I couldn't see — tiny insects perhaps; well, anyway, whatever it was, I decided to fish. I took my line and hook and walked down to the stream.

I lay on a log and dangled my line in the bright water. The fish were not biting. That made me hungrier. My stomach pinched. You know, it really does hurt to be terribly hungry.

A stream is supposed to be full of food. It is the easiest place to get a lot of food in a hurry. I needed something in a hurry, but what? I looked through the clear water and saw the tracks of mussels in the mud. I ran along the log back to shore, took off my clothes, and plunged into that icy water.

I collected almost a peck[1] of mussels in very little time at all, and began tying them in my sweater to carry them back to camp.

But I don't have to carry them anywhere, I said to myself. I have my fire in my pocket, I don't need a table. I can sit right here by the stream and eat. And so I did. I wrapped the mussels in leaves and sort of steamed them

---

[1] *peck:* a measure for fruits and vegetables equal to eight quarts

in coals. They are not quite as good as clams—a little stronger, I would say—but by the time I had eaten three, I had forgotten what clams tasted like and knew only how delicious freshwater mussels were. I actually got full.

I wandered back to Great-grandfather's farm and began to explore. Most of the acreage was maple and beech, some pine, dogwoods, ash; and here and there a glorious hickory. I made a sketch of the farm on my road map, and put *x*'s where the hickories were. They were gold trees to me. I would have hickory nuts in the fall. I could also make salt from hickory limbs. I cut off one and chopped it into bits and scraps. I stuck them in my sweater.

The land was up and down and up and down, and I wondered how Great-grandfather ever cut it and plowed it. There was one stream running through it, which I was glad to see, for it meant I did not have to go all the way down the mountain to the big creek for fish and water.

Around noon I came upon what I was sure was the old foundation of the house. Miss Turner was right. It was ruins—a few stones in a square, a slight depression for the basement, and trees growing right up through what had once been the living room. I wandered around to see what was left of the Gribley home.

After a few looks I saw an apple tree. I rushed up to it, hoping to find an old apple. No apples beneath it. About forty feet away, however, I found a dried one in the crotch of a tree, stuck there by a squirrel and forgotten. I ate it. It was pretty bad—but nourishing, I hoped. There was another apple tree and three walnuts. I scribbled x's. These were wonderful finds.

I poked around the foundations, hoping to uncover some old iron implements that I could use. I found nothing. Too many leaves had fallen and turned to loam, too many plants had grown up and died down over the old home site. I decided to come back when I had made myself a shovel.

Whistling and looking for food and shelter, I went on up the mountain, following the stone walls, discovering many things about my property. I found a marsh. In it were cattails and arrow-leaf— good starchy foods.

At high noon I stepped onto a mountain meadow. An enormous boulder rose up in the center of it. At the top of the meadow was a fringe of white birch. There were maples and oaks to the west, and a hemlock forest to the right that pulled me right across the sweet grasses, into it.

Never, never have I seen such trees. They were giants—old, old giants. They must have begun when the world began.

I started walking around them. I couldn't hear myself step, so dense and damp were the needles. Great boulders covered with ferns and moss stood among them. They looked like pebbles beneath those trees.

Standing before the biggest and the oldest and the most kinglike of them all, I suddenly had an idea.

I knew enough about the Catskill Mountains to know that when the summer came, they were covered with people. Although Great-grandfather's farm was somewhat remote, still hikers and campers and hunters and fishermen were sure to wander across it.

Therefore I wanted a house that could not be seen. People would want to take me back where I belonged if they found me.

I looked at that tree. Somehow I knew it was home, but I was not quite sure how it was home. The limbs were high and not right for a tree house. I could build a bark extension around it, but that would look silly. Slowly I circled the great trunk. Halfway around the whole plan became perfectly obvious. To the west, between two of the flanges of the tree that spread out to be roots, was a cavity. The heart of the tree was rotting away. I scraped at it with my hands; old, rotten insect-ridden dust came tumbling out. I dug on and on, using my ax from time to time as my excitement grew.

With much of the old rot out, I could crawl in the tree and sit cross-legged. Inside I felt as cozy as a turtle in its shell. I chopped and chopped until I was hungry and exhausted. I was now in the hard good wood, and chopping it out was work. I was afraid

December would come before I got a hole big enough to lie in. So I sat down to think.

You know, those first days, I just never planned right. I had the beginnings of a home, but not a bite to eat, and I had worked so hard that I could hardly move forward to find that bite. Furthermore, it was discouraging to feed that body of mine. It was never satisfied, and gathering food for it took time and got it hungrier. Trying to get a place to rest it took time and got it more tired, and I really felt I was going in circles and wondered how primitive man ever had enough time and energy to stop hunting food and start thinking about fire and tools.

I left the tree and went across the meadow looking for food. I plunged into the woods beyond, and there I discovered the gorge and the white cascade splashing down the black rocks into the pool below.

I was hot and dirty. I scrambled down the rocks and slipped into the pool. It was so cold I yelled. But when I came out on the bank and put on my two pairs of trousers and three sweaters, which I thought was a better way to carry clothes than in a pack, I tingled and burned and felt coltish. I leapt up the bank, slipped, and my face went down in a patch of dog-tooth violets.

You would know them anywhere after a few looks at them at the Botanical Gardens and in colored flower books. They are little yellow lilies on long slender stems with oval leaves dappled with gray. But that's not all. They have wonderfully tasty bulbs. I was filling my pockets before I got up from my fall.

"I'll have a salad-type lunch," I said as I moved up the steep sides of the ravine. I discovered that as late as it was in the season, the spring beauties were still blooming in the cool pockets of the woods. They are all right raw, that is if you are as hungry as I was. They taste a little like lima beans. I ate these as I went on hunting food, feeling better and better, until I worked my way back to the meadow where the dandelions were blooming. Funny I hadn't noticed them earlier. Their greens are good, and so are their roots—a little strong and milky, but you get used to that.

A crow flew into the aspen grove without saying a word. The little I knew of crows from following them in Central Park, they always have something to say. But this bird was sneaking, obviously trying to be quiet. Birds are good food. Crow is certainly not the best, but I did not know that then, and I launched out to see where it was going. I had a vague plan to try to noose it. This is the kind of thing I wasted time on in those days when time was so important. However, this venture turned out all right, because I did not have to noose that bird.

I stepped into the woods, looked around, could not see the crow, but noticed a big stick nest in a scrabbly pine. I started to climb the tree. Off flew the crow. What made me keep on climbing in face of such discouragement, I don't know, but I did, and that noon I had crow eggs and wild salad for lunch.

At lunch I also solved the problem of carving out my tree. After a struggle I made a fire. Then I sewed a big skunk cabbage leaf into a cup with grass strands. I had read that you can boil water in a leaf, and ever since then I had been very anxious to see if this were true. It seems impossible, but it works. I boiled the eggs in a leaf. The water keeps the leaf wet, and although the top dries up and burns down to the water level, that's as far as the burning goes. I was pleased to see it work.

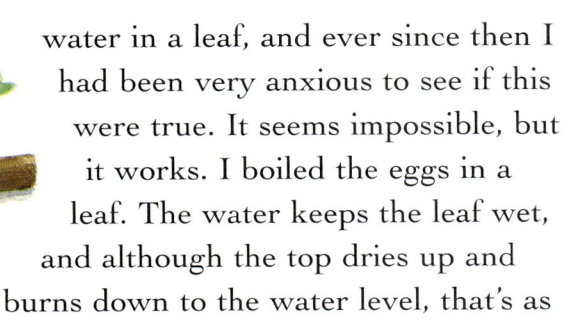

Then here's what happened. Naturally, all this took a lot of time, and I hadn't gotten very far on my tree, so I was fretting and stamping out the fire when I stopped with my foot in the air.

The fire! Indians made dugout canoes with fire. They burned them out, an easier and much faster way of getting results. I would try fire in the tree. If I was very careful, perhaps it would work. I ran into the hemlock forest with a burning stick and got a fire going inside the tree.

Thinking that I ought to have a bucket of water in case things got out of hand, I looked desperately around me. The water was far across the meadow and down the ravine. This would never do. I began to think the whole inspiration of a home in the tree was no good. I really did have to live near water for cooking and drinking and comfort. I looked sadly at the magnificent hemlock and was about to put the fire out and desert it when I said something to myself. It must have come out of some book: "Hemlocks usually grow around mountain streams and springs."

I swirled on my heel. Nothing but boulders around me. But the air was damp, somewhere — I said — and darted around the rocks, peering and looking and sniffing and going down into pockets and dales. No water. I was coming back, circling wide, when I almost fell in it. Two sentinel boulders, dripping wet, decorated with flowers, ferns, moss, weeds — everything that loved water — guarded a bathtub-sized spring.

"You pretty thing," I said, flopped on my stomach, and pushed my face into it to drink. I opened my eyes. The water was like glass, and in it were little insects with oars. They rowed away from

347

me. Beetles skittered like bullets on the surface, or carried a silver bubble of air with them to the bottom. Ha, then I saw a crayfish.

I jumped up, overturned rocks, and found many crayfish. At first I hesitated to grab them because they can pinch. I gritted my teeth, thought about how much more it hurts to be hungry, and came down upon them. I did get pinched, but I had my dinner. And that was the first time I had planned ahead! Any planning that I did in those early days was such a surprise to me and so successful that I was delighted with even a small plan. I wrapped the crayfish in leaves, stuffed them in my pockets, and went back to the burning tree.

Bucket of water, I thought. Bucket of water? Where was I going to get a bucket? How did I think, even if I found water, I could get it back to the tree? That's how citified I was in those days. I had never lived without a bucket before — scrub buckets, water buckets — and so when a water problem came up, I just thought I could run to the kitchen and get a bucket.

"Well, dirt is as good as water," I said as I ran back to my tree. "I can smother the fire with dirt."

Days passed working, burning, cutting, gathering food, and each day I cut another notch on an aspen pole that I had stuck in the ground for a calendar.

Think About It

1. How does the main character use his inventiveness to find food and shelter in the woods?

2. Would you like to live in the woods, as the main character does in the story? Why or why not?

3. How does the author use descriptive language to help you picture the story's setting?

Meet the Author
Jean Craighead George

Award-winning author Jean Craighead George called upon her lifelong interest in nature to help her write *My Side of the Mountain*. Here she answers questions about her childhood experiences.

What was your childhood like?
I grew up in Washington, D.C., and at the old family home at Craighead, Pennsylvania. Both my father and mother were entomologists (scientists who study insects), and my twin brothers were among the first falconers in the country and the first to track grizzly bears using radio collars.

Did you have any memorable times in the wilderness?
My brothers took me with them on hunting and camping trips. We went to the tops of cliffs to look for falcons, down the whitewater rivers to fish and swim, and over the forest floors in search of mice, birds, wildflowers, trees, fish, salamanders, and mammals. My childhood seems like one leaping, laughing adventure into the mysteries and joys of the earth.

Did you have pets when you were growing up?
Our home was always full of pets—falcons, raccoons, owls, and opossums, and dozens of sleeping insects. Hounds and kids ran in and out. It was a rollicking childhood.

Visit *The Learning Site!*
www.harcourtschool.com

Response Activities

Let's Go Camping

MAKE COST ESTIMATES

Sam Gribley has to be inventive to survive. Suppose you and an adult family member are going on a weekend camping trip. Think about ways you could "make do" with what you have and what you could find. List these ideas, and then list the equipment and supplies you would need to buy. Estimate how much you would have to spend. Compare lists with a partner. Decide whose list is the most inventive and requires the least amount of money.

How the Skunk Cabbage Got Its Name

WRITE A FOLK SONG
Choose a plant from the story that has a descriptive name, such as the dogtooth violet, cattail, or skunk cabbage. Write a folk song that explains how the plant got its name. You can use the melody of a song you know or make up a new melody.

Dancing on Air

WRITE A POEM
What do you picture when you read the phrase *birds were dripping from the trees*? Think of imaginative ways to describe other things. Then use your images to write a haiku or another type of poem. Recite your poem to the class.

The Name Game

MAKE FLASHCARDS
Sam is excited to find dogtooth violets because they are a source of food. Choose a plant, and find out what is special about it. Write clues about the plant on one side of an index card, and draw and label its picture on the other. Meet with a group of classmates, and use the cards to play a plant-guessing game.

FOCUS SKILL: Predict Outcomes

As you read "My Side of the Mountain," you probably thought about, or made predictions about, what would happen to Sam Gribley next. You based your predictions on everything you knew about the story up to that point. Your thoughts may have run something like this:

Story Information
Sam needs to find food for himself, but it is hard work.

+

Story Information
He keeps at it and supplies himself with food.

+

Story Information
He starts digging a shelter, but the work is too hard.

=

Prediction
I predict that Sam will find another way to solve his problem, just as he found ways to get food.

Knowing what has happened before and using personal experience can help you predict how characters will act and what will happen next in a story.

Predicting outcomes as you read prepares you for new information. It's as if you've made file folders, or envelopes, in your head. Now you have places to put new information. As you discover new information, ask yourself, "Does this support my prediction?" If not, you might have to make a new prediction. Good readers make predictions all the time. Yet they are ready to rethink them when they receive new information.

Read the paragraph below. Then make a diagram like the one on page 352. Fill it in with information from the passage. Then make a prediction.

Aaron had not only seen Native American tepees, he'd been inside one. His sister had begged him to build one for her for months. Now her birthday was only two days away, and this was to be her gift. The supplies had cost him five weeks' allowance! He remembered the tree house he'd built last summer in the woods. It had been a struggle, but he had finished it, and it looked great!

WHAT HAVE YOU LEARNED?

1. Will Sam Gribley find shelter and survive in the wilderness? Make a prediction. Support it with information from the story and from your own experiences.

2. Think of a science project or an art project that didn't turn out the way you planned it. What information might have helped you predict the outcome?

TRY THIS • TRY THIS • TRY THIS

Predict how well Sam will adjust to living in the wilderness in the winter. Base your prediction on facts in the story. Keep in mind his personality, his food supply, and his shelter. Write your prediction in the middle of an idea web, and add supporting story facts in the outer circles. Compare your prediction with a classmate's.

Visit *The Learning Site!*
www.harcourtschool.com

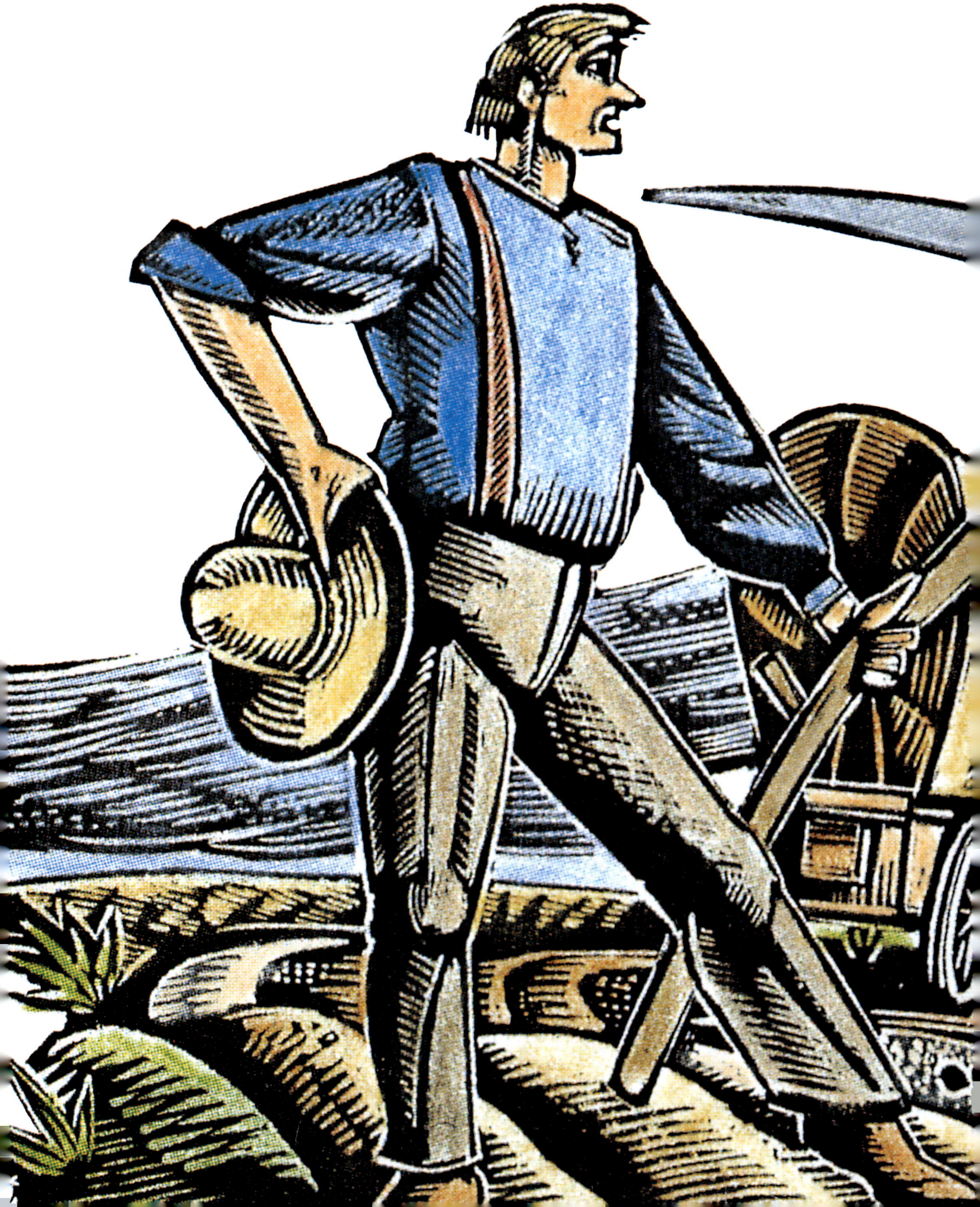

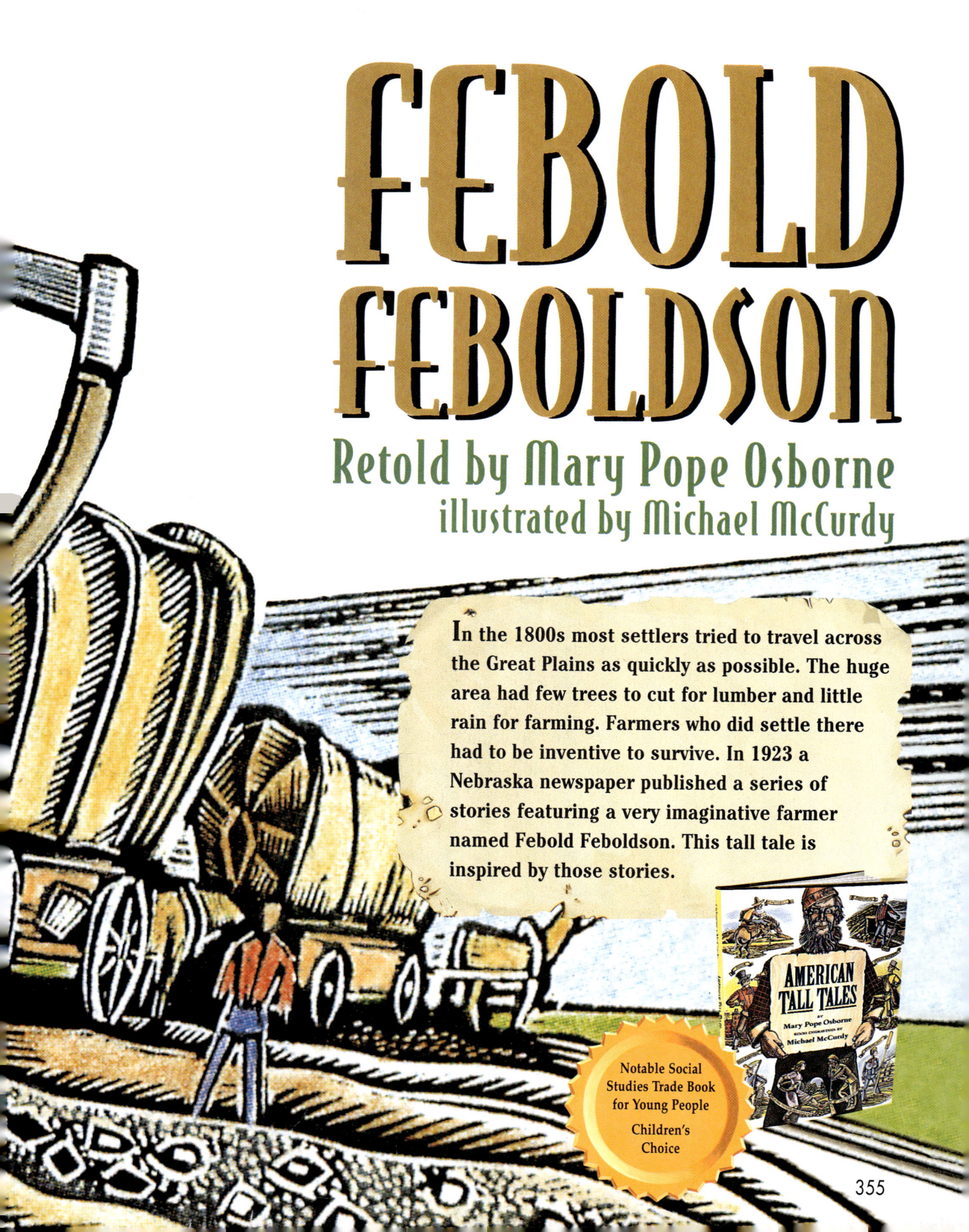

FEBOLD FEBOLDSON

Retold by Mary Pope Osborne
illustrated by Michael McCurdy

In the 1800s most settlers tried to travel across the Great Plains as quickly as possible. The huge area had few trees to cut for lumber and little rain for farming. Farmers who did settle there had to be inventive to survive. In 1923 a Nebraska newspaper published a series of stories featuring a very imaginative farmer named Febold Feboldson. This tall tale is inspired by those stories.

Notable Social Studies Trade Book for Young People

Children's Choice

After living on the Great Plains by himself for a year, a Swedish farmer named Febold Feboldson grew afraid that he might die of loneliness. As he watched wagon trains bump over the prairies on their way to California, he waved his straw hat and shouted, "Stay here! Live here!"

But Febold always got the same answer: "No, thanky. We're going to look for gold!"

Instead of giving up, the broad-shouldered, sunburned Swede sat down and cupped his jaw in his giant hand and tried to figure out a way to make the gold hunters settle near him on the plains. In three seconds Febold came up with about a hundred great ideas. But the idea that made him do a little dance was this: order a thousand goldfish from Peru.

Febold ordered the goldfish, and when they arrived, he dumped all of them in a lake near his sod shanty — the only lake on the whole prairie. Then the crafty farmer hid in the tall grass and waited for the prairie schooners to roll by.

It wasn't long before a small wagon train clattered over the hard-baked earth near Febold's farm.

"Look, look! Gold!" a pioneer woman shrieked when she saw something glittering in the sunlit lake.

Febold grinned as the pioneers jumped off their wagons and charged across the prairie. From the tall grass he watched the pioneers dipping their pans into the water. They chattered like magpies, and Febold's heart soared with joy. He saw wonderful times ahead, sharing his life with good neighbors.

But as the pioneers panned for gold, the terrible dry weather of the plains began to get to them. It was so hot, they were soon forced to jump into the lake to keep from drying up and blowing away altogether.

357

"Folks, this is a terrible place to live," said Olaf Swenson, the wagon master. "It's too hot and dry. It never rains. And we haven't found any gold in this lake all day."

"You're right, Olaf. Let's move on to California," said the others. With their tongues hanging out, they all ran back to the wagon train.

As the pioneers climbed aboard their wagons, Febold saw his precious dream of having neighbors start to evaporate. Before anyone could say giddy-yap, he jumped out of the grass and screamed, "*Wait!* Stay here tonight, neighbors, and I promise you some rain."

A tall order, but Febold was desperate. He thought and thought, until he came up with about a hundred great ideas. But the idea that made him do a little dance was this: build a big bonfire beside the lake.

The bonfire Febold built was so big and burned so hot that soon the water in the lake vaporized and formed clouds over the prairie. The clouds were so big and so heavy that when they rolled into one another, it started to rain. Buckets and buckets of rain!

The problem was, none of the rain hit the ground. Why? Because the air was so hot and so dry that the rain turned to steam before it even touched the land. And what happens when steam and dry land meet? Fog. So much fog covered the plains that the pioneers couldn't see a thing.

"This is awful," said Olaf, groping toward his wife, Anna.

"It sure is. Let's get out of here," said Anna.

But as they stumbled back toward their wagon, Febold shouted, "*Wait!* I'll get rid of the fog." Then he ran into his shanty and came out with a giant pair of clippers.

The pioneers gaped as Febold snipped the fog into long strips. Then they watched him bury the strips in his field. When all the fog was buried, the rain from the clouds crashed to the ground! And everyone shouted with joy.

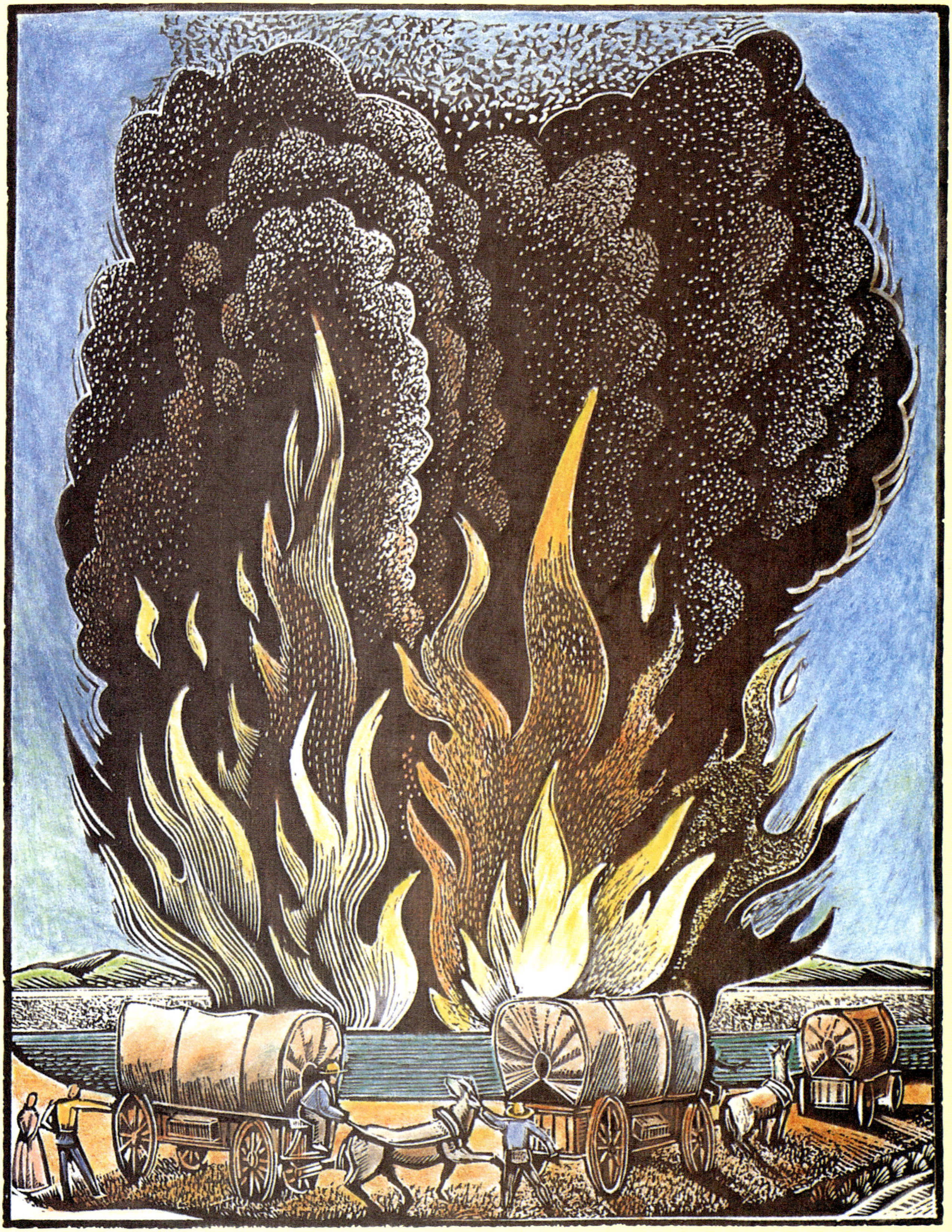

But then a silly thing happened — a thin piece of the fog seeped out of the ground and wafted through the air. When the clouds saw it, they ran away in fright — leaving the day right back where it had begun: unbearably hot and dry.

"We can't live here without rain!" cried Olaf.

"*Wait!*" said Febold. "I'll get more rain. Just give me a minute to think." He cupped his large jaw in his giant hand and thought and thought — until suddenly he came up with a plan.

"Noise!" he announced.

"Noise?" asked Anna.

"Didn't you ever notice it always rains when there's a lot of noise? Fourth of July fireworks? Parades? Battles? Outdoor dances?"

"Well . . ." said Olaf.

"And nothing makes more noise than *frogs*!" Febold said.

The pioneers rolled their eyes at each other, but before they could say anything, Febold ran out into the fields, gathering all the frogs that lived on his farm. Thousands of them! Frogs of all sizes and dispositions!

His plan was not as simple as it looked, though, for he soon discovered that frogs make noise only when they're good and wet. So he grabbed one cheerful-looking frog and whispered in its tiny ear, "It's raining, it's raining, it's raining."

Febold kept this up until he had completely hypnotized the frog. And when it started to croak, the others began to croak too, and soon every single frog was singing its heart out — and the rains came!

As the rains fell, Olaf, Anna, and the others jumped for joy and cried, "Yes! We'll stay on the plains and build our farms! Miracles happen in this land!"

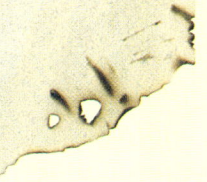

But disaster was just around the corner. The next day the pioneers discovered that they couldn't get their fence posts in the ground because the soil was still hard.

"If we can't fence in our properties, how in the world can we tend to our horses, cows, sheep, oxen, dogs, chickens, and children?" asked Olaf. "We can't stay in this terrible place."

Oh, for goodness' sakes, thought Febold. But he just smiled and said, "*Wait.* And I'll teach you an old prairie trick."

He gathered all the pioneers together for a lesson. "This is how you make and keep postholes on the Great Plains," he said.

"One: Bore a bunch of holes in the hard ground. Two: Let the holes freeze all winter. Three: In the spring, before the ground thaws, dig up the holes. Four: When the frozen holes come out of the ground, slap coats of varnish on them. Five: Slip the varnished holes back into the ground. Six: Insert fence posts."

Well, you might say that this was the beginning of a true change of heart for the pioneers. They were so intrigued with Febold's posthole procedure, they were willing to wait for winter to come to try it out. Before they knew it, Febold was teaching them how to make sod shanties with bricks of matted prairie turf, how to grow corn and wheat, how to plow the barren land, and how to fight grasshoppers, tornadoes, dust storms, and prairie fires.

Olaf and Anna grew quite content with their new life. As they walked through the tall, whispering grass in the twilight, they watched the goldfish slapping the dark waters under the moon. They listened to the frog choruses practicing their rain songs. And they smiled at Febold Feboldson as he waved from his shanty and said, "Evening, neighbors."

Think About It

1. How does Febold Feboldson get people to live on the Great Plains with him?

2. What is the most unbelievable part of the story? Why?

3. How would the story change if the author told it as nonfiction instead of as a tall tale?

ACTIVITIES

Febold in Gold Country

PRESENT A SCENE Work in a small group to create a scene in which Febold joins settlers in California's gold country. For example, you might invent a humorous way for Febold and his friends to find gold. Use details from the story to make Febold's personality come to life. Act out your scene for the class.

Making Connections

WRITE A PARAGRAPH Imagine that Febold and all the characters from the folktale and the fables are in a contest to determine who is the cleverest. As the judge, use evidence from the stories to help you decide. Write a paragraph naming a winner and a runner-up and explaining how you decided.

WHO INVE
THE KID

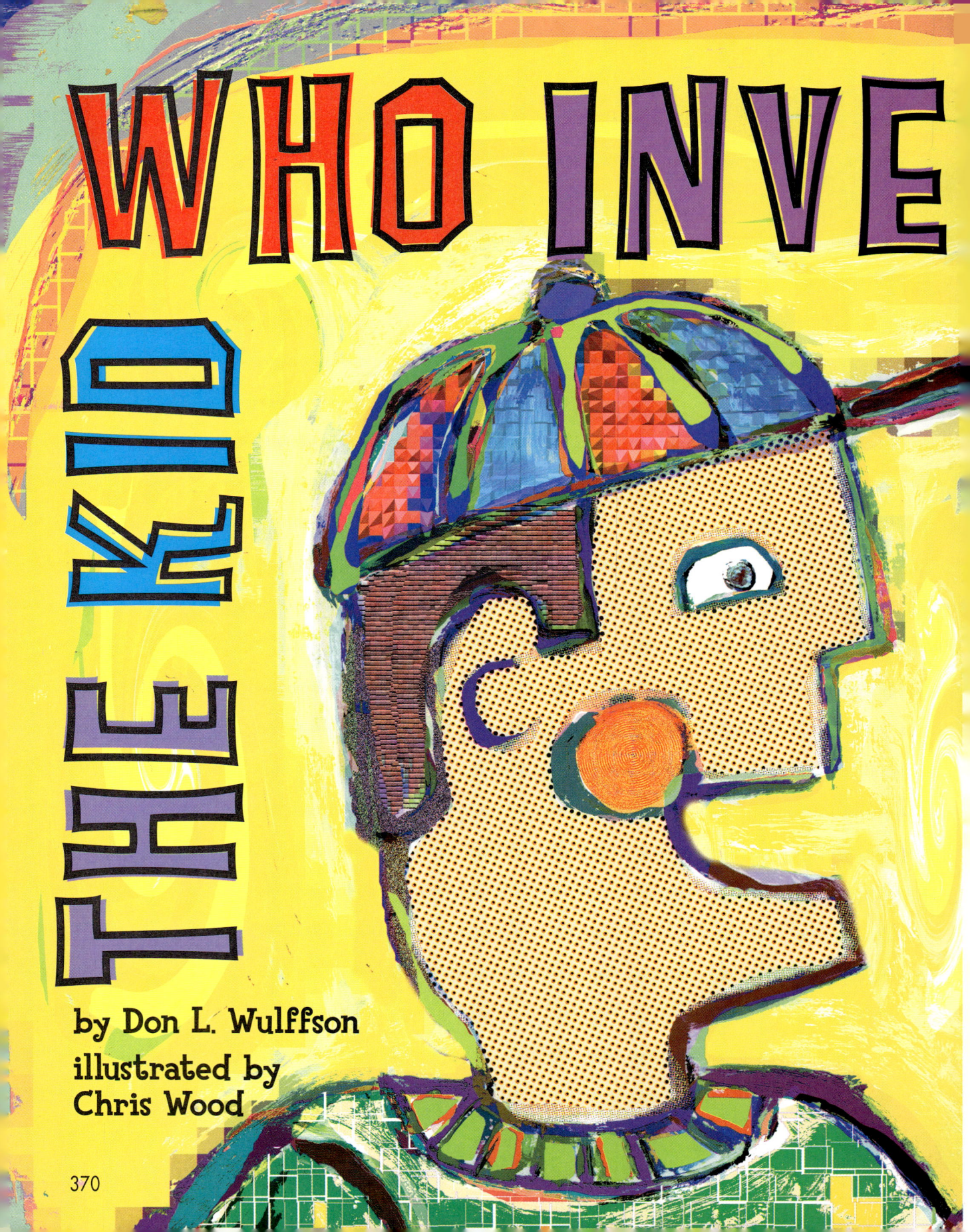

by Don L. Wulffson
illustrated by
Chris Wood

NTED THE POPSICLE

Many people take everyday items like the flashlight and the paper cup for granted. But they would miss these items if they weren't available. Who invented these useful things? How did the inventors get their ideas? The answers may surprise you.

Award-Winning Author

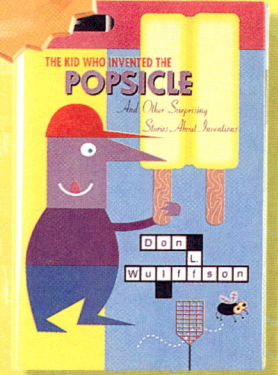

THE KID WHO INVENTED THE
POPSICLE
And Other Surprising Stories About Inventions
Don L Wulffson

POPSICLE

One day in the winter of 1905, eleven-year-old Frank Epperson mixed a jar of powdered soda pop mix and water. Accidentally, he left the mix on his back porch that night. The next morning Frank found the stuff frozen, with the stirring stick standing straight up. Pulling out the frozen soda pop, stick and all, he realized he had accidentally invented something pretty good.

Calling it the "Epperson Icicle" (which he soon changed to "Epsicle"), the next summer he made them in the family icebox and sold them around the neighborhood at five cents apiece. Later, he renamed his product the "Popsicle," since he'd made it with soda pop.

CHEWING GUM

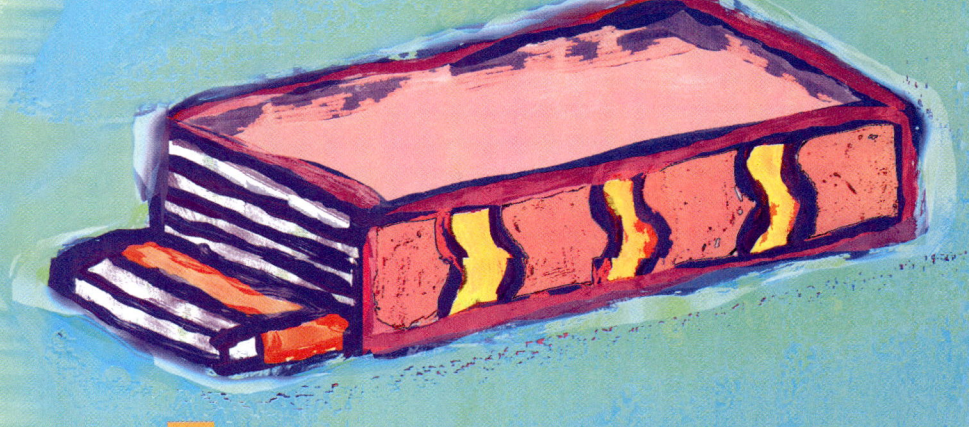

For centuries, the Mayans of Mexico chomped on *chicle*, the dried sap of the sapodilla tree.

In 1845, after he was defeated by the Americans in Texas, Mexican General Santa Anna was exiled to New York. Like many of his countrymen, Santa Anna chewed chicle. One day he introduced it to inventor Charles Adams, who began experimenting with it as a substitute for rubber. Adams tried to make toys, masks, and rain boots out of chicle, but every experiment failed. Sitting in his workshop one day, tired and discouraged, he popped a piece of surplus stock into his mouth. Chewing away, the idea suddenly hit him to add flavoring to the chicle. Shortly after that, he opened the world's first chewing gum factory.

Gum caught on quickly with Americans. Many doctors, however, said it was unhealthy. In 1869, one wrote that chewing gum would "exhaust the salivary glands and cause the intestines to stick together." Despite such weird warnings, people kept chewing. Today, the average American chews 200 sticks a year.

FLYSWATTER

In 1905, schoolteacher Frank H. Rose of Topeka, Kansas, made a fly-smashing device by attaching a square of wire screen to the end of a yardstick. Initially, Rose called his invention the "fly bat," but changed it to "flyswatter" at the suggestion of a friend. The holes in the wire screen were essential because a fly can sense the air pressure of a solid object, such as a rolled-up newspaper, coming at it.

FLASHLIGHT

The flashlight began as a novelty item called the "electric flowerpot." It consisted of a slender battery in a tube with a light bulb at one end. The tube rose up through the center of a flowerpot and illuminated an artificial plant.

When the novelty item bombed, the inventor found himself with a huge overstock. Attempting to salvage a little of his investment, he separated the light and tube (which was made of cardboard) from the pot. He was soon selling what he dubbed the "Portable Electric Light"—and made a fortune.

BARBIE DOLL

A little hard to believe, but the Barbie Doll started out as a human being! She was Barbara Handler, the daughter of Ruth and Elliot Handler, cofounders of the Mattel Toy Company. The idea for the teenage fashion doll came to Mrs. Handler one day when she noticed that her preteen daughter, Barbie, was losing interest in playing with baby dolls. Instead, she preferred paper cutouts of young women in fashion magazines, even changing their attire by snipping and gluing on changes of clothing.

Barbie Dolls were introduced at the New York Toy Fair in 1959. To date, more than 500 million have been sold.

By the way, the Handlers had a son. His name was Ken.

BLUE JEANS

Levi Strauss was a tailor who arrived in San Francisco at the age of seventeen during the Gold Rush of the 1850s. Levi noticed that the miners needed tougher pants, ones that would hold up to the rough work they were doing. Seeing a business opportunity, he stitched tent canvas into overalls. Though coarse and stiff, they held up so well they were soon in great demand.

Not entirely happy with canvas, Levi started using a new fabric, one that was much softer but almost as tough and sturdy. Weavers in the Italian city of Genoa, where the fabric was made called it "genes." Strauss changed the spelling to "jeans." To minimize stains, he found that it was best to dye them indigo blue.

Today, "blue jeans" are the best-selling type of pants in the Western world.

PAPER CUP

The story of the paper cup begins in 1908. A young inventor, Hugh Moore, produced a vending machine to dispense a cup of pure, chilled drinking water at a penny a serving.

To Moore's disappointment, nobody was interested in paying for a cup of water. At that time, people drank water out of a bucket, using a common tin dipper. Because the dipper was used by the sick and the healthy alike, and was seldom washed or sterilized, it was a real health hazard. By chance, Moore met a rich man who greatly disliked the unsanitary dippers, and who, after one meeting, decided to invest $200,000, not in Moore's water-vending machines, but just in his paper cups. Overnight, Health Kups were invented.

Moore's office happened to be in the same building as the Dixie Doll Company. He liked the name, and in 1919 changed Health Kups to Dixie Cups.

BALL-POINT PEN

In the 1930s, in Hungary, Ladislao Biro was getting fed up with his old-fashioned fountain pen. He was tired of the way it leaked and had to be endlessly refilled. Fiddling around in his workshop, Biro filled a pen with printer's ink and on the tip of it he fashioned a little ball that picked up more ink as it rolled.

In England, Biro helped set up a factory to manufacture "high-altitude, nonleaking writing sticks" for the British Air Force. The factory was eventually taken over by Bic, a French company, which developed an even better and cheaper throw-away pen.

In America, following World War II, Milton Reynolds invented his own version of the ball-point pen. As a sales gimmick, he advertised it as the "pen that writes underwater." To attract customers, he arranged a demonstration in the display window of a department store. While sitting in a tank of water, a demonstrator scribbled with a ball-point pen on white plastic. In one day, nearly 10,000 had been sold! The price: $12.50 apiece.

The calculator was invented by a nineteen-year-old French boy named Blaise Pascal way back in the year 1642. Blaise made it to help his father in his work.

The man was a clerk, and all day long he had to do a tremendous number of mathematical calculations. The boy's invention consisted of a wooden box with sixteen dials on it. By turning the dials, one could do simple addition and subtraction very quickly.

CALCULATOR

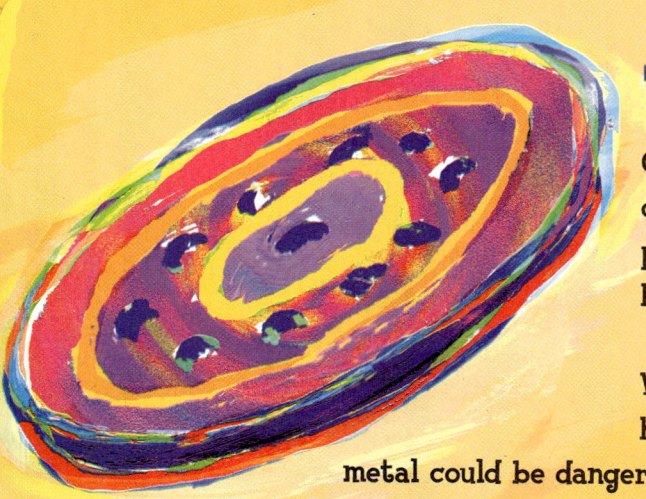

The Frisbee is named after the Frisbie Pie Company, a Connecticut bakery that first opened for business during the 1870s. For fun, people tossed around the empty pie tins, which had the name "Frisbie" embossed on the bottom.

In the early 1950s, a man by the name of Walter Morrison devised a metal tossing toy he called the "Flying Saucer." Soon, because metal could be dangerous, he changed the metal to plastic. Then he changed the name. Morrison, at the time, was living in California, but recalling his younger days in Connecticut where he and his friends had tossed around pie tins from the local bakery, he decided to name his invention the "Frisbee."

FRISBEE

BAND-AID

In the 1920s, the Johnson & Johnson Company was in the business of manufacturing large cotton-and-gauze bandages for hospitals and soldiers wounded on the battlefield. One of the employees of the company, a man named Earle Dickson, had a wife who was very accident-prone, frequently cutting or burning herself in the kitchen. Though the injuries were painful and needed tending to, they were far too small to require the company's large sterile dressings. In a moment of inspiration, Dickson cut a little patch of gauze, placed it at the center of an adhesive strip—and invented the Band-Aid.

Johnson & Johnson was soon marketing them, but sales were poor. In a clever advertising gimmick to popularize their new product, the company distributed an unlimited number of free Band-Aids to Boy Scout troops across the country. Sales skyrocketed. The company estimates that since the product was introduced in 1921 more than 120 *billion* Band-Aids have been sold worldwide.

POTATO CHIPS

In the summer of 1853, American Indian George Crum was a chef at a fancy restaurant in New York. One guest ordered French fries, which at the time were flat wedges of fried potatoes. The man kept sending back his fries, complaining that they were too thick. Annoyed, Crum decided to play a trick on the guest by producing French fries that were ridiculously thin and crisp. Instead of being angry with Crum's little practical joke, the guest was ecstatic over the browned, paper-thin fries. Soon "potato chips" had become a specialty of the restaurant.

In the 1920s, a salesman named Herman Lay began traveling the country selling bags of potato chips out of the trunk of his car. Within a few years, Lay was rich and Americans everywhere were eating the crisp, salty snack that had originated as a practical joke.

Think About It

1. Why do you think the author chose these particular inventions to write about? Give examples to support your answer.

2. Which person in the selection do you think was the most inventive? Why?

3. What important traits do the inventors in the selection share?

MEET THE AUTHOR

DON L. WULFFSON

Don L. Wulffson was inspired to write about inventions when his daughter Jennifer was young. The author says, "She started asking me how just about everything in the world came to be. 'Where do paper cups come from? Who invented bicycles? Who thought up crayons?' I told her what little I knew, and promised to find out the rest."

Wulffson has written stories, plays, poems, nonfiction, and mysteries for young readers. Through his books, the author shares his curiosity about the world. He says, "I have always been intrigued by both the past and the future. I enjoy exploring how the world came to be and trying to anticipate what it might someday become."

Visit *The Learning Site!*
www.harcourtschool.com

ACTIVITIES

RESPONSE

ODDBALL INVENTIONS

DRAW A DIAGRAM The flashlight began its life as part of a now-forgotten invention, the electric flowerpot. Choose a common object in the classroom or at home. With a partner, brainstorm ideas for turning that item into a new invention. Draw a diagram, and give your invention a catchy name. Tell how your invention fits the theme "Creative Solutions."

MEET AN INVENTOR

WRITE A LETTER Review the selection, and decide which of the inventors interests you the most. Write a letter to that person. Ask questions about the development of his or her invention, and tell how the invention has affected your life.

MORE THAN JUST FACTS

RESEARCH AN INVENTION
Choose an invention that is now commonly used, such as the washing machine. Use an encyclopedia to find out when the item was invented. In your report, tell whether you think the item is a necessity or a convenience.

INVENTOR ROUNDTABLE

ROLE-PLAY INVENTORS
With two other students, role-play a meeting of inventors from the selection. Prepare for your roles by reading again about your inventors. Then sit around a table and ask one another questions about your lives and your inventions.

FOCUS SKILL

Draw Conclusions

Part of the fun of reading is figuring out something that the author does not directly state. By using information in a selection and what you already know, you can understand why something happens or why a character says or does something, even if reasons are not given. When you figure out something about a situation or a character, you are **drawing a conclusion**.

In "The Kid Who Invented the Popsicle," you read about inventors Charles Adams and Frank Epperson. Combining what you read about these inventors and what you already know leads you to conclusions about inventions. Your thoughts may have taken the following path:

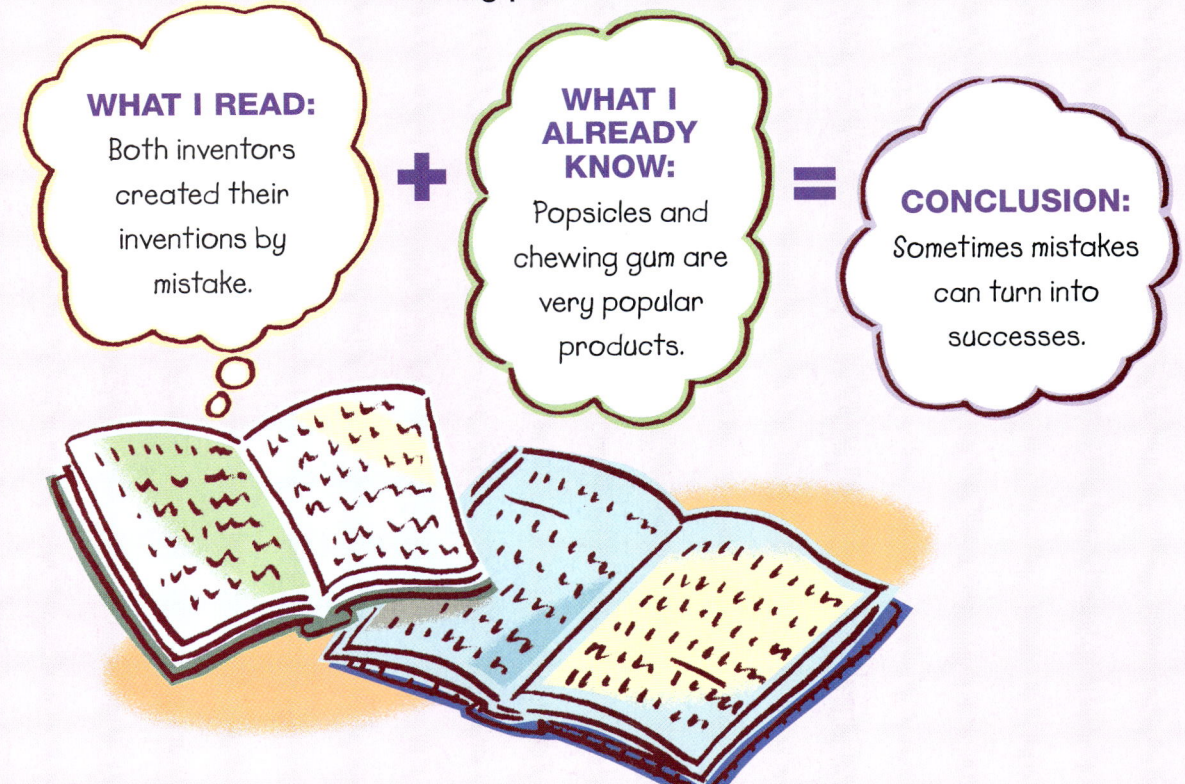

WHAT I READ: Both inventors created their inventions by mistake.

+

WHAT I ALREADY KNOW: Popsicles and chewing gum are very popular products.

=

CONCLUSION: Sometimes mistakes can turn into successes.

386

As you read, you draw conclusions about a character's feelings, motivations, personality traits, and abilities. You can also draw conclusions about why something has happened. Read the following paragraph from the selection. What conclusion can you draw about the success of the flashlight?

Attempting to salvage a little of his investment, he [the inventor] separated the light and tube (which was made of cardboard) from the pot. He was soon selling what he dubbed the "Portable Electric Light" — and made a fortune.

WHAT HAVE YOU LEARNED?

1. What conclusion can you draw about why the Barbie Doll is popular? Give details from the selection that helped you draw your conclusion.

2. You are late for the school bus. You arrive at the stop, and all of the other students are there. What conclusion can you draw? What leads you to draw this conclusion?

TRY THIS • TRY THIS • TRY THIS

Think of a sports figure you consider persistent — a person who has "stick-to-itiveness." What has the person said or done that helps you draw your conclusion? Use a web to jot down the person's words and actions.

Visit *The Learning Site!*
www.harcourtschool.com

387

A Do-It-

Yourself Project

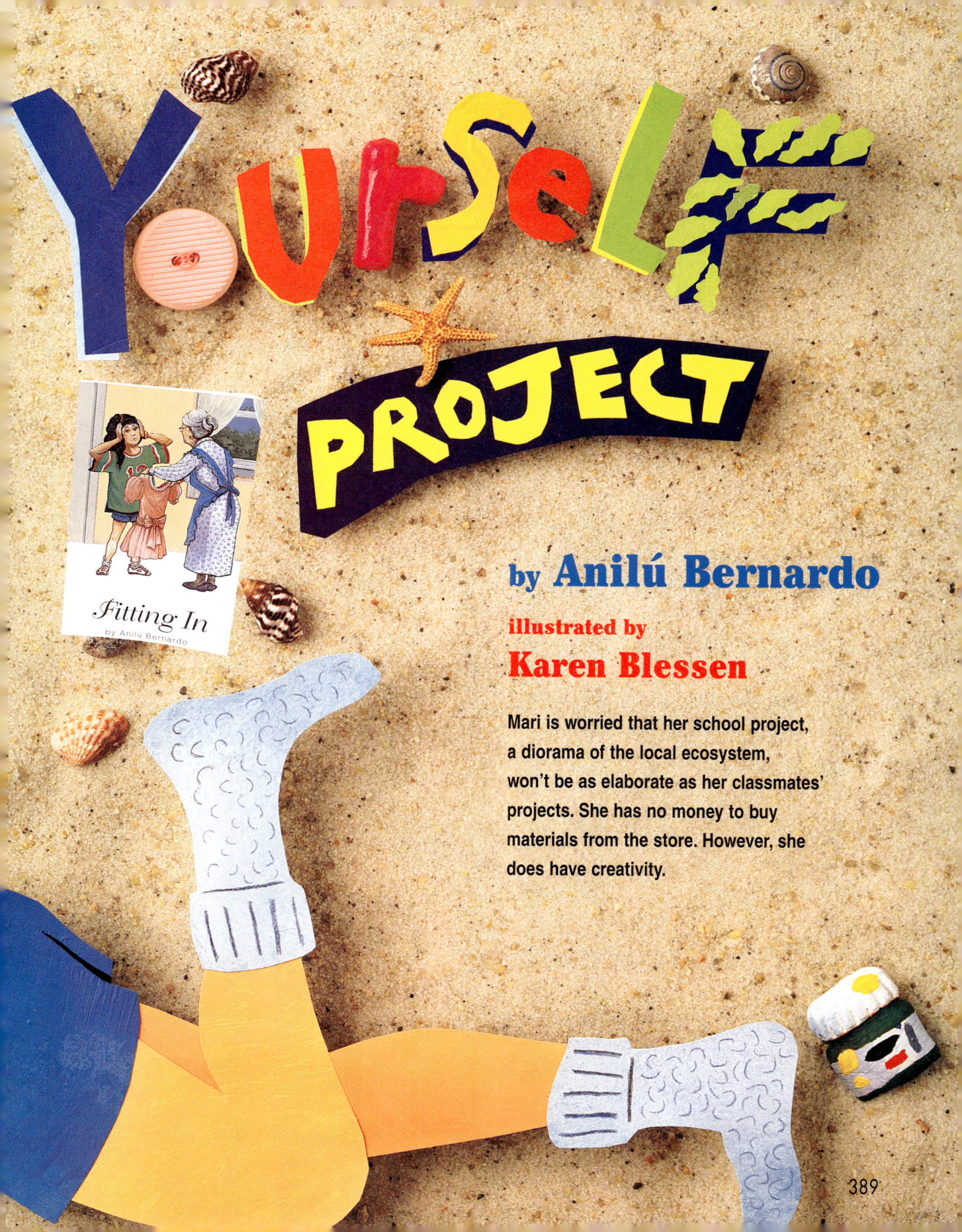

by **Anilú Bernardo**

illustrated by **Karen Blessen**

Mari is worried that her school project, a diorama of the local ecosystem, won't be as elaborate as her classmates' projects. She has no money to buy materials from the store. However, she does have creativity.

The next day, Mari had a chance to visit the library during her English class. Her English teacher usually let four students go to the library during the last fifteen minutes of class. There, she opened a heavy dictionary and searched under 'D.'

"di-o-ram-a: noun. A scene reproduced in three dimensions by placing objects, figures, etc. in front of a painted background."

Finally, she had an answer! Mrs. Graham wanted them to make a miniature scene of the life of the bay. She had to show how each living thing was dependent on another for food by making little models of them. After all the worry, Mari felt a flood of relief. But the work was still ahead. Now, she had to decide how she would do it. She had never seen a diorama before.

When she got up to put the dictionary away, Mrs. Frank, the librarian, asked if Mari needed help. Mari had always turned down her sweet offers, but this time she said yes.

"I have to make a diorama for my Natural Science class," Mari told her. "I have never made one. I have never even seen one," she laughed nervously.

"I have photographs of some that students made in years before. Would you like to see them?" Mrs. Frank led her to her office and took five pictures from her desk drawer.

They were beautiful small scenes of landscapes. One showed a river with a cow pasture on one side and a sugar cane field on the other. The river flowed into a marshy area in which the plants were shown to be dying. A girl glowing with pride and holding a red ribbon stood by the project. In another photo, a pimply-faced boy held a diorama of sand dunes with sea oats growing on them. The ocean was made out of clear dark-blue cellophane. Each project had won a ribbon.

"I'd like to show you my favorite one," said Mrs. Frank. She opened the door to a storage case. "This scene shows the daily life of the Seminoles living in the Everglades."

Mrs. Frank brought the diorama out and set it on a table. "I like it very much because it was made with natural materials."

On a sandy island in the middle of the box, there was a small *chickee* hut, the palm-frond house used by the Native American tribe of South Florida. It was made out of reeds and grasses. A tiny wooden canoe, resembling the kind the Seminoles carved from a single log, rested on the painted water. Straw dolls were dressed in colorful calico clothes Seminole women take pride in making.

"The student made the dolls, too?" Mari asked, amazed.

"No, I think he bought them at a souvenir shop. But he made everything else. He even carved the canoe." Mrs. Frank ran a finger down the side of the rough, miniature boat.

"It's beautiful!" Mari exclaimed. "What kind of box did he use?" She walked around the table to view the back of the four-sided stage.

"Just about any grocery-store carton would do. You can cut out the top and one side and paint a background scene on the in—" The loud sound of the bell interrupted Mrs. Frank's words. She didn't fight the ringing. She waited quietly for it to end. "What is your topic?"

"The food chain in Biscayne Bay," Mari said. She anxiously glanced at the other students, who picked up their books and were moving on to other classes.

"Would you like me to find some books on the subject? I can have them ready for you after school," Mrs. Frank asked, realizing Mari had to go.

"Yes, that would really help me." Mari thanked her and ran out of the library.

Sitting on her bed that afternoon, Mari leafed through the three books Mrs. Frank had selected for her. One was a biology book which had a chapter on food chains. Another was a book on marine life of southern Florida. The third book showed examples of three-dimensional models and directions for making them. Mari's mind raced with ideas on how to design her project. She could buy crinkly cellophane for the light-green water of the bay. And she'd get the beautiful, shiny fish she'd seen at the museum store when they took a school trip. The handmade fish were expensive, but now she had a valid reason to buy them.

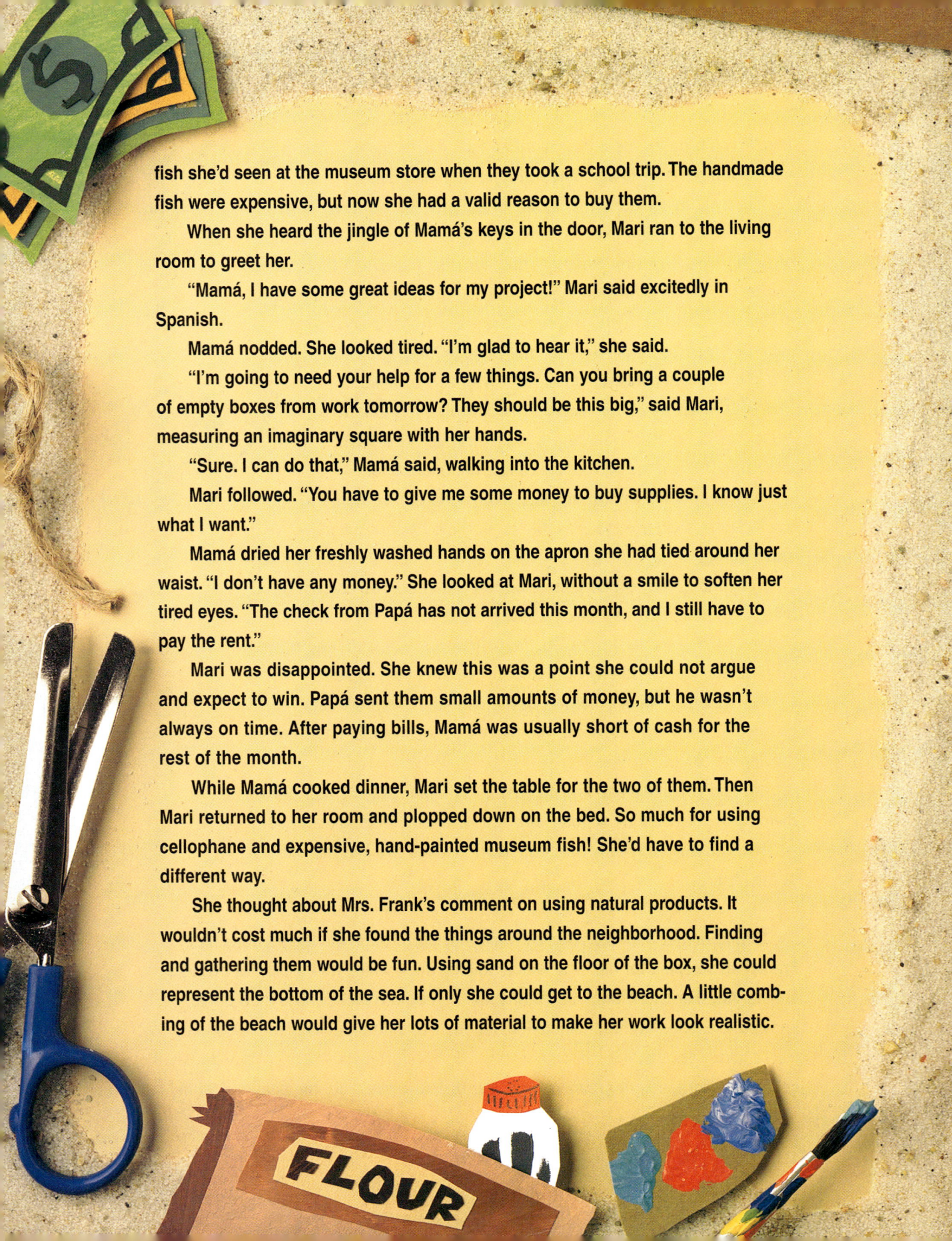

When she heard the jingle of Mamá's keys in the door, Mari ran to the living room to greet her.

"Mamá, I have some great ideas for my project!" Mari said excitedly in Spanish.

Mamá nodded. She looked tired. "I'm glad to hear it," she said.

"I'm going to need your help for a few things. Can you bring a couple of empty boxes from work tomorrow? They should be this big," said Mari, measuring an imaginary square with her hands.

"Sure. I can do that," Mamá said, walking into the kitchen.

Mari followed. "You have to give me some money to buy supplies. I know just what I want."

Mamá dried her freshly washed hands on the apron she had tied around her waist. "I don't have any money." She looked at Mari, without a smile to soften her tired eyes. "The check from Papá has not arrived this month, and I still have to pay the rent."

Mari was disappointed. She knew this was a point she could not argue and expect to win. Papá sent them small amounts of money, but he wasn't always on time. After paying bills, Mamá was usually short of cash for the rest of the month.

While Mamá cooked dinner, Mari set the table for the two of them. Then Mari returned to her room and plopped down on the bed. So much for using cellophane and expensive, hand-painted museum fish! She'd have to find a different way.

She thought about Mrs. Frank's comment on using natural products. It wouldn't cost much if she found the things around the neighborhood. Finding and gathering them would be fun. Using sand on the floor of the box, she could represent the bottom of the sea. If only she could get to the beach. A little combing of the beach would give her lots of material to make her work look realistic.

She opened the book on making models and browsed through it. A section of the book had instructions for making figures out of homemade clay. A portion of flour, a portion of salt, and a little water made a molding dough. Perhaps she could use this dough to shape sea creatures. She had all the ingredients at home. But she would still need paint for the animals and for the background. And this would require money.

Breaking the silence at dinner, Mari brought up the diorama again. "I need you to take me to the beach. Can we go this weekend?"

"*Mi amor*, I work six days a week. How can I spend my only day off at the beach?" Mamá looked at her lovingly, but her eyes were droopy. Mari knew she was tired.

"But Mamá, I need to collect a few things for my project. It won't cost us a thing. And you can help me. It will be fun!"

"Oh, Mari," was all Mamá said as she took another bite of *bistec*, the thin Cuban steak smothered with fried onions. From her tone, Mari knew Mamá was softening.

"We could find some sand for the bottom and some shells, and seaweed, and twigs . . . I promise we can go home right after." She gave her mother an orphaned-puppy-dog look that said, *Take pity on me*. "You told me to figure out a way on my own."

Mamá smiled. "Very well. We'll take a little time Sunday afternoon."

"There is one thing I will still need to buy. Poster paints," Mari said, breaking a small piece of crusty Cuban bread. "They sell them at your store. They're not that much money and with your discount . . ."

Mamá nodded her head and smiled. Mari could tell she was giving in to her request. "There's four dollars in my wallet. You can have three. Meet me at the store tomorrow and we'll see what you need."

---★---

The diorama was taking shape. The store manager where Mamá worked had given Mari a sturdy carton that had held boxed cookies. He even helped her cut off the sides she didn't need.

Mari was pleased with the paints she'd bought. Although only four colors had been in the package, Mari had a knack for mixing them to get all the shades she wanted. She painted a background divided horizontally into sky, water surface, and underwater levels. Using different shades of soft blue and clear light green, it was easy to tell the sea apart from the sky with its puffy, white clouds.

The trip to the beach had been a success. Mari found many colorful shells and cut small bits of sea grass and weeds that had dried up above the surf line. Mari's enthusiasm spilled over to Mamá, who kept her eyes lowered to the sandy beach looking for useful things. Mamá discovered small bits of coral and sponges that had washed up on shore. She handed Mari a large paper cup to bring back sand. Mari was glad Mamá had taken the time to go to the beach and relax. She could tell Mamá had a good time.

Maybe Mrs. Graham was right after all. Making a diorama was turning out to be fun!

After school, she opened her locker and decided which books she would need for homework. As she filled her backpack, Erica and Cathy, the two girls from Natural Science class, came up to their lockers.

"My diorama is looking great!" Cathy said. "We used iridescent paper to show the water and plaster to make the shore. Wait till you see it!"

"My dad is helping me," Erica said. "He takes an underwater camera when he goes diving. He gave me great pictures to use as our background. Maybe I should say I'm helping him!"

Great! Mari thought. Erica is getting help from her father. Her diorama will look perfect, like an adult worked on it. She continued to listen, pretending to be busily sorting through the junk in her locker.

"My dad built a wooden box to display my diorama," said Jake, the smart kid, who had now joined them at the wall of lockers. "He's really handy and has lots of ideas for it. I guess our project will be very scientific."

"Well, my mom is an artist. She's giving me a hand, too," Cathy told them. "If she weren't, my diorama would look awful! I'm not handy at all."

It seemed like everyone's parents were getting in on the act. It wasn't fair. Mari had no one to help her make hers.

"No, I'm not artistic either," Erica told Cathy. "Mine would look homemade without my dad's help. I'd probably just have sand and a few shells."

Mari was devastated. Hers looked homemade! It was decorated with sand and a few shells, just as Cathy had said.

"How's yours coming along, Mari?" Erica asked, turning to her.

The question took Mari by surprise. She had fallen deep into her sad thoughts, regretting her choice of materials and angry that her father was not around to help her.

"Have you started working on it?" Jake asked her.

"Yes. I've been working on it. It's coming along fine," Mari said, her Spanish accent coming through her words and annoying her. She padlocked the door to her locker and picked up her backpack. "I've got to go now."

The school library was almost empty after class the next day. Shyly, Mari approached Mrs. Frank. The librarian put her book down and looked up at her over her reading glasses.

"Hello, Mari. Did you find the books useful?" she asked, smiling sweetly.

"Yes. Thank you. I'm finished with them now." Although Mari was grateful, she could not bring herself to smile. She was too disappointed in her work.

"What did you decide to do about your diorama?" Mrs. Frank questioned her with interest.

"I'm using things found in nature, like you said." Mari saw Mrs. Frank's face light up. But Mari didn't think she had cause to feel proud.

"That sounds like an excellent choice," Mrs. Frank said.

"Well, I'm afraid it wasn't." Mari hung her head. "All the other kids have their parents helping them. My mother can't help me. She hardly speaks English and doesn't understand what the teacher wants. My father moved away. My diorama will look like a kindergartner made it!"

Mrs. Frank removed her glasses and set them on her desk. She took her time to speak, and for a moment Mari thought she had nothing to say. Then the soft-spoken librarian asked, "Why don't you tell me what materials you used?"

"I got beach sand for the bottom of the bay and scattered a few shells and bits of coral in it." Mari examined her fingernails nervously. "To make it look realistic, I put dried sea grass growing from the bottom of the sea. I found some twigs, that I glued to the shallow end, to represent red mangrove. The roots reach into the salt water. I cut tiny leaves from bits of green gift wrap and glued them to the tops of the twigs."

"So far, it sounds wonderful!" said Mrs. Frank.

"I know, but the others are using fancy paints and pictures, and even special wooden boxes instead of grocery-store cartons. My mom says we don't have money to spare for such things."

"Well, it doesn't matter what you use. The teacher will be looking for the amount of care each student puts into her work," Mrs. Frank said, looking into Mari's sad, brown eyes. "What are you using for the animals?"

Mari reached in her book bag and pulled out a small box held together with a rubber band. She opened it and took out a cotton-wrapped figure. It was a little, white fish, unpainted and delicate.

"I made these out of dough, from the recipe in the book you gave me." Mari watched Mrs. Frank for a reaction to her work.

Mrs. Frank took the little fish in her hand gently. She put her reading glasses back on and examined it. "Why, you've carved out little circles for the eyes and tiny half moons for scales. You've even scraped little lines down the length of the fins," Mrs. Frank said, clearly impressed.

Mari smiled. "I used a pin from my mother's sewing basket and carved out the lines and curves while the dough was soft." She removed the cotton from a few other figures and set each one on Mrs. Frank's desk.

"Let's see. You've made bigger fish and a tiny crab." The librarian looked the dough figures over carefully.

"Well, the little crab has no legs yet," Mari said, laughing at the little white shell in Mrs. Frank's hand. "I'm going to make them out of soft, thin wire that I found among my dad's tools. I might even paint it with pink nail polish."

Mrs. Frank nodded her head and smiled. "And this bird is beautiful!" She pointed to the spread wings, too afraid to take the delicate figure in her hand.

"That's an osprey," said Mari proudly. "They hunt for fish as they fly above the bay. I left a ceiling on my display box so I could hang a bird from it."

Mrs. Frank shook her head with disbelief. "Your work is wonderful!"

Mari thanked her. She raised her shoulders, still unsure of herself. "Well, I still have to paint the animals. I hope they look as realistic when I finish."

Mrs. Frank opened her desk drawer. She took out a small bottle and handed it to Mari. "See if you'd like to put glitter on the sides of the fish. It will make them look like the summer sun is reflecting off their scales."

"Thank you. This is great!" Mari shook the silver dust happily. "Maybe I can mix it with the paint I use."

Mrs. Frank helped her wrap the dough creatures back in their protective cotton coats. "You know, Mari," the librarian said, "I wouldn't worry about the work the other students are doing. It seems to me, you're doing a great job all by yourself."

Soon, the big day arrived. Mrs. Graham and Mrs. Frank had arranged tables in the library into a large rectangle. The students brought their projects in the morning and set them up for the judges. They would go to classes and return later in the day, after the dioramas had been examined and judged.

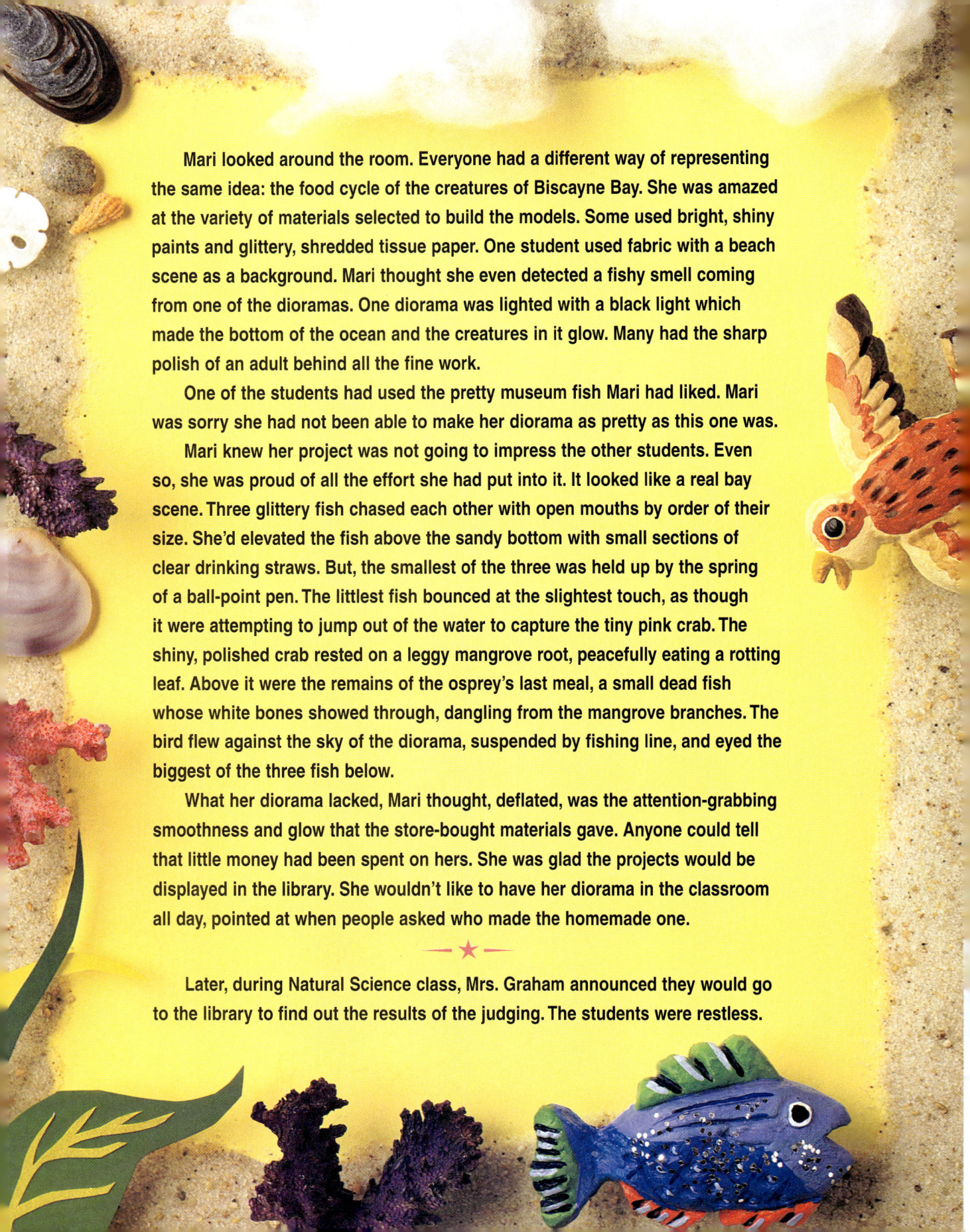

Mari looked around the room. Everyone had a different way of representing the same idea: the food cycle of the creatures of Biscayne Bay. She was amazed at the variety of materials selected to build the models. Some used bright, shiny paints and glittery, shredded tissue paper. One student used fabric with a beach scene as a background. Mari thought she even detected a fishy smell coming from one of the dioramas. One diorama was lighted with a black light which made the bottom of the ocean and the creatures in it glow. Many had the sharp polish of an adult behind all the fine work.

One of the students had used the pretty museum fish Mari had liked. Mari was sorry she had not been able to make her diorama as pretty as this one was.

Mari knew her project was not going to impress the other students. Even so, she was proud of all the effort she had put into it. It looked like a real bay scene. Three glittery fish chased each other with open mouths by order of their size. She'd elevated the fish above the sandy bottom with small sections of clear drinking straws. But, the smallest of the three was held up by the spring of a ball-point pen. The littlest fish bounced at the slightest touch, as though it were attempting to jump out of the water to capture the tiny pink crab. The shiny, polished crab rested on a leggy mangrove root, peacefully eating a rotting leaf. Above it were the remains of the osprey's last meal, a small dead fish whose white bones showed through, dangling from the mangrove branches. The bird flew against the sky of the diorama, suspended by fishing line, and eyed the biggest of the three fish below.

What her diorama lacked, Mari thought, deflated, was the attention-grabbing smoothness and glow that the store-bought materials gave. Anyone could tell that little money had been spent on hers. She was glad the projects would be displayed in the library. She wouldn't like to have her diorama in the classroom all day, pointed at when people asked who made the homemade one.

———★———

Later, during Natural Science class, Mrs. Graham announced they would go to the library to find out the results of the judging. The students were restless.

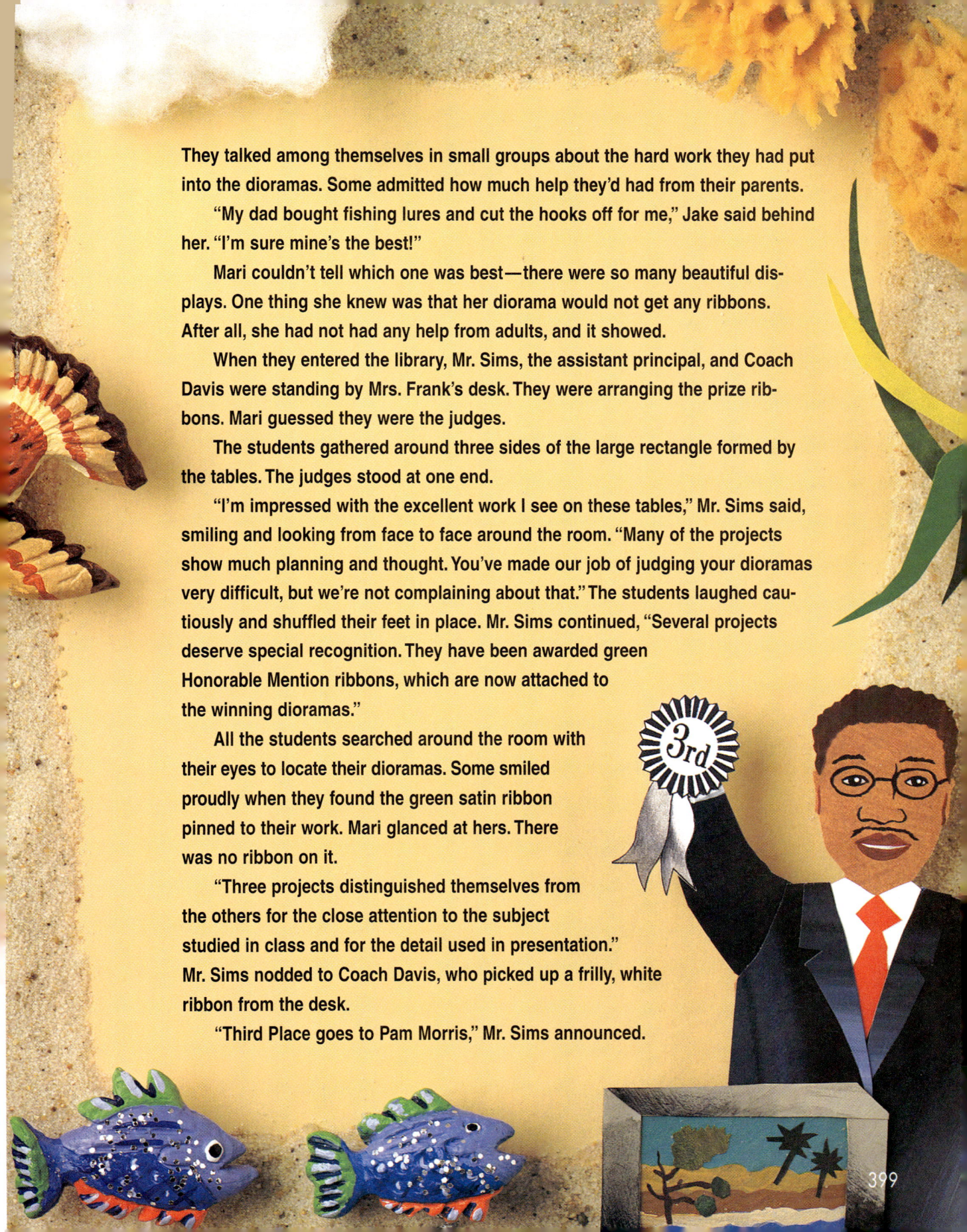

They talked among themselves in small groups about the hard work they had put into the dioramas. Some admitted how much help they'd had from their parents.

"My dad bought fishing lures and cut the hooks off for me," Jake said behind her. "I'm sure mine's the best!"

Mari couldn't tell which one was best—there were so many beautiful displays. One thing she knew was that her diorama would not get any ribbons. After all, she had not had any help from adults, and it showed.

When they entered the library, Mr. Sims, the assistant principal, and Coach Davis were standing by Mrs. Frank's desk. They were arranging the prize ribbons. Mari guessed they were the judges.

The students gathered around three sides of the large rectangle formed by the tables. The judges stood at one end.

"I'm impressed with the excellent work I see on these tables," Mr. Sims said, smiling and looking from face to face around the room. "Many of the projects show much planning and thought. You've made our job of judging your dioramas very difficult, but we're not complaining about that." The students laughed cautiously and shuffled their feet in place. Mr. Sims continued, "Several projects deserve special recognition. They have been awarded green Honorable Mention ribbons, which are now attached to the winning dioramas."

All the students searched around the room with their eyes to locate their dioramas. Some smiled proudly when they found the green satin ribbon pinned to their work. Mari glanced at hers. There was no ribbon on it.

"Three projects distinguished themselves from the others for the close attention to the subject studied in class and for the detail used in presentation." Mr. Sims nodded to Coach Davis, who picked up a frilly, white ribbon from the desk.

"Third Place goes to Pam Morris," Mr. Sims announced.

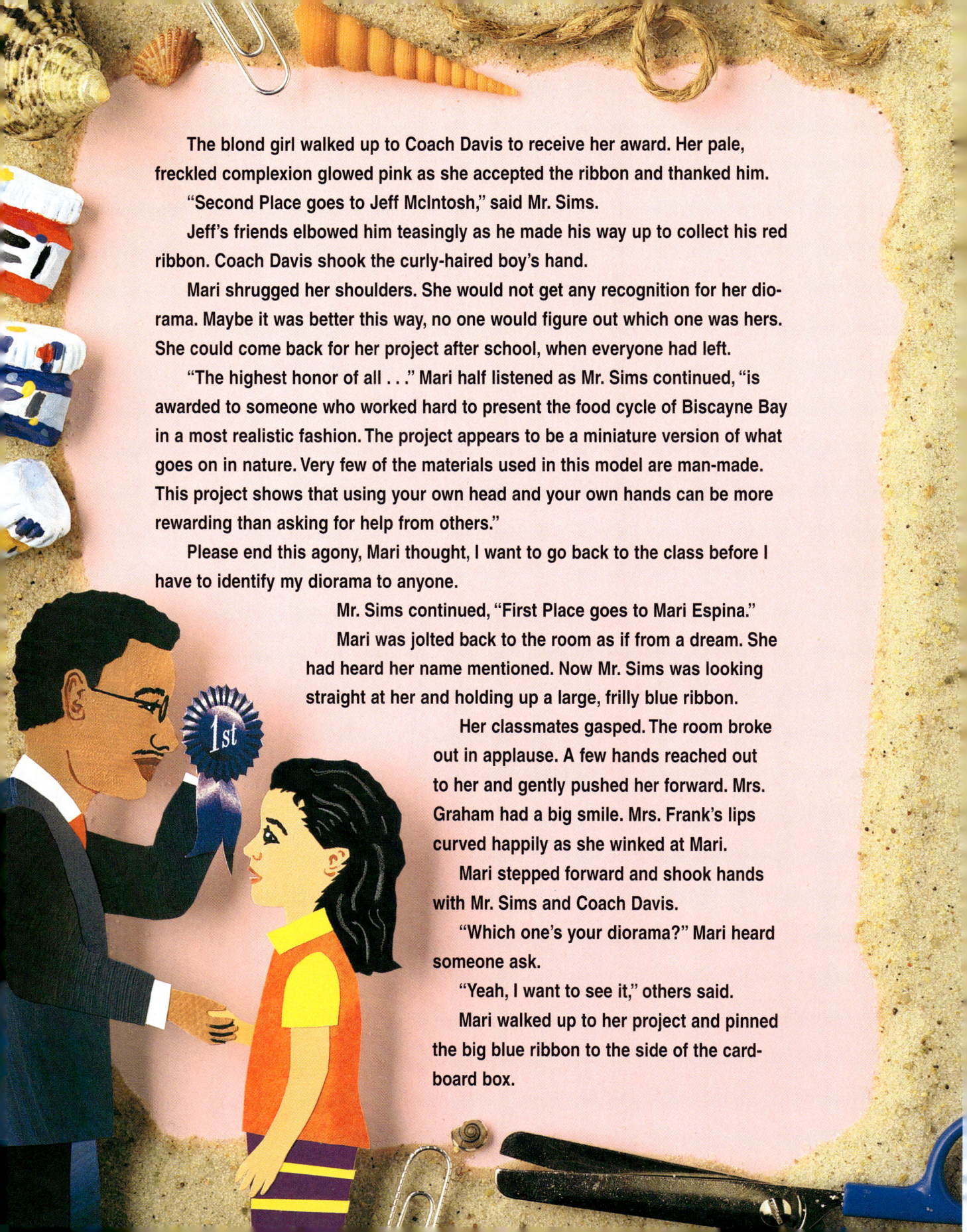

The blond girl walked up to Coach Davis to receive her award. Her pale, freckled complexion glowed pink as she accepted the ribbon and thanked him.

"Second Place goes to Jeff McIntosh," said Mr. Sims.

Jeff's friends elbowed him teasingly as he made his way up to collect his red ribbon. Coach Davis shook the curly-haired boy's hand.

Mari shrugged her shoulders. She would not get any recognition for her diorama. Maybe it was better this way, no one would figure out which one was hers. She could come back for her project after school, when everyone had left.

"The highest honor of all . . ." Mari half listened as Mr. Sims continued, "is awarded to someone who worked hard to present the food cycle of Biscayne Bay in a most realistic fashion. The project appears to be a miniature version of what goes on in nature. Very few of the materials used in this model are man-made. This project shows that using your own head and your own hands can be more rewarding than asking for help from others."

Please end this agony, Mari thought, I want to go back to the class before I have to identify my diorama to anyone.

Mr. Sims continued, "First Place goes to Mari Espina."

Mari was jolted back to the room as if from a dream. She had heard her name mentioned. Now Mr. Sims was looking straight at her and holding up a large, frilly blue ribbon.

Her classmates gasped. The room broke out in applause. A few hands reached out to her and gently pushed her forward. Mrs. Graham had a big smile. Mrs. Frank's lips curved happily as she winked at Mari.

Mari stepped forward and shook hands with Mr. Sims and Coach Davis.

"Which one's your diorama?" Mari heard someone ask.

"Yeah, I want to see it," others said.

Mari walked up to her project and pinned the big blue ribbon to the side of the cardboard box.

"It's so realistic!" Cathy said.

"Look at the materials she used," said Erica, clearly impressed.

Mrs. Frank brought out her camera. "Stand by your diorama and hold up the ribbon," she told Mari.

"I'm sure your picture will be put on the library bulletin board. Everyone will see it when they come in," Liz said.

"Better than that," said Mrs. Graham. "We'll have the diorama on display for a month, right here in the library."

"Can I take it home tonight and show my mother?" Mari asked. "I promise to bring it back tomorrow."

"Sure, dear. But right now I want to see a big, fat smile!" said Mrs. Frank, looking through the camera lens.

Mari couldn't hide her pride. A satisfied smile broke out across her face.

"Mamá, look! Look what I won!" Mari yelled happily in Spanish. She had been controlling her excitement since she got home and now she ran to the door as her mother entered their apartment. "I won a ribbon for my project!" Mari held the frilly medallion against her chest so that the long, blue ribbons hung down to her waist.

401

Mamá reached for the satin streamers and stroked them with her fingers. "It's beautiful! Congratulations!" she told her daughter in Spanish, and smiled lovingly.

"Read what it says," said Mari.

In her best English, Mamá read slowly, "First Place."

"They said mine was the best!" Mari said excitedly in Spanish. "You should have seen the other dioramas. They were so beautiful. But they said mine was the best!"

"Well, I'm not surprised, *mi amor*," Mamá said. "You worked so hard on it every night and it turned out perfect."

"Mr. Sims told everyone they could tell I had worked on the project without any help from others." Mari took a breath and watched her mother's reaction. Mamá smiled and nodded. "You know what, Mamá? Mr. Sims was wrong. I did have some help."

"I don't see how, *mi amor*. You worked alone at this table every night," Mamá said, resting her purse on the kitchen table.

"Well, Mamá," Mari said tenderly. "You gave me the best help anyone could get. You told me to figure things out on my own."

Mamá's eyes filled with tears. "I wish I could have helped more."

"But, Mamá, this was the kind of help I needed. I needed to realize I could do it by myself."

"I'm proud of you." Mamá didn't need to tell her that. Mari already knew. Mamá wrapped her arms around Mari. "Let's take a picture of you standing by your project. In your next letter to Papá, you can send it to him and tell him all about your project and your ribbon."

"Yes," said Mari, grinning happily. "I bet he'll be very proud of me, too!"

Think About It

1. What creative things does Mari do to make her diorama?
2. What does Mari learn by taking part in and winning this contest?
3. What is the author's message? How do you know?

Meet the Author

Anilú Bernardo

Like Mari, author Anilú Bernardo was born in Cuba and moved to the United States when she was very young. It was a challenge fitting in—she spoke very little English, and her classmates could not speak Spanish. Bernardo loved to write, and she began to write poems in Spanish. Later, she drew on her childhood experiences to make her stories about young Cuban immigrants realistic and enjoyable. With a little patience and creativity, Anilú Bernardo has become a successful author of stories for young readers.

Anilú Bernardo

Visit *The Learning Site!*
www.harcourtschool.com

Some Like

from **Contact Kids** magazine

When Curry and his staff aren't checking coral reefs, they might be examining historic shipwrecks.

It Wet!

Richard Curry is all wet. That's because 95 percent of his "office" is underwater! Biscayne is one of America's five undersea national parks. Curry spends much of his time studying and repairing the park's coral reefs: underwater ridges that are home to fish, plants, and other marine life.

Lots of things can be dangerous to the coral reefs. "Anchors that drop on the reefs cause the most damage," Curry told CONTACT KIDS. Fishing lines, spear guns, and debris from boats are also to blame for broken coral.

Damaged coral reefs can throw off the whole marine ecosystem. It's Curry's job to make sure that doesn't happen. To help reverse the problem, he started his own coral reef recovery program.

Growing coral is no easy task. First, Curry places mini concrete pyramids underwater. He glues damaged coral to the pyramids. When the coral matures, Curry attaches it to a real coral reef.

So far, the program's been a success. "One of the sites has had a 100-percent survival rate," says Curry. Spoken like a proud papa!

Curry on his way to build a coral nursery.

Curry and a fellow diver position the pyramid.

Think About It
How does Curry's recovery process work?

Response

You Have a Phone Call

ROLE–PLAY A CONVERSATION Mari plans to tell her father about winning the diorama contest. With a partner, role–play a telephone conversation between Mari and her father. Make sure Mari tells her father about her diorama and the contest.

Judging Contests

WRITE YOUR OPINION Think about the contest in the story. Do you think contests put too much pressure on students, or do you think they encourage them to do their best? Write your opinion in a paragraph, providing supporting details from the story.

Activities

Library Super Sleuth

CONDUCT AN INTERVIEW The school librarian helps Mari begin her diorama project. Interview a librarian at your school or public library. Tell the librarian about the stories in this theme, "Creative Solutions." Ask the librarian for the name of another book that would fit the theme. Read the book. Then write a paragraph telling why you do or do not agree with the librarian's choice.

Making Connections

WRITE A SEQUEL Write a new story in which Mari volunteers to help someone like Richard Curry in "Some Like It Wet" protect the coral in Biscayne National Park. Use details from the story and the magazine article to make your sequel believable. If possible, use a word processing program to type your final draft.

Catching the Fire

Philip Simmons, Blacksmith

by Mary E. Lyons

In 1925, when Philip Simmons was thirteen, he became a blacksmith's apprentice in Charleston, South Carolina. After more than ten years of hard work, Philip had acquired the skills to run his own shop. To find work during hard times, Philip started fixing people's iron gates and fences. Sometimes he added animal figures to bring his ironwork to life. Before long, people started to take notice of his skill and artistry. In 1976 Philip was invited to demonstrate his talent in front of the entire nation.

CATCHING THE FIRE
Philip Simmons, Blacksmith

MARY E. LYONS

Booklist Editors' Choice

"You must be Philip Simmons," the young man said. Sixty-year-old Philip looked up from his pile of scrap iron. The year was 1972, and he was working in his shop yard on Blake Street. Philip shook the visitor's hand. Who was this fellow, anyway? He said he was a graduate student from Indiana, but he had Washington, D.C., plates on his car.

Was he lost? Well, yes, he was. John Michael Vlach had been wandering around the one-way streets near Philip's shop, looking for the man who knew "the old ways of ironwork." John seemed a little nervous, maybe because a scruffy dog named Brownie was barking at him. But the blacksmith liked to talk about old times, so the scholar soon relaxed.

Philip explained the history of his business to John.

Philip Simmons forges a scroll in the early 1970s.

In the late 1930s, the federal government gave Charleston enough money to build two East Side housing projects: one for black citizens and one for whites. So Philip had to move his shop "for the improvement of the city."

The smith moved four times and landed on Blake Street in 1969. It was here that he replaced the spiteful bellows with an electric forge blower.

By the time America entered World War II in 1941, most of the city's blacksmiths were gone. When the Charleston Naval Ship Yard wanted parts for ships, they went to Philip Simmons. But after the war was over in 1945, business slowed down.

"I needed to make some money on the side," Philip told John. He drove a taxi, ran a dry-cleaning business, and opened and closed a restaurant. There must be a faster way to "grab a few more pennies," he thought.

Peter Simmons had died in 1953, two days before his ninety-eighth birthday. About this time, Philip decided to modernize his own shop. He bought an electric arc welder that was three times faster than riveting. And he attached an old washing machine motor to his hand drill. Both tools speeded up the work.

When John Vlach wanted to compare the old ways to the new ones, Philip took him on a tour of Charleston. He led John down a narrow alley to one of his first "fancy" pieces. Philip was proud of the old-time rivets he had used to join the wiggle tail to the gate.

Next, the two men looked at a bird gate. The customer had given Philip a drawing of an egret. "Can you make it?" the fellow had asked.

Sure he could. Philip knew egrets like the calluses on his

hands. He used an acetylene torch to cut the metal talons, and he made a bended knee so the bird was "looking ready to go."

Philip drove John over to East Bay Street to see his Snake Gate. It took him one month to forge that gate. He thought he'd never finish the eye. At first, it stared as if it were dead. Philip "heat and beat, heat and beat, heat and beat," until the snake looked as real as a diamond head rattler. "If it bites you," Philip joked, "you better get to the doctor fast. Blood get up to your heart, you know what happens!"

John Vlach was impressed. These were no ordinary pieces of ornamental ironwork. They were sculpture! Philip Simmons was not just a blacksmith. He was an artist.

John saw Philip often over the next four years. He helped install gates, took photographs, and tape-recorded conversations. And in 1976, John offered Philip the greatest test of his career: an invitation to make a gate at the Festival of American Folklife, a summer-long event in Washington, D.C.

The two men discussed the trip in the dim light of Philip's shop. As they spoke, pinpoints of sun poked through the sheet metal walls. At first the artist didn't want to go.

"No, no, no, no, no," Philip said. He held two scrolls up to the light to see if they matched. "I got business to do."

This wasn't going to be easy. John raked his hands through his dark brown hair. "You'll only be gone fifteen days," he said.

"Any special piece that you want me to make?" Philip asked.

"The choice is yours," John sweet-talked him. "We just want you to come up and demonstrate what you're doing in Charleston."

This offer made sense to the businessman. He could make

Egret Gate, 2 St. Michael's Alley, Charleston, South Carolina

Overthrow of Snake Gate, 329 East Bay Street, Charleston, South Carolina

something small to bring home and "sell for a profit."

"What about the materials? How will I move them?"

"We'll put everything in the trunk of your car."

"Only so much I can do without my 'prentice boys."

"Bring the apprentices with you. We'll pay their expenses, and they can drive the car."

The blacksmith ran out of arguments. "Yes, I'll come," he finally agreed.

There were a few other hurdles. First, Philip needed a portable forge. He always "liked to make the odd thing," so he cut the top off an old hot water heater and packed it with fire clay. He didn't spend more than fifty dollars on his homemade invention.

Second, what kind of gate should he make? Philip "set to

the desk," but nothing came to mind. He lay awake at night. Still no ideas. Six weeks passed. Suddenly he realized he was leaving—tomorrow!

Would this be the first test the blacksmith failed? When the airplane left Charleston the next day, Philip peeked out the small oval window next to his seat. He took a long look at the rivers and marshes that hugged Charleston on three sides.

"I'm just crazy about the water," he thought. "Maybe I'll show the stars in the water."

He considered fish. "Fish represents Charleston. It's known for fishing."

Philip imagined the moon over the Cooper River and decided to show a "quarter-moon, just racing along."

But like the old Sea Island tale says, " 'sidering and 'cidering won't buy Sal a new shirt." The artist pulled out a scrap of paper and began to draw. By the time the plane landed an hour later, he had solved the puzzle.

He would make a fish in the water and a double star in the sky, one inside the other. "Like watchin' a star," he thought, "it get smaller on you." Two quarter-moons would shine over it all.

Maybe this wouldn't be his prettiest gate, but it would be his most important one. It would be his "sacrificial piece." The one made in front of thousands of people and forged with the ancient tools of ironworking: fire, hammer, and a blacksmith's rugged hands.

The Festival

Washington, D.C., was almost as hot as Charleston. Especially the last week of July and first week of August 1976. For these two weeks, Philip and his apprentices, Joseph

Pringle and Silas Sessions, worked on the grassy Mall near the Lincoln Memorial. When the sun grew too bright, they moved under a striped tent.

The United States was two hundred years old, and the festival was a birthday party. It celebrated the skills of people from all over the world. Philip was impressed with the other talented folks he saw on the Mall: singers, dancers, cooks, hairdressers, gospel singers, woodcarvers, and seamstresses.

"Everybody on this ground," he noticed, "is doing it the old way."

At first, he and his helpers forged simple chandeliers and plant stands. The rain of sparks and ring of hammers drew a stream of visitors to the demonstration. Philip answered their questions, just as Peter Simmons had done fifty years before.

Then the blacksmiths began the Star and Fish Gate. They cut lengths of iron bars, forged pecan leaves, welded J-curves inside of S-curves. Philip used several pieces of metal to create an open effect in the spot-tailed bass. Finally he made the striking star within a star.

Toward the end of Philip's stay in Washington, John noticed something curious about the outside star.

"The center point is off by twenty degrees," he commented.

"A star can shine all different ways," the artist explained.

That evening Philip started thinking. Nothing is right until it's right. His grandfather had taught him that as a boy on Daniel Island. Peter Simmons had drilled it into him as a young man. And what about his customers? "If it weren't for them," Philip thought, "I wouldn't even be in Washington."

The blacksmith tossed all night in his dormitory bed at George Washington University. The next day, he hurried to the Mall before anyone else was around. It took him fifteen min-

"In sixty-two years," Philip says, "I never went in the shop and didn't need a hammer."

utes to cut the star out of the gate and weld it back in place.

By the time the demonstrations began at eleven A.M., the star pointed straight up toward the enamel blue sky. Philip Simmons had proved himself once more. And though he didn't know it yet, he had hooked his future to that star.

AFTERWORD

The Star and Fish Gate sparked a national interest in Philip Simmons's work. Festival officials invited him again in 1977, and in 1981 John Michael Vlach published *Philip Simmons, Charleston Blacksmith*. That year John suggested his friend's name for a Heritage Fellowship. The federal government gives this award to artists who are considered "national treasures."

Philip Simmons was one of "fifteen head" of people who

won. He returned to Washington in 1982 to accept the award and to join the festival again. The same year, the Smithsonian Institution bought his Star and Fish Gate. Now it's a national piece that travels to museums around the country.

State awards followed. In 1988 the blacksmith won a South Carolina Folk Heritage Award. He was admitted into the South Carolina State Hall of Fame in 1994.

The city of Charleston was the last to "get on the bandwagon." Some say this is because Charlestonians take African-American craftsmen for granted. Local officials finally followed the example of state and national agencies. In 1995 they gave Mr. Simmons a Conservation Craftsman Award.

Every year, more tributes come the blacksmith's way. He doesn't dwell on the success. Instead, like Peter Simmons, he concentrates on his role as a teacher.

Since 1955, Philip Simmons has taught at least five apprentices. Two of them, Joseph Pringle, a cousin, and Carlton Simmons, a nephew, are now fully trained smiths. Both are the latest in a long line of African-American blacksmiths in Charleston.

The silver-headed Mr. Simmons puts it this way: "I say to people, 'There won't be another Philip, but there will be another Joseph or Carlton.'"

Philip Simmons, 1996

Star and Fish Gate, 1976

Like generations of blacksmiths before him, Mr. Simmons has passed on the tradition. And now the Historic Charleston Foundation plans to open a Philip Simmons training center for young blacksmiths. The center will grant the artist his deepest wish: "to teach more kids."

"You got to teach kids while the sap is young," he believes, "just like you got to beat the iron while it's hot."

Students from Buist Academy on Visitor's Center Gate, Charleston, South Carolina

Think About It

1. What problem did Philip Simmons face before going to the festival, and how did he solve it?

2. Do you think the art of the blacksmith will still exist in the future? Tell why or why not.

3. How can you tell that Philip Simmons cares about his craft?

MEET THE AUTHOR
MARY E. LYONS

Author Mary E. Lyons with Philip Simmons in his blacksmith shop in Charleston, South Carolina.

Problem: Many of Mary Lyons's students wanted to learn more about an African American author named Zora Neale Hurston. They had trouble finding information on her that was written for kids.

Solution: Mary Lyons researched and wrote a biography of Zora Neale Hurston that was both entertaining and informative.

Problem: Little has been written about the work of talented African American craftspeople.

Solution: Mary Lyons created a series called "African American Artists and Artisans." While researching *Catching the Fire*, Mary visited with Philip Simmons to learn as much as she could about this artist and his craft.

Visit *The Learning Site!*
www.harcourtschool.com

The Path by the River, **Ernest Albert**
1936. Oil on canvas 32" x 40". Grand Central Gallery, New York

The Road Not Taken

by Robert Frost

Two roads diverged in a yellow wood,
And sorry I could not travel both
And be one traveler, long I stood
And looked down one as far as I could
To where it bent in the undergrowth;

Then took the other, as just as fair,
And having perhaps the better claim,
Because it was grassy and wanted wear;
Though as for that, the passing there
Had worn them really about the same,

And both that morning equally lay
In leaves no step had trodden black.
Oh, I kept the first for another day!
Yet knowing how way leads on to way,
I doubted if I should ever come back.

I shall be telling this with a sigh
Somewhere ages and ages hence:
Two roads diverged in a wood, and I—
I took the one less traveled by,
And that has made all the difference.

Response

Art Forged from Steel

DESIGN A GATE Philip Simmons designed a personalized gate for a customer using that person's initials and the design of an egret. Design a personalized gate for yourself. You might want your gate to represent a favorite hobby or sport. Write a caption that explains your design.

What You Do Best

WRITE A PARAGRAPH Think of an activity that you do well. Maybe you are a good artist or are great at sports. Write a paragraph that compares and contrasts Philip Simmons's special talent with your special talent.

Activities

Fine Festivals

WRITE AN ARTICLE Philip Simmons's craft gained national attention at the Festival of American Folklife in Washington, D.C. What art, music, or drama festivals take place in your area? Research one of these events, and write an article telling about this festival.

Making Connections

WRITE A LIST At first, Philip Simmons did not want to go to the Festival of American Folklife. Think about the message in "The Road Not Taken." Make a list titled "Two Roads." In the first column, write what might have happened if Philip had not gone to the festival. In the second column, write how his life changed because he did go to the festival.

Celebrate Creativity

MAKE A THEME POSTER In this theme, the people in the selections find creative ways to solve everyday problems. Make a "Creative Solutions" poster. Draw pictures or cut out pictures and words from magazines, and include interesting quotes from the selections. Display your poster in your classroom.

Theme WRAP-UP

Creative Problem Solvers

PROBLEM-SOLUTION CHART What problems or challenges do the people in this theme face? How do they use creativity to solve these problems? Make a chart that displays your answers. Your chart may look like the one here. Share your chart with the class.

Selection	Problem or Challenge	Creative Solution
My Side of the Mountain		
Febold Feboldson		
A Do-It-Yourself Project		
The Kid Who Invented the Popsicle		
Catching the Fire: Philip Simmons, Blacksmith		

A Book Club Meeting

LITERATURE CIRCLE Meet with a small group to discuss the selections in this theme. Use these questions and others like them:

- Which is the most entertaining selection?
- Which character or person do you admire the most?
- Which author's work would you like to read more of? Why do you like that author's style?
- What other books have you read that would fit in this theme?

Be sure to support each of your answers with examples.

THEME
MAKING A

DIFFERENCE

CONTENTS

Seventh Grade 432
by Gary Soto

FOCUS SKILL:
Narrative Elements:
Plot, Character, Setting 448

Fall Secrets 450
by Candy Dawson Boyd

Kids Did It! 464
from *National Geographic World*

Out of Darkness:
The Story
of Louis Braille 468
by Russell Freedman

FOCUS SKILL:
Make Generalizations 482

Anne of
Green Gables 484
by Lucy Maud Montgomery
adapted by Jamie Turner

Tea Biscuits 504
by Carolyn Strom Collins
and Christina Wyss Erikksson

Cowboys:
Roundup on an
American Ranch 508
by Joan Anderson

Home on the Range 522
Traditional Cowboy Song

READER'S CHOICE

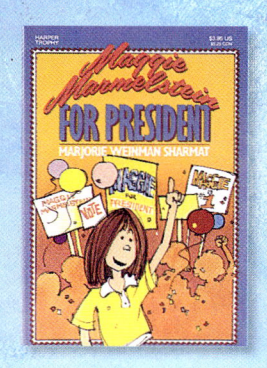

Maggie Marmelstein for President
by Marjorie Weinman Sharmat

REALISTIC FICTION

After Thad Smith refuses to let Maggie be his campaign manager in the race for class president, she decides to run for president herself. Now Maggie must decide if she is really the best person for the job.

Children's Choice
READER'S CHOICE LIBRARY

The World at His Fingertips: A Story about Louis Braille
by Barbara O'Connor

BIOGRAPHY

Louis Braille, blinded by an acccident at age three, changed the world for people who are blind by inventing an alphabet made of raised dots that could be read with fingertips.

READER'S CHOICE LIBRARY

The American Family Farm
by George Ancona and Joan Anderson

PHOTO ESSAY

This photo essay provides an in-depth look at the joys, dreams, and hardships of three different families in the farm community.

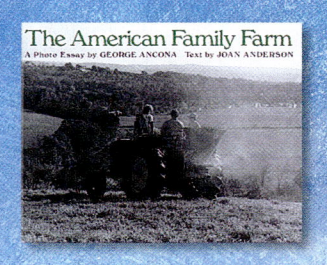

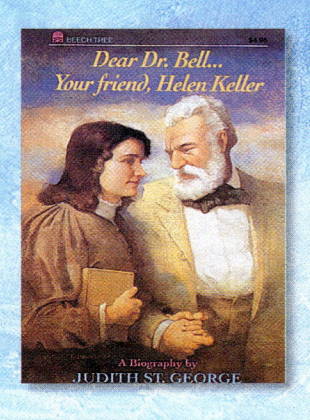

Dear Dr. Bell...Your Friend, Helen Keller
by Judith St. George

BIOGRAPHY

A childhood illness left Helen Keller blind and deaf. With the help of Dr. Bell, Helen's family found a teacher who helped Helen learn to communicate. Helen and Anne Sullivan spent their lives helping other blind and deaf people.

Mop Moondance and the Nagasaki Knights
by Walter Dean Myers

REALISTIC FICTION

The Elks are playing against several international teams in a baseball tournament. The games aren't easy, but the real challenge is communicating with the visiting players.

432

Seventh Grade

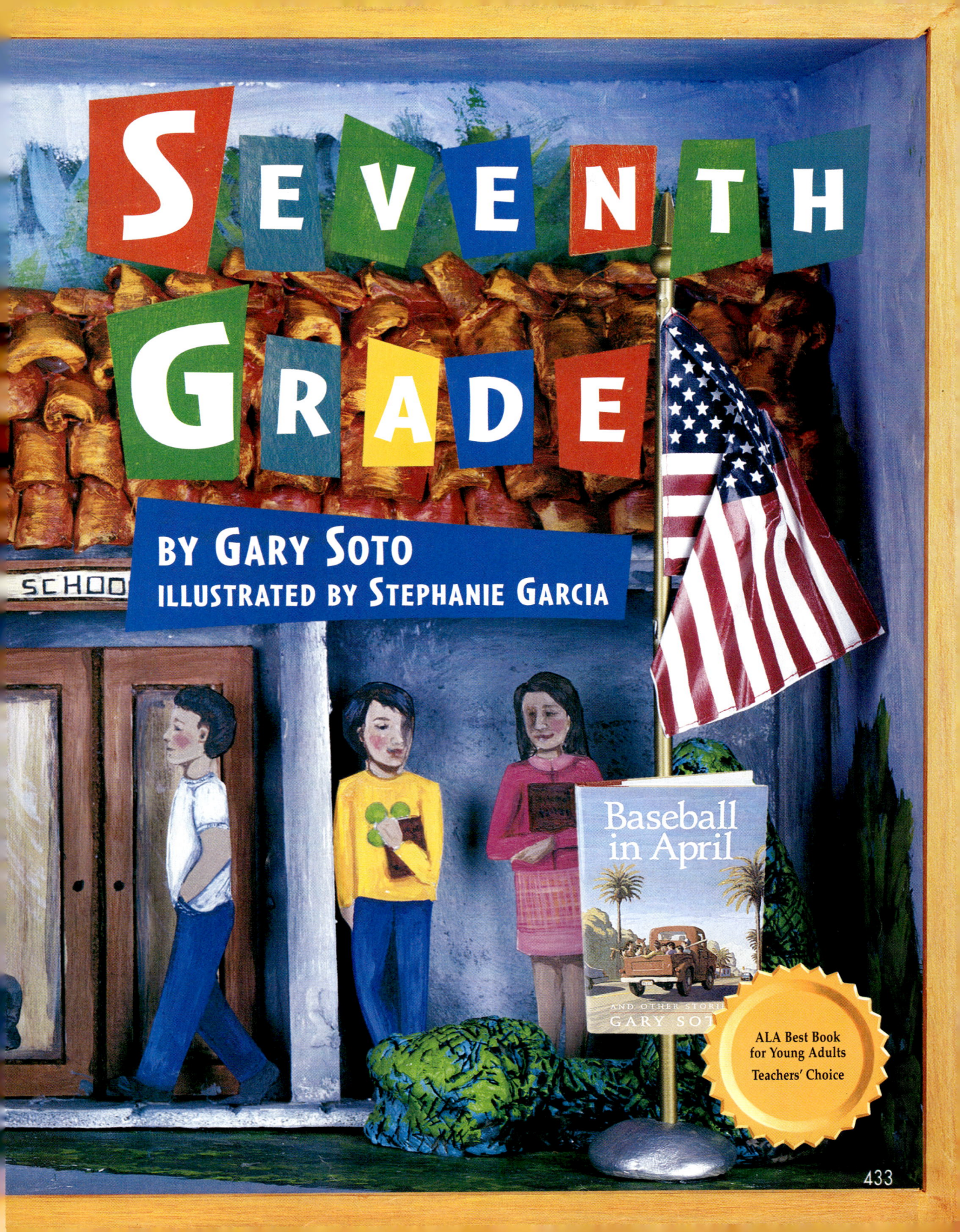

by Gary Soto
Illustrated by Stephanie Garcia

ALA Best Book for Young Adults
Teachers' Choice

On the first day of school, Victor stood in line half an hour before he came to a wobbly card table. He was handed a packet of papers and a computer card on which he listed his one elective, French. He already spoke Spanish and English, but he thought some day he might travel to France, where it was cool; not like Fresno, where summer days reached 110 degrees in the shade. There were rivers in France, and huge churches, and fair-skinned people everywhere, the way there were brown people all around Victor.

Besides, Teresa, a girl he had liked since they were in catechism classes at Saint Theresa's, was taking French, too. With any luck they would be in the same class. Teresa is going to be my girl this year, he promised himself as he left the gym full of students in their new fall clothes. She was cute. And good at math, too, Victor thought as he walked down the hall to his homeroom. He ran into his friend, Michael Torres, by the water fountain that never turned off.

They shook hands, *raza*-style,[1] and jerked their heads at one another in a *saludo de vato*.[2] "How come you're making a face?" asked Victor.

"I ain't making a face, *ese*.[3] This *is* my face." Michael said his face had changed during the summer. He had read a *GQ* magazine that his older brother borrowed from the Book Mobile and noticed that the male models all had the same look on their faces. They would stand, one arm around a beautiful woman, and *scowl*. They would sit at a pool, their rippled stomachs dark with shadow, and *scowl*. They would sit at dinner tables, cool drinks in their hands, and *scowl*.

"I think it works," Michael said. He scowled and let his upper lip quiver. His teeth showed along with the ferocity of his soul. "Belinda Reyes walked by a while ago and looked at me," he said.

Victor didn't say anything, though he thought his friend looked pretty strange. They talked about recent movies, baseball, their parents, and the horrors of picking grapes in order to buy their fall clothes. Picking grapes was like living in Siberia, except hot and more boring.

---

[1] *raza-style:* a special way of shaking hands
[2] *saludo de vato:* greeting
[3] *ese:* man

"What classes are you taking?" Michael said, scowling.

"French. How 'bout you?"

"Spanish. I ain't so good at it, even if I'm Mexican."

"I'm not either, but I'm better at it than math, that's for sure."

A tinny, three-beat bell propelled students to their homerooms. The two friends socked each other in the arm and went their ways, Victor thinking, man, that's weird. Michael thinks making a face makes him handsome.

On the way to his homeroom, Victor tried a scowl. He felt foolish, until out of the corner of his eye he saw a girl looking at him. Umm, he thought, maybe it does work. He scowled with greater conviction.

In homeroom, roll was taken, emergency cards were passed out, and they were given a bulletin to take home to their parents. The principal, Mr. Belton, spoke over the crackling loudspeaker, welcoming the students to a new year, new experiences, and new friendships. The students squirmed in their chairs and ignored him. They were anxious to go to first period. Victor sat calmly, thinking of Teresa, who sat two rows away, reading a paperback novel. This would be his lucky year. She was in his homeroom, and would probably be in his English and math classes. And, of course, French.

The bell rang for first period, and the students herded noisily through the door. Only Teresa lingered, talking with the homeroom teacher.

"So you think I should talk to Mrs. Gaines?" she asked the teacher. "She would know about ballet?"

"She would be a good bet," the teacher said. Then added, "Or the gym teacher, Mrs. Garza."

Victor lingered, keeping his head down and staring at his desk. He wanted to leave when she did so he could bump into her and say something clever.

He watched her on the sly. As she turned to leave, he stood up and hurried to the door, where he managed to catch her eye. She smiled and said, "Hi, Victor."

He smiled back and said, "Yeah, that's me." His brown face blushed. Why hadn't he said, "Hi, Teresa," or "How was your summer?" or something nice?

As Teresa walked down the hall, Victor walked the other way, looking back, admiring how gracefully she walked, one foot in front of the other. So much for being in the same class, he thought. As he trudged to English, he practiced scowling.

In English they reviewed the parts of speech. Mr. Lucas, a portly man, waddled down the aisle, asking, "What is a noun?"

"A person, place, or thing," said the class in unison.

"Yes, now somebody give me an example of a person—you, Victor Rodriguez."

"Teresa," Victor said automatically. Some of the girls giggled. They knew he had a crush on Teresa. He felt himself blushing again.

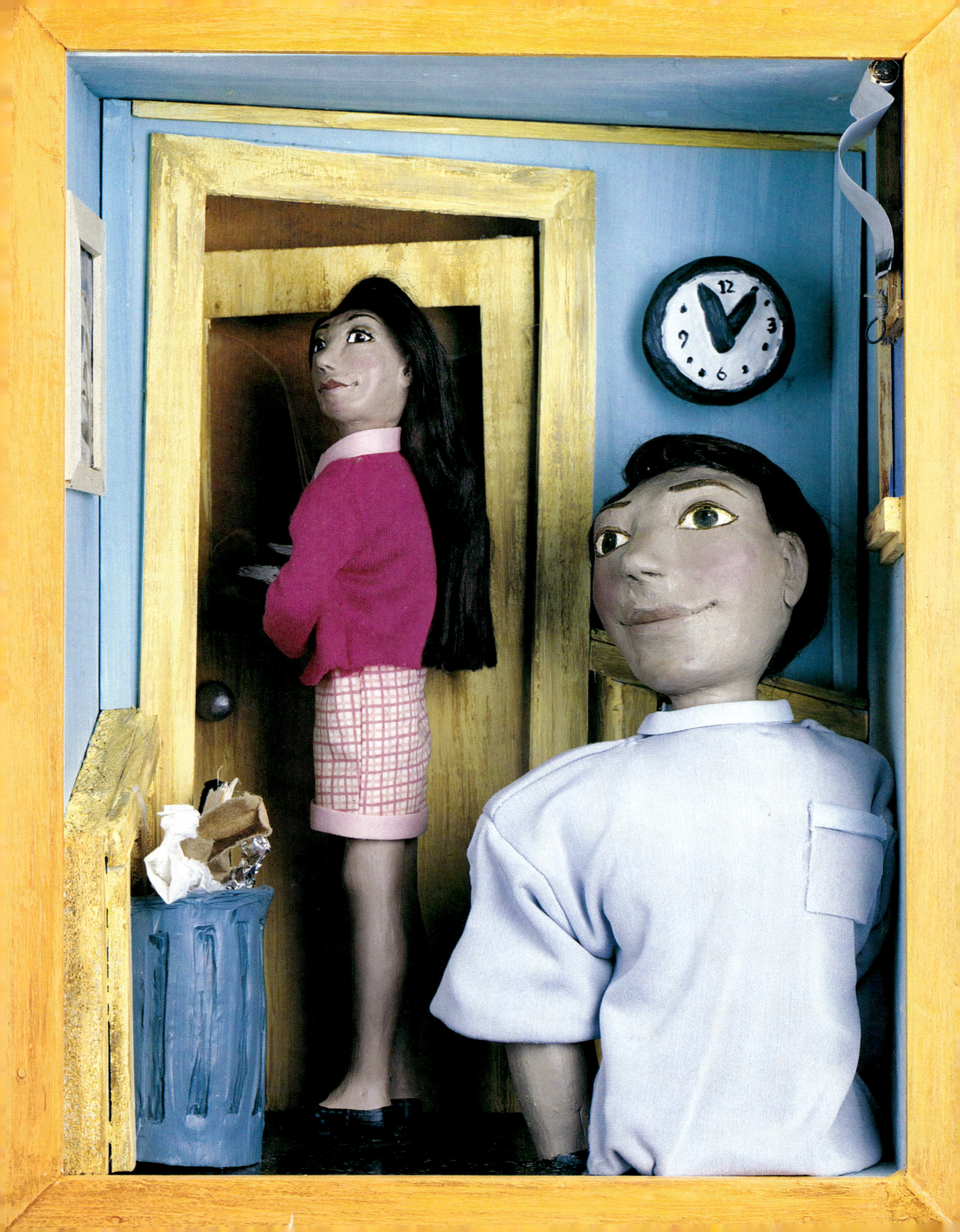

"Correct," Mr. Lucas said. "Now provide me with a place."

Mr. Lucas called on a freckled kid who answered, "Teresa's house with a kitchen full of big brothers."

After English, Victor had math, his weakest subject. He sat in the back by the window, hoping that he would not be called on. Victor understood most of the problems, but some of the stuff looked like the teacher made it up as she went along. It was confusing, like the inside of a watch.

After math he had a fifteen-minute break, then social studies, and, finally, lunch. He bought a tuna casserole with buttered rolls, some fruit cocktail, and milk. He sat with Michael, who practiced scowling between bites.

Girls walked by and looked at him.

"See what I mean, Vic?" Michael scowled. "They love it."

"Yeah, I guess so."

They ate slowly, Victor scanning the horizon for a glimpse of Teresa. He didn't see her. She must have brought lunch, he thought, and is eating outside. Victor scraped his plate and left Michael, who was busy scowling at a girl two tables away.

The small, triangle-shaped campus bustled with students talking about their new classes. Everyone was in a sunny mood. Victor hurried to the bag lunch area, where he sat down and opened his math book. He moved his lips as if he were reading, but his mind was somewhere else. He raised his eyes slowly and looked around. No Teresa.

He lowered his eyes, pretending to study, then looked slowly to the left. No Teresa. He turned a page in the book and stared at some math problems that scared him because he knew he would have to do them eventually. He looked to the right. Still no sign of her. He stretched out lazily in an attempt to disguise his snooping.

Then he saw her. She was sitting with a girlfriend under a plum tree. Victor moved to a table near her and daydreamed about taking her to a movie. When the bell sounded, Teresa looked up, and their eyes met. She smiled sweetly and gathered her books. Her next class was French, same as Victor's.

They were among the last students to arrive in class, so all the good desks in the back had already been taken. Victor was forced to sit near the front, a few desks away from Teresa, while Mr. Bueller wrote French words on the chalkboard. The bell rang, and Mr. Bueller wiped his hands, turned to the class, and said, "*Bonjour.*"[4]

"*Bonjour,*" braved a few students.

"*Bonjour,*" Victor whispered. He wondered if Teresa heard him. Mr. Bueller said that if the students studied hard, at the end of the

---

[4] *Bonjour:* hello; good day

439

year they could go to France and be understood by the populace.

One kid raised his hand and asked, "What's 'populace'?"

"The people, the people of France."

Mr. Bueller asked if anyone knew French. Victor raised his hand, wanting to impress Teresa. The teacher beamed and said, "*Très bien. Parlez-vous français?*"[5]

Victor didn't know what to say. The teacher wet his lips and asked something else in French. The room grew silent. Victor felt all eyes staring at him. He tried to bluff his way out by making noises that sounded French.

"La me vava me con le grandma," he said uncertainly.

Mr. Bueller, wrinkling his face in curiosity, asked him to speak up.

Great rosebushes of red bloomed on Victor's cheeks. A river of nervous sweat ran down his palms. He felt awful. Teresa sat a few desks away, no doubt thinking he was a fool. Without looking at Mr. Bueller, Victor mumbled, "Frenchie oh wewe gee in September."

---

[5] *Très bien. Parlez-vous français?*: Very good. Do you speak French?

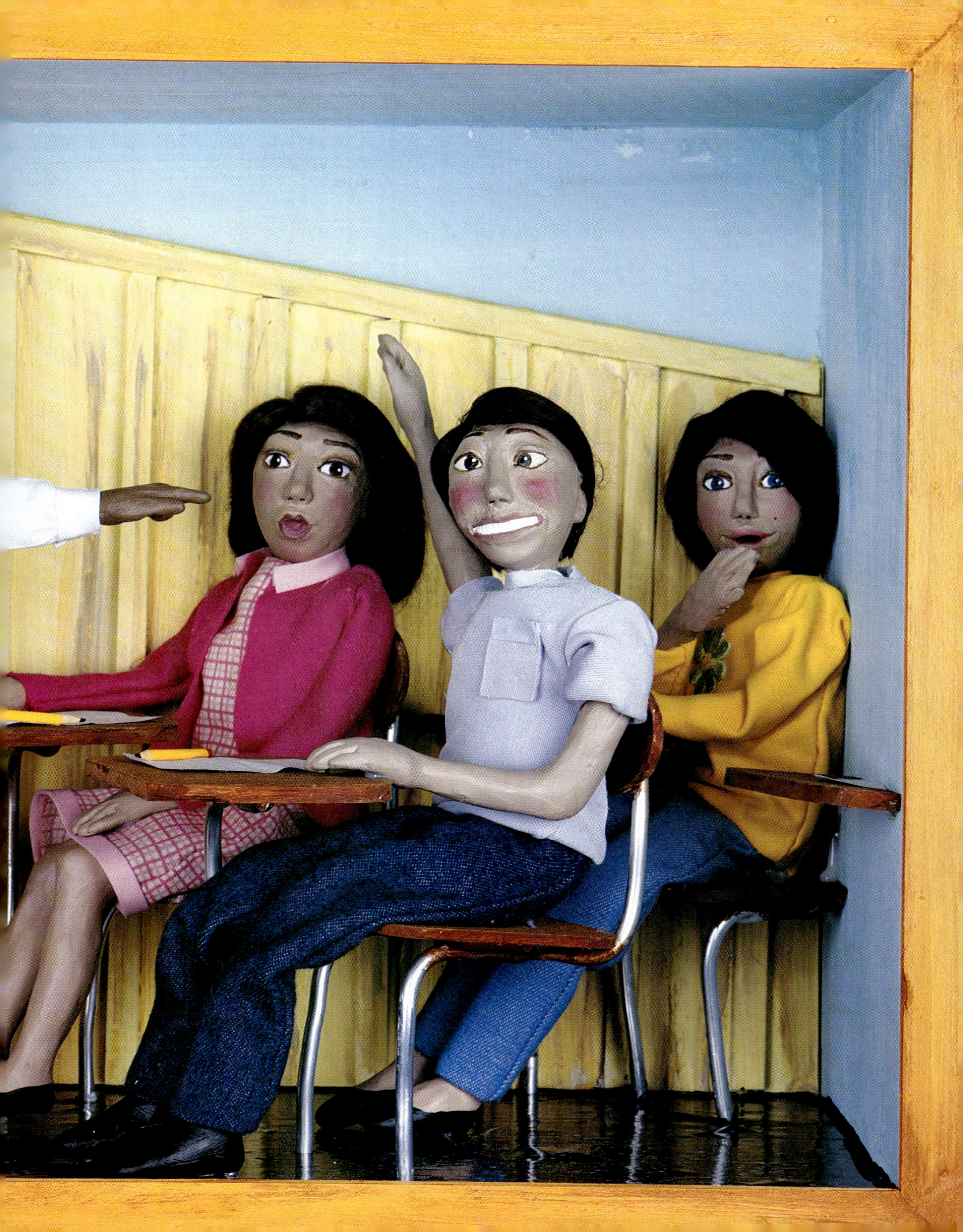

Mr. Bueller asked Victor to repeat what he had said.

"Frenchie oh wewe gee in September," Victor repeated.

Mr. Bueller understood that the boy didn't know French and turned away. He walked to the blackboard and pointed to the words on the board with his steel-edged ruler.

"*Le bateau,*" he sang.

"*Le bateau,*" the students repeated.

"*Le bateau est sur l'eau,*"[6] he sang.

"*Le bateau est sur l'eau.*"

Victor was too weak from failure to join the class. He stared at the board and wished he had taken Spanish, not French. Better yet, he wished he could start his life over. He had never been so embarrassed. He bit his thumb until he tore off a sliver of skin.

The bell sounded for fifth period, and Victor shot out of the room, avoiding the stares of the other kids, but had to return for his math book. He looked sheepishly at the teacher, who was erasing the board, then widened his eyes in terror at Teresa, who stood in front of him. "I didn't know you knew French," she said. "That was good."

Mr. Bueller looked at Victor, and Victor looked back. Oh please, don't say anything, Victor pleaded with his eyes. I'll wash your car, mow your lawn, walk your dog—anything! I'll be your best student, and I'll clean your erasers after school.

Mr. Bueller shuffled through the papers on his desk. He smiled and hummed as he sat down to work. He remembered his college years when he dated a girlfriend in borrowed cars. She thought he was rich because each time he picked her up he had a different car. It was fun until he had spent all his money on her and had to write home to his parents because he was broke.

Victor couldn't stand to look at Teresa. He was sweaty with shame. "Yeah, well, I picked up a few things from movies and books and stuff like that." They left the class together. Teresa asked him if he would help her with her French.

"Sure, anytime," Victor said.

"I won't be bothering you, will I?"

"Oh no, I like being bothered."

---

[6] *Le bateau est sur l'eau:* The boat is on the water.

Le bateau
Le bateau est
sur l'eau

"*Bonjour,*" Teresa said, leaving him outside her next class. She smiled and pushed wisps of hair from her face.

"Yeah, right, *bonjour,*" Victor said. He turned and headed to his class. The rosebushes of shame on his face became bouquets of love. Teresa is a great girl, he thought. And Mr. Bueller is a good guy.

He raced to metal shop. After metal shop there was biology, and after biology a long sprint to the public library, where he checked out three French textbooks.

He was going to like seventh grade.

Think About It

1. How do different people change Victor's outlook during the first day of school?

2. What advice would you give Victor about how to avoid embarrassing situations in the future?

3. Why is Mr. Bueller an important character in the story? Explain.

MEET THE AUTHOR
GARY SOTO

In "Seventh Grade," award-winning author Gary Soto remembers his experiences growing up in Fresno, California. Like Victor in the story, Soto liked a girl who didn't notice him, and he wanted to fit in at a new school. Soto says that "taking the past and reshaping it into a story" is the reason he wrote "Seventh Grade."

MEET THE ILLUSTRATOR
STEPHANIE GARCIA

Before illustrator Stephanie Garcia begins to bring a story to life, she tries to identify with the main characters. Her sixth-grade nephew was the model for Victor in "Seventh Grade." Garcia says that her family and friends often see themselves in her work and that a little part of her is in every illustration.

Visit *The Learning Site!*
www.harcourtschool.com

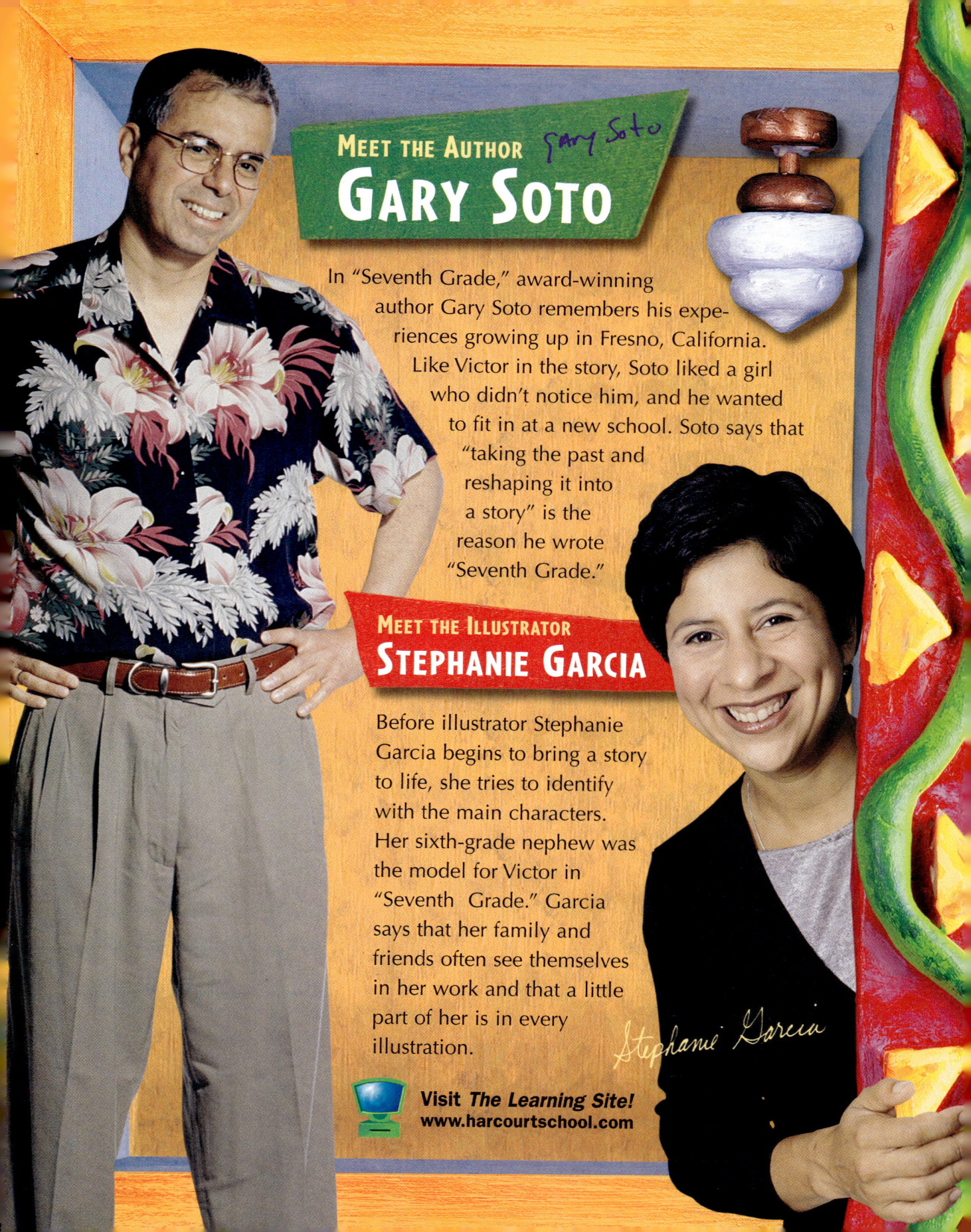

Response Activities

Dear Victor,

WRITE A LETTER Think about a time when you joined a new community. Perhaps you moved to a new neighborhood or changed schools. Write a letter to Victor telling him about your experience in that new community.

Bonjour!

CONDUCT A LANGUAGE SURVEY Victor's French teacher greets his students with *bonjour,* which means "good day." With a partner, survey your classmates to find out any foreign words or phrases they know. Be sure to get the English translations as well. Display your survey results on a poster.

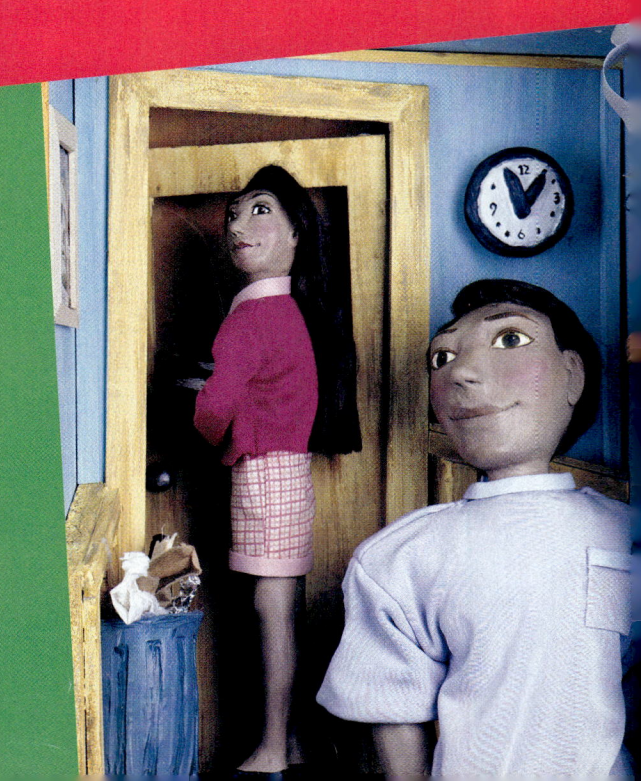

Take a Right at the Gym...

DRAW A MAP The author describes Victor's school. Make a map of how you think the school is arranged. Use story details and what you know from your own school. Add a dotted line that shows Victor's route during the school day.

School's Almost Out

MAKE A COMIC STRIP Think of what Victor does during his first day of school. Now imagine that it is his last day of school. Create a four- or five-frame comic strip that shows a scene between Victor and his friends. Use details from the story to make Victor's words and actions believable.

FOCUS SKILL

Narrative Elements: Plot, Character, Setting

Like every story, "Seventh Grade" has a plot, characters, and a setting. The **plot** is the sequence of events. It often involves a problem that the main character must solve. The **characters** are the people and/or animals in the story. The **setting** is the place and time in which the story takes place.

In most stories, the narrative elements of character, setting, and plot are identified in the first few paragraphs. After reading just the beginning of "Seventh Grade," you could fill in a story map to identify the main characters, the setting, and the beginning of the plot.

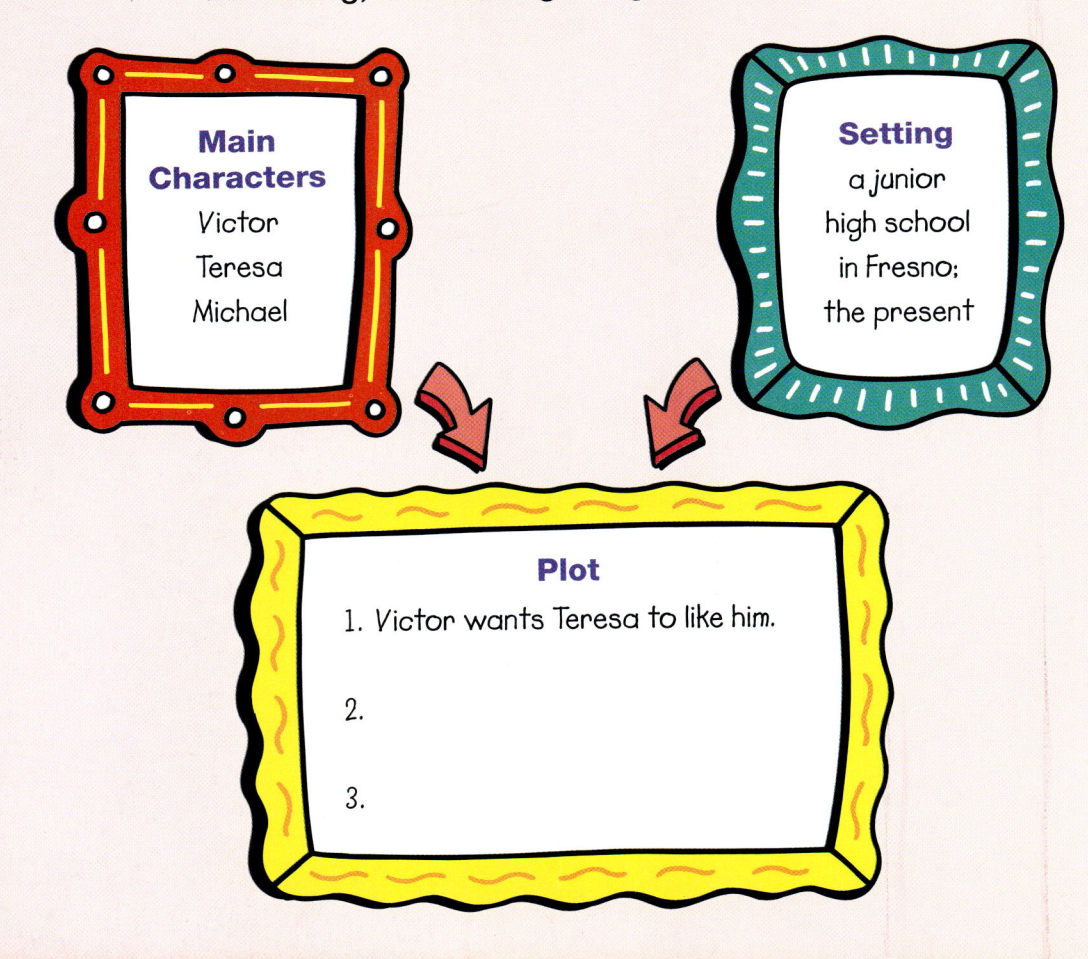

Main Characters
Victor
Teresa
Michael

Setting
a junior high school in Fresno; the present

Plot
1. Victor wants Teresa to like him.
2.
3.

448

By following the plot and noting what characters say and do, you can understand the characters' actions. You can also understand why a character solves a problem in a certain way. Read the following story opener. What can you discover about the characters, the setting, and the plot of the story from this beginning? Record your ideas in a story map like the one on page 448.

Rosalia stood staring at her paintings on the cafeteria wall at Winslow Middle School. A "Best of Show" ribbon hung from one, and two others bore Honorable Mention ribbons. Outside it was snowing, but Rosalia felt filled with the warmth of the Mexican plaza in her paintings. They showed her mother's memories of a time and place Mamá said was simple and beautiful and full of soul. Rosalia wondered what it would be like when she and her family moved to Veracruz next year. Would her *primos*, her cousins, accept her? Would her Spanish be good enough? Would she find a teacher with whom she could continue her art studies?

WHAT HAVE YOU LEARNED?

1. Think about Victor and Michael in "Seventh Grade." What similarities and differences do you see in these characters? Use a Venn diagram to compare and contrast the two boys.

2. Plan a story of your own. Decide on the characters, the setting, and the plot. Fill in a story map with your plan.

TRY THIS • TRY THIS • TRY THIS

Continue the story of Victor and Teresa. Add new characters and think of a plot you'd like to develop. Sketch out the sequence of events. You can number the events or put them in a story map. Then write the opening paragraph of your story.

Visit *The Learning Site!*
www.harcourtschool.com

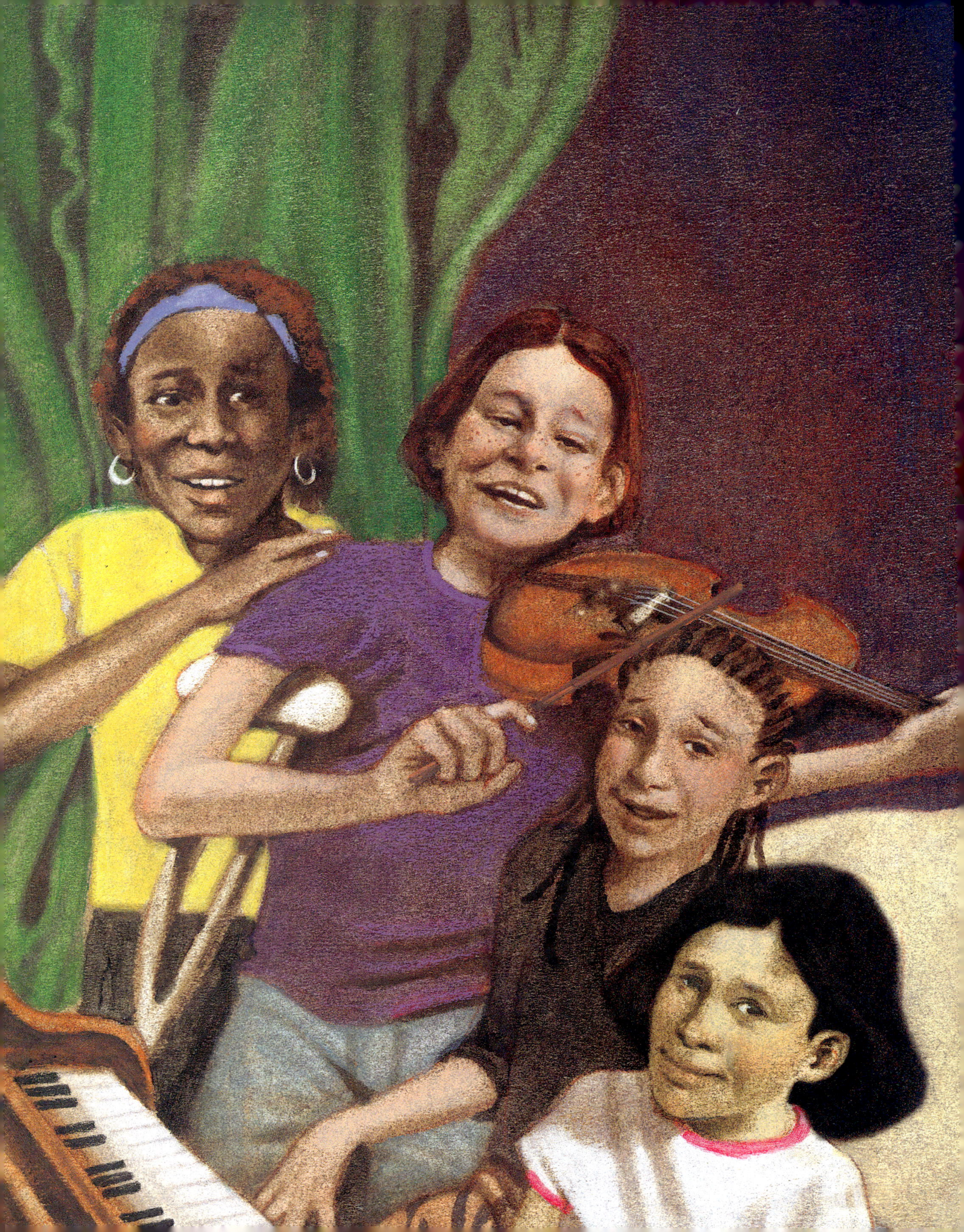

Fall Secrets

by
Candy Dawson Boyd

illustrated by
Floyd Cooper

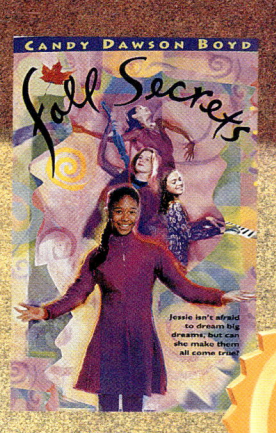

Award-Winning Author and Illustrator

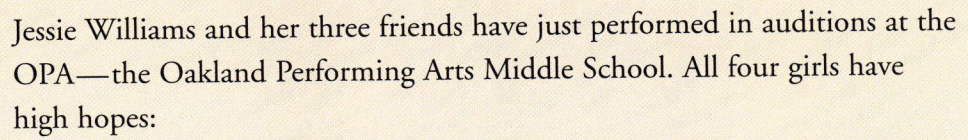

Jessie Williams and her three friends have just performed in auditions at the OPA—the Oakland Performing Arts Middle School. All four girls have high hopes:

- Jessie hopes to get a leading role in a play.
- Mkiwa (mm-KEE-wah) Cooper (also known as Addie Mae) hopes to be placed in the first line of dancers.
- Maria Hernandez hopes to play the piano flawlessly.
- Julie Stone, with her broken leg, just hopes for the best when she stands to play the violin.

In addition to their separate talents, the girls perform together in a group called the Fours. The Fours perform in order to give something to the community. But today, the community will give something to them.

On Wednesday the results of the auditions were posted at various places in the school. Crowds of students gathered around. Groans and whoops of joy were heard up and down the corridors of OPA.

Jessie hung back. At last she got the courage to read the list by the theater door. The part of the elderly Harriet Tubman had gone to Dorothy Foster. Jessie bit her bottom lip. Sylvia Duncan was listed after "Harriet Tubman as a young woman." *That figures.* And Jamar had been selected as Harriet's second husband. Jessie searched for any mention of her name. There it was. The part of Harriet's sister, Mary Ann, went to Jessie Williams.

"Hey. How did you do?" Jamar stood behind her.

Unable to respond, Jessie fled down the hall. What could she tell Dad, Mom, Cass, and Mamatoo? She was a failure. At the front of the school building she saw the other three.

"I didn't get the part of Harriet as an old woman. I got the part of Harriet's younger sister," said Jessie, the words coming out in a rush. "And I wore all of my good-luck clothes and jewelry!"

Tears glistened in Maria's eyes. "I practiced three hours a day! No matter what else I want to do—I practice and then I fall apart!"

"Maria, it can't be that bad!" said Julie, leaning against the wall, one crutch on the floor.

"I tried out for a simple solo part in the Winter Festival concert. Instead I get to play one song that a two-year-old could play, with the rest of the orchestra!" Maria wiped at the tears falling from her eyes.

"Here." Mkiwa handed her some Kleenex. "Maria, everybody blows it sometimes. Even me. Try being placed in not the first, not the second, but the third line of dancers! My mother will be disappointed, but I know that my father will understand. He's always in my corner. No matter what."

The girls just stared at her.

Jessie decided to let any questions about Addie Mae and her family drop. Everybody waited for Julie to say something.

"I don't feel bad. I get to play a short solo. Nothing really exciting. But to tell the truth, I was surprised and happy. I didn't expect to get to do much of anything," she said.

"Like my grandmother says, 'There's always next time.' And next time we'll do better. I'm glad we all tried." Jessie struggled to sound upbeat.

"I feel the same way, Jessie." Maria handed Julie her crutch.

Jessie bit her bottom lip. "Anyway, we have other opportunities. There's the Spring Fund-Raiser. That's the one that counts the most."

"We don't have time to stand around here," said Addie Mae.

Maria nodded. "They're expecting us at Evergreen in fifteen minutes. If we mess this up, there goes our grade."

"I don't feel much like performing," Jessie confessed.

"We have to." Julie added, as she limped off, "If we're serious artists we have to work even when we don't want to."

The girls carried Julie's things with their own. She walked well on the crutches. The sky was overcast. The chill in the air hurried them along.

Once inside Evergreen Residential Manor, they stowed their belongings in a small room off the dayroom. Mrs. Winters had arranged the furniture in the dayroom. Mrs. Hernandez rushed in with the video camera. The girls changed clothes. They had decided to dress up and appear as professional as possible.

Jessie broke the silence. "Julie's right. Professionals give their best, no matter what," she said.

Addie Mae spoke up. "Let's put our hands on top of each other's and say—"

"Four, three, two, one. We're the best. Let's have some fun!" Jessie quipped.

"I like it!" Maria put her hand out.

One after the other they placed their hands on top of each other's. The girls chanted, "Four, three, two, one. We're the best. Let's have some fun!"

Residents and members of the staff crowded the dayroom. The senior citizens sat on chairs or couches, or in wheelchairs. The Fours walked out to smiles and applause. Mrs. Winters introduced them. There was more applause.

The girls took their places. Julie sat on a chair, holding her violin. Her green taffeta dress shimmered. Maria, dressed in a long velvet skirt and white blouse, stood by the piano. Clad in a black bodysuit with a leopard print skirt and head wrap, Addie Mae crouched down on the side. Jessie had on the same black pants, white T-shirt, and *kente* cloth scarf she had worn for the reader's theater performance. The gold hoop earrings glowed against her skin.

"Good afternoon, Evergreen residents. My name is Jessie Williams. My friends and I are sixth graders at the Oakland Performing Arts Middle School. We are very happy to be here. Each one of us has a special dream and talent. We want to share each of our stories with you. Our first Dreamgirl is Maria Hernandez. No one works harder than Maria to make her dream come true. When she succeeds she will open another door for her people." She nodded to Maria, who stepped forward. Jess moved back.

"My name is Maria Hernandez. I live a few blocks from here. When I was five years old, my godmother took me to a piano recital in Mexico City. I saw a beautiful lady sit down at a huge grand piano. The concert hall looked like a castle and she was the queen. She started to play and minutes later I was lost in the most wonderful, magical music I had ever heard in my life. It all came from her mind and hands. When I told my father I wanted to learn how to be a concert pianist, he said that it was not a wise choice. There were few, if any, Mexican female concert pianists. But my godmother and mother persuaded him to let me take piano lessons."

Maria moved to the piano. "My dream is to become a world-class concert pianist. I will now play the audition piece that won me entrance into the castle, the Oakland Performing Arts Middle School." More applause filled the room. Maria nodded.

The lilting strains of the *New World Symphony* flowed over the audience. Jessie listened closely. Maria wasn't making any mistakes. Mrs. Hernandez videotaped the presentation. When Maria finished and took her place by the side of the piano, the room shook with approval. More relaxed, Jessie walked to the center of the room.

"Our next Dreamgirl is Mkiwa Cooper. She has chosen a rough road to dance on. Her heroines represent the most brilliant shining stars in the world of dance. When she succeeds she will continue the legacy they have left behind for her people." Jessie nodded to Addie Mae as she turned on the taped music. African drums and percussion instruments created an exciting mood.

"My name is Mkiwa Cooper. All of my life I have wanted to be a dancer like Judith Jamison of the Alvin Ailey Dance Company. For years I have taken classes in ballet, tap, modern dance, and African dance. I continue to take classes on Saturdays and practice every day. Dance is the only way I can really communicate how I feel and who I am. I'd like to perform the African dance I did when I auditioned for the Oakland Performing Arts Middle School. This is part of a dance by the Kikuyu (ke-KOO-yoo) people to celebrate a good hunt."

Jessie fast forwarded the tape to the number on her script. This music was pulsating and melodious. Addie Mae's movements, combined with the commanding African music, electrified the audience. She stomped, leaped, gestured, and swayed. Jessie saw several of the elderly people lift their hands in appreciation. As the last drumbeat drifted away, Addie Mae sank into a crouch, her head bowed. Again, applause thundered. One man pounded his cane.

This is going a lot better than we hoped. We are talented, thought Jessie.

"Our next Dreamgirl, Julie Stone, selected one of the oldest instruments in the world to master. In the face of enormous hardship, she has persevered."

Jessie moved the chair to the center. She carried Julie's violin and handed it to her after she was seated, the crutches by her side. Keeping Julie's part short had been deliberate. Julie wanted her violin to speak for her. The group had agreed.

"My name is Julie Stone. Like Mkiwa, I can't remember when I didn't want to play the violin. I take lessons on Saturday and practice every night. Whenever I play, I am happy. This is my favorite piece. I hope you like it."

There were moments when Julie's playing touched Jessie so deeply that she wanted to cry. Julie was oblivious to the audience. As her bow moved across the strings for the last time, Jessie saw a tear fall on her cheek. The silence in the audience lasted for several seconds. It ended with applause and shouts of "Brava!" Julie grinned. Addie Mae and Maria helped her move to the back.

Jessie exhaled. No one had made any mistakes. In fact, they had been at their best. *I just hope that I can do my part as well.*

"Now, I switch from narrator to performer. I am still Jessie Williams."

People chuckled.

Jessie continued. "My grandmother, Mamatoo, is the artistic director of a repertory theater company here in Oakland. I've been going to plays since I was born! My dream is to become a famous dramatic actress. I realize that this will be difficult. Not many make it, and there are few parts for African-Americans, but I am determined. To audition for acceptance at the Oakland Performing Arts Middle School, I selected Sojourner Truth's speech, 'Ain't I a Woman?' It is my pleasure to share her powerful words with you."

Like the rest of her group, Jessie delivered a flawless performance. This time she was able to erase everyone before her. In moments she escaped back to 1851 and that packed hall.

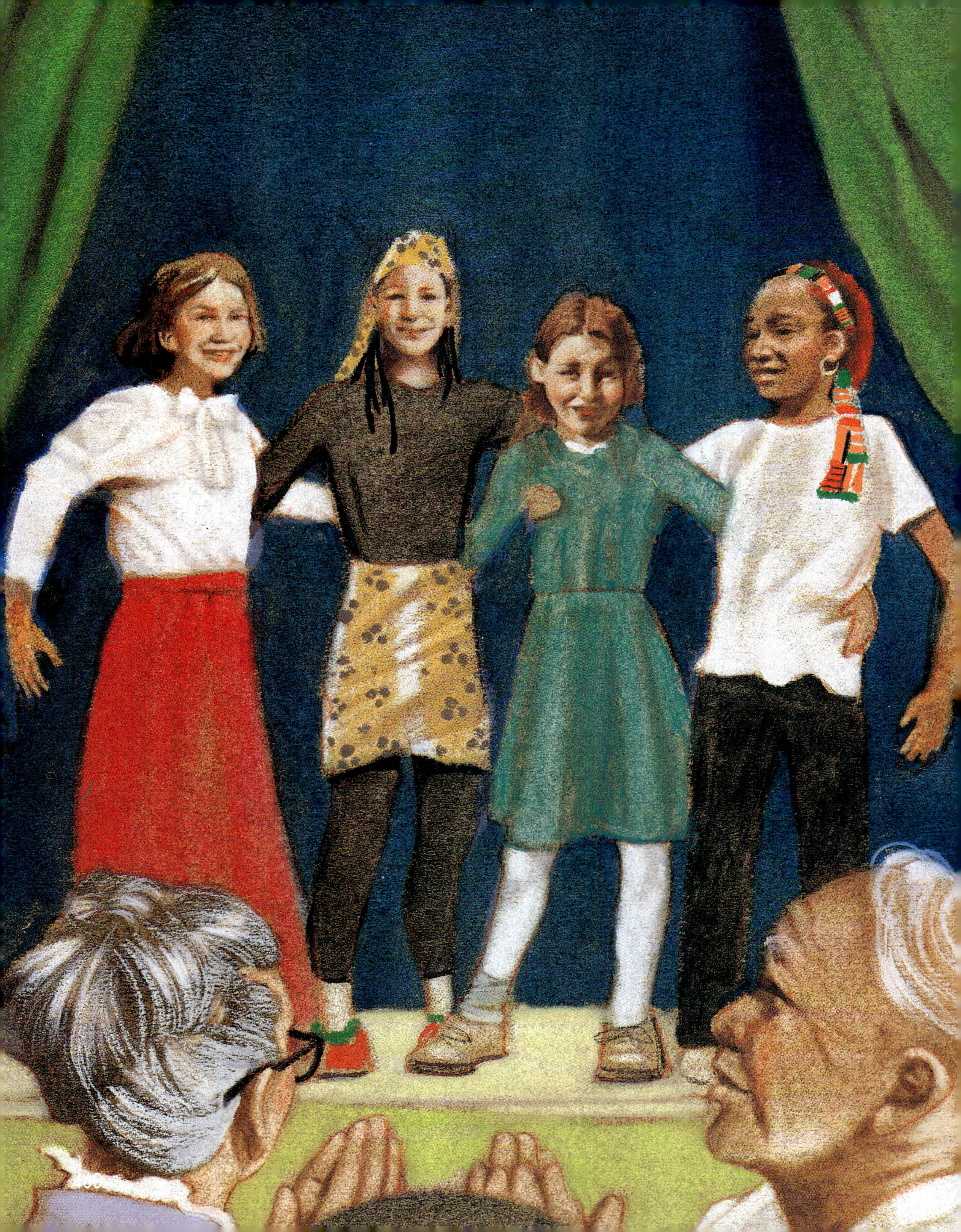

The words and intonations flowed like music. The audience's response startled her. Maria's mother was leading the cheers! Jessie was relieved that their work had been videotaped. Their stories plus the interviews with some of the residents about their lives would make a great project.

After two bows, Mrs. Winters explained that from now on the girls would be entertaining the residents twice a month. A table laden with punch, sandwiches, and cake stood in the corner. She invited everyone for refreshments. Before the girls could even change clothes, people came up to shake their hands and thank them.

Jessie watched an elderly black woman who walked with a cane beckon to Julie. The woman walked with a distinctive style, her eyes clear. The two of them sat down together. So Julie had already begun her interviews. Both Maria and Cooper were talking with certain residents.

For a second, the girls gazed at one another. An understanding passed between them. Going home depressed and dejected about the audition results would have been foolish and irresponsible. Coming here and performing was great.

Think About It

1. What does Jessie learn about herself through performing at Evergreen Residential Manor?

2. Are your dreams like those of Jessie and her classmates? Explain.

3. How does the introduction that each girl gives help you know what her character is like?

MEET THE AUTHOR
Candy Dawson Boyd

Candy Dawson Boyd's writing career began when she was a teacher in Chicago. She was always on the lookout for good books that represented different cultures. They were hard to find, so she decided to write some herself. Boyd's stories often show African American children winning out against the odds they face in life. She believes, "If books help children or give them a safe place to go, then that's the biggest reward for writing." This belief, along with her writing talent, has helped Candy Dawson Boyd become an award-winning author.

MEET THE ILLUSTRATOR
Floyd Cooper

Floyd Cooper drew his first picture as a young child in Tulsa, Oklahoma. He used a piece of Sheetrock to sketch "a duck of some sort" on the side of his father's house. "But I had to erase it," he recalls, "and I've been drawing ever since."

Actually, Cooper still erases quite a bit. He creates his warm, sunny illustrations using a technique called oil-wash-on-board. "What I'll do is cover the board with paint, and then erase the images out of this…paint using these little things called kneaded erasers."

Cooper does not draw many ducks nowadays, but his skillfull illustrations of people in books such as *Grandpa's Face* and *Meet Danitra Brown* have earned him several awards. He currently lives in West Orange, New Jersey, with his wife, his two children, and a fish named Little Foot.

Visit *The Learning Site!*
www.harcourtschool.com

KIDS DID IT!

Keys to Success
Randy Chang, 16

"When I first started piano lessons at age 9, it was quite a struggle," says Randy Chang of **Dover, Delaware.** Randy was born with a disability called Down's syndrome that makes it hard to learn new skills. But little by little, he practiced, learned, and began performing. Today Randy has played more than 30 concerts, performed on TV fund-raisers, and represented Delaware at the International Very Special Arts Festival in Brussels, Belgium.

"Music has inspired me and helped me learn about myself," says Randy. "Performing a piece called 'Waterwheel,' I began to think of myself as a small waterwheel powered by my faith, always spinning, always trying."

Randy loves playing and listening to music by composers such as Mozart and Bach. He is an excellent student in school and has gradually become a skilled public speaker. If something is hard, he advises: "Practice every day. Never give up. Learning is fun!"

Bridging Generations
Kristen DeForrest, 14

After her grandmother died three years ago, Kristen DeForrest noticed that her grandfather was sad and lonely. "He was all alone in his apartment and needed us to visit him," she says. "I wondered if other older people needed companionship, too."

Kirsten organized an Adopt-an-Elder program for kids at her school in **Rowley, Massachusetts.** She matched 20 kids in grades 6–8 with seniors who were patients at a nearby rehabilitation center. The kids phoned their seniors, sent them cards, and visited them at home. "The elders were really happy to see the kids," says Kristen. "But the kids enjoyed it, too."

For her idea Kristen won $3,000 in a contest to help the community. She uses the money to buy gift baskets and other items for the seniors. Kristen says her best reward is "seeing all the smiles of the pairs together."

Kristen still spends a lot of time with her own grandfather (above). He says he loves her idea and is proud to be the one who inspired it.

Think About It
Why are Randy's and Kristen's accomplishments noteworthy?

Response Activities

Celebration Dance

PERFORM A DANCE In the story, Mkiwa performs a traditional celebration dance. With a partner or small group, create and perform a dance that celebrates something important to you. Before your performance, explain what the dance is about.

Take a Deep Breath

MAKE A POSTER Think about how Jessie and her friends encouraged each other before performing at Evergreen Residential Manor. Make a poster of inspirational sayings and practical tips that could help you and your classmates. Display it where students can refer to it before their next public talk or performance.

Be a Volunteer

CONDUCT RESEARCH Jessie volunteers her time and talents at Evergreen Residential Manor. Use an on line Web browser, the telephone directory, or other sources to find places where you can volunteer. Make a chart of your findings, and share what you learn with your classmates. Discuss how your volunteering might change your life and the lives of those you help.

Make Someone Smile

MAKE A LIST Jessie in "Fall Secrets" and Kristen DeForrest in "Kids Did It!" both donate their time to make others happy. Think of some ways you could brighten someone's day. Write them down, and share your list with the class.

Out of Darkness

The Story of Louis Braille

by Russell Freedman
illustrated by Glenn Harrington

Louis Braille was living at a
school for the blind in Paris when he first heard
about Captain Barbier's reading system.
That system, called sonography, used dots and dashes
to stand for sounds. Louis learned the system
eagerly, but he was soon disappointed. It took too long
to use, and it had no spelling or punctuation.
Louis decided that he himself could
create a better system.

Out of Darkness
"THE STORY OF LOUIS BRAILLE"
by RUSSELL FREEDMAN
Illustrated by Kate Kiesler

Award-Winning Author

Visions of dots and more dots danced in Louis's head. He wanted to simplify Captain Barbier's system so that each dotted symbol could be "read" with a quick touch of the finger.

His days were filled with classes and school activities, so he experimented whenever he could find the time—between classes, on weekends, at night in the dormitory. When everyone else had gone to bed, and the only sound was the breathing of his sleeping classmates, he would take out his stylus and paper and begin to juggle dots. Often, he would doze off himself, his head nodding, the stylus grasped in his hand as though he wanted to keep on working in his sleep.

On some nights, he lost all track of time. He would be sitting on the edge of his bed, punching dots, when the rumbling of wagons on the cobblestones outside told him that morning had come.

After staying up all night, he fell asleep in class. And like several other students, he developed a hacking cough. Winter coughs were common at the Institute. The old school building always felt damp and cold.

Louis's mother worried about him when he came home for vacation. He looked so pale and gaunt. She wanted to fatten him up, and she insisted that he go to bed early. Monique would climb the stairs to the garret bedroom, tuck Louis in, and kiss him good-night, as though he were still a little boy.

A few weeks of fresh country air did wonders. Louis's cough vanished. He felt revived. On fine mornings, he would walk down the road with his cane, carrying a stylus, writing board, and paper in his knapsack. He would sit on a grassy slope, basking in the sun and working patiently as he punched dots into paper. People would pass by and call out, "Hello there, Louis! Still making pinpricks?" They weren't sure what he was trying to do, but whatever it was, he was obviously lost in thought.

Gradually, Louis managed to simplify Captain Barbier's system, but he wasn't satisfied. The dotted symbols he came up with were never simple enough. Sometimes he shouted in frustration and ripped the paper he was working on to shreds.

Then an idea came to him—an idea for an entirely different approach. It seemed so obvious! Why hadn't he thought of it before?

Captain Barbier's symbols were based on *sounds*—that was the problem! There were so many sounds in the French language. With sonography, a dozen dots or more might be needed to represent one syllable, as many as a hundred dots for a single word.

Instead of sounds, suppose the dot-and-dash symbols represented *letters of the alphabet*? The alphabet would be so much easier to work with.

Of course, Louis could not simply have one dot stand for *a*, two dots for *b*, and so on. That way, a blind reader would have to count twenty-six dots to read the letter *z*. Additional dots would be needed for numbers and punctuation marks.

But now that he had changed his thinking, Louis made real progress. He invented a simple code that allowed him to represent any letter of the alphabet within the space of a fingertip. At the beginning of the fall term in 1824, he was ready to demonstrate his new system. He had been working on it for three years.

First, he asked for a meeting with the school's director, Dr. Pignier. Louis sat in a big armchair opposite Pignier's desk, a writing board and paper on his lap, a stylus in his hand. He asked the director to select a passage from a book, any book he chose. "Read from it slowly and distinctly," Louis said, "as if you were reading to a sighted friend who was going to write down all your words."

Pignier picked a book from the shelf behind him. He opened it and began to read. Louis bent over his writing board and paper, his hand flying as he punched dots. After a few lines, he told Pignier, "You can read faster."

When Pignier finished reading the passage, Louis ran his finger over the raised dots on the back of the paper, as if to reassure himself. Then, without hesitating, he read every word he had taken down, at about the same speed as the director had read them.

Pignier couldn't believe his ears. He picked out another book, another passage, and asked Louis to repeat the demonstration. Then, rising from his desk with a burst of emotion, the director embraced Louis and praised him.

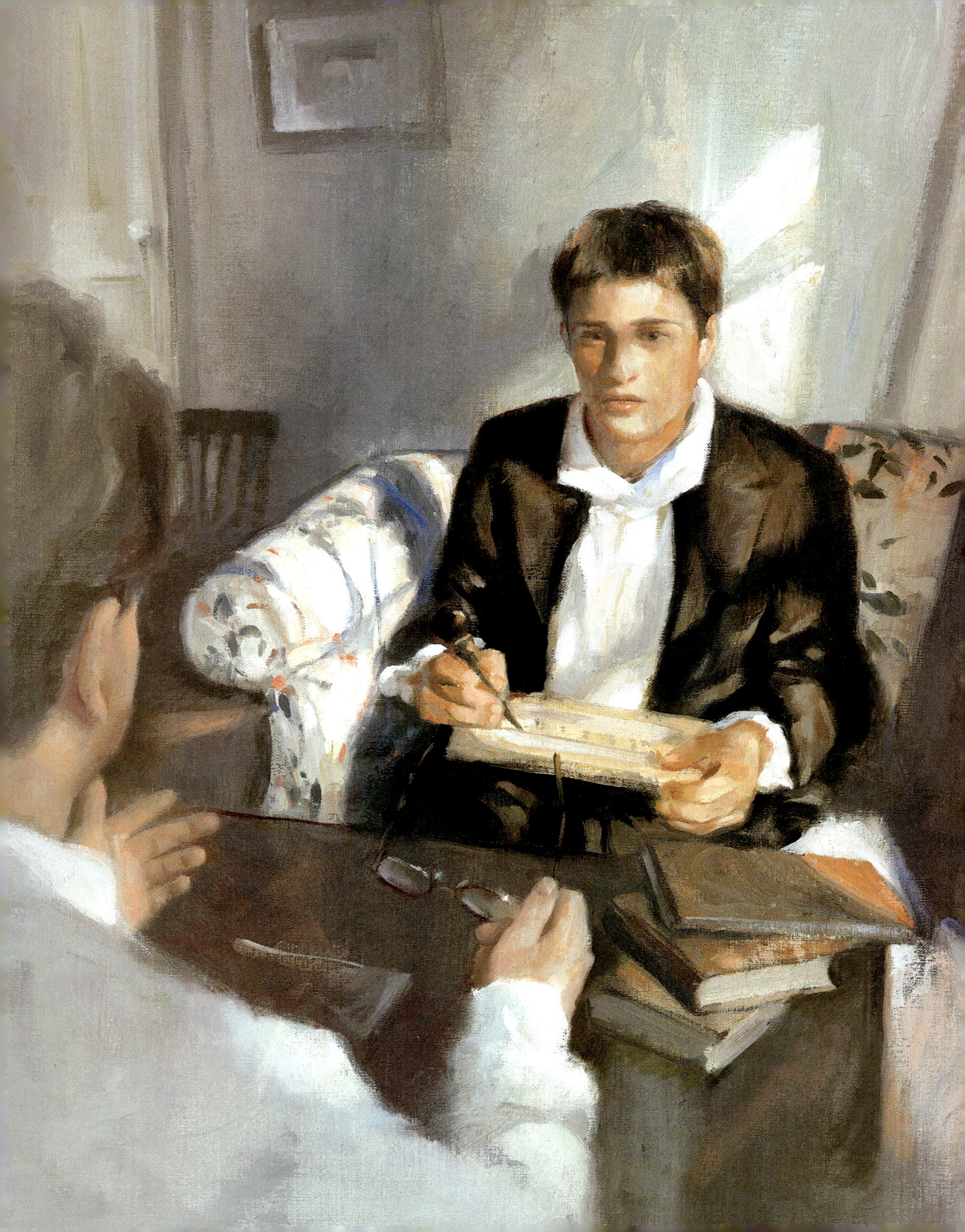

Soon the entire school was talking about Louis's new language of raised dots. Dr. Pignier called an assembly to introduce the students and teachers to the new system. Louis sat in the middle of a big classroom, working with his stylus as one of the sighted teachers read a poem aloud. The other sighted teachers leaned forward in their seats, watching Louis's hand move across the paper. The blind instructors and students cocked their heads and listened as the point of the stylus punched out dots.

Then Louis stood up. He cleared his throat and recited the poem, his fingers moving as he spoke, without missing a word or making an error. When he finished, an excited murmur filled the room and everyone crowded around him.

Louis was just fifteen years old when he demonstrated the first workable form of his system. During the next few years, he would continue to improve and add to his system, but he had already devised the basic alphabet that would open the doors of learning to blind people all over the world.

At first, he used dots combined with small dashes. But as his system was put to use, he found that dashes, while sensitive to the touch, were difficult to engrave with the stylus. Eventually, he got rid of the dashes, perfecting an alphabet made up entirely of dots.

Braille's system seems simple at first glance. That is the true sign of its genius. A simple system is exactly what Louis had spent three years trying to perfect.

To begin with, Louis reduced Barbier's dot clusters to a basic unit small enough to fit within the tip of a finger. This unit, now known as the braille cell, has space for six dots—two across and three down:

1 ● ● 4
2 ● ● 5
3 ● ● 6

Within this cell, Louis worked out different arrangements of dots. Each dot pattern represented a letter of the alphabet. As used today, the first ten characters of the system represent the first ten letters of the alphabet and the ten Arabic numerals:

A   B   C   D   E   F   G   H   I   J
1   2   3   4   5   6   7   8   9   0

Additional letters are formed by adding dots at the bottom of the cells:

K   L   M   N   O   P   Q   R

S   T   U   V   W   X   Y   Z

Using this basic six-dot cell, Louis eventually worked out sixty-three characters, representing the entire alphabet, numbers, punctuation symbols, contractions, some commonly used words, and later, musical notation and mathematical signs.

For use in writing his system, he adapted a device Barbier had used to write sonography—a grooved slate to hold the paper, and a sliding ruler to guide the stylus. The ruler was pierced by little windows. By positioning the stylus in these openings, a blind person could punch dots across the page with precision, then slide the ruler down to the next line.

The stylus produces depressions on the paper. One must therefore write from right to left and turn over the paper in order to read it.

With this system, Louis swept away all the shortcomings of embossing. The raised-dot characters were simple and complete. They could be read quickly with a light touch of a finger. They took up little more space than conventional printed letters. The braille system, as it came to be known, made it possible to place all the world's literature at the fingertips of blind readers.

The new alphabet of raised dots was mastered quickly by Louis's fellow students. Now, they could take notes in class, write letters and essays, keep journals, record their thoughts and feelings on paper. Louis personally transcribed parts of a standard textbook, *Grammar of Grammars*, into his new alphabet. It became the first text that blind students could read with ease.

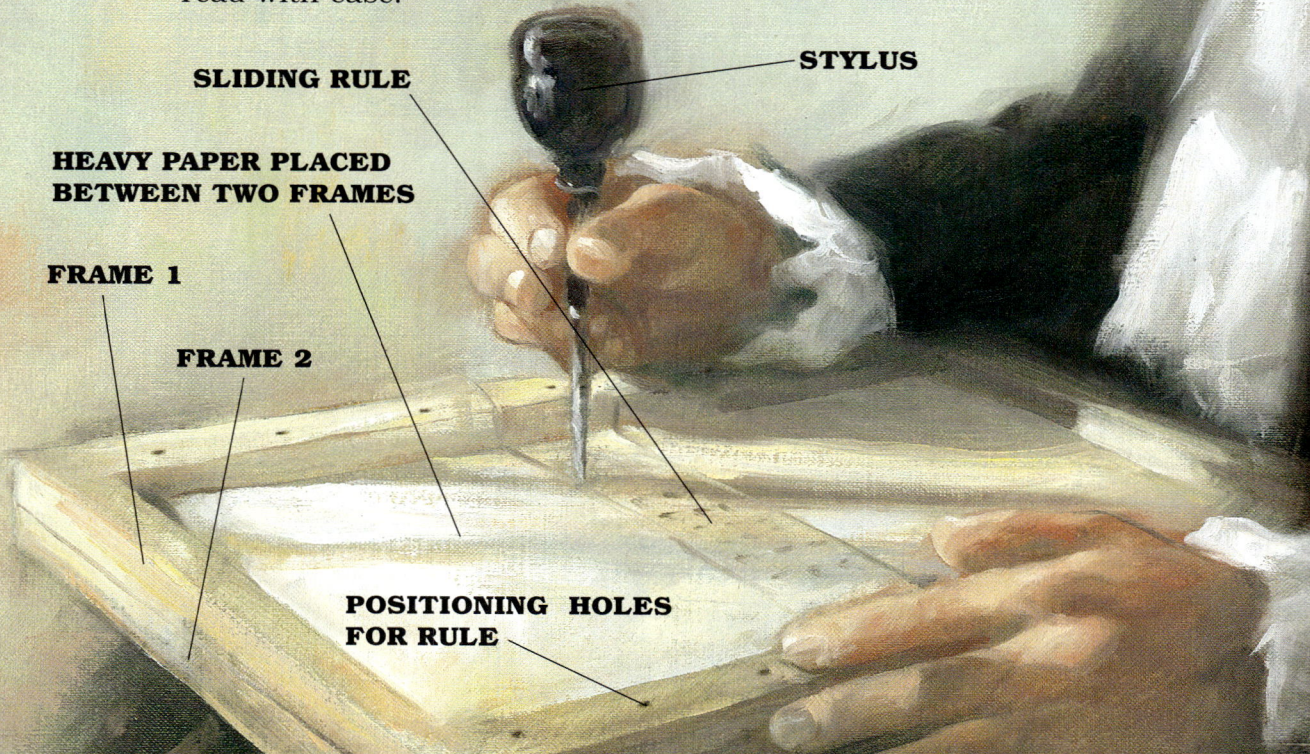

SLIDING RULE

STYLUS

HEAVY PAPER PLACED BETWEEN TWO FRAMES

FRAME 1

FRAME 2

POSITIONING HOLES FOR RULE

Yet he still wasn't satisfied. During his remaining years as a student, he continued to add to his system. Meanwhile, he did not neglect his studies. "Each year," wrote a classmate, "the name of Louis Braille rang out among the winners of the various prizes."

In 1826, while Louis was still a student, both he and his friend Gabriel Gauthier became teaching assistants at the Institute. When Louis graduated in 1828, Dr. Pignier asked him to stay on as a full-time instructor of grammar, geography, and arithmetic. Louis accepted gladly. By now, the school had become a real home to him.

When Louis celebrated his twentieth birthday in 1829, his raised-dot alphabet had been perfected to the point where it was substantially the same as the braille system used today.

Think About It

1. What was Louis Braille's problem and how did he solve it?

2. What do you think were Louis Braille's most important personal traits? Explain.

3. How did Louis affect the lives of the students in his school community?

Meet the Author
RUSSELL FREEDMAN

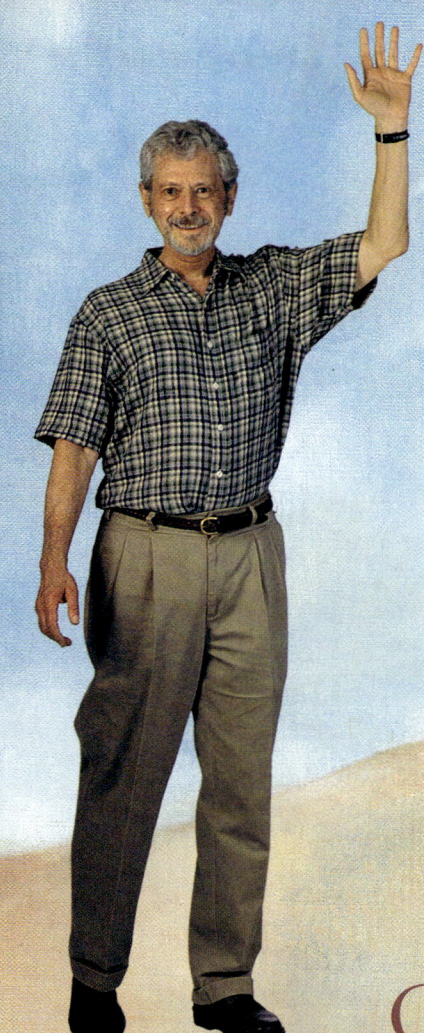

Russell Freedman has written over 30 books for young readers. His work has earned many awards, including the Newbery Medal for *Lincoln: A Photobiography*.

Freedman got the idea for his first book after reading a newspaper article about a blind sixteen-year-old who invented the braille typewriter. He learned that Louis Braille himself was only fifteen when he invented the braille alphabet. Freedman decided to write about Louis Braille and other outstanding young people in *Teenagers Who Made History*. He told Louis Braille's life story many years later in *Out of Darkness*.

Meet the Illustrator
GLENN HARRINGTON

Born and raised in New York, illustrator Glenn Harrington has always had a love of art. He began drawing at a young age and his parents encouraged him to take art lessons.

Much like Louis, who stuck with his invention, Glenn has been illustrating for 20 years. He says that he gets the ideas for his illustrations from the words of the story. He wants his drawings to show the reader what is between the pages.

Glenn enjoys writing poetry and children's books. His hobbies are baseball, spending time with his two sons, and woodworking.

Visit *The Learning Site!*
www.harcourtschool.com

RESPONSE ACTIVITIES

ON THE AIR WITH MR. BRAILLE

ROLE-PLAY A RADIO INTERVIEW With a partner, write a radio interview with Louis Braille. Have the interviewer discuss with Louis how he changed his school for the better. Use details from the selection to make the script realistic. Choose roles, rehearse the interview, and perform it for the class.

HOW TO BE LIKE LOUIS

WRITE A PARAGRAPH In spite of his physical handicap and his youth, Louis Braille developed a writing system that is still in use today. Write a paragraph about a time when you were determined to succeed in spite of obstacles.

On the Big Screen

MAKE A MOVIE POSTER Your job is to make a poster for a movie about Louis Braille. Draw or paint a scene from his life, or create a collage of images. Think of a catchy title for the movie and a description that will grab people's attention. Display your poster on a bulletin board.

Community Heroes

WRITE AN ESSAY Louis Braille is still a hero to people around the world. Read local newspaper articles to find the name of a hero in your community. Write a brief essay telling how that person has made your community a better place in which to live. Read your essay aloud to your class.

FOCUS SKILL: Make Generalizations

In "Out of Darkness," you read about Louis Braille's struggle to invent a reading and writing system for people who are blind.

Based on the information you gathered as you read, you can make a **generalization** about his invention. A generalization goes beyond any conclusion you have drawn. It makes a statement about other similar experiences. The diagram below shows how to make a generalization.

STEP 1	Gather information or evidence from reading and experience.
Example	*Louis Braille created a reading and writing system that is still used today by people who are blind.*
STEP 2	Draw a conclusion based on the evidence.
Example	*Braille wanted to invent a system to help people who are blind to read and write because no system was available.*
STEP 3	Make a generalization based on the evidence.
Example	*Today many people who cannot see can use the braille system to read and write.*
STEP 4	Evaluate the generalization for flaws.
Example	*Is the generalization **valid**, or reasonable? Or is it **invalid** because it goes too far beyond the information in the selection?*

To judge whether your generalization is valid, look for limiting words such as *some, many, most, sometimes,* or *usually*. Your generalization is more likely to be true if you add a limiting word.

To make a generalization based on something you've read, first draw a conclusion about the topic from what the author said. Then go beyond the information the author has given, but not too far. If you make a statement that is too broad, your generalization may be invalid.

Read the paragraph below. Then make a generalization based on what you have read. Be sure that your generalization is valid.

When Benjamin Franklin saw a problem, he tried to solve it with an invention. One problem he solved helped people see better. People had been using eyeglasses for centuries, but the earliest lenses all curved outward. These lenses helped people who couldn't see things up close. Later, inward-curving lenses were invented to help people who couldn't see things far away. Neither type of lens was right for people who needed help seeing both up close and far away. Franklin filled this need by combining the two kinds of lenses to create bifocals.

WHAT HAVE YOU LEARNED?

1. Reread the two paragraphs that describe how Louis Braille demonstrated his new system to the entire school. What generalization can you make based on the information there? What evidence did you use?

2. How can you decide whether a generalization is valid or invalid?

TRY THIS • TRY THIS • TRY THIS

Read a short article in a newspaper or a magazine. Make a generalization based on what you read. Then complete a diagram like the one on page 482.

Visit *The Learning Site!*
www.harcourtschool.com

by **Lucy Maud Montgomery**
adapted by **Jamie Turner**
illustrated by **Mitchell Heinze**

Anne of Green Gables

Characters

MARILLA CUTHBERT
MATTHEW CUTHBERT
ANNE SHIRLEY
MRS. RACHEL LYNDE
MRS. BARRY
DIANA BARRY
PEDDLER
REVEREND ALLAN
MRS. ALLAN

EN

485

Scene 1

Time: *Early 1900's.*

Setting: *Kitchen in Green Gables, a farm on Prince Edward Island. Dining table and chairs are center. Rocking chair, footstool, another chair and lamp are at left. Cupboard or long table across back of stage holds dishes, kitchen utensils, etc. Stove with pots on it is at right. Large window attached to back curtain shows view of trees in bloom, lake, etc. Working door is left.*

At Rise: Marilla Cuthbert *sits in rocking chair, sewing.*

Marilla (*To herself*): Where is that brother of mine? He should be back from the station by now. (*Rises and crosses to stove*) This stew will be cold if he doesn't come soon. (*After a moment,* Matthew Cuthbert *and* Anne Shirley *enter,* Anne *holding a battered suitcase.* Marilla *turns, then gasps.*)

Marilla (*Pointing to* Anne): Matthew Cuthbert, who's *that*? Where's the *boy* we sent for? (*During following conversation,* Anne *looks back and forth at* Marilla *and* Matthew.)

Matthew: There wasn't any boy at the train station, Marilla. Just this girl.

Marilla: But there must be a mistake. We sent word to Mrs. Spencer at the orphanage to bring us a *boy*.

Matthew (*Matter-of-factly*): Well, she didn't. She brought *her*, and I couldn't very well leave her at the station, mistake or not.

Marilla (*Throwing up hands*): Well, this is a pretty state of affairs. How is a *girl* going to be able to help us with all our work on the farm?

Anne (*With spirit*): You don't want me! You don't want me because I'm not a boy! (*Dramatically*) I might have expected it! Nobody ever did want me! I should have known all this was too good to last. Oh, what shall I do? (*Throws herself into chair, buries head in her arms and sobs loudly.*)

Marilla (*Sharply*): Well, well, there's no need to cry about it.

"Where is that brother of mine? He should be back from the station by now."

Anne (*Looking up*): Yes, there is need. You would cry, too, if you were an orphan and had come to a place you thought was going to be home and found they didn't want you because you're not a *boy*. (*Dramatically*) Oh, this is the most *tragical* thing that ever happened to me! (*More sobs*)

Matthew: Marilla, we'd best let her get a night's sleep. She's had a hard day.

Marilla (*To* Anne *a bit soothingly*): Now, now. Don't cry anymore. We're not going to turn you out of doors tonight. What's your name?

Anne (*Wiping eyes*): Well…I wish my name were *Cordelia*. It's such an elegant name. But my real name is Anne — with an *e* on the end. A-n-n-e looks so much more distinguished than plain old A-n-n, don't you agree?

Marilla: I don't see what difference it makes. (*Shakes head, puzzled*) Come, let's have our supper, and then you can get to bed.

Anne: Oh, I couldn't possibly eat, thank you anyway.

Marilla: And why not?

Anne: Because I'm in the depths of despair. Can *you* eat when you're in the depths of despair?

Marilla: I've never been in the depths of despair, so I can't say.

Anne: Well, it's a very uncomfortable feeling indeed. When you try to eat, a lump comes right up in your throat and you can't swallow a thing, not even a chocolate caramel. (*Looks at pot on stove*) Everything looks extremely nice, but I still cannot eat. I hope you won't be offended.

Matthew: I guess she's too tired to eat, Marilla. Come on, Anne, let me show you your room. (*Exits*)

Marilla: Good night, Anne.

Anne (*Starting to exit*): I'm sorry, Miss Cuthbert, but I can't bear to say *good* night when I'm sure it's the very worst night I've ever had! (*Exits.* Marilla *ladles stew from pot to bowl, sets it on table.* Matthew *re-enters, sits at table, and begins to eat.*)

Marilla: Well, Matthew, this is a pretty kettle of fish! The girl will have to be sent back to the orphanage, of course.

Matthew (*Unhappily*): Well, yes, I suppose so.

Marilla: You *suppose* so? Don't you *know* it?

Matthew (*Uneasily*): Well, she's a nice little thing, Marilla.

Marilla (*Sharply*): Matthew Cuthbert! You don't mean to say you think we ought to keep her! We need a boy to help out on the farm. What good would she be to us?

Matthew (*Firmly*): *We* might be some good to *her*, Marilla.

Marilla (*Crossing arms*): I can see as plain as plain that you want to let her stay.

Matthew: It does seem kind of a pity to send her back when she's so set on staying. (*Chuckling*) She's quite an interesting little girl, Marilla. You should have heard her talk coming home from the station.

Marilla: Oh, she can talk, all right, but talk is…

Matthew (*Interrupting*): I can hire a boy to help out with the farm, Marilla.

Marilla: Well, I…(*Exasperated*) Matthew! You're a stubborn one, for sure. (*Sighs heavily*) I can fight forever, but I may as well give in now as later. All right, Matthew. She can stay.

Matthew (*Smiling*): You won't regret this decision, Marilla. It will be nice to have a lively little girl on the farm.

Marilla (*Shaking head*): Marilla Cuthbert, did you ever suppose you'd see the day when you'd be adopting an orphan girl? (*Curtain*)

Scene 2

Time: *Next morning.*
Setting: *Same.*
At Rise: Marilla *is setting food on table for breakfast.* Matthew *is seated at table.*

Marilla (*Calling off*): Anne! Time to be up and dressed for breakfast! (Anne *enters.*)

Anne: Oh, aren't mornings a wonderful thing? Though my heart is still aggrieved, I'm not in the depths of despair anymore. I'm glad it's such a sunshiny morning; it's easier to bear up under afflictions when the sun is shining, isn't it?

Marilla (*Grumpily*): Never mind all your talk now. Let's sit down to eat. (Anne *and* Marilla *join* Matthew *at table. They start to eat.* Marilla *puts down fork and speaks to* Anne *in businesslike tone.*) I suppose I might as well tell you that Matthew and I have decided to keep you (Matthew *smiles.*)—that is, if you will try to be a good little girl. (Anne *looks disturbed.*) Why, child, whatever is the matter?

Anne (*Bewildered*): I'm crying. And trembling. I can't think why. I'm as glad as glad can be. But *glad* doesn't seem the right word at all. I was glad when I saw that wild cherry tree blooming outside my window, but this—oh, Miss Cuthbert, this is something more than glad! (*Sniffs loudly, wipes eyes*)

Marilla: Well, there's no sense in getting so worked up. I'm afraid you're too emotional for a little girl. And you must not call me Miss Cuthbert. That would make me nervous. We'll be just Marilla and Matthew.

Anne: Oh, Miss—I mean, Marilla—I'll try ever so hard to be good — *angelically* good.

Marilla (*Looking toward door*): Well, here comes your first opportunity. Our neighbor Mrs. Rachel Lynde is headed up the path to pay us a visit. Finish your breakfast quickly.

Matthew (*Standing*): I'm going out to plant the rest of my turnip seed. (*Exits right, as knock at door is heard.* **Marilla** *rises, goes to door, and lets in* **Mrs. Rachel Lynde**.)

Marilla: Why, Rachel, you're out early this morning. (*They walk back to table.*)

Mrs. Lynde (*Sitting down with a groan*): Oh, Marilla, I'm coming down with a terrible case of the rheumatics. I can just feel myself stiffening up something fearful! (*Sighs heavily*) Well, well, life is full of suffering. (*Turns to peer over her glasses at* **Anne**) Well! And who is *this*, Marilla?

"Why, Rachel, you're out early this morning."

Marilla: This is Anne Shirley, Rachel. Mrs. Spencer sent her to us from the orphanage. Anne, this is Mrs. Lynde.

Mrs. Lynde: I thought you said you were getting a boy from the orphanage. She's terribly homely and skinny, Marilla. Merciful heavens, did anyone ever *see* such freckles? And hair as red as carrots!

Anne (*Jumping to feet; angrily*): How dare you call me homely and skinny! You are a rude, impolite woman! How would you like to be told that you are fat and clumsy? You've hurt my feelings *excruciatingly*, and I shall never forgive your unkindness! Never! Never! (*Stamps foot and runs from stage, crying.* **Marilla** *and* **Mrs. Lynde** *sit in stunned silence.*)

Mrs. Lynde: Well! Did anybody ever see such a temper? I don't envy you your job of bringing *that* up, Marilla!

Marilla: What Anne just did was very naughty, Rachel, but I wish you hadn't called attention to her looks. (*Sighs*) I'll have to give her a good talking to.

Mrs. Lynde (*Primly*): You'll have trouble with that child, mark my words! (*Rises and goes to door*) Goodbye, Marilla! I'm going to look around in your garden for a few minutes before I go, if you don't mind. I want to have a word with Matthew, too. (*Exits.* **Marilla** *turns, shakes head, and sighs.*)

Marilla (*Calling*): Anne, come here. (**Anne** *enters, head down.*) Now, aren't you ashamed of the way you spoke to Mrs. Lynde?

"*Y*ou'll have trouble with that child, mark my words!"

Anne: She had no right to say those things.

Marilla: And you had no right to fly into such a fury. You must ask her forgiveness.

Anne: Oh, I can never do that, Marilla. (*Dramatically*) You can shut me up in a dark, damp dungeon inhabited by snakes and toads, but I *cannot* ask Mrs. Lynde to forgive me.

Marilla (*Sternly*): Anne, disrespect in a child is a terrible thing. I'm disappointed in you. (**Anne** *hangs her head and is silent for a few moments.*) You did tell me that you would try to be good, didn't you?

ANNE (*Looking up*): Now that my temper has died down, I suppose I am truly sorry for speaking so to Mrs. Lynde.

MARILLA: And you will tell her so?

ANNE: Yes, Marilla. I will. (MARILLA *goes to door.*)

MARILLA (*Calling*): Rachel! Anne has something to say to you. Will you please come back in for a minute? (ANNE *is mouthing words to herself.*) What are you doing, Anne?

ANNE: I'm imagining out what I must say to Mrs. Lynde. (MRS. LYNDE *enters, and* ANNE *approaches, falling down on her knees and extending her hands.*) Oh, Mrs. Lynde, I am so extremely sorry. (*In a quivering voice*) I could never express all my sorrow, no, not if I used up a whole dictionary. You must just try to *imagine* the extent of my grief. I have been dreadfully wicked and ungrateful. Oh, Mrs. Lynde, *please, please* forgive me. If you refuse, it will be a lifelong sorrow to me. (MRS. LYNDE *and* MARILLA *exchange surprised glances.*)

MRS. LYNDE (*Embarrassed*): There, there, child. Get up. Of course I forgive you. I guess I was a little too harsh and outspoken.

ANNE (*Rising*): Oh, thank you, Mrs. Lynde. Your forgiveness is like a soothing ointment to my heart.

MRS. LYNDE (*Patting* ANNE *on head*): Good day, Anne. Good day, Marilla. (*Aside, to* MARILLA) She's an odd little thing, but you know, on the whole I rather like her. (*Exits. Curtain*)

Scene 3

TIME: *Next day.*
SETTING: *Same.*
AT RISE: MARILLA *sweeps floor while* ANNE *dries dishes.*

MARILLA: Anne, the Barrys are coming over this morning. Mrs. Barry is going to return a skirt pattern she borrowed, and you can get acquainted with her daughter, Diana. She's about your age.

ANNE (*Dropping dish towel*): Oh, Marilla, what if she doesn't like me?

MARILLA: Now, don't get into a fluster. I guess Diana will like you well enough. Just be polite and well behaved, and don't make any of your startling speeches.

ANNE: Oh, Marilla, *you'd* be flustered, too if you were going to meet a little girl who might become your best friend. I've never had a best friend in my whole life. My nerves are absolutely *frazzled* with excitement!

MARILLA: I do wish you wouldn't use such long words. It sounds funny in a little girl. (*Knock at door is heard.*) For pity's sake, calm yourself, child. (*Goes to answer door.* MRS. BARRY *and* DIANA *enter.*) Hello, Margaret, Hello, Diana.

MRS. BARRY: How are you, Marilla?

MARILLA: Fine. I'd like you both to meet the little girl we've adopted. (*Gestures*) This is Anne Shirley.

ANNE: That's "Anne" spelled with an *e*.

DIANA: Hello, Anne. I'm Diana.

492

Mrs. Barry (*Taking Anne's hand*): How are you, Anne?

Anne: I am well in body although considerably rumpled in spirit, thank you, ma'am. (*Aside, to Marilla*) There wasn't anything startling in that, was there?

Marilla: Anne, why don't you take Diana outside, and show her the flower garden while Mrs. Barry and I talk? (*Ladies sit down.*)

Anne: All right, Marilla. (*Girls walk stage front, sit side by side with legs hanging over edge, looking at each other shyly.*)

Mrs. Barry (*To Marilla*): I'm glad for the prospect of a playmate for Diana. Perhaps it will take her more out of doors. She spends too much time inside, straining her eyes over books. (*Ladies continue to talk in background as focus shifts to Anne and Diana.*)

Anne (*Fervently*): Oh, Diana, do you think…do you think you can like me well enough to be my best friend?

Diana (*Laughing*): Why, I guess so. I'm glad you've come to live at Green Gables. It'll be fun to have somebody to play with.

Anne (*Seriously*): Will you swear to be my friend for ever and ever?

Diana (*Gasping*): Why, it's dreadfully wicked to swear!

Anne: Oh, no, *my* kind of swearing isn't wicked. There are two kinds, you know.

Diana: I've heard of only one kind.

Anne: My kind isn't wicked at all. It just means vowing and promising solemnly.

Diana: Oh. Well, I guess it wouldn't hurt to do that. How do you do it?

Anne: First, we stand up. (*Girls stand.*) Then we just join hands—so. (*They join hands.*) I'll repeat the oath first. (*Closes eyes*) I solemnly swear to be faithful to my best friend, Diana Barry, as long as the sun and the moon shall endure. Now you say it and put my name in.

Diana: I solemnly swear to be faithful to my best friend, Anne Shirley, as long as the sun and moon shall endure. (*Laughs*) I can tell we're going to have lots of fun together, Anne Shirley! Will you go with me to the Sunday School picnic next week? It's going to be ever so much fun! Everyone takes a picnic basket, and we eat our lunch down by the lake and go for boat rides—and then we have *ice cream* for dessert!

Anne: Ice cream! Oh, Diana, I would be perfectly *enraptured* if Marilla would let me go with you. I'll go ask her right now. Come on. (*Still holding hands, girls approach* Marilla *and* Mrs. Barry.) Oh, Marilla! Diana has invited me to go to the Sunday School picnic with her next week! I've never been to a picnic, though I've dreamed of them often. Oh, and Marilla— think of it— they are going to serve *ice cream! Ice cream*, Marilla! And there will be boats on the lake and everyone will take a picnic basket—and, oh, dear Marilla, may I go, *please*, may I? I would consider my life a graveyard of buried hopes—I read that in a book once, doesn't it sound pathetic?—if I couldn't go to the picnic! *Please* say that I can go, Marilla.

Marilla (*Shaking head and clicking tongue*): Anne, I've never seen the like for going on and on about a thing. Now, just try to control yourself. As for the picnic, I'm not likely to refuse you when all the other children are going.

Anne (*Throwing her arms around* Marilla): Oh, you dear, good Marilla! You are so kind to me.

Marilla: There, there, never mind your hugging nonsense. I'll make you up a nice lunch basket when the time comes.

Mrs. Barry: Anne may ride over to the picnic with Diana if you like, and we'll bring her home, too. (*Rises*) We must be going home now, Diana. Tell Anne goodbye. Maybe you can play together tomorrow. Thank you, Marilla, for the nice visit. (Barrys *exit*.)

Anne: Oh, Marilla, looking forward to things is half the pleasure of them, don't you think? I do hope the weather is fine next week. I don't feel that I could endure the disappointment if anything happened to prevent me from getting to the picnic. (*Curtain*)

Scene 4

TIME: *Several days later.*
SETTING: *Same. Brooch is on floor, under chair. Loose flowers and vase are on table.*
AT RISE: ANNE *sits with patchwork in lap, daydreaming.* MARILLA *enters.* ANNE *begins stitching vigorously.*

ANNE: I've been working steadily, Marilla, but it's ever so hard when the picnic is *this very afternoon*. I keep trying to imagine what it will be like.

MARILLA (*Looking around, puzzled*): Anne, have you seen my amethyst brooch? I thought I put it right here in my pin cushion, but I can't find it anywhere.

ANNE (*Nervously*): I—I saw it last night when you were at the Ladies Aid Society. It was in the pin cushion, as you said.

MARILLA (*Sternly*): Did you touch it?

ANNE (*Uncomfortably*): Yes. I pinned it on my dress for just a minute—only to see how it would look.

MARILLA (*Angrily*): You had no business touching something that didn't belong to you, Anne. Where did you put it?

ANNE: Oh, I put it right back. I didn't have it on but a minute, and I didn't think about it being wrong at the time, but I'll never do it again. That's one good thing about me. I never do the same naughty thing twice.

MARILLA (*Sternly*): You did not put it back, or else it would be here. You've taken it and put it somewhere else, Anne. Tell me the truth at once. Did you lose it?

ANNE (*Upset*): Oh, but I did put it back, Marilla. I'm perfectly certain I put it back!

MARILLA (*Angrily, her voice rising*): If you had put it back, it would be here, Anne. I believe you are telling me a falsehood. In fact, I know you are.

ANNE: Oh, but, Marilla...

MARILLA (*Harshly*): Don't say another word unless you are prepared to tell me where the brooch is. Go to your room and stay there until you are ready to confess. (ANNE *starts to exit, downcast.*)

ANNE: The picnic is this afternoon, Marilla. You *will* let me out of my room for that, won't you? I *must* go to the picnic!

MARILLA: You'll go to no picnic nor anywhere else until you've confessed, Anne Shirley. Now, *go*! (ANNE *exits.*)

MATTHEW (*Entering*): Where's Anne? I wanted to show her the new geese down at the pond.

MARILLA (*Coldly*): She's in her room. The child has lost my amethyst brooch and is hiding the truth from me. She's *lied* about it, Matthew.

MATTHEW: Well now, are you certain, Marilla? Mightn't you have forgotten where you put it?

MARILLA (*Angrily*): Matthew Cuthbert, I'll remind you that I have kept the brooch safe for over fifty years, and I'm not likely to lose track of it now.

Matthew: Don't be too hasty to accuse Anne. I don't think she'd lie to you. (*Exits.* Marilla *begins to arrange flowers in vase on table as* Anne *enters.*)

Anne: Marilla, I'm ready to confess.

Marilla: Well, that was mighty quick. What do you have to say, Anne?

Anne (*Speaking quickly, as if reciting from memory*): I took the amethyst brooch, just as you said. I pinned it on my dress and then was overcome with an irresistible temptation to take it down by the Lake of Shining Waters to pretend that I was an elegant lady named Cordelia Fitzgerald. But, alas, as I was leaning over the bridge to catch its purple reflection in the water, it fell off and went down—down—down, and sank forevermore beneath the lake. Now, will you please punish me, Marilla, and have it over so that I can go to the picnic with nothing weighing on my mind?

Marilla (*Staring at* Anne *in anger*): Anne, you must be the very wickedest girl I ever heard of to take something that wasn't yours and to lose it and then to lie about it and now to show no sign of sorrow whatever! Picnic, indeed! You'll go to no picnic! That will be your punishment, and it isn't half severe enough either for what you've done!

Anne (*Sobbing*): Not go to the picnic! But, Marilla, that's why I confessed! Oh, Marilla, you promised! Think of the ice cream, Marilla! How can you deny me the ice cream and break my heart?

Marilla (*Stonily*): You needn't plead, Anne. You are *not* going to the picnic, and that is final. (Anne *runs to table and flings herself into a chair, sobbing and shrieking wildly.*) I believe the child is out of control. (Marilla *walks around, wringing her hands. She suddenly catches sight of brooch under chair and picks it up with a startled cry.*) What can this mean? Here's my brooch, safe and sound! And I thought it was at the bottom of the lake! (Anne *looks up.*) Anne, child, whatever did you mean by saying you took it and lost it?

Anne: Well, you said you'd keep me in my room until I confessed, so I thought up an interesting confession so I could go to the picnic. But then you wouldn't let me go after all, so my confession was wasted.

Marilla (*Trying to look stern, but finally laughing*): Anne, you do beat all! But I was wrong—I see that now. I shouldn't have doubted your word when you had never told me a lie before. Of course, you shouldn't have made up that story, but I drove you to it. So if you'll forgive me, I'll forgive you. Now, go upstairs and wash your face and get ready for the picnic.

Anne: It isn't too late?

Marilla: No, they'll just be getting started. You won't miss a thing—especially the ice cream. That's always last.

Anne (*Squealing happily*): Oh, Marilla! Five minutes ago I was in the valley of woe, but now I wouldn't change places with an angel! (*Exits*)

"Here's my brooch, safe and sound! And I thought it was at the bottom of the lake!"

Scene 5

Time: *Next day.*
Setting: *Same.*
At Rise: Marilla *is dusting furniture. Anne enters.*

Anne: When I woke up just a while ago, Marilla, I spent a good ten minutes at my window just remembering yesterday's splendid picnic. I could hardly bear to face a plain old ordinary day after such a romantic experience. Words fail me to describe the ice cream, Marilla. I assure you it was *scrumptiously sublime*.

Marilla: I'm glad you had a pleasant time, Anne, but you must come back down to earth. I've invited the new minister, Mr. Allan, and his wife for tea this afternoon.

Anne (*Clasping hands*): Oh, Marilla! How divine! I think Mrs. Allan is perfectly lovely. I've watched her during sermons every Sunday since they've been here. She wears such pretty hats and has such *exquisite* dimples in her cheeks!

Marilla: Hmph! You'd do better listening to the sermon instead of studying hats and dimples.

Anne: Marilla, will you let me make a cake for the Allans? I'd love to do something special for them.

Marilla: Well, I suppose you can — if you'll be very careful to measure properly and then clean up afterward.

Anne: Oh, I will, I will—I promise! Thank you, Marilla! (Anne *starts to measure, stir, etc. As she works, she alternately hums and talks.*) I do hope the minister and Mrs. Allan like layer cake. Diana says she has a cousin who doesn't even like ice cream. Can you *imagine*, Marilla? (*Pause*) I wonder if Mrs. Allan will ask for a second piece of cake? She's probably a dainty eater, judging from her waistline, don't you think? But then, sometimes it's hard to tell. (*Pours batter into pan*) I can eat quite a bit, and I'm awfully skinny, but Diana eats hardly anything and is ever so plump. (*Puts pan into oven*) There, now. The cake's in the oven, Marilla.

Oh, I don't see how I can ever wait till this afternoon! I'm bound to *explode* before the Allans arrive.

MARILLA: Goodness, child, let's hope not. That would be quite a spectacle. Now, why don't you go outdoors and run off a little of your excitement? I'll keep a close eye on your cake and take it out when it's done.

ANNE: Thank you, Marilla! (*Exits and comes out side door,* PEDDLER *comes out other side, and they meet on floor on front of stage.* MARILLA *may work in kitchen or sew during conversation.*)

PEDDLER: Hello there, miss. Would you be interested in buying some of my wares?

ANNE: Uh—well—what kinds of things do you have?

PEDDLER (*Walking around* ANNE, *looking at her hair and shaking his head*): Well, right here in my bag, miss, I have a bottle of Mr. Roberts' Hair Potion that is guaranteed to turn you into the raven-haired beauty of Prince Edward Island. (*Takes bottle from bag, holds it up*) One simple application will give your hair a glossy ebony sheen.

ANNE (*Touching her hair*): My red hair *is* a sore affliction to my soul. And I *have* always dreamed of having beautiful black hair. But I have only fifty cents. (*Fishes in pocket*)

PEDDLER: Well, now, I'll tell you what, miss. The regular price of Mr. Roberts' Hair Potion is seventy-five cents, but just for today I'll give it to you for only fifty cents. (*Takes her money and gives her the bottle; exits quickly*)

ANNE: What a kind-hearted man! (*Excited*) Now I can be the dark-haired beauty I've always wanted to be! I'll go home right now and put the potion on before the Allans come. With my cake and my beautiful new hair, I'm sure to impress them! (*Exits.* MARILLA *takes cake from oven, rearranges flowers in vase, straightens napkins at table.*)

MARILLA: Now, I must call Anne in. The Allans will be here any minute. (*Calls offstage*) It's time for tea! Anne! Anne! (MATTHEW *enters.*)

MATTHEW: I didn't see Anne outside, Marilla. (*Knock on door is heard.*)

MARILLA: Oh, dear. That must be the Allans. Now, where could Anne be? (*Goes to door.* REVEREND *and* MRS. ALLAN *enter.*) Hello, Reverend Allan. Mrs. Allan. Do come in! We're mighty glad you could come.

499

MRS. ALLAN: How lovely of you to invite us for tea, Marilla.

REV. ALLAN: We've been looking forward to it. (*To* MATTHEW) Hello, Matthew.

MATTHEW (*Shaking hands with* ALLANS): Welcome to our home.

MARILLA (*Gesturing to chairs*): Please have a seat. Anne will be right here to greet you. (ANNE *enters, wearing large, floppy hat, head down.*) Here I am, Marilla.

MARILLA (*Startled*): Why, Anne, what in creation are you doing with a hat on your head?

ANNE: Uh—my head feels a little chilly, Marilla. Good day, Reverend and Mrs. Allan. It's an honor to have you come for tea. (*Curtsies with a flourish. Her hat falls off, and* ANNE'S *hair, bright green, tumbles down.*)

MARILLA (*Stepping back; covering mouth*): Anne Shirley! What have you done to your hair?

MATTHEW (*Amused*): Well now, it looks *green*!

ANNE (*Miserably*): Oh, please don't scold me. I'm utterly wretched as it is, and scolding would only make it worse. (*Covers face with hands*) I wanted to have beautiful raven hair—the peddler promised—but...

MARILLA (*Sternly*): Peddler? What peddler?

MATTHEW: I saw one of those traveling peddlers around town this morning. I'll warrant he came out this way after he finished in Avonlea.

MARILLA: Anne, what did you buy from the peddler?

ANNE: Mr. Roberts' Hair Potion. My hair was supposed to turn glossy black, but it turned...(*Holding up a strand*) green.

MARILLA (*Shaking head*): Oh, Anne, goodness only knows what's to be done with you. You can get yourself into more scrapes. It appears to me that you would run out of ideas for mischief one of these days. Now I hope you've learned...(MATTHEW *begins laughing quietly.*) Matthew, what *are* you doing? (ALLANS *join in; soon everyone is laughing.*)

REV. ALLAN (*Smiling, holding hand out to* ANNE): I don't believe we've ever been greeted in such a unique fashion, Anne. We're pleased to be here.

MRS. ALLAN (*Shaking* ANNE'S *hand*): Hello, Anne. Don't be upset. I like little girls with imagination and an adventurous spirit.

MARILLA: Well, I do hope you'll pardon us. I certainly hadn't expected to greet you in such a fashion. Anne, we'll have to try to see what we can do with your hair after tea. But for now, let's all sit down. Everything's ready. (*All sit.*) Let me serve the cake first. Anne made this all by herself.

MRS. ALLAN: My, what an accomplished girl to bake such a lovely cake!

"My hair was supposed to turn glossy black, but it turned...*green*."

REV. ALLAN: Yellow layer cake is my favorite, Anne. (*Everyone takes a bite at the same time. Peculiar looks cross faces; everyone begins to cough, take drinks from cups, fan faces, etc.*)

MARILLA: Anne Shirley! What did you put into that cake?

MATTHEW: Well now, it does taste a mite peculiar.

ANNE (*Forlornly*): I put in what the recipe said. Oh, it must have been that baking powder!

MARILLA: Baking powder, fiddlesticks! What flavoring did you use?

ANNE: Only vanilla.

MARILLA: Go and bring me the bottle of vanilla you used. (ANNE *gets up and brings back small brown bottle from cupboard.*) Mercy on us, Anne, you've gone and flavored our cake with Matthew's cough medicine! (ANNE *utters a cry of distress and runs off stage. Curtain closes.* ANNE *enters in front of curtain and sits down, crying dejectedly.* MRS. ALLAN *enters from other side and stands quietly while* ANNE *talks.*)

ANNE (*Crying*): Oh, I'm disgraced forever and forever. I shall never live this down, not if I live to be a hundred years old. I can never look the Allans in the face again. First my hair and then the cake—oh, I'm doomed to bounce from one tragedy to another! How can I ever tell Mrs. Allan that the cake was an innocent mistake? What if she thinks I tried to *poison* her?

MRS. ALLAN (*Stepping closer*): Oh, I doubt that she'll think that. (ANNE *looks up and rises quickly, wiping eyes.*) You mustn't cry like this, Anne. It's only a funny mistake that anybody might make.

ANNE: Oh, no, it takes me to make such a mistake, Mrs. Allan. And I so wanted to have that cake perfect for you.

MRS. ALLAN: In that case, I assure you I appreciate your kindness and thoughtfulness just as much as if it had turned out all right. Now, you mustn't cry anymore, but come down to the flower garden with me. Miss Cuthbert tells me you have a little plot all your own. I want to see it, for I love flowers. (*They begin walking across stage together.*)

ANNE: Well, I suppose there's one encouraging thing about making mistakes. There *must* be a limit to the number a person can make, and when I get to the end of them, then I'll be through with them for good. (*They exit.*)

Think About It

1. How does Anne change Marilla's and Matthew's lives?

2. If you were an actor in the play, which character would you want to be? Why?

3. How do you know Anne has a good imagination? Give examples from the story.

About the Author
Lucy Maud Montgomery

Lucy Maud Montgomery (1874-1942) grew up in a small town on Prince Edward Island, a province of Canada. At the age of eleven, Lucy began sending her writing to publishers. Four years later, a Canadian magazine published her first poem. She once said she was born with "an itch for writing."

Montgomery had a lot in common with her most famous character, Anne Shirley. Montgomery was raised by grandparents similar to Anne's adoptive parents, Marilla and Matthew Cuthbert. Like Anne, she had an outgoing, lively personality. Instead of getting into trouble, however, Montgomery put her energy into writing. She wrote ten novels about Anne and her family as well as hundreds of stories and poems.

Lucy Maud Montgomery's lively characters and the humor in her stories made her books popular around the world. Today, tourists visit her home in the Canadian province of Ontario, where she did most of her writing as an adult. Many more visit Prince Edward Island to experience for themselves the setting of their favorite story, *Anne of Green Gables*.

Visit *The Learning Site!*
www.harcourtschool.com

Tea Biscuits

Mrs. Rachel and Marilla sat comfortably in the parlour while Anne got the tea and made hot biscuits that were light and white enough to defy even Mrs. Rachel's criticism. (ANNE OF GREEN GABLES)

"The Tea," about 1880, Mary Stevenson Cassatt
M. Theresa B. Hopkins Fund, Courtesy, Museum of Fine Arts, Boston

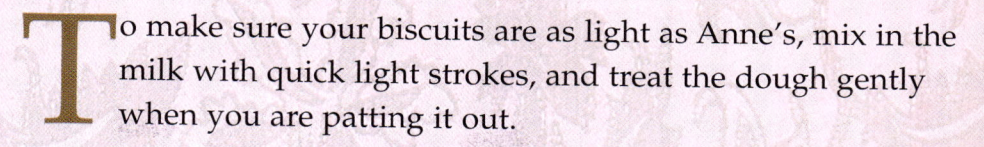

To make sure your biscuits are as light as Anne's, mix in the milk with quick light strokes, and treat the dough gently when you are patting it out.

Ingredients

1¼ cups	all-purpose flour	300 mL
1¼ tsp	baking powder	6 mL
¼ tsp	baking soda	1 mL
pinch	salt	pinch
6 tbsp	cold butter, cut in small pieces	90 mL
6 tbsp	milk or buttermilk	90 mL

1. Preheat your oven to 400°F (200°C).
2. In a large bowl, combine the flour, baking powder, baking soda, and salt.
3. Add the butter to the dry ingredients and, using a pastry blender, your fingers, or a fork, blend it in thoroughly until the mixture has the look of coarse crumbs.
4. Add the milk and mix it in just until blended.
5. Turn the dough out onto a lightly floured board. Flour your hands and pat out the dough until it is about ½ inch (1.25 cm) thick.
6. Cut out biscuits with a 1½-inch (3.75-cm) floured cutter. (Do not twist the cutter.) Place the biscuits about ½ inch (1.25 cm) apart on an ungreased baking sheet.
7. Bake the biscuits for 10 to 12 minutes, or until they are just golden-brown. Butter the tops of the biscuits lightly as soon as they come out of the oven. Serve them hot, if possible, with butter and jam.

Makes about 16 biscuits.

Think About It

What do you think would happen if you didn't follow the directions?

RESPONSE ACTIVITIES

A Scrumptiously Sublime Speech

PERFORM A DIALOGUE
Anne often speaks in an exaggerated way, as when she says, "My nerves are absolutely frazzled with excitement." Find some dialogue from another story you have read, and rewrite it as if Anne speaks it. Use a synonym finder to help you find fancy variations on common words. Perform the new dialogue for the class.

Your Hair Turned *What*?

CONDUCT AN INTERVIEW
Anne is unexpectedly funny when she tries to dye her hair black but it turns green. Interview a classmate about a time when he or she made a humorous mistake. Take notes, and then write a funny story about what happened.

Home Sweet Home

WRITE A POEM
One of Anne's goals is to be happy in her new community. Write a poem about a part of your community that makes you happy. Draw a picture to go with your poem.

Making Connections

WRITE AN INVITATION
Design an invitation for Anne to come to a party that you will host. List in it what you will serve. Be sure to include tea biscuits, which you know Anne likes. You might use the food section of a local newspaper or a cookbook to get interesting menu ideas.

COW

ROUNDUP ON AN

BY JOAN ANDERSON

BOYS

AMERICAN RANCH

PHOTOGRAPHS BY GEORGE ANCONA

Booklist Editors' Choice

It is spring roundup time at the Eby Ranch in Faywood, New Mexico. Leedro and Colter Eby have reported to work to help their father. Their mission: to round up 800 cattle on the 75-square mile range.

Eby Ranch brand

The smell of saddle soap and neat's-foot oil, used to keep saddle leather soft, permeates the air. The cowboys haul saddles and blankets out of the tack room. They brush the snarls out of their horses' backs and speak tenderly to them.

"There's no vehicle that can go where these horses go," says Leedro, pulling the saddle strap tight, making sure the rigging has no extra play. "They give us so much. We've got to take care of 'em."

Just then he notices his horse favoring her hind leg. He rubs his hand gently over her ankle. It feels hot. "You're not goin' anywhere," he says, realizing she must have strained a tendon on yesterday's ride. "You need a couple days' rest." He pats her neck and leads her back to a pen.

The once-tranquil corral is now alive. Boots pound the hardened earth, and spurs clink as the cowboys head for their horses, hiding bridles behind their backs.

"The horses don't like a bridle on," says Leedro, "so we kinda creep up on 'em." Meanwhile, experienced horse trainer Randy Biebelle has cornered the high-spirited filly that he's been breaking for the past thirty days. All eyes are on Randy to see how he handles her. He talks gently to the barely tame horse. After some initial balking, she lets him secure the bit in her mouth.

"I think you're ready to ride," Randy says, patting her and swiftly saddling her up. "We'll soon see," he says, thinking ahead to the challenge of riding her all day. Just then the horse bucks, as if to assert that she's still free.

All the cowboys are mounted and ready to go when Leedro and Colter's mom, Rose Ann, pulls up. She tucks freshly made burritos into saddlebags and grabs the reins of her horse, Tommy. A full-fledged cowgirl herself, Rose Ann would rather work alongside her husband and boys than stay behind.

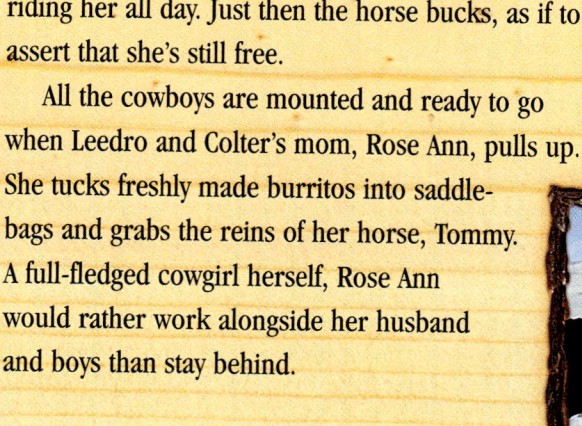

"Time to head out," Larry says. The cowboys gather for their orders, some still shivering in the cool early-morning air. It's been a dry winter and an even drier spring. Larry is anxious to sell off as many cows as he can before he loses them to the drought.

Larry has divided up his territory into sections like a checkerboard. Each cowboy is assigned a section, where he will search for and bring in every last grazing cow.

"Leedro, you head east up the canyon. Colter, you go with Johnny and Abe. The rest of you come with me to the high country. See you at Tom Brown Basin in a couple of hours." They trot off toward the red clay mesas, into the wind, eyes squinting to avoid the dust, felt hats pulled down around their ears. The lilt of voices bounces off the canyon walls for a time and then fades away.

Leedro feels safe mounted on Comanche, a surefooted horse who can handle rugged terrain. They proceed slowly at first, navigating around craggy mesquite bushes and paddle cactus plants.

Leedro keeps his eyes open for rattlesnakes, knowing horses buck when they see one. The buzz of hummingbirds and the clack of Comanche's hooves against the shale rock keep him company. These wide-open spaces are his backyard, a place he's been playing in and riding over since he was a baby. They pass rock caves where Apaches corralled their horses, spots where his dad found weapons left behind by Spanish conquistadores, and rock carvings drawn by Mimbres Indians.

Seconds later his horse stops. She neighs and jumps backward. Leedro looks around to see what is upsetting her. Nearby lies a dead baby calf, probably killed by a hungry predator. Coyotes and mountain lions, desperate for food when there is a drought, ravage anything they can find. Leedro has never seen conditions this bad on the range, and he's worried.

On the other side of the mountain, Larry Eby stares at the brown rubble that was once hearty food for his cattle. He is concerned about the health of his herd as well as the condition of his land.

As he rides, he scans the quiet hills for signs of life, cows grazing or the movement of deer and antelope. It takes a while to find the cattle with Larry's method of ranching. "I spread 'em out, only about eight or ten on each section. That way I'm bein' kinder to the land. It does take a little longer to round 'em up." But Larry doesn't mind.

"Comin' up here, smellin' the sage, breathin' clean air, I forget about everything back in the valley.

"I love this place," he says of the ranch his family has worked for one hundred fifty years. "My dad used to say that you didn't need church when you lived out here under the big sky — you can see God's been here." Even so, Larry would feel much better if the sky turned dark with rain clouds.

The cowboys usually begin to spot cows after about an hour of riding. "It's like findin' a needle in a haystack," Leedro says. "You gotta think like a cow. What would they be feedin' on? Where would they be hidin' their newborns? If they finished breakfast, would they be sleepin' under trees by the waters?"

Just then he sees a momma with a newborn close beside, fur still damp, legs unsteady. Leedro smiles. The new life makes up for the animal that didn't make it.

"When you finally start collectin' them," Leedro continues, "it takes a lot of cow jibberish to get 'em movin'. Hey, hey, hey, yup, yup, c'mon girlie, git up there," he hollers and then prods them with a stick or taps them with his lasso until they get going.

"There's a time to rush a cow and a time to be slow with her. A cowboy's got to know which way a cow's goin' to run, and the shortest way to head her off."

516

It doesn't take long after finding the first cow to have a string of ten or twelve. The trick is to push them along and together.

Just when the riding gets lonely, Leedro spots his dad up above him on a mesa ledge. He hears a whistle and looks below. Randy is chasing a frisky yearling who doesn't want to stay with the others.

"Head 'em off," Larry shouts, just as a heifer breaks free and follows the yearling. Leedro charges after Randy as his dad gallops down from the mesa in hopes of blocking them from straying too far. Before long, half the team is in the chase, six cowboys running after two cows. Three miles and forty-five minutes later, they finally lasso the skittish runaways and drag them back to the rest of the herd.

What can start out as a short day frequently turns into a long one. "You can never tell when they'll break up on you," Leedro says. "You can have a real smooth drive goin', and then somethin' will happen. They'll get spooked, or a bull will get ornery, and boom, they just take off."

Now the fun begins. Each cowboy on his own has found ten or twenty head of cattle, and they are slowly, cautiously moving them toward one of the many corrals that dot the range. With combined herds, the cowboys begin pushing fifty or sixty cows, trying to keep them together even though each cow has a favorite direction.

"There was a stampede down on the flats last week," Leedro says, a smile in his eyes. "The cows are kinda wild there in the open spaces. They don't like bein' bunched and driven. Sure enough, as we neared the pen the lead cow took off. Colter and I followed her, ridin' forever to catch up, when the other cows got the same idea. They went in the opposite direction. We had cows goin' everywhere, hats flyin' off, dust swirlin' . . . all you could hear were poundin' hooves and cowboys yellin'."

Just before noon, half of the cowboys are at a corral called The Box, where they lead the cattle into a pen and close the gate.

They refresh themselves near a windmill, which creaks and rattles as the wind catches its blades and water pours into the tank. As the horses eagerly slurp, Leedro takes off his jacket and grabs his canteen for a drink. It feels good to stop. The corral, tucked between giant rocks and steep embankments, is a cool place to rest from the blazing sun.

These watering spots are vital for the cattle, who are struggling to survive and raise their young. The Ebys have seventeen windmills that pump water up from underground springs. Since the forty natural water holes and creek beds have dried up in the drought, the windmills must be kept in perfect working order if the animals are to survive.

After ten minutes or so, Larry gives the order to move out. "We can't keep the others waitin'," he says, referring to the rest of the crew on the other side of the mountain. Leedro opens the pen containing the newly herded cows, and they rush out, their heavy bodies rubbing up against each other, dust clouds rising from the weight of their hooves. They look confused and angry about being pushed and prodded. One utters a long "moo" and then another, until a chorus of guttural groans fills the valley that was once silent.

"C'mon, girlie, thataway," a cowboy coaxes a big fat momma. "Yo bully, git up there."

This time the cattle are compliant. It only takes half an hour to drive them to Tom Brown, an enormous basin scooped out of the barren landscape. Eyes squinting, the cowboys scan the hills for signs of the rest of the crew. Randy points east, spotting Rose Ann's blue shirt. Leedro sees Colter herding a bunch of cows through a thicket. The hills are now dotted with cowboys leading strings of cattle toward the valley.

And then the cowboys emerge from all directions, proceeding gently, quietly toward the center, each string of cattle becoming like the spoke of a wheel. Larry gallops out ahead to count the cows and determine if the crew has found them all. A good cowman knows precisely how many cows he has in every section of his land. After a quick calculation, Larry shakes his head in amazement. "You got 'em all," he shouts above the bawling. "Let's move 'em out."

The drive is on. "Keep 'em together," Larry shouts above the thunder of hooves. The point is to gather cattle, not scatter them. "It's like keepin' a bunch of marbles on the table," Larry says as he prods them into line.

"Yippee!" Colter shouts, twirling his rope and lassoing first one calf and then another, more for his own amusement than anything else. "Once you get 'em goin' forward, you don't want 'em goin' back," he says.

The cows duck and dodge, startled by the slightest diversion. In order to keep them together, several cowboys ride swing, along the sides of the herd, to keep the line from bulging. Larry rides point, up front, heading them to the next watering place. Colter, Leedro, and their friends and mom ride flank, behind, staring at rear ends and getting most of the dust in their faces.

Even so, this part of the roundup is fun. After hours of riding alone, whistling to themselves, the cowboys can now talk to one another, munch on burritos, and drink soda.

Think About It

1. How do Leedro and Larry solve problems during the spring roundup?

2. What would you enjoy most about living and working on a cattle ranch? What wouldn't you enjoy?

3. The author joins a new community when she rides with the cowboys. What message does she share about this experience?

Meet the Author

JOAN Anderson

What do acting, teaching English, hosting a cable television show, and being a radio reporter have in common? Joan Anderson has drawn on the experiences of each of these former jobs to help her become a better writer. She enjoys writing magazine articles about exotic adventures in Peru, the south of France, and the Grand Canyon. She and photographer George Ancona have worked on fifteen books together.

Meet the Photographer
George
ANCONA

Photographer George Ancona says that making children's books is his own special way of celebrating life. Photographing, filming, or writing about someone or someplace makes him feel alive and in touch with the world around him. Ancona says that when he begins working on a book, he travels to the place where the book will be set. "I meet the people, live with them for a while, listen to their stories, photograph their lives. As the book grows, we become friends, and it's always difficult to say good-bye."

Visit *The Learning Site!*
www.harcourtschool.com

HOME ON THE RANGE

Traditional Cowboy Song

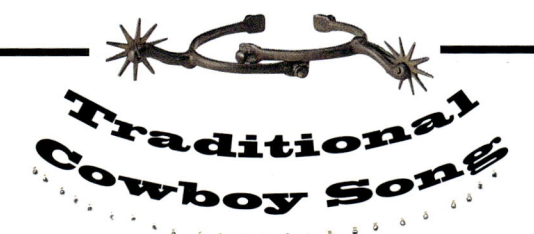

Against the Sunset, **Frederic Remington**
1906. Oil on canvas 22" x 30". Gerald Peters Gallery, Sante Fe

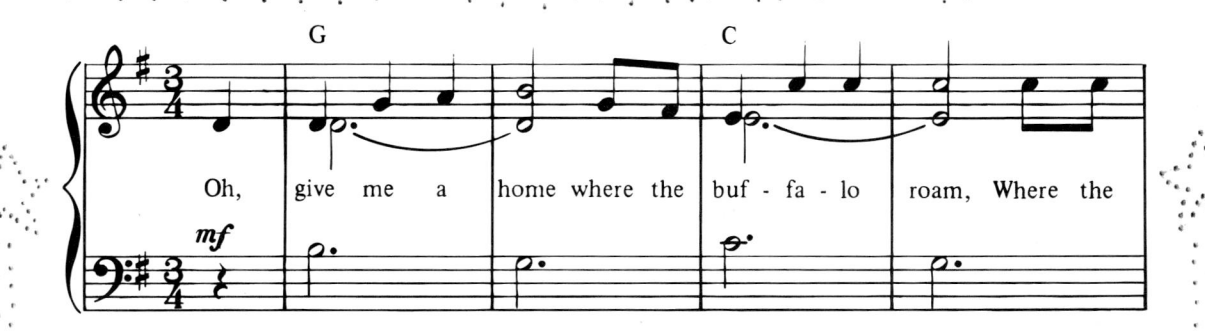

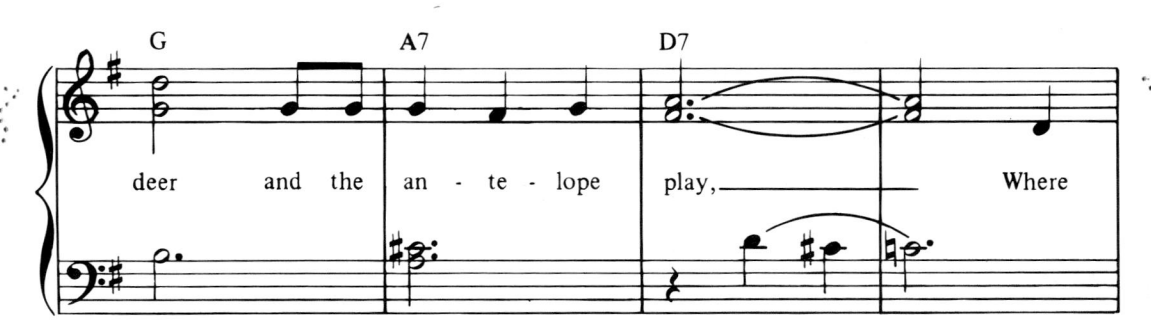

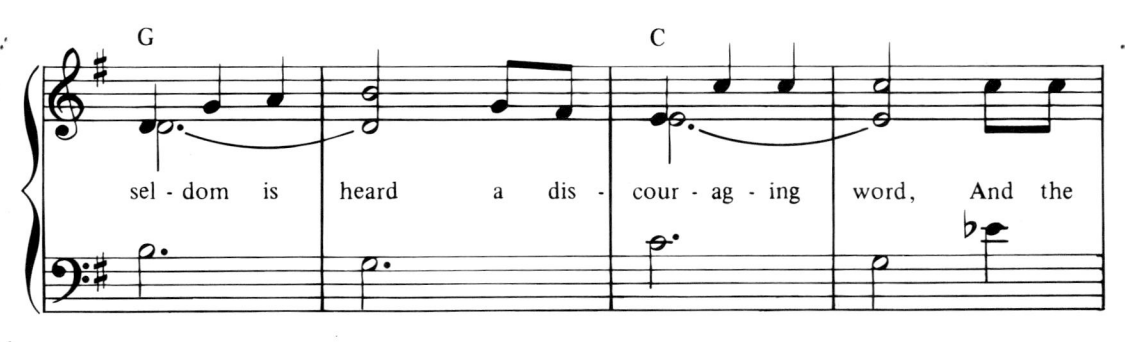

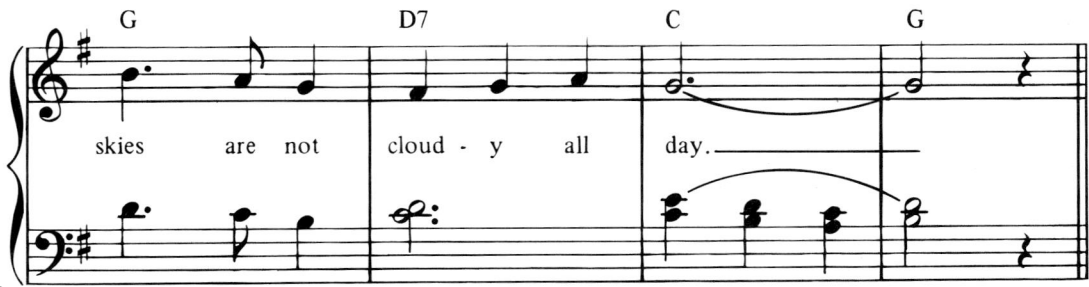

Home, home on the range,
Where the deer and the antelope play.
Where seldom is heard
A discouraging word,
And the skies are not cloudy all day.

RESPONSE

Pounding Hooves and Clinking Spurs

PANTOMIME A SCENE

Find an exciting scene in the selection. Work with a small group to pantomime the scene. Use body movements and facial expressions to show what is happening. Perform your scene, and see if your classmates can guess the scene you are presenting.

Helping Out on the Ranch

WRITE A STORY

Imagine that you have joined a cattle ranch to help during the spring roundup. Write a story about your experience. Your story should show how joining the ranching community changes you and your new friends there.

ACTIVITIES

The Great Outdoors

GRAPH SURVEY RESULTS

The cowboys love the open space on the range. Make a list of different outdoor settings. Conduct a survey in which people rate those settings from 1 to 10, with 10 being the most beautiful or enjoyable. Compile the results of your survey, and use them to create a graph.

Making Connections

WRITE NEW LYRICS

Write a new verse for "Home on the Range." Use a scene from "Cowboys" to help you get ideas. Sing the verse with your lyrics for the class.

THEME WRAP-UP

People Who Care

CHARACTER STUDY The title of this theme is "Making a Difference." Think about the people in the selections you have just read. Write about how each person makes a difference in his or her community.

A Great Place to Visit

COMPARING SETTINGS Choose the settings of three selections in this theme. How does each author appeal to the reader's senses of sight, hearing, touch, taste, and smell? Make a chart like the one shown to jot down your notes. Then write your ideas in a paragraph. End your paragraph by telling which setting is your favorite and why.

Selection	Setting	Vivid Details

What's Your Opinion?

CONDUCT INTERVIEWS With a partner, write four or five questions about the selections in this theme. Here are two examples:

- Which selection best fits this theme? Explain.

- Which do you like better, the selections about real people or the ones with made-up characters? Explain.

Trade questions with another pair of students. Take turns with your partner by asking one another the questions and recording your answers. Remember to support your answers with details from the selections.

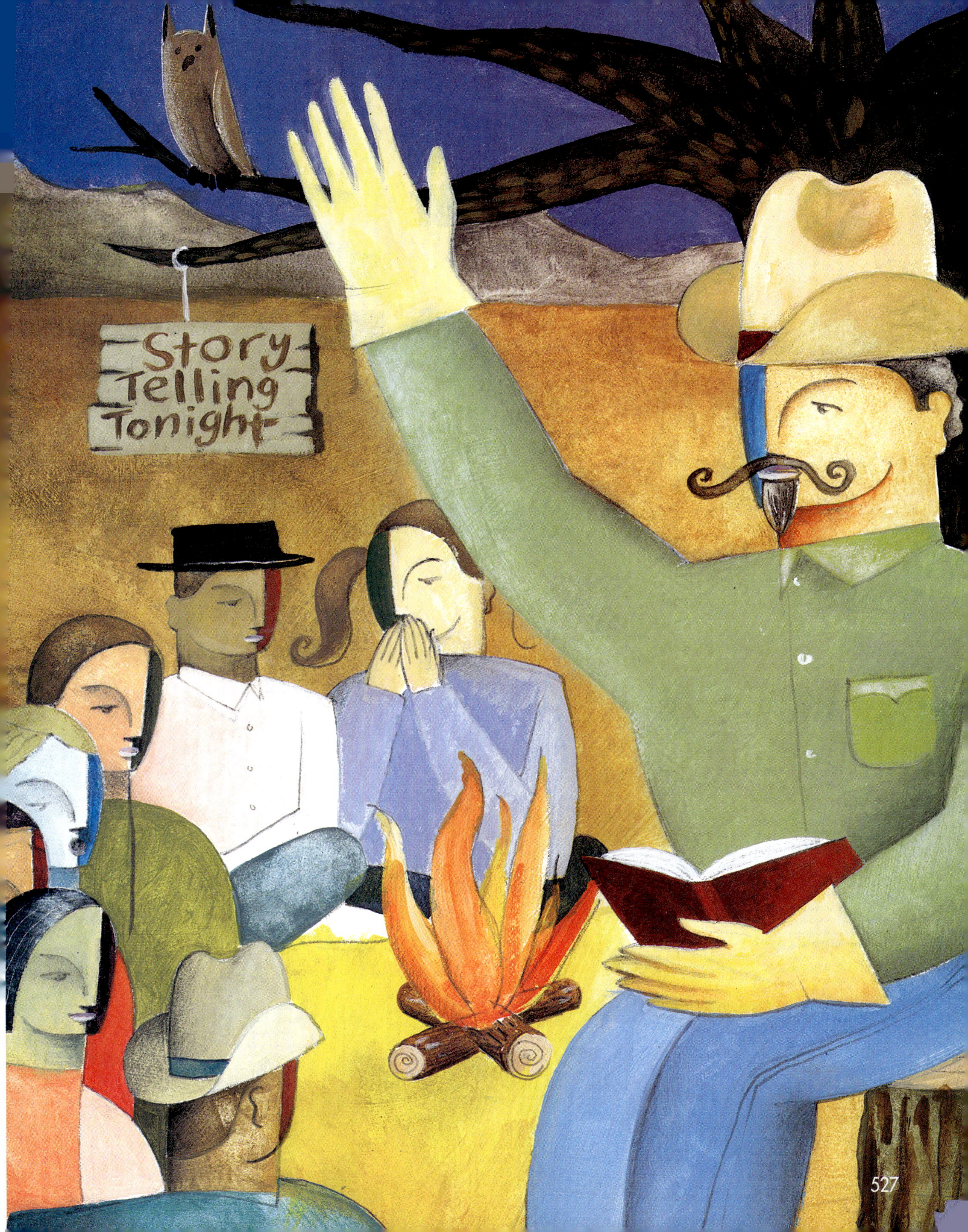
Story
Telling
Tonight

THEME
EXPANDING WORLDS

CONTENTS

The Wright Brothers: How They Invented the Airplane 532
by Russell Freedman

FOCUS SKILL:
Main Idea and Supporting Details 548

I Want to Be an Astronaut 550
by Stephanie Maze and Catherine O'Neill Grace

FOCUS SKILL:
Summarize/Paraphrase 564

Voyager: An Adventure to the Edge of the Solar System 566
by Sally Ride and Tam O'Shaughnessy

The Three Hunters and the Great Bear 584
retold by Joseph Bruchac

CyberSurfer 590
by Nyla Ahmad

In the Next Three Seconds 606
by Rowland Morgan

The Fun They Had 612
by Isaac Asimov

To Dark Eyes Dreaming 622
by Zilpha Keatley Snyder

529

READER'S CHOICE

The Wright Brothers: How They Invented the Airplane
by Russell Freedman

BIOGRAPHY

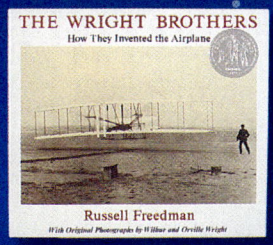

Orville and Wilbur Wright began their careers as bicycle mechanics, but they ended up changing the course of history by inventing the airplane.

Newbery Honor/Outstanding Science Trade Book

READER'S CHOICE LIBRARY

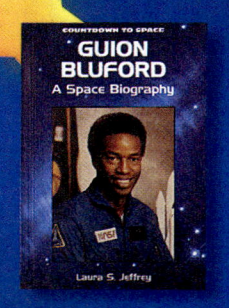

Guion Bluford: A Space Biography
by Laura S. Jeffrey

BIOGRAPHY

As a child, Guion Bluford loved science and airplanes. As an adult, he made history by becoming the first African American to travel into space.

READER'S CHOICE LIBRARY

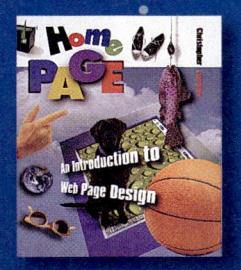

Home Page: An Introduction to Web Page Design
by Christopher Lampton

NONFICTION

Follow step-by-step instructions to become part of the World Wide Web by creating your own Web page.

Flight Through Time: How Airplanes Were Designed, Developed, and Flown
by Chris Oxlade

NONFICTION

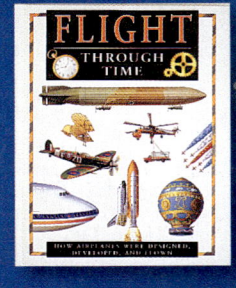

From hot-air balloons to modern aircraft, find out how advancements in technology have changed the way we fly.

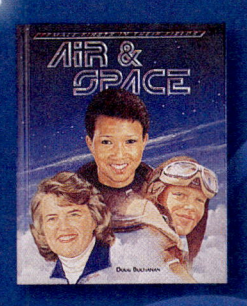

Female Firsts in Their Fields: Air and Space
by Doug Buchanan

BIOGRAPHY

Women have made many exciting contributions to aviation and space exploration. Learn about the remarkable women who have taken their professions to new heights.

532

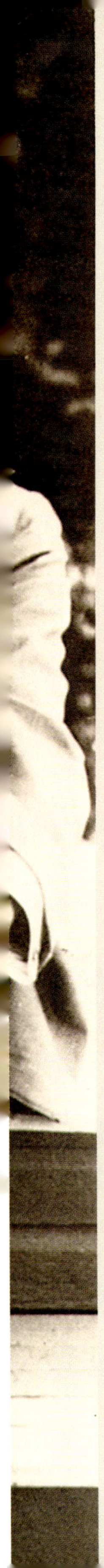

THE WRIGHT BROTHERS

HOW THEY INVENTED THE AIRPLANE

by Russell Freedman

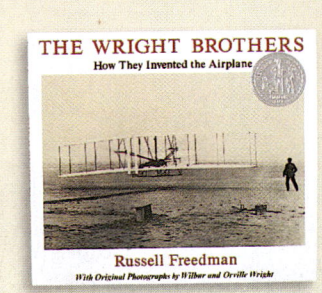

The Aerial Steam Carriage, designed by William Henson and John Stringfield in 1842. Though this aircraft was never built, its forward-looking appearance influenced many future experimenters.

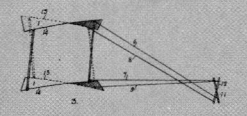

The Wrights' drawing of their 1899 kite — their first experimental aircraft.

No one had ever seen what Amos Root saw on that September afternoon in 1904. Standing in a cow pasture near Dayton, Ohio, he looked up and watched a flying machine circle in the sky above him. He could see the bold pilot lying facedown on the lower wing, staring straight ahead as he steered the craft to a landing in the grass.

The pilot was Wilbur Wright. He and his brother Orville had built the machine themselves in the workroom of their bicycle shop. Now they were testing it out at a farmer's field called Huffman Prairie.

Amos Root had come all the way down from Medina, Ohio, where he ran a beekeepers' supply house. For weeks he had heard rumors about the Wright brothers' flying machine, and being a curious fellow, he wanted to investigate this miracle for himself. So he packed a bag, climbed into his automobile, and drove nearly 200 miles to Dayton — a very long trip at a time when automobiles were still called "horseless carriages."

He was lucky enough to be on hand when Wilbur Wright took off and flew once around Huffman Prairie — the first circling flight ever made by an airplane. The flight lasted 1 minute 36 seconds.

Back home in Medina, Root wrote history's earliest eyewitness account of an airplane in controlled flight. His article appeared in the January 1, 1905, issue of *Gleanings in Bee Culture,* a magazine he published for customers of his supply house.

"Dear friends," he wrote, "I have a wonderful story to tell you — a story that, in some respects, outrivals the Arabian Nights fables." He reported that "two minister's boys who love machinery, and who are interested in the modern developments of science and art . . . began studying the flights of birds and insects. From this they turned their attention to what has been done in the way of enabling men to fly. . . . This work, mind you, was all new. Nobody living could give them any advice. It was like exploring a new and unknown domain."

534

The 1904 Wright Flyer over Huffman Prairie. The Wrights made their first complete circle with this machine on September 20, 1904.

They started the motor. The propellers turned over, paddling loudly. The transmission chains clattered. The motor popped and coughed, and the whole machine seemed to shudder and shake. The two small boys took one look, backed away, and went racing across the sand dunes with the dog at their heels.

Wilbur and Orville tossed a coin to decide who should try first. Wilbur won. He lay down on the lower wing, sliding his hips into the padded wing-warping cradle. Orville took a position at one of the wings to help balance the machine as it roared down the starting track. Then Wilbur loosened the restraining rope that held the Flyer in place. The machine shot down the track with such speed that Orville was left behind, gasping for breath.

After a 35- to 40-foot run, the Flyer lifted up from the rail. Once in the air, Wilbur tried to point the machine up at too steep an angle. It climbed a few feet, stalled, settled backward, and smashed into the sand on its left wing. Orville's stopwatch showed that the Flyer had flown for just 3½ seconds.

Wilbur wasn't hurt, but it took two days to repair the damage to the Flyer. They were ready to try again on Thursday, December 17, 1903.

They woke up that morning to freezing temperatures and a blustery 27-mile-an-hour wind. Puddles of rainwater in the sand hollows around their camp were crusted with ice. They spent the early part of the morning indoors, hoping the wind would die down a little. At 10 o'clock, with the wind as brisk as ever, they decided to attempt a flight. "The conditions were very unfavorable," wrote Wilbur. "Nevertheless, as we had set our minds on being home by Christmas, we determined to go ahead."

They hoisted the signal flag to summon the lifesavers. Then, in the biting wind, they laid down all four sections of the starting track on a level stretch of sand just below their camp. They had to go inside frequently to warm their hands by the carbide-can stove.

By the time the starting track was in place, five witnesses had shown up—four men from the lifesaving station and a teenage boy from the nearby village of Nags Head. They helped haul the Flyer over to the launching site.

The crew of the U.S. Lifesaving Station, located about a mile from the Wrights' camp. These men became the world's first aircraft ground crew.

Now it was Orville's turn at the controls. First he set up his big box camera, focused on a point near the end of the track, and inserted a glass-plate negative. Then he placed the rubber bulb that tripped the shutter in the big hand of John Daniels, one of the lifesaving men, and asked him to squeeze the bulb just as the Flyer took off.

The brothers shook hands. "We couldn't help but notice how they held onto each other's hand," one of the lifesavers recalled, "sort of like two folks parting who weren't sure they'd ever see one another again."

Orville took the pilot's position, his hips in the wing-warping cradle, the toes of his shoes hooked over a small supporting rack behind him. Like his brother, he was wearing a dark suit, a stiff collar, a necktie, and a cap. Wilbur turned to the lifesaving men and told them "not to look so sad, but to . . . laugh and holler and clap . . . and try to cheer Orville up when he started."

"After running the motor a few minutes to heat it up," Orville recalled, "I released the wire that held the machine to the track, and the machine started forward into the wind. Wilbur ran at the side of the machine, holding the wing to balance it on the track. Unlike the start on the 14th, made in a calm, the machine, facing a 27-mile-per-hour wind, started very slowly. Wilbur was able to stay with it till it lifted from the track after a 40-foot run. [John] snapped the camera for us, taking a picture just as the machine had reached the

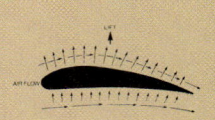

Air streaming across the upper and lower surfaces of a curved wing, or *airfoil*, will keep it aloft.

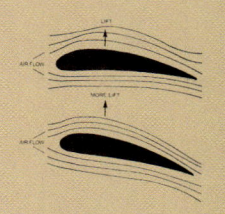

As the leading edge of the wing tilts upward, air moves faster over the top of the wing, increasing its lift and making the wing rise. When the leading edge of the wing tilts downward, the wing loses lift and drops. The angle at which the wing meets the oncoming air is called the *angle of attack*.

537

In one of the most famous photographs ever taken, the Wright Flyer takes off on the world's first successful airplane flight at 10:35 A.M. on December 17, 1903. Orville is at the controls, while Wilbur runs alongside. Estimated distance and time: 120 feet in 12 seconds.

end of the track and had risen to a height of about two feet."

Wilbur had just let go of the wing when John Daniels tripped the shutter. The lifesavers broke into a ragged cheer. The Flyer was flying!

Orville couldn't hear them. He hung on to the control lever and stared straight ahead as the icy wind whistled past his ears and the motor clattered beside him. Buffeted by gusts, the Flyer lurched forward. "The course of the flight up and down was exceedingly erratic," wrote Orville, "partly due to the irregularity of the air, and partly to lack of experience in handling this machine. . . . As a result the machine would rise suddenly to about ten feet, and then as suddenly dart for the ground. A sudden dart when a little over a hundred feet from the end of the track, or a little over 120 feet from the point at which it rose into the air, ended the flight. . . .

"This flight lasted only 12 seconds, but it was nevertheless the first in the history of the world in which a machine carrying a man had raised itself by its own power into the air in full flight, had sailed forward without reduction of speed, and had finally landed at a point as high as that from which it had started."

It had happened so quickly. A boy could have thrown a ball as far as the Flyer had flown. But the Wright brothers were elated. Seven years after Otto Lilienthal's fatal crash, four and a half years after Wilbur's letter to the Smithsonian Institution, they had launched a flying machine that could actually fly.

The group hauled the Flyer back to the starting track. By now everyone was so chilled, they had to go inside the camp building to huddle around the stove.

Wilbur and Orville made three more flights that windswept December morning, taking turns at the controls. The longest flight of the day took place at noon, when Wilbur covered a ground distance of 852 feet in 59 seconds. They were getting ready to try again when a powerful gust of wind struck the machine and began to turn it over.

"Everybody made a rush for it," wrote Orville. "Wilbur, who was at one end, seized it in front, Mr. Daniels and I, who were behind, tried to stop it by holding to the rear uprights. All our efforts were vain. The machine rolled over and over.

"Daniels, who had retained his grip, was carried along with it, and was thrown about head over heels inside the machine. Fortunately he was not seriously injured, though badly bruised in falling about against the motor, chain guides, etc."

For the rest of his life, John Daniels would boast that he had survived the world's first airplane crash. But the Flyer was so damaged that "all possibility of further flights with it for that year were at an end."

Three months earlier, while seeing Wilbur and Orville off at the Dayton train station, Bishop Milton Wright had given his sons a dollar to cover the cost of sending a telegram as soon as their Flyer made a successful flight. Now was the time. That afternoon the brothers walked 4 miles up the beach to the Weather Bureau station at Kitty Hawk and sent a wire to their seventy-four-year-old father, announcing the world's first powered, sustained, and controlled airplane flights.

After receiving his sons' telegram, Bishop Wright made a statement to the press:

"Wilbur is 36, Orville 32, and they are as inseparable as twins. For several years they have read up on aeronautics as a physician would read his books, and they have studied, discussed, and experimented together. Natural workmen, they have invented, constructed, and operated their gliders, and finally their 'Wright Flyer,' jointly, all at their personal expense. About equal credit is due each."

Once back home in Dayton, the brothers issued a press statement of their own:

"As winter was already well set in, we should have postponed our trials to a

This historic telegram was sent from the Kitty Hawk weather station to the weather station at Norfolk, Virginia, then relayed by telephone to the local Western Union office. During transmission, two errors were made: 59 seconds became 57 seconds, and Orville's name was misspelled.

more favorable season, but . . . we were determined, before returning home, to know whether the machine possessed sufficient power to fly, sufficient strength to withstand the shock of landings, and sufficient capacity of control to make flight safe in boisterous winds, as well as in calm air. When these points had been definitely established, we at once packed our goods and returned home, knowing that the age of the flying machine had come at last."

Before their Flyer could be considered a practical invention, the Wrights had to prove that it was capable of more than brief, straight-line flights. That winter they built a new Flyer with a stronger body and a more powerful motor. Now they wanted a flying field closer to home, where they could spend more time testing the machine.

A friend offered the use of Huffman Prairie, the 100-acre cow pasture on the outskirts of Dayton. The brothers immediately set to work on their airfield. First they cut the tall grass with scythes. Then they built a wooden shed in a corner of the meadow. There they assembled their Flyer II in the spring of 1904.

Huffman Prairie had its disadvantages, though. Trees bordering the meadow tended to cut down on the winds necessary for launchings. Cows and horses had to be shooed out of the way before every test flight. "Also the ground is an old swamp and is filled with grassy hummocks some six inches high, so it resembles a prairie-dog town," Wilbur reported. "This makes track-laying slow work."

Their starting track had worked well at Kitty Hawk, but it wasn't as effective at Huffman Prairie, where the bumpy ground made it difficult to lay down the track in the right direction. "While we are getting ready the favorable opportunities slip away, and we are usually up against a rain storm, a dead calm, or a wind blowing at right angles to the track," wrote Wilbur.

A replica of the Wrights' pioneering wind tunnel.

Using this cleverly designed device inside their wind tunnel, the Wrights were able to test the lift and drag of their experimental airfoils.

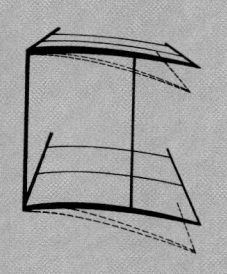

Wing-warping in the 1903 Wright Flyer served the same function as ailerons on a modern aircraft.

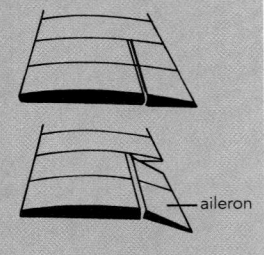

—aileron

The situation improved when they built a new launching device that allowed them to get their Flyer into the air regardless of wind strength and direction. It was a portable derrick—four 20-foot poles forming a pyramid. A 1,600-pound weight was pulled to the top of the derrick and connected to the Flyer by means of ropes and pulleys. When the weight dropped, the Flyer was catapulted along its starting track with enough speed for lift-off.

With this launching system, the Wrights were able to make more than eighty short flights in their 1904 Flyer. Improvement came slowly, however. At first, the airplane was frequently operating out of control. The brothers were still learning to handle the machine, and many flights ended in crash landings as the Flyer bounced across the field and skidded to a stop. They were constantly repairing broken wings, smashed propellers, bent rudders, and splintered skids. They kept a bottle of liniment handy to nurse their bruises and bumps.

With practice their flights grew longer and more reliable. By the end of August, they were making flights of about a quarter of a mile—as far as they could travel in a straight line without crossing the barbed-wire fence separating Huffman Prairie from farmer Stauffer's cornfield. On September 15, Wilbur made his first turn in the air. On September 20, he flew his first complete circle in the sky—the flight witnessed by Amos Root.

After that, the brothers repeatedly flew complete circles. On November 9, in their longest flight of 1904, Wilbur circled Huffman Prairie four times in 5 minutes. Altogether, the Wrights were airborne for about 45 minutes that year.

Their flying practice was often interrupted by foul weather. And even when conditions were ideal, flight tests involved plenty of hard physical work. The Flyer had to be removed sideways from its shed so the tail and forward elevator could be bolted on. Sixty feet of track had to be laid and staked into place, and the 1,600-pound weight hoisted to the top of the starting derrick. After each flight, the 700-pound machine had to be lifted on wheeled supports and hauled back to the starting track across the bumpy meadow.

An electric trolley line ran past Huffman Prairie, and the brothers rode it back and forth between the flying field and Dayton. "I sort of felt sorry for them," recalled a fellow passenger, Luther Beard. "They seemed like well-meaning decent young men. Yet there they were, neglecting their business to waste their time day after day on that ridiculous flying machine. I had an idea they must worry their father."

In the spring of 1905, the brothers completed Flyer III, an improved model of their powered aircraft. The most important change was in the control system. In the earlier Flyers, the tail rudder was linked to the wing-warping system. As a result of their flight experiences, the brothers decided to separate the rudder and warp controls. The pilot's hips remained in the wing-warping cradle, while his hands rested on two levers—one for the elevator in front of the plane, the other for the rudder at the rear. This made the controls more sensitive to the pilot's commands.

That year the Wrights completed more than forty successful flights, spending just over 5 hours in the air. On October 5, Wilbur set a new endurance record when he circled the field thirty times in 39 minutes, covering a distance of 24½ miles.

These flights demonstrated that the Wright Flyer III was the world's first truly practical airplane. It could stay safely in the air as long as the fuel supply lasted. It could bank, turn, circle, and perform figure eights with ease and grace. And it was sturdy enough to withstand repeated takeoffs and landings. Wilbur told a friend: "Our 1905 improvements have given such results as to justify the assertion that flying has been transformed from the realm of scientific problems to that of useful arts."

Even so, people weren't easily convinced that the age of flight had arrived. Newspaper accounts of the Wrights' first flights at Kitty Hawk had been wildly exaggerated. To help clear the air, the brothers had invited local reporters to watch the first test flights of Flyer II back in May 1904. Twice that month, reporters had trooped out to Huffman Prairie, and both times, the Flyer's engine had failed before it could lift off. The reporters left and didn't come back. Wilbur and Orville carried out their flight tests with only a few friends and neighbors as witnesses.

By the autumn of 1905, however, word was getting around that a strange winged contraption was circling noisily in the sky above Huffman Prairie. Newspapers in Dayton and Cincinnati began to carry stories about the flights. And yet the news did not go out over the wires. The rest of the world paid little attention to the historic event taking place in an Ohio cow pasture.

People found it hard to believe in airplanes. Understandably so, as Orville stated plainly years later: "I think it was mainly due to the fact that human flight was generally looked upon as an impossibility, and that scarcely anyone believed in it until he actually saw it with his own eyes."

Think About It

1. What obstacles did the Wright brothers face as they tried to improve their aircraft?
2. Do you think the Wright brothers gained a better understanding of their world? Explain why you feel as you do.
3. How do you know that the Wright brothers were determined to succeed? Give some examples.

MEET THE AUTHOR

RUSSELL FREEDMAN

Russell Freedman often uses original photographs to bring history to life. *The Wright Brothers: How They Invented the Airplane* contains photographs taken by Orville and Wilbur Wright, whose flying experiments changed the world. The inventors took pictures to make a lasting record of their often difficult and frustrating efforts.

To do research for the book, Russell Freedman traveled to Kitty Hawk, North Carolina, and to Dayton, Ohio, where many of the famous first flights took place. He also researched the early Flyers at the National Air and Space Museum in Washington, D.C. After reliving the experiments in his imagination, he set to work to recapture their drama in his book. Speaking of the Wright brothers, Russell Freedman explains, "Their work is what made their lives exciting. Orville once said, 'We could hardly wait for morning to come to get at something that interested us.' *That's* happiness."

Visit The Learning Site!
www.harcourtschool.com

RESPONSE

Amos Speaks His Mind
ROLE-PLAY A CONVERSATION
With a partner, role-play a conversation between Amos Root and a friend. Amos's friend should ask questions about the event Amos witnessed. Amos should tell why he believes Orville and Wilbur's experiments will change the world.

Birds in Flight
PRESENT AN ORAL REPORT
The Wright brothers studied birds and insects to help them design their flyers. Use the Internet or an encyclopedia to research a flying creature. Write a brief report that explains how this creature flies. When you give your oral report to the class, support your words with a visual prop such as a diagram.

ACTIVITIES

The Wright Project
WRITE A LETTER

Wilbur and Orville Wright want you to help raise money for their flying experiments. Write a persuasive letter to a possible donor. Include reasons that the Wright brothers' experiments would be a good investment.

Believe It or Not
WRITE A STORY

Most people wanted to see it for themselves before they would believe that the Wright Brothers could fly. Write a story set in the past. Have a character invent a new item that people find unbelievable.

FOCUS SKILL
Main Idea and Supporting Details

The **main idea** of many paragraphs in "The Wright Brothers" is stated directly. Speaking of their work at Huffman Prairie, the author says, "Improvement came slowly." Then the author **supports** this main idea with **details**. You can use a diagram like this one to identify the main idea and supporting details of the passage.

Main Idea
Improvement came slowly.

↑

Supporting Detail
The airplane was frequently operating out of control.

+

Supporting Detail
The brothers were still learning to handle the machine.

+

Supporting Detail
They were constantly repairing broken wings, smashed propellers, bent rudders, and splintered skids.

The main idea of the entire selection is not stated directly. It is **implied**. What support can you find for the implied main idea that Wilbur and Orville Wright believed in themselves when few others believed their dream was possible?

Figuring out the main idea of a passage helps you understand and remember the most important point about the information you are reading. When the main idea is implied, look for clues in the passage to help you find it.

Read the following passage. Record the main idea and supporting details on a diagram like the one on page 548. Is the main idea stated or implied?

Before Otto Lilienthal fell to his death, neighbors saw him fly nearly 900 feet in the air in a bat-shaped glider. Lilienthal's career was cut short after only five years, but word of his accomplishments spread to other countries. Like Lilienthal, the Wright Brothers first flew in gliders. Their bodies were unprotected in the open structures. Like Lilienthal, the brothers mastered the art of heavier-than-air flight themselves. They knew about Lilienthal's ideas, but they discarded most of them and came up with ideas of their own.

WHAT HAVE YOU LEARNED?

1. Give details from "The Wright Brothers" to support this main idea: *Few people other than Amos Root believed in the Wright Brothers' experiments.*

2. Think of another story you have read. What is its main idea? How could you prove this is the main idea of that story?

TRY THIS • TRY THIS • TRY THIS

Think of something you believe can be done that others believe is impossible. What makes you believe in your idea? List facts and details to support your idea. You can use a diagram like the one on page 548 to help organize your thoughts.

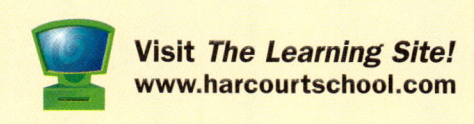

Visit *The Learning Site!*
www.harcourtschool.com

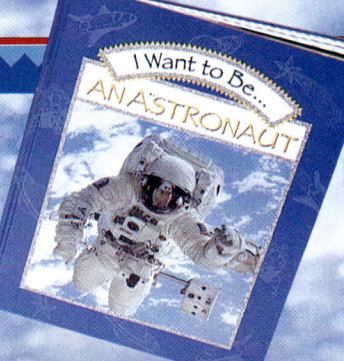

I WANT TO BE an ASTRONAUT

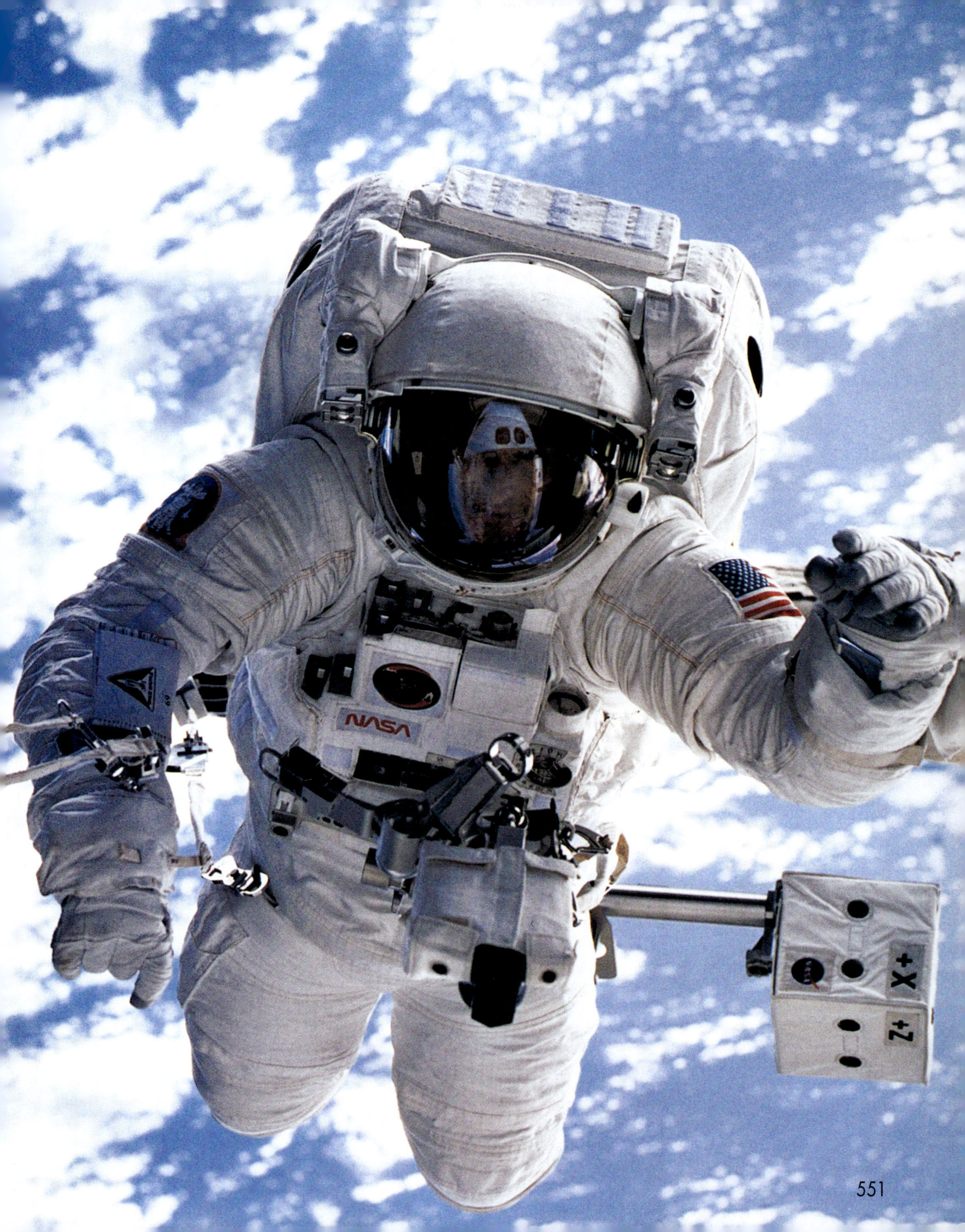
NASA
X+
Z+

● WHERE TO START ✱

Can you picture yourself in a space suit? Do you dream about traveling in space or going to other planets? Can you imagine climbing aboard a space shuttle?

Astronauts Bernard A. Harris and C. Michael Foale had dreams like yours that came true. The astronauts blasted off on the space shuttle *Discovery* in 1995. In this picture, Harris (top) and Foale are on their way out of the shuttle orbiter for some extravehicular activity (EVA). This means that they're getting ready to leave the vehicle for a space walk, protected by their high-tech space suits.

Harris was payload commander and Foale was a mission specialist on the flight. Payload crew members are scientists or engineers who run and analyze experiments during a mission. Mission specialists are technical/scientific astronauts who also run experiments in flight and work with the pilots to keep the shuttle running smoothly.

Whether you hope to fly the shuttle or to supervise experiments on board, taking math and science courses now will help you prepare. These two astronauts studied hard to get into the space program. Harris earned a doctorate of medicine at Texas Tech. Foale earned a doctorate in astrophysics from Cambridge University in England.

Education is essential for astronauts. Fields in which they train include mathematics, astronomy, engineering, geology,

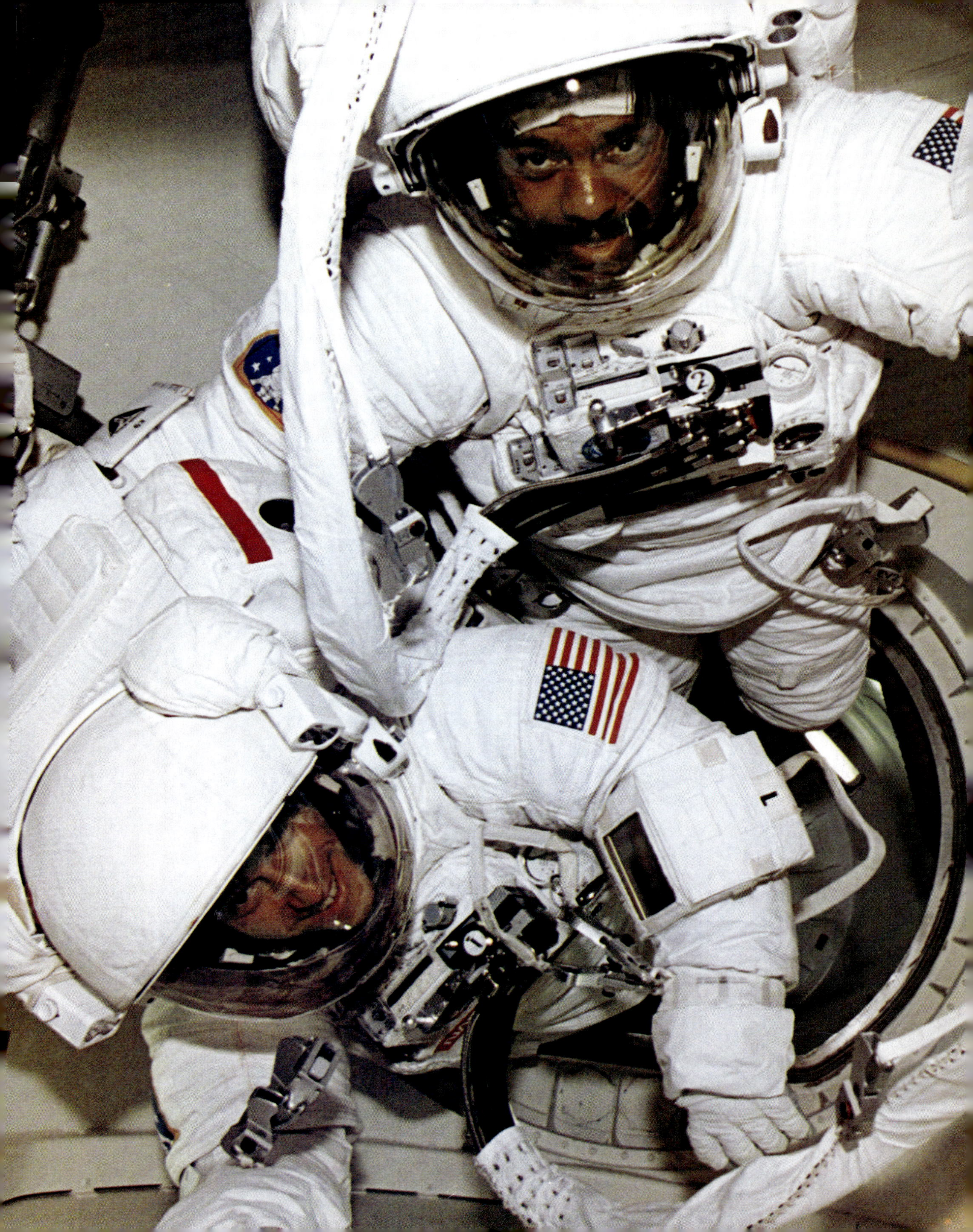

chemistry, biology, physics, and electronics. Although you don't have to be a championship athlete, fitness is important, too. You must be in top physical condition to go into space, so prepare your body with healthful food and exercise.

LIVING IN SPACE

In space you have to take care of yourself as you do on Earth—but it's more difficult. Right, astronaut William B. Lenoir, an electrical engineer by training, tries his hand at being a barber. He trims the sideburns of space shuttle *Columbia*'s pilot, Robert F. Overmyer, during a mission in 1982. Aboard *Endeavour* in 1992, Japanese astronaut Mamoru Mohri (below) lathers up for a dry shampoo.

Washing your hair, brushing your teeth, having a snack, going to the bathroom, getting some exercise, or taking a snooze all sound like ordinary things to do, don't they? How about performing all those daily tasks while you're weightless—and the tools you need to use are weightless, too? That's the challenge astronauts deal with every day while they're on a mission. They use lots of straps to hold things down. Even the toilet has a seatbelt!

Of course, weightlessness can be fun. Sometimes astronauts fool around a bit when they're relaxing during a mission. Astronauts Daniel W. Bursch and Frank L. Culbertson did as they brushed their teeth before going to bed aboard the space shuttle *Discovery* one evening in 1993 (below). No, Culbertson isn't standing on his head. He's floating upside down! In the background you can see sleep restraints attached to the wall. The straps will keep the astronauts from floating around the cabin while they're sleeping.

TRAINING TO BE AN ASTRONAUT

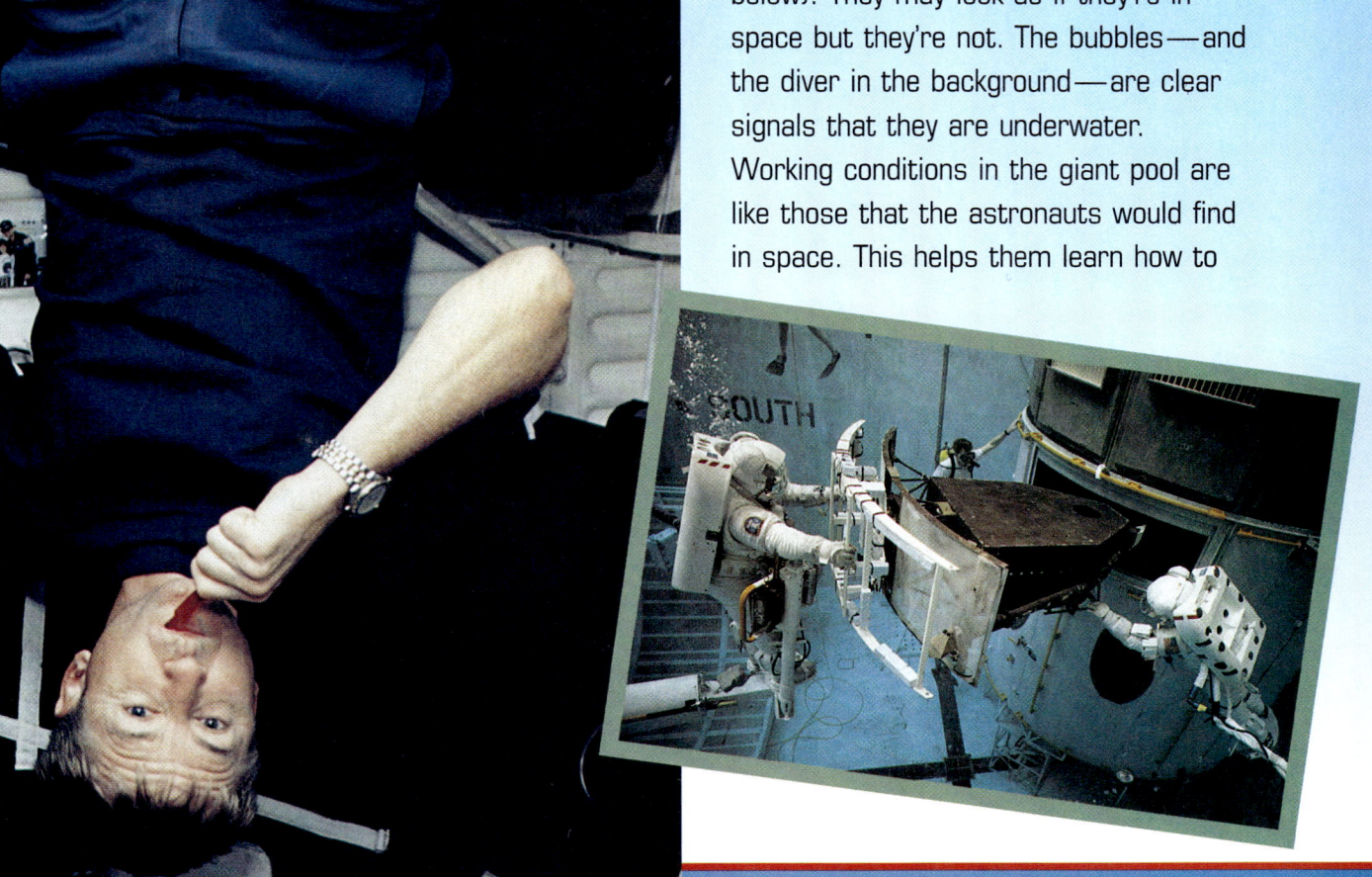

It takes many years of training to become an astronaut. After they are selected, astronauts-to-be train at facilities in Texas, Alabama, and Florida. At the Weightless Environment Training Facility, part of the Lyndon B. Johnson Space Center in Houston, trainees learn everything they need to know to do their extravehicular jobs correctly in zero-gravity conditions in space. Astronauts-in-training wearing extravehicular mobility units (EMUs)—the suits that make it possible to survive outside a spacecraft—practice for the Hubble Space Telescope repair mission (see photo below). They may look as if they're in space but they're not. The bubbles—and the diver in the background—are clear signals that they are underwater. Working conditions in the giant pool are like those that the astronauts would find in space. This helps them learn how to maneuver and to use tools in the bulky space suits.

Trips in a modified jet airplane give astronauts-in-training a chance to actually experience the feeling of weightlessness—if only for a few seconds. The airplane produces weightlessness by diving from thirty-five thousand to twenty-four thousand feet. *Zoom!* People inside are weightless for about twenty seconds during the dive. One of the side effects of this training is airsickness. Some astronauts feel queasy in weightless conditions during missions in space, too. But they get used to it and feel better after a while. During training, the nose dives may be repeated as often as forty times in one day. Riding a roller coaster must seem pretty tame after that!

Astronauts prepare for many different situations they might encounter if their craft landed somewhere other than at a fully equipped space center. Below, astronaut Mae C. Jemison—who in 1992 became the first African American woman in space when she flew on the space shuttle *Endeavour*—takes part in land survival training. Astronaut candidates learn parachute jumping, scuba diving, and sea survival skills, too. When they finally lift off, they are ready to deal with just about anything.

Practicing the checklist run-through in a shuttle cockpit simulator are Charles F. Bolden, Jr. and NASA's Steven A. Nesbitt.

EDUCATION AND TRAINING

You don't have to wait until college to learn more about space science. Tell your teacher or principal about the National Aeronautics and Space Administration's (NASA) Teacher Resource Centers, a nonprofit program that provides videotapes, slides, computer software, and other materials about the space program to schools. Many spaceflight centers, universities, and science-and-technology museums offer hands-on programs for kids. Top right, students from E. Brooke Lee Middle School in Silver Spring, Maryland, try on a space suit at NASA's Goddard Space Flight Center in Maryland. Goddard was the first major U.S. spaceflight lab. It has been operating since 1959. Other students at Patrick Henry Elementary School in Arlington, Virginia (middle right), build space satellites with aluminum foil in class. They are participants in the Young Astronauts program.

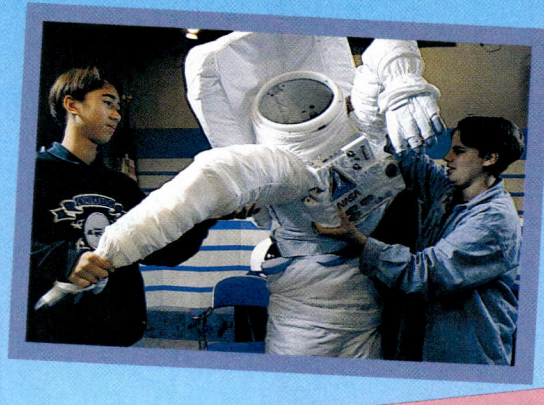

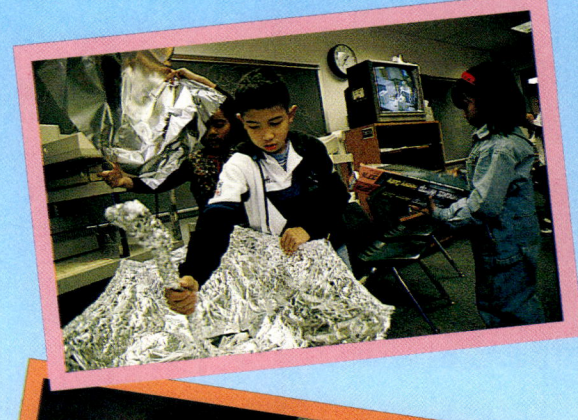

Student Liana Lorigo manipulates a lunar robot, which she built at the Massachusetts Institute of Technology's Artificial Intelligence Lab.

In Huntsville, Alabama, a space camper tries out a mission control station.

Young Astronauts is a national program headquartered in Minnesota. It offers schools around the country a challenging and fun space curriculum that covers astronomy, flight, rocketry, shuttle missions, and life in space. Below, ninth graders at Montgomery Blair High School in Silver Spring, Maryland, learn the fundamentals of physics by building a catapult to launch coins.

☾ LEARNING PROGRAMS ☀

Going to camp means doing crafts, swimming, sitting around a fire and telling stories . . . right? Not at space camp. There you try out astronaut water survival training, launch your own model rocket, and take part in a simulated space shuttle mission.

There are several space camps in the United States. Two of the best known camps are located at the U.S. Space and Rocket Center in Huntsville, Alabama, and in Florida near NASA's Kennedy Space Center. At space camp you learn about the space program and the science of spaceflight. But the programs involve more than that. Space camps focus on teamwork and problem-solving ability, too—skills astronauts need.

Students in Charleston, South Carolina, who got involved with NASA's Can Do program actually launched experiments into space. Their experiments were loaded into one of the shuttles' "Get Away Special" (GAS) cans, which NASA provides for special educational and research purposes. Their work went into space aboard the space shuttle *Endeavour* in 1993.

Below, high school students at NASA's Ames Research Center in Mountain View, California, wear special glasses to observe heat patterns from sources out in the universe.

A space camper tries out a reduced gravity chair.

Christa McAuliffe, the first teacher to prepare for spaceflight—died. After the disaster the families of the seven astronauts did not turn their backs on the space program. Instead, they founded an education program in memory of the *Challenger* crew.

The program, called the Challenger Center, uses space exploration to get kids excited about science, math, and technology. It also encourages young people to pursue careers that use those skills—like becoming an astronaut.

The Challenger Center experience begins in the classroom. Student crews prepare for a simulation of a space mission. They do team assignments in navigation, communication, life support, and space-probe assembly.

CHALLENGER ✷ LEARNING CENTER

In 1986 the space shuttle *Challenger* exploded seventy-three seconds after blastoff. Seven astronauts—among them

The mission itself takes place at one of twenty-five learning centers located in science museums, schools, and other educational institutions throughout the United States and Canada—including

Below, Maria Ibarra checks Jacqueline Zacatales's blood pressure. In space, astronauts monitor their bodies—so Challenger Center students do, too.

The shuttle flight deck is command central during a simulated mission. Above, communications officer Trang Phan unloads data from a computer.

the Challenger Research, Development & Training Center in Washington, D.C., shown on these pages. During their simulated spaceflights, students may launch a space probe into the tail of a comet, land on the Moon, relieve a research team stationed on Mars, or study Earth's environment from space. Student crews work in mission control and aboard a model spacecraft. It's very realistic!

The students in these photographs go to Bailey Elementary School for the Arts and Sciences in Fairfax, Virginia. Above right, classmates John Paez and Michael Osorto work with a glove-box laboratory that's free of contaminants. They're examining rocks and other substances for radioactivity and magnetism. Meanwhile, Trang Phan (below), wearing a headset, serves as a communications officer, linking the space station with mission control.

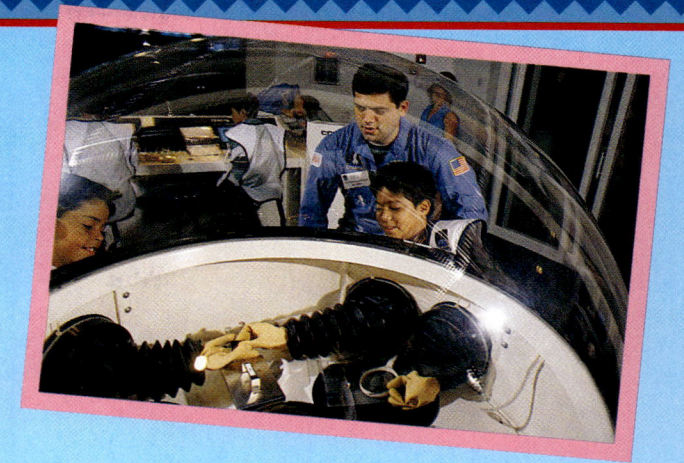

The thousands of young people who take part in Challenger Center programs every year share the mission of astronauts on *Challenger*'s last flight—to learn, to explore, and to inspire.

Think About It

1. How is living in space different from living on Earth? Explain.

2. Would you recommend this selection to a friend? Why or why not?

3. What is the author's purpose in writing this selection? How do you know?

RESPONSE

OUTER SPACE RESCUE

ACT OUT A RESCUE MISSION The selection explains that astronauts take special survival training to prepare for their space missions. With a group, act out a rescue mission in space. Use information from the selection to make your rescue realistic.

INCOMING MESSAGE

WRITE AN E-MAIL Imagine that you are an astronaut on a space shuttle. Write an e-mail to a friend back on Earth. Tell how you are expanding your world by exploring space.

ACTIVITIES

SCUBA 101

TEACH A SKILL Astronauts have to study parachute jumping, scuba diving, and ocean survival. Read about one of these skills. Then present a brief explanation of the skill to your class.

3...2...1...LIFT OFF!

WRITE A SCIENCE FICTION STORY You are an astronaut of the future on a space shuttle mission. Write a humorous story about living and working in zero gravity. Use details from the selection to make the setting realistic.

563

FOCUS SKILL: Summarize/Paraphrase

When you tell just the most important ideas and facts in a selection, you are **summarizing**. If you retell a passage or selection in detail in your own words, you are **paraphrasing**. Read this summary of the first section of "I Want to Be an Astronaut."

> Working as an astronaut is an adventure that requires years of preparation, education, and specialized training. Tasks on a space shuttle include piloting the spacecraft and running experiments. You have to study long and hard to be an astronaut, and you have to be fit.

Here is a paraphrase of the last sentence in the paragraph:

> Astronaut training requires a great deal of study and physical fitness.

Making a chart can help you prepare for writing a summary.

Main Idea	Working as an astronaut requires years of preparation, education, and specialized training.
Most Important Facts	Some astronauts pilot the shuttle, and others run experiments. You have to study long and hard to be an astronaut. You have to be fit.

After listing facts to be included in your summary, you might decide that some of them don't belong. A summary should include only the most important points. When you paraphrase something, however, you can give more details. Read this summary chart. Use the facts and ideas to write a summary. Then paraphrase the main idea.

Main Idea	The launch of *Pioneer 10* began a mission to introduce Earth's civilization to extraterrestrial life.
Most Important Facts	**Launch date** March 2, 1972 **Destination** Jupiter and interstellar space **Purpose** To launch into space a plaque showing human figures, the spacecraft's flight plan (on a solar system diagram), and a pulsar map (to help fix the time between takeoff and discovery)

WHAT HAVE YOU LEARNED?

1. Write a one-sentence summary of the part of the selection that tells about space camps.

2. How is summarizing a passage or a selection different from paraphrasing it?

TRY THIS • TRY THIS • TRY THIS

Think of an educational video, television program, school film, or documentary you have seen recently. Write a one-paragraph summary of it. Prepare for writing by completing a chart like the ones on these pages.

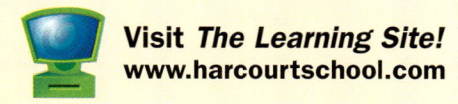

Visit **The Learning Site!**
www.harcourtschool.com

FACE TO FACE WITH SCIENCE™

SALLY RIDE
TAM O'SHAUGHNESSY

VOYAGER

An Adventure
to the Edge
of the
Solar System

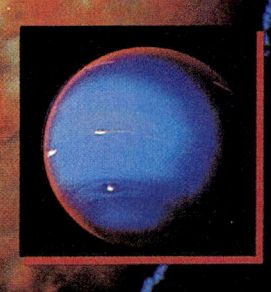

Outstanding Science Trade Book

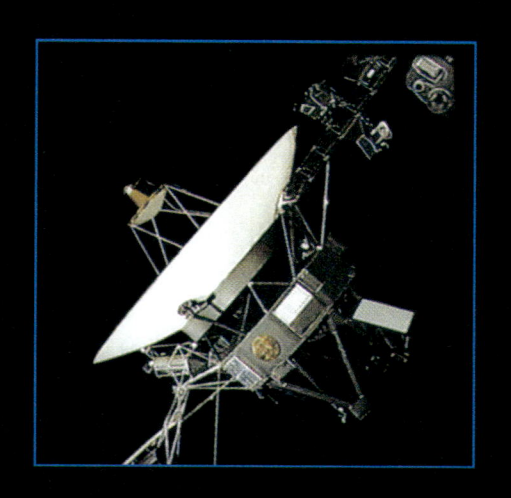

This is the story of two spacecraft:
Voyager 1 and *Voyager* 2.
They were launched from
Earth to explore four distant planets: Jupiter,
Saturn, Uranus, and Neptune.

Earth is the third of nine planets that circle the star we call the Sun. Jupiter, Saturn, Uranus, and Neptune are the fifth, sixth, seventh, and eighth. They are very, very far away. Jupiter, even when it is closest to Earth, is 400 million miles away. Neptune is 3 billion miles away.

All four of these planets are very different from Earth.

The first two, Jupiter and Saturn, are like each other in many ways. Both of them are huge. Jupiter is the biggest planet in the solar system—more than one thousand Earths would fit inside it. Both are made up mostly of hydrogen and helium gas, the two lightest gases in the universe. Toward the center of each planet the gas gets thicker and thicker, until it is so thick that it becomes liquid. Jupiter and Saturn have no solid ground to stand on. Because they are so big, and are made up mostly of gas, they are called "gas giants."

Uranus and Neptune are also giant planets. Although they are not as big as Jupiter and Saturn, both are much, much bigger than Earth. Their atmospheres are also made up mostly of hydrogen and helium gas. Because they are so far away from the Sun, they are cold, dark planets.

Scientists had studied the four giant planets through telescopes and learned a lot about them, but even the most powerful telescopes could not answer all their questions. A spacecraft designed to explore the giant

The four giant planets, Jupiter, Saturn, Uranus, and Neptune, shown to scale. Earth (above) is also shown to scale.

planets would give them a closer view. But it would have been impossible to send astronauts so far. Astronauts have never traveled beyond our own moon. A trip to the giant planets would be thousands of times farther and would take several years. Only a robot spacecraft could make the long journey.

The mission was so important that two spacecraft were built, *Voyager 1* and *Voyager 2*. If one broke down on the long trip, there would still be one left.

The *Voyagers* were not very big—each one was about the size of a small car—but they were the most advanced spacecraft ever designed. The scientific instruments they carried included special cameras with telescopic lenses. These cameras would take close-up pictures of the giant planets and the surfaces of their moons. Other instruments would measure ultraviolet and infrared light. This light, invisible to normal cameras, would tell scientists more about the temperatures of the planets and what they are made of.

During their long trip through space, the *Voyagers* would be controlled from Earth. Scientists would radio commands to the spacecraft telling them what path to follow, what to photograph, and when to send back information. The *Voyagers*' antennas would always be pointed toward Earth, ready to receive instructions.

Radio signals from the *Voyagers* were picked up by large antennas in California, Australia, and Spain. The signals were then relayed by satellite to Mission Control in Pasadena, California.

The pictures and information collected by the spacecraft would be radioed back to Earth. But the *Voyagers*' radio transmitters were not very powerful, and by the time their signals reached Earth, they would be very, very weak. Many large antennas all over the world would be needed to pick them up. It would be like listening for a whisper from thousands of miles away.

Exploring all four giant planets is possible only when the planets are lined up correctly in their orbits. Then each planet's gravity can be used— like a slingshot—to speed up the spacecraft and bend its path toward the next planet. The *Voyagers* would fly to Jupiter, then use Jupiter's gravity to accelerate them toward Saturn. If both *Voyagers* were still working when they got to Saturn, one spacecraft would be sent to study Saturn's largest moon, Titan, and the other would continue on to explore Uranus and Neptune.

The planets do not line up this way often—only once every 176 years! The *Voyager* mission was a rare opportunity.

In the summer of 1977, the *Voyagers* were launched into space by two powerful rockets. Leaving Earth, they were flying so fast that it took them only ten hours to pass the Moon. As it was racing away, *Voyager 1* looked back to take a picture of the Earth and Moon it was leaving behind.

On their way to Jupiter, the two *Voyagers* would have to pass through the asteroid belt. Asteroids are huge, fast-moving rocks that orbit around the Sun. There are thousands of them between the planets Mars and Jupiter, and a collision with one could destroy the spacecraft. Both *Voyagers* made it safely past them. *Voyager 1* led the way to Jupiter, the first gas giant.

The flight paths of the two *Voyagers*. *Voyager* 1 was launched second but took a faster route to Jupiter. After visiting Saturn, *Voyager* 1 took an upward path out of the solar system. *Voyager* 2 continued to Uranus and Neptune.

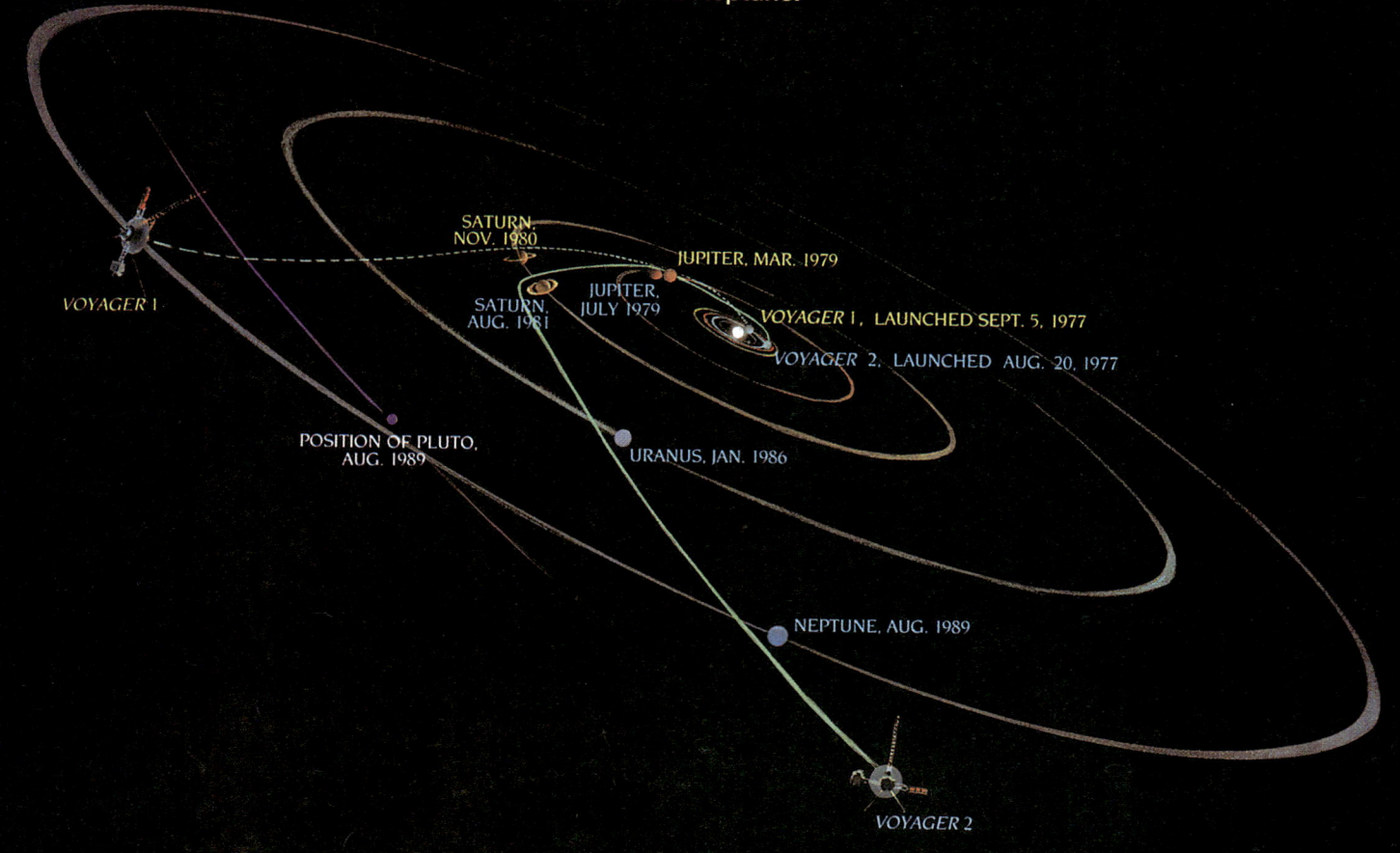

VOYAGER 1

SATURN, NOV. 1980
JUPITER, MAR. 1979
SATURN, AUG. 1981
JUPITER, JULY 1979
VOYAGER 1, LAUNCHED SEPT. 5, 1977
VOYAGER 2, LAUNCHED AUG. 20, 1977
POSITION OF PLUTO, AUG. 1989
URANUS, JAN. 1986
NEPTUNE, AUG. 1989

VOYAGER 2

JUPITER

The *Voyagers* sped closer and closer to Jupiter. As the spacecraft approached the planet, hundreds of scientists crowded into Mission Control to see the close-up pictures of this faraway world.

The radio signals that carry *Voyagers*' pictures travel at the speed of light. So although it had taken the *Voyagers* one and a half years to travel to Jupiter, their pictures traveled back to Earth in about 45 minutes. As soon as the pictures were received by the huge antennas on Earth, they were relayed to Mission Control, then displayed on TV screens. The scientists were stunned by what they saw.

The giant planet has bright colors and complex patterns that scientists had never seen through their telescopes. It is covered with wide bands of yellow, orange, red, and white clouds. Violent storms move through the clouds.

The Great Red Spot is a huge storm in Jupiter's atmosphere that never disappears. Scientists had looked at it through telescopes for over three hundred years, but they had never been able to study its motion. Hundreds of the *Voyagers*' pictures were put together into a movie so that the motions of the Great Red Spot and the other storms could be seen. The movie showed the Great Red Spot swirling violently around its center, with hurricane-force winds around its edges.

Each of the smaller white circles is also a violent, swirling storm. Scientists do not understand why some storms are bright red and others are white. Although the white storms look small next to the Great Red Spot, some of them are as big as the Earth.

Jupiter has 16 moons that circle around it like a miniature solar system. Three of these moons were discovered by the *Voyagers*. Some of the other moons were seen close up for the first time.

Two pictures of Jupiter's Great Red Spot. The distance from top to bottom in the right picture is about 15,000 miles.

573

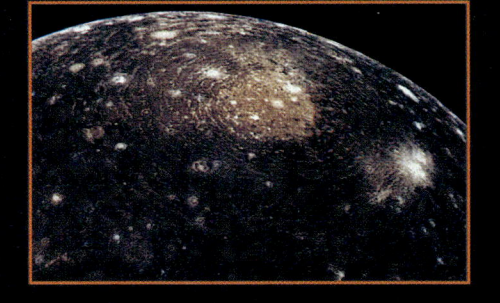

Callisto's surface, showing thousands of craters and the bright patch of ice and faint rings left by a collision with another object.

Jupiter's moon Callisto has been hit by rocks and meteorites for over 4 billion years. Each of these collisions left a crater in Callisto's icy surface. Some of the craters look very bright. These are the newer ones. Each collision sprays fresh ice over the surface, and the freshest ice is the brightest.

Long ago, a very big object—maybe an asteroid—crashed into Callisto. Callisto's icy surface wasn't strong enough to hold the shape of the huge crater left by the collision. Its surface sagged back to its original shape, and now all that's left is a bright patch of ice and a series of faint rings that formed at the time of the collision.

Scientists expected most of the moons in the solar system to look like Callisto—dark, frozen, and covered with craters. They were shocked when they saw the *Voyagers*' pictures of Io, another of Jupiter's moons. There were no craters, and its surface looked orange and splotchy. At first Io was a mystery. But then one of the *Voyagers*' pictures showed something completely unexpected: a volcano erupting! There are active volcanoes on

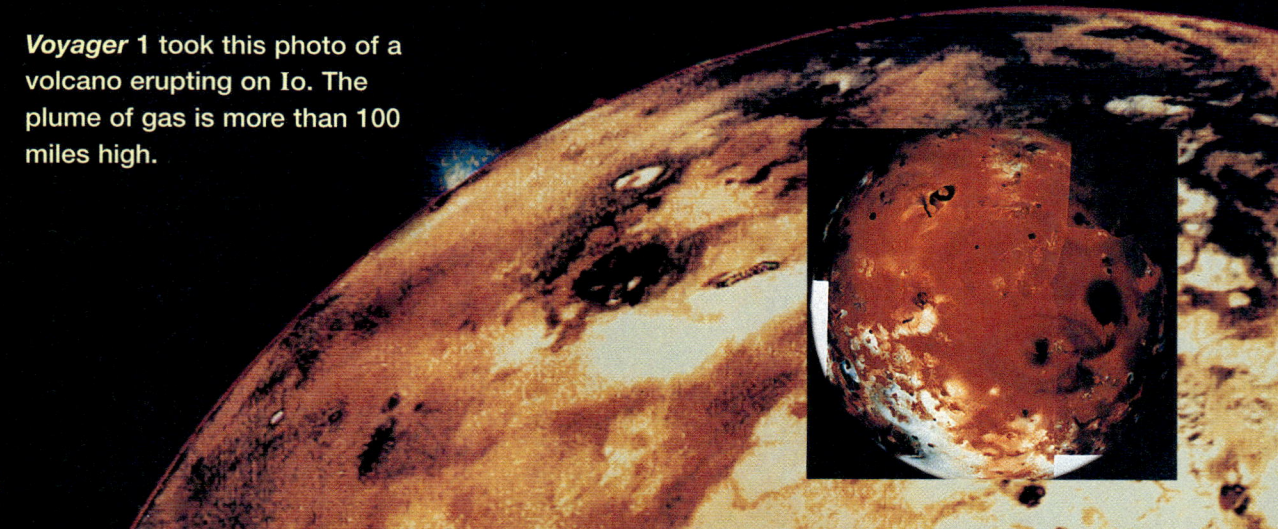

Voyager 1 took this photo of a volcano erupting on Io. The plume of gas is more than 100 miles high.

Earth, but scientists did not expect to find them anywhere else in the solar system. Nine volcanoes were erupting on Io while the *Voyagers* flew past, some throwing hot gas hundreds of miles high. There are no craters on Io because lava from the volcanoes flows over its surface and fills in the craters. The cooled lava contains the chemical sulfur, which gives Io's surface its orange, yellow, red, and black colors.

Europa is Jupiter's brightest moon. Like Io, Europa did not look the way scientists expected a moon to look. It is bright because it is covered with a very smooth layer of ice that reflects the sunlight. Scientists believe that the lines on Europa's surface are cracks in the ice. Fresh ice from below the surface oozes up through the cracks and forms long, flat ridges.

Like Callisto, Europa has been hit by thousands of rocks and meteorites. But there are very few craters left on its surface. Europa's layer of ice must have once been soft, or even liquid, and erased the craters.

For hundreds of years, scientists thought that Saturn was the only planet with rings, but the *Voyagers* discovered a thin ring around Jupiter. The ring could not be seen from Earth. Even the *Voyagers*' sensitive cameras could barely make it out.

The ring is made up of very small dust particles that are circling the planet. Where does the dust come from? The *Voyagers* discovered two tiny moons at the edge of the ring. Scientists think that meteorites hit those moons and knock dust off their surfaces. The dust goes into orbit around the planet and becomes part of the ring.

The *Voyagers* relayed more than 30,000 pictures of Jupiter and its moons back to Earth. As scientists settled down to study the pictures and other scientific information, the spacecraft began their two-year trip to the next planet, Saturn.

Europa's icy surface, covered with cracks and ridges.

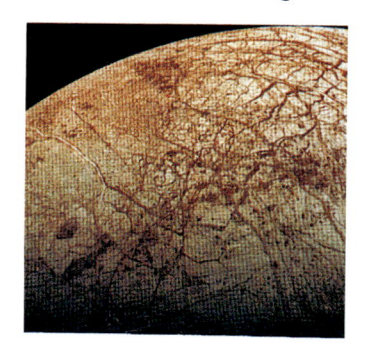

EUROPA

SATURN

Saturn is the second largest planet in the solar system—only Jupiter is bigger. But although Saturn is big, it is very light. It is not like a big rock. A rock would sink in a bucket of water. If you could find a bucket big enough, Saturn would float in it.

When astronomers look at Saturn through telescopes on Earth, they see a yellow, hazy planet with three beautiful rings. But as the *Voyagers* got closer and closer, they showed Saturn as it had never been seen before. The planet turned out to have broad belts of brown, yellow, and orange clouds. Its striped atmosphere reminded scientists of Jupiter, but the colors weren't as bright, and the bands weren't as sharp.

Saturn's atmosphere, photographed by *Voyager* 2. The white band is moving at more than 300 miles per hour.

High winds howl through Saturn's atmosphere, blowing much faster than any winds on Earth. Jet streams near Saturn's equator can reach 1,000 miles per hour. The *Voyagers* also discovered wild, swirling storms, like those in Jupiter's atmosphere.

Saturn's famous rings are made up of countless pieces of rock and ice in high-speed orbits around the planet. If you could scoop up all the particles in the rings, you would have enough rock and ice to make a medium-sized moon. Scientists think that the rings may be what's left of a moon that was shattered by collisions.

As part of an experiment, the *Voyagers* sent radio signals through the rings back to Earth. The radio signals were changed a little bit as they went through the rings. By studying these changes, scientists learned that the pieces of rock and ice that make up the rings come in many different sizes. Some are as small as grains of sand. Some are as big as trucks.

Saturn's rings. Colors have been added to the photographs by a computer to show different parts of the rings.

From Earth, Saturn appears to have three broad rings. In the *Voyagers*' pictures it looked as if there were thousands and thousands of rings. *Voyagers*' other instruments showed that the rings are all part of a huge sheet of particles. There are no completely empty gaps. The thin sheet starts close to Saturn's cloud tops and extends out 40,000 miles. Three very faint rings orbit outside the main sheet.

The *Voyagers* discovered a very small moon, invisible from Earth, at the outer edge of the main sheet of rings. This moon, like the rings themselves, is probably a piece of a larger moon that was shattered when it was hit by a comet or an asteroid. There are other small moons like this one that help shape the rings and sweep the edges clean.

Saturn has at least 18 moons, more than any other planet. Four of them, including the one at the edge of the main sheet of rings, were discovered by the *Voyagers*.

This picture shows Saturn, its rings, and two of its 18 moons, Tethys and Dione.

MIMAS　　HYPERION　　PHOEBE　　TITAN

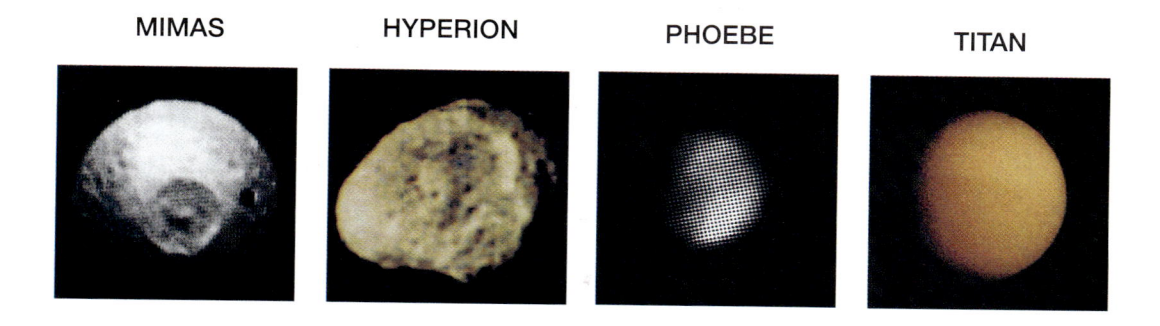

The *Voyagers*' pictures of Saturn's moons show that the solar system can be a dangerous place. One of the moons, Mimas, barely survived a collision that left an enormous crater on its surface. The crater is 80 miles wide, and the mountain at its center is higher than Mount Everest. If the collision had been much harder, Mimas would have split apart.

Another moon, Hyperion, is probably a piece of what was once a larger moon that did break apart.

Most of Saturn's moons are icy balls that were formed at the same time as the planet. But Phoebe is different. It is probably an asteroid that came too close to the planet and was captured by the pull of Saturn's gravity. The picture is blurry because Phoebe is small and *Voyager* was far away.

Titan, Saturn's largest moon, fascinated scientists. Before the *Voyager* mission, it was the only moon in the solar system known to have an atmosphere. From Earth, scientists had detected methane gas around Titan, but they could not tell whether there were other gases in its atmosphere. To find out more, scientists sent *Voyager 1* on a path that would take it very close to this unusual moon.

When the spacecraft arrived at Titan, it found a thick orange haze covering the moon. Titan's atmosphere is very thick—more than one and a half times thicker than the air on Earth. It is made up mostly of nitrogen gas, just like Earth's atmosphere. But unlike the air we breathe, Titan's atmosphere contains no oxygen.

What is below the orange haze? *Voyager* 1's cameras could not see to Titan's surface, but its other instruments sent back clues. The chemical ethane is as abundant on Titan as water is on Earth. Scientists think that Titan might have ethane rainstorms, and maybe even ethane rivers and lakes on its frozen surface.

Because *Voyager* 1's path took it so close to Titan, it would not be able to go on to Uranus and Neptune. Instead, the spacecraft headed up and out of the main plane of the solar system.

Voyager 2 was on a path that would enable it to visit the last two giant planets.

The *Voyagers* are still traveling.

Since leaving Saturn, *Voyager* 1 has been heading north out of the solar system. *Voyager* 2 is now heading south. Although the *Voyagers* are no longer taking pictures, they are still collecting data. They will continue to radio information back to Earth until about the year 2020. Both spacecraft are studying the solar wind, high energy particles that stream out of the Sun. And they are searching for the edge of the solar system—the place where our Sun's influence ends.

The *Voyagers* won't stop there. They will continue on into interstellar space, the empty space between the stars. Although they are traveling at more than 35,000 miles per hour, neither spacecraft will come near another star for thousands and thousands of years.

It is very unlikely that either *Voyager* will be found by space travelers from another world. But just in case, they carry a message from their home planet, Earth. A copper record attached to the side of the spacecraft contains pictures and sounds from Earth. It begins:

"This is a present from a small and distant world, a token of our sounds, our science, our images, our music, our thoughts, and our feelings."

The *Voyagers* are still traveling, heading toward the stars, carrying a message from all of us.

The record attached to each *Voyager* contains greetings in more than 60 languages, music from many different cultures, and other sounds from Earth, such as the songs of humpback whales. The record's cover (inset) has symbols showing where Earth is located in the universe.

Think About It

1. How do the *Voyager* explorations help scientists understand the mysteries of outer space?

2. Which planet or moon that the *Voyagers* visited do you think is the most unusual? Why?

3. Why do you think scientists were stunned by some of the information revealed by the *Voyager*s?

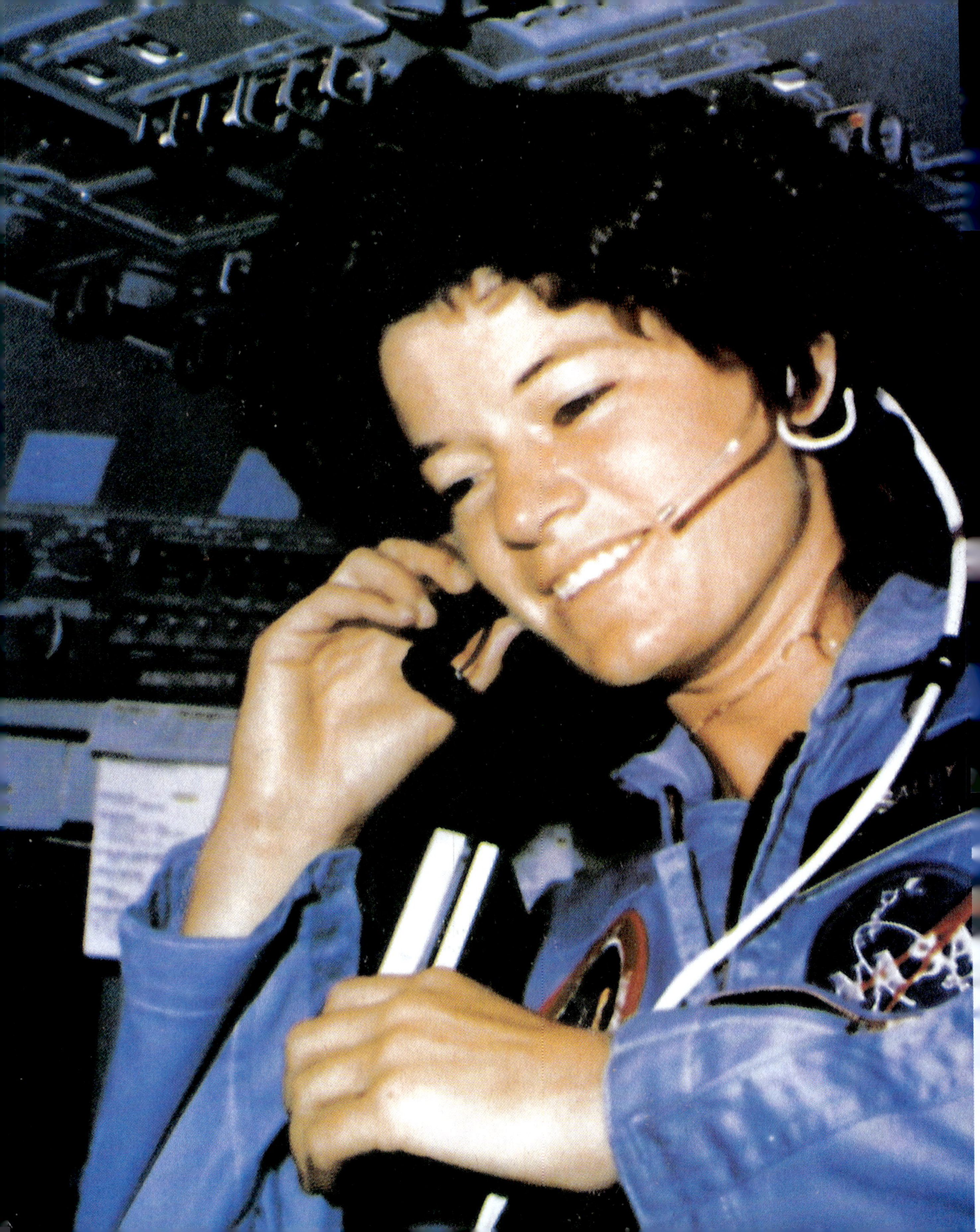

MEET THE AUTHOR

SALLY RIDE

What does it take to be astronaut material? Take a look at some of the interests and personal qualities of author and former astronaut Sally Ride.

A+ student at school—discovered a love of science in high school

Self-reliant—could do her own car repairs

Tennis player—had a high national ranking on the junior circuit

Risk-taker—sent a postcard almost on a whim to apply to enter NASA's space program

Outgoing—loves to speak to students about her experiences

NASA record-setter—at 31 she was the youngest person sent into orbit

Author—has written other books for young readers about space travel and exploration including *To Space and Back* and *The Third Planet*

Unique—the first American woman in space

Team member—worked with another crew member to operate the shuttle's robot arm co-wrote *Voyager* with her friend, science teacher Tam O'Shaugnessy

Visit *The Learning Site!*
www.harcourtschool.com

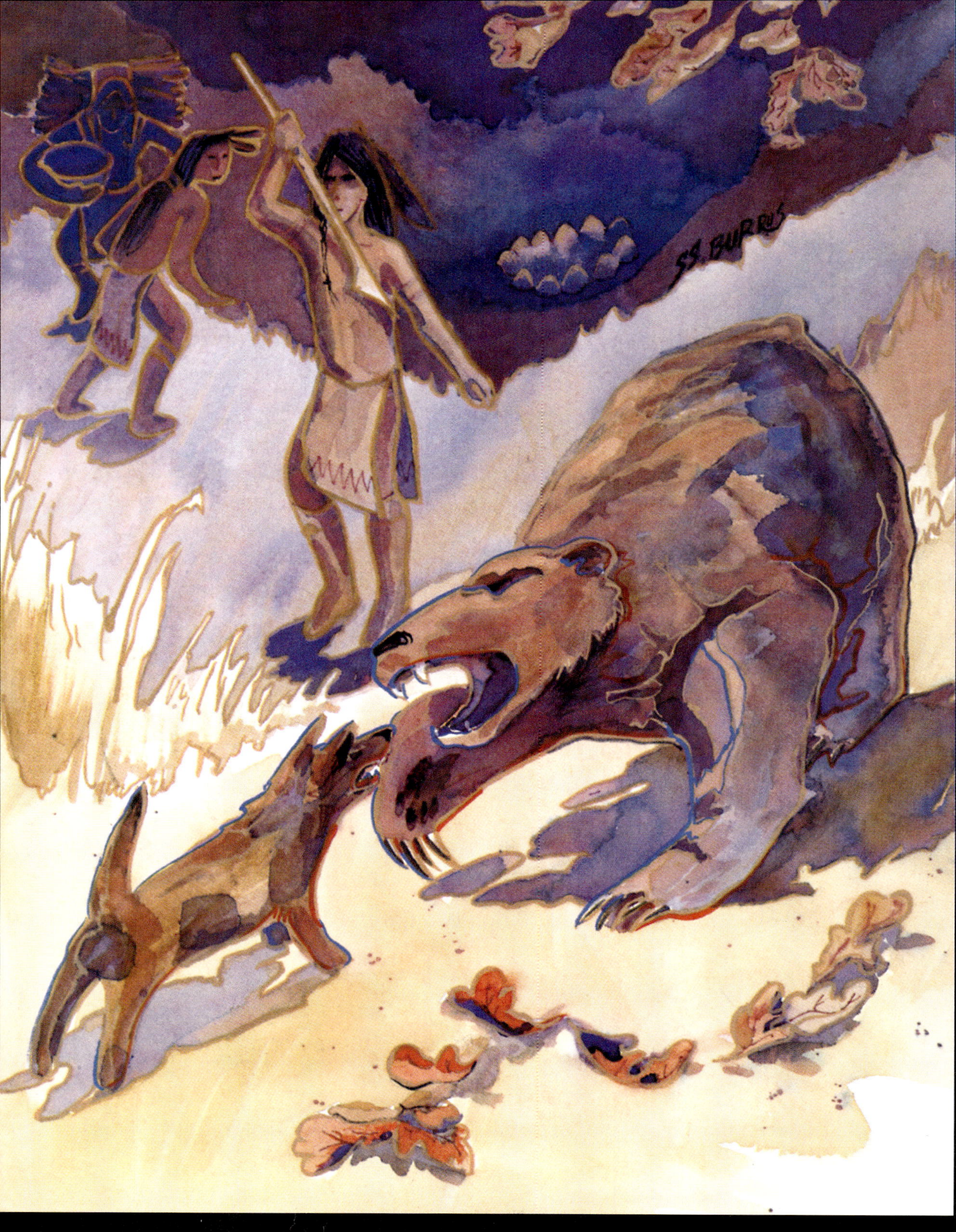
S.S. BURRUS

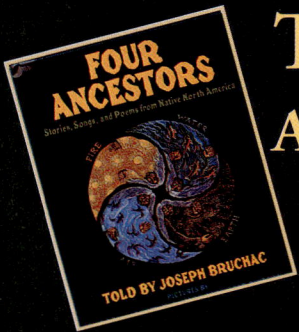

The Three Hunters and the Great Bear

A Seneca myth
retold by Joseph Bruchac
illustrated by S. S. Burrus

Long ago there was a little village. The people in that village lived very well until a strange thing happened. The deer disappeared from the forest, and the fish vanished from the streams. Whenever the men of the village tried to hunt, they found no game.

One day, two hunters went out from the village. One of them went up on a hill to look around while the other followed the trail. Suddenly the one on the trail fell into a hole that had not been there before.

"Where did this hole come from?" called the hunter who had fallen.

The hunter who was up on the hilltop looked down and grew afraid. "That is no ordinary hole," he called back. "Come up here and see."

The first hunter scrambled out of the hole and climbed to the hilltop. When he looked down, he, too, became afraid. The hole into which he had fallen was the paw print of a giant bear.

The two hunters hurried back to the village to tell their story.

"This is why the game has vanished," one of the elders said. "This is why the fish are gone from the streams. This giant bear has eaten all the fish and all the animals."

"We must build fires around the village," said another of the elders. "Now that all the other food is gone, the great bear will come after us."

In that same village, there were three brothers who were the greatest of all the hunters. Whenever they went out hunting with their little dog, they always brought back game. The first brother had such keen eyes that he never lost the trail. The second brother was so strong that he could carry back anything they caught. The third brother was so good at throwing a spear that he never missed. But he was also one of the laziest men in the village.

"We will go out and get that giant bear," said the first brother.

"We will not stop until we have caught it," said the second.

"But first we will take a nap," said the third.

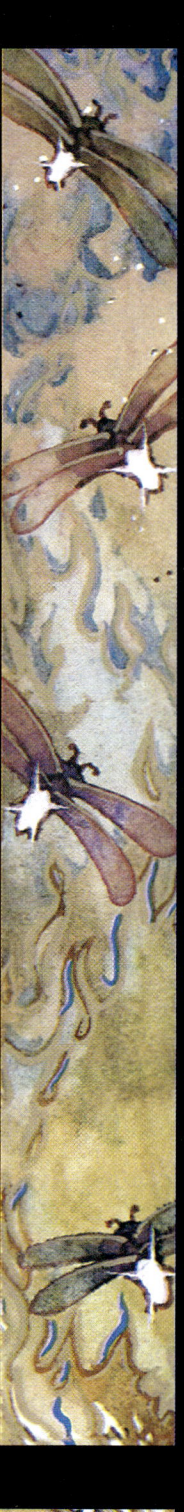

"No," said his brothers, "we will go right now." And even though the lazy hunter protested, they set off on the trail of the giant bear.

The first brother, whose eyes were keen, quickly found the trail. The second brother was close behind him, carrying a big pot and a load of firewood so that they could cook some of the meat from the bear after they caught it. Their little dog was close beside them, sniffing the air. The third brother hung back.

"Brothers," he said, "let us stop and rest for a while."

Just then, the little dog began to bark. It ran into the thick brush by the side of the trail. As soon as it did, the giant bear ran out the other side. It was afraid of that little dog's bark.

"We see you," shouted the first brother.

"We are going to catch you," shouted the second brother.

"Don't run so fast," shouted the third brother.

Then the three brothers ran after the bear as their little dog nipped at its heels. The bear ran through the forest, but they stayed close behind. It ran up the hills, and they still stayed close behind. Then it came to a tall mountain and began to climb. It went higher and higher, but the brothers still followed.

The third hunter, though, was tired of running. "Brothers," he said, "I have hurt my foot and can run no farther. Each of you must grab one end of my spear so that I can sit on it while you carry me."

His two brothers did as he asked. On and on they went as the bear climbed higher and higher up the mountain. It was growing dark, and the third brother was becoming so heavy that they were beginning to fall behind.

"Brothers," said the lazy hunter, "put me down. My foot feels much better now."

So the brothers put him down. Because he had rested, the third brother ran ahead. When he caught up with the bear, he drew back his spear and threw it, killing the giant bear.

The three brothers were very happy. They made a fire, cooked up some of the bear meat, and began to eat. Then the first brother looked around. There were lights all around them in the darkness. Then he looked down.

"Brothers," he said, "we are up in the sky."

The brothers looked around. It was true. That giant bear had fled up into the sky land, and they had followed it up among the stars.

Suddenly they heard their little dog barking. The giant bear had come back to life and was running away. They took up the chase again.

If you look up into the night sky, you can still see the three hunters following the great bear, circling around the sky. They are the stars some call the Big Dipper and others call Ursa Major, the Great Bear. The three stars behind the bear are the hunters, and the faint star with them is their dog. Every year, in the autumn, the Great Bear turns upside down. When Seneca children see that, they say, "Look, the lazy hunter has killed the great bear again."

THINK ABOUT IT
What does this myth try to explain?

RESPONSE

Asteroid Art

PAINT A PICTURE

Choose an interesting planet or moon described in the selection. Look at photographs, and use descriptions and your imagination to make a painting of that place. Title your painting, and hang it in your classroom.

Inventions Through Time

MAKE A TIME LINE

Make a list of important inventions, such as the radio and the telescope, that helped make the *Voyager* missions possible. With a partner, research when these items were invented. Show your findings in chronological order on a time line.

ACTIVITIES

Voices from Earth

WRITE A LIST

On the side of each *Voyager* is a record containing recordings of greetings, music, and sounds from Earth. Make a list for your own recording of voices, messages, sounds, or songs. Give a brief reason why you chose each one. Tell how the recording might help you understand your place in the universe.

Making Connections

WRITE A MYTH

Voyager and "The Three Hunters and the Great Bear" each illustrate a way of understanding the planets and stars. Write your own myth that explains a feature of the night sky.

Cyber

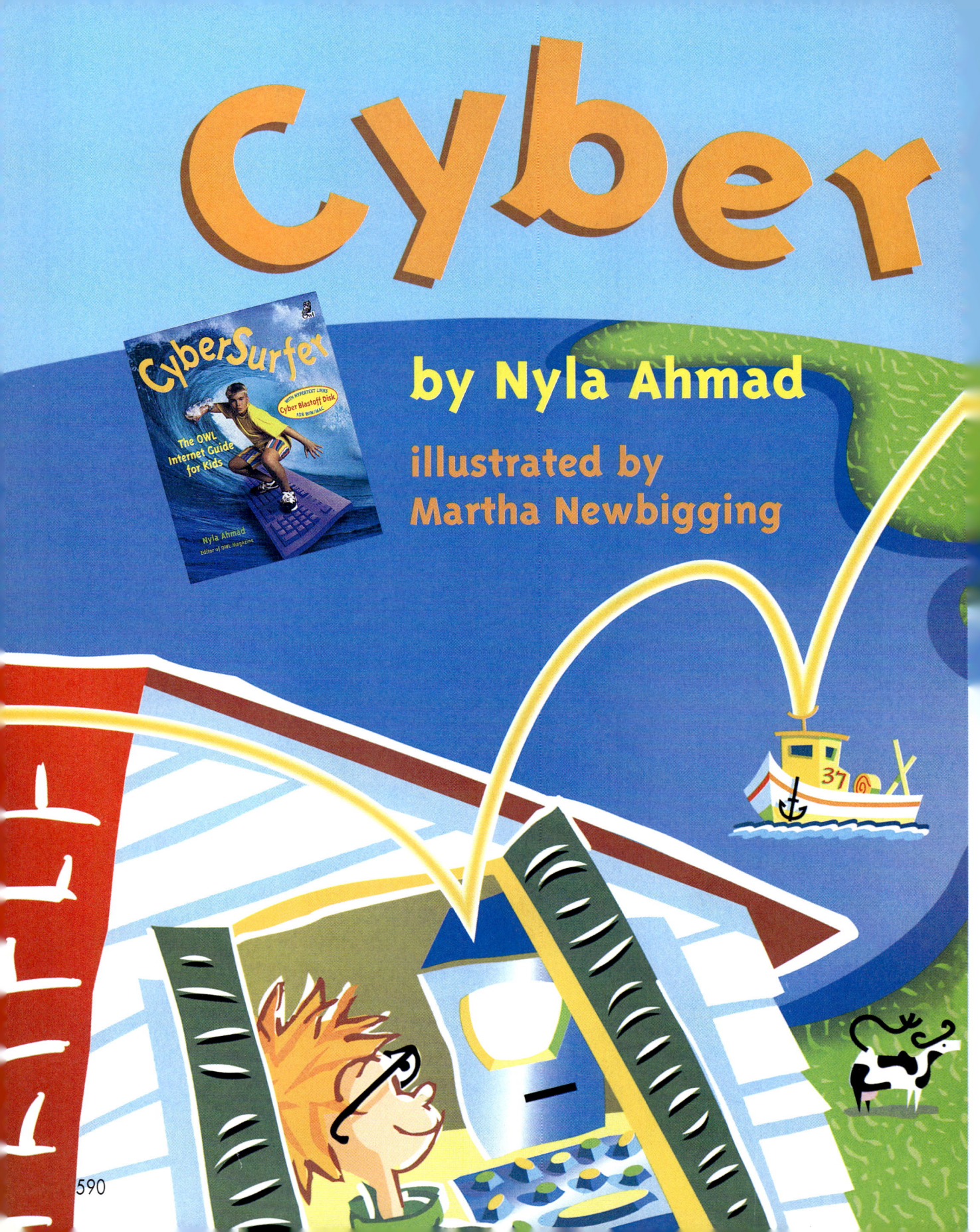

by Nyla Ahmad

illustrated by Martha Newbigging

Surfer

Logging onto the Internet is like entering a new world. On the Internet, you can talk to people from all over, send and receive e-mail, watch video clips, listen to music, and find a lot of great information at the click of a button! The Internet is constantly growing. Since this selection was written, even more advances to Internet technology have been made. The selection you are about to read will get you ready to explore this new world . . . and become a cybersurfer!

Goodbye Snail-mail, Hello E-mail

You've heard about "snail-mail," right? That's the usual way to send a letter—paper, pen, envelope, stamp. Why do cybersurfers call it snail-mail? Because it's s-o-o-o s-l-o-o-o-w! If you send snail-mail to your buddy in France, for example, you must write the letter, stuff it in an envelope, put your address and your buddy's on the front, and slap on a stamp. Then, you walk over to the closest mailbox, toss in your letter—THUMP!—and go home to wait. You could wait for days, maybe even weeks, before your pal gets your letter, reads it, and writes back.

Say "Goodbye snail-mail, hello e-mail." The fastest way to send a letter anywhere in the world is through the Net. With electronic mail, or e-mail for short, your modem can send messages around the Net in just a few seconds. Type a letter on your computer, zip it across the Net to the computer of the person you're trying to reach, and you can be sure that it gets there before you even have time to yawn.

E-mail is quick and lots of fun. In this section, you'll find out how to talk to cyberpals on the Net. There's a new language of symbols you should learn, a netiquette to follow, and some hot flames that you should be aware of. So read on, and get the message.

Who Are You?

In real life, there might be several people in the world with the same name as you—maybe even hundreds. But on the Net, no two users can have the same name. Each user is known by an e-mail address. An e-mail address is a lot like a telephone number—just as there's a different number for every telephone, there's a different e-mail address for every person on the Net.

At first an e-mail address looks like a bowl of alphabet soup. All the letters, numbers, dots, and symbols couldn't possibly make any sense, right? Well, believe it or not, they do. Just as the combination of area code and numbers tells you a lot about where a telephone is located, an e-mail address reveals a lot about who the user is and where the message is coming from. But beware—some people enjoy "spamming," or using your e-mail address to pull a Net prank on someone else! You wouldn't give your phone number to a stranger you meet on the street, and you should also be careful with your e-mail address when dealing with strangers on the Net—but more about that later.

Anatomy of an Address

Any time you see an Internet address—online, in a magazine, here, or in the "Yellow Pages" Directory—it will be a string of letters, numbers, symbols, and sometimes words. Type every character into your computer exactly as you see it. Keep the characters all on one line, even if the address runs over two lines on the page. And don't leave any spaces—Internet addresses never contain spaces.

Take a look at the e-mail address below. When you read it aloud, the address is pronounced: "newbie at cyberguide dot surfcity dot e-d-u." Sounds strange, doesn't it? But it's actually a lot like a regular address, with periods or "dots" separating the different elements. So let's take a look at what this address means—just so you know what you're seeing and saying.

newbie@cyberguide.surfcity.edu

At the beginning of the address is the user ID, the identity of the person sending or receiving the message. It can be a name written in letters, a series of numbers, or a combination of both. In this case, the person is identified as "newbie."

The "at" symbol is one of the most important symbols in an e-mail address. It separates the user ID to the left of it from the location to the right of it.

This tells you where the user is. It could be the name of a school, office, club, or organization. In this case, newbie is at "cyberguide."

In most cases, this part of the e-mail address is the geographic location, called the subdomain. In this example, cyberguide is located in a place called "surfcity."

This is the user's domain. It tells you what kind of user this is. In this case, "edu" means that cyberguide is an educational institution.

Anatomy of E-mail

You can send e-mail from your computer to anyone who has an e-mail address any place in the world. E-mail is faster than regular mail—it only takes a few seconds!—and electronic letters rarely get lost.

Once you've seen one piece of e-mail you've seen them all! All e-mail looks exactly the same, because it follows a standard format, or protocol, that all computers on the Net can understand. Here's how it all works:

1. Sending e-mail is very simple. All you do is type your message, fill in the complete e-mail address of the person you're sending the message to, and then click on "SEND." The Internet will take care of the rest.

2. The Internet breaks down your message into small packets of information that travel individually. Each packet contains the address of the destination of the whole message. In a process known as routing, the Internet chooses the best way to send your message to the destination.

3. Messages going a long distance may need to be amplified, or given a boost, to make sure they get to where they're going.

4. When your message arrives at the destination, its tiny packets are put back in the correct order. The Internet checks that all the packets have arrived, in the correct order, and lets you know by telling you "transmission was successful" or "message sent." Signed, sealed, and delivered!

The **To** line is the address of the person receiving the message. If the address on this line is incorrect, the message will be returned.

The **From** line contains the address of the person sending the message.

The **Subject** line tells you what the message is about in a few words.

Attachments are files that you add to your e-mail message. An attachment can be anything—a story, a picture, a game—you want to pass along on the Net.

The **Message** is the "letter" part of the e-mail. It can be as long as you like. But be nice on the Net, or you might get flamed!

Netiquette and Flames

When you speak to someone face to face or on the phone, it's usually easy to tell when they're joking and when they're not. But on the Net, where you communicate by messages on a computer screen, it's not so easy. And you might send a message to a person you've never met—so they may not understand the way you express yourself or your sense of humor. Getting along with others on the Net requires rules of netiquette. If you don't follow them you might get flamed—receive a barrage of negative responses to your rude behavior—and then it could get difficult to cool things down!

- On the Net, TYPING A SENTENCE IN CAPITAL LETTERS, LIKE THIS, IS LIKE SHOUTING, and it's considered very rude. Type in caps only if you are very angry, or only a word or two if you're expressing a very STRONG point.

- When you receive an e-mail message, try to answer it as soon as possible. Since the message only took a few seconds to get to you, why should it take weeks before you reply?

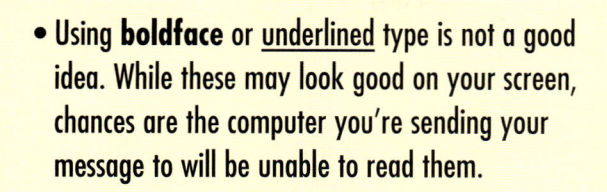

- Using **boldface** or <u>underlined</u> type is not a good idea. While these may look good on your screen, chances are the computer you're sending your message to will be unable to read them.

- E-mail makes it easy—too easy—to send a message you might regret later. Swearing, name-calling, and general rudeness are absolute no-no's on the Net. If you forget your manners, you'll get flamed back—you'll be bombarded with angry messages from unhappy people on the Net. So remember: "Sticks and stones may break your bones, but flames could really hurt you!"

Say It with a "Smiley" :-)

If you're being funny on the Net, or just want to have some fun, try an emoticon. Emoticons show your feelings on faces made up of symbols and letters from your keyboard. Here are a few to help *say* it with a smiley—just tilt your head to the left to *see* it with a smiley!

:-)	Smiley	:-#	My lips are sealed!
:-o	Wow!	I-{	Good grief!
:-I	Hmmm...	8-o	No way!
'-)	Wink	%-)	Bug-eyed
:^D	Great idea!	8-)	I wear glasses
:-*	Ooops!	3:)	My pet
:-(	Frown	I-I	Sleeping
:-,	Smirk	I-O	Yawning
:-V	Shout	:-S	I'm totally confused!
:-T	Keeping a straight face	:-O	Ouch!
:-D	Big smile	<:-D	It's my birthday!

Acronyms FYI—For Your Information

On the Net you may see abbreviations of common expressions or sayings. People use these just for fun, or to save time. Here's a list of some popular Net acronyms. So the next time someone says BBL, you know to say CYA!

BBL	Be back later	**NBD**	No big deal
BRB	Be right back	**NOYB**	None of your business
BTW	By the way	**OIC**	Oh, I see...
CYA	See ya!	**OTL**	Out to lunch
FYI	For your information	**ROFL**	Rolling on the floor laughing
IMHO	In my humble opinion	**TTFN**	Ta-ta for now
IOW	In other words	**TTYL**	Talk to you later
ITC	It's the coolest!	**YMBJ**	You must be joking!
LMHO	Laughing my head off	**WYSIWYG**	What you see is what you get
LOL	Laughing out loud		

Surfing the Net

Sending and receiving e-mail is one fun thing you can do on the Net, but surfing the Net is where it's really at. Surfing the Net means hopping onto the Internet's digital waves and riding the computer network to just about any place in the world. Surfers cruise between computers, databases, and forums around the globe, moving from site to site, in search of the perfect wave . . . er . . . file.

You can log on at the computer in your home, hook up to the Louvre Museum in Paris, jump over to the United Nations in New York, then check out the latest version of your favorite video game—all in the time it takes to suck a cough drop! Getting, sending, and receiving information from the Net can take only a few seconds, as long as you know how to surf.

Surfing the Net, or being able to find what you're looking for, takes a bit of practice. There's so much information on the Net, and so many places to go to get it, that you may not know where to start. Then there's the problem of knowing how to get to where you want to go, once you've decided what you're looking for! But have no fear, this section tells you all you need to know about surfing the Net—without ever getting wet. Surf's up, dude!

A Web of Waves

Once you start exploring the Net in search of cool things to see, download, and explore, it won't be long before you get caught in the WWW, or the World Wide Web. It's called the Web, for short, and it's the main reason surfing the Net has become so popular for millions of scientists, teachers, business people, adults, and kids around the world. It's a part of the Net that's great because it's easy to use. The Web uses graphics and hypertext, and these make all the difference when it comes to smooth surfing.

Grab Graphics and Hyper Surf

Web graphics are more than just pretty pictures that can move around or spin on your computer screen! The pictures, called icons, allow you to click with your mouse instead of typing in commands. Icons are a serious bonus when it comes to surfing the Net because you just point-and-click at certain commands without having to spell them out for your computer. If you can see the icons on your screen and can click your mouse, then you've got what it takes to surf the Web of waves.

Hypertext makes surfing the Net hyper-easy. With hypertext, certain words are underlined or appear in color on your computer screen. These words are linked automatically to related information somewhere else on the Web. To get to this information, you click on the hypertext words with your mouse and your computer jumps to a new site. Let's say you're on the Web reading about monk seals at a zoo Web site. You read: "Monk seals are protected in the Frigate Shoals off the coast of the Hawaiian Islands. . . ." If the words Frigate Shoals are hypertext, clicking on those words with your mouse will get you more information about where they are—and this information might be posted by a tourist office in Hawaii!

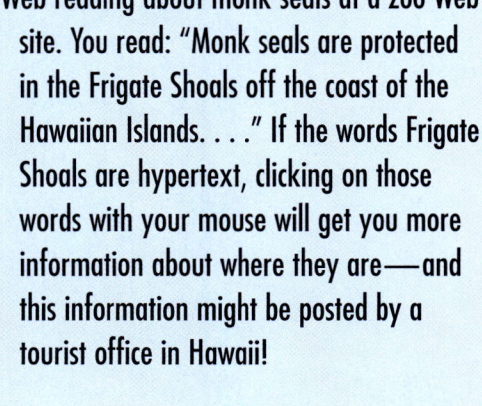

Web Text

Browser: special software that lets you surf or "browse" through the Net, and especially the Web, by letting you use your mouse to point-and-click at icons instead of typing in commands

Home Page: a page or screen that a site on the Web uses as its main base or home

Hypertext: text that appears underlined or in a different color on your screen. Clicking on hypertext will automatically link you to other documents, sites, and information on the Web that are related to that subject

Hypertext Markup Language, or HTML: a computer language used by programmers to design Web Home Pages

Hypertext Transfer Protocol, or HTTP: a special computer code used by programmers that makes it possible for users to get and see documents on the Web

Site: a place you visit on the Web, usually starting with the Home Page, that's filled with lots of things to check out

Uniform Resource Locator, or URL: the address for a site on the Web

Home Sweet Home...

When you get to a site on the Web, the first thing you'll see is a Home Page. This is where you start exploring a site. Some Home Pages have lots of photos or graphics and others don't. Some have a lot of hypertext areas and others don't. But the one thing that every Home Page has in common is that it says, "Welcome to our cyberhome!" Here's an example of what a Home Page might look like.

A Home Page can be as long as you want it to be. Ben's takes up more than three screens as you scroll down. On the first screen, Ben welcomes you and lets you choose a description of what you see: Fantastic, Incredible, Beautiful, or Fantastically Well Made. (Humble, isn't he?) The second screen lets you visit different sections of the site to do some cool stuff: send e-mail, play games, learn more about Ben, chat in real time. It also tells you how many people have visited Ben's Home Page before you—Ben makes a joke that the counter is wrong, and that a lot more people than *that* have checked out his site.

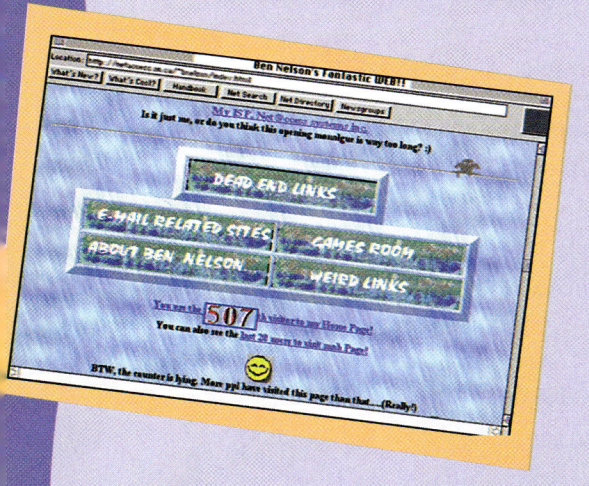

On the third screen, Ben suggests some of the more popular things to do when you visit him at his cyberhome. For example, you can play Hairball, a game Ben invented, and chase a crazy cat through a large hotel in Ben's home town. Ben ends up by inviting you to e-mail your comments to him, if only to let him know how many spelling mistakes or stray paragraphs you can find. Ben's Fantastic Home Page is loads of interactive fun, and has made him lots of cyberpals.

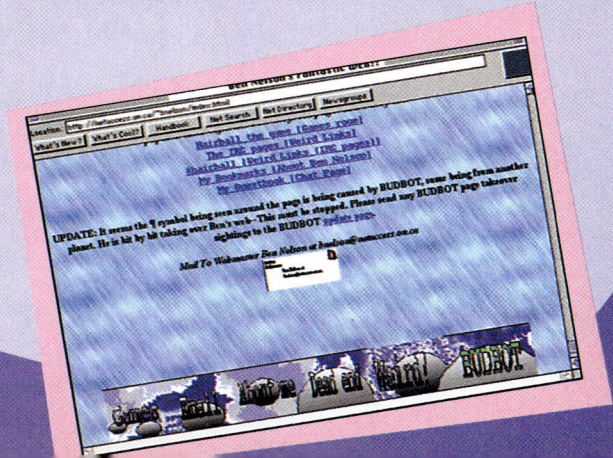

The Safety Net

Don't talk to strangers. Look both ways before you cross the street. Don't play with fire. Be careful. Do these safety rules sound familiar? They should, because you've probably heard them over and over again. All kids get the same warnings from parents, teachers, and other people who care. They're giving you one simple message: play it smart no matter what you do.

Wherever you are, being smart helps you to keep safe, and the Internet is no exception. The Internet isn't really a dangerous place. For the most part, it's lots of fun. On the Net, anything goes—that's why you'll find lots of wonderful stuff to see and do. But this freedom also has its flip side.

Just like dangers in the real world, problems on the Net include theft, intruders, nasty messages, hate literature, and people you want to avoid, who may be dishonest or dangerous or both. Because millions of computers on the Net are hooked up to each other, nasty messages from nasty people spread quickly across the Net. Computer illnesses, or viruses, are also very contagious. If you download a file that contains a virus, your computer can "catch" a virus from Japan, for example, and pass it on to a computer in Boston. In just a few seconds, thousands of computers around the world can become "sick."

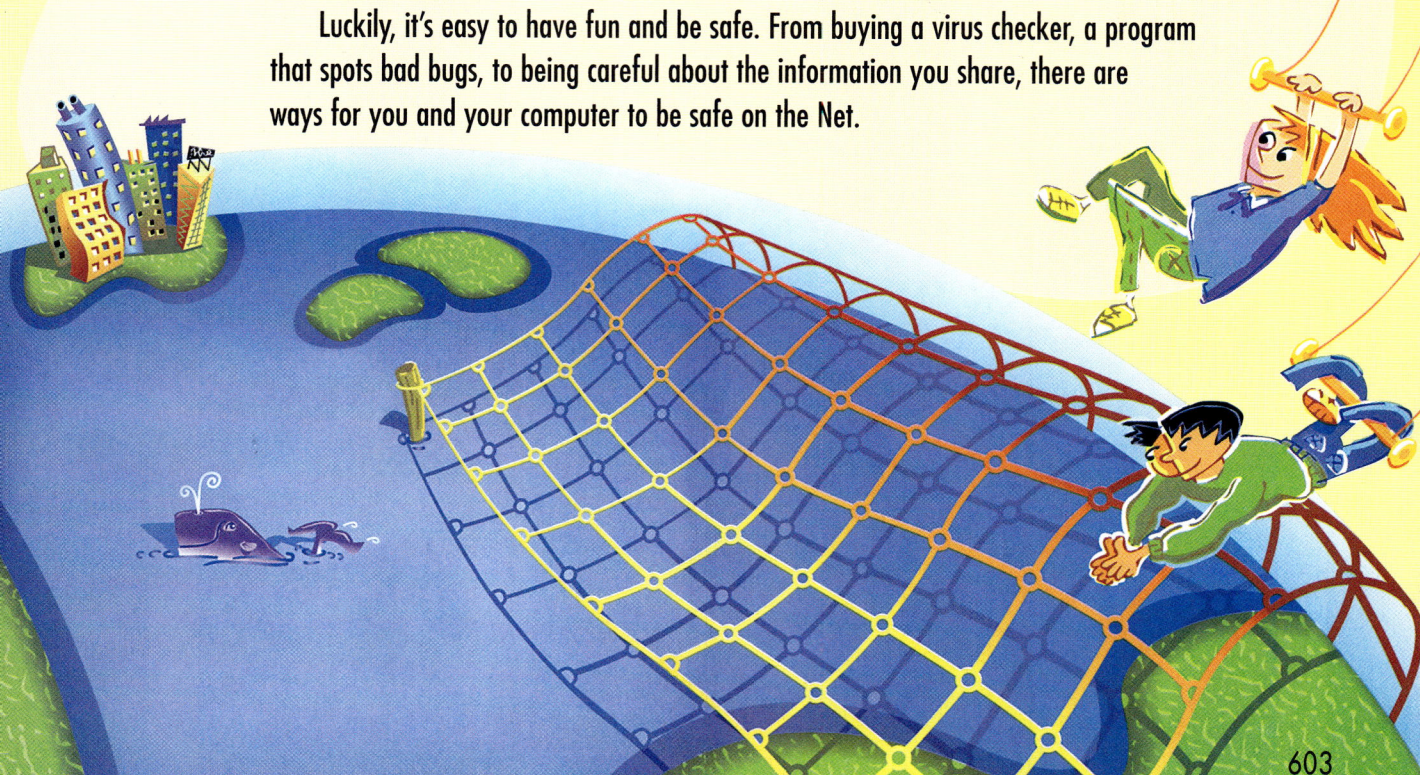

Luckily, it's easy to have fun and be safe. From buying a virus checker, a program that spots bad bugs, to being careful about the information you share, there are ways for you and your computer to be safe on the Net.

Be a Street-smart Surfer

Be cool, not cruel
Play it cool—not cruel—and you'll make more friends than enemies on the Net. Don't be mean to cyberpals and stay away from those who say mean things to you.

Mum is always the word
It's cool to talk to strangers on the Net, but it's not cool to tell them certain things: your home address or phone number; where you go to school; where your parents work or what they do; or anything else about your family or friends. After all, they're still strangers and they could really hurt you.

Go for the good, steer clear of the bad
Most kids go on the Net for the same reason you do—to have fun, make friends, and find cool stuff. But there are bad guys on the Net, too. These people fill the Net with nasty messages, horrible pictures, and dangerous information. You'll know what the bad stuff is when you see it, so you should know that it's better to stay away. Stay out of trouble, go for the good, and you'll be a street-smart surfer.

Think About It

1. How do cybersurfers use the Internet to explore new "worlds"?

2. Do you like the way the author presents information about the Internet? Explain why you feel as you do.

3. What does the author tell readers to persuade them to use the Internet?

Meet the Author
Nyla Ahmad

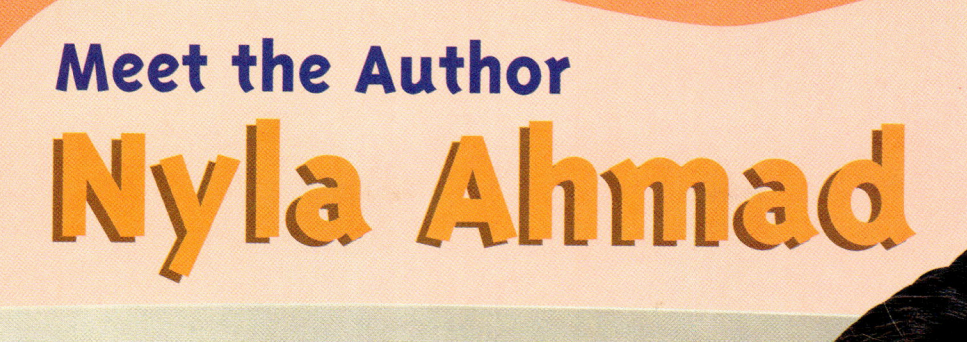

Read this e-mail to find out about author and editor Nyla Ahmad.

To: readers@yourschool.edu
From: cybersurfer@cyberspace.com
Subject: Meet an adventurous writer!

Hi! Have you ever read *OWL* or *Chickadee*? Nyla Ahmad has edited both of these magazines for young readers for more than twenty years. In 1996 she launched an Internet site called OWLkids Online. It was named a Canadian Cool Web site of the Day. Ahmad doesn't just work at her computer, though. She's visited more than sixteen countries and she likes hiking, cycling, and sea kayaking. Nyla Ahmad loves adventure!

Visit *The Learning Site!*
www.harcourtschool.com

Your heart will beat nearly three times.

The planet Earth will orbit 56 miles around the sun.

In The Next Three Seconds...

from *In the Next Three Seconds...* compiled by **Rowland Morgan**
illustrated by **Rod and Kira Josey**

A Sprinting Cheetah will cover three-quarters... the length of a soccer field.

The human population will increase by NINE.

Motor Vehicles will use three tanker trucks of gasoline.

Italians will DRINK a stack of cases of mineral water as HIGH as the Statue of Liberty.

AMERICANS will eat 6,000 eggs.

95 AIRLINERS WILL TAKE OFF.

In The Next Three Hours...

Menu – Americans will eat 600,000 lobsters.

Americans will use paper that requires 375,000 trees to make.

More than 500 baby rabbits will be adopted as family pets.

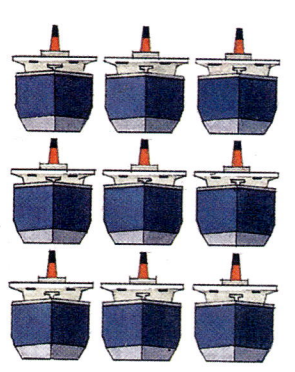

Certain types of bamboo will grow 9.0 in. when exposed to the sun.

It's for you–hoo!

Nine OIL tankers will dock in British ports.

A butterfly will transform from a pupa into a beautiful, fluttering adult.

Americans will throw away 99 miles of plastic pens.

Meteosat, the weather satellite, will take six complete pictures of the clouds over Europe, Africa, and the Atlantic Ocean.

Americans will buy 4,500 pairs of jeans.

Americans will buy one STACK of telephones four times as high as Toronto's CN communications tower.

607

IN THE NEXT THREE DAYS...

More than 2,000 products will be trademarked in the U.S.A.

A blue shark in a hurry could travel 1,600 miles, or from Africa to India.

FRENCH pet dogs will eat the weight of a herd of 700 African elephants in pet food. (WOOF)

More than 2,000 people OR half-mile bumper-to-bumper busloads of people will move to Florida.

WELCOME TO FLORIDA — THE SUNSHINE STATE
TALLAHASSEE · JACKSONVILLE · ORLANDO · TAMPA · MIAMI

MEMO: Enough paper to cover one tennis court will be used per office worker. Signed _____

JOURNEY INTO SPACE
Enough writing will move on the computer Internet to make a stack of THICK paperback books reaching into outer space (37 miles).

A ton of wood in a forest will release a ton of oxygen. O₂

DOCTOR'S NOTE: Your cold virus will multiply itself 10,000 million times before causing your first sneeze.

More than 1,000,000 new bicycles will be wheeled out of factories.

In The Next 3 Three Weeks...

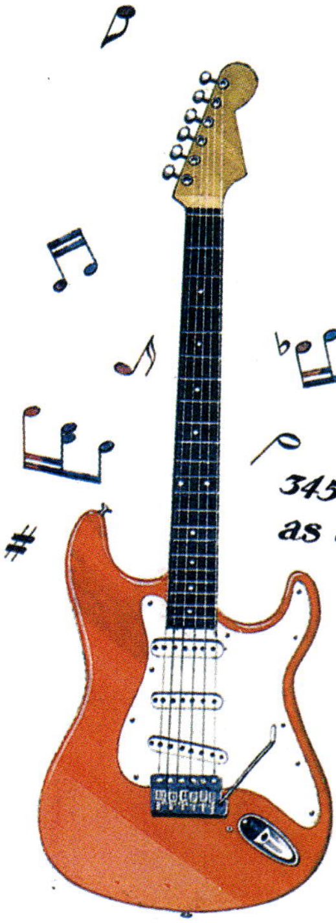

345 pop-songs will be released as singles in the U.K.

132,000 people will visit the Tower of London.

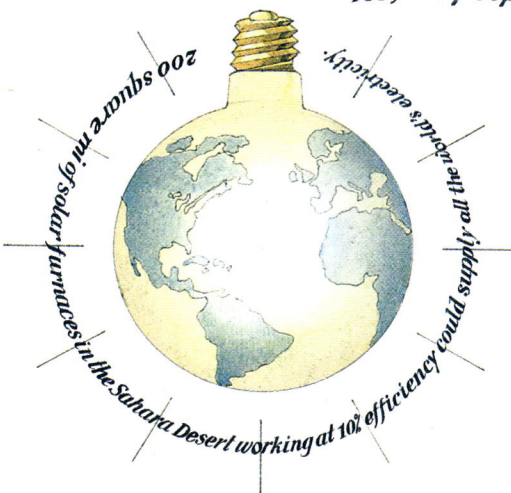

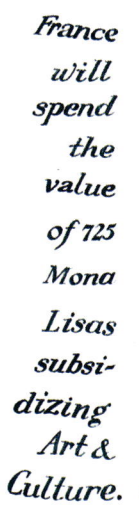

200 square miles of solar furnaces in the Sahara Desert working at 10% efficiency could supply all the world's electricity.

France will spend the value of 725 Mona Lisas subsidizing Art & Culture.

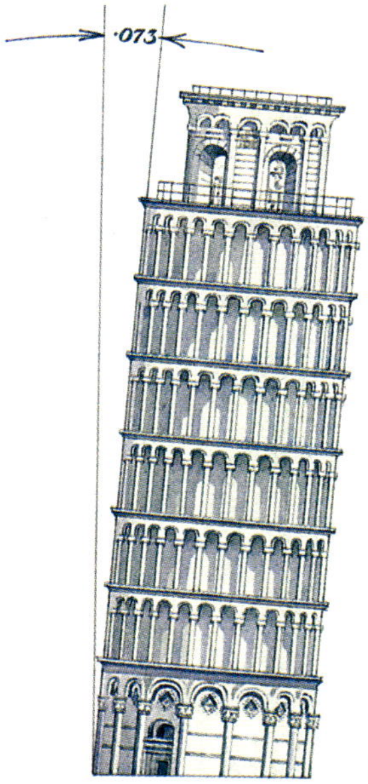

The leaning tower of PISA will move another 0.0028 inch off vertical.

6,575 sightseers will take a flight over the Grand Canyon.

Americans will eat 80 pizzas as BIG as the White House grounds.

The young herb Puya Raimondii will move one-thirteen-hundredth nearer the flowering of its only panicle in at least 80 years' time.

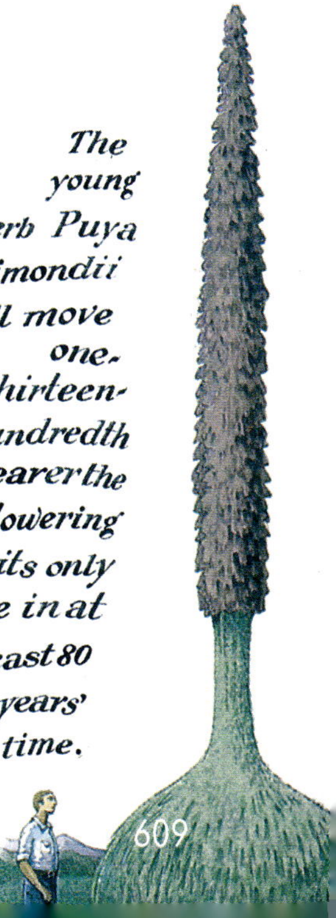

Think About It
Which piece of information did you find most interesting? Why?

Response

That's My Sign!

DESIGN AN EMOTICON
Look at the emoticons on page 598 in the selection. Then make up your own personal emoticon. Write an explanation beneath it. Use your emoticon when you e-mail friends. Invite your friends to create emoticons too!

Snail Mail Versus E-Mail

HOLD A DEBATE
The author of the selection believes that e-mail is better than regular mail. Do you agree? Make a list of the reasons for your opinion. Then work with a partner who takes the opposite viewpoint. Hold a debate about the issue.

Activities

My Home in Cyberspace

DESIGN A HOME PAGE
Many people create home pages based on their favorite hobbies. Design a home page that shows your favorite hobby. Be sure to include some graphics and links to related Web sites. Make a poster of your home page design, and hang it in your classroom.

Making Connections

WRITE AN E-MAIL
Write an imaginary e-mail to a friend or family member. Include *To, From,* and *Subject* lines in your mail. In your message, tell what you like about the selection "In the Next Three Seconds. . . ." Explain how it helps you explore the future.

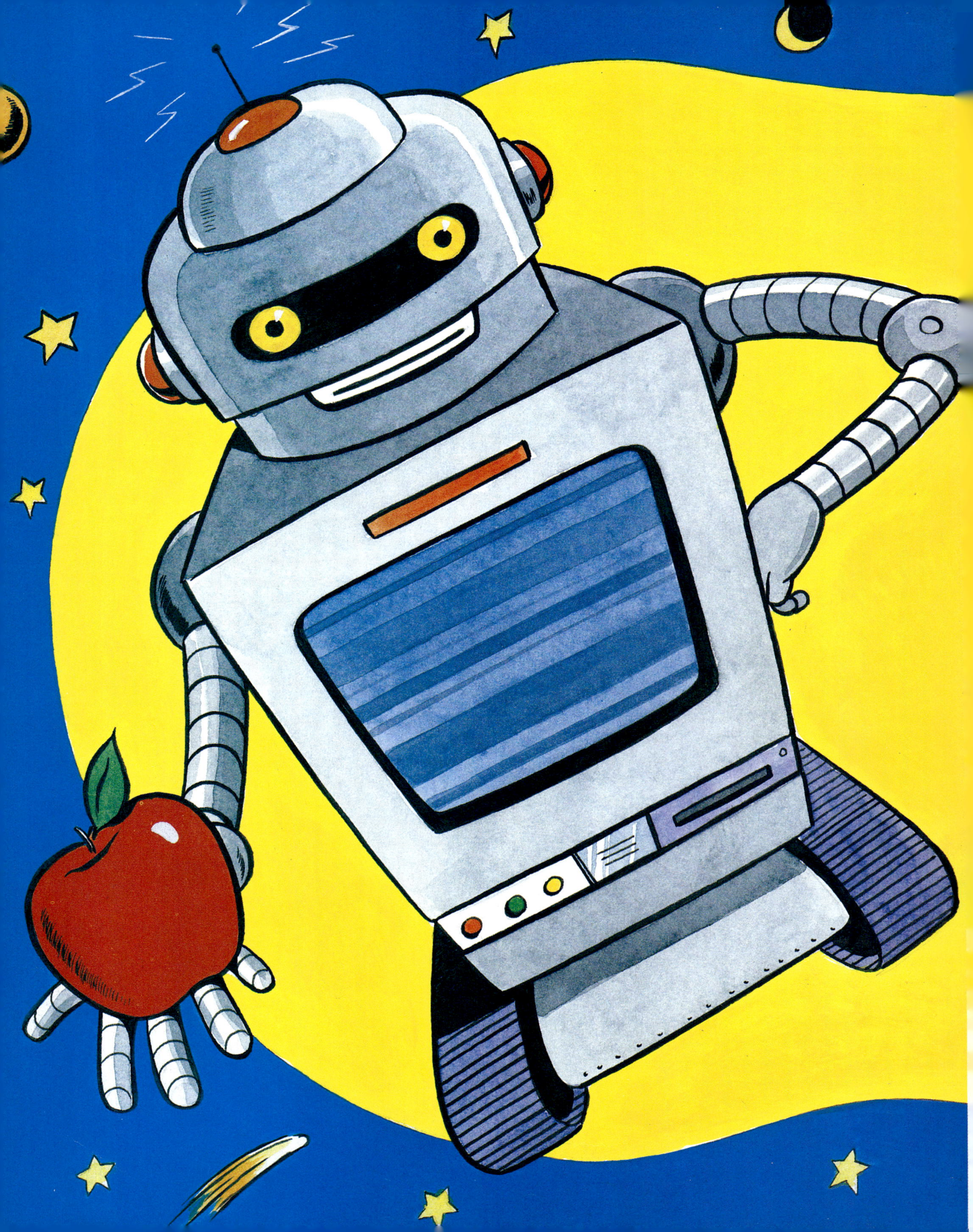

THE FUN THEY HAD

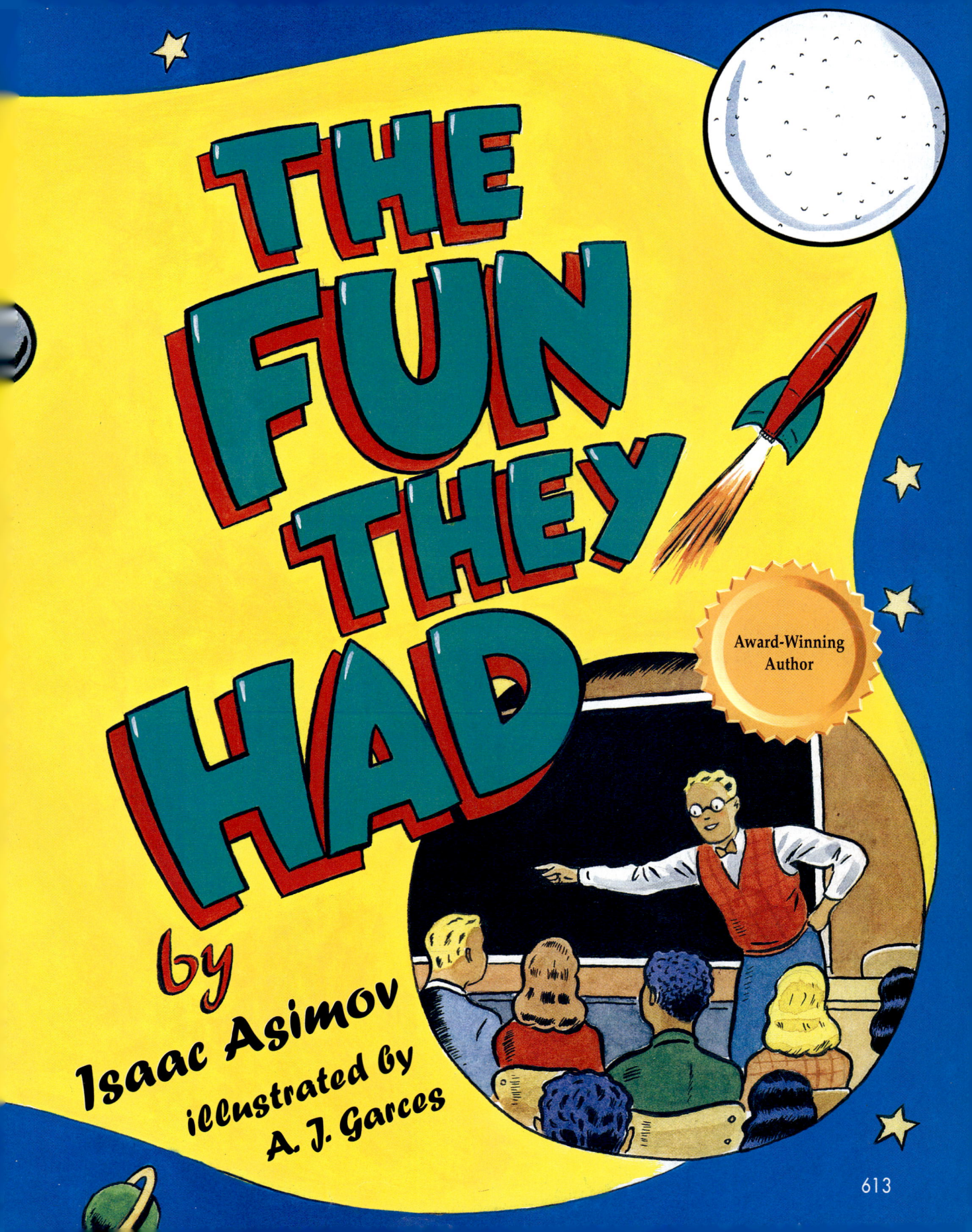

by Isaac Asimov

illustrated by A. J. Garces

Award-Winning Author

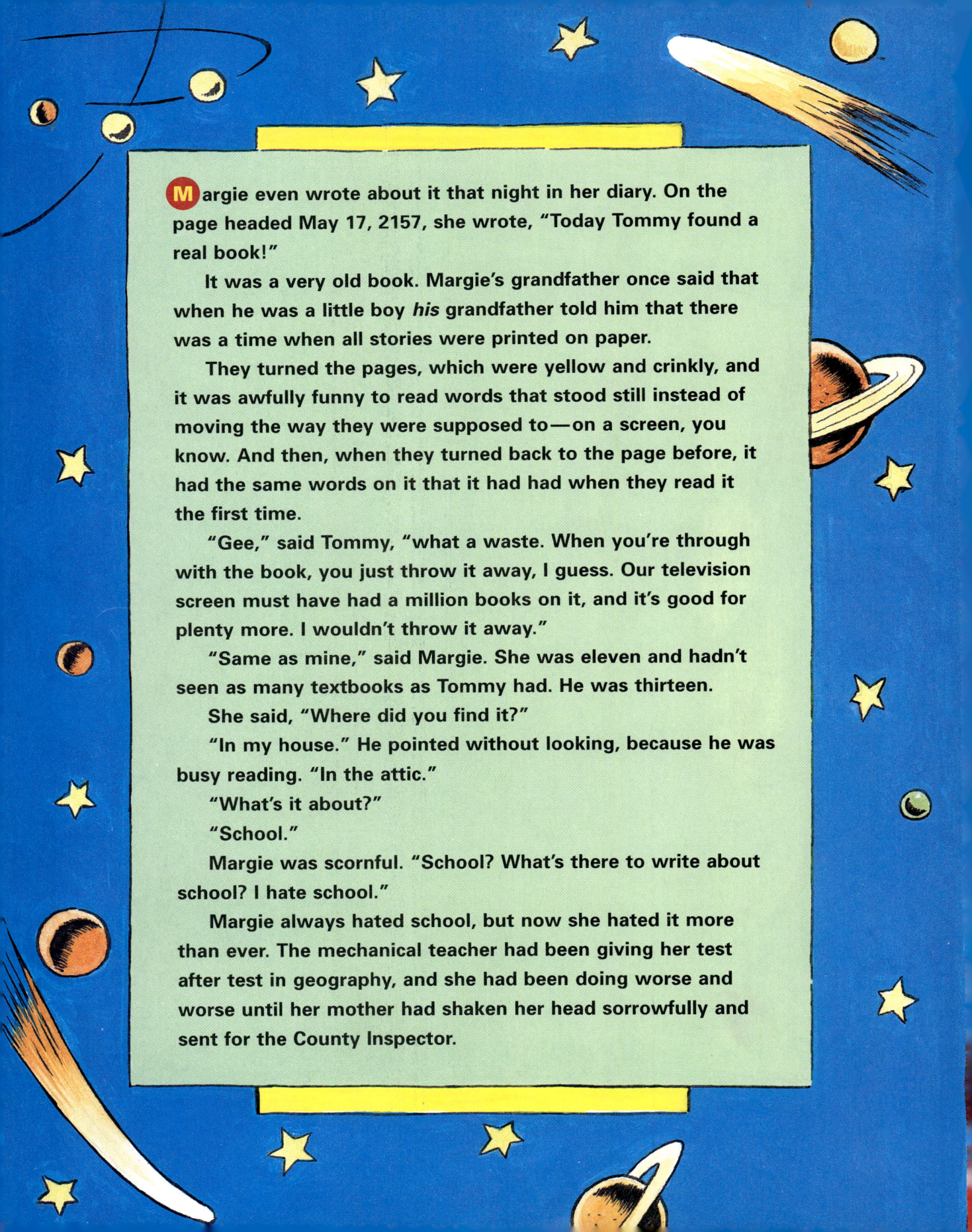

Margie even wrote about it that night in her diary. On the page headed May 17, 2157, she wrote, "Today Tommy found a real book!"

It was a very old book. Margie's grandfather once said that when he was a little boy *his* grandfather told him that there was a time when all stories were printed on paper.

They turned the pages, which were yellow and crinkly, and it was awfully funny to read words that stood still instead of moving the way they were supposed to—on a screen, you know. And then, when they turned back to the page before, it had the same words on it that it had had when they read it the first time.

"Gee," said Tommy, "what a waste. When you're through with the book, you just throw it away, I guess. Our television screen must have had a million books on it, and it's good for plenty more. I wouldn't throw it away."

"Same as mine," said Margie. She was eleven and hadn't seen as many textbooks as Tommy had. He was thirteen.

She said, "Where did you find it?"

"In my house." He pointed without looking, because he was busy reading. "In the attic."

"What's it about?"

"School."

Margie was scornful. "School? What's there to write about school? I hate school."

Margie always hated school, but now she hated it more than ever. The mechanical teacher had been giving her test after test in geography, and she had been doing worse and worse until her mother had shaken her head sorrowfully and sent for the County Inspector.

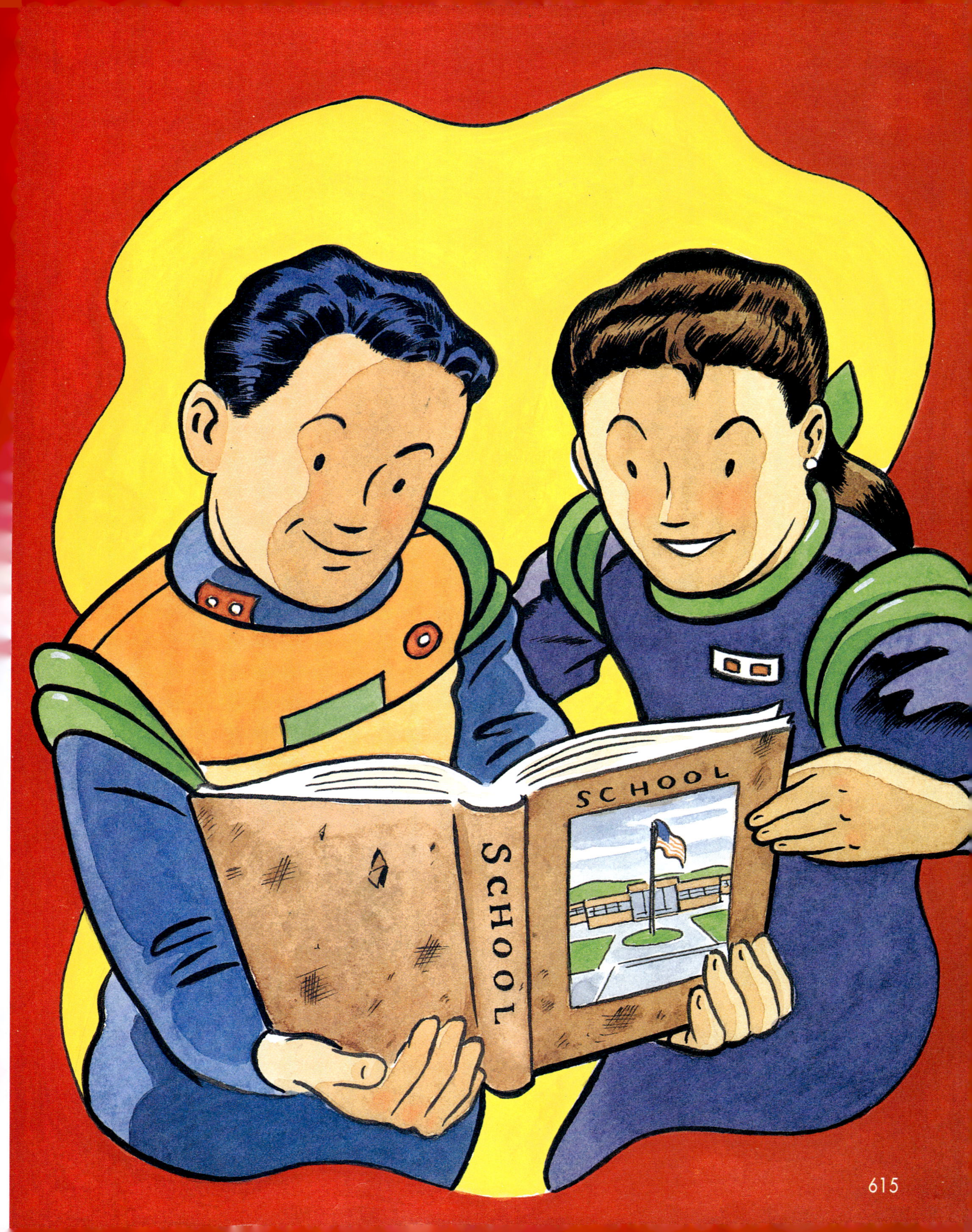
SCHOOL
SCHOOL

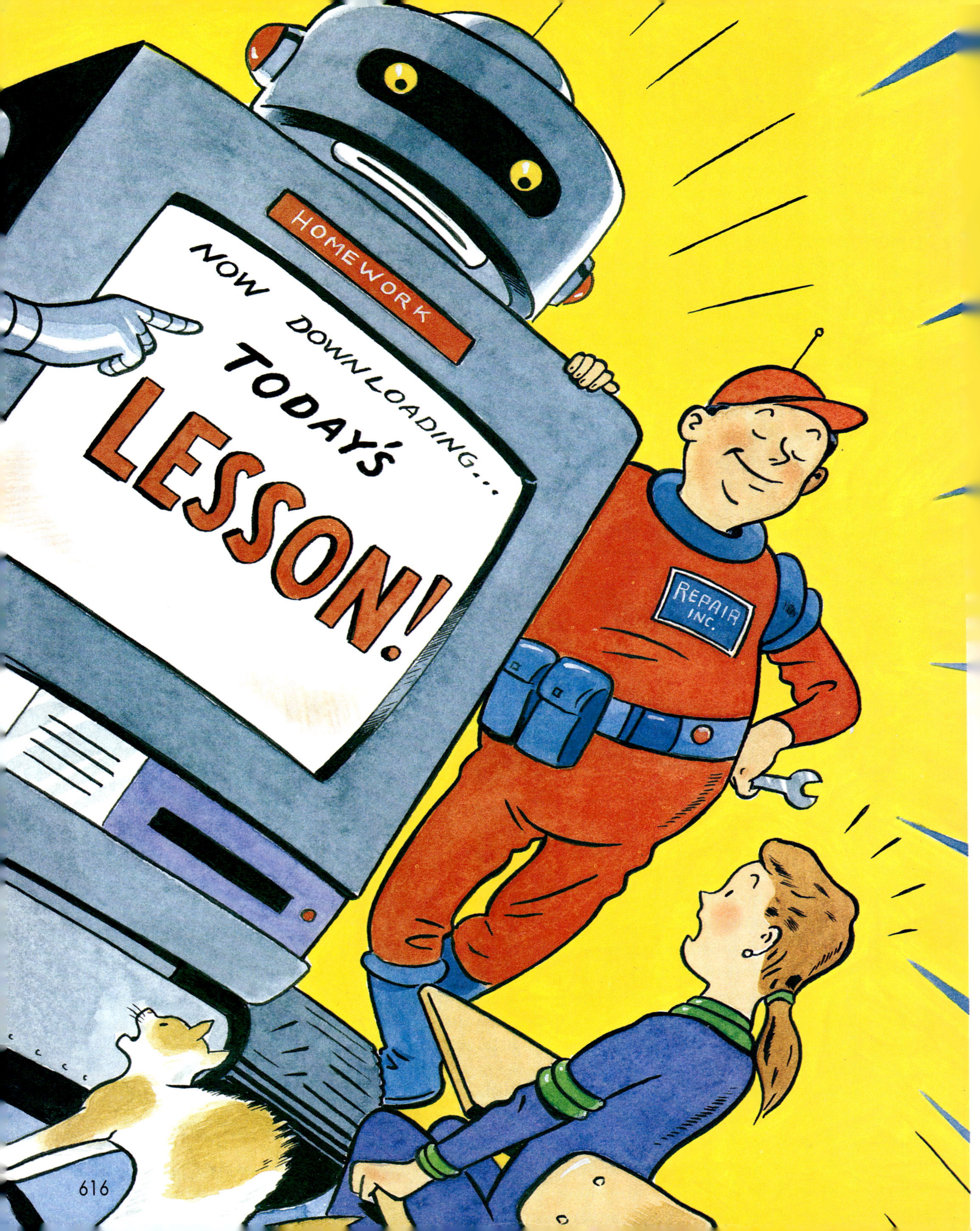
HOMEWORK
NOW DOWNLOADING...
TODAY'S
LESSON!
REPAIR INC.

He was a round little man with a red face and a whole box of tools with dials and wires. He smiled at Margie and gave her an apple, then took the teacher apart. Margie had hoped he wouldn't know how to put it together again, but he knew how all right, and, after an hour or so, there it was again, large and black and ugly, with a big screen on which all the lessons were shown and the questions were asked. That wasn't so bad. The part Margie hated most was the slot where she had to put homework and test papers. She always had to write them out in a punch code they made her learn when she was six years old, and the mechanical teacher calculated the mark in no time.

The Inspector had smiled after he was finished and patted Margie's head. He said to her mother, "It's not the little girl's fault, Mrs. Jones. I think the geography sector was geared a little too quick. Those things happen sometimes. I've slowed it up to an average ten-year level. Actually, the overall pattern of her progress is quite satisfactory." And he patted Margie's head again.

Margie was disappointed. She had been hoping they would take the teacher away altogether. They had once taken Tommy's teacher away for nearly a month because the history sector had blanked out completely.

So she said to Tommy, "Why would anyone write about school?"

Tommy looked at her with very superior eyes. "Because it's not our kind of school, stupid. This is the old kind of school that they had hundreds and hundreds of years ago." He added loftily, pronouncing the word carefully, "*Centuries* ago."

Margie was hurt. "Well, I don't know what kind of school they had all that time ago." She read the book over his shoulder for a while, then said, "Anyway, they had a teacher."

"Sure they had a teacher, but it wasn't a *regular* teacher. It was a man."

"A man? How could a man be a teacher?"

"Well, he just told the boys and girls things and gave them homework and asked them questions."

"A man isn't smart enough."

"Sure he is. My father knows as much as my teacher."

"He can't. A man can't know as much as a teacher."

"He knows almost as much, I betcha."

Margie wasn't prepared to dispute that. She said, "I wouldn't want a strange man in my house to teach me."

Tommy screamed with laughter. "You don't know much, Margie. The teachers didn't live in the house. They had a special building and all the kids went there."

"And all the kids learned the same thing?"

"Sure, if they were the same age."

"But my mother says a teacher has to be adjusted to fit the mind of each boy and girl it teaches and that each kid has to be taught differently."

"Just the same, they didn't do it that way then. If you don't like it, you don't have to read the book."

"I didn't say I didn't like it," Margie said quickly. She wanted to read about those funny schools.

They weren't even half-finished when Margie's mother called, "Margie! School!"

Margie looked up. "Not yet, Mamma."

"Now!" said Mrs. Jones. "And it's probably time for Tommy, too."

Margie said to Tommy, "Can I read the book some more with you after school?"

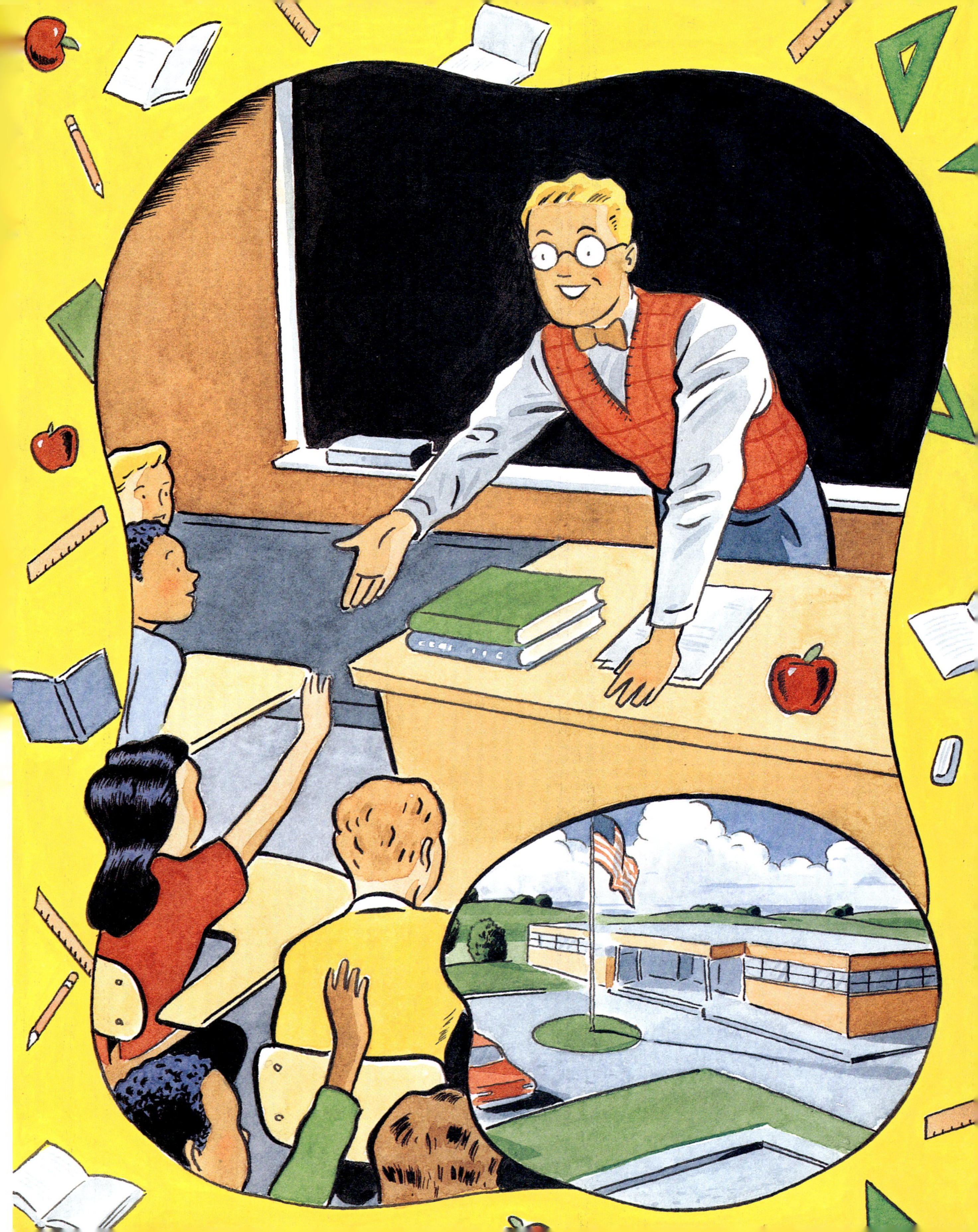

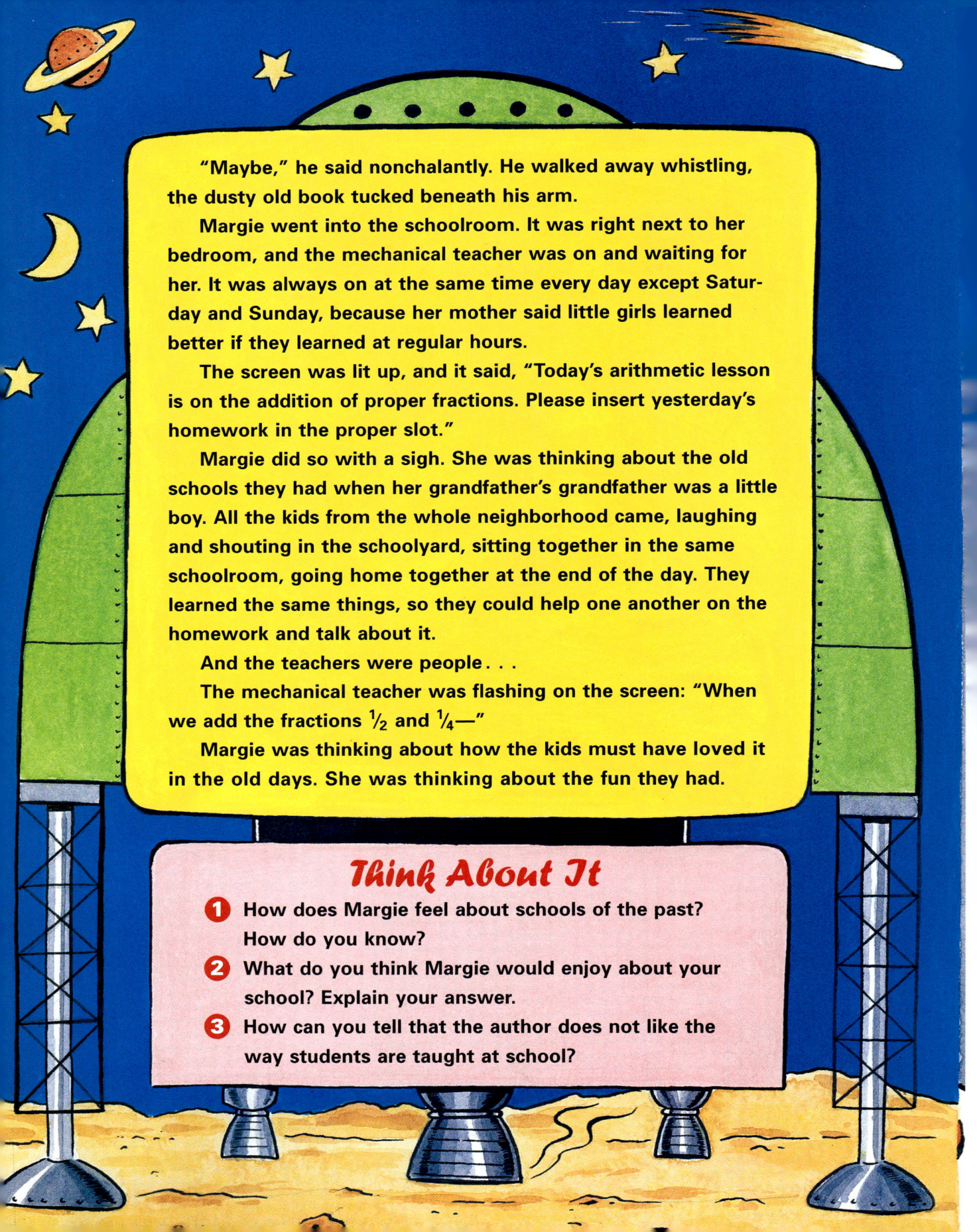

"Maybe," he said nonchalantly. He walked away whistling, the dusty old book tucked beneath his arm.

Margie went into the schoolroom. It was right next to her bedroom, and the mechanical teacher was on and waiting for her. It was always on at the same time every day except Saturday and Sunday, because her mother said little girls learned better if they learned at regular hours.

The screen was lit up, and it said, "Today's arithmetic lesson is on the addition of proper fractions. Please insert yesterday's homework in the proper slot."

Margie did so with a sigh. She was thinking about the old schools they had when her grandfather's grandfather was a little boy. All the kids from the whole neighborhood came, laughing and shouting in the schoolyard, sitting together in the same schoolroom, going home together at the end of the day. They learned the same things, so they could help one another on the homework and talk about it.

And the teachers were people . . .

The mechanical teacher was flashing on the screen: "When we add the fractions $\frac{1}{2}$ and $\frac{1}{4}$—"

Margie was thinking about how the kids must have loved it in the old days. She was thinking about the fun they had.

Think About It

1. How does Margie feel about schools of the past? How do you know?
2. What do you think Margie would enjoy about your school? Explain your answer.
3. How can you tell that the author does not like the way students are taught at school?

About the Author

Isaac Asimov

Read this true-false quiz about Isaac Asimov (1920–1992), one of the most active science fiction writers ever. (He wrote *hundreds* of books!)

1. Asimov started writing science fiction stories because he liked science fiction television shows.

Answer: *False. Most families in the United States did not own televisions until after Isaac was grown up. As a boy, Isaac loved reading the science fiction magazines that were sold in his father's candy store.*

2. Asimov's first science fiction stories were not published.

Answer: *True. The editor of* Astounding Science Fiction *magazine did not accept them, but he gave the young writer many helpful suggestions. Later on, the magazine did publish his work.*

3. Asimov liked to use scientific ideas in his science fiction.

Answer: *True. He often based his stories on one interesting scientific idea.*

Visit *The Learning Site!*
www.harcourtschool.com

To Dark Eyes Dreaming

by Zilpha Keatley Snyder
illustrated by Jui Ishida

Dreams go fast and far
  these days.
They go by rocket thrust.
They go arrayed
  in lights
    or in the dust of stars.
Dreams, these days,
  go fast and far.
Dreams are young, these days,
  or very old,
They can be black
  or blue or gold.
They need no special charts,
  nor any fuel.
It seems, only one rule applies,
  to all our dreams—
They will not fly except in open sky.
  A fenced-in dream
    will die.

623

RESPONSE ACTIVITIES

Celebrate Books

MAKE A MURAL

Margie and Tommy read books on computers, not on printed pages. Think about what they might enjoy about reading printed books. With a small group, make a mural that celebrates some of your favorite books.

Margie's New Adventure

WRITE A SEQUEL

Think about what Margie is like. Then write a sequel to "The Fun They Had." Tell what happens to Margie and how she continues to explore her world.

My Teacher, the Computer

INTERVIEW TEACHERS

With a partner, discuss how Margie and Tommy feel about computers. Talk about how people use computers at your school. List questions to ask your teacher about what he or she likes and dislikes about using computers in education. Conduct your interview and write your story. Then publish it in the school newspaper.

Making Connections

MAKE A LIST

Margie in "The Fun They Had" and the writer of "To Dark Eyes Dreaming" both believe in the importance of dreams and goals. Make a list of dreams and goals that a person your age might have, and tell how he or she might reach them.

THEME WRAP-UP

In My View . . .

COMPARING AUTHORS' VIEWPOINTS Think about how the authors of two selections in this theme feel about exploring new worlds. Do they view it as hard work, exciting, dangerous, or all three? How can you tell? Write a paragraph comparing and contrasting the authors' viewpoints. Include examples from the selections to support your statements. Share your paragraph with your class.

An Out-of-This-World Performance!

WRITE A PLAY Work with a small group to write a short play based on one or more of the selections in this theme. You may use facts from the other selections in the theme. Create a program for your play that lists the characters, plot, and setting. Then perform your play for the class. After each group's performance, discuss how the characters in each play explore new worlds.

Far-Out Facts

MAIN IDEAS AND DETAILS Suppose you want to share what you have learned about exploration with someone who has not read the selections in this theme. Make a chart such as the one shown for the four nonfiction selections. For each selection, identify one main idea about exploration and two supporting ideas.

Selection	Main Idea	Detail	Detail
The Wright Brothers			
I Want to Be an Astronaut			
Voyager			
CyberSurfer			

Using the Glossary

Like a dictionary, this glossary lists words in alphabetical order. To find a word, look it up by its first letter or letters.

To save time, use the **guide words** at the top of each page. These show you the first and last words on the page. Look at the guide words to see if your word falls between them alphabetically.

Here is an example of a glossary entry:

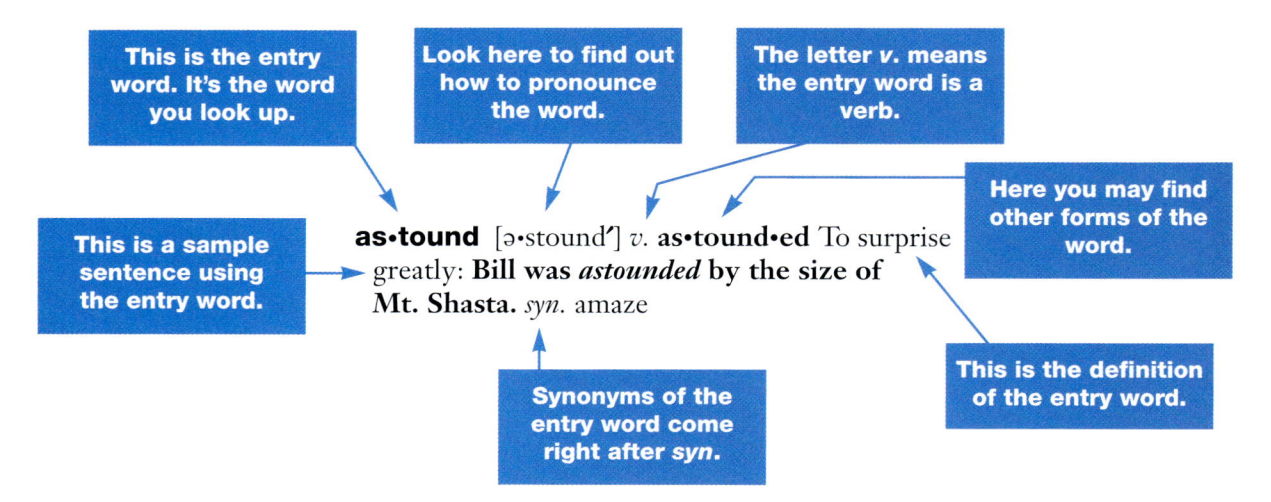

- This is the entry word. It's the word you look up.
- Look here to find out how to pronounce the word.
- The letter *v.* means the entry word is a verb.
- Here you may find other forms of the word.
- This is a sample sentence using the entry word.
- Synonyms of the entry word come right after *syn*.
- This is the definition of the entry word.

as·tound [ə·stound′] *v.* **as·tound·ed** To surprise greatly: **Bill was** *astounded* **by the size of Mt. Shasta.** *syn.* amaze

Word Origins

Throughout the glossary, you will find notes about word origins, or how words got started and changed. Words often have interesting backgrounds that can help you remember what they mean.

Here is an example of a word-origin note:

> **endurance** The word *endurance* has as its root the Latin word *durus*, meaning "hard." The word *durable*, meaning "long-lasting," also has this root. The meanings of both these words fit with the idea of something tough or hard.

628

Pronunciation

The pronunciation in brackets is a respelling that shows how the word is pronounced.

The **pronunciation key** explains what the symbols in a respelling mean. A shortened pronunciation key appears on every other page of the glossary.

PRONUNCIATION KEY*

a	add, map	m	move, seem	u	up, done
ā	ace, rate	n	nice, tin	û(r)	burn, term
â(r)	care, air	ng	ring, song	yo͞o	fuse, few
ä	palm, father	o	odd, hot	v	vain, eve
b	bat, rub	ō	open, so	w	win, away
ch	check, catch	ô	order, jaw	y	yet, yearn
d	dog, rod	oi	oil, boy	z	zest, muse
e	end, pet	ou	pout, now	zh	vision, pleasure
ē	equal, tree	o͝o	took, full	ə	the schwa, an unstressed vowel representing the sound spelled
f	fit, half	o͞o	pool, food		
g	go, log	p	pit, stop		
h	hope, hate	r	run, poor		
i	it, give	s	see, pass		*a* in *above*
ī	ice, write	sh	sure, rush		*e* in *sicken*
j	joy, ledge	t	talk, sit		*i* in *possible*
k	cool, take	th	thin, both		*o* in *melon*
l	look, rule	th	this, bathe		*u* in *circus*

Other symbols
- separates words into syllables
- ʹ indicates heavier stress on a syllable
- ʹ indicates light stress on a syllable

Abbreviations: *adj.* adjective, *adv.* adverb, *conj.* conjunction, *interj.* interjection, *n.* noun, *prep.* preposition, *pron.* pronoun, *syn.* synonym, *v.* verb

* The Pronunciation Key, adapted entries, and the Short Key that appear on the following pages are reprinted from *HBJ School Dictionary* Copyright © 1990 by Harcourt Brace & Company. Reprinted by permission of Harcourt Brace & Company.

accelerate | cavity

A

ac·cel·er·ate [ak·sel′ə·rāt] *v.* To speed up; go faster: **Step on the gas pedal to make the car *accelerate*.**

ad·just [ə·just′] *v.* **ad·just·ed** To change something so it fits better or works better: **Simma *adjusted* the radio dial to tune in the station more clearly.** *syn.* modify

ad·min·is·tra·tive [əd·min′is·trā′tiv] *adj.* Having to do with how something is run or managed: **John's *administrative* duties include hiring new employees.** *syn.* organizational

a·gen·da [ə·jen′də] *n.* A list of things to accomplish: **The first item on the *agenda* is reading the minutes of our last meeting.** *syn.* program, schedule

air·borne [âr′bôrn] *adj.* In flight: **The plane taxied down the runway and was soon *airborne*.** *syn.* aloft

an·guish [ang′gwish] *n.* Great pain or suffering: **Sue felt *anguish* when her grandmother passed away.** *syn.* torment, grief

aq·ue·duct [ak′wə·dukt′] *n.* A large pipe or tunnel for supplying water, especially over long distances: **The *aqueduct* ensured that the city would have enough water.**

aqueduct

ar·chae·ol·o·gist [är·kē·äl′ə·jist] *n.* Someone who studies ancient civilizations: **An *archaeologist* studied the ruins of the ancient city.**

as·tound [ə·stound′] *v.* **as·tound·ed** To surprise greatly: **Bill was *astounded* by the size of Mt. Shasta.** *syn.* amaze

at·mos·phere [at′məs·fir] *n.* **at·mos·pheres** The layer of gases that surrounds a planet: **The *atmospheres* of Venus and Jupiter consist of thick clouds of gas.**

awe [ô] *v.* **awed** To overwhelm with greatness: **Dale was *awed* by the size of the cathedral.** *syn.* amaze

awk·ward [ôk′wərd] *adj.* Not graceful: **The baby's first steps were *awkward*.** *syn.* clumsy

B

bar·rage [bə·räj′] *n.* A physical or verbal onslaught: **Liana was not prepared for the *barrage* of phone calls that came in response to her sharp editorial.** *syn.* volley

bel·lig·er·ent·ly [bə·lij′ər·ənt·lē] *adv.* With a quarrelsome or hostile attitude: **The passenger spoke *belligerently* to the ticket clerk when she found that the airline had overbooked her flight.** *syn.* argumentatively

Word Origins
belligerently We often use the term *belligerently* to speak of people not getting along. The word is related to the Latin word *bellum*, meaning "war"—in this case a war of words.

bel·low·ing [bel′ō·ing] *n.* A loud, deep sound, like an animal's call: **The zoo was full of the animals' *bellowing* as feeding time grew near.** *syn.* roar

be·wil·dered [bi·wil′dərd] *adj.* Thoroughly confused: **The boy wore a *bewildered* expression when he first tried to solve the maze puzzle.** *syn.* mystified, puzzled

bom·bard [bäm·bärd′] *v.* **bom·bard·ed** To send a number of objects or a great deal of information at a very rapid pace: **The students *bombarded* the teacher with questions on the first day of school.**

brisk [brisk] *adj.* Quick-moving, full of energy: **Take a *brisk* walk and you will feel energized.** *syn.* lively

browse [brouz] *v.* To glance through something or to quickly explore a place: **Dan likes to *browse* through the library stacks.** *syn.* skim

brute [broot] *n.* **brutes** A person who acts coarsely, like an animal: **The actors fought onstage like *brutes*, crashing into everything on the set.** *syn.* boor

buf·fet [buf′it] *v.* **buf·fet·ed** To hit with something; to toss about: **The ship was *buffeted* by wind and rain.** *syn.* thrash

bus·tle [bus′əl] *v.* **bus·tled** To be busy and active: **The train station *bustled* with people.**

C

cav·i·ty [kav′ə·tē] *n.* A hollow place in a solid thing: **A woodpecker made a *cavity* in the tree and moved in.** *syn.* hole

charge [chärj] *v.* **charg·ing** To run at something: **Soldiers on horseback were *charging* the fort.** *syn.* attack

civ·i·li·za·tion [siv′ə·lə·zā′shən] *n.* The culture and history of a group of people: **Roman *civilization* affected most of Europe.**

col·li·sion [kə·lizh′ən] *n.* The forceful coming together of two or more things: **No drivers were hurt in the *collision* because everyone wore a seat belt.** *syn.* crash

com·pli·ant [kəm·plī′ənt] *adj.* Yielding, giving in to others: **The flight attendant was *compliant* with our requests.** *syn.* agreeable, submissive

com·pli·ment [käm′plə·mənt] *n.* Praise for a job well done: **Kaitlyn received a *compliment* for the quilt she had made.** *syn.* tribute

com·pul·sion [kəm·pul′shən] *n.* A feeling that one must do something, whether one wants to or not: **His *compulsion* to eat chocolate made losing weight difficult.** *syn.* urge

con·sole [kən·sōl′] *v.* To give comfort: **The mother kissed the toddler to *console* him when he fell.** *syn.* soothe

con·vic·tion [kən·vik′shən] *n.* A firm belief in the rightness of something: **She spoke with such *conviction* that others agreed.** *syn.* fervor

cor·ral [kə·ral′] *v.* **cor·ralled** To drive animals into a fenced area: **The wranglers *corralled* the frightened ponies.** *syn.* herd

crag·gy [krag′ē] *adj.* Bumpy and rugged, such as rocky land: **The ledges of the *craggy* cliffs were good nesting places for the puffins.** *syn.* jagged, rough

crest [krest] *v.* **crest·ed** To reach the highest point before going back down: **The waves *crested* close to shore.** *syn.* peak

cur·rent [kûr′ənt] *n.* A definite, regular stream of water or air: **The Gulf Stream is an ocean *current* that flows northeast across the Atlantic Ocean.** *syn.* stream

D

dem·o·crat·ic [dem′ə·krat′ik] *adj.* According to the rules of a democracy: **In a *democratic* society, people vote to choose who will govern them.**

dem·on·stra·tion [dem′ən·strā′shən] *n.* A display that shows how something is used: **There was a *demonstration* about how to do computer animation.** *syn.* presentation

de·pen·dent [di·pen′dənt] *adj.* Affected by something else: **Our going to the picnic is *dependent* on whether or not it rains.** *syn.* determined

de·sign [di·zīn′] *v.* To plan or sketch, such as a piece of art or clothing: **The play's cast will *design* and paint their own scenery.** *syn.* conceive

de·vise [di·vīz′] *v.* **de·vised** To work out an idea; to invent something: **Fran thought about the problem until she *devised* a solution.** *syn.* formulate

dis·be·lief [dis′bi·lēf′] *n.* Refusal to accept that something is true: **When Todd got the bad news, he stared in *disbelief*.**

dis·cour·ag·ing [dis·kûr′ij·ing] *adj.* Causing someone to lose hope or confidence in reaching a goal: **The news that Juan did not make the team was *discouraging*.** *syn.* daunting, dismaying

dis·dain·ful·ly [dis·dān′fəl·lē] *adv.* In a manner that shows scorn or contempt for something: **The haughty king spoke to his servant *disdainfully*.** *syn.* haughtily

dis·guise [dis·gīz′] *v.* **dis·guised** To hide something by making it look different: **The insect's camouflage *disguised* it from its predators.** *syn.* cloak

dis·pute [dis·pyo͞ot′] *v.* To argue about: **The lawyers will *dispute* the facts of the case.** *syn.* challenge

di·ver·sion [də·vûr′zhən] *n.* Something that takes one's attention from one thing and refocuses it on something else: **The performer creates a *diversion* so that you don't see how the trick is done.** *syn.* distraction

dor·mi·tor·y [dôr′mə·tôr′ē] *n.* A building or part of a building where many people sleep; the place in an institution, such as a school, where on-campus students live: **Sal and Nick shared a room in the *dormitory*.**

dra·mat·i·cal·ly [drə·mat′ik·lē] *adv.* In a manner that shows a lot of feeling or action: **Rachel pounded *dramatically* on the table.** *syn.* theatrically

E

ed·i·ble [ed′ə·bəl] *adj.* Able to be eaten: **Not all plants are *edible*; some are poisonous.** *syn.* consumable

---

a	add	e	end	o	odd	o͞o	pool	oi	oil	th	this		*a* in *above*
ā	ace	ē	equal	ō	open	u	up	ou	pout	zh	vision	ə =	*e* in *sicken*
â	care	i	it	ô	order	û	burn	ng	ring				*i* in *possible*
ä	palm	ī	ice	o͝o	took	yo͞o	fuse	th	thin				*o* in *melon*
													u in *circus*

631

effective

ef·fec·tive [ə•fek′tiv] *adj.* Producing the desired result: **Eating right is an *effective* way to stay healthy.** *syn.* practical, constructive

e·lab·o·rate [i•lab′ər•it] *adj.* Intricate, complex: **Nan made *elaborate* plans about what to plant in her garden.** *syn.* detailed

e·lec·tive [i•lek′tiv] *adj.* Optional; not required: **Aimee took two *elective* courses this year—Greek and gymnastics.** *syn.* voluntary

em·bar·rass·ment [im•bar′əs•mənt] *n.* A feeling of self-consciousness or shame: **Allowing the other team to score a goal caused him great *embarrassment*.** *syn.* shame

em·blem [em′bləm] *n.* A symbol, often with a motto, that stands for an institution or a place: **The fire department's uniform includes an *emblem*.** *syn.* symbol

en·a·ble [in•ā′bəl] *v.* **en·a·bling** To make it possible to do something: **Her hard work is *enabling* her to get better grades.** *syn.* permit, empower

en·dur·ance [in•dyŏŏr′əns] *n.* The ability to perform a difficult task over a long period of time: **Elena's *endurance* increased the more she worked out.** *syn.* durability

> **Word Origins**
> **endurance** The word *endurance* has as its root the Latin word *durus*, meaning "hard." The word *durable*, meaning "long-lasting," also has this root. The meanings of both these words fit with the idea of something tough or hard.

en·gulf [in•gulf′] *v.* To swallow up; to make something disappear as if it fell into a gulf: **Rachel scoots under the big quilt and lets it *engulf* her.** *syn.* envelop, surround

en·ter·pris·ing [en′tər•prīz′ing] *adj.* Showing energy and a will to succeed: **The twins' *enterprising* efforts to earn money paid off.** *syn.* industrious, ambitious

es·sen·tial [ə•sen′shəl] *adj.* Absolutely necessary: **Food, air, and water are *essential* to life.** *syn.* required, indispensable

ex·as·per·ate [ig•zas′pə•rāt′] *v.* **ex·as·per·at·ed** To annoy or push to the limits of one's patience: **The coach became *exasperated* as he argued with the referee's decision.** *syn.* irritate

ex·haus·tion [ig•zôs′chən] *n.* Extreme tiredness to the point of collapse: **The runner fainted from *exhaustion* at the end of the race.** *syn.* weariness

ex·panse [ik•spans′] *n.* A wide-open space: **The girls stood in the vast *expanse* of the empty gym.** *syn.* stretch

full-fledged

F

fa·cil·i·ty [fə•sil′ə•tē] *n.* **fa·cil·i·ties** An institution where a particular kind of task takes place: **A new eye care unit opened at one of the city's medical *facilities*.**

fam·ine [fam′ən] *n.* A serious shortage of food: **The people were starving due to the *famine*.**

fa·vor [fā′vər] *v.* **fa·vored** To prefer over others: **The star of the show was *favored* over the rest of the cast.** *syn.* preferred

flaw·less [flô′ləs] *adj.* Without blemish or mistake; perfect: **The violinist performed a *flawless* solo.** *syn.* impeccable

flex [fleks] *v.* **flexed** To bend, such as a body part: **The runner *flexed* her legs to warm up before the race.**

flood·plain [flud′plān′] *n.* A low, flat area on each side of a river that gets flooded if the river's level rises: **Because the *floodplain* is fertile, it is good for farming.**

flour·ish [flûr′ish] *v.* **flour·ished** To do well in an environment: **Tropical plants *flourished* in the warm, humid climate.** *syn.* thrive

flus·ter [flus′tər] *n.* A state of being upset: **Rushing to the airport put Steve's parents into their usual *fluster*.** *syn.* tizzy

forge [fôrj] *n.* A place where metal is heated and worked into shapes: **The blacksmith heats iron until it is red-hot and shapes it into useful objects at his *forge*.** *syn.* smithy

for·mal [fôr′məl] *adj.* According to proper ceremony and custom: **A *formal* invitation is usually mailed, not phoned.** *syn.* decorous

forge

foun·da·tion [foun•dā′shən] *n.* A base that supports a building: **The *foundation* of this house is cement, but the house itself is made of wood.** *syn.* groundwork

full-fledged [fŏŏl′-flejd′] *adj.* Fully developed and ready to operate at full capacity: **Karen practiced at the skating rink until she became a *full-fledged* figure skater.**

632

fume [fyoom] *v.* **fumed** To feel anger or annoyance: Don *fumed* when he found out that Lee had lost his favorite book. *syn.* seethe

fund [fund] *v.* **fund•ing** To provide money for a worthy cause: The city is *funding* a project to build more parks. *syn.* sponsor

G

gim•mick [gim′ik] *n.* An attention-getter: "Buy one, get one free" is a sales *gimmick*. *syn.* ploy

glare [glâr] *v.* To stare angrily: He whispered so the librarian would not *glare*. *syn.* frown

grad•u•al•ly [graj′oo•wə•lē] *adv.* Step-by-step: Tammy *gradually* increased the number of situps she did each day.

H

high-tech [hī′-tek′] *adj.* Based on the most up-to-date technology: *High-tech* appliances are soon made obsolete by other high-tech appliances. *syn.* cutting-edge

hoist [hoist] *v.* **hoist•ed** To pull something up, particularly by using a pulley or a similar machine: Two men pulled the rope that *hoisted* the piano up to the second floor. *syn.* raise

hy•brid [hī′brid] *adj.* Usually in reference to plants, describing the offspring that result from two varieties being mixed together: This *hybrid* corn has features from each of the parent plants. *syn.* combination

hy•giene [hī′jēn] *n.* The daily tasks and habits that preserve health: Proper tooth care is an important part of *hygiene*.

I

im•mune [i•myoon′] *adj.* Protected, such as from disease or damage: This vaccine makes people *immune* to chicken pox.

in•gen•i•ous [in•jēn′yəs] *adj.* Creative, inventive, and imaginative: Jenna's *ingenious* plan for raising money worked. *syn.* brilliant

in•hab•it•ant [in•hab′ə•tənt] *n.* **in•hab•i•tants** People or animals that dwell in a certain place or environment: Gorillas are *inhabitants* of the jungle. *syn.* occupant

in•her•it [in•her′it] *v.* To become the owner of someone's property after that person dies: Malvina will *inherit* her parents' house one day, as they did from her grandmother. *syn.* acquire

in•sep•a•ra•ble [in•sep′ər•ə•bəl] *adj.* Unable to be parted from one another: Joey and his best friend Josh were *inseparable*.

in•stall [in•stôl′] *v.* To put something in its proper place so it can be used: A worker came to *install* the stove before we moved into our new home.

in•stinct [in′stinkt] *n.* An ability to sense one's surroundings; a natural ability or impulse: Her *instinct* told her that trouble was near. *syn.* intuition

in•ter•ac•tive [in′tər•ak′tiv] *adj.* Having to do with two-way electronic communication, as when a computer prompts the user to give a response: This *interactive* program asks what you want to know and then answers your questions.

in•trigue [in•trēg′] *v.* **in•trigued** To catch one's interest or curiosity: The story *intrigued* its readers. *syn.* fascinate

in•ven•tive [in•ven′tiv] *adj.* Able to plan and create new ideas: She was so *inventive* that, by the age of 15, she was already creating new toys for a toy company. *syn.* creative

ir•re•sist•ible [ir′i•zis′tə•bəl] *adj.* Causing so much emotional pull that something can't be avoided: Some people find chocolate to be *irresistible*. *syn.* overpowering

i•so•late [ī′sə•lāt] *v.* **i•so•lat•ed** To keep away from everything else: The hospital *isolated* the patient with the disease to keep it from spreading to others. *syn.* separate

is•sue [ish′oo] *n.* An important matter to be handled or discussed: The *issue* between Philip and his parents was balancing his schoolwork with his outside activities. *syn.* concern

L

leg•a•cy [leg′ə•sē] *n.* Something that has been handed down from one's ancestors or from the past: The founders of the country gave us a *legacy* of democracy. *syn.* heritage

lev•ee [lev′ē] *n.* **lev•ees** The side of a river that has been built up to prevent flooding: During the rainstorm workers reinforced the *levees* with sandbags.

a	add	e	end	o	odd	oo	pool	oi oil	th this	
ā	ace	ē	equal	ō	open	u	up	ou pout	zh vision	ə = { *a* in *above*, *e* in *sicken*, *i* in *possible*, *o* in *melon*, *u* in *circus* }
â	care	i	it	ô	order	û	burn	ng ring		
ä	palm	ī	ice	oo	took	yoo	fuse	th thin		

lilt·ing [lilt′ing] *adj.* Having a light grace and rhythm: **The sound of the waltz was fast and *lilting*.**

loft·i·ly [lôf′tə·lē] *adv.* With the qualities of noble thought: **The politician spoke *loftily* of what changes she would make if she were elected.** *syn.* high-mindedly

lunge [lunj] *v.* **lung·ing** To suddenly surge forward, as if without control: **The two dogs were *lunging* toward each other, growling and barking, but their owners held them back.** *syn.* charge

M

man·eu·ver [mə·nōō′vər] *v.* To move something skillfully: **Irita can *maneuver* the sailboat through strong winds and light winds.** *syn.* manipulate

me·lo·di·ous [mə·lō′dē·əs] *adj.* Having a pleasant tune: **Her *melodious* voice cheered up the whole house.** *syn.* tuneful, lyrical

me·men·to [mi·men′tō] *n.* An object for reminding oneself about a place or thing: **Judy brought home several beautiful shells as a *memento* of her trip.** *syn.* souvenir

mi·gra·tion [mī·grā′shən] *n.* A large group of the same type of animal making a seasonal journey to a specific place: **The southward *migration* of geese is a regular sight in the October skies.**

min·i·a·ture [min′ē·ə·chər] *adj.* Very small; greatly reduced: **Dad's toy train set had *miniature* versions of everything you'd find in an old-time station.** *syn.* tiny

mis·sion [mish′ən] *n.* In space terminology, a specific flight and all the activities related to it: **It takes more than a year to prepare for a space *mission*.**

mo·dem [mō′dəm] *n.* An electronic device that translates a computer's data into electric impulses that can be sent and received along a telephone line: **The computer's *modem* allows you to connect to the Internet.** *syn.* interface

mo·sa·ic [mō·zā′ik] *n.* A decorative work made by cementing small bits of colored tile: **Builders discovered a very old *mosaic* in his grandmother's attic.**

mosaic

N

nav·i·ga·tion [nav′ə·gā′shən] *n.* The science of knowing how to plot a course for a ship, an aircraft, or a spacecraft: **Early methods of *navigation* were based on the stars' positions in the sky.** *syn.* piloting

new·fan·gled [nōō′fan′gəld] *adj.* A slightly insulting term for a new, improved item or concept: **At first, people thought automobiles were *newfangled* contraptions that would never replace the horse.**

non·cha·lant·ly [nän′shə·länt′lē] *adv.* Without a strong reaction: **Gina answered her mother *nonchalantly*, but inside she was very worried.** *syn.* calmly

nour·ish·ing [nûr′ish·ing] *adj.* Including elements that produce health: **The juice of fresh vegetables is very *nourishing*.** *syn.* healthful

nov·el·ty [näv′əl·tē] *n.* An item that is very interesting for a short time; sometimes cheaply made: **The new game in the toy store was a fun *novelty* at first but didn't last long.** *syn.* trinket

nui·sance [nyōō′səns] *n.* A bothersome, annoying thing: **Flies are a *nuisance* at a barbecue.** *syn.* bother, aggravation

O

oc·cu·pa·tion [äk′yə·pā′shən] *n.* One country's presence in and military control over another country: **Latin spread throughout Europe because of the Roman *occupation* of many lands.** *syn.* foreign rule

of·fi·cial·ly [ə·fish′əl·ē] *adv.* With permission from the authority of an organization to do something: **The club voted, and Alex was *officially* invited to become a member.** *syn.* formally

on·line [än·līn′] *adj.* Connected through a modem to a server—an electronic device that allows many people to access its files at the same time: **You can access today's news on the *online* newspaper.**

opportunity — recognition

op·por·tu·ni·ty [äp′ər·tōō′nə·tē] *n.* A time or occasion that is good for a certain purpose: **Keri's new job offers her an *opportunity* to use her talents.** *syn.* occasion

> **Word Origins**
> **opportunity** The word *opportunity* contains the word parts *ob* (of which *op* is a variation), meaning "at" or "before," and *portus*, meaning "the port." A *port* is a place from which ships come and go. The word *port* also means "a door." The phrase *opportunity knocks* means that an opportunity presents itself at the door.

or·di·nance [ôr′dən·əns] *n.* A rule for a city or town: **The town *ordinance* states that only residents may park at the town's beach.** *syn.* regulation

o·rig·in·ate [ə·rij′ə·nāt] *v.* **o·rig·in·at·ed** To bring something into being, such as an idea: **Pat *originated* the fad of wearing hand-painted T-shirts.** *syn.* conceived

or·na·ment·al [ôr·nə·ment′əl] *adj.* Serving as a decoration: **An *ornamental* vase held the extravagant bouquet.** *syn.* decorative

or·ner·y [ôr′nər·ē] *adj.* Having a mean or disruptive attitude or nature: **The *ornery* dog was kept chained up.** *syn.* ill-tempered

P

pas·sage·way [pas′ij·wā] *n.* **pas·sage·ways** A narrow path, corridor, or tunnel: **Sleeping quarters on the ship opened onto various *passageways* below deck.**

peak [pēk] *adj.* The highest level of accomplishment: **The athlete displayed her *peak* performance in the Olympic event.**

per·me·ate [pûr′mē·āt] *v.* **per·me·ates** To fill every space with a substance: **When it rains, water *permeates* the soil and reaches roots deep underground.** *syn.* infiltrate

per·se·vere [pûr′sə·vir′] *v.* **per·se·vered** To continue working toward a goal regardless of difficulties or obstacles: **The scientists *persevered* in their search for a cure for the disease.** *syn.* persist

port·a·ble [pôr′tə·bəl] *adj.* Able to be carried: **The campers found it easy to travel with a *portable* stove.** *syn.* movable

post·pone [pōst·pōn′] *v.* To put off until later: **If it rains, they will *postpone* the parade.** *syn.* delay

pounce [pouns] *v.* **pounced** To spring out at something: **The cat crouched down, waited, and then *pounced* on a mouse.** *syn.* ambush

pre·cious [presh′əs] *adj.* Having great monetary or emotional value: **His photographs were his most *precious* treasure.** *syn.* cherished

pre·ci·sion [pri·sizh′ən] *n.* The quality of doing something exactly as it should be done: **The clock keeps time with great *precision*.** *syn.* accuracy

pre·sen·ta·tion [prē′zen·tā′shən] *n.* Something that is performed: **Our rehearsal went more smoothly than the actual *presentation*.** *syn.* show

pre·serve [pri·zûrv′] *v.* **pre·served** To keep something in good condition: **Miri *preserved* an antique lace collar by wrapping it in tissue paper.**

pro·ce·dure [prō·sē′jər] *n.* The steps one takes to do a complicated action: **Lawrence learned the correct *procedure* for setting up his tent.** *syn.* method

pro·pel [prō·pel′] *v.* **pro·pelled** To use a force to push forward: **The jet engine *propelled* the plane down the runway.** *syn.* drive

prov·ince [präv′ins] *n.* **prov·in·ces** A territory that is far from the center of government: **When the Roman Empire controlled most of Europe, France was one of its *provinces*.** *syn.* district

Q

qual·i·ty [kwäl′ə·tē] *n.* A characteristic or typical feature of someone or something: **Rocks have the *quality* of hardness.** *syn.* trait

quar·ry [kwôr′ē] *n.* **quar·ries** A place where stones are mined to be used as building material: **Vermont is famous for its granite *quarries*.**

R

re·al·is·tic [rē·ə·lis′tik] *adj.* Having the quality of looking real without being real: **The plastic flowers were so *realistic* that no one could tell the difference.** *syn.* lifelike

reck·less [rek′ləs] *adj.* Without control; causing a dangerous situation: ***Reckless* driving is the cause of many accidents.** *syn.* rash, careless

re·cog·ni·tion [rek′əg·nish′ən] *n.* Knowing something well enough to identify it after a previous encounter:

a	add	e	end	o	odd	oo	pool	oi	oil	th	this		a in *above*
ā	ace	ē	equal	ō	open	u	up	ou	pout	zh	vision	ə =	e in *sicken*
â	care	i	it	ô	order	û	burn	ng	ring				i in *possible*
ä	palm	ī	ice	oo	took	yoo	fuse	th	thin				o in *melon*
													u in *circus*

An expression of *recognition* lit up the old dog's face whenever its owner came home.

re·con·struct [rē·kən·strukt′] *v.* To build again: **The earthquake victims began to *reconstruct* their lives.** *syn.* rebuild

re·li·a·ble [ri·lī′ə·bəl] *adj.* Something that can be depended upon: **This *reliable* old clock always tells the correct time.** *syn.* trustworthy

re·luc·tant·ly [ri·luk′tənt·lē] *adv.* With an unwilling attitude: **James left his best friend's party *reluctantly* and got back home later than he had planned.** *syn.* unwillingly

re·mote [ri·mōt′] *adj.* Faraway: **The explorers set up camp at a *remote* site, far from the main landing party.** *syn.* distant

re·pre·sent [rep′ri·zent′] *v.* To portray or exhibit in art: **He used cotton to *represent* clouds for his science project.** *syn.* depict

res·er·voir [rez′ər·vwär] *n.* **res·er·voirs** An artificial lake made to hold the water supply for all the people of a particular area: **The city's *reservoir* received runoff from melting ice and snow as well as rainwater.**

re·source·ful [ri·sôrs′fəl] *adj.* Having good ideas; able to handle situations effectively and creatively: **The *resourceful* artist made a sculpture out of old rubber tires.** *syn.* ingenious

romp [rämp] *v.* **romp·ing** To run and leap in a playful way: **Baby lambs were *romping* in the grassy field.** *syn.* frolic

rouse [rouz] *v.* To cause someone or something to get up: **Julian was hard to *rouse* every morning, and he often missed the school bus.** *syn.* wake

rug·ged [rug′id] *adj.* Tough and rough as a result of use or exposure to wind, water, or heat: **The pioneers' *rugged* faces were no longer as soft as they had been when the pioneers first arrived on the Plains.** *syn.* coarse

rum·mage [rum′ij] *v.* **rum·maged** To look for something by digging energetically through a pile: **Searching for a pen, Mike *rummaged* through his backpack.** *syn.* search

scorn·ful [skôrn′fəl] *adj.* Showing disregard and disrespect: **Pete was *scornful* of his sister's drawing ability.** *syn.* contemptuous

scour [skour] *v.* **scour·ing** To search through a place: **Mandy continued *scouring* the field in search of her grandmother's lost pin.** *syn.* examine

scowl [skoul] *v.* To make a facial expression that shows displeasure: **The policeman continued to *scowl* at the driver of the speeding car.** *syn.* frown

seep [sēp] *v.* **seep·ing** To leak or ooze, as a liquid would: **Water began *seeping* through the crack in the ceiling.** *syn.* soak, trickle

shan·ty [shan′tē] *n.* A shack or a hut: **A *shanty* can be made of sod, wood, or even tin.** *syn.* dwelling

shat·ter [shat′ər] *v.* **shat·tered** To hit so hard as to break into pieces: **The windshield was *shattered* when a baseball crashed into it.** *syn.* smashed

sheep·ish·ly [shēp′ish·lē] *adv.* With feelings of shyness or embarrassment: **The child stood *sheepishly* in front of the audience when he forgot his lines.** *syn.* self-consciously

Fast Fact
sheepishly Sheep are characterized in many stories and images by their docility and fearfulness. The similarity between sheep and people also is reflected in the idea that if everyone in a group does the same thing, they are behaving as a flock of sheep might behave.

shrewd [shrood] *adj.* Clever, with a hint of cunning: **The manager made a *shrewd* deal that rocketed the business to first place in its field.** *syn.* calculating

sim·u·la·tion [sim′yoo·lā′shən] *n.* An artificial setup that imitates a real situation: **Scientists can use a computer *simulation* to understand how a change in habitat would affect the living things there.** *syn.* fabrication

skew·er [skyoo′ər] *v.* To pierce with a thin, pointy stick before cooking: ***Skewer*** **the marshmallows before you toast them over the coals.**

so·cia·ble [sō′shə·bəl] *adj.* Friendly, able to get along with others: **Dolphins are *sociable* mammals that live in groups.** *syn.* outgoing

so·lemn·ly [säl′əm·lē] *adv.* With great seriousness: **The witness *solemnly* took the stand.** *syn.* gravely

sooth·ing·ly [sooth′ing·lē] *adv.* In a calm or comforting way: **The police officer spoke *soothingly* to the frightened child.** *syn.* comfortingly

sor·row·ful·ly [sär′əf·lē] *adv.* Showing signs of sadness: **The soldiers hung their heads *sorrowfully* when their fallen comrade passed by.** *syn.* mournfully

spe·cial·ty [spesh′əl·tē] *n.* A famous, favorite thing that someone does: **Mike's hamburgers are the diner's *specialty*.** *syn.* trademark

styl·us [stī′ləs] *n.* A pointy tool used for writing in braille: **Nora held the *stylus* and began to write the braille alphabet.**

sub·lime [sə·blīm′] *adj.* Wonderful, awe-inspiring: **The music at the concert was *sublime*.** *syn.* majestic

stylus

swol·len [swō′lən] *adj.* Made larger because of pressure from inside: **The boy's *swollen* ankle was an indication that it had been sprained.** *syn.* enlarged

T

ta·per [tā′pər] *v.* **ta·pered** To gradually get smaller or less powerful: **The pain *tapered* off until it was completely gone.** *syn.* decrease

tel·e·scop·ic [tel′ə·skäp′ik] *adj.* Made of sections that fit into each other the way a telescope does: **The *telescopic* ladder on the hook-and-ladder truck can extend up to three stories.** *syn.* collapsible

ter·race [ter′əs] *n.* **ter·rac·es** A series of stepped parcels of land, such as used for farming: **The hilly farmland was covered in *terraces*.**

three-dimensional [thrē-də·men′shən·əl] *adj.* Having the three dimensions of height, width, and depth: **You can hold a *three-dimensional* box in your hand, but a picture of the same box is flat.**

tran·scribe [tran·skrīb′] *v.* **tran·scribed** To represent in a new but related way, especially with sounds or symbols: **The famous guitarist Andrés Segovia *transcribed* pieces for other instruments into music that could be played on the guitar.**

trans·mis·sion [tranz·mi′shən] *n.* A message that has been sent across a distance from one place to another: **The radio *transmission* started at the radio station and ended up in our dining room.** *syn.* message, signal

trans·mit·ter [trans·mi′tər] *n.* **trans·mit·ters** The equipment that sends a radio or television signal from its point of origin to another piece of equipment that can receive it: **The satellite's *transmitters* send back information about objects in space.**

trib·ute [trib′yo͞ot] *n.* **trib·utes** A present or a compliment in honor of something that someone has done: **Emily received *tributes* in the town paper for her caring volunteer work.** *syn.* praise

trot [trät] *v.* **trot·ted** To run with a jogging gait: **The horse *trotted* across the meadow.**

U

un·cer·tain·ly [un·sûrt′in·lē] *adv.* In a manner that shows a lack of confidence: **Sean answered *uncertainly* because he hadn't heard the question.** *syn.* doubtfully

un·wav·er·ing [un·wāv′ər·ing] *adj.* In a steady, unchanging way: **She cast her *unwavering* gaze toward the horizon for sight of any ship.** *syn.* unfaltering

V

va·por·ize [vā′pər·īz] *v.* **va·por·ized** To change from a liquid or a solid to a gas: **The heated water *vaporized* into steam.**

vi·o·la·tion [vī′ə·lā′shən] *n.* **vi·o·la·tions** The breaking of a law: **Exceeding the posted speed limit and driving without a license are *violations* of the traffic laws.** *syn.* infringement

vir·tue [vûr′cho͞o] *n.* **vir·tues** A positive character trait: **Honesty and steadfastness were among his many *virtues*.** *syn.* merit

W

waft [wäft] *v.* **waft·ed** To float or to be carried by the air: **A feather *wafted* gently down from the nest.** *syn.* drift

wail [wāl] *v.* **wailed** To cry in grief or pain, or to make a sound such as the cry of grief or pain: **The child *wailed* when she stubbed her toe.** *syn.* weep

wa·ver [wā′vər] *v.* To get stronger and weaker by turns: **The swimmer's strength began to *waver* after the fourth lap.** *syn.* fluctuate

wedge [wej] *n.* **wedg·es** A sharp, triangular piece of wood or metal: **Use *wedges* and a sledgehammer to split the logs.**

Y

yarn [yärn] *n.* **yarns** An exaggerated story: **The crew of the fishing boat told many *yarns* about "the ones that got away."** *syn.* tall tale

yearn [yûrn] *v.* **yearned** To feel a strong desire to do something: **After several weeks, the traveler *yearned* to return home.**

a add	e end	o odd	o͞o pool	oi oil	th this		*a* in *above*
ā ace	ē equal	ō open	u up	ou pout	zh vision	ə =	*e* in *sicken*
â care	i it	ô order	û burn	ng ring			*i* in *possible*
ä palm	ī ice	o͝o took	yo͞o fuse	th thin			*o* in *melon*
							u in *circus*

Index of Titles

Page numbers in color refer to biographical information.

Ahmad, Nyla, 590, 605
Ancient China, 256
Anderson, Joan, 508, 520
Anne of Green Gables, 484
Armour, Richard, 73
Asimov, Isaac, 612, 621
Austin, Mary, 328
Bernardo, Anilú, 388, 403
Best School Year Ever, The, 22
Boyd, Candy Dawson, 450, 462
Bruchac, Joseph, 584
Byars, Betsy, 146, 163
Catching the Fire: Philip Simmons, Blacksmith, 408
Chinese Dynasties, The, 270
Clark, Margaret, 366
Collins, Carolyn Strom, 504
Cowboys: Roundup on an American Ranch, 508
CyberSurfer, 590
Darnell Rock Reporting, 94
Dividing the Horses, 364
Do-It-Yourself Project, A, 388
Erikksson, Christina Wyss, 504
Fall Secrets, 450

Febold Feboldson, 354
Flood: Wrestling with the Mississippi, 208
Fox and the Crow, The, 367
Freedman, Russell, 468, 479, 532, 545
From the Autograph Album, 72
Frost, Robert, 422
Fun They Had, The, 612
George, Jean Craighead, 338, 349
Gipson, Fred, 166, 180
Good Sportsmanship, 73
Grace, Catherine O'Neill, 550
Hicks, Peter, 294
Home on the Range, 522
I Want to Be an Astronaut, 550
In the Next Three Seconds, 606
Kid Who Invented the Popsicle, The, 370
Kids Did It!, 464
Knots in My Yo-yo String, 60
Konigsburg, E. L., 40, 55
Lauber, Patricia, 208, 223
Look Into the Past: The Greeks and the Romans, 294
Lowry, Lois, 120, 140
Lyons, Mary E., 408, 421

and Authors

Macdonald, Fiona, 236, 251
Marble Champ, The, 76
Maze, Stephanie, 550
Montgomery, Lucy M., 484, 503
Morgan, Rowland, 606
My Side of the Mountain, 338
Myers, Walter Dean, 94, 109
Naylor, Phyllis Reynolds, 184, 202
Nicholson, Robert, 256
Nolan, Paul T., 314
North Wind and the Sun, The, 366
Number the Stars, 120
Old Yeller, 166
Osborne, Mary Pope, 354, 363
O'Shaughnessy, Tam, 566
Out of Darkness: The Story of Louis Braille, 468
Puppies with a Purpose, 204
Pyramids, 274
Ride, Sally, 566, 582
Road Not Taken, The, 422
Robinson, Barbara, 22, 35
Saving Shiloh, 184
Saving the Day, 110
Seventh Grade, 432
Shannon, George, 364

Skill of Pericles, The, 314
Smoke Jumpers, 224
Snyder, Zilpha Keatley, 622
So Long, Michael, 90
Some Like It Wet, 404
Song of Greatness, A, 328
Soto, Gary, 76, 88, 432, 445
Spinelli, Jerry, 60, 71
Stone Age News, The, 236
Summer of the Swans, The, 146
Tea Biscuits, 504
Three Hunters and the Great Bear, The, 584
To Dark Eyes Dreaming, 622
Turner, Jamie, 484
View from Saturday, The, 40
Voyager: An Adventure to the Edge of the Solar System, 566
Watts, Claire, 256
Williams, A. Susan, 294
Wright Brothers: How They Invented the Airplane, The, 532
Wulffson, Don L., 370, 383

Copyright © 2001 by Harcourt, Inc.

All rights reserved. No part of this publication may be reproduced or transmitted in any form or by any means, electronic or mechanical, including photocopy, recording, or any information storage and retrieval system, without permission in writing from the publisher.

Requests for permission to make copies of any part of the work should be mailed to the following address: School Permissions, Harcourt, Inc., 6277 Sea Harbor Drive, Orlando, Florida 32887-6777.

HARCOURT and the Harcourt Logo are trademarks of Harcourt, Inc.

Printed in the United States of America

Acknowledgments

For permission to reprint copyrighted material, grateful acknowledgment is made to the following sources:

Arte Público Press – University of Houston: "A Do-It-Yourself Project" from *Fitting In* by Anilú Bernardo, cover illustration by Daniel Lechón. Copyright © 1996 by Anilú Bernardo.

Atheneum Books for Young Readers, an imprint of Simon & Schuster Children's Publishing Division: From *The View from Saturday* by E. L. Konigsburg, hand lettering by Bobbi Yoffee. Text and cover illustration copyright © 1996 by E. L. Konigsburg. From *Saving Shiloh* by Phyllis Reynolds Naylor. Text copyright © 1997 by Phyllis Reynolds Naylor. Cover illustration by Zena Bernstein from *Mrs. Frisby and the Rats of Nimh* by Robert C. O'Brien. Copyright © 1971 by Robert C. O'Brien; copyright renewed 1999 by the Estate of Robert O'Brien. Cover illustration from *Tutankhamen's Gift* by Robert Sabuda. Copyright © 1994 by Robert Sabuda.

Blackbirch Press, Inc.: Cover photograph from *Wilma Rudolph: Olympic Gold!* by Wayne Coffey. © 1993 by Blackbirch Press, Inc.

The Broadway Ballplayers, Inc., P.O. Box 597, Wilmette, IL 60091: Cover illustration by Rebecca Havekost from *Left Out by Rosie* by Maureen Holohan. Illustration copyright © 1998 by Rebecca Havekost.

Candlewick Press, Inc., Cambridge, MA: From *The Stone Age News* by Fiona Macdonald, cover illustration by Gino D'Achille. Text © 1998 by Fiona Macdonald; illustrations © 1998 by Walker Books Ltd.

Carolrhoda Books, Inc., Minneapolis, MN: Cover illustration by Rochelle Draper from *The World at His Fingertips* by Barbara O'Connor. Copyright 1997 by Carolrhoda Books, Inc.

Chelsea House Publishers, a division of Main Line Book Co.: Cover illustration by Cliff Spohn from *Female Firsts in Their Fields: Air & Space* by Doug Buchanan. Copyright © 1999 by Chelsea House Publishers, a division of Main Line Book Co. From *Journey into Civilization: Ancient China* by Robert Nicholson and Claire Watts. Text copyright © 1994 by Two-Can Publishing Ltd.

Chicago Review Press, Inc., 814 N. Franklin St., Chicago, IL 60610: Cover illustration from *Women Invent!* by Susan Casey. © 1997 by Susan Casey.

Children's Television Workshop, New York: "Some Like It Wet" from *Contact Kids* Magazine, July/August 1998. Text copyright 1998 by Children's Television Workshop.

Clarion Books/Houghton Mifflin Company: From *Out of Darkness: The Story of Louis Braille* by Russell Freedman, cover illustration by Kate Kiesler. Text copyright © 1997 by Russell Freedman; cover illustration © 1997 by Kate Kiesler.

Cobblehill Books, an affiliate of Dutton Children's Books, a division of Penguin Putnam Inc.: From *The Kid Who Invented the Popsicle and Other Surprising Stories About Inventions* by Don L. Wulffson, cover illustration by Todd Graveline. Text copyright © 1997 by Don L. Wulffson; cover illustration copyright © 1997 by Todd Graveline.

Delacorte Press, a division of Random House, Inc.: Cover illustration by Joe Csatari from *Make Like a Tree and Leave* by Paula Danziger. Illustration copyright © 1990 by Joe Csatari.

Dell Publishing, a division of Random House, Inc.: Cover illustration by Raúl Colón from *Radiance Descending* by Paula Fox.

Doubleday, a division of Random House, Inc.: "The Fun They Had" from *Earth Is Room Enough* by Isaac Asimov. Text copyright © 1957 by Isaac Asimov. Cover illustration by John O'Brien from *Mistakes That Worked* by Charlotte Foltz Jones. Illustration copyright © 1991 by John O'Brien.

Dutton Children's Books, a division of Penguin Putnam Inc.: From *My Side of the Mountain* by Jean Craighead George. Text and cover illustration copyright © 1959, renewed © 1987 by Jean Craighead George.

Michael Garland: Cover illustration by Michael Garland from *My Side of the Mountain* by Jean Craighead George. Published by Dutton Children's Books, a division of Penguin Putnam Inc.

Greenwillow Books, a division of William Morrow & Company, Inc.: Cover illustration by Frank Modell from *Journal of a Teenage Genius* by Helen V. Griffith. Copyright © 1987 by Helen V. Griffith. "Dividing the Horses" from *Stories to Solve: Folktales from Around the World* by George Shannon, illustrated by Peter Sis. Text copyright © 1985 by George W. B. Shannon; illustrations copyright © 1985 by Peter Sis.

Greey de Pencier Books Inc.: Adapted from *Cybersurfer* by Nyla Ahmad, Directory researched and written by Keltie Thomas, illustrated by Martha Newbigging, cover photo illustration by Bob Anderson. Text and directory compilation © 1996 by Owl Books; illustrations © 1996 by Martha Newbigging; cover photo illustration © 1996 by Bob Anderson.

Harcourt, Inc.: Cover photograph by George Ancona from *The American Family Farm* by Joan Anderson. Photograph copyright © 1989 by George Ancona. From *I Want To Be…An Astronaut* by Stephanie Maze. Text copyright © 1997 by Maze Productions. "Seventh Grade" and "The Marble Champ" from *Baseball in April and Other Stories* by Gary Soto. Text copyright © 1990 by Gary Soto.

HarperCollins Publishers: Cover from *The Riddle of the Rosetta Stone* by James Cross Giblin. Cover back ground photograph courtesy of the Trustees of the British Museum. From *Old Yeller* by Fred Gipson, cover illustration by Carl Burger. Text and cover illustration copyright © 1956 by Fred Gipson; text and cover illustration copyright renewed. Cover illustration from *The Fool and the Phoenix* by Deborah Nourse Lattimore. Copyright © 1997 by Deborah Nourse Lattimore. From *The Best School Year Ever* by Barbara Robinson, cover illustration by Michael Deas. Text copyright © 1994 by Barbara Robinson; cover illustration copyright © 1994 by Michael Deas. Cover illustration by Alan Tiegreen from *Maggie Marmelstein for President* by Marjorie Weinman Sharmat. Illustration © 1991 by Alan Tiegreen; cover © 1991 by HarperCollins Publishers. Cover illustration by Tom Pohrt from *A Child's Anthology of Poetry*, edited by Elizabeth Hauge Sword with Victoria Flournoy McCarthy. Copyright © 1995. Originally published by The Ecco Press.

John Hawkins & Associates, Inc.: "Good Sportsmanship" by Richard Armour. Text copyright © 1958 by Richard Armour. Published by McGraw-Hill.

Holiday House, Inc.: Text and cover photograph from *The Wright Brothers: How They Invented the Airplane* by Russell Freedman. Text copyright © 1991 by Russell Freedman. Photograph courtesy of The Smithsonian Institution.

Henry Holt and Company, Inc.: "The Road Not Taken" by Robert Frost from *The Poetry of Robert Frost*, edited by Edward Connery Lathem.

Houghton Mifflin Company: "A Song of Greatness" from *The Children Sing in the Far West* by Mary Austin. Text copyright 1928 by Mary Austin; text copyright © renewed 1956 by Kenneth M. Chapman and Mary C. Wheelwright. From *Number the Stars* by Lois Lowry. Text and cover photograph copyright © 1989 by Lois Lowry. From *Catching the Fire: Philip Simmons, Blacksmith* by Mary E. Lyons. Text copyright © 1997 by Mary E. Lyons. Cover illustration from *City: A Story of Roman Planning and Construction* by David Macaulay. Copyright © 1974 by David Macaulay.

Kids Discover: From "The Pyramids of Egypt" in *Kids Discover: Pyramids*. Text and cover © 1993 by Kids Discover. From *Kids Discover: Ancient China* (Retitled: "The Chinese Dynasties"). Text and cover © 1998 by Kids Discover.

Alfred A. Knopf, Inc.: From *American Tall Tales* (Retitled: "Febold Feboldson") by Mary Pope Osborne, illustrated by Michael McCurdy. Text copyright © 1991 by Mary Pope Osborne; illustrations copyright © 1991 by Michael McCurdy. From *Knots in My Yo-Yo String: The Autobiography of a Kid* by Jerry Spinelli, cover photograph by Penny Gentieu. Text and photographs copyright © 1998 by Jerry Spinelli; cover photograph copyright © 1998 by Penny Gentieu.

Lee & Low Books Inc., 95 Madison Avenue, New York, NY 10016: Cover illustration by Dom Lee from *Passage to Freedom: The Sugihara Story* by Ken Mochizuki. Illustration copyright © 1997 by Dom Lee.

Little, Brown and Company (Inc.): "The Fox and the Crow" and "The North Wind and the Sun" from *The Best of Aesop's Fables* by Margaret Clark, illustrated by Charlotte Voake. Text copyright © 1990 by Margaret Clark; illustrations copyright © 1990 by Charlotte Voake.

Lodestar Books, an affiliate of Dutton Children's Books, a division of Penguin Putnam Inc.: From *In the Next Three Seconds* by Rowland Morgan, illustrated by Rod and Kira Josey. Text copyright © 1997 by Rowland Morgan; illustrations copyright © 1997 by Rod and Kira Josey.

Alan Mazzetti: Cover illustration by Alan Mazzetti from *Taking Sides* by Gary Soto.

The Metropolitan Museum of Art, New York: Musical arrangement from "Home on the Range" in *Go In and Out the Window*, arranged and edited by Dan Fox. Musical arrangement © 1987 by The Metropolitan Museum of Art.

Barry Moser: Cover illustration by Barry Moser from *Saving Shiloh* by Phyllis Reynolds Naylor. Illustration copyright © 1997 by Barry Moser. Published by Atheneum Books for Young Readers.

National Geographic Society, 1145 17th St., N.W. Washington, DC 20036: "Keys to Success" by Laura Daily from "Kids Did It!" in *National Geographic WORLD* Magazine, August 1998. Text copyright © 1998 by National Geographic Society. "Smoke Jumpers" by Janice Koch from *National Geographic WORLD* Magazine, March 1997. Text copyright © 1997 by National Geographic Society. From *Flood: Wrestling With the Mississippi* by Patricia Lauber. Text copyright © 1996 by Patricia Lauber; maps and illustrations copyright © 1996 by National Geographic Society. "Bridging Generations" by Judith E. Rinard from "Kids Did It!" in *National Geographic WORLD* Magazine, January 1999. Text copyright © 1999 by National Geographic Society. "Puppies with a Purpose" by Christina Wilsdon from *National Geographic WORLD* Magazine, March 1997. Text copyright © 1997 by National Geographic Society.

Penguin Books Canada Limited: "Tea Biscuits" and cover illustration from *The Anne of Green Gables Treasury* by Carolyn Strom Collins and Christina Wyss Eriksson. Text copyright © 1991 by Carolyn Strom Collins and Christina Wyss Eriksson; cover illustration copyright © 1991 by Pronk & Associates.

Plays, Inc.: *Anne of Green Gables* by Lucy M. Montgomery, adapted by Jamie Turner from *Plays: The Drama Magazine for Young People*, March 1987. Text copyright © 1987 by Plays, Inc. *The Skill of Pericles* from *Folk Tale Plays Round the World* by Paul T. Nolan. Text and cover illustration copyright © 1982 by Paul T. Nolan. These plays are for reading purposes only; for permission to produce, write to Plays, Inc., Publishers, 120 Boylston St., Boston, MA 02116.

Puffin Books, a division of Penguin Putnam Inc.: Cover illustration by Lino Saffioti from *The Summer of the Swans* by Betsy Byars. Illustration copyright © 1991 by Lino Saffioti.

G. P. Putnam's Sons, a division of Penguin Putnam Inc.: Cover illustration by Ellen Thompson from *Dear Dr. Bell…Your friend, Helen Keller* by Judith St. George. Illustration © 1992 by Ellen Thompson.

Random House Children's Books, a division of Random House, Inc.: From *Darnell Rock Reporting* by Walter Dean Myers, cover illustration by Mark Smollin. Text and cover illustration copyright © 1994 by Walter Dean Myers. Cover illustration from *Mop, Moondance, and the Nagasaki Knights* by Walter Dean Myers. Copyright © 1992 by Walter Dean Myers. *Voyager: An Adventure to the Edge of the Solar System* by Sally Ride and Tam O'Shaughnessy, illustrated by Gaylord Welker. Copyright © 1992 by Sally Ride.

Marian Reiner: "From the autograph album" in *At the Crack of the Bat*, compiled by Lillian Morrison. Published by Hyperion Books for Children.

Barry Root: Cover illustration by Barry Root from *Baseball in April and Other Stories* by Gary Soto. Illustration copyright 1990 by Barry Root.

Scholastic Inc.: From *Cowboys: Round Up on an American Ranch* by Joan Anderson, photographs by George Ancona. Text copyright © 1996 by Joan Anderson; photographs copyright © 1996 by George Ancona.

Zilpha Keatley Snyder: "To Dark Eyes Dreaming" from *Today Is Saturday* by Zilpha Keatley Snyder. Text copyright © 1969 by Zilpha Keatley Snyder.

Sports Illustrated for Kids: From "So Long, Michael" in *Sports Illustrated for Kids*, March 1999. Text copyright © 1999 by Time Inc.

Steck-Vaughn Company: From *Look into the Past: The Romans* by Peter Hicks. Text copyright © 1993 by Wayland (Publishers) Ltd.; U.S. revision text copyright © 1994 by Thomson Learning. Cover illustration from *Flight Through Time* by Chris Oxlade. From *Look into the Past: The Greeks* by Susan Williams. Text copyright © 1993 by Wayland (Publishers) Ltd.; U.S. revision text copyright © 1993 by Thomson Learning.

Tomorrow's Morning, Inc.: "Saving the Day (and the Lake)" from *Tomorrow's Morning*, Volume 6, Number 240.

Troll Communications, L.L.C.: "The Three Hunters and the Great Bear" from *Four Ancestors: Stories, Songs, and Poems from Native North America*, told by Joseph Bruchac, illustrated by S. S. Burrus. Text and illustrations copyright © 1996 by Joseph Bruchac and S. S. Burrus. Published by Bridgewater Books, an imprint and trademark of Troll Communications, L.L.C.

Viking Penguin, a division of Penguin Putnam Inc.: Cover illustration by Melodye Rosales from *My Sister, My Science Report* by Margaret Bechard. Illustration copyright © 1990 by Melodye Rosales. From *Fall Secrets* by Candy Dawson Boyd, cover illustration by Jim Carroll. Text copyright © 1994 by Candy Dawson Boyd; cover illustration copyright © 1994 by Jim Carroll. From *The Summer of the Swans* by Betsy Byars. Text copyright © 1970 by Betsy Byars. Cover illustration by Lane Smith from *Tut, Tut* by Jon Scieszka. Illustration copyright © 1996 by Lane Smith.

Franklin Watts, a division of Grolier Publishing Co., Inc.: Cover photographs from *Home Page: An Introduction to Web Page Design* by Christopher Lampton. Copyright © 1997 by Christopher Lampton.

Albert Whitman & Company, Inc.: Cover photograph from *Small Steps: The Year I Got Polio* by Peg Kehret. Photograph courtesy of Renée Anderson.

Photo Credits

(t), top; (b), bottom; (c), center; (l), left; (r), right

Page 35, Rick Friedman/Black Star; 55, Ron Kunzman; 60-71, all baseball cards courtesy of Topps; 62(t), 65, courtesy, Jerry Spinelli, 70, Sal DiMarco/Black Star, 71, 73, courtesy, Jerry Spinelli; 88, Dale Higgins; 90(l), John McDonough; 90(tr), Buck Miller Photography; 90(cr), Bill Smith/Sports Illustrated; 91(tl), Chuck Solomon/Sports Illustrated; 91(cl), Manny Millan/Sports Illustrated; 91(bl), Warner Brothers; 109 (t), Christopher Myers; 110, Tom Stack/National Geographic Image Collection; 163, Kelly Culpepperl; 204-205 (all), Steve Winter/National Geographic Image Collection; 208-209, Cameron Davidson; 210(t), Annie Griffiths Belt/National Geographic Image Collection; 210(b), Army Corp of Engineers; 212(both), EOSAT; 213, Jim Richardson/National Geographic Image Collection; 214, Scott Dine/St. Louis Post Dispatch; 215, Michael Kipley, Quincy Herald Whig; 216, Jim Rackwitz/St. Louis Post Dispatch; 217, Cameron Davidson; 218, James L. Stanfield/National Geographic Image Collection; 219, Karen Elshout/St. Louis Post Dispatch;220, Rick Rickman; 221, Rich Sugg/Kansas City Star; 222, Wes Paz/St. Louis Post Dispatch; 228-229, Cameron Davidson; 253, David Levensen/Black Star; 256-257, Werner Forman; 270(shang), Giraudon/Art Resource; 270(zhou), Giraudon/Art Resource; 270(qin), Asian Art & Archaeology; 270(han), Pierre Belzeaux/Photo Researchers; 270(sui), Giraudon/Art Resource; 271(tang), Art Resource; 271(song), Pierre Belzeaux/Photo Researchers; 271(yuan), Pierre Belzeaux/Photo Researchers; 271(ming), Laurie Platt Winfrey, Inc.; 271(qing), Werner Forman; 274-275, Gerard Champlong/The Image Bank; 278(r), The British Museum; 279(bl), Newsweek Books/Laurie Platt Winfrey, Inc.; 279(br), Michael Holford; 284, Stock Connection/FPG; 286 (r), Museum of Fine Arts, Boston; 287 (jars), The British Museum; 287(tl), Photofest; 287(tr), Newsweek Books/Laurie Platt Winfrey, Inc.; 287(br), Archives Photographiques/Laurie Platt Winfrey, Inc.; 288(Tut), Lee Boltin Picture Library; 288(Carter), Photograph by Egyptian Expedition. The Metropolitan Museum of Art; 288 (right hand side), Lee Boltin Picture Library; 209(l), Stock Connection / FPG; 290(c), (r), Lee Boltin Picture Library; 291(c), Michael Holford; 291(bl), Newsweek Books/Laurie Platt Winfrey, Inc.; 291(br), Michael Holford; 294(all), Michael Holford; 295(r), C.M. Dixon; 297, Michael Holford; 298, The British Museum; 298-99, The British Museum; 299, British Museum/Michael Holford; 300(t), Gerry Clyde/Michael Holford; 300(b), The Mansell Collection/Time Inc. Picture Collection; 301(b), The Mansell Collection/Time Inc. Picture Collection; 302, The Mansell Collection/Time Inc. Picture Collection; 303(t), C.M. Dixon; 304, C.M. Dixon; 305, Robert Harding; 306-307, C.M. Dixon; 306, C.M. Dixon; 307(l), C.M. Dixon; 307(r), Focal Point; 308(both), Robert Harding; 309(t), Peter Hicks; 309©, Robert Harding; 309(b), C.M. Dixon; 310, Peter Hicks; 311(t), The Mansell Collection/Time Inc. Picture Collection; 311(b), Sonia Halliday; 312(ct), The British Museum; 312(cb), The Mansell Collection/Time Inc. Picture Collection; 312(b), The British Museum; 313(t), The Mansell Collection/Time Inc. Picture Collection; 312(br), Robert Harding; 327, Tom Stack & Associates; 383-403, Sugarman Productions, Inc.; 403, Ron Kunzman; 404-405, Photo courtesy of Biscayne National Park/John Brooks; 405, Mark Baker/WPBT; 408-409, John Michael Vlach/Philip Simmons Foundation; 410, Philip Simmons Foundation; 413, Mannie Garcia/Philip Simmons Foundation; 414, Mannie Garcia/Philip Simmons Foundation; 417, Philip Simmons Foundation; 418, Philip Simmons Foundation; 419, Smithsonian Institution; 420, Mannie Garcia/Philip Simmons Foundation; 421, Philip Simmons Foundation; 424(t), Philip Simmons Foundation; 424(b), Mannie Garcia/Philip Simmons Foundation; 425(t), Philip Simmons Foundation; 425(b), Mannie Garcia/Philip Simmons Foundation; 449(l), Dale Higgins; 463, Tom Sobolik/Black Star; 464, Richard T. Nowitz; 465(both), Paula Lerner/Aurora; 488(t), Lisa Quinones/Black Star; 508-519, George Ancona; 522, Frederic Remington, Against the Sunset, Photo courtesy of Gerald Peters Gallery, Inc., Sante Fe, New Mexico; 524-525, George Ancona, 532, Smithsonian Institution; 534-544, Wright State University Archives; 545, Lisa Quinones/Black Star; 546-547, Wright State University Archives; 546(inset), Smithsonian Institution; 550-556, NASA; 557(tr), (cr), Karen Kasmauski; 557(br), Cary Wolinsky; 558(t), Mike Clemmer; 558(b), Stephanie Maze; 559(t), Roger Ressmeyer/Corbis; 559(b), Mike Clemmer; 560(t), (c), Barbara Ries; 560(b), NASA; 561(t), Barbara Ries; 561(bl), Karen Kasmauski; 561(br), Barbara Ries, 562-563, Barbara Ries; 562(tl), NASA; 562(bl), Karen Kasmauski, 563(bl), (br), NASA, 566-583, NASA, 611, Ray Boudreau, 621, Liaison Agency.

Illustration Credits

Phillip Singer, Cover Art; Cameron Clement, 4-5, 18-21, 114-115; Tracy Sabin, 4-5, 18-21, 114-115; Karen Barbour, 6-7, 116-119, 230-231; Raphael Lopez, 8-9, 232-235, 332-333; Roger Chouinard, 10-11, 334-337, 426-427; Andrew Powell, 12-13, 428-431, 526-527; Chris Lensch, 14-15, 528-531, 626-627; Ethan Long, 16-17, 548-549, 564-565; Tom Newson, 22-37; Mary Anne Loyd, 38-39; Marc Burckhardt, 40-57; Stephen Schudlich, 58-59, 448-449; Gary Davis, 60-71; Kathy Lengyel, 60-71, 74-75; Mike Gardner, 72-73; David Diaz, 76-89, 92-93, 166-181; James Ransome, 94-109, 112-113; Russ Wilson, 120-143; Catherine Ross Crowther, 144-145, 292-293; Lori Lohstoeter, 146-165; Charlene Potts, 182-183, 254-255; Murray Kimber, 184-203, 206-207; Stephen Wirt, 256, 330-331, 355, 403, 407, 423, 464-465, 508-509, 524-525, 624; David Scott Meier, 314-327, 330-331; Bernie Fuchs, 328-329; Allen Garns, 338-351; Becky Heauner, 352-353; Chris Wood, 370-385; Joe Van Der Bros, 386-387, 482-483; Karen Blessen, 388-403, 406-407; Klaus Heesch 404-405; Stephanie Garcia, 432-447; Floyd Cooper, 450-463, 466-467; Glenn Harrington, 468-481; Mitchell Heinze, 484-503, 506-507; A.J. Garces, 612-621, 624-625; Joi Ishida, 622-623.